American Government

American Government

FIFTH EDITION

Alan R. Gitelson
Loyola University of Chicago

Robert L. Dudley
George Mason University

Melvin J. Dubnick
Rutgers University—Newark

Houghton Mifflin Company
Boston   New York

For Laura and Rachel, who light up my life and teach me my lessons.   A. R. G.

For Pat, my love as well as my royalties go with you.   R. L. D.

For Heather and P. D.—and the wisdom of motherhood.   M. J. D.

Sponsoring Editor: Melissa Mashburn
Assistant Editor: Lily Eng
Project Editor: Nicole Ng
Production/Design Coordinator: Jennifer Meyer
Manufacturing Manager: Florence Cadran
Marketing Manager: Sandra McGuire

Cover Design: Tony Saizon
Cover Image: Regatta Series #17 by Thomas Gruenebaum

Illustration Credits

Chapter 1: p. 5, Reprinted with special permission of King Feature Syndicate; p. 7, Jacques M. Chenet/Gamma Liaison; p. 9, Grantwood, *Parson Weem's Fable,* 1939, oil on canvas, #1970, 43, Amon Carter Museum, Fort Worth, Texas; p. 13, A. Ramey/Stock Boston; p. 14, Will & Deni McIntyre/Photo Researchers; p. 19, Owen Franken/Stock Boston.

Credits continue on page C–1.

Printed in the U.S.A.

Library of Congress Catalog Card Number: 97-72979

ISBN: 0-395-88734-8

123456789-VH-01 00 99 98 97

Contents

7 Campaigns and Elections   190

8 Interest Groups   225

15 Foreign and Defense Policy   447

Appendixes

Preface

In the preface to the fourth edition, we wrote of the many changes that took place in American government since the first edition was published in 1988. These changes addressed transformations in our subject matter—from Reagan to Bush to Clinton in the White House, from Democratic to Republican party majorities in Congress, from a world preoccupied with contending superpowers to one where nationalism and religious fanaticism seem to pose the greatest threats. We sensed that behind those changes there might be something more fundamental at work. "While the system is not broken," we argued, "it certainly is not operating in the ways that many of the experts have expected it to work."

Another two years have passed, and we are no less convinced that "new realities [are] taking shape that we don't quite understand as yet but which touch on the fundamental nature of government and the changing roles that it will play in our lives." The form and details of those new realities are still unclear, but in this edition (as in the previous four) we remain committed to the task of clarifying American government for our student readers.

As in the previous editions, we have kept two major goals in mind. First and foremost, we present a concise yet comprehensive picture of American government and politics. Through a traditional organization of fifteen chapters, the text covers the basic information essential for understanding today's political affairs. In the fifth edition, we have refined the presentation of this basic information in many crucial areas throughout the book.

Our second goal is closely tied to the first. A textbook should help students to think critically about politics. We encourage the reader to think critically by highlighting and confronting myths that they or other Americans may hold about government. Thus each chapter begins with a vignette and a short statement of one or two preconceptions found in discussions of politics. A myth, as defined in Chapter 1, is a shorthand way of thinking about the role and activities of government and politics. Myths often take the form of stories, stereotypes, proverbial sayings, or pervasive and popular attitudes that help us comprehend "the way things are"—or at least, the way we believe them to be. Examples of typical myths include the myth of the all-powerful president and the myth that courts are above politics.

While often helping us make sense of American government and politics, many myths also reflect and promote some of the misunderstandings that ordinary citizens have about the political system and how it works. It is our hope that through understanding some of the myths of American politics and how they evolved, students will be able to think more critically and systematically about our complex political system.

The Fifth Edition

There are two arenas of change that we attempt to treat with greater clarity in this edition. The first is the growing influence and impacts of *devolution* on the role of government in our lives. Over the past two decades, the typical American government course and textbook has focused increasingly on the national government and its politics and institutions. While not intending to do so, this focus on Washington has taken its toll on what students of American government think about state and local government. At the same time, the role of states and communities has gone through a resurgence of sorts, and the need to pay greater attention to subnational politics is evident to a growing number of American government instructors. To that end, we have introduced a new feature in each chapter—"Closer to Home" boxes—that draw more focused attention to the state and local dimensions of American government.

The second arena of change is the obvious impact of the information *revolution* on what we know—or can find out from the many web sites maintained by anyone from news organizations to official government agencies to lobbying groups to private individuals and groups—about government and hundreds of related topics. The appellation "revolution" is not used lightly here, for there is no other way to signify what the personal computer, the Internet, and the World Wide Web are doing to our access to government and policy issues. The impact of this revolution on the form and content of the American Government classroom over the next two to four years will be significant, and the role of the textbook is bound to change. With this edition we have taken the first steps toward an integration of our textbook with the vast resources of the Internet. Our goal: nothing less than to develop *American Government* as a dynamic textbook suitable for the classroom of the future.

The future of American government courses and reading material has entered a new age with the growth of the Internet and other digital media. In this edition we enter that new world by providing students with access to a World Wide Web site designed to expand and enhance the material found in these pages. With this in mind, the reader will find, throughout each chapter, icons indicating where additional information about the topic being discussed can be found on the **Gitelson/Dudley/Dubnick web site** of the Houghton Mifflin Company World Wide Web site. The site, which can be accessed from the Houghton Mifflin College Home Page at **http://www.hmco.com/college,** offers three features: supplementary material, updates, and topical links. The supplementary material expands the coverage of each chapter through added features, case studies, and commentary on chapter-relevant topics. In Chapter 2, for example, students will find a history of efforts to pass an equal rights amendment. Chapter updates offer students an opportunity to get the latest word on recent election results, Court decisions, or important legislative developments. And in the topical links section, the site provides students with up-to-date access to relevant and useful Internet resources for each major subject covered in the textbook.

In preparing the fifth edition, we have thoroughly reviewed and updated all chapters, in terms of both research and current events. As a result, in this edition, we have included thorough coverage of the 1996 elections, and we have given additional emphasis to the media, public opinion, the Supreme Court, and domestic and international policy. We have also carefully scrutinized every chapter, refining, clarifying, and tightening the text.

Additional Highlights of the Fifth Edition

Chapters 2 and 3, "Constitutional Foundations" and "Federalism and Intergovernmental Relations," respectively, have been reorganized, with constitutional foundations of federalism now discussed in Chapter 2. Changes in Chapter 3 focus more on intergovernmental relations and the practical dimensions of federalism. In Chapter 4, "The Heritage of Rights and Liberties," we cover recent Supreme Court decisions on the right to die and affirmative action as well as other important cases.

Changes in Chapter 5, "Public Opinion and Political Participation," include new polls on the changing attitudes of Americans to a variety of issues regarding the role of government. Chapter 6, "Political Parties," updates the role of third parties in the 1996 elections and the ongoing and changing roles that the Republican and Democratic parties play in the electoral process. Chapter 7, "Campaigns and Elections," includes timely coverage of the 1996 elections and campaign financing. Chapter 8, "Interest Groups," updates our coverage of interest groups and political action committees (PACs). Chapter 9, "Media and Politics," has been revised and updated to cover the 1996 elections and the rise of the new media.

In Chapter 10, "Congress," we discuss the several structural changes that the Republican majority has instituted in the U.S. House of Representatives. In Chapter 11, "The Presidency," we provide new discussions of presidential power in the Clinton administration and the latest analysis on the line-item veto. Chapter 12, "Bureaucracy," retains its balanced perspective on the role of public administration on our constitutional system. In Chapter 13, "Courts, Judges, and the Law," we provide more coverage of the "original intent" approach to constitutional interpretation and counterarguments to this approach. We also discuss the Clinton administration's appointments to the federal courts.

Both policy chapters—Chapter 14, "Domestic Policy and Policymaking," and Chapter 15, "Foreign and Defense Policy"—have been updated. In Chapter 14 the section on welfare policy has been revised in light of the 1996 Welfare Reform Act. Chapter 15 gives special attention to the dynamic changes that have occurred in both foreign and defense policy.

In addition to these content revisions, we have also thoroughly revised other features of the book. Many chapter-opening vignettes and "Myths in Popular Culture" boxes have been updated, focusing on the way different forms and transmitters of popular culture—the movies, cartoons, popular music—reflect and shape popular myths about the way government and politics function.

To help students understand the various topics, we include several pedagogical features in each chapter. Each chapter opens with a highlighted myth-and-reality question and a preview outline, and ends with a point-by-point summary, an expanded list of key terms and concepts, as well as a conclusion that provides a retrospective glance at the myths in light of the whole chapter discussion.

At the end of the book, in addition to the appendix containing the Declaration of Independence, the Constitution, Federalist Papers Nos. 10 and 51, and a list of presidents, an updated chapter-by-chapter listing of references and suggested readings on topics covered throughout the text is included.

Ancillary Package

The fifth edition of *American Government* offers an extensive package of supplementary materials for both the instructor and the student:

- *New!* The **Gitelson/Dudley/Dubnick web site** is a new and unique approach to using the vast resources of the World Wide Web by integrating the web with materials from the textbook. The site, which can be accessed from the Houghton Mifflin College Home Page at **http://www.hmco.com/college,** includes additional information on topics such as recent developments in campaign financing and regulatory reform, as well as information on pending Supreme Court rulings, corresponding to the web icons in the margins, and chapter summaries and outlines, as well as web links connecting students to various interesting and useful web sites such as the National Conference of State Legislature and the Library of Congress.

- The **Instructor's Resource Manual,** written and revised by the authors, includes for each chapter a chapter overview and one or two lecture outlines. One lecture outline parallels the text; the other (where provided) is a bonus lecture that explores a specific chapter theme or concept in greater detail. Each chapter also includes learning objectives, critical thinking activities, classroom activities, a list of transparencies and videos related to topics covered in the chapter, and a list of suggested readings.

- A **Test Bank,** written by Jonathan Webster of Walla Walla Community College, is included with the Instructor's Manual and provides approximately 55 multiple-choice test items and 10 short essay questions for each chapter. The test questions have been extensively revised for the fifth edition.

- A **Computerized Test Bank** for IBM and Macintosh computers is available to adopters. This program enables instructors to prepare custom examinations using the test items in the printed Test Bank as well as test items they have produced themselves.

- The **Study Guide,** also written by Jonathan Webster, is keyed closely to the text. Each chapter contains learning objectives. These objectives are keyed to chapter outlines, which are to be completed by the student. The Study Guide also includes key terms and critical thinking exercises, and practice multiple-choice and essay questions, all of which have been extensively revised for the fifth edition. An introductory section focuses on study skills, such as outlining, reviewing, and analyzing charts, graphs, and tables, and on how to write good answers to essay questions. A computerized version of the Study Guide is available for IBM computers.

- Thirty multicolor **Transparencies** of all charts and graphs from the text are assembled in a separate package.

- *New!* The **Houghton Mifflin American Government web site,** located at **http://www.hmco.com/college,** contains a complete array of resources to accompany our American Government titles, including an extensive *Documents Collection* with accompanying discussion questions and web exercises, various instructor's resources, web-based research activities, an annotated collection of links to innovative and useful web sites, as well as a downloadable, updated version of the award-winning *Crosstabs,* a computerized software program allowing students to crosstabulate survey data on the 1996 presidential election and the 1994–95 voting records of members of Congress in order to analyze voter attitudes and behavior.

Acknowledgments

Many people contribute to the success of a textbook, and such is the case with the fifth edition of *American Government.* We happily acknowledge the many helpful comments of the following reviewers: Ronald Rubin, Borough of Manhattan Community College; Charles Sewall, Jr., Robert Morris College; Kenneth Wink, Western Carolina University; William Gorden, Redlands Community College; John R. Baker, Wittenberg University; Sarbjit Johal, Merritt College; Douglas Costain, University of Colorado, Boulder. We would also like to thank Jonathan Webster for writing another first-rate revision of the Study Guide and Test Bank.

In a venture of this magnitude, authors realize that the success of a textbook is closely tied to the editors associated with the project. We have been fortunate enough to work with a dedicated, creative, and sensitive editorial staff at Houghton Mifflin. For the fifth edition, we are indebted to Melissa Mashburn, Lily Eng, Jean Woy, Nicole Ng, Carol Newman, Leah Strauss, and Vikram Mukhija.

We want to give an unqualified thanks, with love, to Idy, Laura, and Rachel Gitelson; Judy, Pat, and Michael Dudley; and Randi, Heather, and P. D. Dubnick, for all of their support and patience during the writing of this book.

Finally, we would like to emphasize the equal role played by all three authors in the writing of this textbook. There was no junior partner in this project. Alan Gitelson's name appears first on the cover because he administered the project. A flip of the coin determined the order of the names for Bob Dudley and Mel Dubnick.

A. R. G.   R. L. D.   M. J. D.

American Government

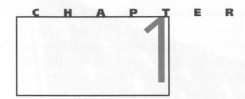

Myth and Reality in American Politics

See **Political Science** at
http://www.hmco.com/college

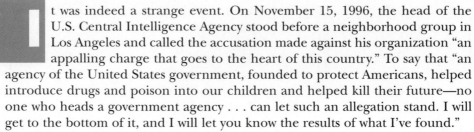

t was indeed a strange event. On November 15, 1996, the head of the U.S. Central Intelligence Agency stood before a neighborhood group in Los Angeles and called the accusation made against his organization "an appalling charge that goes to the heart of this country." To say that "an agency of the United States government, founded to protect Americans, helped introduce drugs and poison into our children and helped kill their future—no one who heads a government agency . . . can let such an allegation stand. I will get to the bottom of it, and I will let you know the results of what I've found."

The then CIA director, John Deutsch, had come to South-Central Los Angeles to respond to a growing controversy spawned by a series of newspaper articles published in the *San Jose Mercury News* starting August 18.[1] For three days the paper carried a reporter's investigation into the crack cocaine epidemic, which had spread throughout the United States and which had its most devastating impact on black neighborhoods like South-Central. It was a story that traced the drug's trail back to a San Francisco–based drug ring, which "sold tons of cocaine to the Crips and Bloods street gangs of Los Angeles and funneled millions in drug profits to a Latin American guerrilla army run by the U.S. Central Intelligence Agency."

For those in the African-American community trying to understand the roots of the suffering brought on by the crack cocaine epidemic, the stories confirmed what many suspected all along—that once again they were victims of a conspiracy in which government played a key role. It did not matter that the *Mercury News* reporter found no explicit evidence of a government-based conspiracy. Yes, there were links and associations between the drug ring and a CIA-supported rebel group from Nicaragua, which seemed to benefit from the profits of crack sales, but there was nothing to indicate CIA knowledge or involvement. Nevertheless, it was clear to many in the black community that such a conspiracy did occur. Agency denials and internal investigations meant little or nothing. The local U.S. representative, Juanita Millender-McDonald, put the situation bluntly: it was "not up to us to prove the CIA was involved in drug trafficking in South-Central Los Angeles. Rather, it is up to them to prove that they were not."

The members of the African-American community who believe that a federal agency would conspire to bring drugs into their community are not alone. Members of the right-wing militias believe the bombing of the federal building in Oklahoma City in 1995 was a government conspiracy intended to frame their followers. Conspiracy theories about government involvement in the assassinations of President John F. Kennedy, Martin Luther King, Jr., and Malcolm X remain popular subjects for magazine stories, movies, and books.

In fact, conspiracy theories are not new to American government. Historian Richard Hofstadter wrote in 1963 about a "paranoid style" in American politics traceable to at least the late 1700s. Rumors of a conspiracy among members of the secretive Freemason societies—who included such notables as George Washington, Benjamin Franklin, Thomas Jefferson, and Andrew Jackson—were widespread throughout the nineteenth century. By the 1850s those believing in a Catholic conspiracy involving papal bribery of top government officials were having a political impact among various segments of the citizenry. Pre–Civil War abolitionists spoke of conspiracies among slaveholding southern politicians, and western state populists focused on a perceived conspiracy of international bankers, which supposedly shaped American currency policies at the turn of the century.

This paranoid style of politics continued into the twentieth century. Munitions manufacturers were said to have started the First World War, and communists and socialists were increasingly viewed with suspicion between the wars. By 1951 Senator Joseph McCarthy spoke openly of a communist-led "great conspiracy" at the highest levels of the national government. In these and other forms, conspiracy theories have played a constant role in American politics. The accusations regarding CIA involvement in bringing crack cocaine to inner city African-American communities are merely the latest in a long line of such theories.

Why have Americans been so prone to adopt conspiracy theories about their government? Some might argue that it is because such conspiracies have existed in the past and might in fact be at work today. Of greater importance for Hofstadter and other students of American history, however, is the existence of an underlying myth about the workings of American government. The most significant fact about the paranoid style is not that some Americans "see conspiracies or plots here and there in history," but that they see such grand and elaborate conspiracies as the central "motive force" in history and in the operations of government.

This "grand conspiracy myth" has been more visible in some periods than in others. A number of observers of the American political scene believe that we have entered a period where conspiracy theories are being taken seriously by a growing number of citizens. We see the results in such events as the CIA director's visit to South-Central Los Angeles and numerous other actions taken to counter the rumors of elaborate government conspiracies. We also see the power of the grand conspiracy myth in popular cultural images (see Myths in Popular Culture 1.1).

Like other Americans, you or someone you know may feel that there is something to the grand conspiracy myth. Such beliefs are understandable given the facts behind the headlines. The actions or inactions of the CIA can be brought into question in the crack cocaine case, as can the decisions of federal law enforcement agents at the Branch Davidian Church tragedy in Waco, Texas, in 1994 and a number of similar episodes over the past decade. But are those beliefs warranted given the realities of American government and politics? Or are they just being driven by the power of the grand conspiracy myth?

We believe it worthwhile for every American to confront such questions directly. Doing so requires that you be knowledgeable about the U.S. political system. Only then will you be able to sort out the realities from the myths of American government. This book is intended to help you gain that knowledge.

MYTHS
IN POPULAR CULTURE

1.1   Mirrors and Shapers of Images

Popular culture—the music and movies and stories that we hear and see in the mass media every day of our lives—plays an important role in American social life. At times words and images generated and marketed by the "pop culture" industry reflect the realities of American life; at other times they help shape that reality.

For example, over the past fifty years the American fascination with conspiracies has shown up in Hollywood movies. At first the conspiracies took the form of alien invasions from outer space, the most notable being the 1956 classic, *Invasion of the Body Snatchers.* In a 1967 spy spoof, *The President's Analyst,* the telephone company is behind a grab for total control. During the 1970s the conspiracy thriller took a more serious form. In 1974 Warren Beatty starred in *The Parallax View* as a journalist who was being hunted down by those who thought he knew too much about a Kennedyesque assassination, and in 1976 the real-life conspiracy behind Nixon's cover-up of the Watergate break-in was the subject of *All the President's Men,* starring Robert Redford and Dustin Hoffman. Three years later Jane Fonda and Michael Douglas coproduced and costarred in *The China Syndrome,* a movie that suggested a conspiracy among large utility companies and the government to hide the dangers of nuclear power. Just coincidentally, the movie was released as the Three Mile Island accident brought the issue of nuclear power safety to the front pages of every newspaper in the country. Oliver Stone's controversial *JFK* (1991) was based on the long-standing view that there were more people involved in President John F. Kennedy's assassination than merely Lee Harvey Oswald, and a later political movie of his, *Nixon* (1995), contains scenes implying the existence of a right-wing conspiracy to control the highest levels of U.S. government.

More recently, movies such as *Mission Impossible* (1996), *Extreme Measures* (1996), and *Shadow Conspiracy* (1997) have been based wholly or partly on conspiracies, while films such as *A Few Good Men* (1992), *Courage Under Fire* (1996), and *Absolute Power* (1997) build on the premise that government cover-ups are possible and even commonplace.

Beyond conspiracy and the movies, popular music has also mirrored the politics of the day— and at times actually taken the lead in trying to influence and shape political action. Starting in the early 1960s, folk singers gained a significant audience for their performances of songs that protested injustice and war. Woody Guthrie's tunes from the 1930s (e.g., "This Land Is Your Land") and songs by Pete Seeger ("Where Have All the Flowers Gone?" and "If I Had a Hammer") made it to the top of the *Billboard* charts in 1962. In 1963 the folk trio of Peter, Paul, and Mary sold millions of recordings of "Blowin' in the Wind," a song by a very young Bob Dylan. The music itself became a political force as these and other popular "hits" were heard again and again at civil rights and anti-war rallies over the next decade.

Throughout our history, popular culture has played a major role in reflecting and shaping public opinion, political activity, and even the development of governmental institutions in our nation. To some degree, it has described, distorted, enhanced, and shaped our images of government and politics in the United States.

The political cartoon, for example, has often satirized and parodied politicians and government activity. Around the turn of the century, the "muckraking" novel was used to shape public opinion about the evils of economic robber barons and machine politics. Music, as well, was a partner in political protest and dissent—long before Guthrie and Seeger and Dylan set their lyrics to music. And movies have been an important part of our political culture since the beginning of the twentieth century when, as a nation, we first viewed one of the earliest popular silent films, *Birth of a Nation*, a 1915 epic saga of the Civil War that aggrandized the Ku Klux Klan.

It is important to recognize the role popular culture plays in our political lives, for today the music and movies and words we hear or read are a major source of the images and myths we have about government and politics. Throughout this book, in special boxes labeled "Myths in Popular Culture," we will use this theme to describe how mythic images of politics and government are occasionally shaped, reinforced, and subsequently distorted by movies, cartoons, and other vehicles of popular culture that have such an important impact on how we, as Americans, view the governmental process.

There are a number of books that you can read to help you understand how popular culture affects our views of politics and society in general. For example, see S. Robert Lichter, Linda Lichter, and Stanley Rothman, Prime Time: *How TV Portrays American Culture* (Washington, D.C.: Regnery Publishing, 1994). For a perspective on how popular music has played a role in our culture, see Bruce Pollack, *Hipper Than Our Kids* (New York: Shirmer Books, 1993).

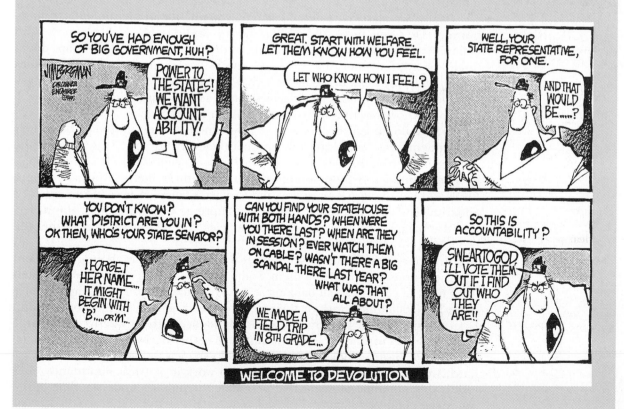

We will not try to fool you: learning about American government and politics is no easy task. As you will see in the chapters that follow, the framers of the U.S. Constitution designed a complicated system of government, and more than two hundred years of use have made that system even more elaborate and sometimes difficult to understand. Thus, learning to appreciate the dynamics of the American constitutional system and the many forces that shape its form and actions can be a challenging task. We hear you ask: Is this "learning" really necessary? Is it really necessary to take a formal course on American government? Can't we Americans just rely on what we already know and the information we receive through the news media and discussions with family and friends?

An informed American public should at least have some basic knowledge about its system of government. Can you identify the vice president of the United States? Do you know how many years a U.S. senator serves between elections, or how we determine how many U.S. senators represent each of the fifty states? In a 1991 survey, only 25 percent of those polled knew that senators serve six-year terms. In 1994, 35 percent of those asked in a national survey could not identify the vice president, and almost one-third of high school seniors surveyed believe that the size of a state's population determines the number of senators it has.[2]

In the overall scheme of modern life, you might consider these facts unimportant. However, these and similar survey findings often shock those who believe that Americans should know about their government. Others are not as disappointed, for Americans have often proven themselves to be good citizens without knowing some of the more "trivial" details of government. Despite a lack of basic knowledge, many Americans seem to sense what is going on in government and know how they feel about the major issues.

Where do we get that "sense" of government? When thinking about their government, most Americans rely on what they see and hear. They draw on the images they see on the nightly news or in daily newspapers as well as on the opinions and attitudes of those around them. Using these images, they are able to think and talk about the president and Congress haggling over health issues or anticrime laws, about recently announced Supreme Court decisions, about election campaigns, or about government policies and statements concerning the economy or foreign affairs.

Another source of understanding is the stories we hear about government and the lessons we learn from them. Some of those stories are as fresh as yesterday's news of congressional banking scandals or how a government agency purchased $10,000 toilet seats; or they are as old and familiar as the story of John Hancock signing the Declaration of Independence with an inscription so large that the British monarch could not miss it. Whether derived from today's headlines or our history books, these stories help shape our views and attitudes toward American government and those who work in it. Most importantly, they reflect the multitude of myths that permeate the public's understanding of the American political system.[3]

America's Government Discontent

American voters have become increasingly angry and frustrated with their government and traditional politicians. Talk radio personalities, such as Rush Limbaugh, have become important political actors in the 1990s because they seem to articulate the feelings of many disaffected citizens.

Myths and American Government

What are **myths?** In ancient times, myths were stories about a civilization's gods and heroes that helped members of those societies explain and understand the world around them. The ancient Greeks relied on stories about the gods on Mount Olympus to make sense of both the good and bad things happening to them. Similarly, myths created by ancient Romans played a critical role in shaping their daily lives.[4] Many cultures still celebrate mythical traditions with holidays. In early October, for example, Koreans celebrate the birth of their nation's ancient founder, Tan-gun, the son of a heavenly prince who came to earth and married a bear that had turned into a woman.

The term *myth* is applied more broadly in our times. Myths are still associated with stories, but the focus of modern tales is not necessarily on gods and heroes. The story of George Washington admitting to his father that he could not tell a lie and did indeed chop down the cherry tree is mythical in the classic sense, as is the rags-to-riches story of Horatio Alger with its message that hard work leads to success. But today there are equally powerful stories about our nation's leaders—about the lives and accomplishments of political families like the Roosevelts and the Kennedys, about individual presidents like Richard Nixon and Bill Clinton, and about institutions like the U.S. Senate and the Pentagon.

Such stories remain a powerful force in shaping the public's views about government, as are stories about the actions of bureaucratic agencies and historical figures. For some people, the story about a government agency buying $10,000 toilet seats, for example, might confirm the widely held belief that government bureaucracy is inefficient and wasteful; on a different level, the story of John Hancock signing the Declaration of Independence supports the popular images of the American Revolution, what it stood for, and the risks and sacrifices made by those who chose to break with England in 1776. In each case, the myth helps shape our understanding of and attitudes toward our system of government.

Today, however, it is not the myth-as-story that is important. Instead, some of today's most important myths take the form of stereotypes such as "All Democrats are big-spending liberals" and "Republicans are the party of big business"; proverbial sayings such as "You can't fight city hall"; and pervasive attitudes such as "All politicians are crooks" that have an impact on the way we think about government and the American political system.

What roles do these myths play in our understanding of American government and politics? To what extent do these myths reflect reality? Are they merely innocent falsehoods that are used to make the complex world of American government seem simpler? Or are they distortions and untruths that help perpetuate the rule of a few?

Although the elaborate religious mythologies of ancient Greece and Rome are gone, modern societies, including our own, are no less influenced by myths. We rely on myths for a variety of reasons. First, like the ancients, *we sometimes use myths to help us simplify the complex world in which we live.* Myths help us "to live in a world in which the causes" of our problems "are simple and neat and the remedies are apparent."[5] During the recession of the early 1990s, many Americans blamed the Japanese for the economic woes of the United States. Stories about unfair pricing strategies used by Japanese firms as well as widely publicized remarks by Japanese officials regarding poor American work habits helped fuel a myth about an "economic war" with Japan.[6] The popularity of both Japan-bashing and "buy-American" campaigns reflected a tendency among too many Americans to seek easily targeted scapegoats. In the meantime, these same Americans ignored the more complex national and international economic transitions that were responsible for the problems.[7]

Second, *myths often help us define our place in the world and provide us with a common social and political identity.*[8] Many of us perceive the United States in mythical terms "as a community of free and equal self-governing citizens pursuing their individual ends in a spirit of tolerance for their religious and other forms of diversity."[9] This and other myths held by Americans are supported by stories— of the first Thanksgiving, of Washington cutting down the cherry tree, of the deeds of young Abe Lincoln—that reinforce our national "belief in innocence, in honesty, in freedom, in the use of the wilderness, in adaptability, in the right of the individual to act freely without restraint. . . . Like all myths, their function is to say this is the way it was with Americans, this is the way it is, and this is the

The Cherry Tree Myth

In this painting, titled *Parson Weems' Fable,* Grant Wood makes fun of the famous patriotic myth that George Washington could tell no lies. The painting of young Washington with an adult face is to emphasize the mythmaking of the adoring parson, who invented the story.

www.

For more information on myths and American government, see the **Gitelson/Dudley/Dubnick** web site.

way it ought to be."[10] Without such myths, the political system might crumble as it did in the former Soviet Union in 1991.[11]

Third, we frequently *depend on myths to help guide and rationalize our behavior.* The "myth of good citizenship" tells us that we ought to vote because that is the only effective way to influence the behavior of government officials.[12] Myths also have an impact on how we conduct our foreign policies. Many critics of American foreign policy, for example, feel that our behavior in international affairs is shaped by a national myth of progress—a vision of "America as the wave of the future."[13] "Americans see history as a straight line," comments essayist Frances FitzGerald, "and themselves standing at the cutting edge of it as representatives for all mankind. . . ."[14]

By their very nature, myths influence our views of reality. But are they always outright lies? Americans often assume that myths are the opposite of truths and facts. That was the view expressed by President John F. Kennedy in a 1962 speech in which he suggested that the "great enemy of truth is very often not the lie— deliberate, contrived, and dishonest—but the myth—persistent, persuasive, and unrealistic." Many myths have indeed been outright lies, such as the long-held myth that women and blacks are intellectually or morally incapable of exercising the political judgment necessary to vote.[15] But *many myths are oversimplifications rather than outrageous falsehoods.* The myth that any boy or girl can grow up to be president of the United States is neither true nor false, but it does offer a naive picture of the possibilities for most of America's children.

Another important aspect of myths is that many of the most significant ones *reflect views of the past or the future.* Many of the myths surrounding our most important government institutions—the U.S. Constitution, the presidency, Congress, and the Supreme Court—reflect historical judgments of those bodies and the people who served in them. For example, although Abraham Lincoln is regarded today as one of the nation's great presidents, he was highly criticized by other politicians and the media while he occupied the White House. His status as a "great" president—much of it reflected in stories and myths—is well established in our eyes despite the low regard with which he was held by many of his contemporaries.

We also adopt many future-oriented myths that *often shape our expectations of what government officials can or will do.* For example, among military professionals the failure of America's military venture in Vietnam during the 1960s and early 1970s was often blamed on the lack of enough commitment to the military's efforts. What emerged from that experience can be called the "Vietnam War myth," a widely held belief among our nation's top military leaders that American military forces could not be successful in the future unless enough forces were sent to do the job and military commanders were allowed to act without interference from the politicians back in Washington. This myth had a significant influence on President George Bush's decisions on the use of military force against Iraq in 1991: he committed more than 500,000 U.S. troops and gave military commanders considerable freedom to determine how to deal with the forces of Saddam Hussein that had invaded Kuwait.[16] Given the relative success of that mission, some would argue that the myth was proved correct. However, for our purposes it is important to note that the Vietnam War myth had a significant impact on the attitudes and decisions of key policymakers as well as the American public.

And, of course, many of our myths *focus on the present to help us deal with what is taking place* in Washington, Topeka, or Sacramento right this moment. For example, many people believe in the "myth of special-interest government," which, correctly or incorrectly, helps many of us understand why Congress or the state legislature passes a law providing a new tax break for some major or local industry that will ultimately increase the general taxpayer's burden. According to this myth, such laws are passed because special interests are able to hire high-priced lobbyists in Washington or the state capital who are effective in influencing legislators, whereas the general public has no one representing its interests (see Chapter 8, on interest groups).

From these examples, it should also be obvious that myths focus on a wide range of subjects—from the nature of American society and our national Constitution to everyday political and governmental activities. Individually, many of us have adopted myths about whether American society is racist or sexist, about the efficiency and effectiveness of local firefighters and law enforcement personnel, and about how important our participation in the political system is or can be. The wide range of topics covered by myths will become increasingly evident as you read through this textbook.

As a student of American government, it is essential that you understand the role that myths play in our governmental and political systems. By taking myths into account, you will be able to make sense of some features of the American system that might have puzzled you in the past. The fact that some myths are lies should put you on notice that we all must focus critical attention on what we hear and believe about government and politics. The fact that other myths help us get things done or resolve complicated problems should also be factored into your approach. In any case, you must also have a clear picture of the institutional and political reality that underpins our national government. Before we learn to run, however, we must learn to walk. Therefore, let us turn to some fundamental questions.

The Nature of Government and Politics

What is government, and how does it accomplish its varied responsibilities? In brief, **government** comprises *those institutions and officials whose purpose it is to write and enact laws and execute and enforce public policy.* The goal of government in the United States is to maintain order through the rule of law, provide goods and services that benefit the lives of all citizens, and promote equality among members of society. These activities are conducted by legislators, presidents or other chief executive officers (such as governors and mayors), judges, bureaucrats, and other elected and appointed officials who work in the institutions that make up the executive, legislative, and judicial branches of federal, state, and local governmental systems. Ultimately, these officials carry out their responsibilities through the authority to enact and enforce laws crucial to the functioning of government.

What is politics? In its most general sense, **politics** refers to the *activities of influencing or controlling government for the purpose of formulating or guiding public policy.* We will be discussing the politics of running for or being appointed to office; choosing policy alternatives; and bargaining, negotiating, and compromising to get policies enacted and executed. The politics of federal student loan programs, for example, involves presidents and legislators—influenced by students, parents, bankers, and college administrators—negotiating the issue of who receives loan benefits and who pays the bills.

Has government always been important in the lives of most Americans? Despite some popular feelings to the contrary, the answer is probably yes. Historian Arthur M. Schlesinger, Jr., has pointed to a "cherished national myth" ascribing the economic development of the nation "to the operations of unfettered individual enterprise."[17] In contrast, history shows that American government has always affected economic and social life. As early as colonial times, citizens expected government to perform such traditional functions as ensuring law and order and resisting foreign aggression. But even then government often did more.

From the time the first European settlers established communities in America, colonial governments, under the general authority of the British government, played a major role in developing and regulating local economies. Colonial (and later state) governments helped finance new enterprises, build ports, construct turnpikes and canals, and even control wages and prices in local markets.

Shortly after the United States gained its independence, a series of laws written by Congress during the 1780s, collectively called the Northwest Ordinance, established rules for selling land and organizing local governments in the large territory stretching from the Ohio River to the Mississippi and north to the Great Lakes. Land was even reserved to support public schools. One of the earliest examples of the national government's role as "an active promoter of the economy" was its 1803 purchase of the Louisiana Territory. That vast region was vital to the prosperity of farmers working the lands along the entire length of the Mississippi.[18] Historians have also found other examples of early government efforts to plan, manage, and promote the new country's resources.[19]

The role of government continued to expand during the 1800s and early 1900s. Attempts to solve the economic and social problems of the Great Depression of the 1930s, a depression that left millions of Americans jobless and homeless, led to an explosion of new programs. Soon an army of bureaucrats was managing the economy, promoting stable economic growth by helping find jobs for the unemployed, and enforcing price controls designed to hold down the prices of goods and services.

As the United States became a more complex society, Americans demanded that the national government pay more attention to problems once solved by families and communities—problems of the poor, the handicapped, the elderly, and others. Between 1932 and the present, all Americans have been touched directly or indirectly by programs covering early childhood nutrition, health care, unemployment benefits, food stamps, or social security.

The government, however, has not limited its interest to the economy and social welfare programs. As destruction threatened the vast American forests and pollution tainted air and water, Americans turned to government for environmental management, ranging from conservation programs to regulations affecting many polluting industries. In support of such goals as preventing environmental damage and securing a steady supply of energy, government has lowered speed limits on highways, pushed for the development of nuclear energy, and implemented a variety of other policies.

In recent years, a growing number of Americans have concluded that perhaps they have depended too much on government for solving their problems. The 1994 congressional election results made it clear to many officials that the

The Environment

To protect Americans, the government is becoming increasingly more involved in environmental management, ranging from conservation programs to regulations affecting many polluting industries. Here a worker removes illegally dumped corrosive chemicals in Orange County, California.

public wanted a change, if not a redirection, in government priorities. By 1996 the White House too was admitting it was time for a change. "The era of big government is over," declared President Bill Clinton in his State of the Union address. No one, however, denies that government has played an important role in the development of the modern American social and economic system.

Fundamental Issues of Government and Politics

The fact that government has always played an important role in the lives of Americans does not mean that its activities have been uncontroversial. Several basic questions about government and politics have constantly emerged—questions about who should govern, where governmental authority should be located, and how much government should be doing.

Who Should Govern?

The fact that government plays a critical and pervasive role in everyone's life should automatically raise the question of who should control the use of this

Government Regulation of the Workplace

For these textile workers and other Americans, regulation of the workplace is an important issue. The question is often asked as to who should govern, where government activity should be located, and what the scope of government activity should be in our public and private lives.

important social institution. In other words, who should govern? The answer to that question has taken two forms, one focused on governmental authority and the other on the wielding of governmental power.

Authority.   For many students of government, the question "Who should govern?" focuses on who is officially authorized to control governmental institutions. In other words, who should exercise formal authority in government? **Authority** can be defined as the capacity to make and enforce public policies possessed by individuals who occupy formal government roles.

As we already noted, government comprises institutions and officials who make and enforce public policies. The roles those officials play in conducting the business of government derive from a variety of sources. Some are defined in constitutions and other legal documents (see the discussion of constitutional foundations in Chapter 2), whereas others may be the result of long-standing traditions. In either case, when we are concerned with who should occupy those official roles, we are dealing with the issue of authority.

Among the first to try to answer the question of who should govern through the exercise of authority was the ancient Greek philosopher Aristotle. He classified governments into three types: government by one, by the few, and by the many. For each type, he believed, there is a good, or "right," form and a bad, or "wrong," form. A right form of government serves the common interests of the people, whereas a wrong form of government serves the personal interests of the ruler or rulers.

CLOSER TO HOME

1.1   Who Governs?

When you think about government, what comes to mind? Like most Americans, you probably think about Washington, D.C., the White House, and even the Supreme Court. This is understandable since most of the political news we read or hear about is national. When Americans do turn to local or state news, it is typically about some major crime or scandal. Rarely does the daily news of state and local government get the attention it merits.

How much attention do state and local governmental affairs deserve? When you consider the degree to which state and local governments impact our lives, it is clear that we should be paying a lot more attention to them. Indeed, in addition to the fifty state governments, there are over eighty-six thousand local governments in the United States. Everything from streets to schooling to water to trash collection comes from local government service providers. Highways, airports, and mass transit systems are usually operated and maintained by regional or state authorities. And to find such governmental services as law enforcement, public health inspections, and environmental protection you again have to look closer to home.

Although this book focuses on the national government in almost all its chapters, we are including a Closer to Home feature in each chapter to highlight some aspect of state and local government relevant to the topic under discussion. Although only touching the surface, it is intended to give you an appreciation of an extremely important part of the American political system. We hope that this feature also whets your appetite to learn more about state and local governments.

Consider, for example, how the question "Who should govern?" is answered at the local government level. You will read in Chapter 2, on constitutional foundations, how that question is answered at the national level through the establishment of three distinct branches of government. For the most part, state governments also follow that model. At the local level, however, Americans have selected a wide range of responses to the question "Who should govern?"

In small-town New England, for example, local governments rely on a very democratic form of governance called the town meeting. At least once a year, all the town's voting citizens gather to vote on local ordinances, tax levies, and the town budget. Having made those decisions, they elect town officials from among their number to carry out the town's business until the next meeting.

In contrast, some forms of local government are run by an executive director hired by a body of nonelected officials who owe their positions to a governor or some influential state legislator. This seemingly undemocratic answer to the question "Who should govern?" is not that uncommon. Numerous "special district" governments can be found throughout the United States—many providing public housing and others operating major bridges and tunnels (see Chapter 3 on Federalism).

Between the extremes of town meetings and appointed special district government, local communities have selected a broad range of answers to the "Who should govern?" question. In New York City, the government is in the hands of a strong mayor, who takes the lead in government policymaking and program management. In Dallas, Texas, however, the day-to-day tasks of governing are in the hands of an appointed city manager, who serves at the pleasure of an elected city commission.

Why such variations among local government structures? The answer lies in the fact that situations and traditions vary across the nation. Any attempt to make one size fit all will be doomed to failure. That is one of the reasons it is important for us to pay attention to what is going on in the governments closer to home.

Aristotle called the government by the many that serves the common interests of the people a *polity* and a government by the many that serves their personal interests a *democracy*. Like many other political thinkers through the ages, Aristotle feared democracy, for he assumed that self-interest would rule if government were turned over to the "rabble in the streets." In fact, his other term for democracy was "mobocracy," or rule by the mob.

Americans admire democracy as much as Aristotle feared it, and most believe that it is the most appropriate type of government for the United States. Americans' idea of **democracy** can best be summed up as a belief in government where authority is based on the consent and will of the majority. If they were asked the question "Who should govern?" a vast majority would state that the people should govern.

Nevertheless, the American concept of democracy does not mean a commitment to direct rule by the majority. As we will see, the framers of the Constitution did not believe that government authority should be directly in the hands of the people. They envisioned the United States as a **republic,** or **representative democracy,** in which the people govern indirectly by electing individuals—the president, members of Congress, governors, mayors, state legislators, and others —to make decisions. Thus the people do not vote on or directly make specific policy decisions; they do so indirectly, through those they elect to represent their interests.

Despite this general acceptance of representative democracy, controversies still arise about the need for greater or lesser citizen participation in government decision making. Some argue that much more should be done to increase public input into policy decisions through procedures called **initiative and referendum.** The initiative process allows members of the general public to place questions of public policy on the ballot for voters to consider directly. In contrast, it is the state or local legislative body that places a referendum on the ballot for public consideration.

Others believe that too much public input through direct participation can be damaging. Many local school districts, for example, have faced budgetary crises in recent years because local voters have constantly turned down requests to increase revenues.

Power.   The question "Who should govern?" can also be approached from the perspective of politics. As defined above, politics involves activities intended to influence or control what goes on in government. Those who have the ability to wield such influence are said to possess **power.** From this perspective, the question about who governs should really be "Who should wield power over the operations of government?"

What does it take to possess power? Reduced to its basics, power is a relationship between two parties, A and B. We say that A—let's call her Alice—has power relative to B—let's call him Bob—if Alice can influence Bob's choices or decisions. To do that, Alice should probably possess something that Bob finds desirable or irresistible. That something, called a resource, can be some special knowledge or expertise, a dynamic and winning personality, the promise of financial reward, or even an outright threat to do Bob harm if he does not co-operate. Just as important, Bob must find Alice's knowledge, rewards, or threat credible. If Bob, for instance, does not believe that Alice is an expert, then Alice will lose her influence over Bob.

From the perspective of power, the answer to the question "Who should govern?" rests on how dispersed the resources for wielding power are in a society. Those who believe in democracy want to see such resources distributed as widely as possible. For them the ideal situation would exist if each and every citizen was able to exercise the same degree of influence over government actions. Under such conditions, government would do what the majority of citizens want done. This is called the **majoritarian view of power.**

But most students of government agree that politically influential resources are unequally distributed in society; consequently, some members of society will be able to influence government actions more than others. Thus the question really becomes whether it is more desirable to have those resources concentrated in the hands of a few ("elitism") or dispersed as widely as possible ("pluralism").

Those who advocate the **elitist view of power** would argue that the general public is best served when there is a basic consensus among a country's top leaders regarding fundamental issues. Although these leaders might disagree on minor issues or even compete against one another for positions of authority in government, the fact that they share a common view on issues that might otherwise split the nation is regarded as an important foundation for governing.

In contrast, while not denying that power-relevant resources are unequally distributed in society, those who support the **pluralist view of power** advocate a political system where many elites, instead of just one, influence government. For pluralists, it is not important that members of some small elite agree on fundamental issues. Rather, it is crucial that membership in the elite be open to all in society and that they need only agree to abide by the rules of the game in government and politics. From the pluralist perspective, members of this open elite serve the public good by competing among themselves for the attention of government, as well as for control of public offices.

Whether focused on authority or power, the issue of who should govern is an important one. It helped shape the American political system, and remains a critical question in today's hotly contested political environment.

Where Should Government Authority Be Vested?

Should government authority be vested in local communities, in governments close to the people? Should it be vested in the political center of the nation, Washington, D.C.? Or should it be vested in the fifty state capitals—in Harrisburg,

Springfield, Austin, Sacramento, Columbus, Tallahassee, and all the others? These questions do not have simple answers because of the broad range of government activities.

To illustrate, would it make sense for the national government to run your town's fire department? Who should be responsible for collecting garbage, running your town's parks, and hiring schoolteachers? Many people trust local government to deal with these important issues. There is no way, however, that towns and cities or even states can deal effectively with foreign policy, national defense, regional unemployment, and other major economic and social issues. Consequently, most Americans also believe that the national government, with its vast economic resources and national perspective, should tackle such issues. Many also argue that national policies can better reflect the general will and values of the American people and are less likely to discriminate against racial, religious, and political minorities than local policies.

Most complex societies have found that to ensure effective governance they need intermediate levels of government as well. Different nations have solved this problem in different ways. The United States has developed a unique solution that allows national, state, and local governments to share power. But even this solution is incomplete, and the debate continues over the role of each level of government in delivering services to the American public. We discuss the struggles over the vesting of power in greater detail in Chapter 3, on federalism and intergovernmental relations.

How Much Should Government Do?

What should be the scope of government activity? The answers to this question vary from society to society and from era to era. We can gain a partial answer by examining the dominant ideologies of our nation. If myths help orient us toward our government by shaping our attitudes and understanding about what government does, ideologies provide us with the tenets for assessing the world of politics and the work of government. **Ideologies** are the *conceptual tools we use to think about whether government is doing what it ought to be doing.* They offer us general priorities and principles about what government could or should do and suggest the means for doing it.[20] Whereas myths help us understand and deal with the world, ideologies *reflect our beliefs about the way we think the political world does or ought to operate.*

Although some governments have attempted to establish an official ideology, in most democratic nations there is competition among two or more dominant ideologies. Until the middle 1980s, the leaders of the Soviet Union endorsed and enforced a Marxist-Leninist ideology that made opposition to the government a crime.[21] More common, however, is the experience of many Western European democracies, where competition among followers of different ideologies is at the heart of the representative system. In France, Italy, Belgium, Denmark, and even Great Britain, differences in ideology are often reflected in differences among the political parties.[22]

Government Affects Private Lives

A major issue dividing Americans along ideological lines is the degree to which government should intervene in the private lives of U.S. citizens. The debate over abortion rights is, in part, a reflection of differing ideological views on that issue.

Although the American approach has been less overtly ideological, ideology does play an important—and increasingly controversial—part in shaping our political life. The American ideological landscape has been molded by two central issues regarding the question of how much government should do. The first is the issue of how much government should intervene in economic affairs. For many Americans, government should not interfere in the marketplace unless absolutely necessary; for others, government regulation and management of the economy are crucial for the nation's health.

The second issue focuses on the degree to which government should meddle in the private affairs of Americans. At one extreme are those who believe that government has no right to intrude in their personal choices and that the areas of personal freedom must be extended as much as possible. At the other end are those who believe that government sometimes has a moral obligation to intercede in the private lives of people who might otherwise make unwise decisions. From that perspective, governments should be permitted to make and enforce laws related to smoking, abortion, sexual activity, and so on.

Taken together, the intersection of American beliefs on these two issues has generated four ideologies that seem to represent four general answers to the question of how much government should be doing (see Figure 1.1).[23] **Liberalism** is the label typically applied to those who favor increased government intervention in the economy but oppose increased limits on personal freedoms. In contrast, **conservatism** is the label usually given to those who favor increased

FIGURE 1.1

Issues and Ideologies

The four major ide-
ologies of American
politics have been
shaped by debates
over government's
role in economic and
personal matters.

Source: Adapted from
William S. Maddox and
Stuart A. Lilie, *Beyond
Liberal and Conservative:
Reassessing the Political
Spectrum* (Washington, DC:
The Cato Institute, 1984),
p. 5. Reprinted by permission.

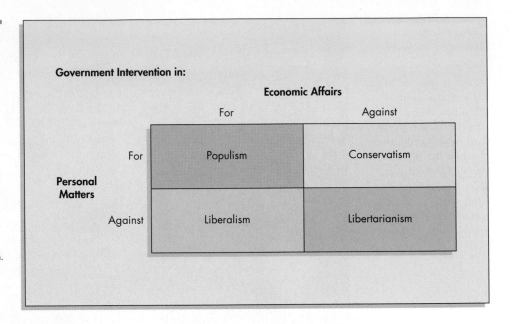

regulation of private lives for moral purposes but oppose government interference in the economy.

    Traditionally, liberals and conservatives have constituted the mainstream ide-
ological positions of most Americans. But in recent years many Americans have
found that their views do not fit neatly into either perspective. They found that
they are "liberal" on certain issues and "conservative" on others. As a result, two
other popular ideological perspectives have emerged. Modern-day **populists** are
inclined to favor government intervention in both economic and personal matters, whereas **libertarians** take a strong stand against both.

    The growing popularity of both the populist and libertarian ideologies re-
flects some fundamental problems and potential shifts in the American
ideological landscape. Some observers of American government and politics have
noticed that our dominant ideological perspectives, liberalism and conservatism,
seem increasingly inconsequential to Americans. Some argue that there is a growing gap between the dominant ideologies and the realities of American political
life. "The categories that have dominated our thinking for so long are irrelevant
to the new world we face," contends E. J. Dionne, Jr.[24] Others see our contemporary problems as rooted in a widening "discrepancy" and tension between our
dominant ideologies and the myths of American government that help define
our expectations of how our political system should be operating.[25] In either case,
ideological responses to questions about what government does are important to
understanding American government.

Overview of This Book

American government and politics is a complex subject involving more than a knowledge of the institutions and people who make our systems work. The choices made through the governmental and political systems are greater in number than the fundamental issues described above. Yet these—institutions, people, and issues—form the "basics" of what we must know in order to understand American government. As the political turmoil of recent years in Eastern Europe and the former Soviet Union has demonstrated, we must also understand and appreciate how myths operate in our own governmental and political systems. These are the objectives of the chapters that follow.

The first step in developing an understanding of American politics is to become informed about the major constitutional institutions and processes of government. Chapters 2 through 4 offer an overview of the historical and constitutional basis for the organization and functioning of the American governmental system. Chapter 2 focuses on the Constitution—its creation and its principal features. Chapter 3, on federalism and intergovernmental relations, considers the relationships among the various levels of government. Chapter 4 looks at some limits on government power: the civil liberties protected by the Constitution and the civil rights guaranteed to citizens by the Constitution and by law.

The next five chapters consider the activities and institutions that link citizens to their government. In Chapter 5, we discuss the opinions that people have about government and how these opinions affect their participation in nongovernmental politics. Chapter 6 deals with the role of political parties, and Chapter 7 examines the most widespread forms of participation: nominations, campaigns, and elections. That discussion is followed by an analysis of two important institutions that influence the political system: interest groups, in Chapter 8, and the media, in Chapter 9. Interest groups shape politics by making it possible for people with similar goals to band together to influence public policy. The media have an impact on the way people perceive politics.

Chapters 10 through 13 examine the four central institutions of government: Congress, the presidency, the bureaucracy, and the courts. Finally, in Chapters 14 and 15, we probe the relationship between politics and policymaking in domestic and foreign policy.

In each chapter, we point out a myth or myths associated with each topic. In some instances, as in Chapter 2, we focus on a myth (the "timeless and perfect Constitution") that distorts the truth but that has helped generate popular and consistent support for our governmental institutions. In other instances, we consider myths that seem closer to the truth but that have misrepresented the reality of American government. For example, in Chapter 10, on Congress, we tell you about the myth of congressional ineffectiveness, quoting one political commentator who suggested that it would take Congress thirty days to make a cup of instant coffee. Then we ask whether this myth misrepresents not only what Congress does but also what it is supposed to do. As we consider that myth and others, we show you the nuggets of truth that have given rise to them, as well as the ways in which they distort reality—sometimes for good, sometimes not. Only through an understanding of these and related myths can we comprehend the nature and work of our system of government.

We hope that you will find this approach stimulating and that it will provoke thought, discussion, and debate on your basic assumptions about government and politics. We also hope that our discussion will prompt you to ask additional questions about the dynamics of our exciting political process. Like the classic tales of the Greek gods, the myths of American politics reflect the rich imagination and the anxieties of those who created them.

Key Terms and Concepts

Myths Stories, stereotypes, proverbial sayings, and pervasive attitudes that have an impact on the way we think about government and the American political system.

Government Those institutions and officials involved in enacting laws and executing and enforcing public programs. In the United States, government consists of the executive, legislative, and judicial branches of federal, state, and local governmental systems.

Politics The act of influencing or controlling government for the purpose of formulating or guiding public policy.

Democracy A system of government, in the American sense, derived from belief in government based on the consent and will of the majority.

Republic A constitutional form of government in which decisions are made democratically by elected or appointed officials.

Representative democracy See republic.

Initiative and referendum Two means used to enhance the role of citizens by giving them a direct voice in making policy decisions. The initiative process allows members of the general public to place questions of public policy on the ballot for voters to consider directly. In contrast, it is the state

or local legislative body that places a referendum on the ballot for public consideration.

Authority The capacity to make and enforce public policies possessed by individuals who occupy formal government roles.

Power The capacity and ability to influence the behavior and choices of others through the use of politically relevant resources. In the context of this book, it is the capacity and ability to wield influence over government.

Majoritarian view of power The view that political power should be distributed as equally as possible in a political system in order to facilitate meaningful majority rule.

Elitist view of power The view that political power should be in the hands of a relatively small part of the general population that shares a common understanding about the fundamental issues facing society and government.

Pluralist view of power The view that political power should be dispersed among many elites that share a common acceptance of the rules of the game.

Ideologies Conceptual tools used to help us think about whether government is doing what it ought to be doing. Ideologies offer us general priorities and principles about what government could or should do and suggest the means for doing it.

Liberalism A set of ideological beliefs usually favoring government intervention in the economy, but disinclined toward government interference in the private lives of individuals.

Conservatism A set of ideological beliefs tending to resist government interference in economic matters while favoring government action in private affairs for moral purposes.

Populism A set of ideological beliefs that tends to favor government intervention in both economic and personal affairs.

Libertarianism The ideological belief that government should do no more than what is minimally necessary in the areas of economic affairs and personal freedom.

Constitutional Foundations

MYTH & REALITY

Is the Constitution a perfect and timeless document?

See **Political Science** at
http://www.hmco.com/college

Thomas Jefferson and James Madison—every schoolchild in the United States knows them as the third and fourth American presidents. They were also lifelong friends and close political allies who contributed much to their country. Jefferson authored the Declaration of Independence, and Madison is known as the "Father of the Constitution" for the important role he played in shaping that document. Together they founded the country's first political party, and as presidents they led the young nation through difficult times.

There was at least one issue, however, on which they differed: the need for constitutional stability. Madison thought the key to any effective government was for the people to develop a strong emotional attachment to its basic law—the constitution. As a result, he advocated using public events and patriotic celebration to build long-term support for the U.S. Constitution.[1] In contrast, Jefferson regarded such "sanctimonious reverence" for the U.S. Constitution—or any other such document—with disdain. Instead, he favored major constitutional change every generation or so to refresh the public interest in government. "I hold it that a little rebellion now and then is a good thing, & as necessary in the political world as storms in the physical."[2]

The opposing views of those close friends have found a home in the American political landscape. Thus, an astute foreign visitor to the United States may likely be struck by contradictions in the attitudes of Americans toward their government. Most Americans, reflecting Madison's wish for public adoration of their constitutional system, believe theirs is the best of all possible governments and would readily tout the American constitutional system as a model for modern

James Madison & Thomas Jefferson

Despite their close friendship and shared views on politics, Jefferson and Madison disagreed about the need for radical constitutional change.

democracy. However, the observant visitor is likely to hear many other citizens, following in Jefferson's footsteps, call for major changes in a system of government they claim is too cumbersome and moves too slowly, if at all, and cannot meet the needs of our modern society.

A case in point emerged after the 1994 elections. Leaders of the victorious Republican party saw the overwhelming vote for their candidates in those elections as a mandate from the electorate to bring about what many of them have termed a "revolutionary" shift in the size and direction of American government. High on the list of priorities for the newly elected Republican majority in Congress were proposals to add to the Constitution of the United States amendments on balanced budgets and congressional term limits. The Republicans were also committed to passing legislation that would make it more difficult for Congress to raise taxes (by requiring a three-fifths majority vote on such issues) and easier for a president to control excessive or frivolous congressional spending (by giving him a line-item veto over congressional spending legislation). If adopted, these proposals would have a significant and fundamental impact on the way American government operates.

Despite this push to radically transform the basic institutions of government, *none of those supporting such changes felt they were fundamentally altering the basic nature of the Constitution.* Rather, they saw such changes as a means for restoring the promise and premise of America's Constitution. "The [U.S.] Capitol once stood as a shining example for the entire world of free people governing themselves," noted a highly partisan document released by the Republican leadership after the election.

> Republicans want to return that trust to the American people. For more than forty years, the Democrats ran Congress with an iron fist, *ruining the tradition and trust created by our Founding Fathers.* Republicans have taken this responsibility seriously, and want to prove to the American people that our system of government *can work as intended,* with free people responsibly governing themselves (italic emphasis added).[3]

To understand that apparent contradiction, one must consider the influence of one of the most fundamental myths of American government: the *myth of the timeless and perfect Constitution.* It is a myth so deeply ingrained in the American view of government that it influences the attitudes of those who seek fundamental change as well as those who want to maintain the system as it is. Holders of that myth regard the U.S. Constitution as an almost sacred blueprint for an ageless and nearly flawless "machine that would go of itself"—a device so wisely crafted that it has needed only occasional adjustment during its more than two hundred years of constant operation. Yes, twenty-seven times the blueprint has been modified through the amendment process. But to those who adhere to the myth of the timeless and perfect Constitution—whether they advocate change or not— the framers' magnificent creation continues to provide the basic machinery and principles of government.[4]

The power of that myth can be found throughout the nation's history. In 1791, just two years after the U.S. Constitution was ratified and began operating, a senator commented that one would think that "neither Wood grew nor Water run in America, before the late happy Adoption of the New Constitution."[5] In 1861, leaders of the seceding Confederate States of America adopted the text of the 1787 Constitution and its amendments as their own, making only minor corrections for style. Thus, the confederate president, Jefferson Davis, was able to proclaim that, in fact, it was the so-called "rebels" of the South who "were upholding the true doctrines of the Federal Constitution."[6]

In this chapter we will look closely at the U.S. Constitution through a lens that attempts to penetrate the myth of the timeless and perfect Constitution. We will look at the political and intellectual conditions that influenced the framers of the Constitution in order to understand the political world from their perspective. Then we will describe the document itself, and how it has changed over the past two centuries. Finally, we will pay special attention to the enduring principles of government found in the Constitution and consider the central role these play in sustaining the myth of the timeless and perfect Constitution.

The Setting for Constitutional Change

Why do people develop constitutions? The obvious and simple answer is that when two or more people work together to resolve mutual problems, their efforts eventually require that they organize and establish rules under which to operate. At minimum, constitutional structures and procedures help sustain collective efforts and prevent the deterioration of social relationships into violent clashes over who is in charge and how things get done.

For the framers of the U.S. Constitution, that question is not so clearly or simply answered. For one thing, when they met in Philadelphia in May 1787 there was already a constitution in place.

The **Articles of Confederation** were written in 1777 and ratified in 1781 as America's first constitution. They established a loose union of states (a "firm league of friendship") and a relatively weak national congress. The national congress comprised a single body in which each state had one vote. That body could exercise significant powers if it could muster the nine-thirteenths majority it took to pass any major legislation. For instance, under the Articles the congress was empowered to make war and peace, send and receive foreign ambassadors, borrow money and establish a monetary system, build a navy and develop an army in cooperation with the states, fix uniform standards of weights and measures, and even settle disputes among the states. However, it was powerless to levy and collect taxes or duties, and it could not regulate foreign or interstate commerce. There was no executive to enforce acts of the congress and no national court system. As for amending the Articles themselves, it took a unanimous vote of the member states to make such fundamental changes in the national government.

The meeting at Philadelphia was convened because many of the country's political leaders saw that the national government under the Articles lacked the strength to cope with the young republic's problems. For example, by 1787 it was clear to many officials that the national government under the Articles could not conduct an effective foreign policy. Despite the colonists' victory in the American Revolution, the British did not relinquish the Northwest Territories along the Great Lakes. Furthermore, the Spanish remained a hostile presence in Florida and what was then the Southwest. Encouraged by both Britain and Spain, Native American tribes harassed Americans all along the new nation's frontier.

The national government was just as ineffective within its borders. One group of North Carolinians declared an independent "State of Franklin" in 1784 and actively sought annexation by the Spanish; and while New York and New Hampshire argued over claims to the territory of Vermont, residents of that area attempted to have themselves annexed by the British as part of Canada.[7]

Even worse was the Confederation's inability to deal with the nation's financial problems. Without the power to tax, the national congress had to rely on funds provided by the states. Its requests for funds from the states were increasingly ignored. The country had accumulated a large public debt during the Revolutionary War, and much of it remained unpaid. When some states began to print worthless paper money to pay off their debts, spiraling inflation hit the economy.

Economic conditions under the Articles were not good. Within the states, many small farmers faced bankruptcy and the loss of their farms. In western Massachusetts, where the situation was particularly bad, a group of farmers led by a former revolutionary war officer, Daniel Shays, disrupted court foreclosure proceedings in September 1786 and several months later tried unsuccessfully to seize a national government arsenal. That incident, known as *Shays's Rebellion*, convinced many of the young nation's leaders that changes had to be made in America's governmental system.[8]

The Framers

Who were those leaders? What do we know about them? We know there were fifty-five of them who came to Philadelphia in 1787, all white males. Women and African-Americans, as well as other racial minorities, were excluded from this momentous gathering. Although we frequently honor these men as the nation's "Founding Fathers," most of their names are unfamiliar to us. Among them were merchants, physicians, bankers, planters, and soldiers. Their average age was forty-three; the youngest was Jonathan Dayton of New Jersey at twenty-six, and the oldest was Benjamin Franklin at eighty-one. More than half were trained in the law, and more than two-thirds had served in the Continental Congress, which had governed the new nation during the Revolutionary War. At least twelve were receiving a major portion of their income from public office at the time the Philadelphia convention assembled. That summer they took part in a rare moment of "decisive political creation": they applied their knowledge and experience of government to the design of a new constitution.[9]

According to observers at the time, the delegates included some rather interesting personalities. Gouverneur Morris, a delegate from Pennsylvania, played a major role in drafting the Constitution. A member of a well-known family who lost a leg in a childhood accident, Morris had been active in New York State politics before relocating to Philadelphia. A contemporary noted that he possessed "one of the best organized heads on the continent, but without manners, and, if his enemies are to be believed, without principles." Hugh Williamson, a delegate from North Carolina, was a Pennsylvania-born physician, preacher, mathematician, astronomer, and businessman. A "leading light" at the convention, Williamson was regarded as "extremely bizarre, loving to hold forth, but speaking with spirit." And Nicholas Gilman, a bachelor delegate from New Hampshire who played a relatively minor role in the proceedings, was characterized as a "pretentious young man; little loved by his colleagues."[10]

Mostly well educated and wealthy, the delegates included at least two men of international reputation: George Washington and Benjamin Franklin. A popular and imposing figure, Washington was unanimously elected to chair the meeting. A tight-lipped person, the fifty-five-year-old general contributed little to the convention's debates but could enforce its strict rules because the delegates feared his anger.

Constitutional Convention

The Constitution was shaped by several compromises reached through debates of the 1787 convention.

Benjamin Franklin was well regarded by the other delegates, and many constantly sought his opinions. At eighty-one years of age, his physical powers were failing him. He was so ill at times that prisoners from the city jail were assigned the task of carrying him from his home to the nearby sessions in a specially designed sedan chair. Despite being well prepared for the meetings, he was not always attentive during the convention's debates and rarely spoke. Nevertheless, his influence helped in the eventual adoption of the document. During the final days of the convention, he expressed his support by noting that whenever a group of men are gathered to write a constitution, "you inevitably assemble with those men all their prejudices, their passions, their errors of opinion, their local interests, and their selfish views." One can hardly expect, he argued, that any such gathering would produce a "perfect" government. "It therefore astonishes me," he continued, "to find this system approaching so near to perfection as it does. . . . Thus I consent . . . to this Constitution, because I expect no better, and because I am not sure that it is not the best."[11]

The Roots of the Constitution

From a historical perspective, Franklin's astonishment is itself surprising, for the framers of the Constitution were hardly as diverse in their "prejudices" and "passions" as he thought. Despite many disagreements and debates over specifics, the framers shared a common legal and intellectual heritage. In that sense, the roots of the Constitution run deep. To understand the unique circumstances that led to its creation, we must explore the traditions that guided its authors.[12]

The British Constitutional Heritage

With few exceptions, the leaders of the American Revolution respected the British constitutional system. Indeed, many of them saw the Revolution as a fight to secure the rights they had assumed to be theirs as Englishmen.[13] Therefore, when the time came to devise their own system of government, the framers relied heavily on the British constitutional tradition.[14]

What was that tradition? The question is not easy to answer. The British constitution was not then—and is not now—found in any single document. Rather, the British constitution consists of three British legal institutions with deep historical roots: charters, common law, and several major statutes.

Charters.   During the Middle Ages, **feudalism** dominated European society: it involved social, political, and economic arrangements through which landless families secured farmland and protection in exchange for providing services and resources to the land's owner. These arrangements were sometimes written down in agreements called charters. A **charter** described the rights and duties of both the landowner and those bound to him. It was usually drawn up to settle or avoid disputes in the feudal relationship.

In 1215 such a disagreement about the rights of those who served under the British Crown caused a major conflict between King John and the English nobility. After losing on the battlefield, John signed the **Magna Carta,** a document that reaffirmed long-standing rights and duties of the nobility and defined the limits placed on the king. The charter stands for the principle that everyone, including the king, must obey the law. Over the centuries it became an almost sacred guarantee of law and justice among citizens of the United States as well as England.[15]

Common Law.   During medieval times, monarchs, not legislatures, made laws. A king or queen would proclaim the law of the land, sometimes (but not always) after seeking the advice of a legislative body. Legislatures did not become a major source of laws in England until the 1600s. In the meantime, a large gap remained between the broad coverage of most royal proclamations and the details of legal disputes.

Into that legal breach stepped judges appointed by the British Crown to settle such disputes, and from their work came common law. **Common law,** also called judge-made law, represents the collection of legal doctrines that grew out of the many cases heard by those judges. Over an extended period of time, some of those doctrines developed into basic principles of law applied throughout England and its expanding colonial empire.

When the British Parliament eventually began to pass laws, conflicts arose between its statutes and the common law being applied by the British courts. They emerged, in part, because many English judges and lawyers believed that common-law principles represented a set of "immutable and eternal" rules against which Parliament's actions should be measured.[16] These conflicts came to a head in 1610, when an English court held that an act of Parliament could be overturned if a judge determined that the law violated the basic tenets of common law.

Even though legal reforms have reduced the high status of common-law rules in both England and the United States, that tradition contributed two important constitutional principles. First, it established the idea that there was a higher law against which legislative actions should be measured. In the United States, the Constitution itself became that higher standard.[17] Second, this common-law tradition provided a basis for the power of courts to apply those standards and to nullify statutes and government actions that they judged to be in violation of a higher-law standard. That became the foundation of judicial review, which is a key ingredient in the operations of the American constitutional system.[18] (See the discussion of checks and balances later in this chapter.)

Major Statutes.   Several major acts of Parliament have also shaped the British constitutional tradition. The *British Bill of Rights* (1689), for instance, established some basic principles of constitutional government: Parliament's supremacy over the monarchy, guarantees of a jury trial, and prohibitions against excessive bail and cruel and unusual punishment. Other laws asserted the independence of the judicial branch from the monarchy (*Act of Settlement,* 1701) and the right of representation in determining taxes (*Petition of Right,* 1629)—an issue that would be central to the complaints of the North American colonists.

The Colonial Heritage

Most British colonies were established under royal charters allowing settlers to govern themselves in many matters. In several colonies, the settlers modified or supplemented these agreements. For example, the **Mayflower Compact,** written by the Pilgrims, set forth several major principles for the Plymouth Colony's government. That agreement and similar ones found throughout the colonies became part of the colonial heritage that helped shape the Constitution.[19]

When thinking about colonial rule, we often picture an oppressed people dominated by foreign rulers. We rarely think of colonial government as a breeding ground for self-government and openness. Yet from the 1630s until the American Revolution, England let its North American colonies govern themselves, making no major effort to establish a central administration for its growing empire.[20]

Each of the colonies remained primarily a self-governing entity, and by the early 1700s most had developed similar governmental structures. A typical colony had three branches of government: a governor appointed by the king, a legislature, and a relatively independent judiciary. Local government consisted of self-governing townships and counties. The future leaders of the American Revolution gained political experience and an understanding of how governments operate through participation in these colonial institutions.[21]

Intellectual Roots

The intellectual atmosphere of the time also influenced the framers of the Constitution. Raised in a society that took its religion seriously, they grew up with such concepts as equality before God and the integrity of each human life—concepts rooted in their *Judeo-Christian religious traditions.*[22] The idea of a covenant, or contract, among members of society developed from those traditions, as did the distrust of the monarchy and the need for a system of laws to protect individual rights.

The framers were also children of the **Enlightenment.** Usually dated from the 1600s through the 1700s, that period in European intellectual history was dominated by the idea that human reason, not religious tradition, was the primary source of knowledge and wisdom. On issues related to government and politics, a number of writers set the tone of discussions among the framers and their peers in the colonies.

Among the most controversial Enlightenment writers was Thomas Hobbes. Writing in the middle 1600s, Hobbes argued that governments were not formed because God had conferred political authority on a specific ruling family. In his most famous work, *Leviathan* (1651), Hobbes contended that governments were formed by an agreement among rational individuals who, living without government in a brutish state of nature, realized it was in their self-interest to subject themselves to an all-powerful ruler. Thus Hobbes argued that government depended on the consent of the governed. Although he was no advocate of democracy (he wrote in defense of the British monarchy), his views proved helpful in establishing the rational basis of government.[23]

Another British political philosopher, John Locke, was perhaps the most influential of the Enlightenment authors among the colonists. He offered an explanation of political life that carried Hobbes's argument further by asserting that people possess an inherent right to revolution. In *Two Treatises on Government* (1690), Locke argued that individuals form governments as a matter of convenience to deal with the depraved behavior of some individuals. Thus, any government can continue to exist as long as it proves convenient to its citizens and does not interfere with their pursuit of life, liberty, and property. But if the government violates this arrangement, then the citizens have a right to emigrate or resist. Ultimately, this view sanctions the right of citizens to replace that government with another.[24]

The work of a French aristocrat, Charles de Montesquieu, clearly influenced those who wrote the Constitution. The framers relied especially on his book *The Spirit of the Laws,* which was first published in Paris in 1748. In that work Montesquieu argued that the best government is so designed that no person or group can oppress others. This end is best achieved, Montesquieu wrote, by separating the legislative, executive, and judicial functions into three distinct branches of government.[25]

Finally, just as the seeds of the American Revolution were being planted in the 1750s and 1760s, a Swiss-born philosopher, Jean-Jacques Rousseau, published several works arguing for a more extreme version of popular sovereignty than that offered by Locke. According to Rousseau, the best form of government is one that reflects the general will of the people, or **popular sovereignty,** which is the sum total of the interests that all citizens have in common. Rousseau's major writings influenced the French Revolution of 1789 much more than the American Revolution, and most of the framers probably regarded him as too radical. Nevertheless, he was read widely and had many followers in the American colonies. Among them was Thomas Paine, a British-born American revolutionary whose pamphlets had a great influence during the American Revolution. His best-known work, *Common Sense* (1776), is among the most often cited writings to come out of the American Revolution.

The Onset of Revolution

In the 1760s British policies toward the North American colonies changed. After nearly 150 years of relative freedom from direct interference from England, the colonists found themselves under increasing pressure from London. Britain needed men and resources to fight the French and so began to impose demands and commercial restrictions on the American colonists. Given their legal, political, and intellectual heritage, it is not surprising that some colonists responded with calls for revolutionary actions.

In 1765 the British passed the *Stamp Act*—the first tax levied directly on the colonists by Parliament. Relying on their view of the rights granted all British subjects under English law, colonial leaders protested against this "taxation without representation." The Stamp Act was repealed within a few months, but other controversies soon arose. For instance, the British granted a monopoly over the sale of tea to a British firm, thus interfering with the interests of many colonial merchants. In 1773 a group of Boston citizens responded by raiding a ship loaded with tea and dumping its contents overboard. That incident, now known as the *Boston Tea Party,* caused the British to close Boston Harbor and tighten control over the colonial government in Massachusetts. The events leading to rebellion soon escalated, and by 1774 even some of the moderate voices in colonial politics were calling for change.

Representatives from the colonies gathered as the First Continental Congress in Philadelphia in September 1774. After passing resolutions protesting recent British actions, the delegates set a date for reconvening the next year and adjourned. By the time they met again as the Second Continental Congress in May 1775, colonists and British troops had exchanged gunfire at Concord and Lexington.

The Second Continental Congress took a number of steps that officially launched the American Revolution. It organized itself as a provisional government, and in June 1775 it created a continental army, to be headed by George Washington. In May 1776, the congress voted to take the final step of drawing up a statement declaring the colonies free and independent states. On July 2, 1776, it adopted the **Declaration of Independence.** Two days later independence was formally declared.

The Declaration of Independence accomplished several objectives. It denounced the British for abusing the rights given the colonists under the British constitution and long-standing traditions of self-government. It proclaimed the intention of the colonial revolutionaries to sever their ties with England and explained the reasons for such drastic action. Most important, it articulated two fundamental principles under which the newly formed nation would be governed. First, the Declaration held that governments have one primary purpose: to secure the "unalienable rights" of their citizens, among which are "life, liberty, and the pursuit of happiness." Second, it stated that such governments derive their powers and authority from the "consent of the governed." The signers of the Declaration asserted that when any government violates the rights it was established to secure, "it is the Right of the People to alter or to abolish it" and to create a new government in its place.[26]

What They Did

As noted before, the "new government" created in the immediate aftermath of the American Revolution—the Articles of Confederation—had developed some significant flaws by 1787, thus leading to the Philadelphia meeting. Although originally charged with recommending changes to the Articles, the delegates soon assumed the broader task of constructing an entirely new set of institutions and rules.

The framers designed a system of government that met several of the basic requirements of any constitution. To shape a viable national government, they needed to establish its legitimacy and work out its basic structures. Through the Constitution, they created the three branches of government and defined and limited their powers. They also devised formal procedures by which the Constitution itself could be amended.

Establishing Legitimacy

A government cannot be effective unless it possesses power—that is, the ability to carry out its policies and enforce its laws. Even more important, government should have its citizens believe that it possesses the ability to exercise authority and power (see the discussion in Chapter 1). How many Americans would voluntarily file their federal income taxes each year with the Internal Revenue Service by April 15 if they thought the government could not collect those revenues? How many car manufacturers would include pollution-reducing devices in their vehicles if they believed the government could not enforce its environmental protection laws?

The power and authority of any government is enhanced by the willingness of its citizens to obey government officials. A government is most effective when its citizens believe that those officials have a right to pass and enforce laws. That is why the establishment of government **legitimacy** is so important. It provides government with the effective authority it needs to govern.

The legitimacy of the U.S. government is rooted in the Preamble to the Constitution. In a few words, the framers make clear the source of authority for the republic. "We the People . . ." begins the Preamble. The choice of words is important. The government created under the Articles of Confederation in 1777 was called a "firm league of friendship" among the states. Ultimately, all authority was retained by the states. The Constitution, in contrast, leaves no doubt that the national government's right to exercise authority—its legitimacy—comes directly from the people and not from the states (see Table 2.1).[27]

Structuring Authority

The framers of the Constitution faced two challenges when deciding how to structure the authority of the new government. First, they had to create a stronger national government while allowing the states to retain their authority. Second, they had to deal with the issue of how to allocate authority within the national government itself.

cut to the chase

TABLE 2.1

Comparing America's
Two Constitutions

	Articles of Confederation	Constitution of the United States
Establishing legitimacy	Through a "firm league of friendship" among the states	Through "We the People"— all citizens of the nation
Structuring authority	Through a confederacy, with ultimate authority residing in states	Through a federal arrangement, with national and state governments dividing and sharing authority
	Within the national government, in a single body—the congress	In three distinct branches of government: legislative, executive, judicial
Describing and distributing powers	Number of foreign and domestic powers listed in Article IX, many limited to not interfere with state authority	Delegated and implied powers for national government in Article I Concurrent and reserved powers for states
Limiting powers	Many limitations on national powers, with deference to states	Provision in Article I Bill of Rights
Allowing for change	Amendments require unanimous vote of states No national courts to interpret meaning of Articles	Elaborate amendment process requiring significant majorities rather than unanimity Judicial review implied

Balancing National and State Authority.   The framers knew they had to create a stronger national government in order to contend with the problems plaguing the country under the Articles of Confederation. At the same time, they needed to make certain that their new constitution did not threaten the traditional authority of the thirteen states.

Under the Articles, ultimate government authority rested with the states that constituted the union. Whatever power the national government had was derived from the states' willingness to give up some of their authority to a central government. Such an arrangement is called a **confederation;** hence the title of the Articles.

In considering alternatives, the framers could have proposed a constitution based on a **unitary system** of government. In unitary governments, the ultimate authority rests with the national government, and whatever powers state or local governments have are derived from the central government. The framers would not have had to look far for examples, as each of the thirteen states was in fact a unitary government. Although each state contained towns, counties, and boroughs, those local governments exercised only such powers as were granted to them by a charter issued by the state government.

While seeking to move toward a stronger national government, the framers realized that their new constitution would not be ratified if it included a unitary form of government. In the end they created a hybrid—a mixture of confederation and unitary systems now called a **federation.** In a federation, the authority of government is shared by both the national and state governments. In its ideal form, a federal constitution gives some exclusive authority over some governmental tasks to the national government, while giving the states exclusive authority over other governmental matters. There would also be some areas where the two levels of government shared authority. Which areas of government would be distributed to the national government and which to the states is discussed below.

Structuring Authority Within the National Government.   Having established a national government with authority, the framers also had to develop structures of authority within the national government so that it could exercise its powers. Under the Articles of Confederation, whatever powers the national government possessed were exercised by a single body: the congress. In contrast, and following the model elaborated by Montesquieu in his *Spirit of the Laws,* the framers created three branches of government: Congress, the presidency, and the courts. They did so in the first three articles of the Constitution, which define these primary structures of government and outline the roles, powers, and responsibilities of the public officials who occupy these offices.

The basic structure of American government emerged from a series of compromises reached among the delegates to the Constitutional Convention. When the convention opened, the delegation from Virginia offered a series of resolutions for the meeting to consider. Under the *Virginia Plan,* there would be a **bicameral** (two-house) congress in which each state's representation would be based on its population relative to other states. Under the Articles of Confederation, a state could send several representatives to congress, but each state had only a single vote. The Articles of Confederation also did not provide for separate executive or judicial branches of government at the national level; the Virginia Plan called for both.

Delegates from states with larger populations welcomed the Virginia Plan's provisions. But after lengthy debate, some delegates from the smaller states put forward a counterproposal. Known as the *New Jersey Plan,* it called for strengthening the existing Articles by adding executive and judicial offices. It also increased the powers of the Articles' **unicameral** (one-house) congress, especially its ability to force reluctant states to cooperate with the national government.

The delegates voted to reject the New Jersey Plan. However, the discussions about it drew attention to the many delegates who remained uncomfortable with key provisions of the Virginia Plan, especially on the question of representation. To avoid a stalemate, the delegates adopted what has become known as the **Great Compromise.** That proposal, offered by the Connecticut delegation, led to acceptance of the structure of American national government as we know it today. It called for the establishment of a bicameral congress consisting of a House of

Representatives in which states would be represented according to their population size, and a Senate where each state would have an equal voice. Article I of the Constitution outlined the composition of Congress and described the rules and restrictions that apply to both legislative bodies.

Furthermore, the Great Compromise contained provisions for executive and judicial branches of government. Article II of the Constitution established the executive offices of president and vice president and specified their qualifications for office. It also detailed the method for selecting those officials, but those provisions have since been changed by the Twelfth Amendment. Later sections of Article II described the president's general responsibilities and provided guidelines for relations with Congress. Article III created a judicial branch of government that is composed of "one supreme Court, and . . . such inferior Courts as the Congress may from time to time ordain and establish."

The Great Compromise was just one of many agreements among the framers to resolve the complex issues they faced (see Table 2.2). Out of such compromises came major provisions of the Constitution. Most important, each compromise made it possible for the framers to complete their work and create a document that had some hope of ratification.

TABLE 2.2 The Major Compromises	**Demands**	**Compromises**	**Demands**
		Great Compromise	
	States to have equal representation in Congress (New Jersey Plan)	Bicameral Congress with equal representation in Senate and population-based representation in House	States to be represented in Congress on the basis of population (Virginia Plan)
		3/5ths Compromise	
	Slaves to be counted for representation purposes, but not for taxation purposes	All slaves to be counted as 3/5ths of a person for both representation and taxation purposes	Slaves not to be counted for representation purposes, but to be counted for taxation purposes
		Commerce/Slave Trade Compromise	
	National government not to regulate slave trade or exports	Congress given power to regulate interstate and foreign commerce but not to impose tax on exports from any state; Congress not to act on slave trade until 1808	National government to have authority over all interstate and foreign trade
		Federalism	
	States to retain their legitimate authority in the government system	Division of legitimate authority between states and national government	An effective national government to be established

Distributing and Describing Government Powers

Having established a two-level structure of authority in the federal system, and having created the three branches within the national government, the framers next faced the task of dividing up the powers among the various institutions.

Powers in the Federal System.   The history and present-day operations of the federal system designed by the framers will be discussed in greater detail in Chapter 3, which focuses on federalism and intergovernmental relations. It is important at this juncture to understand how the framers allocated governmental authority between the national government and the states.

The powers given to Congress in Article I are central to the operations of the national government. They include a detailed list of responsibilities, such as the authority to tax, borrow money, regulate interstate commerce, coin money, declare war, and raise and support an army and navy. These and other powers identified in Section 8 of Article I constitute the **delegated powers** of American national government (see Figure 2.1). Many of these powers—such as the power to coin money, make treaties, and lay import duties—are granted exclusively to the national government; that is, they are denied to the states. Other delegated powers, however, are granted to the national government but not denied to the states—for example, the power to lay and collect taxes or to define criminal behavior and set punishments. These are called **concurrent powers.**

Article I, Section 8, of the Constitution also provides Congress with the authority "to make all Laws which shall be necessary and proper for carrying into Execution the foregoing Powers, and all other Powers vested by this Constitution in the Government of the United States." This **necessary and proper clause,** found in paragraph 18 of Section 8, establishes **implied powers** for Congress that go beyond those listed elsewhere in the Constitution. The U.S. Supreme Court, in *McCulloch* v. *Maryland* (1819), resolved the constitutionality of implied powers.

In that case, the Court considered whether Congress had the right to charter a Bank of the United States. The national bank was a controversial institution from the moment it was created by the first Congress, especially in the South and West, where bank policies were blamed for the nation's economic woes. Several states decided to challenge the constitutionality of the bank by imposing a tax on its local branches. When Maryland officials assessed a tax of $15,000 on the bank's Baltimore branch, the head cashier took state officials to court, charging that they did not have the authority to tax an agency of the national government. Maryland countered that the Bank of the United States was not a legally constituted agency of the federal government because no provision in the Constitution explicitly gives Congress the power to establish a national bank. The bank's lawyers, however, insisted that power to charter a bank is implied in the constitutional authority to collect taxes, borrow money, and regulate commerce.

The Supreme Court unanimously sided with the national government. "Let the end be legitimate," stated Chief Justice John Marshall, "let it be within the

Powers Granted by the Constitution

To the national government ("delegated" or "enumerated" powers; "implied" powers)	To both national and state governments ("concurrent" powers)	To the state governments ("reserved" powers)
• To "lay and collect taxes, duties, imposts, and excises" • To regulate interstate and foreign commerce • To borrow and coin money • To declare war • To raise and support an army • To maintain a navy • To provide for a militia • To govern territories and national property • To define and punish piracies and other high sea felonies • To establish post offices and post roads • To grant patents and copyrights • To set standards of weights and measures • To "make all laws necessary and proper to carry out the foregoing powers" (the "elastic clause" that grants "implied powers")	• To levy and collect taxes • To borrow money • To charter banks and corporations • To make and enforce laws • To establish courts • To take property for public purposes	• To conduct elections • To establish local governments • To regulate commerce within the state • To protect public health, safety, and morals • To ratify amendments to the Constitution • And all other powers not delegated to the national government nor denied to the states

Powers Denied by the Constitution

To the national government	To both national and state governments ("prohibited" powers)	To the state governments
• To tax commerce within a state • To give preference to one state over another in matters of commerce • To change state boundaries without state permission • To violate the Bill of Rights	• To grant titles of nobility • To tax exports • To permit slavery (added through 13th Amendment) • To deny citizens the right to vote because of race, color, sex (added through Amendments 15 and 19)	• To tax imports and exports • To coin money • To make treaties • To wage war • To deny due process and equal protection of the laws (added through 14th Amendment)

FIGURE 2.1

Constitutional Basis of the Federal System

The top middle box lists powers shared by the two levels of government; the bottom middle box shows powers denied to both. Powers on the upper left belong to the national government exclusively; those on the upper right are the states'.

scope of the Constitution, and all means which are appropriate, which are plainly adapted to that end, which are not prohibited, but consistent with the letter and spirit of the Constitution, are constitutional." In that decision, Marshall was agreeing with the national government that by giving Congress the explicit power to regulate commerce the framers of the Constitution implicitly granted Congress the right to charter a bank. This broad interpretation of the necessary and proper clause (also called the "elastic clause") altered the position of the states by greatly expanding the potential powers of the national government. That bank survived until President Andrew Jackson's opposition caused it to close in the 1830s. In 1913 Congress once again set up an agency for managing the banking system. That agency, the Federal Reserve System, still regulates the nation's major banks.[28] The right of Congress to establish such banks is implied in the necessary and proper clause.

The Constitution does not provide a specific list of the powers left to the states. In fact, there is no evidence that the framers of the Constitution even considered the issue. Writing in defense of the Constitution, James Madison noted that the framers felt there was no need to do so because the only powers given to the newly formed national government were those "enumerated" in the body of the Constitution. This approach left to the states the power over "all other objects."[29] This position was made explicit in the Tenth Amendment, which was added to the Constitution in 1791 (see the discussion of the Tenth Amendment in Chapter 3). That amendment declares that "powers not delegated to the United States by the Constitution, nor prohibited by it to the States, are reserved to the States respectively or to the people." Historically, these **reserved powers** have included such responsibilities as providing for public education, building local roads and highways, and regulating trade within a state's borders.

Powers Within the National Government.   Following Montesquieu's prescription, the framers gave each of the three branches of the national government a distinct part of the functions that any government must perform. According to this model, any government must do three things. It must pass laws (legislate), enforce those laws (execute), and settle disputes or controversies arising from application of the laws (adjudicate).

In Article I of the Constitution, the framers established Congress as the legislative branch. It is notable and important that they also chose Article I as the place to locate the delegated powers of the national government. That placement reflects the framers' desire to make certain that the representative parts of the national government—the House of Representatives and the Senate—would be the primary fount of authority at the national level.

In contrast, the description of executive power in Article II takes the form of noting what roles the president will play and what duties he or she will carry out. Chapter 11, on the presidency, describes in greater detail how those roles and duties have expanded over the two centuries.

Finally, Article III says little more than that the "judicial power of the United States shall be vested in one Supreme Court" and in whatever lower courts Congress establishes. As we discuss later in this chapter and again in Chapter 13, on the judiciary, the meaning of "judicial power" would be articulated in the landmark case of *Marbury* v. *Madison* in 1803.

Limiting Government Powers

The Constitution also sets limits on the powers of both the national and the state governments. For example, Section 9 of Article I forbids Congress to suspend the privilege of a writ of habeas corpus except in time of rebellion or invasion. A **writ of habeas corpus** is a court order that individuals can seek to protect themselves against arbitrary arrest and detention. By issuing such a writ, a court can order public officials to bring a suspect or detainee before a judge to determine whether he or she is being held on legal grounds. Another provision prohibits the national government from passing a bill of attainder or an ex post facto law. A **bill of attainder** is a legislative act that declares a person guilty of a crime and sets punishment without the benefit of a formal trial. An **ex post facto law** makes an action criminal even though it was legal when it was performed.

Perhaps the best-known limits on the powers of the national government are provided in the **Bill of Rights,** a term usually applied to the first ten amendments, which were added to the Constitution in 1791 (see Table 2.3). Most of these amendments guarantee the fundamental liberties of citizens (see Chapter 4, on rights and liberties). They were added to the Constitution to satisfy the demands of critics who complained during the ratification process that the original document did not adequately protect individual rights.[30]

The First Amendment protects freedom of expression—speech, press, assembly, and religion. Other amendments prohibit national officials from infringing on the right to bear arms (Second), from arbitrarily ordering families to quarter soldiers (Third), from conducting unreasonable searches and seizures (Fourth), from forcing any person to testify against himself or herself in a criminal trial (Fifth), and from requiring excessive bail or inflicting "cruel or unusual punishment" (Eighth).

The Fifth Amendment also forbids the national government to take any action that might deprive a person "of life, liberty, or property" without "due process of law" or "just compensation." The Sixth ensures a "speedy trial, by an impartial jury" in criminal cases, and the Seventh extends the right of jury trial to civil cases.

The Constitution also places limits on the powers and actions of the states. Section 10 of Article I, for instance, contains a list of powers denied to the states. Other sections set limits on the power of the states in relation to each other and to the national government. Article IV requires that each state give **full faith and credit** to the "Acts, Records, and judicial Proceedings of every other state." Thus a divorce granted in Nevada must be honored in New York, and vice versa. It also mandates that the "Citizens of each State shall be entitled to all Privileges and

TABLE 2.3	Rights Addressed	Amendment
The Bill of Rights Adopted in 1791	Freedom of expression	1. Freedom of religion, speech, press, assembly, and petition
	Personal security	2. Right to bear arms
		3. No quartering of troops without consent
		4. Protection against unreasonable search and seizures
	Fair treatment under law	5. Right to presentation of indictment; guarantee against double jeopardy, self-incrimination; guarantee of due process of law and just compensation
		6. Right to speedy and public trial
		7. Right to jury trial in civil cases
		8. Guarantees against excessive bails, fines, and punishments
	Reserved rights and powers	9. Powers reserved to the people
		10. Powers reserved to the states

Immunities of Citizens in the Several States." Under this **privileges and immunities** guarantee, the right you have as a twenty-one-year-old resident of New Jersey to purchase and consume alcohol in New York (where the legal age for alcohol purchase and consumption is twenty-one) cannot be denied to you just because you are from out of town. We take these provisions of the Constitution for granted today, but they were the source of considerable debate and compromise at the convention as the framers sought to create a strong national government while maintaining state autonomy.

Another problem the framers faced was how to ensure that the laws of the national government would take priority over the laws of the states. One proposal called for giving Congress the power to declare state laws illegal if they interfered with congressional policies. Another asked for a constitutional provision allowing national officials to use armed force if necessary to obtain state compliance. In the end, the delegates settled for a statement found in Article VI. It declares that the Constitution and all laws and treaties "made in Pursuance thereof" would be considered "the supreme Law of the Land." Commonly referred to as the **supremacy clause,** this provision was to be enforced through both national and state courts.

Allowing for Change

Like all constitutions, the American document also describes the way it can be changed through an amendment process. The framers did not make amending the Constitution easy. The procedures require action at both the state and the national level (see Figure 2.2). Amendments can be proposed in either of two ways: by a two-thirds vote of both houses of Congress or by a national convention

FIGURE 2.2

How the Constitution Can Be Amended

The framers created four methods for amending the Constitution. With the exception of the Twenty-first Amendment, only the Congress/state legislature route (at top) has so far been used.

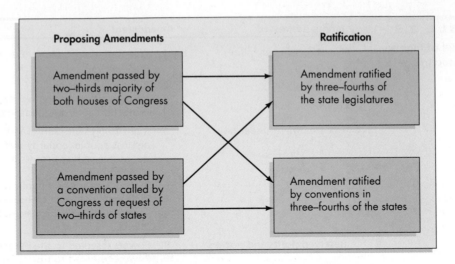

Proposing Amendments

Ratification

Amendment passed by two–thirds majority of both houses of Congress

Amendment ratified by three–fourths of the state legislatures

Amendment passed by a convention called by Congress at request of two–thirds of states

Amendment ratified by conventions in three–fourths of the states

called by Congress at the request of two-thirds of the states. Congress then decides how the amendment will be ratified: by three-fourths of the legislatures or by ratifying conventions in three-fourths of the states.

The method used for all but one of the Constitution's twenty-seven amendments has involved a proposal by Congress and ratification by state legislatures. The single exception was the Twenty-first Amendment, which repealed the Eighteenth (see the discussion of the "prohibition" amendments on page 47). In that case, the amendment was proposed by a two-thirds vote of Congress but was ratified by state conventions.

How difficult is this amendment process? Over the past two centuries, more than six thousand constitutional amendments have been proposed in Congress. Yet only twenty-seven have passed. Some proposed amendments are introduced in Congress but never come to a vote in either body. Some come to a vote in Congress, but fail to get the required two-thirds majority needed in each chamber. In June 1992, for example, a constitutional amendment requiring a balanced federal budget received a majority of votes in the U.S. House but still fell nine votes short of the two-thirds required for passage. At that point, a pending vote on the amendment scheduled for the U.S. Senate was withdrawn, but supporters vowed to renew their efforts the next year. In 1993, another balanced-budget amendment was introduced in the Senate. It too went down to defeat and was taken off the House agenda.

In 1995, leaders of the Republican majority in the House made passage of the amendment their first legislative priority as part of fulfilling their "Contract with America." Joined by many House Democrats, they sent the amendment to the Senate, where it was defeated by a single vote. The balanced budget amendment was one of the first items on the agenda of the U.S. Senate in 1997. Once again, the Senate could not muster the necessary votes to pass the amendment. Most observers believe the proposal will reemerge again.

WWW•

For more information on the long history of the Equal Rights Amendment, see the **Gitelson/ Dudley/Dubnick web site.**

CLOSER TO HOME

2.1   Changing State Constitutions

Changing the U.S. Constitution is no easy task. Of the more than ten thousand proposed amendments introduced in Congress since 1791, only thirty-three made it through the first step in the process and were submitted to the states for ratification. Of those, only twenty-seven were actually adopted.

The situation is quite different at the state level. For example, since its adoption in 1901, the Alabama state constitution has been amended 556 times. California's constitution is a bit older (adopted in 1879), and it has been amended 485 times. This is slightly more than South Carolina's 1896 constitution, which has been modified through amendments 463 times.

The oldest constitutions in the country are all found in New England. The constitution of the Commonwealth of Massachusetts is the oldest. In effect since 1780, it has been amended 117 times. New Hampshire's somewhat younger state charter has been modified 143 times. Vermont's constitution, which is next in age, is the shortest at 6,600 words—yet even it has been changed 50 times.

Louisiana holds the distinction not only of having the youngest constitution (1975), but also of having had the greatest number of constitutions—eleven different ones since it became a state in 1812. Although less than twenty-five years old, the Louisiana constitution has already been amended 54 times.

Historically, the trend in the states has been to make constitutional change easier and to give the general public a bigger role in initiating or approving amendments or other forms of constitutional revision. Today only Delaware does not provide a means for the public to participate in the process. In all states, the legislatures can propose an amendment, and almost all require voter approval of the legislative recommendations. Some states also allow a constitutional convention to be convened, either by the legislature or by petition. In some states, a question about whether a state constitutional convention should be called is required to be put before the voters every ten or twenty years. In other states, a constitutional study commission may be convened to consider and recommend changes.

In at least eighteen states, a constitutional amendment can be initiated through a petition circulated among voters. The number of valid voter signatures needed to get a proposal on the ballot varies: in California, for example, it must equal at least 8 percent of the total votes cast for governor in the last election. In Arizona, the requirement is 15 percent, whereas in North Dakota an amendment must gain the support of 4 percent of the entire state population to get on the ballot.

Sources: On the history of amending the national Constitution, see Richard B. Bernstein, with Jerome Agel, *Amending America: If We Love the Constitution So Much, Why Do We Keep Trying to Change It?* (New York: Times Books, 1993). On constitutional change in state governments, see Ann O'M. Bowman and Richard Kearney, *State and Local Government*, 3rd ed. (Boston: Houghton Mifflin, 1996), chap. 3.

Other proposals are not adopted because they fail to get the required number of states to ratify them. And in at least one instance it took more than two centuries for an amendment to obtain the ratification of enough states to actually become an amendment. The cases of the Equal Rights Amendment (ERA) and the Twenty-seventh Amendment show how difficult the amending process can be. The ERA stated that "equality of rights under the law shall not be denied or abridged by the United States or by any State on account of sex." The ERA was introduced in Congress at almost every session since 1923, but it remained tied up in the legislative process until 1972, when it finally received the needed approval of both the House and Senate. As proposed, the ERA needed to be ratified by thirty-eight states by June 30, 1982,[31] to become an amendment to the Constitution. Thirty-five states had given their approval of the ERA by 1978, but supporters could not muster enough votes in three other state legislatures to pass the proposed amendment. Despite that defeat, the ERA has been reintroduced in Congress at each session since 1983.

As for the Twenty-seventh Amendment, it took 203 years before it received the ratification of enough states to become part of the Constitution. Originally proposed as part of the Bill of Rights in 1789, it set limits on the power of sitting members of Congress to increase their own compensation. By the end of 1791, only six of the ten states needed for adoption at that time had voted to ratify the proposal. But the effort to pass the amendment was revived in the 1980s, and on May 7, 1992, the Michigan legislature formally ratified the amendment, giving it the support of the thirty-eight states required for adoption.

The Constitution has been successfully amended seventeen times since the Bill of Rights (see Table 2.4).[32] Five of those amendments have extended voting rights to a variety of groups: to all men, regardless of race (Fifteenth); to women (Nineteenth); to residents of Washington, D.C. (Twenty-third); and to all citizens eighteen years of age or older (Twenty-sixth). In addition, the Twenty-fourth Amendment eliminated the practice of using poll taxes to stop a citizen from voting.

Another group of amendments changed some of the rules for electing officials as well as the period of time and conditions under which they serve in office. The Twelfth Amendment spells out the process for electing the president and vice president. The Seventeenth Amendment calls for the direct election of senators; before its adoption, senators were elected by state legislatures. The Twentieth Amendment changes the dates for the inauguration of the president and the convening of Congress, and the Twenty-fifth clarifies the procedures for presidential succession in cases of disability, death, or resignation. The Twenty-second Amendment limits the tenure of elected presidents to two full four-year terms. The Twenty-seventh Amendment prohibits a sitting Congress from giving itself a raise.

Other amendments altered the constitutional powers of government institutions. For example, the Eleventh Amendment limits the power of federal courts to hear cases involving the states, and the Sixteenth Amendment gives Congress the power to establish a national income tax.

The Thirteenth and Fourteenth Amendments address the rights of citizens. The Thirteenth Amendment ended slavery. The Fourteenth forbids states to deny individuals the rights guaranteed under the Constitution; these rights include due process and equal protection of the law for all. In Chapter 4, on rights and liberties, we discuss the important role that last amendment has played in the development of American civil liberties and civil rights.

TABLE 2.4

Amendments to the
Constitution 11–27

Amendment	Year Proposed by Congress	Year Adopted	What It Does
11	1794	1798	Gives states immunity from certain legal actions
12	1803	1804	Changes the selection of president and vice president through the electoral college
13	1865	1865	Abolishes slavery
14	1866	1868	Defines citizenship and citizen rights; provides due process and equal protection of the laws
15	1869	1870	Extends the right to vote to African-American males
16	1909	1913	Gives Congress power to impose income tax
17	1912	1913	Provides for direct election of U.S. senators
18	1917	1919	Outlaws alcoholic beverages
19	1919	1920	Extends the right to vote to women
20	1932	1933	Changes the dates for the start of congressional and presidential terms
21	1933	1933	Repeals Eighteenth Amendment
22	1947	1951	Limits presidential tenure in office
23	1960	1961	Extends the right to vote in presidential elections to residents of the District of Columbia
24	1962	1964	Prohibits the use of tax payment (poll tax) as a basis for qualification to vote
25	1965	1967	Establishes procedures for presidential succession, for determining presidential disability, and for filling vacancy in vice-presidency
26	1971	1971	Lowers the voting age to eighteen
27	1789	1992	Limits Congress's ability to change its own compensation

Only two amendments have actually addressed questions of public policy explicitly. In fact, both focused on the same issue: the production and consumption of alcoholic beverages in the United States. In 1919 the states formally ratified the Eighteenth Amendment, prohibiting the manufacture, sale, or transportation of alcoholic beverages in the United States. In 1933, however, the Twenty-first Amendment repealed that prohibition.

While making the formal amendment process difficult, the framers left the door open to changes that might occur through interpretation of constitutional provisions.[33] One of the framers, Alexander Hamilton, stated that a constitution "cannot possibly calculate" for changing conditions and must therefore "consist only of general provisions."[34] By interpreting those "general provisions," public officials have given meaning and shape to the Constitution over the last two centuries (see Chapter 4, on rights and liberties).

In summary, as originally designed, the U.S. Constitution provides five critical foundations on which today's American government operates:

- It establishes the legitimacy of the national government.

- It describes the basic institutional structures of American government.

- It defines the powers of those institutions.

- It places limits on those powers.

- It specifies the procedures used to make changes in the government system.

From the perspective of the myth discussed earlier, has the Constitution of 1787 endured as timeless and perfect, or has American government emerged as a completely different entity despite the existence of that document?

As you continue to learn about the reality of American government and politics in the chapters that follow, it will become increasingly evident that the details and actual operations of American government today bear little resemblance to those outlined in the U.S. Constitution, even as amended. Certainly, the major institutions established by the framers can be recognized, but in many respects Congress, the presidency, and the judiciary are quite different in structure and process from those laid out in Articles I, II, and III. Thus, some might argue that the written Constitution is only a national symbol, like the flag or the bald eagle. It can hardly be regarded as an accurate description or a set of governmental operating instructions. If that is the case, then perhaps we might consider calling a national convention to rewrite that document to reflect the way American government actually operates.

However, there is another side to the written Constitution that we need to consider before taking such a radical step. The Constitution of 1787 did more than establish the machinery of American government. It also contains several basic principles that have served the nation well for more than two centuries.

The Enduring Principles

It would be incorrect to think that the U.S. constitutional system has succeeded because it is an efficiently operating, perfectly crafted, and carefully maintained machine. Instead, American citizens have benefited from a living constitution that has thrived because of *five enduring principles* that have allowed our system of government to adapt to the changing conditions of the last two hundred years. These principles—the rule of law, republicanism, the separation of powers, checks and balances, and national supremacy—are at the heart of that living constitutional system.

The Rule of Law

Although the words **rule of law** are never mentioned in the Constitution, the idea is one of the most important legacies of the framers. As a general concept, the rule of law has its roots deep in western civilization, but it emerged in its modern form during the 1600s in Europe. According to the rule-of-law concept, there exists "a body of rules and procedures governing human and governmental behavior that have an autonomy and logic of their own." Under such rules and procedures, government and public officials are bound by standards of fairness, impartiality, and equality before the law.[35]

The rule-of-law principle, which can be found in a number of constitutional provisions, implies that those provisions limit the powers of both national and state governments. For example, in Article IV of the Constitution the framers included a provision that the "Citizens of each State shall be entitled to the Privileges and Immunities of Citizens in the several states." The privileges and immunities clause was intended to prevent any state from using its legal powers to discriminate against out-of-staters. Similarly, states are prohibited from passing any "Law impairing the Obligation of Contracts," thus preventing any governing group from arbitrarily voiding earlier agreements. That last provision was especially important to those among the framers who feared the passage of debtor-relief laws. The Bill of Rights added strength to the rule-of-law principle through the Fifth Amendment by requiring "due process of law" and "just compensation" whenever government initiates adverse actions against a citizen. The "equal protection of the laws" clause in the Fourteenth Amendment is still further evidence of how important this principle has been throughout our history.[36]

Another way of thinking about the rule-of-law principle is that in American government the rulers, like those they rule, are answerable to the law. No individual stands above the law, regardless of the background of that person or the office that he or she holds. Just as there are laws that address the behavior of general citizens, so there are laws that focus on the behavior of public officials. Those laws generally set limits on the powers of the officials or prescribe the procedures they must use in carrying out their jobs. Under the rule-of-law principle, those limits and prescriptions must be adhered to if the American constitutional system is to function properly.

How important is this constitutional principle? The rule of law has its greatest impact on the day-to-day operations of American government. Almost every action government agencies undertake, from the routine task of issuing monthly social security checks to dramatic efforts to help those surviving earthquakes and other disasters, is carefully designed to meet the requirements of due process of law and other constitutional standards that are the foundation of the rule of law.

Nixon Resigns

The 1974 resignation of President Richard M. Nixon demonstrated the power of the rule-of-law principle as a fundamental tenet of our constitutional system. Under that principle, no one—not even the president of the United States—stands above the law.

Violations of those procedures or standards are likely to lead to legal challenges. In fact, both state and federal courts are constantly hearing criminal cases and civil lawsuits in which possible violations of the rule of law are at issue.[37]

No one is exempt from the rule-of-law principle. The most powerful political officials have had to bend to its force. In August 1974, for example, President Richard M. Nixon resigned in the face of charges that he took part in a criminal cover-up of White House involvement in a break-in into the Democratic party's national headquarters at the Watergate office complex in Washington, D.C. Although Nixon and many of his supporters perceived the *Watergate cover-up* as a relatively minor offense, the president's attempt to circumvent the law resulted in enough political pressure to bring about the first presidential resignation in American history. Nixon and others learned that no public official, not even the president, stands above the law.

Republicanism

Despite the phrase "We the People," the Constitution's framers had questions about the ability of the American people to rule themselves directly. In turning to **republicanism,** the framers created a government in which decisions are made by elected or appointed officials who are ultimately answerable to the people. The framers opposed a direct democracy because they distrusted human nature and the capacity ordinary citizens have to govern themselves.

We know something about the framers' views on democracy thanks to documents such as the *Federalist Papers,* a series of editorials that James Madison, Alexander Hamilton, and John Jay wrote in 1788 to support the ratification of the Constitution. In the "Federalist No. 10" (which is reprinted in the Appendix), for instance, Madison argued that democracies "have ever been spectacles of turbulence and contention; have ever been found incompatible with personal security, or the rights of property; and have ever been as short in their lives, as they have been violent in their deaths."

What did the framers see in republicanism that they did not see in direct democracy? Again, we turn to the "Federalist No. 10," where Madison argued that the problems of government can be traced to the "mischiefs of faction." He defined a faction as a group that puts its shared interests ahead of the rights of others or the interests of the community as a whole. These self-serving factions can be small or large; they can even include a majority of the people. According to Madison, all factions pose a threat to the general well-being of society. Because the causes of faction are basic to human nature, eliminating them is impossible. Thus, if any government is to serve the general interest of the people, it must be designed so that the potentially destructive power of factions can be eliminated or controlled.

Madison and the framers favored a republican form of government in which the people had some voice—but a voice filtered through their representatives. The community was to be governed "by persons holding their offices . . . for a limited time or during good behavior." And although all officials would be answerable to the people, some would be more insulated from public pressure than others. Members of the House of Representatives were to have the most exposure: they alone would be elected directly by the American voters and have comparatively brief terms, two years. Senators and the president were assigned longer terms, and under the original provisions of the Constitution, the people did not elect them directly. Instead, state legislators selected senators, and an electoral college, with members selected by the states, chose the president. These methods were later changed by constitutional amendments and by the action of state legislatures. Supreme Court judges received additional protection from the whims of constantly changing public opinion. They were given lifetime appointments and could be removed only through the lengthy and difficult process called impeachment (see discussion below).

Although the framers felt impelled to take these precautions, they never lost sight of the basic principle of republicanism: that the ultimate responsibility of government officials is to the American public.

Separation of Powers

The principle of the **separation of powers** is also linked with the effort to control factions. By splitting government authority among several branches of government and giving each an area of primary responsibility, the framers sought to

MYTHS IN POPULAR CULTURE

2.1   A Paper Constitution in the Television Age

In contrast to the myth of a timeless and perfect constitution, some critics argue that just the opposite is true—that the Constitution is outdated and irrelevant in today's fast-moving and swiftly changing times. They point out that the number and composition of the American people have changed significantly over the past two centuries. Equally important, they say, is the extent to which basic social relationships—including the way Americans think about social problems and communicate with each other—have also changed radically.

The framers grew up during the Enlightenment, or the "Age of Reason." They matured in a time when the principal vehicle for exchanging ideas was the written word. It was, in the words of media critic Neil Postman, the Age of Paper.

Why is the medium of the period important? In the 1960s, Marshall McLuhan, another student of popular culture and media, wrote a book that radically transformed the way we look at modern society. In *Understanding Media,* McLuhan argues that *what* we say is not as important as the *medium through which* we say it. In a phrase that has become central to the study of popular culture, McLuhan boldly posits: "the medium is the message!"

The written word had considerable impact on the way the framers thought. "To engage the written word means to follow a line of inference-making and reasoning," argues Postman. "It means to uncover lies, confusions, and overgeneralizations, to detect abuses of logic and common sense. It also means to weigh ideas, to compare and contrast assertions, to connect one generalization to another."

That the Constitution was written in the Age of Paper tells us a great deal about the form, content, and debate that surrounded the document's birth. The framers would not be satisfied with the type of "unwritten" constitution found in England, where

tradition and several different documents were considered sufficient; nor would they want to merely create a patchwork of institutions through amendments to the Articles of Confederation. Instead, they insisted on having the Constitution take the form of words set forth on a freshly drawn legal document that contained relatively coherent provisions for the operations of American government.

Although much of the debate over the Constitution took place in taverns and other public meeting places, both supporters and opponents used newspapers and pamphlets to make their points. As noted in this chapter, a great deal of our knowledge about what the framers meant to say comes from *The Federalist Papers,* which were originally published in New York newspapers as part of the campaign for ratification in that state. The antifederalists' opinion was also found in the popular medium of the day. As a result of that medium, we have a record of some of the most intelligent political debate to occur on these shores.

We can only wonder what the Constitution would have been like if it were drawn up and debated during the middle of the nineteenth century—what Postman terms the "Age of Telegraphy"—or during our own time—in the "Age of Television." The written word is now subordinate to pictures on small screens, which seek more to entertain than inform and which provide little or no opportunity for intelligent discourse. What form would a new constitution take in this Age of Television? Would we insist on a written legal document, or would we rather have a collection of sights and sounds on videocassette or laser disc? Would the content reflect the crafting of carefully selected and meaningful words, or would it rely on images that generate more "heat" than meaning? And what kind of debate would we have: a well-reasoned discussion on the pros and cons of important issues, or speeches filled with symbolic gestures and empty sound bites?

As critical as Postman and others are of the Age of Television, one must also wonder what will happen as we enter the Age of the Computer. Some look at the revolution in word processing, telecommunications, and publishing and see the computer as a vehicle for returning to a "reasoning world" in which words are at the center of discourse and debate. Others, however, are not so sanguine. The Age of the Computer also promises even more reliance on sights and sounds, and information moving too fast to allow logical and reasoned thought.

Of course, at present the myth of the timeless and perfect Constitution is so strong that we are un-

likely to witness any movement to replace it with a new one. But the idea of an outdated and irrelevant Constitution highlights the dilemma of operating under a constitution developed during the Age of Paper. As we see in this chapter, the principles established in the Constitution have been adaptable to the changing media through two centuries of technological innovation. We can only speculate whether these principles can be adapted to the new challenge posed by the Age of the Computer.

Sources: For the quotation above and further discussion of these points, see Neil Postman, *Amusing Ourselves to Death: Public Discourse in the Age of Show Business* (New York: Penguin Books, 1985), especially pp. 44–63; 125–141. See also Marshall McLuhan, *Understanding Media: The Extensions of Man* (New York: McGraw-Hill, 1964).

minimize the possibility that one faction could gain control. "The accumulation of all powers, legislative, executive, and judiciary, in the same hands," states Madison, "may justly be pronounced the very definition of tyranny."[38] Thus, to help avoid tyranny, the power to make, to execute, and to judge the law was divided among the three branches: Congress, the presidency, and the courts.

This principle was an important one for the framers, who debated many hours about the design of the national government. The idea was not to distribute powers among the three branches in order to increase government efficiency, but to prevent efficiency that they regarded as potentially dangerous.[39] Each branch was to stand independent of the others when exercising its governmental authority. In this way, the American public would be protected against the tyranny that Madison and others so feared.

The framers reinforced this principle in several ways beyond just giving each institution a distinct role in government. The Constitution makes certain that those holding a position in one branch will not serve in either of the others. This prohibition has been both tightened and loosened in practice over the years. During the 1960s, Supreme Court Justice Abe Fortas resigned his position after it was revealed that he had provided advice to his old friend, Lyndon Johnson, and sat in on political meetings at the Johnson White House. In contrast, during the Cold War several sitting members of Congress retained their high-ranking positions in the military reserve forces—a seeming violation of the prohibition against holding positions in more than one branch of the national government because the military is part of the executive branch of government.

The separation of powers was also reinforced by the framers through the different constituencies and term lengths assigned to each branch of the national government. Members of the House of Representatives, for example, are directly elected by the eligible voters of their respective districts every two years. U.S. senators, on the other hand, were originally selected by the legislatures of their states for six-year terms, implying strongly that they represented the interests of the state governments that sent them to Washington. The design of the electoral college that was to select the president (see Chapter 7, on campaigns and elections) was intended to guarantee that the winner would regard the nation as his or her constituency during a four-year term in office. Along with the lifetime appointment, the elaborate process set up for naming federal court judges—nomination by the president and confirmation by the Senate—was intended to guarantee that those positions were filled by people more accountable to the law than to shifting political moods.

Checks and Balances

While separation of powers provides independent roles for Congress, the presidency, and the courts, the principle of **checks and balances** forces them to work together. By giving each institution the capability of counterbalancing the authority of the other branches, the Constitution makes these institutions interdependent.

The key element in the system of checks and balances is found in the distribution of shared powers among the three government branches. Each branch depends on the others to accomplish its objectives, but each also acts as a counterpoint to the others (see Figure 2.3). The president's power to **veto,** or reject, legislation checks the legislative actions of Congress. The veto, in turn, can be overridden by a two-thirds vote of both chambers of Congress.

While the veto has proven a powerful tool for the president in the checks and balances system, some have complained that it is of limited value because it leaves the president with no alternative to vetoing an entire bill. If the president does not like a specific provision of a bill, he cannot veto that troublesome clause. Many state constitutions have given their governors such power in the form of a **line-item veto,** which permits them to strike a particular clause of a bill that comes before them. During the 1980s, President Ronald Reagan repeatedly asked Congress to consider a constitutional amendment or legislation that would provide presidents with the line-item veto, especially as a means for striking congressional actions that funded wasteful, or "pork barrel," projects or unnecessary tax breaks for a special-interest group. While Reagan did not get his wish, Congress passed a limited version of line-item veto legislation in 1995. Under the provisions of that bill, the president could exercise veto power over specific appropriation or tax bills that he concluded served the interest of individuals or designated groups. As with the constitutional veto, Congress would have the power to override the president's action with a two-thirds vote.

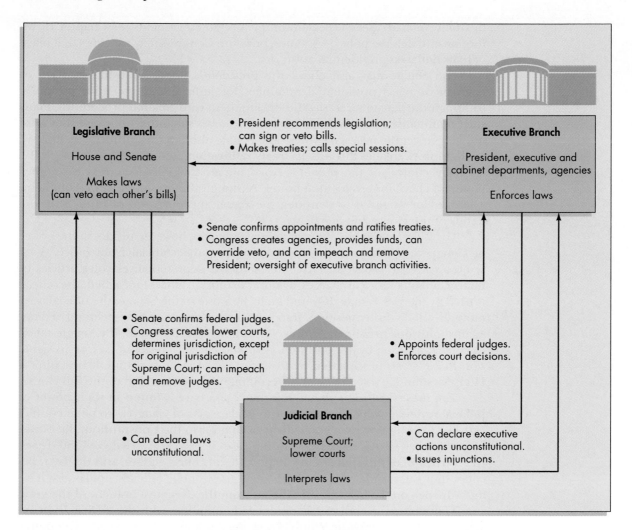

FIGURE 2.3

Separation of Powers and Checks and Balances

Under *separation of powers,* government authority is divided among the three branches: Congress exercises the power to make laws, the president exercises the power to execute laws, and the courts have the power to judge disputes arising under the laws. A system of *checks and balances* provides each branch with a means to counterbalance the authority of the other two, thus making the three branches interdependent.

Congress can restrict presidential power in a variety of other ways. Beyond the powers granted to the president in the Constitution, presidents must have **congressional authorization** to undertake any official course of action. In recent decades Congress has often provided the White House with considerable flexibility in many areas, especially in the foreign policy field (see Chapter 15, on foreign and defense policy). At times, however, Congress may pass laws that place narrow limits on presidential authority.

The Senate may also check the president's power by using its right to confirm or reject presidential nominees for judicial and executive positions. Although the Senate rarely says no during these **confirmation** procedures, many such nominations have been withdrawn (or never submitted) because they were unlikely to get the necessary votes. The Senate also has the authority to approve or disapprove treaties through its **treaty ratification** powers.

The control of the public sector's purse strings by Congress is another powerful check on presidential power. Although the president can recommend a budget for Congress to consider, the actual appropriation of funds is in the hands of the House and Senate.

The ultimate restraint on presidential authority, however, resides in the power of Congress to remove a president or other public official from office. Such removals involve two steps. First, the House of Representatives votes articles of **impeachment,** or formal charges, against the official. Once impeached, the official is tried by the U.S. Senate. If found guilty by a vote of the Senate, the official is removed from his or her position. Impeachment proceedings have been carried out against only one president, Andrew Johnson. In the 1868 trial, the Senate failed to convict Johnson by just one vote. As noted earlier, President Nixon's resignation in 1974 was precipitated by the prospect of an impeachment trial after a House committee voted in favor of recommending such action to the full House.

The most significant check that the courts have is found in their power of **judicial review,** by which the courts can declare acts of Congress to be in conflict with the Constitution. Not explicitly provided for in the Constitution, the power of judicial review was established in the case of *Marbury* v. *Madison* (1803) (see the discussion of this concept in Chapter 13, on courts, judges, and the law). Because they can hear lawsuits about the actions of public officials, courts also have an influence on the behavior of officials from the executive branch. At the same time, the president's power to appoint federal judges with the advice and consent of the Senate gives the White House some power over the courts. The power of Congress over the courts derives in part from its constitutional authority to create or abolish any court other than the Supreme Court. Congress can also impeach and remove judges and has done so in several recent cases.

The principle of checks and balances is strengthened by the different methods of selecting officials, which the framers believed would ensure that the different branches represented different public perspectives. Variations in terms of office were intended to add a further check. For example, senators, responding from the perspective of their six-year terms in office, were expected to act in a more measured and conservative way than their peers in the House, who had only two-year terms.

In setting up the elaborate system of checks and balances, the framers pitted the three branches of government against one another. This has resulted in a slow and ponderous system that often frustrates officials trying to deal quickly with critical issues. Too rapid decision making is what the framers feared, however. More often than many of us like, the system works the way they planned it—deliberately and with care.

National Supremacy

Earlier we pointed out that the U.S. Constitution provides for a federal system in which national and state governments divide the authority of American government. Such a complex arrangement can work only if there is some principle that helps government officials settle fundamental disagreements among the different levels of government. If such a principle did not exist, then "the authority of the whole society" would be "everywhere subordinate to the authority of the parts." That, argued Madison, would have created a "monster" in which the head was under the control of its member parts.[40]

In the American constitutional system, that principle is **national supremacy.** As noted earlier in this chapter, the supremacy clause of Article VI of the Constitution makes the Constitution and those laws and treaties passed under it the "supreme Law of the Land." As you will see in Chapter 3, on federalism and intergovernmental relations, that principle has been a central factor in the evolution of the American federal system. Understanding the operations of American government today would be impossible without grasping the meaning of federalism and the role of the national supremacy principle in American government.

Conclusion: Neither Timeless nor Irrelevant

In public opinion polls and in other forums, Americans continue to express pride in their constitutional system, and few advocate radical changes in the structure of government established by the Constitution.[41] For most, in fact, the document represents the American people as a nation.[42] According to historian Theodore H. White, the American nation is united by a commonly accepted idea rather than by geography—an idea about government embodied in the U.S. constitutional system.[43] Yet Americans familiar with the way their government operates know that the specific provisions of the Constitution do not really reflect how their government functions most of the time.

Why do we maintain the myth of a timeless and perfect constitution in light of the changes it has and will continue to undergo? Our written Constitution is a wonderfully crafted document that deserves the accolades it receives from its admirers worldwide. Nevertheless, the written Constitution does not necessarily reflect the real operational constitution of the United States that is applied daily in this country. Jefferson was correct in noting that if our constitutional system is to survive, it must change with the times. Of necessity, our government operates on the continual interpretation and reinterpretation of the Constitution's provisions and its implicit principles. In the words of William Penn, written more than a century before the framing of the Constitution, "Governments, like clocks, go from the motion men give them; and as governments are moved and made by men, so by them they are ruined too. Wherefore governments rather depend upon men than men upon governments."[44] As you will see in later chapters, government also depends on laws, policies, court decisions, political attitudes and behavior, customs, traditions, and even the myths that surround the exercise of public authority in America.

And yet Madison was also correct, for there are a number of excellent reasons for maintaining the document and the myth of timelessness and perfection that accompanies it. Although the Constitution may not be timeless and perfect, it does provide a stable foundation of principles for our system of government. Furthermore, the Constitution is undeniably more than a legal document or instrument. It is a symbol, a unifying force that provides a common identity for Americans. One can hardly overlook the observation of commentator Irving Kristol that the Constitution stands with the American flag and the Declaration of Independence as part of the American "holy trinity."[45] In a nation that offers few unifying symbols, the Constitution performs that function extremely well.

Summary

1. The framers of the Constitution came together to solve fundamental problems that had arisen under the Articles of Confederation.

2. The roots of the Constitution can be found in the British legal tradition, including the principles that government officials, as well as ordinary citizens, must obey the law and that there exists a higher (constitutional) standard against which laws made by legislatures can be measured. The colonial experience of self-government and the political philosophy of the Enlightenment espoused by such writers as Hobbes and Locke also helped guide the Constitution's framers.

3. The Constitution's framers sought to establish the legitimacy of the government of the United States as coming directly from the people and to create the institutions that would carry out that authority.

4. The framers considered alternative solutions to the problem of how to divide authority within the new national government. Their final decision, laid out in Articles I, II, and III, established legislative, executive, and judicial branches of government.

5. The Constitution describes the specific, or delegated, powers of the national government in Article I and establishes the implied powers of the national government in the "necessary and proper" clause. It also sets limits on national and state power and specifies the rules for making amendments.

6. The framers established in the Constitution the following fundamental principles of American government: the rule of law, republicanism, separation of powers, the system of checks and balances, and national supremacy. These principles

have provided our constitutional system with the flexibility that has made it work for more than two hundred years.

7. Although in reality the Constitution does not live up to the myth of being timeless and per-fect, neither is it irrelevant to today's American government. In addition to the basic principles it embodies, its veneration as a symbol of national identity is important to the success of American government.

Key Terms and Concepts

Articles of Confederation Ratified in 1781 as the United States' first constitution. They established a loose union of states and a congress with few powers.

Feudalism A medieval political economic system in which landless families secured protection and the use of farmland in exchange for providing services and resources to the land's owner.

Charter A British legal institution that originated during the Middle Ages and formed part of the British constitution. Specifically, a formal agreement that describes the rights and duties of both the landowner and those bound to that person.

Magna Carta A document signed by King John in 1215 that reaffirmed the long-standing rights and duties of the English nobility and defined the limits placed on the king. It stands for the principle that government is limited and that everyone, including the king, must obey the law.

Common law Part of the British constitution, it is also called judge-made law. It represents the collection of legal doctrines that grew out of the many cases heard, beginning in medieval times, by judges appointed by the British Crown.

Mayflower Compact A document written by the Pilgrims setting forth major principles for the Plymouth Colony's government.

Enlightenment The period from the 1600s through the 1700s in European intellectual history. It was dominated by the idea that human reason, not religious tradition, was the primary source of knowledge and wisdom. Among the Enlightenment writers who most influenced the framers were Thomas Hobbes, John Locke, Charles de Montesquieu, and Jean-Jacques Rousseau.

Popular sovereignty The concept that the best form of government is one that reflects the general will of the people, which is the sum total of those interests that all citizens have in common. First described by writer Jean-Jacques Rousseau around the time of the American Revolution.

Declaration of Independence The document declaring the colonies to be free and independent states that was adopted by the Second Continental Congress in July 1776. The Declaration also articulated the fundamental principles under which the new nation would be governed.

Legitimacy The belief of citizens in a government's right to pass and enforce laws.

Confederation An arrangement in which ultimate government authority is vested in the states that make up the union. Whatever power the national government has is derived from the states being willing to give up some of their authority to a central government.

Unitary system A form of government in which the ultimate authority rests with the national government. Whatever powers state or local governments have under this type of government are derived from the central government.

Federation (federal system) A mixture of confederation and unitary systems in which the authority of government is shared by both the national and state governments. In its ideal form, a federal constitution gives some exclusive authority over some governmental tasks to the national government, while giving the states exclusive authority over other governmental matters. There would also be some areas where the two levels of government would share authority.

Bicameral Refers to a legislature that is divided into two separate houses, such as the U.S. Congress.

Unicameral Refers to a legislature that has only one house.

Great Compromise The proposal offered by the Connecticut delegation to the Constitutional Convention in 1787. It called for establishment of a bicameral congress, consisting of a house where states were represented according to their population size, and a senate where each state had an equal voice.

Delegated powers Sometimes referred to as "enumerated powers," these are the powers the Constitution gives the Congress that are specifically listed in the first seventeen clauses in Section 8 of Article I.

Concurrent powers Those powers the Constitution grants to the national government but does not deny to the states, for example, to lay and collect taxes.

Necessary and proper clause The eighteenth clause of Article I, Section 8, of the Constitution, which establishes "implied powers" for Congress that go beyond those listed in the Constitution.

Implied powers Those powers given to Congress by Article I, Section 8, clause 18, of the Constitution that are not specifically named but are provided for by the "necessary and proper clause."

Reserved powers Sometimes called "residual powers," these are the powers that the Constitution provides for the states, although it does not list them specifically. As stated in the Tenth Amendment, these include all powers not expressly given to the national government or denied to the states.

Writ of habeas corpus A court order that protects people against arbitrary arrest and detention.

Bill of attainder A legislative act declaring a person guilty of a crime and setting punishment without the benefit of a formal trial.

Ex post facto law A law declaring an action criminal even if it was performed before the law was passed to make it illegal.

Bill of Rights The first ten amendments to the Constitution, which collectively guarantee the fundamental liberties of citizens from abuse by the national government.

Full faith and credit Article IV of the Constitution requires that each state respect in all ways the acts, records, and judicial proceedings of the other states.

Privileges and immunities A provision in Article IV of the Constitution stating that the citizens of one state will not be treated unreasonably by officials of another state.

Supremacy clause A provision in Article VI declaring the Constitution the supreme law of the land, taking precedence over state laws.

Rule of law The principle that there is a standard of impartiality, fairness, and equality against which all government actions can be evaluated. More narrowly, the concept that no individual stands above the law and that rulers, like those they rule, are answerable to the law. One of the most important legacies of the framers of the Constitution.

Republicanism A doctrine of government in which decisions are made by elected or appointed officials who are answerable to the people; decisions are not made directly by the people themselves.

Federalist Papers A series of editorials written by James Madison, Alexander Hamilton, and John Jay in 1788 to support the ratification of the Constitution in New York State. Now regarded as a major source of information on what the framers were thinking when they wrote the Constitution.

Separation of powers The division of the powers to make, execute, and judge the law among the three branches of American government: Congress, the presidency, and the courts. This principle was adopted by the framers to prevent tyranny and factionalism in the government.

Checks and balances The principle that lets the executive, legislative, and judicial branches share some responsibilities and gives each branch some control over the others' activities. The major support for checks and balances comes from the Constitution's distribution of shared powers.

Veto An important presidential check on the power of Congress. It is the president's power to reject legislation passed by Congress. The veto can be overruled, however, by a two-thirds vote of both chambers of Congress. In 1995, Congress passed a limited **line-item veto** that gave the president power to strike specific provisions of appropriation and tax bills.

Congressional authorization The power of Congress to provide the president with the right to carry out legislated policies.

Confirmation The power of the U.S. Senate to approve or disapprove a presidential nominee for an executive or judicial post.

Treaty ratification The power of the U.S. Senate to approve or disapprove formal treaties negotiated by the president on behalf of the nation.

Impeachment Formal charge of misconduct brought against a federal public official by the House of Representatives. If found guilty of those charges by the Senate, the official is removed from office.

Judicial review The power of the courts to declare acts of Congress to be in conflict with the Constitution. This power makes the courts part of the system of checks and balances.

National supremacy The principle, stated in Article VI as the "supremacy clause," that makes the Constitution and those laws and treaties passed under it the "supreme law of the land."

CHAPTER

3

Federalism and Intergovernmental Relations

Is the national government too weak or too dominant?

WWW•

See **Political Science** at
http://www.hmco.com/college

I t was a campaign promise kept. While running for president in 1992, Bill Clinton promised to bring about "an end to welfare as we know it" if elected. On August 22, 1996, he signed into law perhaps the most sweeping changes in welfare programs since the early 1960s. The *Personal Responsibility and Work Opportunity Reconciliation Act of 1996* significantly altered the system of assistance to the needy, which had generated criticism from both sides of the political spectrum (see the discussion of welfare policy and reform in Chapter 14, on domestic policy).

The new law was designed as one means of ending the cycle of poverty and dependence that had caused concern among even the most ardent supporters of government assistance to the poor. But for those who administered the vast web of federal programs that had developed over several decades, the law represented even more important changes. In many respects, the new welfare law involved an end to the federal system as they had known it for more than half a century.

Before the passage of the reform legislation, assistance to the poor was effectively a set of national programs administered by the states. For example, Aid to Families with Dependent Children (AFDC), Emergency Assistance (EA), and JOBS (offering employment and training for AFDC recipients) involved states in the implementation of programs for which a federal agency established eligibility criteria. The states determined the benefit levels and were required to apply them uniformly to all families in similar circumstances. All three were **entitlement programs**—that is, recipients remained eligible for benefits as long as they met program eligibility rules. And while states received federal matching dollars for all expenditures, there was no cap on the obligation they entered into under these programs. Benefits were guaranteed to eligible individuals even when the state suffered from recessions and budgetary crises.

Thus, until the 1996 reforms were implemented, these and other programs of assistance to the poor involved both national and state governments. But there was an unmistakable national flavor to the welfare system. As in many other policy areas and programs—from education to environmental protection to highway construction and maintenance—states and localities took on significant financial and administrative burdens but were severely limited in deciding on such matters as who was eligible for the programs or how the funds would be spent.

After the 1996 reforms, the role of the states in welfare policy was radically transformed. AFDC, EA, and JOBS were replaced by the Temporary Assistance to Needy Families (TANF) program. Instead of the open-ended federal funding associated with entitlement programs, TANF gave each state a set amount of federal funds, determined through a formula derived from historical spending patterns for the eliminated programs. Each state, in turn, was required to spend on welfare programs at least 80 percent of what it spent in 1994. Welfare recipients were no longer "entitled" to welfare benefits under TANF, and how each state spent its TANF money was a decision for state officials to make within some very broadly defined criteria and limits set by the national government.

For example, under TANF individuals could receive no more than five years of cash support derived from federal funds. Once that limit is reached, it is up to the state to assume full responsibility (if it wishes to do so) for the recipient's needs. States can make some exceptions to this five-year limit for specific groups of welfare recipients, but the limit must apply to at least 80 percent of those receiving federally funded assistance. In addition, each state has the option of restricting eligibility for federal assistance to less than five years—a step it might take to free up the limited federal funds for other uses. Under the new law, the states also have to develop and implement programs that would move welfare recipients into jobs. Thus anyone receiving federal funding from the states must also be required to work at least part time after two years. How states achieve this is up to them, but the level of future federal funding for a state will be reduced if its state program fails to meet targeted numbers for finding employment for these individuals. Dozens of other provisions in the new law reinforce the basic changes in the nation's welfare policy.

As we discuss in greater detail in Chapter 14, on domestic policy, many of the provisions of the 1996 welfare reform act were a response to a growing consensus among policymakers across the political spectrum that something was fundamentally wrong with America's welfare system. It needed to be fixed. But the reforms were also a result of a strong political movement, led by state and local officials: they sought greater freedom from what they perceived as the heavy hand of the federal government. The act thus did more than transform welfare; it transformed American federalism. Indeed, the welfare reforms of 1996 were merely the latest act in a two-century-old drama that had been playing on the federalism stage constructed by the framers. In this drama, at least two groups of protagonists—federal officials and those representing state and local government—have each tried to get the upper hand in nation-state relationships.

The federalism stage has been the site for controversies since it was first used in 1789. Early in the nation's history, the issue of which would play the starring role in America's political dramas—the states or the national government—provided a common theme for most debates of the period.[1] The issue of slavery was probably the most significant political drama presented on the federalism stage until the controversy moved to the battlefields of the Civil War. Government's role in regulating the growing American economy and dealing with social problems created by industrialization (for example, child labor) was at the center of the federalism stage by the turn of the century. By the 1950s and 1960s, the weekly playbill varied from civil rights and civil liberties to social policies (see discussions in Chapters 4 and 14). During the 1970s, environmental concerns joined the list of issues for American governments at all levels. In the 1980s and 1990s, it was welfare's turn. In all these eras and debates, the vaguely defined federalism of the framers was central to determining how each drama played out.

Federalism, it must be recalled, was a compromise between those desiring a stronger national government and those wanting government authority retained within the states. The framers provided no definitive answer to questions about which level of government should do what. As a result, federalism has evolved into a complex arrangement of relationships among the national, state, and local governments.

The old controversy of national versus state and local authority remains, however. Supporters of a stronger national government and those seeking more power for state and local governments keep their debate alive through two contrasting myths: one is based on the assumption that the national government has been too weak and that more power should be given to officials representing the interests of the whole nation; and the other is based on the belief that state and local governments, being closest to the people, can best serve their needs and therefore should be the driving force in American government. From this perspective, the problem is one of national government dominance rather than national government weakness.

The *myth of national government weakness* has had many adherents dating back to Alexander Hamilton. Hamilton, and those who followed him, argued for a stronger central government to help Americans face their problems—whether those problems deal with building a new nation, developing a national economy, protecting the civil rights and liberties of all Americans, or maintaining a clean environment. In contrast, the *myth of national government dominance* reflects a fear of relying too much on Washington, D.C., to solve essentially regional and local problems. Its adherents can trace that myth's roots back to Thomas Jefferson and James Madison. According to the myth, the once highly decentralized federal system of nation-state relationships has slowly eroded over the past two centuries. State and local governments have not disappeared, the myth contends, but their powers have significantly declined. National officials, it seems, now wield the real public authority in this country. As one newspaper editorial noted, "One cannot conceive of an example of public policymaking that the states can engage in . . . without fear of contradiction by the Federal Government."[2] For those believing in this myth, it seems clear that state and local governments are being integrated into a single, national system of government, in which public policies made in Washington, D.C., are carried out by state and local officials.

Public attitudes toward the issue of which level of government should have the power reinforce both myths. According to public opinion polls, many Americans feel a great attachment to state and local governments. A 1981 survey found that 64 percent of those polled regarded state governments as more effective than the national government in dealing with the problems facing America. In a 1987 survey, 59 percent of those responding said that they had "the most trust and confidence" in state and local governments, whereas only 19 percent said the same of the national government. A national survey conducted in late 1995 found that 61 percent of respondents felt they could trust their state government to do a better job of "running things," while only 24 percent said the same of the national government.[3] In short, Americans still give their trust to the public officials closest to them, although that support fluctuates at times.[4]

Indications are equally clear, however, that Americans are less likely to turn to state and local officials when significant problems arise; instead, they look to Congress, the Supreme Court, and the Washington bureaucracy. By the 1960s the national government was already engaged in a wide range of programs that had once been state and local responsibilities alone—for instance, helping to fund education for the young and the construction of roads and sewage-treatment plants. And when new problems arise, such as those dealing with auto emissions and the environment, people often look first to Washington and then to their states. According to Terry Sanford of North Carolina, a former governor who later served in the U.S. Senate, the "people seem to conclude that the state vehicle is not so driveable as the federal vehicles."[5]

What is played out on the federalism stage frequently reflects the ongoing debate among adherents to those conflicting myths. In the rest of this chapter we trace the historical development of those debates and then discuss the various actors who play important roles on the federalism stage.

The Evolution of American Federalism

As noted in Chapter 1, myths influence how we view the complex world of government and how we see history. This is especially true for how we understand the history of American federalism.[6] Each of the two myths concerning the national government presents a different picture of how the federal system has evolved. The myth of national government weakness depicts federalism as a continuous struggle of the nation's leaders to overcome the parochialism and active opposition of state and local interests, whereas the myth of national government dominance pictures federalism as a constant expansion of national power. A more realistic view shows the emergence of an increasingly complex set of relationships among all three levels of government—national, state, and local—as well as a variety of public and private interests.

Battles over Meaning (1790s–1860s)

The Constitution is not completely clear on the powers of the national government relative to those of the states. This lack of precision caused conflict in the early years of the republic. Was the national government primary, or could states ignore the laws of Congress when they chose? Two competing answers emerged, one centered on the states and the other on the nation.[7]

Supporters of **state-centered federalism** would allow the national government only limited powers. Led by Thomas Jefferson and James Madison, they argued that states could overrule national laws if they believed that those laws violated provisions of the U.S. Constitution.[8]

Proponents of **nation-centered federalism** argued that the authority of the national government goes beyond the responsibilities listed in Article I, Section 8, of the Constitution. They contended that the necessary and proper clause and the principle of national supremacy give the national government additional powers to act. Alexander Hamilton and, later, Daniel Webster took this position, as did Chief Justice of the Supreme Court John Marshall in *McCulloch* v. *Maryland* (1819) (see the discussion of that case in Chapter 2, on constitutional foundations). Five years later, in *Gibbons* v. *Ogden* (1824), the Supreme Court dealt another blow to the proponents of state power. It held that a New York law establishing a steamboat monopoly between New York City and New Jersey was not constitutional. Only the national government, the Court ruled, could regulate "commercial intercourse" (**interstate commerce**) between states.

The supporters of the state-centered approach did get some relief starting in the late 1830s when the Supreme Court made a number of rulings that established the existence of sovereign **police powers,** which a state could exercise as part of its duty "to advance the safety, happiness and prosperity of its people. . . ."[9] The existence of these police powers was used to justify state jurisdiction over economic matters.

The debate between advocates of state-centered and nation-centered federalism was also conducted on the floor of Congress. Much of it focused on the issue of slavery, and at times the heated discussions turned bitter and even

Brooks Beating Sumner in Senate

Prior to the Civil War, disputes over federalism and slavery were taken quite seriously. Senator Charles Sumner, an ardent abolitionist from Massachusetts, was nearly caned to death on the Senate floor by Preston Brooks, a member of the U.S. House from South Carolina. Brooks had taken exception to remarks Sumner had made about some pro-slavery members of Congress.

violent. In one particularly notable episode leading up to the Civil War, Charles Sumner of Massachusetts was severely beaten on the floor of the U.S. Senate by Representative Preston Brooks, a member of the House from South Carolina who took exception to remarks made by the senator. Sumner would not return to the Senate chamber for three years, and never really recuperated from the attack. Brooks resigned from the House but was reelected by his constituents, who regarded him as a hero.[10] Ultimately, the conflict over slavery was settled on the battlefields of the Civil War. Out of that bloody confrontation between the North and the South, nation-centered federalism emerged victorious. If state and national laws and policies clashed, national legislation was to have priority. In that sense, the Civil War made it formally possible for the national government to achieve a dominant position in the federal system. In reality, however, the story was quite different.

From Separation to Cooperation (1860s–1920s)

Instead of national government domination, what emerged after the Civil War was a system of **dual federalism,** whereby the national and state governments were regarded as equal partners. Under dual federalism, each level is perceived as responsible for distinct policy functions and each is barred from interfering with the other's work. Thus, whereas earlier cases had established that the states could not interfere with the national government's regulation of interstate trade, post–Civil War decisions held that the national government could not interfere with the power of the states to regulate the sale or manufacture of products or services within their own borders. Starting immediately after the Civil War, the Supreme Court declared in a series of rulings that insurance, fishing, lumbering, mining, manufacturing, building, banking, and a variety of other economic activities were not subject to federal regulation, but rather could be regulated under the police powers of individual states.

The most explicit statement of dual federalism was issued in 1871, when the Court held that within the borders of each state there are "two governments, restricted in their sphere of action, but independent of each other, and supreme within their respective spheres." Neither, the Court said, can intrude on or interfere with the other's action.[11] By 1918 the Court was declaring that those powers "not expressly delegated to the National Government are reserved" to the states.[12] This was an expression of dual federalism at its height.

Despite the Court's reliance on dual federalism during this period, the formal separation between the two levels of government was breaking down in the world of practical politics. The first step in this process was **grant-in-aid programs,** through which state policies and programs were partially funded or provided with other support. The Morrill Act (1862) gave federal land grants to states for the purpose of establishing agricultural colleges.[13] Later on, cash grants helped states with agricultural experiment stations, textbook programs for the blind, marine schools, forestry programs, agricultural extension services, state soldiers' homes, vocational schools, road construction, and a variety of other projects. By 1927 these grant programs were bringing state governments $123 million in national funds annually.[14]

Toward Cooperation and Local Participation (1930s–1950s)

The Great Depression of the 1930s significantly altered the relationship between Washington and the states. Demand for public services grew. At the same time, state and local governments faced tight finances because tax revenues had fallen in the declining economy. The national government was expected and willing to respond. There was an explosion of new and cooperative programs in which the national and state governments shared an increasing number of functions. A new kind of federalism had emerged that recognized the interdependence of Washington and state and local governments. Called **intergovernmental relations** (or IGR), it is a system in which the various levels of government share functions, and each level is able to influence the others.

The emergence of intergovernmental relations was an important development in the history of American federalism. It meant that the formal and highly legalistic nature of federalism was being replaced by a more flexible and informal approach to nation-state relations. Furthermore, by treating interactions among various levels of government as IGR rather than as federalism, the door was open for greater participation by many more actors on the federalism stage. Local and regional governments and even private and community groups could now find a role to play.

The new system offered a variety of grant-in-aid programs covering a wide range of policy concerns. The number and size of these programs grew dramatically during this period, increasing from $100 million in 1930 to $6.8 billion in 1960.[15] Initially, the emergence of intergovernmental relations was the foundation for this period of **cooperative federalism.** Conflict between Washington and the states diminished as public officials worried less about the level of government that performed certain functions and more about their specific program responsibilities. State and national officials began to see each other as "allies, not as enemies."[16]

At the heart of the system of intergovernmental relations was a variety of grant-in-aid programs that financed highways, social and educational projects, and other programs. Many were **categorical, or conditional, grants-in-aid,** under which state governments received federal funding for specific purposes only if they met certain general requirements. For example, state highway departments were expected to operate in an efficient and businesslike fashion, free of corruption and undue political influence. Similar standards were applied to welfare programs. If states failed to meet those standards, support was withdrawn or sometimes the program was taken over. Thus during the Depression, Washington took charge of public assistance programs in six states where officials could not meet federal requirements. Public welfare programs in other states were closely watched to make sure that they were following federal rules.

Under other federal programs, states received **formula grants** based on population, number of eligible persons, per capita income, and other factors. One of the largest of these grants, the Hill-Burton program, used a formula heavily weighted to favor states with substantial low-income populations. By 1986 more than $3 billion of Hill-Burton funds had been used to construct and modernize health care facilities throughout the United States.

Project grants are awarded only after submission of a specific project or plan of action. The Housing Act of 1937 was one of the earliest and largest of such programs. Under provisions of that act, local governments could obtain funds to build public housing. By the 1960s there were more than four thousand such projects, with more than half a million dwelling units. In many instances, the national government required recipient governments to provide a certain percentage of the funds needed to implement the programs. Among these **matching grants** were a program that provided aid to dependent children under the Social Security Act of 1935 and one that gave states $9 for every dollar spent to build interstate highways.

Cities and other local governments also became participants in the federal system during this period. Before the 1930s American cities were regarded as merely subdivisions of the states. Grants or other forms of support came from state capitals, not from Washington. In 1932, for instance, only the nation's capital received aid from the national government. By 1940, however, the situation had changed. That year the national government handed out $278 million in direct grants-in-aid to local governments for a variety of public housing and public works programs. In the 1950s the national government expanded support to include slum clearance, urban renewal, and airport construction. By the start of the 1960s local governments were receiving $592 million worth of direct grants.[17]

The Urban Focus (1960s–1970s)

The intergovernmental relations system continued to grow during the 1960s and 1970s, and by 1980 grant-in-aid programs to state and local governments had surpassed $85 billion. Starting in 1960, other notable changes took place.[18] For example, grant systems expanded into new policy areas. The percentage of funds devoted to highways and public assistance declined, and funding for programs in education, health care, environmental protection, manpower training, housing, and community development increased significantly.

In a shift in the flow of funds, a growing number of intergovernmental programs were targeted at local, rather than state, governments. President Lyndon B. Johnson's Great Society policies included dozens of new and innovative grant programs with an urban focus. For the first time, community-based programs for feeding the urban poor, training the unemployed, and educating the children of low-income families received support. One important initiative, the Model Cities program, was designed to help cities develop projects addressing a variety of economic and social problems. In 1974, many of these and related programs were consolidated under community development grants. By 1985 the national government was disbursing nearly $5 billion directly to local governments through these programs.

Until the early 1960s Washington used federal grants simply to help states and localities perform their traditional government functions. State and local governments might be asked to modify their personnel policies or their methods of bidding for contracts but rarely had to take on new policy responsibilities as a requirement for receiving federal funds. In contrast, the grant programs of the 1960s and 1970s were increasingly designed to involve these governments in achieving national policy objectives. States or localities that initiated new or special programs promoting national goals received substantial grants. The Model Cities program, for example, encouraged cities to institute programs for improving the quality of life for poor and low-income groups. In other instances, Washington threatened to reduce or cut off funding to governments that failed to change old policies or to adopt new ones that complied with national standards. It was during this period, for example, that the national government used the threat of withholding highway funds from states that did not lower their maximum speed limits to 55 miles per hour.[19]

Reforming and Reducing the Grant System (1970s–1980s)

Inevitably, the rapid spread of grant programs and their requirements led to problems. Local recipients criticized federal officials for administering programs without regard to the unique circumstances and dilemmas they were facing. State officials complained that the national government ignored them in designing and implementing many new programs. Both state and local officials complained about the increasing number of strings attached to federal grants, especially the policy mandates tied to the funds, which many recipient governments regarded as costly, irrelevant, and inappropriate. At the same time, members of Congress reacted impatiently to the poor coordination and cooperation in the massive intergovernmental relations system. As a result, there was almost constant pressure to reform the grant system.

Responding to pressures for an increased role for state and local officials, Washington took a number of steps designed to loosen its control over grant programs and to enhance state and local authority. During the early 1970s, for instance, the federal government provided funds to support the formation of local and regional **councils of governments.** These associations of local governments helped their member governments contend with such common problems as co-ordinating local applications for federal grants. In addition, President Johnson and his successor, Richard M. Nixon, reorganized the administration of the grant system, increasing the power of federal regional offices in order to ease the burdens of both state and local governments.

In two additional reform efforts, the national government introduced new funding systems designed to further reduce its control and make procedures more flexible. Most of the established programs were based on categorical, or conditional, grants, in which money given to the states and localities was to be used for limited purposes under specific rules. In the mid-1960s, however, Congress introduced block grants. **Block grants** were a way of consolidating categorical grants in a given area so that the recipients would have greater freedom to spend funds and so that paperwork would be reduced. By 1974 seven major block grants covered such areas as health, education, and other social services. These grants did give state and local officials greater discretion over programs and freed them from some annoying mandates attached to categorical grants. Nevertheless, in financial terms, they constituted only a small portion of the total amount of federal aid flowing to states and localities.

The other new form of federal aid was called **general revenue sharing.** This small but innovative grant-in-aid program had no significant conditions attached to it. State and local governments received funds according to a complex formula based on population and related factors. The program was modified considerably and its funding was reduced late in the 1970s. By 1988 it had disappeared from the intergovernmental system.

The late 1970s and early 1980s produced major changes in intergovernmental relations. Most obvious was the reduction in federal funding to states and localities through grants-in-aid. As shown in Figure 3.1, grant money (measured in constant 1992 dollars to control for inflation) began to decline after 1978. The most significant drop, however, occurred during 1981—Ronald Reagan's first year in office—and represented a larger effort to radically alter government-spending patterns. Significant cuts were made in 1981, and the amount of funds sent to states and localities dropped more than 12 percent from its 1980 levels! It took nearly a decade for federal aid to return to its pre–Reagan administration levels.[20]

In addition to these initial spending cuts, Reagan also attempted a major overhaul of the intergovernmental system. He formally proposed to Congress that many government functions be returned to the states. In exchange, the national government would assume most public welfare programs. When that strategy failed, Reagan administration officials tried to bring about changes by adjusting the way in which grant-in-aid programs were administered. These efforts had a major impact on the federal system.[21]

At the same time, Congress worked toward consolidating more categorical programs into broad block grant programs. During the first half of the 1980s, Congress converted dozens of categorical programs into about a dozen block

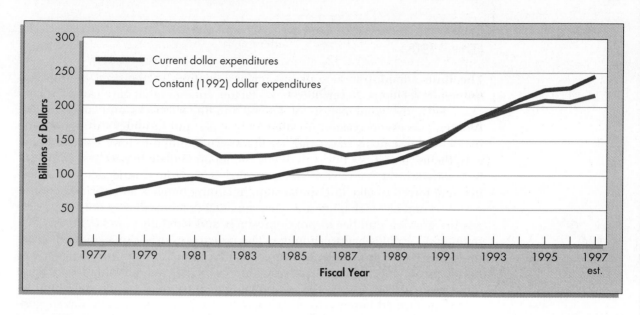

FIGURE 3.1

Federal Expenditures
for State and Local
Governments,
1977–1997

Source: U.S. Office of Management and Budget, *Budget of the United States Government, Fiscal Year 1998 Historical Tables* (Washington, D.C.: USGPO, 1997), tbl. 12.1.

grants.[22] Despite these efforts, hundreds of categorical grant programs remained on the books. By 1988—the last year of the Reagan administration—the national government was spending an estimated $116 billion on grants-in-aid to states and localities.[23]

There is little dispute, however, that the Reagan administration significantly changed the direction of intergovernmental relations, at least for the short term. Although the absolute amount of federal dollars going for grant-in-aid programs increased through most of the 1980s, the total amount in "constant dollar" terms (adjusted for inflation) remained relatively stable during the period (see Figure 3.1). Only after Reagan left office did grant expenditures increase in both absolute and constant terms. More important was that states and localities were becoming less dependent on federal dollars for carrying out their work. For example, 26.5 cents of every dollar spent by state and local governments in 1978 came from the national government. By 1990, however, only 17.9 cents of every dollar spent by states and localities could be linked to a federal grant-in-aid. As one observer put it, the Reagan years represented the years of "fend-for-yourself" federalism.[24]

Crises, Burdens, and Devolution
(The 1990s)

The Bush administration took no major initiatives in the area of intergovernmental relations. Nevertheless, two factors emerged that gave cause for concern. First, the combination of federal funding cutbacks and an extended economic recession created fiscal crises in states and localities throughout the nation. Because many states and localities were required to have balanced budgets, the fiscal crises of the early 1990s had an immediate impact and could not be resolved through government borrowing. States from Connecticut to California were forced to take unpopular steps in cutting budgets and raising taxes.

A second factor shaping intergovernmental relations during the early 1990s was the growing number of policy pressures and federally mandated costs that states and localities had to shoulder. The policy pressures came primarily from the White House as President Bush made education and a war on drugs two of his top priorities. Although Bush called for major reforms and initiatives in these areas, he made no request for additional federal funding for the states and localities that would have to carry out many of the policy changes he was suggesting. Thus, while holding conferences and making speeches on the need for local schools to engage in costly educational reforms, President Bush did not support funding for any major new or special programs to accomplish those objectives. Similarly, his much-touted "War on Drugs" required nearly $500 million in federal funds, but most were earmarked for federal law enforcement efforts and aid to foreign countries. State and local officials complained bitterly that they needed more money to do their part. After all, they argued, it was the states and localities that had to deal with drug use and its consequences.

Congress was also the source of problems. Members offered and passed well-intentioned legislation requiring state and local action but failed to deal with the associated costs of the new programs. In addition to the previously passed requirements for environmental cleanup, Congress in 1991 passed a much-heralded Americans with Disabilities Act, which included provisions for greater public access to services, transportation facilities, and so forth that would result in millions of dollars in additional state and local expenditures for years to come.

Known as *unfunded mandates,* these unfinanced or underfinanced burdens on states and localities became a major issue in national politics and policymaking. By 1994 greater sensitivity developed concerning these burdens. Legislation, such as that dealing with clean water, increasingly generated debate that included consideration of those responsibilities and who should pay for them. As one part of the Republican party's "Contract with America" agenda that was supported by the Clinton administration, the issue of unfunded mandates became the first substantive item passed by the 104th Congress in January 1995. Clearly, the days were gone when Congress could impose mandates on states and localities without addressing the critical problems those requirements caused (see the discussion about Congress that follows).

President Clinton was also sensitive to the growing demands being made on states and localities when he came into office in 1993. As governor of Arkansas for twelve years, he had developed a national reputation as an innovative leader who understood and appreciated the role of states in the federal system.[25] After less than two weeks in office, Clinton held a meeting with the nation's governors to hear their complaints and suggestions. While his administration did not propose any major reforms of the intergovernmental system during his first two years in office, Clinton did establish a policy that permitted federal officials to loosen program requirements in order to allow states and localities greater flexibility to innovate. In addition, his initial proposals to reform America's health-care and welfare systems relied heavily on changes in state policies and administration. This approach of giving states and localities more room to determine the policies they were to enforce became part of a more general movement toward "devolution" in the intergovernmental relations system. **Devolution** involves the process of having the national government turn over more functions with greater responsibility to state and local governments. When joined with the desire to alter the traditional way of providing government assistance to the poor, devolution proved to be central to the 1996 welfare reform policies discussed at the outset of this chapter.

WWW•

For more information on devolution, see the **Gitelson/Dudley/Dubnick** web site.

The Actors of American Federalism

The growing chorus of states and local voices in debates about congressional policies represents part of the ever-changing roles played by those who are actors on the federalism stage. Although considerable historical evidence supports the view that the national government has been playing a more important part in intergovernmental relations, there is also substantial support for the argument that state and local actors remain just as critical to the system as before. In fact, today's federalism is an intergovernmental relations system involving a cast of hundreds of agencies, thousands of political and administrative personnel, and millions of citizens who depend on government for daily public services. In short, the underlying story is an American federal system that has grown wider and deeper as interactions among the different levels of American government have increased and become more complex. Here we briefly describe the many actors who occupy the modern stage of American intergovernmental relations.

National Government Actors

Formally, only one national government exists in the American federal system. In practice, however, dozens of national-level actors play out daily dramas on the intergovernmental relations stage.

The Supreme Court.   In the two centuries of American federalism, no national institution has been more important than the U.S. Supreme Court. We have already seen how in *McCulloch* v. *Maryland* the Court helped establish the national government's dominant role and how the post–Civil War Court supported the notion of dual federalism.

Until recently, Supreme Court rulings seemed to be reducing the role of the states as effective policymakers.[26] In contrast, some Supreme Court decisions handed down in the late 1980s indicated a growing willingness to give state and local governments more power to shape public policies for a wide range of issues—from abortion rights and the right to die to local campaign financing and the use of sobriety tests for drivers suspected of drunk driving. In some areas, such as civil rights, the Court has been more reluctant to defer to states, and it continues to uphold national laws that require states and localities to follow national minimum wage and hour laws. Nevertheless, during the early 1990s, the Supreme Court was definitely leaning more toward support of innovative and unique state actions.[27] And in June 1992, the Court handed down a decision in *New York* v. *United States* indicating its willingness to accept constitutional limits on the national government's ability to mandate state policies and actions.

Whether one accepts or disputes the wisdom of individual Supreme Court rulings, there is little doubt that through these and other cases the Court has helped shape and direct the American federal system.

Congress.   Although presidents often receive credit for major policy innovations, Congress has always played a central role in the evolution of the federal system. This has been especially true in the past thirty years, during which Congress has increased its authorization of grant programs.

Some students of Congress point to strong incentives for members of the House and Senate to create and fund federal grant-in-aid programs for state and local governments.[28] These programs give almost every state and local government an opportunity to obtain federal funding. Therefore members of Congress can claim credit for passing and supporting their constituents' grant applications. As a result, even fiscally conservative members of Congress often find it hard to avoid supporting requests for new and larger intergovernmental grant programs. "Philosophically, I have not been one to jump rapidly to new programs," commented one member of the House of Representatives from Virginia. "But if programs are adopted, my district is entitled to its fair share. And I do everything I can to help—if they decide to apply for aid."[29]

In what may turn out to be a major shift in the way Congress uses the federal system, the Republican majority in the 104th Congress made explicit promises to reform the system. For example, in an effort to help members of Congress avoid the temptation of instituting "pork-barrel" programs, the 104th Congress gave the White House a limited line-item veto (see Chapter 2, on constitutional foundations). Under that act, the president could strike from an appropriation or tax bill any provision that gives special treatment to a particular

3.1   Governing Education

Among the governmental activities that touch the lives of almost every American is the public provision of primary and secondary education. This function is so important that it is the sole objective of over 14,400 special-purpose districts. The number of school districts in each state ranges from one in Hawaii to 1,044 in Texas (California comes in second with 1,001). Twenty-two of those districts serve more than 100,000 students, whereas 1,742 enroll fewer than 150.

A number of educational issues trouble many American citizens. The performance of public schools, for instance, presents a mixed picture. While the dropout rate for high school students has declined overall since the 1970s, it started to go up again in 1990. Furthermore, according to reports issued in 1995, verbal scores on the Scholastic Aptitude Test (SAT) have been dropping steadily for more than three decades, and mathematical scores have also been declining, though at a slower rate. A 1994 national assessment of fourth, eighth, and twelfth graders' knowledge in reading, geography, and history showed mixed results. While 75 percent of the twelfth graders demonstrated proficiency in reading and 70 percent in geography, only 43 percent scored at a sufficient level on tests of historical knowledge.

The issue of educational equity also causes concern. At the heart of this issue is whether each student has access to the same educational resources as every other student. The problem is both sociological and constitutional. Sociologically, research has shown that students enrolled in poor, inner-city school districts do not receive the same quality of education as those who live in suburban areas. These disparities have reinforced racial and class divisions in American society—a disturbing fact to

those who see education as the means of helping individuals overcome the barriers of discrimination and affordability. On constitutional grounds, the inequitable funding that generates more money for per-student spending in the suburbs than in the central city violates the guarantee of equal protection of the laws, which is part of the federal and many state constitutions. The courts are closely scrutinizing the funding formula for education as litigants seek more money for underfinanced areas.

This issue raises two others: how education is funded and what are the implications for control of educational policy. Many school districts get a significant portion of their funds from local property tax revenues—a situation that has added fuel to the taxpayer rebellions that took place throughout the United States during the last two decades. Reliance on local taxes, however, gave some legitimacy to calls for unimpeded local control of school policies. The movement away from property taxes has lessened the justification for local control.

Still, funds coming from state government revenue sources (such as sales and income taxes) stir controversy because of arguments over the appropriate formula for distributing the monies across the state. This controversy is expanding as states gain importance as funding sources (see Figure 3.2) for local districts. In many states, too, statewide performance measures have also become significant questions.

Much less threatening, though no less controversial, is educational funding from the federal government. The issue regarding these funds usually centers on the degree of control the local district can retain over its policies once it accepts federal monies. For example, Title IX of the

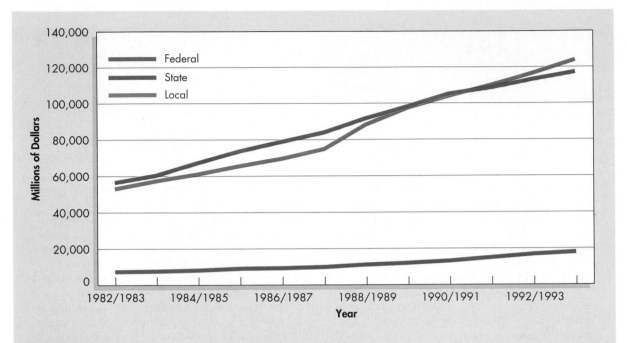

FIGURE 3.2

Funding for
Elementary and
Secondary Education

Although education issues are significant at the national government level, it is the states and local levels that continue to invest the most in this area.

Source: National Center for Education Statistics, *The Digest of Education Statistics 1996,* tbl. 157 (http://www.ed.gov/NCES/pubs/d96/D96T157.html)

Education Amendments of 1972 states that "No person in the United States shall, on the basis of sex, be excluded from participation in, be denied the benefits of, or be subjected to discrimination under any program or activity receiving federal financial assistance. . . ." In the process of enforcing this act, the U.S. Department of Education has informed individual school districts that, with a few exceptions, all classes must be coeducational and the standards for evaluating student performance must be adjusted accordingly.

This particular rule has been especially controversial in the physical education curriculum. Federal regulations, for example, permit segregation of girls and boys in elementary and secondary school classes where the major activity involves

bodily contact (for example, wrestling or football). In physical education classes enrolling both sexes, the federal government allows teachers to form distinct male and female groups, but only if the separation is based on "objective standards of individual performance. . . ." Furthermore, where these or related standards produce an "adverse effect on members of one sex, schools must use appropriate standards that do not have such an effect. For example, if the ability to lift a certain weight is used as a standard for assignment to a swimming class, application of this standard may exclude some girls. The school would have to use other, appropriate standards to make the selection for that class." Regulations such as these often stir resentment and reaction from local school boards

and parents who perceive it as too much interference in local matters.

Thus, although local in nature, education continues to be a complex intergovernmental public
sector function—and a very controversial one in
many parts of the country.

Sources: Ann O'M. Bowman and Richard Kearney, *State and
Local Government*, 3rd ed. (Boston, Mass.: Houghton Mifflin,
1996), chap. 15. Also visit the web site of the National Center
for Education Statistics at http://nces01.ed.gov/pubsearch/
indreport.idc for up-to-date reports and statistics on education
in the United States. For information on Title IX requirements,
see http://inet.ed.gov/offices/OCR/ocrttl9.html.

taxpayer or class of taxpayers. Such powers were intended to stop members of
Congress from using spending or revenue-raising bills to mandate certain portions of federal grant funds for some pet project.

The White House.   American presidents have proposed new federal grant programs and worked to reform the intergovernmental system. Johnson's Great
Society agenda, for example, emphasized the Model Cities program and other
new and innovative projects. As previously noted, the administrations of both
Johnson and Nixon strove to improve the coordination of federal grant programs. In the late 1970s President Jimmy Carter issued several executive orders
aimed at simplifying the complicated grant application and reporting procedures, which by then had grown very complex.

Other White House initiatives sought to expand the role of state and local
governments in the federal system. Johnson called for the establishment of a
"creative federalism" involving a partnership of all levels of government as well
as community and private organizations. Nixon proposed a "new American Revolution" that would give "power to the people" by turning many national domestic programs back to state and local governments. Reagan announced a "new
federalism" that would have revamped the intergovernmental grant system over
a ten-year period. Clinton ordered members of his administration to administer
programs that allow states to experiment with innovative ways of dealing with the
nation's health and welfare problems. Some changes in the American federal system emerged from each of these presidential initiatives, but none led to radical
alterations in intergovernmental relationships until passage of the 1996 welfare
reform act discussed at the beginning of this chapter.

The Federal Bureaucracy.   Perhaps the greatest increase in the numbers of
national-level actors on the intergovernmental stage has been in the bureaucracy, especially in such agencies as the U.S. Departments of Housing and Urban
Development, Health and Human Services, Agriculture, Interior, Transportation, and Education. Some bureaucrats in these agencies determine the eligibility of state and local grant applicants and the appropriateness of their

proposals. Others monitor the use of grant-in-aid funds and constantly consult with other actors in the intergovernmental system about the need to modify specific grant programs.

The emergence of these intergovernmental bureaucracies has added a new dimension to U.S. government. On the one hand, the bureaucrats of such agencies are expected to disburse funds and assist state and local government officials in making effective use of those resources. On the other hand, these federal administrators are expected to ensure that state and local programs meet federal standards and live up to federal requirements. In other words, the growing federal bureaucracy assigned to intergovernmental programs is supposed to both facilitate the grant process and regulate state and local grant recipients. These bureaucrats are actors on the intergovernmental stage with dual, and often contradictory, roles (see Chapter 12, on the bureaucracy).

States in the Federal System

The states have remained extremely active participants in the contemporary intergovernmental arena. They have retained significant responsibilities in the areas of education, public health, criminal justice, and the regulation of gambling and liquor. They also play major roles in enforcing statewide environmental, safety, and health regulations. For years they have been the chief regulators of public utilities and savings banks.

States empower and determine the organization of local governments. Legally, local governments are created by the actions of state legislatures. Thus, theoretically, they can be legally terminated by state officials. In practice, however, states rarely use this life-and-death power over the legal existence of local governments, although they have on occasion eliminated entire city governments through legislative action. City governments cannot impose their own sales or income taxes unless state laws grant them that authority. There are examples of state governments taking over or shifting local government functions because of severe financial problems or unbridled corruption and inefficiency. In Missouri, for instance, the state assumed control of the police forces in both Kansas City and St. Louis earlier this century because of widespread corruption.[30] And in the 1970s, the state of New York helped New York City deal with its critical financial problems by assuming responsibility for all four-year colleges in the city's municipal university system. In recent years, some states have taken control of inner-city school districts that were failing to perform up to state standards.

The states have also made their mark in creative and innovative approaches to solving public problems and meeting challenges; in fact, often the states have led the way. For example, Wisconsin regulated railroads and democratized the political nomination process long before such policies were adopted nationally. Recently, California led the way in developing building-construction standards to help reduce energy costs and establishing auto-emission standards to help reduce air pollution. Such state-initiated innovations are common in almost every major area of domestic policy.[31] In discussions about welfare and education reform, one of the strongest arguments for giving more responsibility to the states was their ability to come up with novel and effective programs, even in the face of budgetary cuts.[32]

Most important today, however, is the states' pivotal role as liaison in the intergovernmental relations system. As noted earlier, the national government uses state agencies to administer its grants in a wide variety of policy areas. Furthermore, local governments rely on state officials for technical assistance, as well as for financial aid. In short, state governments may be the key link—not necessarily the weak link—in the U.S. federal system.[33]

The role of states in the intergovernmental relations system is always changing. When their influence wanes, students of American government tend to pronounce their doom. According to one observer in the 1930s, the American state was "finished." He said, "I do not predict that the states will go, but affirm that they have gone."[34] At other times states have been so important that one can hardly imagine how American government might operate without them.[35]

What accounts for these gains and losses in power? First, the states' authority changes dramatically as the Supreme Court shifts between strict and flexible interpretations of the Constitution. Second, the states' role depends on the actual political power they can mobilize. During certain periods of American history, state officials have managed to exercise considerable influence in Washington through their representatives in the House and Senate. At other times state governors and legislators have carried relatively little weight either in the White House or in the halls of Congress.

Third, public opinion plays a role in determining the extent of states' influence. Although state governments have always been important policymakers, the American public has not always looked to the states for solutions to its collective problems. At times the public has depended on local governments, and more recently it has expected Washington to help.

The question of public support for state government is complicated by citizens' attitudes toward their state governments, which tend to vary from place to place and over time. Between 1981 and 1991, for example, residents of the northeastern United States were less likely to give high marks to their state governments than residents in other regions. In addition, citizen surveys reflect shifting patterns of public attitudes toward state government. The number of western residents who were favorably inclined toward their states fell from 30 percent in 1981 to 21 percent in 1982; by 1991, the figure had again climbed to 30 percent. Similar annual shifts are seen in other regions as well.[36]

Fourth, the role of states in the federal system depends on their administrative capabilities. If states lack the administrative resources and managerial talent to deliver the goods and services demanded by the public, then they cannot play a major role for very long. Most observers believe that state administrative capabilities improved markedly during the 1970s and 1980s.[37] Ironically, much of that improvement has come as a result of pressures imposed by Washington during the past several decades—the pressures of requirements attached to the grant-in-aid programs.

Local Governments

When you think of local governments, you probably picture city halls and county courthouses occupied by small councils of elected officials and a few offices occupied by record-keeping clerks, who collect taxes and issue dog tags and automobile licenses. American local governments are much more than that, however, and their role in the intergovernmental relations system is a major one.

As noted earlier, all local governments are creations of the individual states. Under the formal provisions of the federal system established in the Constitution, governmental powers are divided between the national government and the states. Local governments, in other words, have no constitutional standing. Their very existence and legal authority are derived from legal charters granted to them under state laws.

In practice, however, Americans have always treated local governments as if they had separate and legitimate standing in the federal system.[38] As of 1992, there were 86,692 local governments in the United States. This figure includes county (3,043), municipal (19,296), township (16,666), and other **general service governments,** which provide a wide range of public services to those who live within their borders. There were also 14,556 school districts in 1992, as well as more than 33,000 other **special district governments,** dealing with one or two distinctive government functions, such as fire protection, public transportation, or sewage treatment. Each of these local governments can participate in some way in the intergovernmental relations system—and a great many do.[39]

The problems of local governments are not all alike because those governments reflect a variety of physical, social, cultural, political, or economic conditions. Between the extremes of small, rural, sparsely populated townships and huge, densely populated metropolitan areas are cities, towns, counties, and districts of every conceivable size and shape. To understand the distinctive role played by local governments in the intergovernmental system, we need to perceive their differences.

Of particular importance are wide economic disparities among various local governments. These differences in wealth influence the way community leaders approach the intergovernmental system. In 1988, for example, the per capita income in Laredo, Texas, was just under $7,500—less than half the per capita income of Tulsa, Oklahoma, or Bremerton, Washington, and nearly one-third the per capita income of residents of Naples, Florida, who earned $21,600 that year. A city such as Laredo or Newark, New Jersey, would want more federal aid programs targeted for job-training programs, public housing, public health facilities, and similar projects aimed at helping the urban poor. Naples's government, in contrast, would seek more federal funding for new highways, construction of new recreation facilities, and other amenities.

Besides the economic status of the citizenry, age and ethnic background also bear on local problems and needs. The interests and concerns of Bradenton, Florida, are unique compared with those of many other communities because more than a fourth of its residents are over sixty-five years old. In

Denver International Airport

During the 1950s and 1960s, the federal government provided large grants to help cities build major airports. The controversial and expensive Denver International Airport, opened in 1995 after much delay, was the first major facility to be built since the early 1970s.

Bakersfield, California, a fourth of the population is fourteen years old or under. Thus the people of Bradenton would seek federal and state help in funding special programs for the elderly, whereas the citizens of Bakersfield would be more interested in state and federal aid for elementary and secondary school programs. Ethnic concerns might also be a factor. The very large Hispanic community in El Paso, Texas, is relevant to what that city wants from Washington. The intergovernmental relations system, for instance, can offer El Paso's schools funding for bilingual education programs. Such funds might not be available if the schools had to depend on local resources.[40]

These and other factors make it difficult to generalize about the roles played by local government actors on the intergovernmental relations stage. Nevertheless, local officials have undoubtedly become major participants in the federal system during the post–World War II period and will remain important. They exercise much of their influence through local members of Congress, who are responsive to the needs of the constituents back home. They also exert influence through membership in intergovernmental lobbying groups, which make up an increasingly important set of actors in the federal system.

The Intergovernmental Lobby

The **intergovernmental lobby** includes individuals and groups that have a special interest in the policies and programs implemented through the growing intergovernmental relations system (for more on interest groups, see Chapter 8).

Some of these lobbyists represent private interests that hope to benefit from or expect to be harmed by some intergovernmental program. For example, environmental lobbyists push for effective state and local enforcement of national air quality and water quality standards. Other intergovernmental lobbyists support social regulations to strengthen automobile safety, consumer protection, or occupational health. Representatives of businesses seek to reduce these regulations and to weaken state and local enforcement.

Lobbyists for the poor or the disabled are also active on the federalism stage. In many instances their goals are to ensure federal funding of social welfare and educational programs. In June 1994, for example, the National Associations of Community Health Centers (NACHC)—representing 2,000 medical clinics that serve the health-care needs of nearly 7 million poor Americans—sued the Clinton administration to halt efforts to allow state governments to experiment with the way they provide health care to the poor through Medicaid, the federal program designed to provide health care for America's poor.

In their lawsuit, NACHC officials contended that the waivers being granted by the Clinton administration were illegal because the experimental programs effectively reduced the health care provided to Medicaid recipients in those states.[41] By bringing suit in federal court, the NACHC was not only taking formal legal action on the federalism stage, but was also drawing attention to an intergovernmental issue that has an impact on millions of Americans.

In recent years a new kind of intergovernmental lobby has emerged: **public-sector interest groups,** which represent the interests of elected officials and other major governmental actors involved in the intergovernmental relations system. For example, the National Governors' Association and the U.S. Conference of Mayors are two of the most active groups in Washington that lobby on domestic policy issues. The American Society for Public Administration and the International City and County Management Association represent the interests of public administrators and other nonelected public-sector workers. Still others—such as the National League of Cities, the National Association of Counties, and the Council of State Governments—lobby on behalf of their own government jurisdictions.

A growing number of individual governments also hire lobbyists to represent their interests. In 1969 Mayor John V. Lindsay of New York City took the brash step of opening a Washington, D.C., office to lobby on behalf of the Big Apple. Two decades later, New York City had eight full-time lobbyists looking after its interests in Washington. Similar offices have been opened by just about every major government in the United States.

The increasing number of public-sector interest groups, as well as their political influence, paralleled the growth of the intergovernmental system itself during the 1960s and 1970s.[42] In recent years, however, the reduction in federal aid for states and localities has led several of these public-sector interest groups to reconsider their priorities and roles. Many have cut back their Washington-based staffs and focused more attention on lobbying state legislatures or on providing technical assistance to their members who must adapt to Washington's reductions in grant-in-aid funding.[43]

The Role of the Citizen

The largest group of actors on the intergovernmental stage are the citizens of the United States—the intended beneficiaries of all the policies and public services of American government. Hardly an area of American domestic policy remains untouched by the intergovernmental relations system; yet many Americans remain unaware of the role of intergovernmental relations. Every person who drives a car on the highways, attends public schools, uses city buses, or receives emergency care at the community hospital benefits from intergovernmental programs.

Of course, the American people are more than just the beneficiaries of the many goods and services provided through the intergovernmental system. As taxpayers, citizens also pay for those programs, often indirectly. Most intergovernmental programs are paid for with general tax revenues collected by the various levels of government. However, a portion of the money comes from special trust funds established for a particular program. For instance, each time you

Intergovernment Relations

The U.S. Interstate Highway System is a major example of what has been accomplished through cooperative intergovernment relations since the 1950s.

purchase a gallon of gasoline for your car, you pay a special federal tax. That tax is deposited in the Highway Trust Fund, which is used primarily to pay for the construction and maintenance of interstate highways and other roads.

Most important, the American people generate the demand for intergovernmental programs. The pressures that the public brings to bear on the system are most evident when popular grant programs are threatened with major cuts or when a community faces a crisis that cannot be handled with local resources. Consider, for example, social service programs for the elderly or handicapped. When members of the Reagan administration suggested cutbacks in social security in 1982, the public reacted so negatively that President Reagan felt compelled to promise never to cut those benefits. And when a crisis or tragedy strikes some community—when a tornado or flood devastates a small town or when buried hazardous wastes contaminate a community's soil and water supply—the call for action goes out to Washington as well as to the state capitol and city hall. These kinds of actions generate intergovernmental activity.

Many Dramas on the Stage

Obviously, the federalism stage would be extremely crowded if all the actors were involved at the same time. That rarely, if ever, happens, for few issues exist that interest everyone in the federal system. In fact, only twice in recent history did a great many actors stream onto the intergovernmental relations stage: when Presidents Nixon and Reagan suggested major reforms of the federal system itself.

More typically, the dramas of the federal system are played out on different parts of the stage by relatively few actors. For example, before 1974 the money in the Highway Trust Fund—raised through federal taxes on gasoline purchases—was used exclusively to build and maintain interstate and other federal highways. For years, however, a coalition of environmentalists and local officials from major urban areas pushed Congress to divert some of those funds to building and maintaining urban mass transit systems. Though the political battle was not highly publicized, it was fiercely fought in a corner of the intergovernmental stage. Finally, Congress passed the National Mass Transportation Act of 1974, allowing state officials to spend some of the Highway Trust's funds on mass transit. By 1991, instead of arguing over whether trust fund revenues would be spent on mass transit, the congressional debate focused on what portion should be devoted to highways and what portion to other transportation needs.

Similar instances of intergovernmental politics and policymaking take place daily in Washington, in state capitols, in county courthouses, and in city halls. In this sense, the story of issues surrounding welfare reform and highway policies are typical of today's federalism. Who is involved in those dramas on the various sections of the intergovernmental stage depends to a great extent on what is at stake.

MYTHS IN POPULAR CULTURE

3.1   The Political "Image" of the South

Federalism serves as a means for satisfying the need for a stronger central government while maintaining the authority of state and local government. At the same time, it has provided a stage upon which differences among the states can be played out. For example, state size was a major difference early in the nation's history, as small states such as Rhode Island and New Hampshire used the federal system to protect themselves from the power of larger states such as New York and Virginia. Another important difference has been the division between urban/industrial and rural states. Regional differences (North vs. South, East vs. West), however, have proven the most important over the years.

Modern popular culture has reflected these differences in a variety of forms and formats, especially as they relate to the division between northern and southern states. Despite the natural cleavages that separate westerners from easterners in the United States, it has been the north/south differences that have drawn the public's attention since at least the 1930s. The image of the South offered has ranged from a region victimized and embittered after the Civil War to a hostile place where racism runs rampant.

In 1939 it was the image of a defeated South pillaged and plundered by Northern forces that emerged from the classic movie *Gone With the Wind.* From the 1940s through the 1950s films portrayed a culturally distinct South, stressing the region's innocence and backwardness. This image turned quite negative by 1960 when a Broadway hit play, *Inherit the Wind,* was made into a movie. A fictionalization of the famous "Scopes Monkey Trial," held in Tennessee during the 1920s, it pictures the South as a bastion of backward fundamentalist thinking—more to be pitied than hated.

The image of a South confronting its racism has also been the subject for moviemakers. In the 1967 film, *In the Heat of the Night,* Rod Steiger portrayed a local police chief who grudgingly accepts the reluctantly given help of a black police detective from Philadelphia (Sidney Poitier). Both the film and Steiger won Academy Awards, and the show's plot later turned up as a television dramatic series. In 1988 director Alan Parker revisited that era and image of the South in a critically acclaimed movie, *Mississippi Burning.* The film dramatized the 1964 FBI investigation into the disappearance of four civil rights workers.

In the realm of popular music, rock singer Neil Young wrote two songs promoting the image of the racist South. In the late 1960s his "Southern Man" lyrics spoke of southerners in terms that conjured up images of cracking whips and lynch mobs. Although less simplistic in its imagery of southerners, his 1972 song, "Alabama," still pointed an accusatory finger at the region as the home of racists who needed to change their ways. As if to say "enough is enough," the members of one southern band, Lynyrd Skynyrd, wrote a musical response in their 1974 hit song, "Sweet Home Alabama":

> Well I heard Mr. Young sing about her.
> Well I heard old Neil put her down.
> Well I hope Neil Young will remember,
> Southern Man don't need him around anyhow.
> . . .
> In Birmingham they love the governor.
> Now we all did what we could do.
> Now Watergate does not bother me.
> Does your conscience bother you?
> (Tell me true.)

Images such as these are directly related to the changing myths of American government and politics in the federal arena. Just as southern politicians have emerged as leading "liberals" in the Democratic party (e.g., Jimmy Carter and Bill Clinton), so has the popular image of a racist, ignorant, and backward South significantly changed. The first indications of that shift came during the late 1970s with the shift toward a cinematic image of a "New South" comprising hard-working blue-collar Americans. During the late 1970s, for instance, Burt Reynolds starred in two box office hits—*Gator* and *White Lightning*—in which progressive "New South" southerners worked with federal agents to triumph over corrupt "Old South" southerners, represented by the local sheriff and other officials. The music also changed, with southern bands like Lynyrd Skynyrd becoming part of the mainstream of the popular sounds that emerged during the 1980s.

Conclusion: The Myths Versus the Dramas

The image of intergovernmental relations being played out on different parts of the federalism stage poses a challenge to the widely held myths of national government weakness and national government dominance. Both myths oversimplify the reality of intergovernmental relations. On closer examination, intergovernmental relations emerge as a complex system in which the role of all governments—national, state, and local—changes over time depending on a variety of political, economic, and social factors. The role that national government plays depends on the issues and circumstances surrounding the federalism stage at the time the curtain rises. National government officials fill important and often highly visible roles on this stage, but so do state, local, and even private actors.

For example, the federalism stage changed considerably after the 1994 election. That was evident on the evening that President Clinton presented his 1995 State of the Union address. Normally, a prominent Republican senator or member of the House would respond to the address. On that evening, however, Trenton, the capital of New Jersey, was the setting for the response. There, Governor Christine Todd Whitman stood before the cameras to address the nation. The fact that a state rather than a Washington official assumed that task said a great deal about the changing stage of intergovernmental relations in the mid-1990s.

Of course, the drama metaphor used in this chapter has its shortcomings, for the American federal system today is too complex to be summarized in such an image. To call intergovernmental relations merely a staged play or say that there is a trend toward or away from national government domination distorts an ever-changing reality. Rather, the American federal system is a flexible arrangement among different levels of government; it adapts as problems and circumstances change. In that sense, American federalism is very much like the constitutional system from which it emerged.

Summary

1. Relationships among national, state, and local officials are becoming increasingly complex. This growing complexity is central to the changing nature of the American federal system.

2. The evolution of the American federal system has been shaped by the distinctive challenges that have faced the United States during the past two centuries. Out of that evolution has emerged a complex system of intergovernmental relations based on a variety of grant-in-aid programs. The intergovernmental relations system has been characterized by periods and episodes of conflict and cooperation.

3. The dynamics of American federalism are best understood as a number of dramas being played out on various parts of the intergovernmental stage by several groups of actors, including the courts, the Congress, the White House, the federal bureaucracy, local and state officials, intergovernmental lobbies, and the American people.

4. The complexities and dramas of American intergovernmental relations challenge simplistic views of U.S. federalism that characterize it in terms of how much influence the national government has.

Key Terms and Concepts

Entitlement programs Government programs that pay benefits to all eligible recipients. The amount of money spent depends on the number of those eligible rather than on some predetermined figure.

State-centered federalism The view that the Constitution allowed the national government only limited powers and that the states could overrule national laws if congressional acts were determined to be in violation of the Constitution.

Nation-centered federalism The view that the authority of the national government goes beyond the responsibilities listed in Article I, Section 8, of the Constitution. Based on the necessary and proper clause and the principle of national supremacy.

Interstate commerce Trade across state lines; in contrast to intrastate (within state boundaries) trade and foreign trade. During the early years of the republic, interstate commerce was determined to be within the jurisdiction of the national government.

Police powers The powers of state governments over the regulation of behavior within their borders. These police powers were used to justify state jurisdiction over economic matters.

Dual federalism The perspective on federalism that emerged after the Civil War. It saw the national and state governments as equal but independent partners, with each responsible for distinct policy functions and each barred from interfering with the other's work.

Grant-in-aid programs Federal appropriations that are given to states and localities to fund state policies and programs. The Morrill Act (1862) was the first instance of such a program.

Intergovernmental relations The style of federalism which recognized the interdependence of Washington and state and local governments. The various levels of government share functions, and each level is able to influence the others.

Cooperative federalism A period of cooperation between state and national government that began during the Great Depression. The national government began to take on new responsibilities, and state and local officials accepted it as an ally, not an enemy.

Categorical, or conditional, grants-in-aid Money given to the states and localities by Congress that was to be used for limited purposes under specific rules.

Formula grants Grants given to states and localities on the basis of population, number of eligible persons, per capita income, or other factors.

Project grants Grants awarded to states and localities for a specific program or plan of action.

Matching grants Programs in which the national government requires recipient governments to provide a certain percentage of the funds needed to implement the programs.

Councils of governments Local and regional councils created in the early 1970s by federal funds to help solve problems such as coordinating applications for federal grants.

Block grants Money given to the states by Congress that can be used in broad areas and is not limited to specific purposes like categorical grants. A

means introduced in the mid-1960s of giving states greater freedom.

General revenue sharing A small but innovative grant-in-aid program, used in the 1970s and 1980s, that had no significant conditions attached to it. State and local governments received funds according to a formula based on population and related factors.

Unfunded mandates Required actions imposed on lower level governments by federal (and state) governments that are not accompanied by money to pay for the activities being mandated.

Devolution A term indicating the effort to give more functions and responsibilities to states and localities in the intergovernmental system.

General service governments Local governments, such as counties, municipalities, and townships, that provide a wide range of public services to those who live within their borders.

Special district governments Local governments that deal with one or two distinctive government functions, such as education, fire protection, public transportation, or sewage treatment.

Intergovernmental lobby The many individuals and groups that have a special interest in the policies and programs implemented through the growing intergovernmental relations systems. These lobbyists represent private, consumer, and business groups.

Public-sector interest groups A lobby that represents the interests of elected officials and other major government actors involved in the intergovernmental relations system. An example is the National Governors' Association.

The Heritage of Rights and Liberties

MYTH & REALITY

Is liberty, as defined by the U.S. Constitution, absolute?

See **Political Science** at
http://www.hmco.com/college

The Supreme Court's 1989 ruling that flag burning is a protected form of free speech filled the press with criticisms of the decision. In one such instance, the *Today* show invited a representative of the American Legion (the nation's largest veterans' organization) to appear and explain the group's reaction to the decision. As expected, the American Legion spokesman denounced the Court's decision. The interview did not end there, however. Jane Pauley, one of the show's hosts, asked the legionnaire to explain what the flag meant to him and other veterans. In response, the guest noted simply that "The flag is the symbol of our country, the land of the free and the home of the brave." Not satisfied with the answer, Pauley pressed further, asking, "What exactly does it symbolize?" Puzzled and perhaps a little annoyed by such a question, the guest responded, "It stands for the fact that this is a country where we have a right to do what we want."[1]

Obviously the legionnaire did not mean what he said because that would have justified supporting the rights of flag burners. Nevertheless, he was expressing the commonly held view that in America the guarantee of civil liberties means that we can do what we want. (**Civil liberties,** most of which are spelled out in the Bill of Rights, protect individuals from excessive or arbitrary government interference.) As we will see, that belief is a myth, the *myth of absolute or complete liberty;* liberty is not absolute, nor was it intended to be. Moreover, few Americans really believe in complete liberty when it applies to unpopular groups. When asked general questions about First Amendment liberties, Americans almost universally support them. But support for exercising these liberties drops significantly in regard to flag burners, for instance. As you read this chapter, notice how our understanding of liberty has changed. It is not just a static concept enshrined in the Bill of Rights and other constitutional provisions. Instead, like the Constitution, it has been altered by time and circumstances.

Public attitudes toward **civil rights** (guarantees of protection by government against discrimination or unreasonable treatment by other individuals or groups) tend to reflect a second widely held myth, the *myth of guaranteed political and social equality.* According to that myth, participation in the political and social system is open equally to all. Yet discrimination still marks American society. Indeed, national, state, and local governments have often enforced discrimination instead of guaranteeing individual civil rights. The rights of minorities have often been ignored in favor of the interests of the majority. Our understanding of civil rights—like our understanding of civil liberties—is constantly changing. Even as our nation struggles to live up to the promise of political equality for African-Americans and women, there are new demands for civil rights.

In this chapter, we consider how choices are made regarding the rights and liberties protected by the Constitution. We briefly explore the expansion and contraction of liberties as the courts have interpreted and reinterpreted the Bill of Rights. We also look at the way the Supreme Court has treated minorities, noting particularly its interpretation of the Fourteenth Amendment as it affects the rights of African-Americans and women.

Applying the Bill of Rights to the States

The original Constitution, unlike several state constitutions, made no mention of a bill of rights. Why no such protection was specified is unclear. Most historians argue that the framers simply felt that a listing of rights and liberties was unnecessary. The national government was to have only the powers granted to it, and the Constitution did not give the new government any power to infringe on the people's liberties. Therefore, many delegates reasoned that there would be no problem. No doubt they also assumed that the separation of powers and the system of checks and balances would thwart any effort to diminish individual liberties.

The failure to include a bill of rights in the Constitution caused clashes at state ratifying conventions. State after state ratified the Constitution only with the understanding that the new Congress would strengthen the document with a guarantee of certain personal liberties. Consequently, the First Congress, meeting in September 1789, proposed twelve amendments to the Constitution; within two years the states ratified ten. These ten amendments, collectively referred to as the Bill of Rights, constitute a list of specific limits on the power of the national government.

Originally, the provisions of the Bill of Rights were understood to only limit the actions of the national government. States were restricted only by the provisions of their individual constitutions. The Supreme Court decision in *Barron* v. *Baltimore* (1833) clarified that view.[2] John Barron, the owner of a wharf in Baltimore, sued city officials who had redirected several streams that fed into the harbor where his wharf was located. By redirecting the streams, the city had caused large deposits of sand to build up, making the wharf inaccessible to ships. Because the city had destroyed his business, Barron claimed that city officials were required by the Fifth Amendment to provide just compensation.

After reviewing the precise wording and historical justification for adopting the Bill of Rights, Chief Justice John Marshall, writing for a unanimous Court, ruled against Barron. According to Marshall, the Bill of Rights applied only to the national government. That is why, Marshall argued, the first word of the First Amendment is *Congress*. That position remained unchallenged until the ratification of the Fourteenth Amendment in 1868.

Drafted chiefly to provide equality before the law to the recently emancipated slaves, the Fourteenth Amendment contains much broader language. Its very first paragraph includes this statement: "nor shall any State deprive any person of life, liberty, or property, without due process of law." The statement is critically important for understanding the role of the Bill of Rights in modern society. To some, this "due process" clause clearly indicates that the framers of the Fourteenth Amendment intended to reverse the *Barron* v. *Baltimore* decision. For instance, throughout his long career, Supreme Court Justice Hugo Black steadfastly maintained that the Fourteenth Amendment *incorporated* (that is, made applicable to the states) the entire Bill of Rights.[3]

Although a majority of the Supreme Court has never accepted Black's sweeping interpretation of the Fourteenth Amendment, most provisions of the Bill of Rights have since been applied to the states. Beginning in 1925, the Supreme Court slowly increased the number of provisions applicable to the states. It did so through **selective incorporation**—the application to the states of only those portions of the Bill of Rights that a majority of justices believed to be fundamental to a democratic society. The 1937 case of *Palko* v. *Connecticut* illustrates that approach.[4]

Frank Palko was found guilty of second-degree murder and sentenced to life in prison. The prosecutor, desiring a conviction for first-degree murder, successfully appealed the trial court's decision and retried him. This time, Palko was found guilty of first-degree murder and sentenced to death. Palko then appealed his case to the Supreme Court, claiming that the second trial was unconstitutional because the Constitution protected an individual from being tried twice for the same crime. Writing for the Court, Justice Benjamin Cardozo acknowledged that the Bill of Rights contains guarantees so fundamental to liberty that they must be protected from state as well as national infringement. He did not include among these guarantees the protection against being tried twice for the same crime. Cardozo granted that the protection against being placed in double jeopardy was valuable and important, but it was not "the essence of a scheme of ordered liberty." Consequently, Frank Palko was executed.

In 1969 the *Palko* decision was overturned, and by the early 1970s the Supreme Court had incorporated almost all provisions of the Bill of Rights. As Table 4.1 shows, only a handful of protections remain unincorporated. The most

TABLE 4.1

Selective Incorporation of the Bill of Rights

Although the Bill of Rights was designed to protect individual freedom, it was not immediately clear whether the protection extended to the states. In a series of decisions—mostly in the 1930s through the 1960s—the Supreme Court ruled that the states as well as the national government are barred from infringing on citizens' constitutional rights.

Provision	Amendment	Year	Case
"Public use" and "just compensation" conditions in the taking of private property by government	V	1896 and 1897	*Missouri Pacific Railway Co.* v. *Nebraska,* 164 U.S. 403, 17 S.Ct. 130; *Chicago, Burlington & Quincy Railway Co.* v. *Chicago,* 166 U.S. 226, 17 S.Ct. 581
Freedom of speech	I	1927	*Fiske* v. *Kansas,* 274 U.S. 380, 47 S.Ct. 655; *Gitlow* v. *New York,* 268 U.S. 652, 45 S.Ct. 625 (1925) (dictum only); *Gilbert* v. *Minnesota,* 254 U.S. 325, 41 S.Ct. 125 (1920) (dictum only)

(continued)

TABLE 4.1

Selective
Incorporation
(cont.)

Provision	Amendment	Year	Case
Freedom of the press	I	1931	*Near* v. *Minnesota,* 283 U.S. 697, 51 S.Ct. 625
Fair trial and right to counsel in capital cases	VI	1932	*Powell* v. *Alabama,* 287 U.S. 45, 53 S.Ct. 55
Freedom of religion	I	1934	*Hamilton* v. *Regents of Univ. of California,* 293 U.S. 245, 55 S.Ct. 197 (dictum only)
Freedom of assembly and, by implication, freedom to petition for redress of grievances	I	1937	*De Jonge* v. *Oregon,* 299 U.S. 353, 57 S.Ct. 255
Free exercise of religious belief	I	1940	*Cantwell* v. *Connecticut,* 310 U.S. 296, 60 S.Ct. 900
Separation of church and state; right against the establishment of religion	I	1947	*Everson* v. *Board of Educ.,* 330 U.S. 1, 67 S.Ct. 504
Right to public trial	VI	1948	In re *Oliver,* 333 U.S. 257, 68 S.Ct. 499
Right against unreasonable searches and seizures	IV	1949	*Wolf* v. *Colorado,* 338 U.S. 25, 69 S.Ct. 1359
Freedom of association	I	1958	*NAACP* v. *Alabama,* 357 U.S. 449, 78 S.Ct. 1163
Exclusionary rule as concomitant of unreasonable searches and seizures	IV	1961	*Mapp* v. *Ohio,* 367 U.S. 643, 81 S.Ct. 1684
Right against cruel and unusual punishments	VIII	1962	*Robinson* v. *California,* 370 U.S. 660, 82 S.Ct. 1417
Right to counsel in all felony cases	VI	1963	*Gideon* v. *Wainwright,* 372 U.S. 335, 83 S.Ct. 792
Right against self-incrimination	V	1964	*Malloy* v. *Hogan,* 378 U.S. 1, 84 S.Ct. 1489; *Murphy* v. *Waterfront Com'n,* 378 U.S. 52, 84 S.Ct. 1594
Right to confront witnesses	VI	1965	*Pointer* v. *Texas,* 380 U.S. 400, 85 S.Ct. 1065
Right to privacy	Various	1965	*Griswold* v. *Connecticut,* 381 U.S. 479, 85 S.Ct. 1678
Right to impartial jury	VI	1966	*Parker* v. *Gladden,* 385 U.S. 363, 87 S.Ct. 468
Right to speedy trial	VI	1967	*Klopfer* v. *North Carolina,* 386 U.S. 213, 87 S.Ct. 988
Right to compulsory process for obtaining witnesses	VI	1967	*Washington* v. *Texas,* 388 U.S. 14, 87 S.Ct. 1920

(continued)

Provision	Amendment	Year	Case
Right to jury trial in cases of serious crime	VI	1968	*Duncan* v. *Louisiana*, 391 U.S. 145, 88 S.Ct. 1444
Right against double jeopardy	V	1969	*Benton* v. *Maryland*, 395 U.S. 784, 89 S.Ct. 2056
Right to counsel in all criminal cases entailing a jail term	VI	1972	*Argersinger* v. *Hamlin*, 407 U.S. 25, 92 S.Ct. 2006

Other Incorporated Provisions

Provision	Amendment	
Right of petition	I	Included by implication of other First Amendment incorporations
Right to be informed of the nature and cause of the accusation	VI	Included by implication of other Sixth Amendment incorporations

Amendments Not Incorporated

Provisions of the First Eight Amendments Not Incorporated		Provision(s) Not Incorporated
	II	All
	III	All
	V	Right to indictment by grand jury
	VII	All
	VIII	Right against excessive bail; right against excessive fines

Source: Craig R. Ducat and Harold W. Chase, *Constitutional Interpretation*, 5th ed., pp. 845–846. Copyright © 1992 by West Publishing Company. Used by permission of Wadsworth Publishing Company.

controversial is the Second Amendment, which provides that "a well-regulated Militia, being necessary to the security of a free State, the right of the people to keep and bear Arms, shall not be infringed."

Incorporating the Bill of Rights is one thing, but defining the scope of the provisions is another. We turn now to the Court's interpretation of several provisions of the Bill of Rights, beginning, naturally, with the First Amendment.

The First Amendment Freedoms

Because the First Amendment is written in absolute terms ("Congress shall make no law . . ."), it is more likely to be subject to the myth of absolute liberty than the other amendments. But as we will see, the exercise of First Amendment freedoms often conflicts with other highly desirable goals of society. Most justices have found it unworkable to protect all liberties without qualification. Instead, the issue has been one of balance. Sometimes the Court has interpreted the safeguards of the First Amendment strictly, giving maximum protection to individual liberties. At other times, it has allowed the government great latitude in pursuing its interests. Drawing the lines has never been easy, but it has always been necessary.

Free Speech

Freedom of speech is essential for a democracy. As Justice Black observed, "Freedom to speak and write about public questions is as important to the life of our government as is the heart to the body."[5] The First Amendment states that "Congress shall make no law . . . abridging the freedom of speech or of the press." Nevertheless, the freedom to speak has often been the target of government regulation. No matter how highly we value free speech, each of us is likely at some time to see its exercise as dangerous. This is simply a recognition that ideas have consequences—consequences that we may disapprove of or even fear.

Changing Standards.   Although the First Amendment is phrased in a way that seemingly prohibits any limitations on speech, the Supreme Court has never

Liberty for the Unpopular

Although Americans take great pride in the nation's abstract commitment to political liberty, they are often unwilling to extend constitutional protections to highly unpopular groups such as the Ku Klux Klan.

viewed freedom of speech as immune from all governmental restriction. Justice Oliver Wendell Holmes once noted that freedom of speech does not protect someone who is "falsely shouting fire in a crowded theater." The Court has tried to define the circumstances under which the government may limit speech. To that end, it has employed a series of tests designed to strike a balance between the constitutional protection and the need for public order or security.

The first of these tests was developed by Justice Holmes in *Schenck* v. *United States* (1919).[6] Charles T. Schenck had been convicted under the Espionage Act of 1917 for distributing leaflets urging young men to resist the World War I draft. Writing for a unanimous Court, Justice Holmes rejected the proposition that speech was always protected from government restriction and instead expounded the **clear and present danger test.** The question, Holmes said, was whether speech would cause evils the government had a right to prevent. If the speech could be shown to present grave and immediate danger to its interests, the government had a right to punish it. The justice admitted that in ordinary times the defendant would have been within his constitutional rights, but these were not ordinary times. Urging young men to resist the draft during a war was, he said, a serious threat to the nation's safety.

Almost immediately after Holmes's decision, the majority of the Court began to substitute for clear and present danger the **bad tendency test.** That test allowed the government to punish speech that might cause people to engage in illegal action. Announced in *Gitlow* v. *New York* (1925),[7] the bad tendency test removed the need to prove a close connection between speech and the prohibited evil. To justify a restriction of speech, the government only needed to demonstrate that the speech might, even at some distant time, present a danger to society. Thus Benjamin Gitlow, a member of the Socialist party, could be convicted under a criminal anarchy law that prohibited anyone from advocating the overthrow of the government, even though no evidence showed that his efforts had any such effect.

During the 1960s, questions of free speech became numerous as the civil rights movement and the movement against the Vietnam War generated a succession of mass protests. Sit-in demonstrations, protest marches, and draft-card burnings raised new issues of free speech. The Supreme Court of that era, led by Chief Justice Earl Warren, rejected the bad tendency test of the earlier period. It substituted the **preferred freedoms test,** which proposed that some freedoms—free speech among them—are so fundamental to a democracy that they merit special protection. The government can restrict these freedoms only if they present a grave and immediate danger to the larger society. Theoretically, then, government may limit speech, but in practice it is difficult to design a law that passes the test. The preferred freedoms doctrine comes close to banning all government restriction of speech.

Symbolic Speech.   Not all speech is verbal. In fact, one may engage in what is called symbolic speech without uttering a word. Gestures and even the wearing of garish clothing may convey opinion, perhaps even more effectively than

Burning Old Glory

The congressional act of 1989 banning desecration of the flag prompted several protests challenging the law. Pictured here is a man, identified only as Dred Scott, being arrested by Capitol Hill police after he set fire to a flag on the steps of the Capitol.

speech. Because symbolic speech is a form of communication, the Supreme Court has generally accorded it the protection of the First Amendment. In 1989, for instance, the Court upheld the right of protesters to burn the American flag. Writing for the majority in *Texas* v. *Johnson,* former Justice William Brennan argued that laws that prohibit the burning of the flag infringe on a form of constitutionally protected speech.[8] Brennan's opinion was greeted by a storm of outrage. Saying that "flag burning is wrong, dead wrong," President George Bush called for a constitutional amendment to overturn the decision. Although Bush's proposed constitutional amendment failed in the Senate, Congress did pass the Flag Protection Act of 1989, which provided criminal punishments for anyone who knowingly "mutilates, defaces, physically defiles, burns, maintains on the floor or the ground, or tramples upon any flag of the United States." But in 1990, with Justice Brennan again writing the majority opinion, the Court, in *U.S.* v. *Eichman,* ruled that the new law also violated the Constitution's guarantee of freedom of speech.[9]

Not all symbolic acts have gained protection from the Court. In 1968, for example, the Court ruled that burning a draft card was not a protected form of symbolic speech, despite the obvious political message conveyed by the act.[10] Rejecting the view that "an apparently limitless variety of conduct can be labeled 'speech' whenever the person engaging in the conduct intends thereby to express an idea," Chief Justice Warren concluded that the government's vital interest in having a system for raising armies justified this incidental limitation on the First Amendment. More recently, the Court upheld a lower court's order prohibiting protesters from blocking the entrance to an abortion clinic. Writing for the Court in *Madsen* v. *Women's Health Center* (1994)[11] Chief Justice William Rehnquist argued that the state's interest in protecting the well-being of the clinic's patients justified the burden on free speech.

The First Amendment's guarantee of free speech, including symbolic speech, also covers the freedom not to engage in symbolic action, such as saluting the flag. This freedom not to speak, in words or symbols, was first articulated by the Court in *West Virginia State Board of Education* v. *Barnette* (1943). In that case, Walter Barnette, a parent of school-aged children, challenged a West Virginia statute that required all teachers and schoolchildren to recite the Pledge of Allegiance while maintaining a stiff arm salute. Barnette, a Jehovah's Witness, claimed that the action violated a religious commandment against worshiping graven images. Speaking for the majority, Justice Robert Jackson claimed that the state could not compel any student to salute the flag. To those who argued that a compulsory flag salute was necessary to foster national unity, Jackson answered: "If there is any fixed star in our constitutional constellation, it is that no official, high or petty, can prescribe what shall be orthodox in politics, nationalism, religion, or other matters of opinion, or force citizens to confess by word or act their faith therein."[12]

A Free Press

The same language protects the freedom of the press, which is closely linked with freedom of speech. Because the rights at stake are so similar, many of the interpretations applied to free speech cases also fit freedom of the press. As with free speech, however, the majority of Supreme Court justices have rejected the proposition that freedom of the press is an absolute.

Prior Restraint.   Even though the Supreme Court has never accepted complete freedom of the press, it has repeatedly struck down laws imposing a prior restraint on newspapers. **Prior restraint** means blocking a publication from reaching the public. The First Amendment has stood as a strong check against would-be censors. The first significant prior restraint case, *Near* v. *Minnesota* (1931), illustrates the point.[13]

At issue in *Near* was a state statute that provided for the banning of "malicious, scandalous and defamatory" newspapers or periodicals. After he had printed a series of articles criticizing the local police department, Jay Near, the publisher of the Minneapolis-based *Saturday Press,* was ordered to cease publication of the weekly scandal sheet. Aggravating his attacks on city officials was a constant anti-Semitic, pro–Ku Klux Klan theme that appeared in each edition of the paper.

Clearly, the *Saturday Press* was malicious, scandalous, and defamatory. Yet the Supreme Court lifted the ban on publication, with Chief Justice Charles E. Hughes observing that prior restraint could be applied only in "exceptional cases." Hughes did admit that under some circumstances the government might prohibit the publishing of truly harmful information—for example, information about troop movements in wartime. But in ordinary circumstances, the presumption should be to favor publication.

A more serious challenge to freedom of the press arose in *New York Times* v. *United States* (1971), also known as the Pentagon Papers case.[14] Both the *New York Times* and the *Washington Post* published portions of a classified report on the history of American involvement in Vietnam. Citing a breach of national security, the government sought an order to prevent further publication of the materials by the two newspapers. A divided Court (6 to 3) ruled that the newspapers could continue publishing the report because the government had not justified the need for prior restraint. Still, only Justices Black and William Douglas took the position that the government could never restrain a publication. The four others in the majority assumed that in extreme cases national security could justify an injunction, thus raising the possibility of a constitutional exercise of prior restraint.

The great leeway granted to the press by the Court in questions of prior restraint does not mean that the press is free to do as it pleases without regard to consequences. The press can be punished *after* publication. Two forms of expression—libel and obscenity—are particularly open to punishment.

Libel.   **Libel** is the use of print or pictures to harm someone's reputation, whereas **slander** is injury by spoken word. Traditionally, these actions have been outside First Amendment protection; therefore, they have been punishable by criminal law and subject to civil prosecution for damages.

Until 1964 a plaintiff could win a libel suit simply by proving that the statements in question were substantially false. But in 1964 the Court expanded press protection by requiring that public officials claiming to be libeled prove that the statements were made with "actual malice."[15] In order to recover damages, an official must prove not only that the accusation is false but also that the publisher acted "with knowledge that it was false or with reckless disregard of whether it was false or not." This "actual malice" standard was later extended to cover public figures—private citizens who, because of their station in life or their activities, are newsworthy. Actual malice is very difficult to prove, and therefore the Court's decisions virtually immunized the press against libel suits by public officials and public figures.

Perhaps the Court sensed that it had gone too far in protecting the press at the expense of private individuals who had been victimized by irresponsible attacks because in 1976 it narrowed the category of public figures. In *Time, Inc.* v. *Firestone* (1976), the Court awarded damages against the news magazine *Time*.[16] A *Time* article about a divorce proceeding referred to the divorcee as an adulteress, a finding not substantiated in the trial court's decree. Ruling against the magazine, the Court redefined a public figure as one who voluntarily enters "into the forefront of public controversies." Because parties to a divorce do not meet such a test, Mary Alice Firestone did not need to prove actual malice, but only negligence—a lack of care in checking the facts. In 1988, however, the Court reaffirmed its "actual malice" standard for public figures when it ruled that the Reverend Jerry Falwell was not entitled to compensation for the emotional distress he suffered as a result of a vulgar parody of him published in *Hustler Magazine*.[17]

Obscenity.   Obscenity has never been considered deserving of First Amendment protection. Any work judged obscene may be banned. But what is obscene? Again and again the Court has confronted that question, and each time the justices have struggled to give meaning to the elusive concept. Indicative of the difficulty is Justice Potter Stewart's admission that he could not define hard-core pornography, but "I know it when I see it."

In the first of the modern obscenity cases, *Roth* v. *United States* (1957),[18] Justice Brennan observed that sex and obscenity are not synonymous. Consequently, Brennan tried to formulate a legal test for obscenity that would protect the right to deal with sexual matters and yet reserve to the government the power to prohibit what was truly obscene. The test he proposed was "whether to the average person, applying contemporary community standards, the dominant theme of the material taken as a whole appeals to prurient interest." Later cases attempted to clarify the test by describing the community standards as national standards, not local ones, and requiring proof that the work was "utterly without redeeming social value."[19] This latter aspect of the test made it virtually impossible for prosecutors to obtain pornography convictions.

As a presidential candidate in 1968, Richard M. Nixon vigorously criticized the rulings on pornography as overly permissive. Thus it came as no surprise that the Supreme Court led by Chief Justice Warren Burger, which included four Nixon appointees, moved to limit the spread of sexually explicit materials. In *Miller* v. *California* (1973), the Court ruled that prosecutors no longer need demonstrate that the work is "utterly without redeeming social value."[20] From *Miller* on, prosecutors must prove only that the work "lacks serious literary, artistic, political, or scientific value."

In the *Miller* decision, the Court also rejected the previous rulings that community standards mean national standards. Arguing that it is unrealistic to require the same standard in Maine or Mississippi as in Las Vegas or New York, Chief Justice Burger expressed faith in the ability of jurors to draw on the

**MYTHS
IN POPULAR CULTURE**

4.1 The Final Frontier: Cyberspace and the First Amendment

Navigating the superhighway, surfing the net, e-mailing, and posting messages on one of the thousands of newsgroups of the Usenet have become familiar activities and even preoccupations for millions of Americans. Whether through the Internet or the commercial on-line services, a rapidly growing number of Americans are becoming "jacked in" to cyberspace.

Among the many alluring qualities of cyberspace is that it facilitates person-to-person contact that is not mediated by large organizational structures. The Internet, for instance, is an open system; no single organization owns it. Instead it is operated by the almost 5 million members (called hosts) who freely function across international borders and answer to no single nation or corporation. Disdaining the top-down hierarchical structures of traditional institutions, the Internet is a grassroots system whose users are often fervently dedicated to keeping it that way. There are protocols of behavior, but these are created and enforced by the users. (Those who violate convention may be subject to flaming—being bombarded by insulting messages.) Hierarchical controls and limitations, on the other hand, are for many users an abomination to be fiercely resisted.

Nevertheless, the First Amendment is not an absolute, even in cyberspace. The most significant effort to date to restrict speech in cyberspace occurred with the passage of the 1996 Communications Decency Act (CDA). As part of a larger effort to amend the 1934 Federal Communications Act, the CDA replaced the word "telephone" in the 1934 law with "telecommunications equipment," thus bringing cyberspace under the act's coverage. Further, the CDA made it a crime to transmit, "any . . . image or other communication which is obscene or indecent knowing that the recipient is a minor." Violation of the act is punishable by two years in prison and/or a $250,000 fine.

Contending that the act violated the First Amendment, a coalition of groups including the American Civil Liberties Union, the American Library Association, and the United States Chamber of Commerce challenged the law. The subsequent Supreme Court decision in *Reno* v. *ACLU* produced a partial victory for CDA opponents. Writing for the majority, Justice John Paul Stevens struck down that portion of the act prohibiting knowingly sending indecent materials to a minor. Although Justice Stevens acknowledged that the government had a legitimate interest in protecting children from exposure to indecent materials, the CDA, he argued, threatened to suppress too much speech among adults. According to Justice Stevens, "the interest in encouraging freedom of expression in a democratic society outweighs any theoretical but unproven benefit of censorship."

Still, cyberspace is not an unregulated forum since the court let stand that portion of the CDA that prohibited transmitting obscene materials. Moreover, the pressure to regulate cyberspace is likely to continue and grow more intense as the popularity of cyberspace increases.

standards of their local community. Nevertheless, the question of what constitutes obscenity remains a perplexing judicial and social issue, with the Court's decisions allowing considerable variability among communities.

Religious Freedom

The freedom to worship was one of the dominant motives behind the founding of the American colonies. Yet, surprisingly, the original Constitution makes only one mention of religion. Article VI states in part: "no religious test shall ever be required as a qualification to any office or public trust under the United States." Not until the First Amendment do we find guarantees of religious freedom. The amendment begins: "Congress shall make no law respecting an establishment of religion, or prohibiting the free exercise thereof."

As we have seen, the myth of absolute liberty has seldom been upheld because First Amendment rights have often conflicted with other important social values. The problem is particularly acute in the case of religious freedom. The guarantee of the free exercise of religion clearly means that the state must avoid coercion with regard to religious beliefs. But what about social policies that offend particular religious beliefs? Does the state have the right to require school attendance and vaccinations of those whose religious beliefs forbid such practices? Of course, the easy answer is to make an exception, but exceptions run the risk of violating another First Amendment provision—the establishment clause—by showing favoritism to one religion.[21]

Establishment of Religion.   What does the establishment clause mean? Years of debate have produced two distinct opinions. One view, known as the **accommodationist interpretation,** holds that the clause was meant to be interpreted narrowly, merely barring Congress from establishing an official, publicly supported church, such as the Church of England. Proponents of this view contend that nothing in the establishment clause forbids state support of religion as long as all religions are treated equally.

Others see the establishment clause as a broad-based prohibition against any governmental support of religion. Accordingly, they read the First Amendment as banning government involvement in all religious affairs, even in a completely evenhanded way. Advocates of this view claim that the First Amendment requires a complete separation of the government and religion, or as Thomas Jefferson put it, a **"wall of separation"** between church and state.

The Supreme Court has consistently espoused the "wall of separation" view. Yet in many cases the Court's decisions appear contradictory. They indicate that the justices have not completely rejected the idea of government aid to religious institutions so long as the government does not favor one religion over others. Thus intense debate continues over the establishment clause. It usually focuses on two questions: aid to religious schools and prayer in public schools.

The question of government aid to church-supported educational institutions has long been a knotty problem for the Court. In 1947, the Court allowed to stand a New Jersey plan for providing free bus transportation for children attending parochial schools.[22] Justice Black, writing for the Court, reasoned that the plan was designed to aid the children and their families, and not the religious institutions. Using this so-called child benefit theory, the Court has sustained state programs providing parochial schools with textbooks on secular subjects, school lunches, and public health services normally available in public schools.

In *Lemon* v. *Kurtzman* (1971), however, the Court declared unconstitutional those state programs that used public funds to supplement the salaries of parochial schoolteachers.[23] Chief Justice Burger argued that supplementing teachers' salaries would require an "excessive entanglement" of government with religion.

Currently, the Court seems divided over establishment-clause questions. Some members seek an accommodation of secular and religious practices, whereas others are intent on maintaining a high wall between church and state. A third group on the Court seeks to present a middle position. As a result, the Court has had difficulty drawing a clear line between permissible and impermissible aid programs.

Two cases are illustrative of that division: in 1993, the Supreme Court ruled that the state of Arizona could provide, at state expense, a sign-language interpreter for a deaf student who attended a private religious school. The following year, however, the Court ruled unconstitutional a New York State school district created solely for the disabled children of a Satmar Hasidic village. Without invoking the "excessive entanglement" standard of *Lemon,* Justice David Souter wrote that New York had violated the establishment-clause principle that "government should not prefer one religion to another, or religion to irreligion."

The Court's decisions on prayer in public schools have created intense controversy. In 1962, public protests followed a ruling that a nondenominational prayer of twenty-two words composed by the New York State Board of Regents for daily recitation by New York schoolchildren violated the establishment clause.[24] One year later, the Court added to the controversy by declaring unconstitutional a Pennsylvania law requiring public schools to begin each day with a short reading from the Bible.[25]

Despite the fierce opposition of many religious and political leaders, the Court has maintained its stance that government-sponsored prayers in the classroom violate the First Amendment. The Court, however, has never prohibited prayer in public schools; rather it has forbidden government encouragement or involvement in prayer. Nevertheless, none of the frequent efforts to institute voluntary prayer in schools has met with the Court's approval.

We must stress, though, that the Court has not opposed all exercises of religion in public life. For example, the Court has sustained the practice of opening sessions of Congress and state legislatures with a prayer.[26] Similarly, using what critics have called the "St. Nicholas-too" test, the Court ruled in 1989 that communities may erect nativity scenes and other religious symbols as long as they are part of a larger display that includes secular objects, such as Santa's house and reindeer.[27]

Free Exercise of Religion.   The First Amendment also guarantees that Congress shall not prohibit the free exercise of religion. This straightforward command means that the practice of religious beliefs must be free of government censure. The Court has consistently refused to examine the content of religious beliefs. Thus we are free to adopt any set of beliefs and to call anything a religion.

Freedom to believe, however, is not the same as freedom to act. You can believe in a religion that demands human sacrifice, but the state has a right to make such sacrifices a crime. Consequently, the Court upheld a law that made it a crime to have more than one husband or wife at the same time, despite objections from Mormons.[28] It has also sustained Sunday-closing laws that have caused problems for Orthodox Jews[29] and laws that require children to be vaccinated despite their parents' religious objections.[30]

In each of these cases the Court argued that the guarantee of free exercise cannot be absolute. The justices did, however, recognize that laws applying to the general population but unduly burdening the free exercise of religion violate the First Amendment, unless the state demonstrates an especially important and compelling interest in the regulations. Illustrative of this approach was the Court's 1972 decision in *Wisconsin* v. *Yoder,* which exempted Amish children from compulsory school attendance laws.[31] Writing for the Court, Chief Justice Burger concluded that Wisconsin's general interest in an educated population did not justify restricting the free exercise of Amish religious beliefs.

Radically departing from this precedent, the Court in *Employment Division* v. *Smith* (1990) ruled that state drug laws need not make exceptions for the sacramental use of drugs by religious sects.[32] Specifically, the Court concluded that the state of Oregon did not have to provide unemployment benefits to a worker who was fired for violating state drug laws because he had ingested peyote as part of a ceremony of the Native American Church. Although the Oregon Supreme Court reasoned that the use of the hallucinogenic plant was protected by the free-exercise clause, the U.S. Supreme Court disagreed. Such restrictions on the exercise of religion were, according to Justice Antonin Scalia, permissible as they were "merely the incidental effect of a generally applicable and otherwise valid provision." In other words, so long as the restrictions applied to all persons and were not intended to deny the free exercise of religious belief, the states needed to offer no compelling justification for the restraints. Congress, in 1993, attempted to overturn the *Smith* decision by enacting the Religious Restoration Act. Under the terms of the act no law may burden the exercise of religion unless it furthers a compelling governmental interest. The Congressional effort failed, however, when the Court, in *City of Boerne* v. *Flores* (1997), declared the act unconstitutional.

For more information on religious freedom, see the **Gitelson/Dudley/Dubnick web site.**

Due Process and Crime

Like the liberties discussed earlier, the rights of persons accused of crimes are rooted in the Bill of Rights, especially the Fifth Amendment's guarantee of "due process of law." These rights are meant to protect the individual from the arbitrary use of police power. When it comes to criminal suspects, however, there is little public support for the myth of absolute liberty. The Court has tried to balance the majority's demand for protection from the criminal against the individual's need to be protected from excessive government power.

Right to Counsel

The Sixth Amendment to the Constitution guarantees an accused person the right to representation by a lawyer. But for most of our history, the states were not required to extend that protection, even though most prosecutions occur in state courts. In 1932, the Supreme Court did allow a limited right to representation by counsel in state courts by declaring that in capital offenses—those carrying the death penalty—the state was obligated to provide a lawyer to those unable to afford one (*Powell* v. *Alabama*).[33] The occasion for the ruling was a famous trial known as the Scottsboro case. In that trial, lasting only one day, Ozie Powell and seven other young black men were charged with and convicted of raping two young white women. Before the trial, the local magistrate appointed all members of the local bar to represent the defendants. Not surprisingly, no lawyer stepped forward to defend them, and they were sentenced to death without ever having had adequate time to secure effective counsel.

Not until 1963 did the Supreme Court extend that right to everyone charged with a felony (*Gideon* v. *Wainwright*).[34] Nine years later the Court broadened the guarantee to cover any penniless defendant being tried for an offense for which there is a jail term.[35]

Considerably more controversial, and some would say more effective, were the Court's decisions providing for the right to counsel before trial. Even the most gifted lawyer is unlikely to be of much help to a client who has, during police questioning, given incriminating statements. In view of that fact and the likelihood that pretrial questioning plays upon the fear and ignorance of suspects, the Warren Court expanded the right to counsel to include the investigative stages preceding the trial. Justice Arthur Goldberg, speaking for the Court in *Escobedo* v. *Illinois* (1964), announced that the right to counsel applied whenever the investigation turned from a general inquiry to a focus "on a particular suspect."[36]

Two years later the Court bolstered the *Escobedo* decision by requiring that police officers inform suspects of their constitutional rights. In overturning the rape-kidnapping conviction of Ernesto Miranda, the Court, in *Miranda* v. *Arizona* (1966), created specific guidelines for police interrogations.[37] Accordingly,

The Scottsboro Defendants

Pictured here with Sam Leibowitz, an out-of-state lawyer provided by a labor organization, are the Scottsboro defendants. The young men underwent four trials and the last of the group remained in jail in 1950.

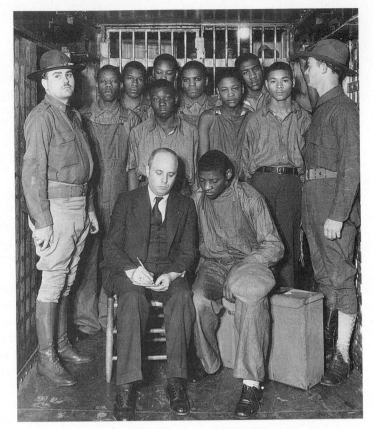

suspects must be told that (1) they have the right to remain silent; (2) anything they say may be used against them in a court of law; and (3) they have the right to the presence of an attorney, and if they cannot afford an attorney, one can be appointed prior to any questioning. These warnings do not have to be given in this exact form, however. Police officers need only provide their equivalent.[38]

Recently, the Court has been willing to allow some exceptions to the *Miranda* decision. For instance, it let stand the rape conviction of Benjamin Quarles in 1984. Before the *Miranda* warnings were read to him, Quarles, at the request of the police, implicated himself in the crime by pointing to the place where the weapon he had used in the attack could be found. In upholding Quarles's conviction, the Court argued that considerations of public safety may outweigh the need to strictly adhere to the *Miranda* decision.[39] Carving out an even more important exception, the Rehnquist Court ruled that the admission at a trial of an illegally coerced confession does not require overturning the conviction if, given all the other evidence, the impact of the confession was harmless.[40] The admission of an illegally acquired confession may be considered simply a harmless error if other evidence, gathered independently of the confession, substantiates a guilty verdict.

Searches and Seizures

The Fourth Amendment states that "the right of the people to be secure in their persons, houses, papers, and effects, against unreasonable searches and seizures, shall not be violated." Notice that only unreasonable searches are prohibited. Unfortunately, the amendment does not tell us what is reasonable, making an absolute application of the amendment impossible.

As a general rule, a search may be conducted after a neutral magistrate issues a **search warrant,** which grants written permission. The authorities must fill out an application that describes what they expect to find and where they expect to find it. In addition, the officers must set out facts that enable the magistrate to conclude that there is "probable cause" to justify issuing the warrant. Over the years, however, the Court has recognized certain exceptions to the warrant rule.

If a suspect consents, a warrantless search is legal, even if the suspect was unaware of the right to refuse.[41] Recognizing that cars are mobile and relatively public places, the Court has allowed them to be searched without a warrant if the officer has "probable cause." In 1991, the Court significantly expanded that exception by ruling that police officers may conduct warrantless searches of closed containers found in automobiles if they have probable cause to believe that they conceal contraband or evidence. Somewhat paradoxically, a suitcase may not be subjected to a warrantless search if it is being carried down the street. But that same suitcase may be searched, without a warrant, if found in an automobile.

Instances of hot pursuit also constitute an exception to the warrant requirement. Thus police officers chasing a suspect need not turn back and acquire a warrant. In 1989, the Court created an additional exception by allowing drug agents, without warrants or probable cause, to use "drug courier" profiles to stop and search people who look like possible drug dealers. Finally, a police officer need not ignore evidence accidentally discovered; the officer may seize that which is in plain sight.

Before 1961, there were few effective checks on police searches. An individual subjected to an illegal search could sue the police for civil damages, but juries rarely sympathized with criminal suspects. Evidence was admissible in state trials even if it had been gathered illegally. In 1957, police officers in Cleveland, Ohio, broke into the home of Dollree Mapp and seized pornographic materials while looking for a fugitive. Later, Mapp was convicted of possession of the pornographic materials seized in the warrantless search. On appeal, the Supreme Court overturned Mapp's conviction, ruling that evidence gathered illegally was inadmissible in state trials (*Mapp* v. *Ohio,* 1961).[42] This **exclusionary rule** means that evidence, no matter how incriminating, cannot be used to convict someone if it is gathered illegally.

Perhaps no other criminal law ruling stirred as much controversy as the exclusionary rule. Law enforcement officials and political leaders around the country accused the Court of coddling criminals. The exclusionary rule provoked such furor precisely because it dramatizes the conflict between the due process rights of individuals and the interests of a society attempting to control crime. Despite the intense controversy, the Court continues to enforce the exclusionary rule, although the justices have limited its reach by creating some broad exceptions. In 1984, for instance, the Court adopted what is called an "inevitable discovery exception": it permits the introduction of evidence collected illegally when such evidence would have been discovered anyway.[43] More important, that same year the Court allowed what is called the "good faith exception." If the police conduct a search using a warrant that later turns out to be invalid, the evidence discovered during the search is admissible at trial.[44]

Cruel and Unusual Punishment

In the 1962 case *Robinson* v. *California,* the Supreme Court made the Eighth Amendment's protection against the imposition of "cruel and unusual punishments" applicable to the states.[45] But beyond noting that the punishment must fit the crime, the justices did little to explain what the terms *cruel* and *unusual* meant. Lawrence Robinson had been convicted under a statute that made it a misdemeanor to be addicted to narcotics. Robinson was not, at the time of his arrest, under the influence of narcotics, nor were any found on him. The police officer made the arrest after observing needle marks on Robinson's arms. Likening this situation to being punished for having an illness, the Court argued that even one day in jail would be excessive.

Recent Court decisions have, however, cast doubt on whether the punishment must fit the crime. In 1991, for instance, a majority of the Court upheld a Michigan law that mandated a prison term of life without the possibility of parole for a defendant found guilty of possessing 650 grams of cocaine.[46] Writing for Chief Justice Rehnquist and himself, Justice Scalia argued that nothing in the text or the history of the Eighth Amendment supported the belief that the harshness of the penalty must be proportional to the severity of the crime. According to Justice Scalia, the Court's Eighth Amendment analysis should be limited to death penalty cases. Justices Sandra Day O'Connor, Anthony Kennedy, and David Souter agreed that the Eighth Amendment did not require proportionality, but they did conclude that it prohibited extreme sentences that are "grossly disproportionate" to the crime. It is unclear what constitutes a grossly disproportionate sentence, but the Court will certainly revisit that issue as litigants begin to appeal the state and federal laws requiring mandatory life sentences for repeat offenders—the so-called three-strikes-you're-out statutes.

In 1972 the Court addressed the most controversial of punishments: the death penalty. A divided Court concluded, in *Furman* v. *Georgia,* that capital punishment was, in that particular case, a violation of the Eighth Amendment.[47] The Court did not reject the death penalty itself as unconstitutional; instead the justices focused on what one justice referred to as the "wanton and freakish" pattern of its imposition. Thus, although the Court declared Georgia's death penalty unconstitutional, it also encouraged states to draft more precise laws that would guide judges and juries.

After the *Furman* decision, several state legislatures rewrote their death penalty statutes in an effort to conform to the Court's guidelines. This turned out to be difficult, however, as the Court seemingly zigzagged through the cases, allowing one statute to stand while ruling another unconstitutional. The justices continued to demand precise standards for the application of the death penalty and yet declared unconstitutional a state law that mandated capital punishment for specific crimes because it denied judges and juries the ability to consider mitigating circumstances.[48] Recently, the Court has declared the death penalty for those under sixteen to be unconstitutional but has permitted the execution of older teenagers.[49] Mentally retarded individuals may also be subject to the death penalty for capital offenses, so long as the jury is allowed to consider the defendant's retardation as a mitigating factor.[50]

Although the precise constitutional standards controlling executions remain unclear and controversial, the Supreme Court handed down two 1991 decisions favoring the imposition of the death penalty. In the first of these cases, the Court moved to speed the execution of condemned defendants by limiting them to only one request for a writ of habeas corpus from the federal courts, unless there is good reason why a new constitutional issue was not raised in the first appeal.[51] (A writ of habeas corpus is a court order to release an individual from unlawful detainment.) An inmate's repeated requests for writs of habeas corpus can delay executions by several years.

In the second of the 1991 decisions, the Court reversed a four-year-old precedent and declared that victim impact statements were admissible at the sentencing phase of a capital trial. The case at issue, *Payne* v. *Tennessee*, arose out of Pervis Payne's conviction for the particularly brutal murder of Charisse Christopher and her two-year-old daughter.[52] Payne had also been found guilty of assaulting Christopher's three-year-old son, Nicholas. At the sentencing stage of the trial, the state called Nicholas's grandmother, who testified that the child continued to call out for his dead mother and sister. The grandmother also detailed the effect that the killings had on other family members. In urging that the jury sentence Payne to death, the prosecutor commented on the continuing effect the murders had on the family—an action clearly unconstitutional under previous decisions of the Supreme Court. While admitting that adherence to precedent is generally the wisest course, Chief Justice Rehnquist argued that the four-year-old precedent that had barred victim impact statements in capital cases was wrongly decided. Thus Rehnquist concluded that the Eighth Amendment did not preclude states from using evidence of the impact of the murder on the victim's family when seeking the death penalty.

Privacy

In a classic law review article published in the 1890s, Charles Warren and Louis Brandeis first articulated the notion of a right to privacy.[53] They hoped to establish the "right to be let alone," but the concept did not easily find a place in American law. In fact, the Supreme Court did not recognize or create such a right until the 1965 decision in *Griswold* v. *Connecticut.*[54] Dr. Estelle Griswold had been convicted under a Connecticut law that made it illegal to provide birth control devices or even give instruction on their use. When the case was appealed to the Supreme Court, Justice William O. Douglas, writing for the majority, argued that the law unduly interfered with married couples' right to privacy. Because the Constitution does not specifically mention a right of privacy, Douglas took great pains to demonstrate that, taken together, several provisions of the Bill of Rights created such a right.

In one of the most controversial decisions it ever delivered—*Roe* v. *Wade* (1973)—the Supreme Court extended the right of privacy to cover abortions.[55] The Court ruled that in the first trimester of a pregnancy the decision about abortion rested with the woman. In the second trimester, the state could, in order to protect the health of the woman, dictate general rules governing the procedure, such as requiring that it be performed in a hospital. Only in the third trimester could the state prohibit abortion altogether.

For sixteen years the Court continued to apply the trimester approach developed in *Roe.* In 1989, however, the Court signaled a clear change in direction. Writing for a five-member majority in *Webster* v. *Reproductive Health Services,* Chief Justice Rehnquist let stand state regulations that significantly limit a woman's right to an abortion.[56] The Missouri law at issue in *Webster* requires doctors to conduct tests of viability—tests to determine whether the fetus can survive outside the womb—whenever there is reason to believe that the woman is twenty or more weeks pregnant. Because twenty weeks are within the second trimester, the Court, by upholding the law, placed the trimester structure developed in *Roe* in grave doubt. Another provision that the Court let stand bans the use of public facilities for abortions and prohibits state employees from performing abortions. Although the Rehnquist decision stopped short of overturning *Roe,* the case demonstrated that the majority were willing to uphold a wide array of restrictions. Moreover, four justices made it clear that the trimester formula of *Roe* was, in their view, unworkable and unacceptable.

The *Webster* decision led many to assume that a constitutionally protected right to abortion could not survive further Court scrutiny. Expecting a definitive overturning of *Roe,* supporters and opponents of abortion rights anxiously awaited the Court's 1992 decision in *Planned Parenthood of Southeastern Pennsylvania* v. *Casey.*[57] The Court disappointed both sides, however. The five-to-four decision in *Casey* upheld several restrictions on abortions, including a requirement that a woman first be counseled on the risks and alternatives to abortion and then wait at least twenty-four hours after the counseling to have the abortion. The narrow majority also upheld the state's ban on abortions after twenty-four weeks of pregnancy unless it was necessary to protect the woman's life. More importantly, the Court rejected the trimester framework developed in *Roe*. Nevertheless, the Court fell short of overturning *Roe*, declaring that a woman's right to terminate her pregnancy "is a rule of law and a component of liberty we cannot renounce." In place of the trimester formulation of *Roe*, the Court substituted the "undue burden" test. An undue burden is any law that "has the purpose or effect of placing a substantial obstacle in the path of a woman seeking an abortion of a nonviable fetus." Thus states were granted substantially new powers to regulate abortion but were prohibited from outlawing it entirely. The only clear outcome of *Casey* is that the Court will continue to hand down more abortion rulings as it seeks to define undue burden.

Closely related to the abortion issue is the equally controversial question of doctor-assisted suicide. Dramatized by the tenacious actions of a Michigan doctor, Jack Kevorkian, state laws making assisted suicide a criminal offense have come under attack. In recent years referendums allowing some forms of assisted suicide were narrowly defeated in California and Washington, while voters in Oregon approved, by a slim margin, a statute permitting doctor-assisted suicide.

This rising turmoil over euthanasia has once again thrust the courts into an intensely divisive issue of morality. In 1996 the Ninth Circuit of the U.S. Court of Appeals ruled that Washington State's law prohibiting assisted suicide was unconstitutional (*Compassion in Dying* v. *State of Washington*).[58] Drawing on the abortion decisions, Judge Reinhardt wrote that the right of the terminally ill to die with dignity was, like the decision to terminate a pregnancy, an aspect of liberty protected by the Fourteenth Amendment. A month later, the Second Circuit of the U.S. Court of Appeals, in *Quill* v. *Vacco*, ruled that a similar law in New York was unconstitutional.[59] The Second Circuit took a different line of argument, however. According to the Second Circuit, laws prohibiting doctor-assisted suicide violated the Fourteenth Amendment's guarantee of equal protection of the laws. Judge Miner of the Second Circuit reached this decision by noting that in 1990 the U.S. Supreme Court, in *Cruzan by Cruzan* v. *Director, Missouri Dept. of Health*, ruled that citizens have a right to determine when life-support systems should be turned off—provided they are competent to make the decision.[60] Thus the terminally ill on life-support systems were effectively given the right to choose death. The judge argued that to deny patients not on life-support systems the opportunity to end their lives with assistance from a doctor constituted a denial of equal protection of the laws. On appeal to the Supreme Court in 1997 both decisions were overturned. Writing for the majority in both cases, Chief Justice Rehnquist argued that the right to doctor assisted suicide was not a fundamental liberty protected by the Fourteenth Amendment. Moreover, Rehnquist held that the distinction between withdrawing life support systems and administering lethal doses of drugs constituted a rational distinction serving a legitimate state interest. The result of these decisions is to leave it to the states to decide the issue.

WWW•

For more information on doctor-assisted suicide, see the **Gitelson/Dudley/ Dubnick web site.**

Equal Protection of the Laws

The Declaration of Independence tells us that all men are created equal, and the Fourteenth Amendment provides for equal protection of the laws. The fact is, however, that all laws discriminate. Discrimination in its broadest sense involves treating particular categories of people differently, and that is what most acts of public policy do. The important question then is, what categories are constitutionally impermissible? Invidious, or unconstitutional, discrimination occurs when a category is based on characteristics not fundamentally related to the situation. As you will see, race is such a category. That realization has come slowly to a society dedicated to the myth of guaranteed equality, and so racial discrimination persists. Can the same conclusions be drawn with regard to distinctions based on sex? Here the answer given by the Court is not so clear.

The Continuing Struggle
Against Racism

An important element of post–Civil War Reconstruction was the adoption of three key amendments: the Thirteenth, Fourteenth, and Fifteenth. The Thirteenth abolished slavery and involuntary servitude. The Fourteenth, as we have seen, affected several aspects of individual freedom, but its key provision on civil rights is the clause declaring that no state shall "deny to any person within its jurisdiction the equal protection of the laws." The Fifteenth guarantees that the right to vote cannot be denied on "account of race, color, or previous condition of servitude."

These three amendments, plus the congressional acts passed under their authority, promised the recently freed slaves a future of political and civil equality. Indeed, as C. Vann Woodward pointed out in his classic study, *The Strange Career of Jim Crow,* the period immediately following the Civil War was a time of great progress in assimilating the former slaves.[61] But the gains made did not last.

In 1883 the Supreme Court struck down the Civil Rights Act of 1875, which forbade the separation of the races in public accommodations—transportation, hotels, and theaters. Congress had assumed it had the power to pass the act under the equal protection clause of the Fourteenth Amendment. In disagreeing, the Court argued that the Fourteenth Amendment applied only to state-imposed segregation, not discrimination practiced by private individuals. This interpretation implied that Congress could act if a state affirmatively discriminated, but not if it simply allowed segregation to exist. Thirteen years later the Court dealt another blow to those fighting segregation when it ruled, in *Plessy* v. *Ferguson,* that the Fourteenth Amendment did not even prohibit segregation.[62] On the contrary, the Court argued, separation of the races is permitted as long as they receive equal treatment. This is the infamous "separate but equal" doctrine.

Jim Crow

Under the various statutes known as the Jim Crow laws, racial separation was required in all aspects of life. Nothing was too trivial to escape their reach, not even, as this picture shows, drinking fountains.

The Court's narrow ruling on the Fourteenth Amendment, along with presidential disinterest in racial equality, gave rise to Jim Crow laws. Community after community decreed the separation of the races, and almost no aspect of life was too trivial to escape the reach of these laws. Not only did states require separate drinking fountains and public bathrooms for blacks and whites, but some went so far as to require different courtroom Bibles.[63] The stress was on separation. Even the Court paid little heed to equality. Three years after *Plessy*, the Court let stand as a local matter a Georgia school board decision to close the black high school while leaving open the all-white high school.[64] "Separate but equal," then, meant separate.

Public Education.   Despite such setbacks, the struggle to end segregation in American society continued. The National Association for the Advancement of Colored People (NAACP), formed in 1909, became the driving force in these efforts. At first the NAACP tried to persuade Congress to pass federal legislation forbidding segregation. Failing in the legislative arena, the organization created a separate unit, the Legal Defense Fund, directed by Thurgood Marshall (who later became a justice of the Supreme Court). The primary tactic of the Legal Defense Fund was to attack segregation in the courts.

In the late 1930s the Legal Defense Fund began a series of court battles that challenged segregation in all areas of American life. It was most successful in the realm of education. As a result of the fund's efforts, the Court struck down a Missouri law that reimbursed black law students for out-of-state tuition rather than admit them to the University of Missouri.[65] Then, in 1950, the Court ruled that a separate University of Texas law school for blacks was not equal to the University of Texas law school attended by whites because the former lacked certain intangible factors such as prestige and reputation.[66] Although the Court failed to overturn the "separate but equal" doctrine in its Texas decision, it came close to doing so.

Finally, on May 7, 1954, the Supreme Court startled the nation by a unanimous decision in *Brown* v. *Board of Education of Topeka* that the Fourteenth Amendment prohibits a state from compelling children to attend racially segregated public schools.[67] In a brief opinion that specifically overturned *Plessy* v. *Ferguson,* the Court simply declared that "in the field of public education the doctrine of 'separate but equal' has no place." No other conclusion was possible, the justices argued, because "separate educational facilities are inherently unequal."

Pronouncing segregation unconstitutional was one thing; compelling desegregation another. Recognizing that fact, the Court set the case for reargument the following term in order to consider remedies, and *Brown II* (1955) required desegregation of public schools to proceed with "all deliberate speed."[68] "All deliberate speed," however, was interpreted by many school districts and lower courts as "all deliberate delay."

Between 1955 and 1969 little change occurred in public schools, and progress that was made exacted a high cost. For instance, in 1957 President Dwight D. Eisenhower used federal troops to protect black students enrolled in a Little Rock, Arkansas, high school. The admission of the University of Mississippi's first black student sparked riots that resulted in the deaths of two men. Responding to this resistance, the Court proclaimed in 1969 that "'allowing all deliberate speed' is no longer constitutionally permissible." Every school district was "to terminate dual school systems at once."[69]

Implementing the *Brown II* decision was hard enough in southern schools, but in the 1970s the Court began to confront seemingly more difficult problems of segregation in the North. By the 1970s many urban school systems in the North were more segregated than their counterparts in the South—because of housing patterns rather than state laws. Having ruled that courts may order remedial action, such as busing, only to correct instances of state-imposed segregation,[70] the Supreme Court made it extremely difficult to remedy segregation caused by the movement of white families out of the central cities to the suburbs. This movement created in the North a pattern of largely white suburban school districts surrounding increasingly black and Hispanic city schools. Thus public school integration remains an elusive goal in many cities.

Public Accommodations.   The *Brown* decision had little bearing on the widespread practice of private discrimination in public accommodations. As court efforts to eliminate discrimination against blacks continued, public protest against discrimination began to mount. In December 1955, Rosa Parks, a Montgomery, Alabama, seamstress, was arrested for refusing to give up her seat on a bus to a white man. Her arrest sparked a yearlong boycott of the Montgomery bus system—a boycott led by Dr. Martin Luther King, Jr. Eventually the system was integrated, but not before Dr. King's home was bombed and he and several others were arrested for "conspiracy to hinder the operations of business."

The Montgomery boycott was only the beginning, however. In the early 1960s, unrest grew among the opponents of segregation: blacks and white sympathizers increasingly turned to public protest. Marches and sit-in demonstrations received wide publicity as police reacted to the protests with greater force. In 1963, President John F. Kennedy proposed legislation to desegregate public accommodations, which Congress finally passed at the urging of Kennedy's successor, President Lyndon B. Johnson.

When passed, the Civil Rights Act of 1964 made it a crime to discriminate in providing public accommodations. The statute barred racial discrimination in hotels, restaurants, and gas stations; at sporting events; and in all places of entertainment. The act also included provisions against discrimination in employment. Though covering similar ground as the Civil Rights Act of 1875, the 1964 statute invoked congressional power over interstate commerce rather than the Fourteenth Amendment. The 1964 act made discrimination a crime because it interfered with the flow of interstate commerce. To justify an attack on discrimination by reference to commerce may seem strange and even dehumanizing, but it was an effective way of getting around the narrow reading of the Fourteenth Amendment given by the Supreme Court in the Civil Rights Cases of 1883.

Voting Rights. As we noted earlier, the Fifteenth Amendment guarantees that the right to vote cannot be denied on account of race. Nevertheless, after 1877—the year the federal government stopped supervising elections in the South—southern states excluded the vast majority of blacks from the voter registration rolls. They did so through diverse and inventive means that commonly involved the use of some type of highly subjective test. Potential voters might, for instance, be given portions of the Constitution to read and explain. Because the examiners had complete freedom in selecting questions and answers, rejecting applicants was an easy matter. Even black lawyers sometimes failed the Constitution test. So effective were these efforts that in 1961 less than 10 percent of the black population was registered to vote in 129 counties of the South.

To counter this situation, Congress passed the Voting Rights Act of 1965. In states and subdivisions covered by the act, all tests were suspended, and the attorney general was empowered to assign federal registrars to enroll all applicants meeting state requirements. Extensions of the act in 1970 and 1975 banned literacy tests nationwide and broadened coverage to areas where Spanish, Asian, Indian, and Alaskan languages are spoken by large numbers of people.[71] After a protracted struggle between Congress and the White House, in 1982, portions of the act were extended for twenty-five years. Finally, in 1991, the Supreme Court expanded the reach of the act by ruling that its provisions covered the election of state and local judges as well as legislative and executive officials.[72]

Sex Discrimination

White women have always held citizenship, but from the beginning it was citizenship without political rights. Women could not vote and were recognized by law as subservient to their husbands. A married woman could not own property, contract debts, or even keep the money she might earn. In return for giving up her separate existence, the law guaranteed the wife that the husband would provide for her necessities. He was not responsible, however, for anything beyond what he decided were the necessities of life.

Women first organized in the effort to abolish slavery. The first generation of feminists, led by Lucy Stone, Elizabeth Cady Stanton, Susan B. Anthony, and others, were dedicated abolitionists. In the organized opposition to slavery, the feminist leaders developed political skills that laid the foundation for the first women's movement.

Crucial to the movement was the first women's rights conference, held in 1848 in Seneca Falls, New York. But suffrage—the most dramatic of the many reforms proposed by the Seneca conference—was submerged in the Civil War effort and then in the struggle over the post–Civil War amendments. Although some feminists wanted to add sex to the provisions of the Fifteenth Amendment's guarantee of the right to vote, others opposed such an effort. Many supporters of the Fifteenth Amendment maintained that the issues of race and sex had to be treated separately if they were to be successfully resolved.

Among the many groups that continued to press for suffrage, none was more dedicated than the Congressional Union. Using techniques that would become more common in the 1960s, its members held marches, picketed the White House, and staged hunger strikes. Several members were jailed and beaten for their protests. Finally in 1920 the Nineteenth Amendment was ratified. After years of struggle, the Constitution now contained the guarantee that "the right of the citizens of the United States to vote shall not be denied or abridged by the United States or by any State on account of sex."

After the adoption of the Nineteenth Amendment, the women's movement lost steam. The movement had always been broader than the issue of suffrage, but the long and difficult battle for the vote had displaced most other issues. Not until the early 1960s did the women's movement revive. This "second wave" has been seeking the eradication of sexism in all aspects of life.

Paternalism and Discrimination.   The ratification of the Nineteenth Amendment did not eliminate sex discrimination from American society, partly because sex discrimination, even more than race discrimination, stems from a strong tradition of paternalism. Discrimination against women has been routinely defended as a means of protecting them, even when the goal was exploitation.

For many years the Supreme Court rather uncritically accepted distinctions based on sex if they appeared to benefit women. The Court's 1948 decision in *Goesaert* v. *Cleary* illustrates that approach.[73] The Court upheld a Michigan law that prohibited women from working as bartenders unless they were the wife or daughter of the owner. They could, however, work as waitresses. The Court accepted the argument that the statute protected women from the unwholesome elements encountered by bartenders. The exception for wives and daughters was reasonable because the husband or father would protect them. What the Court overlooked was that the statute maintained male domination of the better-paying jobs, while women were relegated to the less lucrative role of server.

Even the Warren Court, which did so much to open American society to racial minorities, accepted the paternalistic treatment of women. In *Hoyt* v. *Florida,* the Court upheld the conviction of a woman charged with murdering her husband. Gwendolyn Hoyt claimed that the conviction by an all-male jury violated her rights under the Fourteenth Amendment. Florida law required that both men and women serve on juries, but it also provided that no woman would be called for jury duty unless she had previously registered with the clerk of the court her desire to be placed on the jury list. In declaring the Florida statute constitutional, Chief Justice Earl Warren noted that "woman is still regarded as the center of home and family life."[74] A woman had a right but not a duty to jury service. Any vitality that *Hoyt* may have had as precedent was eliminated in *J.E.B.* v. *Alabama* (1994), in which the Court ruled that lawyers may not exclude people from a jury based solely on sex.

In the last twenty years or so the Court has been less tolerant of statutes that supposedly benefit women. Thus the Court struck down an Oklahoma law that set a lower drinking age for women than for men.[75] Nevertheless, the Court continues to accept some classifications that treat men and women differently. For instance, the Court accepted as constitutional Florida's tax exemption for widows but not widowers. Noting the economic inequality that existed between men and women, the Court argued that the law was designed to compensate for past discrimination.[76]

Despite the Court's willingness to include sex discrimination under the equal protection clause of the Fourteenth Amendment, many questions remain. Gender discrimination has traditionally not received the same strict scrutiny as racial and ethnic discrimination. That may be changing, however.

Indications of a change in the Court's approach appeared in the Court's 1996 decision on the status of the Virginia Military Institute (VMI) as an all-male school. VMI is a state-supported, four-year institution of higher education providing a unique experience. Students at VMI are subjected to an educational environment emphasizing "physical rigor, mental stress, absolute equality of treatment, absence of privacy, minute regulation of behavior, and indoctrination in desirable values." In order to stave off a constitutional challenge to the all-male admissions policy, the state of Virginia proposed the creation of a parallel military leadership program at nearby Mary Baldwin College. This Virginia Women's Institute for Leadership (VWIL) would not offer the same disciplined

Scandal in the Army

Proud of its success in integrating women into its forces, the U.S. Army was, in 1996, rocked by numerous charges of sexual harassment within its ranks. The ongoing scandal began when female recruits at the Army's ordinance school in Aberdeen, Maryland charged that several noncommissioned officers at the training center harassed and even raped young female trainees under their charge.

approach that characterized VMI, but it would, the state argued, provide women with an education as citizen soldiers.

When this matter was appealed to the Supreme Court, Justice Ruth Bader Ginsburg, writing for the seven-member majority in *U.S.* v. *Virginia,* ruled that the all-male policy violated the equal protection clause of the Fourteenth Amendment.[77] Furthermore, Justice Ginsburg argued, the establishment of the VWIL fell far short of the necessary remedial action required. Virginia could comply with the equal protection clause only by opening VMI to women as well as men.

Most important, Justice Ruth Bader Ginsburg seemingly elevated the rigor of review employed by the Court. Although the justice denied that gender classifications were to be treated like classifications based on race or national origin, she went on to announce a very high standard of review. Accordingly, Ginsburg noted that when reviewing classifications based on gender, "the reviewing court must determine whether the proffered justification is 'exceedingly persuasive.'" To most observers "exceedingly persuasive" seems to be another way of saying "strictly scrutinized." Whether this is true or not only future cases will tell. It may be, however, that in the future questions of gender discrimination will receive the same scrutiny as those involving race and national origin.

Women in the Work Force.   One of the most dramatic changes in society has been the growing importance of women in the work force. In 1987, for instance, the Census Bureau reported that for the first time in American history more than half of all women with children under the age of one were either working or actively seeking employment. Yet women's wages still lag behind those of men. To some extent the wage gap between men and women represents the failure of employers to abide by the Equal Pay Act of 1963, which requires "equal pay for equal work." A large part of the difference, however, is explained by the fact that so many women work in low-paying, traditionally female occupations, such as teaching, nursing, and secretarial work.

The recognition that traditional women's work has long been underpaid has led to calls for a new approach to wage setting, referred to as **comparable worth.** Advocates of comparable worth contend that women should receive equal pay for work demanding comparable skill, effort, and education. To date, comparable-worth plans have been introduced in several local governments and in the personnel system of Washington state, but resistance to the idea has been strong. Indeed, President Reagan's chairman of the Council of Economic Advisers called comparable worth "a ridiculous idea," and the Bush administration continued opposition to the concept.

Although Title VII of the Civil Rights Act of 1964 prohibits discrimination in employment on the basis of "race, color, religion, sex, or national origin," its application to women has been slow in coming. Initially, the national government was reluctant to apply the act to cases of sex discrimination. In fact, Herman Edelsberg, a former executive director of the Equal Employment Opportunity Commission, portrayed the ban on sex discrimination in the workplace as a "fluke . . . conceived out of wedlock."[78] The federal courts often tolerated discrimination based on sex plus some other characteristic. For example, the Court used the "sex-plus" distinction to justify company policies that provided for compensation for all non-job-related disabilities except pregnancy. Such policies, the Court argued, do not constitute sex discrimination because they are not based simply on sex but rather on sex plus the characteristic of pregnancy.[79] Congress overturned that decision, however, by passing the Pregnancy Discrimination Act of 1978.

Eventually Title VII also became the vehicle used to attack sexual harassment in the workplace, but judicial acceptance of harassment as discrimination was slow in developing. Initially, courts refused to view sexual harassment as a form of discrimination, ruling instead that such matters were private matters not covered by Title VII. In 1974, for example, the district court for the District of Columbia dismissed a case brought by an employee of the Environmental Protection Agency who claimed that her job had been abolished because she refused to have an affair with her supervisor. According to the court, the supervisor's actions did not constitute sex discrimination because they were motivated not by her sex but by her refusal to have sexual relations with him. Title VII, the court concluded, did not prohibit that kind of sex-plus discrimination.

Slowly, however, courts began to accept that at least some types of sexual harassment constituted sex discrimination. In the 1976 case of *Williams* v. *Saxbe* the district court for the District of Columbia became the first court to rule that sexual harassment could violate Title VII.[80] Diane Williams brought suit against the U.S. Department of Justice alleging that she was fired less than two weeks after refusing her supervisor's sexual advances. In finding in Williams's favor, the district court ruled that the type of sexual harassment known as *quid pro quo* constituted sex discrimination. (*Quid pro quo* harassment occurs when a supervisor demands sexual favors from an employee in exchange for some employment advantage.)

Although several lower courts followed the *Williams* decisions by permitting Title VII suits for sexual harassment, the U.S. Supreme Court did not rule on the issue until 1986. Writing for the majority in *Meritor Savings Bank* v. *Vinson,* Chief Justice Rehnquist argued that sexual harassment need not result in promotion or job loss to be prohibited.[81] Sex discrimination could also be the result of a hostile environment. The creation of an offensive or hostile working environment is, Rehnquist said, sufficient to satisfy the definition of sex discrimination. Not every instance of offensive or annoying behavior in the workplace constitutes harassment, but the Court argued that a pattern of behavior that includes such things as requests for sexual favors, sexual innuendoes, or sexual insults creates a condition of employment disparity that Title VII prohibits. The Court's 1993 decision in *Harris* v. *Forklift* broadened this ruling. The Court decided that a woman claiming sexual harassment need not prove that she was psychologically injured in order to receive a damage award. She need only prove that the work environment was such that a reasonable person would find it hostile or abusive.[82]

Emerging Issues of Discrimination

Among the emerging interests seeking coverage under the equal protection clause of the Fourteenth Amendment, none are more controversial than the claims of homosexuals and illegal immigrants. For over a decade gay rights organizations and the Christian right have waged an ideological battle over the constitutional rights of homosexuals. The results, at least in the courts, have been somewhat mixed. Similarly, a growing anger at illegal immigration has prompted a national re-examination of the U.S. immigration policy and the rights accorded immigrants.

Equal Protection and Sexual Orientation.   Initially, the Supreme Court was reluctant to extend judicial protection to homosexuals. In the 1986 case of *Bowers* v. *Hardwick,* the Court ruled that state laws prohibiting homosexual sodomy, even among consenting adults, did not violate the constitutional right to privacy.[83] Writing for the five-member majority, Justice Byron White argued that whatever residual rights to the privacy of the bedroom existed were clearly outweighed by the majority's belief that homosexual sodomy is "immoral and unacceptable." Although the *Bowers* decision, based as it was on the right to privacy, did not involve an equal protection claim, neither did it suggest a Court open to the advocates of gay rights. After all, if the majority's belief in the immorality of homosexuality outweighs the right to privacy, it stands to reason that it may also constitute grounds for discrimination.

Thus the Court surprised both sides of the issue when, in the 1996 case of *Romer* v. *Evans,* it struck down an amendment to the Colorado constitution that prohibited any law protecting homosexuals from discrimination.[84] The amendment (known as Amendment 2) was the voters' response to ordinances in three Colorado cities that made it illegal to discriminate against homosexuals, as well as women and racial minorities, in housing, education, employment, and health and welfare services. Ignoring the *Bowers* decision, Justice Anthony Kennedy argued that Amendment 2 violated the Fourteenth Amendment by depriving homosexuals of the right to seek legal protection against any form of discrimination except by the extraordinary method of a constitutional amendment. In overruling Amendment 2, Justice Kennedy very carefully avoided defining homosexuals as a constitutionally protected class entitled to strict judicial scrutiny. Discrimination against homosexuals could, Kennedy argued, be justified so long as it serves a legitimate state interest. But the justice went on to argue that the majority's "animus" toward a group does not constitute a legitimate governmental interest. No group, Kennedy argued, could be put at an electoral disadvantage simply because a majority disapproved of the group. As Justice Antonin Scalia pointed out in a biting dissent, the juxtaposition of *Bowers* and *Romer* means that a practicing homosexual may be jailed but not put at an electoral disadvantage.

Even as the courts were struggling with the question of discrimination against homosexuals, Congress and the Clinton administration waded into the issue. Early in Clinton's first term, he proposed and Congress passed the "Don't Ask, Don't Tell" policy for the armed services. Under this policy, the armed services may discharge an acknowledged homosexual; however, they may not question a member of the uniformed services about sexual preferences. A member may be discharged for homosexuality only if the individual makes his or her sexual preference known by word or deed. The constitutionality of this policy remains murky. Some lower courts have ruled it unconstitutional, whereas others have found it constitutional. In the meantime, according to a 1997 study, the number of discharges for homosexuality has increased. Ultimately, it is likely that the issue will makes its way to the Supreme Court.

Three years after passing "Don't Ask, Don't Tell," Congress again entered the fray, this time to minimize the effects of a decision of the Supreme Court of Hawaii. Like the other forty-nine states, Hawaii limited marriage to individuals of the opposite sex, but in 1996 the state's Supreme Court ruled the law unconstitutional. Even before the Supreme Court of Hawaii announced its decision, Congress rushed through and the president signed the 1996 Defense of Marriage Act. The act provides a definition of marriage as "the legal union between one man and one woman as husband and wife." More important, the act relieved the states of the legal responsibility to recognize same-sex marriages granted in any other state. Under the full faith of credit clause of the Constitution (Article IV, Section 1), states must give full legal effect to the laws and judicial decisions of every other state. Consequently, a marriage granted in Hawaii would have to be recognized in all other states. To counter this, the Defense of Marriage Act provides that no state need acknowledge a same-sex marriage granted in another state. Thus the decision of the Supreme Court of Hawaii is binding on Hawaii only.

Nevertheless, a few communities have adopted domestic partnership acts that grant most of the benefits of traditional marriage to same-sex couples. Stretching these further, San Francisco's domestic partnership act requires that all companies doing business with the city must recognize these arrangements by providing the same benefits (for example, health insurance) to domestic partners as they provide to legal spouses. These domestic partnership arrangements promise a rich source of litigation.

Equality and Citizenship Status.   Although it may seem ironic in a nation of immigrants, immigration policy and the legal status of immigrants have often been hotly debated in American politics. In recent years the debate over the rights of both legal and illegal immigrants has gained new urgency. The state of California, a major destination point for both legal and illegal aliens, has spearheaded this re-examination of the legal status of immigrants. On November 8, 1994, California voters opened a nationwide debate over the rights of illegal aliens by adopting Proposition 187. Among its many provisions, Proposition 187 required police officers, health care professionals, social service workers, and public school teachers to verify the immigration status of persons with whom they came in contact and report to state and federal officials any individuals lacking proper documentation. The proposition also denied health care, education, and social services to those illegally in the country. This broad denial of benefits and services to illegal aliens raised legal issues never before fully addressed. In 1982 the U.S. Supreme Court, in *Plyler* v. *Doe,* had ruled unconstitutional a Texas law that empowered local school districts to deny educational services to children illegally in the country.[85] Proposition 187 went well beyond the *Plyler* decision in denying public services.

www•

For more information on emerging rights claims, see the **Gitelson/Dudley/Dubnick** web site.

Even before Proposition 187 was to become effective, the U.S. District Court in Central California issued an injunction preventing enforcement. Significantly, though, the court did not rely on the decision in *Plyler.* Instead, it ruled that California's actions were preempted by federal law, which did not at that time require the denial of benefits. Since the issuance of the injunction, however, Congress has passed and the president has signed a welfare reform bill that, among other things, allows states to cut off all cash assistance and social services to noncitizens—legal and illegal. Thus the stage has been set for a legal showdown. Is *Plyler* applicable? Can it be extended beyond public education to cover other social services, such as health care?

Affirmative Action

Affirmative action is a set of procedures that attempts to correct the effects of past discrimination against racial minorities and women. In its least controversial form, affirmative action seeks only to ensure that members of minority groups are fairly considered for educational and employment opportunities. Much more subject to dispute are the affirmative action plans that establish specific goals and quotas for hiring minority applicants. Attacked by opponents as reverse discrimination, such plans have increasingly provoked criticism.

In its first full review of the affirmative action issue, *Regents of the University of California* v. *Bakke* (1978), the Court sent mixed signals as to the constitutionality of affirmative action measures. In 1973 and 1974, Alan Bakke had sought admission to the medical school at the University of California at Davis. Both times he was denied admission, even though the school accepted others with lower admission scores under its special admissions program for disadvantaged students. Bakke finally sued the school, claiming that he was a victim of reverse discrimination.

A majority of the justices agreed with Bakke and ordered the school to admit him. They argued that because it lacked a history of racial discrimination, the medical school could not establish numerical quotas for minority students. It could not, as was done on the Davis campus, set aside seats for minority candidates. The Court held, however, that the school could take minority status into account when deciding on admissions; to ensure a diverse student body, the university could treat the applicant's status as a member of a minority group as a plus.[86]

Even though in the Bakke case the Court did seem to conclude that affirmative action was constitutional, the confusion surrounding the decision encouraged opponents to continue challenging affirmative action procedures. During the Reagan administration, the Department of Justice repeatedly argued that affirmative action programs were unconstitutional. According to the government's view, remedies for discrimination must always be limited to the actual victims of discrimination and not apply to all members of a class subjected to discrimination. Initially, the Court rejected the Reagan administration's argument that affirmative action was inherently unconstitutional. In 1989, however, the Court seemed to retreat from its support of affirmative action. By widening the ability of white employees to file "reverse discrimination" suits, the Court raised questions about long-established affirmative action programs. Specifically, it concluded that white firefighters in Birmingham, Alabama, who had not been parties to a 1981 suit that resulted in an agreement establishing hiring and promotion goals for black employees could sue the city, charging reverse discrimination.[87] Thus the Court provided the opportunity to reopen previously agreed-on affirmative action plans. Even more controversial was the 1989 ruling in *Wards Cove Packing Company* v. *Atonio*. In *Wards Cove* the Court reversed previous decisions and ruled that employees filing discrimination suits bore the

CLOSER TO HOME

4.1   Civil Rights and Liberties in State Constitutions

With such strong focus on the Bill of Rights and the Fourteenth Amendment, it is easy to forget that state constitutions also provide for individual rights and liberties. Indeed, state constitutions often give more extensive and explicit guarantees than the U.S. Constitution. But the attention paid to state guarantees declined substantially in the 1960s. During those years the Warren Court, applying selective incorporation, federalized criminal procedure, required states to respect national standards of basic freedoms, and applied the Supreme Court's interpretation of the equal protection clause across the nation.

In the 1970s, however, the U.S. Supreme Court became more conservative in its approach to civil rights and liberties. Many states responded by developing what has been called the "new judicial federalism." Dissatisfied with the conservative trend of the Burger and then the Rehnquist Courts, state courts began to rely on interpretations of their own constitutions. As the U.S. Supreme Court has often recognized, state courts may interpret their own constitutions in ways that go beyond the minimal requirements of the U.S. Constitution.

For instance, in the 1986 case of *Bowers* v. *Hardwick,* the U.S. Supreme Court ruled that state laws criminalizing homosexual sodomy do not violate any constitutionally protected right. Nevertheless, courts in more than a half dozen states have ruled that such laws are unconstitutional restrictions of liberty or property guaranteed by their respective state constitutions. Similarly, although the U.S. Supreme Court has refused to rule that reliance on property taxes to fund local schools violates the equal protection clause of the Fourteenth Amendment, almost half of the state supreme courts have considered such challenges. Relying on their state constitutions, three states—California, Massachusetts, and Connecticut—have expanded a woman's right to an abortion beyond that guaranteed by the U.S. Supreme Court. These states have even required state funding for abortions.

Of course, state courts are often guided by the more explicit language contained in their constitutions. The right to privacy is not specifically mentioned in the U.S. Constitution, but ten state constitutions have an explicit guarantee of privacy. Perhaps more surprisingly, given the failed attempt to amend the U.S. Constitution, seventeen state constitutions contain an equal rights amendment that expressly forbids sex-based discrimination. On the lighter side, California's constitution guarantees the right to fish, while New Hampshire's ensures the right to revolution.

Even this brief sampling of the array of constitutional provisions and interpretations demonstrates the vitality of state governments in American life. Guaranteeing the rights and liberties of individuals is not simply a function of the U.S. Supreme Court or the U.S. Constitution; states also play an important role.

WWW•

For more information on your state's constitution, see the **Gitelson/Dudley/Dubnick web site.**

burden of proof in demonstrating that hiring practices and standards that adversely affected women and minorities were not job related.[88] Prior to this decision, employers were required to meet the tougher standard of proving that employment practices that adversely affected women and minorities were necessarily related to job performance.

Although the Court seems to be retreating from its previous commitment to affirmative action, the controversy continues. Indeed, changes in Court decisions have prompted wider argument over job discrimination and affirmative action. Reacting to the more conservative Court decisions, Congress began an extended debate over job discrimination and affirmative action, which finally ended with the passage of a 1991 civil rights bill. Characterized by its supporters as a civil rights restoration bill but attacked by opponents—especially within the Bush administration—as a quota bill, the act overturned, in whole or part, seven recent Supreme Court decisions. Thus the act directly overturned the *Wards Cove* decision and limited the ability of employees to re-open previously agreed-on affirmative action plans.

Despite this congressional endorsement of at least a limited application of affirmative action, several states have begun to prohibit state-sponsored affirmative action plans. Shortly before the 1996 elections, for instance, the regents of the University of California system repealed a race-based admissions policy on its campuses. Moreover, in 1996 California voters amended their constitution to prohibit any preferential treatment in public education, public employment, or public contracting. Shortly afterward, a lower court issued an injunction against applying the amendment. All these proceedings guarantee that affirmative action will continue to be a highly divisive issue. Affirmative action remains so contentious because it represents a basic conflict inherent in Americans' ideas about equality.

Conclusion: Absolutes and Qualifications

In this chapter, we have seen how inaccurate and inappropriate the myth of absolute liberties is. As we have noted, the Supreme Court—the government institution most directly responsible for reconciling conflicting values—has never accepted the myth. For many citizens, however, the myth lives on in regard to First Amendment freedoms and occasionally inspires movements to thwart the Supreme Court by amending the Constitution.

In contrast, there is little public belief in the myth when it comes to the liberties of criminal suspects. The Court has tried to balance the majority's demand for protection against appropriate constitutional protections for suspects. A society that disregards the rights of defendants risks creating a police state that ignores all individual rights. Yet all societies must be able to prevent lawless behavior.

Finally, we have seen how in recent years the Court has recognized the reality behind the myth of guaranteed equality. Using the equal protection clause of the Fourteenth Amendment, it has done much to ensure civil rights for African-Americans, although equality is yet to be achieved. But the Court has not expanded the concept of equality to cover other minority groups. Thus women, the aged, the handicapped, homosexuals, and others still face considerable discrimination.

Summary

1. Civil liberties are the protections individuals have against excessive or arbitrary government interference. Civil rights are guarantees by the government of protection against discrimination or unreasonable treatment by other individuals or groups.

2. Originally, the Bill of Rights did not restrict the actions of state governments. Through a process known as selective incorporation, however, the Supreme Court has made most provisions applicable to the states as well as to the national government.

3. Rejecting the position that all forms of speech are protected, the Court has attempted to balance conflicting interests, using a series of tests that consider the impact of the speech. Sometimes the Court has favored free speech, but at other times it has not.

4. As with freedom of speech, the Court has rejected the argument that freedom of the press is an absolute, but the justices have been unwilling to permit prior restraint, that is, blocking a publication from reaching the public. After publication, the press can be punished for libel and obscenity.

5. The First Amendment prohibits the government from establishing a religion, and it also guarantees the free exercise of religion. The Supreme Court's interpretation of these provisions has generated considerable controversy in American society.

6. Although it has made some exceptions recently, the Court continues to require that a suspect in a crime be allowed representation by counsel and be informed of that right, as well as of the right to remain silent. Evidence seized illegally cannot be used to convict, although the Supreme Court has recently made broad exceptions to that rule.

7. Racial and sexual discrimination has burdened many in American society. The struggle for equality has led to the end of the separate-but-equal doctrine and some decreases in discrimination, particularly in education, public accommodations, and voting. But African-Americans and women are still subject to discrimination's effects.

8. Even as Americans struggle with racial and sexual discrimination new equal protection claims command the nation's attention.

9. Among the most controversial of the equality issues is affirmative action. Though many view it as an essential means to ensure equality, others attack it as reverse discrimination.

Key Terms and Concepts

Civil liberties Freedoms, most of which are spelled out in the Bill of Rights, that protect individuals from excessive or arbitrary government interference.

Civil rights Rights that guarantee protection of individuals by the government against discrimination or unreasonable treatment by other individuals or groups.

Selective incorporation The Supreme Court's practice of making applicable to the states only those portions of the Bill of Rights that a majority of justices felt to be fundamental to a democratic society.

Clear and present danger test The proposition proclaimed by the Supreme Court in *Schenck* v. *United States* (1919) that the government had the right to punish speech if it could be shown to present a grave and immediate danger to the government's interests.

Bad tendency test The principle that the Supreme Court began to prefer, in First Amendment cases, over the clear and present danger test. It allowed the government to punish speech that might cause people to behave illegally.

Preferred freedoms test The principle that some freedoms—such as free speech—are so fundamental to a democracy that they merit special protection. The test was instituted by the Warren Court of the 1960s and in effect banned all government restrictions on speech.

Prior restraint The government's blocking of a publication before it can be made available to the public. The Supreme Court has repeatedly struck down laws imposing prior restraint on newspapers.

Libel The use of print or pictures to harm someone's reputation. An offense that is punishable by criminal law and subject to civil prosecution for damages.

Slander Injury by spoken word, which, like libel, is outside First Amendment protection and punishable by criminal law and civil prosecution.

Accommodationist interpretation A reading of the establishment clause that bars only the establishment by Congress of an official public church. Accommodationists agree with state support of religion so long as all religions are treated equally.

Wall of separation An interpretation of the establishment clause that requires a complete separation of government and religion.

Search warrant A written grant of permission to conduct a search that a neutral magistrate issues to police authorities. Police must describe what they expect to find and must show "probable cause."

Exclusionary rule The principle that evidence, no matter how incriminating, cannot be used to convict someone if it is gathered illegally. Established by the Supreme Court in *Mapp* v. *Ohio* (1961).

Comparable worth The idea that employers should offer equal pay for jobs that require comparable skill, effort, and education.

Affirmative action A set of procedures that attempts to correct the effects of past discrimination against minority groups and that can include specific goals and quotas for hiring minority applicants.

C H A P T E R

5

Public Opinion and Political Participation

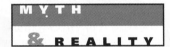

M Y T H

& R E A L I T Y

Is there such as thing as majority opinion?

WWW•
See **Political Science** at
http://www.hmco.com/college

The issue seemed clear-cut. Citing polling data indicating that between 68 and 78 percent of the American people were in favor of a balanced budget amendment to the Constitution, an amendment that would require the federal budget to be balanced by the year 2002, Senator Orrin Hatch (R-Utah) proclaimed that "[Supporters] come from all walks of life, from every group." Indeed, a New York Times/CBS News poll backed up the Hatch assertion: it found that 76 percent of the public favored a balanced budget amendment to the Constitution.[1] But did the poll results accurately reflect the importance of this issue to Americans and their intensity of feeling toward it? Did the American people have conflicting views and competing demands?

The role public opinion plays in public policy decisions is often complex for elected officials. That was certainly true of the balanced budget amendment. In general, policymakers feel compelled to pay close attention to public opinion. Yet public opinion is often difficult to assess, and survey results often appear contradictory. Such was the case early in 1997 when public opinion seemed ambivalent about the importance of a balanced budget amendment—an amendment that would first need the support of two-thirds of the Senate and the House of Representatives before it could be ratified by three-fourths of the states. While the New York Times/CBS News poll showed strong support for a constitutional amendment, a poll taken that same month gave a mixed message about the degree of public support for such action. A plurality of the public, 49 percent, indicated that it did not "think requiring the Federal Government to balance the budget is the kind of issue you would like to change the Constitution for" (39 percent said it was). An earlier poll found that seven out of every ten Americans would forgo balancing the federal budget in order to prevent major cuts in social security.[2] Ultimately, such ambivalence in public opinion on this issue helped thwart any action by Congress early in 1997.

The problem of interpreting polls has been escalating over the past decade. Political pollsters and pundits argue over the reasons for differences in poll results, and particularly over the ability of polls to predict election outcomes. Some assert that voters lie to pollsters. Others believe that more and more people are refusing to answer pollsters' questions, thus distorting the final estimates with large numbers of undecided or noncommittal voters. But, as respected pollster and political scientist Everett Carll Ladd has pointed out, we simply do not know why pollsters have been having so much difficulty predicting elections.[3] Only further systematic study will help us understand the issues better.

We do know that polls have become ingrained in the political process—not only in predicting election outcomes but also as a tool used by politicians, scholars, and the media for measuring and assessing the public's opinions on everything, from its favorite presidential candidate to its attitudes on specific issues or laws. That reliance on polls comes about, in part, because of the widespread misconception that public opinion is majority opinion. Elected officials who claim that they are following majority opinion when they vote on legislation share this

Demonstrations Against California Proposition 187

Not surprisingly, opinions of Americans on any given issue often vary in intensity, saliency, stability, and direction. Public opinion in California in 1994 favored the passage of Proposition 187, which limited the rights and benefits accorded immigrants living in the state. This did not stop many individuals from protesting against the proposition, although it eventually was supported by a majority of the public in the November 1994 elections.

misconception. This view of public opinion is strongly influenced by a widely held myth: the myth of majority opinion.

The *myth of majority opinion* occasionally surfaces in high school civics books. According to that myth, public opinion "is generally used to refer to the opinion held about any issue by a majority of the people."[4] In reality, the public cannot be viewed as a monolith with a single, or even a majority, viewpoint. Rather, the public must be viewed as a mixture of groups with varying viewpoints that typically arrive at a consensus through compromise. Such compromise potentially allows government to produce reasonably satisfactory public policies.

Consider, for example, the public's views on balancing the national budget. Most Americans recognize the problem—that the deficit is too high and that reforms are necessary—but few agree on any one solution. While four out of five Americans agree in principle that the national budget should be balanced by the year 2002, support for this goal drops dramatically when the public is confronted with some of the hard choices required to do just that. Thus in trying to manage the deficit, public officials must balance a diverse set of opinions voiced by a variety of groups. On many such issues, "majority opinion" is often unclear, unstable, or nonexistent.

In this chapter, we look at the origins of public opinion and its content. By understanding the facts behind the myth of majority opinion, you can gain a sense of how the public influences the decisions made by government.

We also examine different forms of participation in the political system, for it is often the strength and intensity of public opinion that lead to political activism and participation on the part of citizens. Many journalists, social scientists, and others argue that citizen participation in politics in the United States is very low, based on low voter turnout. Participation in politics can, however, take many forms other than the act of voting, from joining the school board, the PTA, or other community groups to attending political rallies and discussing politics with family and friends. It is important to examine not only the origins and content of public opinion but also the many ways in which Americans act on their beliefs and opinions.

First of all, however, we define public opinion and describe its characteristics. Then we discuss the way political beliefs develop and the use of polls in measuring public opinion. Finally, we turn our attention to different avenues of political participation and the factors that promote activism in the political system.

Public Opinion: Definition and Characteristics

V. O. Key, a respected scholar of public opinion, said that "to speak with precision of public opinion is a task not unlike coming to grips with the Holy Ghost."[5] And yet no democratic government can afford to ignore public opinion, for it is public opinion that links the values, demands, and expectations of the citizens of any country to the actions of their government. What then is this elusive concept? Stated formally, **political public opinion** is the collective evaluations expressed by people on political issues, policies, institutions, and individuals.

Public opinion varies in **intensity, saliency, stability,** and **direction.** Not every issue evokes intense feelings, and not every issue is equally salient or stable. In turn, public opinion varies in terms of direction, that is, in favor of or against a particular issue. Much of the time there are various levels of support for an issue, with no clear and precise direction of public opinion.

For example, many Americans share a concern about the treatment of laboratory animals. But few feel intensely about this issue, and many may not view it as a salient or relevant issue, because it matters little in their everyday lives or they believe that other issues are more important to focus on. In contrast, most people feel strongly, or intensely, about unemployment and rising interest rates. These issues are salient, or important, to them because they affect them directly. On other issues, the shades of opinion in favor of or against, for example, abortion, are so numerous as to confuse the policy direction favored by the public.

Public opinion also varies in stability. For example, one poll dealing with national health care found that 61 percent of those surveyed were "willing to pay higher taxes so that all Americans have health insurance that they can't lose, no matter what." A survey taken just one week later found 65 percent of the respondents to be against "raising additional money from taxes" to pay for a national health care plan.[6] Thus, far from being stable, public support on many issues, especially on difficult issues, is often vulnerable to the expectations and demands of the people. On less-complex and confusing matters, however, such as public funding of congressional campaigns or federal funding of higher education, public opinion has remained generally favorable over the years.

Many public officials use measures of intensity, saliency, stability, and direction as a guide to the public's political preferences. If a majority, or even an active minority, of the public seems indifferent, or if opinions are unstable and shifting, officials may discount the public's views or not act at all. In contrast, salient issues that arouse intense feelings and popular passions are likely to generate action.

How Public Opinion Develops

What factors influence the intensity and stability of public opinion? People's long-term political convictions—particularly whether they think of themselves as Democrats or Republicans—constitute one important factor. Some of the other key determinants are people's views on the role of women and minorities in politics, the value of compromise in the political process, the appropriate use of money in political campaigns, and the effectiveness of the democratic process. When we recently asked our students about their views on terrorism, we found that most based their opinions on such long-term values as the sanctity of life, concern about the random killing of innocent human beings, and faith in the democratic process. These beliefs affected even students who felt some sympathy for the political concerns of terrorists in the Middle East and in Northern Ireland.

How do long-term political values and beliefs develop? According to social scientists, they are based on the different experiences that people undergo throughout their lives. Growing up or living in Boston, Tampa, Pittsburgh, Houston, Cincinnati, San Diego, or Oklahoma City is very different from growing up or living in rural Wyoming, Texas, Vermont, or Appalachia. These differences translate into regional variations in what people believe and value; further differences in opinion derive from gender, race, and other factors.

As we indicated in Chapter 1, political ideologies frequently shape our attitudes and opinions about specific political issues and institutions. As the political scientist Max Skidmore suggests, **"Political ideology** is a form of thought that presents a pattern of complex political ideas simply and in a manner that inspires action to achieve certain goals."[7]

Most Americans have a common, or core, **political culture:** that is, a set of shared values, beliefs, and traditions with regard to politics and government.

These shared values include a general faith in democracy, in representative government, in the free-market system, in freedom of speech, and in the rights of individuals. The process by which people acquire these important values and gain knowledge about politics is known as **political socialization.** It is strongly influenced by persons with whom people have contact from early childhood through adulthood.

Agents of Political Socialization

Children are influenced by many variables as they grow up and are exposed to the political world around them. They learn from songs, the celebration of holidays, the honoring of heroes, and a variety of patriotic rituals that we as Americans practice. Some institutions play a particularly strong role in our acquisition of political values and knowledge.

Family and Friends.   Families, especially parents, transmit to their children basic attitudes, beliefs, and values that mold their children's views of the political world. These general values include perceptions of right and wrong and attitudes toward authority figures—parents, teachers, police officers, judges, and political officeholders. They also include perceptions of one's **political efficacy,** that is, one's ability to have an impact on the political system. Family and friends also have an impact on our attitudes about the political system, including how trusting or cynical we may be toward government and politicians, and the degree to which we may feel alienated from government.

One specific belief often passed from parent to child is particularly important in understanding political opinions and behavior: **party identification,** or whether people think of themselves as Democrats, Republicans, or independents. Studies in the 1960s and 1970s found that children have a strong tendency to adopt the party identification of their parents. Despite a significant number of eighteen- to thirty-year-olds who call themselves political independents, children tend to choose the same party as their parents when both mother and father share the same identification.

Peer groups and friends have relatively little influence on a person's party identification or voting behavior at the age of eighteen. As we get older, however, our peers tend to reinforce our already established beliefs because we tend to associate with friends and colleagues who share similar values and attitudes.

School.   Another institution that potentially has a great impact on political socialization is the school. At any given time, about a quarter of the population is enrolled, full- or part-time, in degree-granting educational programs. Public schools teach such political virtues as patriotism, compliance with the laws, the importance of voting, and the peaceful changeover of presidential administrations. By repeating many of the lessons we learn at home regarding our beliefs

I Pledge Allegiance

Like schoolchildren all over America, these second-grade students in Austin, Texas, begin their day with a recitation of the Pledge of Allegiance. Schools are an important influence in learning about politics, often reinforcing such political virtues as patriotism and support of our government system.

about government, the school serves to reinforce many of the values we already hold about politics and government.

The amount of schooling greatly influences the way a person forms opinions and views the political world. Differences between the better educated and the less well educated cover a wide range of attitudes and behavior. Better-educated men and women know more about politics. Those who have been to college are more likely than others to hold liberal views on civil liberties and rights, foreign policy, and social questions.[8] Education also brings confidence that one can affect political and governmental policy—what we earlier called political efficacy—which leads to a relatively high level of participation in politics.[9]

There are limits on what the schools can do, however. For example, the educational system does not seem to create civil libertarians who are tolerant of minorities or of others who are perceived as different. Similarly, education does not foster wide support for others who believe in forms of government that differ from our representative democracy.[10]

The Media.   The media, particularly television, are also important socializing agencies. Ninety-eight percent of households in the United States have at least one television. By age sixteen, a person has spent about a quarter of his or her waking hours watching television. Because the average family television is on about seven hours a day, its potential effect as an agent of political socialization is enormous. But what is its actual influence?

Although television teaches and reinforces general beliefs and attitudes,[11] it has limited political impact, chiefly because such a small proportion of programming has direct political content. For example, during the 1992 presidential primaries and the general election, only 38 percent of the television campaign coverage focused on policy issues, whereas the remaining time was spent covering news concerning candidate character and the "horse race" nature of the campaigns—who was ahead and who was behind.[12] Television coverage of the 1996 presidential race also chiefly focused on the candidates' character and the horse race.

Even if the content of television focused more on governmental and political news, there is no guarantee that it would have a greater political impact on the public. For example, among eighteen- to twenty-four-year-olds, only about 7 percent watch the early network evening news, the lowest viewing rate among all age groups. While a larger percentage—about 22 percent—watch the all-news CNN station coverage during a given week, only about 3 percent watch the late-night evening news in any week. About 28 percent of eighteen- to twenty-four-year-olds read a newspaper daily.[13]

Clearly, the media in all its forms, including broadcast and print, play an important role in the socialization of Americans. But a careful examination of that role suggests that its impact is varied and dependent on our viewing and reading habits. (We say more about the impact of the media, including the press, in Chapter 9.)

Religion.   Religion can often serve, both directly and indirectly, as an important agent of political socialization. Indirectly, religion teaches morality and values— values that are often also learned from family, schools, and the media—that can apply to the way we think about government and politics. Later in life we may view the acts of politicians through the "value lenses" afforded us by attending a church, synagogue, or mosque of our choice. Religion also takes overt positions on political issues that may affect our political beliefs. Some denominations, for example, strongly oppose abortion and voice that position in political campaigns. Others support a woman's right to choose an abortion. An individual's religious training can influence his or her attitudes about many political issues and thus have an impact on the political socialization process.

Political Culture.   Although Americans share a common political culture, a variety of political subcultures flourish in this vast country.[14] Individuals grow up and live in one region; have different religious, ethnic, and racial backgrounds and customs; and undergo different economic and social experiences from those living in other parts of the country. A carpenter who grew up and still lives in the rural poverty of West Virginia is likely to view the political system as far less responsive than a Florida lawyer who grew up and prospered in a state that has experienced great economic growth. Such influences help shape the way a person views the political world.

Indeed, variations in life experience inevitably result in differing political, social, and economic views. The work of pollsters and public officials would be made easier if the myth of majority opinion were true. But reality, it seems, is never that simple.

Adult Socialization

Not surprisingly, political socialization is not just a childhood experience. Coworkers, neighbors, and friends reinforce—and sometimes shape—adults' opinions as parents' influence declines. Television, of course, affects adults' political views more than children's because adults, more than children, rely on it for the news. And a variety of additional media—newspapers, magazines, and radio—provide wider exposure to political information.

In addition, adults bring their own established ideas to their assessment of new situations. They are also likely to be influenced by the current conditions of their life. For example, parents may see more merit in a tax increase to support local schools than do childless adults. Thus the development of public opinion is clearly a process that continues throughout adulthood.

Public Opinion Polls

Formal and systematic public-opinion polling began about sixty years ago. Informal public-opinion surveys date back to 1824, when a reporter from the *Harrisburg Pennsylvanian,* standing on a street corner in Wilmington, Delaware, asked 532 men whom they planned to vote for in the presidential race that year. But it was not until the 1930s that George Gallup and Elmo Roper began to experiment with scientific measures of public opinion. By taking into account differences in age, gender, ethnic background, race, religion, social class, and region, pollsters such as Gallup and Roper were able to measure opinion on many issues with a high degree of accuracy.

Pollsters choose their interviewees by the method of **random probability sampling,** in which every person in the population theoretically has a chance of being selected. While that system of sampling is not perfect (in any population, some individuals have little or no chance of being selected for interview), and the procedure is fairly complicated, the basic idea—that the opinions of individuals selected by chance will be representative of the opinions of the population at large—is highly effective and reliable. Since 1936, for example, the Gallup poll has correctly predicted the winner in all but one presidential election and has been within a few percentage points of the actual results each time.[15]

In contrast, **straw polls** rely on an unsystematic selection of people. People are questioned in shopping centers or on street corners, with little or no effort

For more information on public opinion polls, see the **Gitelson/Dudley/Dubnick** web site.

made to ensure that respondents are representative of the population at large. The results are often inaccurate and unreliable. For instance, in 1936 a highly respected magazine, the *Literary Digest,* using a straw poll of 2.5 million people, predicted that Republican Alfred Landon would defeat Democrat Franklin D. Roosevelt in the presidential election; Roosevelt won overwhelmingly. The *Digest* poll failed because it selected its respondents from telephone directories and automobile registration lists. In the midst of the Great Depression, that sample had too many middle- and high-income individuals and excluded voters who could not afford telephones or cars. Gallup's survey for the same election—his first presidential poll—was quite accurate.

Currently, polls are essential to effective campaign strategies. Candidates who can afford their high cost typically survey prospective voters to learn their concerns. In fact, a national or statewide candidate who does not use a poll is probably not a serious candidate or at least does not face serious opposition.

Major television stations and newspapers also survey the public on issues and candidates. When elections are under way, poll results are frequently the bread and butter of the evening news and the daily newspaper. In the months before major elections—and on election night—these reports often have a horse-race quality; that is, they focus on who is ahead or behind in a contest. That was true in the 1996 presidential and congressional elections, when the media spent significant amounts of time and money tracking voter preferences. How people feel about the real issues of the campaign often goes unreported or under-reported in election coverage.

Many elected officials, including the president, use polls to assess the public's views on a variety of issues. Presidents Carter, Reagan, Bush, and Clinton each employed pollsters and used the results to help increase support for their positions or to fine-tune or eventually abandon policies. During the 1992 and 1996 presidential campaigns and throughout Clinton's first term of office, he steadfastly called for a rejuvenation of family values as the basis for welfare reform policy in 1996. The president may have been sincere in his beliefs, yet his call for greater discussion of family values also appeared to be a response to public opinion during his first campaign for the presidency; at that time 68 percent of the public expressed a strong belief that "[P]olitical candidates should talk about family values."[16]

The use of polls by public officials, however, should not imply that presidential or congressional decision making is based solely on evaluation of public opinion. Although polls are an important source of feedback in making policy decisions, representatives also rely on their own values and on both their own and others' experience, knowledge, and expertise. In effect, polls represent one glimpse of the public's attitudes at the time that the poll is taken. Events, both personal and public, may have a significant impact on those opinions a day, week, month, or year later, making opinions susceptible to change.

What makes a good poll? As the failure of the *Literary Digest* poll demonstrates, the sample must be chosen with care. In addition, questions must be worded in such a way that their form or content does not influence the response. For example, starting a question on a farm issue with the phrase "Most people believe that farms should be family owned" will increase the likelihood that a respondent will agree with what "most people" believe. A more neutral, unbiased opening phrase, such as "People have different beliefs regarding support for family-owned farms," avoids the suggestion, on the part of the pollster, that there is a right and wrong answer to the question.

Good questions are another important ingredient. Many surveys ask many questions and allow for only brief answers, often a simple yes or no. Although such questions may improve survey efficiency, they do so at the expense of more thorough information. Consequently, the intensity, saliency, stability, and direction of opinion may be distorted and complex shades of opinion may be obscured, giving support to the myth of majority opinion when, in fact, there is no such view.

Finally, pollsters must measure what people know about an issue, as well as what their opinions are, in order to distinguish between informed and uninformed responses. Many Americans recognize the difficulties of keeping up with the issues. In recent polls, as many as 71 percent of the public indicated that government was "so complicated that a person like me can't understand what's going on."[17] Americans continue to find government often baffling and mysterious. Still, failure to understand does not keep people from answering questions. In a 1989 poll, 83 percent of those interviewed rated the president's cabinet appointments as excellent, good, fair, or poor. Yet when asked to name a cabinet member, four out of five Americans could not name a single appointee.[18] Although the public may be ignorant on an issue, it is hardly shy about expressing an opinion about it.

Poorly designed and poorly administered polls provide inaccurate and misleading findings. But when carefully done, professional polls can help link citizens with the officials who represent them, amplifying, not distorting, the public's voice.[19]

The Content of American Public Opinion

Answering the question "What is American public opinion?" is not a simple task. Americans hold strong, weak, or ambivalent opinions—or none at all—on a variety of political issues. Indeed, as we suggest in our discussion of the myth of majority opinion, public opinion is frequently difficult to divide into neat categories. To complicate matters further, public opinion changes as conditions change (see Figure 5.1).

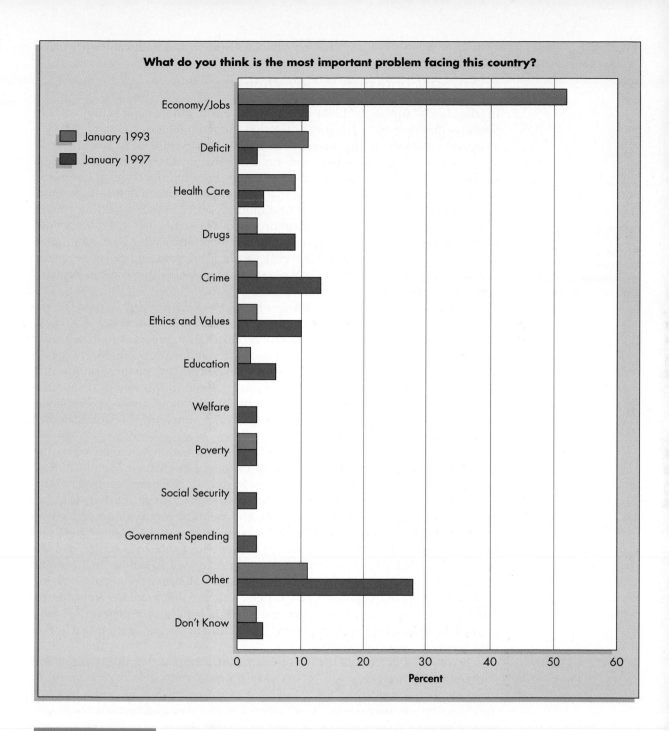

FIGURE 5.1

Changing Concerns of
the American Public

While issues such as the economy, jobs, health care, and crime are seen as important
problems facing this country, the public's priorities can and do change over time.

Source: Copyright © 1997 by The New York Times Company. Reprinted by permission.

Confidence and Trust in Government

WWW●

For more information on confidence and trust, see the **Gitelson/Dudley/Dubnick** web site.

In the 1950s and early 1960s Americans viewed government optimistically. Seventy-eight percent of Americans felt that the national government tended to improve conditions in the nation.[20] The nation had triumphed in World War II, the economy was flourishing, and no domestic or foreign policy problem seemed too difficult to solve. By the late 1960s, however, the country was mired in a seemingly endless war in Vietnam, a war in which more than fifty-eight thousand American lives and hundreds of thousands of Asian lives were lost. Americans' confidence in their government dropped. On September 4, 1974, Richard M. Nixon became the first president to resign from office after insurmountable evidence proved he condoned the cover-up of a break-in and burglary of the headquarters of the Democratic National Committee in the Watergate apartments in Washington, D.C.

The 1970s also brought the Iranian hostage crisis, and then in 1986 the nation was jolted by exposure of the Reagan administration's covert sale of arms to Iran in exchange for hostages. Reagan had previously promised that he would never negotiate for the release of hostages with nations supporting terrorist activities, and Iran was regarded as one of those nations. What further complicated the situation was the illegal transfer of money gained in this sale to revolutionaries fighting in Nicaragua, because aid to the Nicaraguan Contras was explicitly prohibited by a law of Congress. As a consequence, a majority of Americans felt that Reagan had lied to them.

Crises persist. During the 1990s, we face a major national budget deficit, the widespread use of drugs, such major health issues as the AIDS epidemic, and an ongoing battle against crime on the streets. Moreover, there are complicated foreign policy issues, including peace in the Middle East, Africa, Eastern Europe, and Central America, and the economic and political revitalization of Eastern Europe and Russia. President Clinton faced troubling accusations of personal financial irregularities regarding an investment he made in a real estate development called Whitewater while he was governor of Arkansas. In turn, the Democratic National Committee and the White House were accused of improper soliciting of campaign funds in 1996, a charge that some Republican candidates also faced. Many journalists and scholars believe that these crises have eroded the public's confidence in government and in the people that run it. Poll data seem to support their view.

In 1964, 76 percent of the American people claimed that they trusted and had confidence in "the government in Washington to do what is right" most of the time. By the mid-1990s, only 25 percent expressed such confidence (see Figure 5.2). Indeed, over two-thirds of Americans feel that government wastes taxpayers' money.[21] When asked whether government should be doing more or less to solve national problems, 68 percent of the public say that government is doing many things that would be better left to business and individuals. Interestingly,

Public Opinion and Trust in Government

While Americans strongly support our democratic form of government, public opinion remains skeptical regarding many elected officials who serve in government. Here, Arkansas Governor Jim Guy Tucker leaves the federal courthouse in Little Rock, Arkansas on May 28, 1996. Tucker was found guilty of crimes committed while he served in public office.

the most trusting age group in the United States is eighteen- to twenty-nine-year-olds, 27 percent of whom trust government to do the right thing most of the time.[22]

The decline in confidence and trust in government has been matched by a rise in cynicism among many Americans regarding the ethics of elected officials. A 1994 poll found that 51 percent of the public—as against 32 percent in 1984—felt that "quite a few of the people running the government are crooked."[23] By the 1990s, two-thirds of Americans felt that most elected officials did not care "what people like me think." The cumulative impact of Vietnam, Watergate, and the Iran-Contra affair, in addition to a number of government scandals at the local and state level, seems to have taken its toll.

FIGURE 5.2

How Much Do
You Trust the
Government?

Over the last three
decades, Americans'
trust and confidence
in their government's
ability have steadily
decreased.

Source: University of Michigan National Election Study
(NES) for years 1960–1992;
1996 data from the CBS/*New
York Times* poll, December
1996.

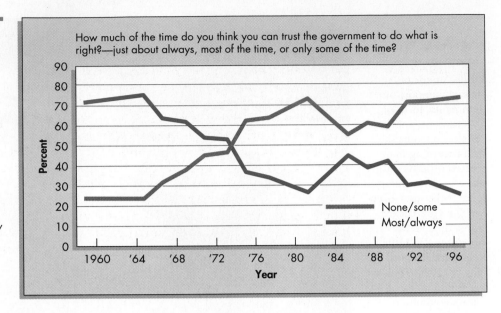

How much of the time do you think you can trust the government to do what is right?—just about always, most of the time, or only some of the time?

The Paradox in Public Opinion

Do these findings suggest that the public no longer believes in democracy and representative government? Interestingly, the answer is no. Most citizens are proud to be Americans. When asked if they would like to move and settle in another country, an overwhelming majority—90 percent—said no.[24] A significant majority feel optimistic about the opportunities for getting ahead in their lives.[25] In fact, the legitimacy of the system—that is, the acceptance by the people of the authority of government—has been in jeopardy only once in the nation's history: during the Civil War.

Most contemporary Americans believe that no other country or government provides the opportunities found in the United States. That perception is shared even by minorities who have suffered centuries of discrimination.[26] Ninety percent of Americans consider themselves patriotic.[27] Even on specific issues, pride in America seems to be the norm. When Americans were asked in 1991 whether they felt proud of the United States' role in the Persian Gulf War, more than 80 percent responded with a resounding "yes."[28] In 1993, 79 percent of Americans approved of the presence of U.S. troops in Somalia, Africa, and were proud of the humanitarian role that the United States played in halting the starvation and violence.[29] By 1996, three-quarters of Americans felt proud to live under our political system.[30]

Opinions on Issues

www•

For more information on the public's opinion on issues, see the **Gitelson/Dudley/Dubnick** web site.

Issues, however, change over time, as does public opinion. For example, during the 1990s support grew significantly for federal funding of social programs that deal with crime, child care, education, and health care. At the same time, strong public backing of military spending declined.

But despite opposing substantial cuts in social and military programs, the public overwhelmingly favors a reduction in the national deficit. How that reduction is to be accomplished remains a major point of debate among Americans and their elected officials. (See Chapters 14 and 15, on domestic and foreign policy, for additional discussion of public opinion and policymaking.)

On other topics opinion is often lacking. For example, at different times over the past ten years, few people have given much thought to such issues as the nation's involvement in Central America, the role of government in ensuring employment and a good standard of living for all, or the need for school busing in order to achieve integration.[31]

Group Opinion

The differences both among and within groups in our society further fragment opinion. Political views may differ between men and women, African-Americans and whites, young and old. Of course, not all women or all African-Americans or all members of any group are necessarily unified in their views. Nevertheless, some generalizations are possible.

Gender.   Compared with men, women express greater concern about the problems of poverty and hunger, drug abuse, moral and religious decline, genetic engineering, and international tensions. Men are more concerned about the budget deficit, the cost of living, and the trade deficit.[32]

Surprisingly, no strong gender differences exist regarding welfare reform, the death penalty, and the right to choose abortion; a majority of men as well as women supports the three positions.[33] In 1992, Democratic presidential candidate Bill Clinton, challenging Republican George Bush, received an overall advantage of 9 percentage points from female voters, although that advantage was accounted for almost entirely by the strong support of African-American women. In the 1996 elections, President Clinton received an overall advantage of 15 percentage points from female voters.

Within the two groups, however, opinions are anything but uniform. In 1996, for example, married women and men were more likely than single people to support the Republicans, in part because they prized the Republicans' strong public declarations of support for traditional family values.[34] For single women (and many, although not all, single men), the Democrats' promise to support equal pay for men and women may have had greater appeal. A similar pattern had evolved in the 1994 elections, with married men and women more likely than single people to vote Republican. This diversity raises additional doubts about the reality of majority opinion.[35]

College Students and "Twentysomethings."   Despite popular images of youthful extremism, most college students and people in their twenties hold middle-of-the-road political views—opinions that are not much different from those of older generations (see Table 5.1).[36] Their interest in political affairs is weaker, however. A recent survey of freshman college students found that fewer than 17 percent discussed politics and only a little over 6 percent had worked in a political campaign.[37]

In the last decade students have moved away from the views held by college men and women of the 1960s and 1970s. Today's undergraduates worry more about their future economic well-being and the right of employers to do drug testing; they also think that there is too much concern for criminals. They show little support for legalizing marijuana or raising taxes to reduce the national deficit, but they register relatively strong support for the death penalty.[38]

As Figure 5.3 makes clear, not all their views are conservative, however. Many students favor stronger government action regarding pollution control, legalized abortions, gun control, and a national health care plan to cover everybody's medical costs.[39] Thus the opinions of college students, like those of the rest of the population, present a diversified picture.

Race and Ethnicity.   Diversity and divergence also hold true when people are grouped by race and ethnicity, although whites, African-Americans, Hispanics, and others manifest some group consciousness on important issues.

Most African-Americans feel that they are making economic and social progress.[40] Nevertheless, they cite taxes, welfare reform, and Medicare reform as three key issues facing the nation.[41] Whites agree with that evaluation but differ sharply from African-Americans on how best to tackle these problems. Compared with whites, African-Americans favor greater government participation in

TABLE 5.1

The Political
Orientation of
College Freshmen

	Total	Male	Female
Far left	2.9%	3.5%	2.5%
Liberal	21.7	18.8	24.1
Middle of the road	52.7	50.5	54.4
Conservative	21.0	24.6	18.0
Far right	1.7	2.5	1.0

Source: Data from Linda J. Sax, Alexander W. Astin, William S. Korn, and Kathryn M. Mahoney (1996). *The American Freshman: National Norms for Fall 1996.* Los Angeles: Higher Education Research Institute, UCLA, December 1996, pp. 28, 46, 64.

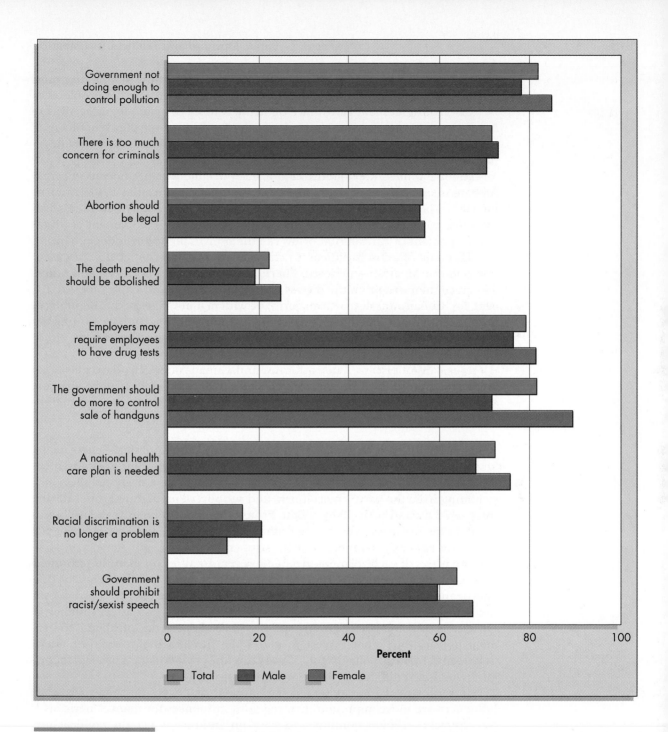

FIGURE 5.3

What Do College Freshmen Think?

Source: Linda J. Sax, Alexander W. Astin, William S. Korn, and Kathryn M. Mahoney (1996). *The American Freshman: National Norms for Fall 1996.* Los Angeles: Higher Education Research Institute, Graduate School of Education, UCLA, December 1996, pp. 28, 46, 64. Reprinted with permission.

resolving economic and social issues. For African-Americans, federal programs remain a key strategy in dealing with civil rights and other pressing problems.

There is agreement across race on many issues. For example, most African-Americans and whites favor the death penalty for murder, harsher sentencing of criminals, and school prayer. Both groups also describe themselves as middle-of-the-road politically.[42]

Among whites, Republicans hold a narrow edge over Democrats, whereas African-Americans have been more heavily Democratic since the 1940s. Approximately 16 percent of both whites and African-Americans described themselves as "independents" in 1950, but in the 1990s approximately 35 percent of whites and 24 percent of African-Americans call themselves politically independent.

Hispanic opinion is difficult to characterize because the label serves as an umbrella for Mexican-Americans, Puerto Ricans, Cuban-Americans, and others who trace their origins to the diverse cultures of Central and Latin America. Except for Cuban-Americans (a majority of whom identify with the Republican party), Hispanics tend to be Democratic in their politics. But they are not as solidly Democratic as African-Americans[43] and are more likely than either African-Americans or whites to call themselves conservative.

Mexican-Americans, Puerto Ricans, and Cuban-Americans have played an important role in local politics in such states as Florida, Texas, and California and in the Southwest. They will certainly gain political strength in other regions and cities around the country, including New York and Chicago.

Religion.   Although religion does not necessarily shape political beliefs, members of the same religious groups do share opinions. Given their liberal to moderate bent, Jews and Catholics lean toward the Democratic party, an allegiance stemming from the party's recruitment and support of immigrant groups during the late 1800s and early 1900s. White Protestants tend to identify themselves as Republicans (39 percent), whereas Catholics (29 percent) and Jews (15 percent) constitute smaller percentages of that party's members.[44]

Members of each religious group, however, do differ on many important issues. Catholics are divided on abortion, public support of birth control programs, and the public funding of parochial schools. Many Jews are divided over the Israeli-Arab conflict and U.S. policy toward the Middle East. A number of Protestant fundamentalist groups oppose a broad spectrum of liberal government policies, but other Protestants decry the fundamentalist stand on social welfare and nuclear policy as too conservative and reactionary. Once again, majority opinion is difficult to define within groups.

In recent years some observers have argued that economic and social class influences are more important than religious influences for many Americans.[45] Nevertheless, religion continues to have an indirect effect on political life, influencing tolerance toward disadvantaged groups, moral and ethical opinions regarding political behavior, and conformity with the rules of the system— attitudes related to all the political issues of the day.[46]

MYTHS IN POPULAR CULTURE

5.1   The Voice of the People or Just Hot Air?

As a form of contemporary popular culture, nothing could appear to be more American than call-in radio and television shows. Howard Stern, Rush Limbaugh, Oprah Winfrey— all provide Americans with the opportunity to tune in and speak out on dozens of topics, many centering on politics and government. Is this talk truly the voice of the people in a democratic system? Or is it just hot air?

In the 1970s, many radio-station owners quickly capitalized on the fact that a multitude of Americans wanted to vent their opinions over the airwaves. Dozens and then hundreds of stations across the country offered this multitude its chance. By the 1980s and 1990s, television caught the call-in show fever, boosting local television talk shows and eventually producing national programs, hosted by Phil Donahue, Larry King, and other television personalities—all prepared to let the American people speak out on just about any topic. Even the all-news television network, CNN, would host a national call-in show, giving the American public the opportunity to "talk back" to public officials and others—over the telephone, by fax, or by e-mail—on any topic, from politics, Congress, and the presidency to O. J. Simpson.

Besides making money for radio and television stations, the call-in shows have attempted to provide a forum for public opinion and even for political activism. Some citizens, no doubt, have used this forum to discuss serious issues. Yet such call-in programs often distort both public debate and the view of U.S. public opinion. For instance, many call-in shows use a screener, who decides, by asking a series of questions, which callers will actually get on the air. Your odds of being chosen usually increase if you fall (or at least claim to fall) into these categories: you are between twenty-five and forty years old and thus project maturity, as well as fit a prime age target for many advertisers; you are an out-of-towner (talk-show hosts have well-developed egos and are impressed by long-distance calls); you are calling on a cellular telephone (they don't want you to run up your telephone bill); and you want to talk on the topic of the day and manage to convince the screener that you have something different and exciting to say, as well as a relevant personal experience to share. It is also a good idea to have a subject to talk about that is both controversial and mainstream.

Although some call-in talk shows provide an interesting and productive forum for the expression of public opinion, the planned and biased selection of a very limited number of callers on any day or in any week can distort the image of what public opinion is on any given issue. As important, myths about how the public views an issue can lead to distortions about how we, as a people, think about a complex problem or policy. One has to ask oneself if call-in radio and television is truly the "voice of the people" in a democratic system . . . or is it all just "hot air."

Sources: Peter Laufer, *Inside Talk Radio* (New York: Birch Lane Press, 1995); Howard Kurtz, *Hot Air: All Talk All the Time* (New York: Times Books, 1996).

Public Opinion and Public Policy

Even though public opinion can often be vague and unstable, it can be informed and strong enough to guide policymaking in our political system. A study on American and British health policy by Lawrence Jacobs reminds us that the public can and does have "a significant impact on broad policy goals and administrative details."[47] Public opinion, even on issues that are complex and difficult to resolve, serves as an important guide for policymakers to a broad range of issues. When public opinion exists on an issue, rarely is it ignored by our elected officials.

In turn, our elected representatives have the responsibility of enlarging, refining, and helping shape the public will. For the link between public opinion and public policy to be effective, elected officials must present the public with clear and precise alternatives to the issues of the day and engage in public debate over those issues.

Avenues of Political Participation

The development of public opinion is a long and complex process, and having opinions is just the beginning. We must also consider whether Americans act on their opinions by participating in the political system. **Political participation** encompasses a broad range of activities—from learning about politics to engaging in efforts that directly affect "the structure of government, the selection of government authorities, or the policies of government."[48]

Most Americans participate in limited ways, for example, by discussing politics with family and friends and following campaigns, elections, and other political events on television and in the newspapers. Others are more active; they write letters to government officials (the number of writers has more than doubled since the 1960s), attend community meetings and legislative hearings, and join in interest-group activities. In 1996, 49 percent of the eligible electorate voted in the presidential election. In 1994, 38 percent of the eligible electorate voted in the congressional elections. Those who are deeply involved in politics contribute money to campaigns, attend political rallies and speeches, take part in campaigns, and run for political office. A smaller but growing number bypass traditional avenues of action and engage in **civil disobedience,** the willful, and at times violent, breach of laws that are regarded as unjust.

Indeed, one major study found "a populace in the United States [that] is highly participatory in most forms of political activity (giving money to political organizations, contacting government officials, etc.) and even more so in non-political public affairs (from a vast variety of organizational memberships to charitable giving and volunteer action)." The study, carried out in the 1990s, found that 44 percent of Americans reported being members of a political

5.1   Whom Do You Trust More: The Federal or State Government?

In recent years, the role that the federal and state governments should play in our lives has been a point of significant debate for both the public and our elected officials. For example, as a result of that debate, in 1996 Congress shifted control of a number of major social welfare programs from the federal to the state governments, a move intended, in part, to bring government closer to home. Much of the sentiment regarding efforts to limit the role of our national government is rooted in our level of trust in government. And that trust clearly centers more on state and local, rather than on national, power.

A recent poll conducted by the highly respected Pew Research Center for the People & the Press found that 17 percent of those interviewed in a national sample felt that they had a "good deal" of trust and 53 percent declared a "fair amount" of trust in the ability of state governments to carry out their responsibilities. How does this 70 percent margin of support match up against public opinion regarding the federal government? One recent poll found that only 25 percent of the public thought that they could "trust the government in Washington to do what is right" "always" or "most of the time."

Americans feel that the federal government can and should play a central role in a number of key areas, including, among other issues, the protection of civil rights, services to immigrants, and provision of health care for the disabled, poor, and elderly. However, when it comes to issues such as job training, welfare, early education for low-income children, and crime, public opinion clearly favors bringing government closer to home—and that means the state and local government.

Source: Richard Morin, *Washington Post*, February 3, 1997, national weekly edition, p. 35; New York Times/CBS News poll, October 30–November 2, 1996.

organization, 36 percent gave money to political organizations, 25 percent had contact with public officials, and 18 percent gave money to political campaigns.[49] Recent studies tend to support high levels of participation.[50]

Political inactivity, however, does not necessarily indicate a lack of interest. Threats of violence kept some groups, particularly African-Americans in the South, out of politics until the 1960s. Work and family responsibilities can also leave little time for political involvement. For people between the ages of eighteen and twenty-six, adjusting to new academic challenges or to being independent, self-supporting adults undoubtedly contributes to political inactivity. Still others feel that their participation will have no impact on government, or they are satisfied with what they see and therefore feel they have no reason for action.

Acting on Opinions

Those who do act on their opinions fall into six general categories, according to political scientists Sidney Verba and Norman Nie.[51] Inactives participate by occasionally casting a vote. Voting specialists vote regularly in presidential, state, and local elections but seldom join other political activities. Parochial activists vote and contact public officials only when their own self-interest is involved. Community activists work to solve problems in their localities and vote regularly but do not otherwise participate in party activities or elections. Campaigners, the mirror image of the community activists, immerse themselves in partisan politics and campaigns rather than in community organizations. Complete activists engage in activities ranging from community affairs to voting, campaigning, and running for political office.

WWW•

For more information on political participation, see the **Gitelson/Dudley/ Dubnick web site.**

Verba and Nie's categories represent traditional forms of political participation. What happens when such tactics do not work? In the early 1960s, African-Americans in the South organized sit-ins at segregated lunch counters, boycotted buses, and engaged in other acts of civil disobedience. Antiwar protests were a common occurrence during the Vietnam War in the 1960s and 1970s. Since that time, protest has become an increasingly common form of participation among those who find traditional avenues of action ineffective or closed. In the 1970s and 1980s, farmers marched on Washington, D.C., to protest government farm policies. In the 1980s and 1990s, both pro- and antiabortion groups marched in cities and towns around the nation arguing their policy positions. Many of these individuals had never been active in politics before, often not voting in elections. In at least one case, the antiabortion group "Operation Rescue" has advocated violent disobedience including physically blocking access to health clinics that perform abortions. As you may recall from Chapter 4, many of these groups have also gone to court to try to influence the political system.

Finally, the impact of limited participation should not be overlooked. In presidential elections, almost 90 percent of the electorate watch programs about the campaigns on television. Two out of every three voters read about campaigns in a newspaper. And a third of the electorate engage in persuading others to vote for or against one of the parties or candidates.[52] These forms of political activity may be less dramatic than voting and running for office, but they represent an important form of participation in the political process.

Despite this evidence, there is certainly room for skepticism, as well as for improvement of Americans' activism. Relatively few people work for parties or candidates. Turnout for presidential elections has dropped over the past thirty years, with only about 49 percent of the eligible electorate voting in 1996. Fewer than 40 percent of the eligible electorate voted in the 1994 off-year elections. We cannot ignore the reality that active political participation in the United States is lower than many political observers believe it should be.

Yet this apparent apathy is balanced by activity. When election time rolls around, many political meetings are jammed with people, campaign buttons and bumper stickers decorate lapels and automobiles, and money pours into campaign headquarters. Political parties, particularly at the national level, thrive on millions of small contributions—most under $50. Tens of thousands of people participate in social and political movements that range from government involvement in Eastern Europe and the Middle East to abortion rights. In addition, volunteerism in the United States is alive and well: in 1996, 58 percent of Americans felt that volunteering time to community service was an essential or very important obligation of citizens.[53] Levels of teenage volunteerism have reached a new high, with 61 percent of that population claiming to participate in volunteer activities.

In fact, historically, Americans have engaged in as much or more campaign and community activity than citizens of many other nations.[54] In a study comparing participation in five democracies—the United States, the Netherlands, Great Britain, Germany, and Japan—the United States ranked first in a variety of activities, including signing political petitions, attending public meetings, contacting officials or politicians, and writing to newspapers.[55] In terms of volunteering and giving money to nonpolitical public affairs programs, Americans significantly outdistanced France and Germany in the amount of time and financial support contributed.[56]

What Influences Participation

Why do people participate in politics? After all, an individual act of participation rarely has much impact. One answer is that people participate if the action does not take much effort. Sending a check or watching the nightly news is easy. People also participate if they care a lot about the outcome. Black college students who took part in sit-ins at lunch counters and marched in demonstrations in the 1960s had a big stake in the success of the civil rights movement. Likewise, many women (and men) participated in demonstrations and marches during the 1970s and 1980s for equal rights and opportunities for women. Finally, participation depends on life circumstances. Thus recent increases in political participation in the South can be attributed to rising educational and socioeconomic levels, as well as to enforcement of voting rights laws; in the past, poll taxes, literacy tests, and other barriers to registration prevented African-Americans from voting.

Participation breeds more participation. For example, people who work in community and fraternal organizations are more likely than the average citizen to participate in politics. A strong sense of party identity also seems to encourage activism. Indeed, even such passive participation as having an interest in politics or holding strong opinions on issues and candidates can serve as a catalyst for political action.

Political activism also depends on age. Those between eighteen and twenty-four are less likely to vote or engage in other forms of political participation, for example, discuss politics, work for a political party, run for political office, than any other age group through the age of seventy-five. Proportionally more people aged forty-five and older register and vote in national elections than those younger than forty-five.[57] As we indicated earlier in this chapter, these statistics reflect the unsettled lives of young people, who are working, starting families, attending school, or adjusting to their status as independent, self-supporting adults. To some extent, too, political activism is a function of the responsibilities of age. As taxpayers, parents, and homeowners, older people have more immediate reasons to get involved in politics.

A Closer Look at Women, African-Americans, Hispanics, and Asian-Americans

Women.   Women have a long history of activism in local and community work; it goes back to Abigail Adams and Judith Sargent Murray during the 1780s and 1790s. Nineteenth-century feminists who fought for equal rights, economic opportunity, and the right to vote included Sarah Grimké, Elizabeth Cady Stanton, Lucretia Mott, and Charlotte Perkins Gilman. Yet their roles in the partisan political arenas of the time were somewhat limited. In recent years barriers against women in national and state politics have diminished. Currently, as party leaders, candidates, voters, and community organizers, women are entering politics in greater numbers. The number of female voters has exceeded the number of male voters in every presidential election since 1964.[58] Their activity at the state and national level has increased significantly.[59]

Since 1975, the number of women holding local or state office has risen dramatically (see Figure 5.4). The 1984 nomination of Geraldine Ferraro as the Democratic candidate for vice president was apparently a breakthrough for women in politics. Two years later an unprecedented 130 women were contesting national and state offices. In the 105th Congress (1997–1998), a record 60 women served in the House of Representatives and the Senate. In 1998, 1,593 women were members of the fifty state legislatures (although that constituted only 21.5 percent of the 7,424 state legislators in the United States).[60] Of the delegates to the 1996 Democratic National Convention, 53 percent were women, a significant increase over the 33 percent that attended the 1976 convention. Female dele-

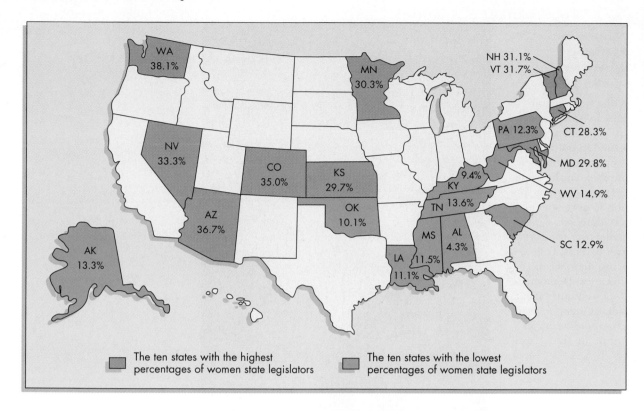

The ten states with the highest percentages of women state legislators

The ten states with the lowest percentages of women state legislators

FIGURE 5.4

Percentages of Women State Legislators

While women are more successful in getting elected to some state legislatures than others, their participation overall is proportionately lower than for men in all of the states.

Source: National Conference of State Legislatures.

gates to the Republican National Convention in 1996 totaled 36 percent, a decrease of 7 percent from the 1992 attendance.[61] Four women serve in President Clinton's cabinet, including Secretary of State Madeleine K. Albright, the highest-ranking female cabinet appointee in U.S. history.

Progress regarding the appointment of women as judges to the federal courts, however, has been slow. In recent years, the percentage of women appointed to the federal district and appeals courts has remained small, ranging from 19.6 percent during the Carter administration and dropping to 19 percent and 5.1 percent, respectively, during the Bush and Reagan administrations.[62] Thirty percent of President Clinton's appointments to the federal district and appeals courts were women, a record high for any president.[63] Two women presently serve on the U.S. Supreme Court: Sandra Day O'Connor and Ruth Bader Ginsburg.

No doubt, women's activism will keep expanding as elected and appointed officials become role models for other women, and as barriers to the inner circles of politics continue to break down. Nevertheless, in absolute numbers, it is disappointing how few women in the 1990s have been able to break into the male-dominated Congress; the state legislatures; city councils; and the national, state, and local executive and judicial branches of government.

Women and African-Americans in Public Office

While women and African-Americans are still underrepresented in politics, proportional to their numbers in the population, their participation in government has increased significantly over the past twenty years. One active member of Congress, Democratic Representative Sheila Jackson Lee, holds a press conference in her home state, Texas.

African-Americans.   Discrimination, along with alienation from and lack of faith in the electoral process, has historically contributed to African-Americans' low rates of participation in politics. African-American voter turnout has increased greatly during the past three decades—in good part because of voting rights laws, key Supreme Court decisions, registration drives, and a rise in educational achievement and economic well-being. In 1960, only 29 percent of African-Americans in the South were registered to vote, compared with 61 percent of whites. By 1988, racial differences in voter registration in the South had nearly disappeared, with 65 percent of African-Americans registered versus 67 percent of whites. By the 1990s, approximately two-thirds of African-Americans across the nation reported being registered to vote; the percentage for whites was 70 percent.[64]

Since the 1970s increasing numbers of African-American candidates have won political office. In 1970, 1,469 African-Americans held local, state, and national offices. By the mid–1990s, that number had increased to 8,015, although it still constituted approximately 2 percent of elected officials in the United States.[65] Besides significantly increasing their numbers as city council members, sheriffs, and county officials, African-Americans have won mayoral races in Atlanta, Chicago, Dallas, Denver, Detroit, Los Angeles, Newark, New Orleans, Philadelphia, Richmond, Seattle, and Washington, D.C., and in Oakland, California, and Gary, Indiana. In 1989, David Dinkins was elected the first African-American mayor of New York City and Douglas Wilder of Virginia became the first African-American governor in the United States. In 1991, the North Carolina legislature elected Daniel Blue, Jr., its first African-American Speaker of the House. Blue joined the only other African-American state legislative leader at that time, Willie Brown, the powerful Speaker of the House in the California legislature.[66]

Thirty-eight African-Americans serve in the 105th Congress (1997–1998), including one U.S. senator. Seventeen percent of the delegates to the 1996 Democratic National Convention were African-American; in 1996 only 3 percent attended the Republican National Convention. President Clinton's second-term cabinet includes three African-Americans. As with women, however, the record is mixed. Although African-Americans participate in growing numbers on the federal bench (19 percent of President Clinton's appointments to the federal district and appellate courts were African-Americans), the number of appointments over the past twenty years has represented a relatively small proportion of the total appointments (2 percent of President Reagan's appointments; 6 percent of President Bush's).[67] The only African-American serving on the Supreme Court is Clarence Thomas. In the contest for public office in the United States, African-Americans have still not been given the opportunity to enter and compete that is proportional to their numbers in the general population.

Hispanics.   Mexican-Americans and Puerto Ricans have also faced major barriers to participation, including language problems, low levels of education and income, literacy tests, and residency requirements. Recently, registration drives in Florida, Texas, and California, where many Cuban-Americans and Mexican-Americans live, have produced increases in voter turnout. In the 1996 elections, an estimated 75 percent of registered Latinos voted in the city of Los Angeles and 70 percent voted in the state.[68] During the 105th Congress, eighteen Hispanics served in the House of Representatives. Miami's mayor is Cuban-American. One of the highest-ranking Hispanic women in local government is Chicago's city treasurer, Miriam Santos. And President Clinton, after his re-election in 1996, appointed Federico F. Peña (former secretary of transportation) as secretary of energy. In addition, U.S. Representative Bill Richardson (D-N. Mex.), a Hispanic, was appointed United Nations representative, the first Latino to serve in that office. There are 176 Hispanics who serve in the state legislatures. By 1994, 2,215 elected Latino officials served in Texas state and local offices; 796 Latinos were elected to offices in California.[69] Seven percent of

Citizenship

Every year, thousands of immigrants come to the United States seeking the opportunity to live and participate in our democratic system. Here, hundreds of immigrants take the oath of citizenship in ceremonies held in San Antonio, Texas.

President Clinton's appointments to the federal bench were Hispanic; 4 percent of Reagan's appointments and 4 percent of Bush's. Although Hispanic participation is still very limited in the United States, the 1990s may lay the groundwork for serious Hispanic activism.

Asian-Americans.   Although only limited data are available regarding the political participation patterns of different Asian-American groups, some tentative conclusions can be drawn. Most Asian-Americans, including Japanese-, Korean-, Vietnamese- and Filipino-Americans, are less likely than either whites or African-Americans to participate in the political system. Chinese-Americans are as likely to vote as white Americans. It is also true that "members of Asian-American ethnic groups are less likely to contact public officials than are whites, but Japanese-Americans are more likely to contribute money than are whites."[70] In the 1996 presidential elections, members of Asian-American ethnic groups supported

President Clinton with 43 percent of their vote. Republican presidential candidate Robert Dole received 48 percent of the Asian-American vote, and Ross Perot 8 percent. That was a significant reversal of the Asian-American vote in 1992 when Clinton received 31 percent of the Asian-American vote.

Presently, five members of the U.S. Congress have Asian or Pacific Island backgrounds. Almost 2 percent of President Clinton's nominations to the federal courts have been Asian-Americans. As many ethnic groups from Asia and the Pacific Basin settle in the United States, learn the language, and assimilate to the political system, it is likely that we will see increases in political participation by members of many of these different groups.

Conclusion: Many Minorities, Much Activity

In this chapter we have looked at the myth of majority opinion. What is the reality behind this myth? Is there a majority opinion? The answer is yes—and no. Many Americans do share beliefs about the political system, including the importance of democracy and representative government, majority rule, and concern for minority rights. An overwhelming majority—in most polls, much more than 90 percent of the respondents—support a democratic form of government. Polls and elections demonstrate every four years that a majority of the electorate favor one presidential candidate over another. And public officials pay attention to public opinion when it has strength and direction on a given issue.

The myth, however, obscures an important attribute of public opinion: that it is often difficult to define clearly. Public opinion, which is usually fuzzy and unstable, is also frequently uninformed and sometimes does not exist at all. It rarely comes packaged in neat, easy-to-understand categories. In this vast and varied nation, differences in religious background, region of residence, education, gender, race, and ethnicity produce a broad spectrum of views about the political world. To complicate matters further, even when people have similar backgrounds, they often do not share the same views.

Thus, in defining majority opinion on any issue, policymakers must tread carefully. Often the answers to a single survey question or even a series of such questions do not capture the diversity or ambiguity of public opinion. Clearly, the generalization that there is a majority opinion in the United States on many issues is a myth.

In this chapter, we also discussed political participation in the United States. Americans are frequently criticized for their lack of participation in the political process. That criticism often focuses on the relatively low voter turnout in the United States, particularly when compared with higher-turnout figures in many other nations.

We agree that if activism is defined by voting, the American public seems apathetic indeed. But by broadening the definition to include nonelectoral activities, including learning forms of participation such as political discussions, we depict a reality of a more politically and socially concerned citizen, a citizen that is more active in the political system than previously thought.

Summary

1. Public opinion is defined as the shared evaluations expressed by people on political issues, policies, and individuals.

2. Four important characteristics of public opinion are its intensity, saliency, stability, and direction.

3. Political socialization is the process by which people acquire political values and opinions about the political world. The socialization process is strongly influenced by people and events from early childhood through adulthood. Family and friends, school, the media, religion, and political culture are five important factors that mold our political beliefs and opinions.

4. Polls are a major instrument for measuring public opinion. Poorly designed and administered public-opinion polls can provide inaccurate and misleading findings. When carefully designed and administered, however, professional polls offer sound and meaningful information about public opinion. Nevertheless, on many issues a clear and unambiguous majority opinion is often difficult to assess from polls.

5. Americans show a lack of confidence and trust in government and politics but an overwhelming faith in the political system.

6. The opinions of Americans are often influenced by sex and by ethnic, religious, racial, regional, and educational backgrounds, although opinions can and do vary widely within any group.

7. Political participation can range from activities that involve taking part in the learning process about politics to engaging in activities that directly influence the structure of government, the selection of government authorities, or the policies of government. Participation in politics in the United States is more extensive if we include not just voting, but all forms of political participation.

8. Minority groups have made some important gains but are still not given opportunities proportional to their numbers. It is likely that we will see increases in political participation and activism by members of many of these groups as we move into the new millenium.

Key Terms and Concepts

Political public opinion The collective preferences expressed by people on political issues, policies, institutions, and individuals.

Opinion intensity The strength of one's opinion about an issue.

Opinion saliency One's perception of the importance of an issue.

Opinion stability The degree to which public opinion on an issue changes over time.

Opinion direction One's position in favor of or against a particular issue. Much of the time we have various shades of support for an issue, with no clear and precise direction of public opinion.

Political ideology A pattern of complex political ideas presented in an understandable structure that inspires people to act to achieve certain goals.

Political culture A set of values, beliefs, and traditions about politics and government that are shared by most members of society. Political culture in the United States includes faith in democracy, representative government, freedom of speech, and individual rights.

Political socialization The process by which individuals acquire political values and knowledge about politics. It is strongly influenced by people with whom the individual has contact from early childhood through adulthood.

Political efficacy The perception of one's ability to have an impact on the political system.

Party identification The tendency of people to think of themselves as Democrats, Republicans, or independents.

Random probability sampling A method by which pollsters choose interviewees, based on the idea that the opinions of individuals selected by chance will be representative of the opinions of the population at large.

Straw polls Polls that rely on an unsystematic selection of respondents. The respondents in straw polls frequently are not representative of the public at large.

Political participation Encompasses a broad range of activities, from involvement in learning about politics to engagement in efforts that directly affect the structure of government, the selection of government authorities, or the policies of government.

Civil disobedience Refusal to obey civil laws that are regarded as unjust. May involve methods of passive resistance such as sit-ins and boycotts.

Political Parties

Is there little difference between the Democratic and Republican parties?

See **Political Science** at
http://www.hmco.com/college

It was not a very auspicious beginning for political parties in the United States. In fact, it would be an understatement to say that the views of many of our nation's founders toward parties were downright hostile. In his farewell address to Congress, George Washington warned his fellow politicians of the "baneful effects of the spirit of party." John Adams, his vice president, complained, "There is nothing I dread so much as the division of the Republic into two great parties, each under its own leader." And in the early 1790s Thomas Jefferson, often referred to as the "father" of the American party system, declared, "If I could not go to heaven but with a party, I would not go there at all."

One Philadelphian who wrote in a local paper at the time of the nation's founding reflected the widespread fear that parties would split the government into factions: "We want no Ticket Mongers: let every citizen exercise his own judgment, and we shall have a good representation—intrigue, favoritism, cabal and party will be at rest."[1] Indeed, so strong was the antiparty fever that no mention was made of political parties in the Constitution.

More than two hundred years after that May 1787 meeting in Philadelphia at which the framers began to chart a course for the new nation, the American people are still questioning the relevance of political parties. The charge that there is not "a dime's worth of difference between the two major parties," attributed to former Alabama governor George Wallace, a disaffected Democrat who ran for president in 1968 under the American Independent party, mirrors in many respects the public's attitude toward parties. According to some scholars, the last three decades have been an "antiparty age," marked by public alienation from parties.[2] Most Americans identify with one of the two major parties but claim that such identification does not sway their vote.

What is the source of these contradictions? Americans' views of the Republican and Democratic parties seem to stem from two misconceptions: that the parties are alike and that they have little impact on domestic and foreign policy. Indeed, when asked to evaluate the Democratic and Republican parties, between 26 and 45 percent of the respondents in recent surveys had unfavorable attitudes about parties.[3]

Apparently, many Americans see limited value in parties even at election time, when two-thirds of the voters indicate that they typically split their ticket, voting for candidates from different parties.[4] Furthermore, over two-thirds of the public regard themselves as either political independents or "soft" (weak) partisans.[5] In the words of one observer of political parties, "Virtually all surveys that tap popular understanding and appreciation of the parties indicate that the public has little confidence in the parties."[6]

How can we explain this deep-seated skepticism about parties? We argue that public criticism of the Democrats and Republicans reflects the *myth of party irrelevance*. This myth holds that the Democratic and Republican parties are unnecessary, perhaps even worthless, in our political system. If that is a myth, what is the reality? In this chapter, we demonstrate that the two major parties are

Political Party Appeal

One of the most important tasks of a political party is to recruit new members. Here, both Republicans and Democrats vie for the attention of prospective party loyalists.

different in several important aspects and that parties still matter in the country's politics, even though fewer people now strongly identify with them.

What Parties Are and What They Do

The structure and functions of political parties differ from country to country. In most Western European democracies, parties are highly centralized, stable, and tightly knit coalitions of men and women who share opinions based on commonly held beliefs. In these countries, parties take clear-cut, sometimes extreme, ideological positions. As you may recall from Chapter 1, ideologies are coherent sets of beliefs about what government should do. For example, in a number of Scandinavian nations, strong socialist parties of the Left face a spectrum of ideologically conservative parties on the Right.

In the United States, some minor parties are strongly ideological—for example, the Libertarian party, the Conservative party, and the Socialist Workers party. However, there is no clear-cut Democratic or Republican ideology. Historically, the two major parties have not strictly based their positions on ideology but on a set of guiding principles, most of which focus on the role that government should play in supporting and enhancing our democratic system. Each party's position includes supporters with a wide range of beliefs about what government should do, and each party seeks to attract a broad spectrum of supporters. Because some of the beliefs overlap, the Democratic and Republican parties may seem alike, especially since they share a strong democratic, capitalist tradition. But they differ on many economic and social issues, and they draw differing proportions of liberals, moderates, and conservatives to their political folds.

Political parties in the United States are coalitions of people organized formally to recruit, nominate, and elect individuals to office. Besides organizing elections, political parties are instrumental in running the government, creating and implementing shared political goals through the election of officials to the executive and legislative branches of government, and bringing stability to the political system. They serve as a major link between the public and government officials.

The Republicans and the Democrats, the two major parties, are decentralized organizations, regulated at the state level.[7] **Decentralization** in this context means that the decision-making power is dispersed. One might appropriately argue that we have two national party organizations and a hundred state party organizations divided equally between the two major parties. No single individual or organization controls the entire system. The comments of one local party leader perhaps best describe that structure: "No state leader, not even the president of the United States, is going to dictate to us whom we slate for local office. They can't even tell us what issues are important." All state party organizations and most local party organizations operate more or less independently of each other, although the authority of one party organization may overlap that of another. Compared with other nations, the United States has one of the most loosely integrated party systems in the world.[8]

American parties are loosely regulated as well as loosely structured. The Constitution makes no mention of parties, and Congress has passed few laws restricting party activities. By and large, individual states are free to define the characteristics and rules for their own state parties, although recent Supreme Court decisions have enhanced the power of the national parties to regulate some aspects of state party activity.

The Three-headed Giant

In describing political parties, we might best characterize them as "three-headed political giants."[9] The heads represent three different alliances of members: the party-as-organization, the party-in-the-electorate, and the party-in-government. Sometimes the heads cooperate, and sometimes they pull in different directions.

The **party-as-organization** has few members. Unlike many European parties, which have enrolled, dues-paying members and extensive professional staffs, American party organizations are small and relatively informal. They consist primarily of state and county chairpersons and ward and precinct captains (sometimes paid, but more often volunteers) who work for the party throughout the year, recruiting candidates and participating in fundraising activities.

The **party-in-the-electorate** includes everyone who identifies with the particular party, tends to vote for that party's candidates, and may even contribute to its campaigns. Anyone of voting age can choose to be a member of the party-in-the-electorate. American parties depend for their electoral strength on such public support.

The **party-in-government** comprises the individuals who have been elected or appointed to a government office under a party label. Contrary to the myth of party irrelevance, parties play a major role in organizing government and in setting policy. When the Republican party gained control of both the U.S. Senate and the House of Representatives in 1995, both houses were reorganized, and the Republicans supported policies different from the Democrats.

A successful party can attract people to its fold. Parties need paid and volunteer workers to ring doorbells, distribute campaign literature, register voters, and staff party headquarters. They need voters who will support the party's candidates, donate money to campaigns, and volunteer their services around election time. Finally, parties need candidates who can successfully run for office and, once elected, work to attain the party's policy goals.

Who Belongs to the Major Parties and Why?

Despite the widespread belief that the two major parties are alike, almost 70 percent of the population identifies with one or the other. As you can see in Figure 6.1, attachment to the Democratic party is stronger than to the Republican party, although the percentages tend to fluctuate, month to month, between elections. Among young adults aged eighteen to twenty-nine who have a high school education, independents (42 percent) outnumber Republicans (28 percent) and Democrats (30 percent).[10] However, across all age groups, only about one-third of the voters consider themselves independents, and roughly two-thirds of those independents characterize themselves as being closer to either the Republican or the Democratic party.

What difference does party identification make? Clearly, it often determines citizens' political choices. In a typical election, for example, a voter may face a ballot listing candidates for ten, twenty, thirty, or more offices. Because no one can thoroughly study every issue and every office seeker's record, many voters select candidates along party lines. Sometimes they find, to their disappointment, that the candidate does not represent their views, but often the party label indicates with reasonable accuracy a candidate's political philosophy and positions on issues. As one party loyalist in Michigan recently put it, "If you are

FIGURE 6.1

Changes in Party Identification 1984–1996

During this period, the Democrats have held their own, while independents and identification as a Republican have decreased.

Source: Inter-University Consortium for Political and Social Research, University of Michigan, Ann Arbor, Michigan, 1984, and New York Times/CBS poll, December 1986, September 1989, May 1992, April 1994, December 1995, and November 1996.

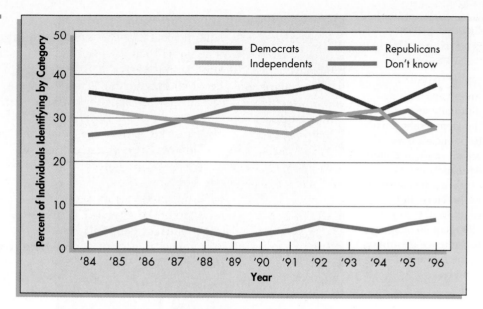

a Democratic candidate in this state and don't support labor, you won't be a Democratic candidate for very long."

WWW•

For more information on Democratic and Republican party activities, see the **Gitelson/Dudley/Dubnick web site.**

Democrats and Republicans

Who are the Democrats and the Republicans? The parties tend to attract different groups of supporters. Democrats maintain their greatest strength among African-Americans and Hispanics, Catholics and Jews, women, members of the working class, and individuals over the age of fifty. White southerners, once a critical part of the Democratic coalition, have voted as a majority for the Republicans in recent elections, although Democrats still maintain a majority foothold in the South among African-Americans.

Republicans are scattered across the country. They tend to be white, Protestant, and middle to upper class, and their views are comparatively conservative.

The issue that most sharply divides Democrats and Republicans is the role of government. Since the 1930s Democrats have favored a large government role in such policy areas as social welfare and business regulation. For example, in the 1930s Democrats took the lead in supporting the social security program. They are also more willing than the Republicans to support nonmilitary foreign aid programs and domestic environmental issues. Republicans, on the other hand, are more likely to favor reducing government services, including aid to minorities and social welfare programs. They also prefer a lesser government role in regulating business but are more likely than Democrats to support government spending on the military.

Courting Non-traditional Party Constituents

While African-Americans have traditionally supported the Democratic party, Republicans have, in recent years, attracted African-American office holders to their ranks. Here, Representative J. C. Watts (R-Oklahoma), speaks to audience members at the Library of Congress.

Although the polling data presented at the beginning of this chapter describe a public that feels political parties are irrelevant in the political system, people tend to view Republicans and Democrats differently in regard to which party can best handle a variety of national issues. Republicans are viewed as better at dealing with such issues as the reduction of the deficit, foreign policy, crime, and control of government spending. Democrats are seen as more competent in handling such problems as the protection of social security and Medicare. They are also thought to care about the needs of women and to be better at dealing with education, the environment, and health care.[11]

Independents

Independents—individuals who do not identify with any party—often claim that their voting patterns are influenced by issues and leadership qualities, not by party labels. The increase in independents during the 1960s and 1970s and their leveling off in the 1980s and 1990s parallel the belief in the myth of party irrelevance—that is, the tendency of many Americans to question the ability of party and government to solve the nation's major problems. The United States has faced a series of major crises in the last three decades. The Vietnam War, Watergate, the Iran-Contra scandal, political assassinations and terrorist attacks, urban decay, crime, environmental pollution, the energy crisis in the 1970s, nuclear proliferation, and the national deficit in the 1980s and 1990s have all contributed to a general feeling that the political system is ineffective and to a corresponding increase in indifference toward both parties.[12]

Independents make up an important part of the voting population, especially in presidential elections. There is less evidence, however, that they maintain an independent position in state and local elections.[13] In these contests, voters often lack information on candidates' policy positions or leadership qualities. It is difficult, however, to find many voters who are pure independents and who totally avoid using party labels to identify candidates for whom they will vote.[14] Thus party label remains one of the best predictors of voter choice in many elections.

A majority of Americans appear to accept the Democratic and Republican parties as relevant symbols, particularly when it comes to voting. In fact, when independents who lean toward one of the parties are included, close to 90 percent of the electorate identify to some extent with either the Democratic or the Republican party.[15] As the data in Figure 6.1 indicate, the number of self-declared independents in the United States has leveled in the 1990s.

What Parties Do

A basic task of political parties is to win elections. Once parties have successfully run candidates for political office, they offer a way to organize the political world and provide elected officials with a means to organize the government. Had parties not developed as a link between the public and the institutions of government, they would have had to be invented.[16] Let us look more closely at some of the functions of parties.

Building Electoral Coalitions.   Parties exist to organize people into **electoral coalitions:** groups of loyal supporters who agree with their party's stand on most issues and vote for its candidates for office. As we have said, party labels remain an important electoral symbol in the United States, and for many Americans no other institutions or organizations embrace as broad a range of issues and goals on the national level as the Democratic and Republican parties.

Developing Public Policy.   Parties also play a role in developing positions on what government should do about various problems and in seeing those positions translated into legislation. Research on presidential and state platforms indicates that opposing candidates usually differ distinctly on specific policies. **Platforms,** which are statements of party goals and specific policy agendas, are taken very seriously by the candidates and the parties, although they are not

MYTHS IN POPULAR CULTURE

6.1   Cartoons and the Parties

William "Marcy" Tweed, the legendary boss of New York City's Tammany Hall Democratic machine during the 1860s and 1870s, hated political cartoons. After viewing a cartoon by Thomas Nast, highly critical of Tweed's corruption in New York politics, Tweed was said to have ordered his lieutenants to "Stop them damned pictures. I don't care so much what the papers say about me. My constituents can't read. But, damn it, they can see pictures!" Nast's cartoons about Tweed were thought to have contributed to Tweed's eventual downfall. In the words of one scholar, they also "established once and forever . . . cartooning as an enduring presence in American [popular] political culture."

Indeed, many an early-rising, coffee-drinking, sleepy-eyed newspaper reader turns every morning to the editorial page, where political cartoons are often featured. One particular editorial cartoonist, Jeff Stahler, has frequently captured the mood of the nation through his artful and often satirical critiques of politicians and political parties. A good example is a cartoon he drew in August 1996, satirizing the Republican and Democratic parties during their national presidential nominating conventions in San Diego and Chicago, respectively. Stahler's message is clear: based on the issues, there is no difference between the two national party programs and platforms. All that a vendor selling campaign T-shirts and political buttons has

to do is change his or her sign from Republican to Democrat. The message on the shirts and buttons can remain the same.

Stahler's stereotyping of political parties—that there are no differences between the Republican and Democratic promises and platforms—is, no doubt, shared by many Americans. And, of course, satire is a purposefully exaggerated art, used to make a strong point. But as we point out in this chapter, and as is clear in a reading of the two party platforms (see Table 6.1), the Republican and Democratic parties differ on many issues and policies. For the most part, though, they do provide Americans with distinct policy and issue positions.

To be sure, we appreciate Stahler's humor and must even acknowledge the partial accuracy of his cartoon, for the two major parties do indeed share similar positions in some policy areas. Yet the myth that the two parties are identical—a distortion the editorial cartoon often creates—also feeds and reinforces the stereotype of U.S. political parties that much of the public clings to.

Source: Roger A. Fischer, *Them Damned Pictures: Explorations in American Political Cartoon Art* (North Haven, Conn.: Archon Books, 1996), esp. chaps. 1 and 6. The quotations are from pp. 2 and 3.

TABLE 6.1

Comparison Between the 1996 Democratic and Republican Party Platforms

As these excerpts indicate, the two platforms differed markedly, giving the voters a clear choice on the solutions to relevant issues.

| Policy Areas | Platform Planks | |
	Republicans	Democrats
State of the economy	"We cannot go on like this. For millions of families, the American dream is fading."	"Today, America is moving forward. The economy is stronger, the deficit is lower and the Government is smaller."
Taxes	Support a 15 percent reduction in tax rates, a $500-per-child tax credit, a 50 percent cut in the capital gains rate, expansion of I.R.A.'s and lower taxes on Social Security benefits. These are "interim steps toward comprehensive tax reform." The Internal Revenue Service "must be dramatically downsized."	"America cannot afford to return to the era of something-for-nothing tax cuts." Support a "$500 tax cut for children" and additional reductions for college tuition payments, small businesses and the self-employed. Allow money in individual retirement accounts to be used to buy a first home and to pay education and medical expenses.
Abortion	Support a Constitutional amendment that would outlaw abortion in all circumstances. No specific mention of tolerance for other views on abortion.	Support a woman's right to choose to have an abortion in all circumstances currently legal. "Respect the individual conscience of each American on this difficult issue."

(continued)

TABLE 6.1

Democratic and
Republican Platforms
(cont.)

Policy Areas	Republicans	Democrats
Affirmative action	"We will attain our nation's goal of equal rights without quotas or other forms of preferential treatment."	"We should mend it, not end it."
Immigration	Prohibit the children of illegal immigrants from attending public schools; restrict welfare to legal immigrants; support a constitutional amendment denying automatic citizenship to children born in the United States to illegal immigrants and legal immigrants who are in this country for a short time.	Permit the children of illegal immigrants to attend public schools; allow legal immigrants to receive welfare and other benefits; make it easier for eligible immigrants to become United States citizens.
Balanced budget	Support a Constitutional amendment requiring a balanced budget.	Promise to balance the budget by 2002.
Education	Favor using Federal money to help parents pay private school tuition.	Support strengthening public schools.
Homosexual rights	"Reject the distortion" of civil rights laws that would "cover sexual preference."	Support efforts "to end discrimination against gay men and lesbians and further their full inclusion in the life of the nation."
Trade	Oppose using trade policy to pursue "social agenda items."	Insist that international trade agreements include standards to protect children, workers and the environment.
Gun control	"Defend the constitutional right to keep and bear arms" and favor mandatory penalties for crimes committed with guns.	Support a waiting period for buying handguns and a ban on the sale of certain assault weapons.
Arts and broadcasting	End Federal financing for the arts and the Corporation for Public Broadcasting.	Favor public support of the arts and the Corporation for Public Broadcasting.
Environment	Emphasize consideration of private property rights and economic development in conjunction with environmental protection.	Emphasize Government regulation to protect the environment.
Star wars	Favor development of the missile defense system.	Oppose revival of the land-based missile defense system, known as Star Wars.

Source: Copyright © 1996 by The New York Times, August 27, 1996, p. A11.

binding on candidates or elected officials.[17] As political scientists Gerald Pomper and Susan Lederman argue,

> The parties do not copy each other's pledges, but make divergent appeals, thereby pointing to the differences in their basic composition. [The platform] is important because it summarizes, crystallizes, and presents to the voters the character of the party coalition. We should take platforms seriously because politicians seem to take them seriously.[18]

As you can see in Table 6.1, despite some similarities, the Republican and Democratic platforms differed significantly in 1996. While party platforms do serve as a form of propaganda—an attempt to put a positive light on the programs and goals of the party—they also represent a serious declaration of policy. The Democrats' positions were relatively liberal, with strong support for social spending, and the Republicans' positions were relatively conservative, with emphasis on individual enterprise.

Winning Elections.   A party's ability to recruit the best-possible candidates and to win elections determines its success. Party organizations do not monopolize that process because many candidates seek nomination on their own. In recent years, however, parties have offered their candidates a growing list of services. Party organizations, particularly at the state and national levels, offer candidates training and support, help them raise funds, and encourage voter turnout on election day. But many candidates in highly visible races also rely heavily on paid professional consultants to manage and finance their campaigns.

Today the nomination of many candidates rests in the hands of the voters who take part in **primaries**—elections to select candidates to run for office under the party banner. (We discuss primaries in detail in Chapter 7, which covers elections.) Although primaries limit the direct role of the party-as-organization in the nomination process, partisanship prevails as the party-in-the-electorate makes its choices. It is important to note, however, that in parts of the country local party organizations are still instrumental in recruiting candidates for political office and in assisting those candidates in their efforts to serve in government.

Organizing Government.   Parties also organize the legislative and executive branches of government. Congress and most state legislatures are structured along party lines. Leadership and committee assignments in those bodies are usually by party, and executives—including mayors, governors, and the president— often work closely with party leaders to pass bills and implement programs.

Although members of Congress often vote along party lines, the changes in the internal processes of Congress have in some ways made it difficult for party leaders to control members. Looking ahead to the next election, many members of Congress are more committed to their constituents than to their party. In addition, self-recruitment and the use of independent campaign consultants decrease reliance on the party as the source of nomination and campaign support.

As a result, members of Congress do not necessarily put their party first and ignore their district's or their own interests. (See Chapter 10, which covers Congress, for a detailed discussion.)

In short, party control over the vote of a member of Congress is far from absolute, in contrast to countries such as the United Kingdom of Great Britain and Northern Ireland, where the party's domination of the nominating process often guarantees the loyalty of its legislative members. Nevertheless, most members of Congress have a pronounced sense of party loyalty and share common values and policy positions with their party colleagues. The average Democrat or Republican often votes along party lines for issues on which the party has taken a strong partisan stand.[19]

Mitigating Conflict.   Parties also serve to allay and control conflict among and between different groups and interests in our society. When opinions differ among people, the Democratic and Republican parties provide a stage for mediation, reminding us that in a nation of over 260 million people, compromise on many issues is a necessity in our representative system of government.

The Two-Party System

As noted earlier, the Constitution makes no mention of parties, and in fact, many of the founders viewed them as dangerous. Yet the debate and controversy that evolved as our nation struggled to deal with complex domestic and foreign issues slowly brought about the rise of divisions in the population and in the government—divisions that would lead to political factions.

The fears of the founders diminished as political parties formed in response to economic and philosophic differences between the merchants and traders in the northern half of the new republic and the planters in the South. By 1828, the United States had a two-party system. In the years that followed, parties evolved into a mechanism for expressing public opinion and organizing support among the citizenry. By 1908, New Jersey governor Woodrow Wilson, soon to become president, argued that parties are "absolutely necessary to . . . give some coherence to the action of political forces" and that they "have been our real body politic."[20]

The Federalists and the Jeffersonians

American parties grew slowly and cautiously at first.[21] Early political organizations were stable but short-lived coalitions of like-minded individuals who were drawn together in a conflict over the power of the national government.[22] The Federalists, led by Alexander Hamilton, favored a strong central government with taxing powers, a national bank, and a favorable foreign policy toward England. They attracted most of their support from the Northeast and the Atlantic seaboard, chiefly among bankers, industrialists, northern landowners, and merchants, who believed that a strong central government would produce a stable economy.

The Jeffersonians (also known as the Democratic-Republicans), organized by Thomas Jefferson and James Madison, favored limited national government and strong states' rights. They argued for a foreign policy that supported France rather than England, and they opposed a national bank. Although the Jeffersonians drew considerable support from the Middle Atlantic states, their greatest strength came from the South, particularly Virginia. They attracted small farmers, business owners, and artisans.

The Federalists elected their last president, John Adams, in 1796. In the years following, the party was torn apart by internal disputes between Adams and Hamilton over the direction of the party (particularly regarding foreign policy). As their base of support narrowed, the Federalists gradually faded from national politics. Thus from 1800 to 1820 the United States was a one-party nation.

The Democrats and the Whigs

The Jeffersonians and their heirs dominated national politics from 1800 to 1860, but their reign was not peaceful.[23] A crucial split occurred with the election of Andrew Jackson in 1828. Known as "Old Hickory," Jackson was a tough, ambitious man, and the first American president to rise from humble beginnings.

The Jacksonians, who now called themselves Democrats, favored increased participatory democracy, limited central government, and strong state power. Jackson's supporters attracted farmers and other working people to the party. By the end of his presidency, the Democrats were truly a national party. Many of the members of the opposition party, the Whigs, were former Federalists who opposed Jackson's attempts to decentralize the government. Supported by commercial and manufacturing interests, the Whigs successfully elected two presidents during the 1840s. Later the Whigs collapsed in the conflict over slavery, which eroded their support in the North and also split the Democrats into northern and southern factions.

The Whigs and the Democrats laid the foundation for the American two-party system. Like modern parties, they were well organized, with local and state committees. They held national conventions, constructed national party platforms, and had a relatively broad base of support, with participation by an expanded white male electorate. Although the period of strong rivalry between the two parties lasted only twenty years, it marked the real beginning of the two-party system in the United States.

The Democrats and the Republicans

The Republican party was born in 1854 in opposition to slavery. It drew its support from former elements of the Whig party, including businesspeople and merchants, abolitionists, and small farmers in the North and West. With the 1860

Two years after the
Republican party, also
known as "the Grand
Old Party" (GOP), was
born in opposition to
slavery, the party held
its first national con-
vention in Pittsburgh
on February 22, 1856.
This relatively sedate
scene would be re-
placed by the 1960s
with conventions
dominated by media
coverage and much
campaign hoopla.

FIRST REPUBLICAN CONVENTION HELD AT LAFAYETTE HALL, PITTSBURG, PA, FEB, 22ᴅ 1856.

election of Abraham Lincoln from Illinois, the Republicans established themselves as a major party. Since then the Republicans and the Democrats have al-
ternately dominated party politics. The Republicans won most (fourteen out of
eighteen) presidential races between 1860 and 1928. Their dominance was
largely due to their probusiness policies, which attracted a strong base of support
in the industrial North. The Democrats remained powerful in the South, although in 1924, when their popularity was at its lowest, they were able to win only
four of the former Confederate states.

The party balance changed in 1932 with the election of Franklin D. Roosevelt of New York, whose victory stemmed from the Republicans' inability to
deal with the hardships of the Great Depression. The Democrats' new power
rested on a coalition of voters from the urban North and the white South. Attracted by Roosevelt's New Deal policies, African-Americans also joined the coalition. With one interruption (the two-term presidency of General Dwight D.
Eisenhower in the 1950s), this coalition held on to the White House until Republican Richard M. Nixon became president in 1969. Since the late 1960s,
scholars, reporters, and political pundits have raised questions about the future
of the two-party system. Before Nixon's triumph, the Republican party seemed
doomed to fail in presidential elections. His victory turned the tide, with the Republicans winning five of the last eight presidential races. When the Democratic

presidential candidate, Bill Clinton, won in 1992, and was re-elected in 1996, questions still remained about the ability of the Democratic party to sustain majority party status at the presidential level.

Realignment of Parties

Are we experiencing a major shift from one party to another? Do the Republicans' presidential victories in the 1980s and their capture of both houses of Congress in 1994, and again in 1996, mark a realignment of power? **Party realignments** occur (1) when a political, social, or economic development prompts those groups that traditionally support one party to shift their support to another party or (2) when large numbers of new voters enter the electorate, causing a shift to a new majority party.[24] For a party realignment to take place, one party must become dominant in the political system, controlling the presidency and Congress as well as many state legislatures. The democratization of parties, slavery, and the Great Depression were three of the economic and social issues that precipitated major party realignments of the past. There have been four major American realignments altogether, marked by the election of Andrew Jackson in 1828, Abraham Lincoln in 1860, William McKinley in 1896, and Franklin D. Roosevelt in 1932.

The realignment that brought Roosevelt's Democrats to power was, in part, the result of a shift in population away from rural small towns, where traditional Republican support rested, to the big cities. New immigrants living in the big cities strongly rejected the Republicans' traditional pattern of nonintervention in economic and social problems. They joined Catholics and other traditional Republicans in a new coalition that gave the Democrats an overwhelming victory in 1932. Together with blacks, they formed a lasting reservoir of support for the Democratic party.

You can see from Table 6.2 that realigning elections seem to occur approximately every thirty years or every generation. If history provides an accurate picture of the future, a realigning election, projecting the Republican party into the majority, should have occurred around 1968. Indeed, many observers thought that Nixon's victory marked the beginning of a new realignment.

Conditions favored a Republican resurgence that year. The Democratic party was bitterly divided over the Vietnam War, and riots marred its national convention. Urban unrest, particularly in African-American ghettos, spelled disaster for the Democrats. Some unusual events, however, may have worked against a shift of power to the Republicans. As the result of the civil rights movement of the 1960s, many southern African-Americans joined the electorate, and their entry strengthened the Democrats' position. People were also living longer, which meant that New Deal Democrats remained in the electorate to support their party's candidates. On the other hand, the Watergate scandal eroded the Republicans' position in the 1970s and contributed, in part, to Georgia governor Jimmy Carter's election to the presidency in 1976. The Democrats continued to dominate both houses of Congress until 1981.

TABLE 6.2

Electoral Party
Systems in the United
States

Despite the shifts documented in this table, the American party system has been remarkably stable. The Democratic party has been around for more than one hundred
and fifty years, and the Republican party has been in existence for more than a century.

Stage of Development	Period	Leading Parties	Events and Developments
First party system	1790s–1824	Federalists Jeffersonians	Parties evolved; powers of national government grew.
Second party system	1824–1860	Whigs Democrats	National nominating conventions; national bank; regional conflicts; national party committees; state and local party committees.
Third party system	1860–1896	Republicans Democrats	Urban political machines; states' rights; role of political bosses.
Fourth party system	1896–1932	Republicans Democrats	Nonpartisan local elections; government reform; U.S. role in world affairs; formal voter registration systems; use of direct primary; weakening of congressional party controls.
Fifth party system	1932–?	Republicans Democrats	Changes in convention rules; civil rights; Vietnam; welfare state policies; nominating rules (Democrats). In 1994 Republicans won the Senate and captured the House after forty years of Democratic control, holding on to both the Senate and the House in 1996. Clinton became the first Democratic president since Franklin D. Roosevelt (1933–1945) to win re-election to the presidency (1993–2001). The question arises as to whether we are entering a new stage of party development.

Source: Alan R. Gitelson, M. Margaret Conway, and Frank B. Feigert, *American Political
Parties: Stability and Change* (Boston: Houghton Mifflin, 1984), pp. 26–27. Adapted by
permission.

Have recent successful electoral victories by Republican presidential candidates and the Republicans' capture of the Senate and the House of Representatives in 1994 and 1996 meant that a realignment has occurred? Three
characteristics of our contemporary political scene warn us against any quick
judgments regarding realignment. First, despite the Republicans' success in
dominating the presidency and gaining control of Congress and thirty governorships in 1994, the Democrats won the presidency in 1992 and again in 1996.
Second, realignments tend to occur over a period of time, and while the Republicans had significant victories in the 1994 and 1996 elections, any permanent

realignment will have to face the test of time. Third, some scholars have suggested that we may be going through a period of **party dealignment,** in which the public disassociates itself from either party and divides its votes among them and strong third-party or independent movements.[25] The relative increase during the past thirty years in the number of independents and weak party identifiers tends to support this argument. If the pattern prevails, neither party may be able to regain a solid hold on the title of "majority party" in the near future.

At present, however, no clear realignment has occurred. Although some scholars do argue that we appear to be moving through a dealigning period, the concept of dealignment does not satisfactorily explain all citizen sentiment regarding parties and politics in the United States.

Why Two Parties?

One thing is clear: for most of its history, the United States has had a two-party system. We have many minor parties, but they rarely elect anyone to a major office. Why has this been the case? Other democracies, including Israel, Holland, France, and Italy, have several important parties. What factors limit significant party activity in the United States to the Republicans and the Democrats?

Winner Takes All. According to one explanation, the rules that govern the electoral system in the United States are responsible for the two-party system.[26] Early in our history we adopted what is known as a **single-member district, winner-take-all electoral system.** In all federal and state elections and in most local elections, we elect officials from districts served by only one legislator. In order to gain office, a candidate has to win a plurality—the most votes. (In certain states a candidate in a given election must win a majority of the votes, that is, more than 50 percent.) Thus only one U.S. representative or state legislator is elected from each congressional or legislative district, no matter how close the vote.

By contrast, most European nations use a system of **proportional representation.** In this system, legislative seats are assigned to party candidates in proportion to the percentage of the vote that the party receives within electoral districts. If a party receives 35 percent of the vote in a district, it is allocated approximately 35 percent of that district's legislative seats. Thus minor or third parties may accumulate enough votes to gain representation in the legislature even if they are not able to attract a plurality or only have strong pockets of support.

The winner-take-all system in the United States has worked against the development of minor parties. Because it is so difficult for even the most successful minor parties to accumulate pluralities, their candidates rarely win. Recognizing that minorities have so little chance, voters tend to be drawn to the major party coalitions at election time, and those parties try hard to maintain middle-of-the-road positions that will attract voters.[27] The result has been two broad-based party coalitions, such as the Republicans and the Democrats of today.

A Division of Interests.   A second explanation, advanced by political scientists V. O. Key, Jr., and Louis Hartz, points to a natural division of interests in our nation as the source of the two-party system.[28] From the time of the country's founding until recently, divisions have existed between eastern manufacturers and western frontier interests, slaveholders and abolitionists, urban and rural interests, and various regional interests. The division has stemmed from tensions over the power of the national government and over questions of economic and social policy. That situation, according to Key and Hartz, has fostered the two-party competitive system, which is really a response to the national duality of interests.

A Similarity of Goals.   Still another view focuses on the overriding consensus in the United States regarding our political, social, economic, and governmental systems. For example, most Americans believe in capitalism, virtually no Americans want to institute a monarchy, and most Americans regard religion as a private matter. By contrast, in many European countries, the people support a variety of radically different social and economic alternatives, ranging from socialism to anarchy, and differences in social class and religion have given rise to a broad range of parties.

Divisions do exist in the United States as well—for example, between the poor and the wealthy. But a basic acceptance of the political and governmental system by most Americans makes compromise possible. As a result, according to this view, the two major parties can adequately serve us all, and we do not need a complex multiparty system.

State Laws.   As there is no mention of political parties in the U.S. Constitution, the definition of what a party is and the laws that regulate parties have been left, for the most part, to the individual states. Since the two major parties, the Republicans and the Democrats, have dominated the state legislatures, with the exception of Nebraska, state laws, in general, have historically made it difficult for third parties to get on the ballot. These restrictive state laws have helped perpetuate the two-party system in the United States (although recent court challenges have eliminated some of those restrictions in the various states).

WWW•

For more information on third parties, see the **Gitelson/Dudley/Dubnick** web site.

Third Parties in the United States

Despite the strength of the two-party system, minor parties have always existed in the United States. There have been more than nine hundred of these "third" parties, yet only one former minor party—the Republicans in 1860—has developed into a permanent national party. Occasionally, third parties even do well in national elections. As Table 6.3 shows, the American "Know-Nothings" party received more than 21 percent of the popular vote in the 1856 presidential election, and the Bull Moose Progressives received more than 27 percent of the popular vote in the 1912 presidential election.[29] In 1992, independent candidate Ross Perot had a highly visible campaign for the presidency and received 19 per-

TABLE 6.3

Major Third Parties in
Elections

Minor parties with a real chance of electoral success are a rarity in American politics, but that does not stop them from trying. Theodore Roosevelt, the most successful third-party candidate, outpolled the Republican incumbent and ensured the election of a Democrat, Woodrow Wilson.

Party	Year	Percentage of Presidential Vote
Anti-Mason	1832	8.0
Free Soil	1848	10.1
American "Know-Nothings"	1856	21.4
Breckinridge Democrats	1860	18.2
Constitutional Union	1860	12.6
Populists	1892	8.5
Bull Moose Progressives (Theodore Roosevelt)	1912	27.4
Socialists	1912	6.0
Robert La Follette Progressives	1924	16.6
George Wallace American Independent	1968	13.5
John Anderson National Unity*	1980	6.6
H. Ross Perot**	1992	19.0
Reform party (H. Ross Perot)	1996	8.0

*Anderson ran as an independent candidate in most states. The National Unity party did not have any formal organizational structure other than as a vehicle for slating the candidate in most states.
**Perot ran as an independent candidate in fifty states.

Source: Daniel A. Mazmanian, *Third Parties in Presidential Elections* (Washington, D.C.: The Brookings Institution, 1974). Data are from *Statistical Abstract of the United States,* U.S. Department of Commerce, Bureau of the Census. Reprinted by permission of The Brookings Institution.

cent of the popular vote in the election. In 1996, however, running as the Reform party presidential candidate, he received only about 8 percent of the vote.

Sometimes a minor party forms around a single issue, such as prohibition, or an ideology, such as socialism. Others are splinter groups that leave a major party because they feel that their interests are not well represented. An example is George Wallace's American Independent party, which split off from the Democrats in 1968.

Independent and Third-Party Candidates

Over the past two hundred years, many third-party and independent candidates have run for president. Here we see Reform Party presidential candidate Ross Perot addressing the television studio audience of *Larry King Live* during the 1996 presidential campaign.

Third parties succeed in elections mostly at the state and local level. But even at that level, they must overcome many barriers. Dominated by the two major parties, state legislatures have created complicated electoral rules that make it hard for the minor parties to obtain funding and to place their candidates on the ballot. In California, for example, a new party must submit a petition containing more than seven hundred thousand signatures before its candidates can be listed on the general election ballot. In Florida, a third party must pay the state 10 cents for every signature submitted.[30]

Federal election laws also work against the minor parties. For example, major parties automatically receive guaranteed funding for presidential campaigns. A third party cannot obtain such funding until its candidate has demonstrated the ability to garner a minimum (5 percent) of the popular vote.

Despite these obstacles, third parties persist, attracting devoted members and serving as a force for change in American politics. Third parties put new issues on the political agenda—issues that the major parties may overlook in their search for the broad middle ground, where most voters are perceived to be. For example, social security, unemployment insurance, the five-day workweek, workmen's compensation, national health insurance, and government aid to farmers were first introduced by the Socialist party in its 1932 party platform and only later recognized as important programs by both the Republicans and the Democrats.

**CLOSER
TO HOME**

6.1   Where Have All the Parties Gone?: Third Parties in our Towns and States

Perhaps no characteristic of political parties is more familiar to the American public than our two-party system, dominated by the Democrats and Republicans (see pages 174–180 in this chapter for a discussion of two-party dominance). Every presidential election year, the two major parties face off in a contest that marks our nation as firmly committed to only two serious contenders fighting it out for the most powerful political office in the world. And while Americans in increasing numbers state that they have voted for third-party (or independent) candidates (37 percent in one recent poll), the fact remains that even a highly visible third-party candidate like H. Ross Perot (Reform party) was able to garner only 8 percent of the vote in the 1996 presidential elections.

Are third parties dead? They may not be very successful in the national electoral arena, but they are alive and active at the state and local levels of government, supporting various issues, presenting policy agendas, and even running candidates for local and statewide offices. In the 1996 elections, over fifty minor political parties fielded candidates in states from Alabama to Wyoming.

One of those third parties that has been particularly active at the local level of government is the Libertarian party. The Libertarian party extols an ideological belief that government should do no more than what is minimally necessary in the areas of economic affairs and the personal freedoms of the people. Libertarians condemn the role of federal, state, and local government in most aspects of a citizen's life, professing the sanctity of individual choice and decision making. Even on the hotly debated issue of cloning—the ability to scientifically reproduce exact genetic duplicates of animals, including human beings, from animal cells—the party's chair, Steve Dasbach, has argued that government should be prohibited from any regulatory role.

The Libertarian party has experienced some limited electoral successes at the local level of government. In recent elections in California, Florida, Pennsylvania, and Texas, Libertarian candidates won the offices of mayor and county supervisor; seats on the city council and public utility boards; and judgeships. For example, Villa Park, California, has a Libertarian mayor, Robert Pachin, and Dayton, Texas, a Libertarian city manager, Robert Ewart. Libertarians Steve Perfect and David Curtis serve, respectively, as a member of Florida's Sarasota County Charter Review Board and as tax assessor for Ashland Township, Pennsylvania.

Indeed, as we get closer to home and state and local government, it is clear that third parties, such as the Libertarians, play a role in our governments and, subsequently, in our lives.

Sources: Survey by the Media Studies Center/Roper Center, February 1996; *Congressional Quarterly Weekly Report*, 54, No. 45 (November 9, 1996), 3250; *San Mateo Libertarian* newsletter, 7, No. 3 (March 1997), 1.

With so many possible issues of significance to small groups of voters, why do we not have more minor parties? Why, for example, did the civil rights movement not produce a minor party? The answer is that those involved in the movement (like many other underrepresented groups) found support within a major party. Democratic presidents John F. Kennedy and Lyndon B. Johnson responded to the movement's strategy of civil disobedience and became strong advocates for civil rights. Of course, the Democrats wanted to retain the support of a growing African-American constituency. When issues are narrower and voter support less widespread, third-party advocates may have few political options except to form a minor party. Future elections will no doubt provide voters with a number of third-party candidates for the presidency, as well as for Congress and state and local offices. In 1996, over fifty minor parties ran candidates in Senate, House, and gubernatorial races and in the presidential race. (See Closer to Home 6.1.)

Party Structure

Decentralization is the key word to remember when thinking about the structure of parties. Just as in our governmental system, power in the parties is fragmented among local, state, and national organizations. The two national parties are loose confederations of state parties, and state political parties are loose confederations of city and county political organizations.

For a long time the most influential party leaders were heads of local party organizations. Bosses, such as Mayor Richard J. Daley of Chicago and Jack Parr in southern Texas, ruled towns and cities and even states with an iron hand, distributing favors and flattening any opposition. It was said of Daley that he controlled even the assignment of the job of running the elevators in city hall. There are still strong local politicians and mayors today, although Daley, who died in 1976, was the last of the old-style, undisputed bosses.

Local Parties

At the bottom of the typical local party structure is the **precinct,** a voting district generally covering an area of several blocks. An elected or appointed precinct captain may oversee electoral activities in the precinct, including voter registration, distribution of leaflets, and get-out-the-vote efforts. Above the precinct level, several different organizations exist. **Wards,** or city council districts, are important in big cities such as Chicago. Elsewhere, party organizations exist at the city, county, congressional district, state legislative, or even judicial level. Members of these committees may be elected or appointed. Their responsibilities include raising money, recruiting candidates, conducting campaigns, getting out the vote, and handling **patronage**—that is, jobs—and **preferments**—providing services or contracts in return for support.

In many places around the country, local parties scarcely exist at all. Nonpartisan elections are the rule, a result of antiparty reforms at the turn of the century, and politics is relatively informal. Indeed, two-thirds of cities with populations of more than five thousand use the nonpartisan form of election. In many of these communities, formal or informal "political clubs" raise money and run campaigns. These clubs actively compete with each other in elections and may identify with either major party.[31]

Even in communities where partisan elections are the rule, party organization and strength vary tremendously. If one party dominates, the weaker party may find it impossible to recruit workers and candidates and to raise money for elections. Until its recent resurgence, the Republican party had to cope with this kind of handicap throughout a previously Democrat-dominated South. In communities that show little interest in politics, neither party may be able to put together a strong local organization.

Nevertheless, it is at the grassroots local community level where party organization often finds its greatest strength and where in recent years we have seen growth in party organizations. Indeed, recent research suggests that local party organizations are becoming increasingly active in various aspects of the campaign process in communities.[32]

State Parties

The influence and power of state party organizations vary from state to state. State parties in Alabama, California, and Maryland, for example, have almost nothing to say about which candidates run for office or how they run their campaigns. In contrast, parties in states like Connecticut, Indiana, and Michigan wield considerable power.[33] Often a good deal of that power is in the hands of the state chairperson. It is not unusual for the governor of a state to control the state's party organization, although, as we shall see in Chapter 7, on elections and campaigns, governors are often motivated to establish their own candidate-centered organization devoted to their campaign for re-election. Party organization varies from state to state, however, and depends on the preferences of officeholders and other influential party members and on state laws and party rules and regulations.

In recent years state party organizations have assumed an important role on the political scene.[34] State parties have increasingly begun to offer fundraising, polling, and research services to state and local candidates. They may also provide computer analyses of voting behavior. In addition, most state party organizations help orchestrate the state presidential campaigns.

National Parties

The national party organizations come into their own every four years when they organize the national conventions and support candidates for major office. Although less visible the rest of the time, the national party staffs, directed by the national chairpersons and the national committees, which include representatives from all the states, are hard at work. They raise money for national and state elections, run workshops on campaigning and fundraising techniques for congressional candidates, and maintain the loose, decentralized structure that is the national party. The Democrats and the Republicans, by devoting greater resources to the national party organizations, have undergone a national resurgence during the past fifteen years.

The electoral role of the national party organizations has been challenged in recent years by interest groups and their **political action committees (PACs).** Because federal laws, as well as many state laws, prohibit various interest groups from donating money to political campaigns, such groups have set up affiliated PAC organizations for the purpose of contributing money to the campaigns of candidates who sympathize with their aims. (See Chapter 8, on interest groups, for a more detailed discussion of the role of PACs.) The involvement of professional consultants and the media in the campaign process has also challenged the role of the national organizations. (See Chapter 7, on elections, for more on this topic.)

Despite these challenges, both national organizations have refused to accept a secondary role in national politics and during the past twenty-five years have worked to revitalize themselves.[35] The Republicans, in particular, have strengthened their fundraising and candidate support systems. They now provide sophisticated technical campaign expertise to state and local parties.

The Democrats have redefined the rules governing the selection of presidential convention delegates to make the party's decision-making structure more democratic and to increase grassroots participation in the party. That process has involved, among other things, systematic efforts to achieve broad-based representation of women and minorities at the national conventions. The Democrats also increased the number of U.S. senators and representatives who attend the national convention as delegates. Since the early 1980s the national Democratic party has also tried to offer more fundraising and campaign support to its own candidates.[36]

Conclusion: Decline or Transformation of Political Parties?

What is the future of the Democratic and Republican parties? Some scholars insist that both parties are in a period of decline and see them as weak, inconsistent in their policies, lacking accountability for their actions, disorganized in pursuing their goals, and less effective than in the past in organizing government.[37] In recent presidential campaigns, we have seen both the Democratic and the Republican party faced with contentious battles over which factions of the party—moderate, liberal, or conservative—will control the nomination of candidates and the writing of the party platform. We seem to be moving from **party-centered campaigns** to **candidate-centered campaigns,** reflecting the shift in control over the candidate recruitment and campaign process from the political parties to candidate-controlled campaign organizations. Given the decrease in party identification and the weakening of party control over some aspects of the campaign and election process, it is not surprising that many people believe in the myth of party irrelevance.

Are the parties identical? It often seems that way because some of their policies can be difficult to distinguish. On certain broad issues, such as supporting reductions in the national deficit, and narrow issues, such as social security for the elderly, their positions are often the same. To confuse matters further, groups of legislators from both parties occasionally join forces to support or oppose legislation.

Nevertheless, the evidence suggests that the parties are not irrelevant. The fact that they attract different coalitions of voters and office seekers and that Democrats and Republicans in the electorate and in government tend to view many issues differently attests to their relevancy in the political system.

The significant number of independents, along with the increase in ticket splitting, suggests that parties may be less relevant than in the past, as does the takeover of some traditional party roles by interest groups, political action committees, the media, and professional political consultants. These issues will be discussed further in Chapters 7, 8, and 9. The parties, however, have changed in response to such challenges. Furthermore, although parties attract fewer strong supporters, particularly among college students, a significant majority of voters still feel some attachment to either the Democrats or the Republicans and believe that one party can do a better job than the other in tackling the nation's most serious problems.[38]

If parties are still viable, what kind of change is taking place? How can we explain, for example, the growing independence of political candidates and legislators from their parties? Some scholars have suggested that a transformation is taking place in the roles and functions of parties in our society.[39]

Although parties are now sharing many traditional functions with other groups, they have taken on new tasks, as our discussion in this chapter has shown. Both national and state organizations have enhanced their roles in the campaign process and have continued to play an important role at the local level. In fact, most of the elections held in our nation during the four years between presidential races—and they number more than five hundred thousand—are not touched by any other organized group. Party influence in the Senate and House remains strong, and on many partisan issues the members vote along party lines more often than not. This pattern is also typical of state legislators.

Thus, despite the myth of party irrelevance, parties remain a key institution in American politics and are still one of the most important cues for voters making electoral decisions. They also play a dominant role in organizing and coordinating public policy on literally thousands of issues. Finally, parties represent many individuals and groups that are not adequately served by other organizations. These groups include the poor, the aged, and minorities. All of them have benefited from strong party platforms and legislative action. Challenged by the entry of new and competing institutions into the electoral process, parties have increasingly adapted to these challenges and have maintained their unique role in our political system.

Summary

1. American political parties are coalitions of people organized formally to recruit, nominate, and elect individuals to office and to use elected office to achieve shared political goals.

2. Parties represent three different alliances of members: the party-as-organization, the party-in-the-electorate, and the party-in-government.

3. Although many Americans' identification with the Republican or Democratic party seems to be weak, the parties remain relevant symbols, particularly when it comes to voting.

4. Parties organize citizens into electoral coalitions, develop policy positions, work to win elections, and organize government.

5. Parties developed slowly in the United States, but by the mid-1800s the Whigs and the Democrats had laid the foundation for the two-party system. There have been four major party realignments, or major shifts in party coalitions, in

U.S. history. Currently, scholars are debating whether we are in a period of realignment or dealignment.

6. Explanations for the existence of the two-party system include winner-take-all electoral rules, a division of social and economic interests, a basic consensus on political goals, and restrictive state laws regarding third parties.

7. Despite the strength of the major parties, minor parties thrive and present program alternatives that are often adopted by the Democratic and Republican parties.

8. Both local and state political parties have grown in importance in recent years. Although the national party organizations have been challenged by competing groups, they have responded to the challenge and in changing have revitalized themselves.

Key Terms and Concepts

Political parties In the United States, a coalition of people organized formally to recruit, nominate, and elect individuals to office and to use elected office to achieve shared political goals.

Decentralization A term used to describe the Republican and Democratic parties, meaning that

decision-making power is dispersed, the party is regulated at the state level, and no single individual controls the system.

Party-as-organization With few members, it primarily consists of state and county chairpersons and ward and precinct captains, who work for the party throughout the year, recruiting candidates and participating in fundraising activities.

Party-in-the-electorate Includes anyone who identifies with a particular party, tends to vote for that party's candidates, and may even contribute to its campaigns.

Party-in-government The individuals who have been elected or appointed to a government office under a party label. They play a major role in organizing government and in setting policy.

Electoral coalitions Groups of loyal supporters who agree with the party's stand on most issues and vote for its candidates for office.

Platforms Statements of party goals and specific policy agendas that are taken seriously by the party's candidates but are not binding.

Primary An election in which party members select candidates to run for office under the party banner.

Party realignment A major shift by voters from one party to another that occurs when one party becomes dominant in the political system, controlling the presidency and Congress as well as many state legislatures.

Party dealignment A period in which the public disassociates itself from either party and splits its votes between the parties.

Single-member district, winner-take-all electoral system The system of election used in the United States in all national and state elections and in most local elections. Officials are elected from districts that are served by only one legislator, and a candidate must win a plurality—the most votes.

Proportional representation The electoral system used by many European nations whereby legislative seats are assigned to party candidates in proportion to the percentage of the vote that the party receives in the election.

Precinct The bottom of the typical, local party structure—a voting district generally covering an area of several blocks.

Wards City council districts that are, in the party organization, a level below that of the citywide level.

Patronage The provision of jobs in return for political support.

Preferments The provision of services or contracts in return for political support. Party committee members use patronage and preferments to court voters and obtain campaign contributions.

Political action committee (PAC) An independent organization that interest groups, officeholders, and political candidates can establish for the sole purpose of contributing money to the campaigns of candidates who sympathize with its aims. PACs are the result of federal laws that prohibit most interest groups from donating money to political campaigns.

Party-centered campaign A campaign in which the party coordinates activities, raises money, and develops strategies.

Candidate-centered campaign A campaign in which paid consultants or volunteers coordinate campaign activities, develop strategies, and raise funds. Parties play a secondary role.

C H A P T E R 7

Campaigns and Elections

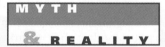

Do **politicians always break their campaign promises?**

WWW●
See **Political Science** at
http://www.hmco.com/college

The excitement of the election was exhilarating. Millions of people turned out to see and hear the presidential candidates as they traveled around the nation speaking on the issues of the day. Between July and November the Democratic candidate "made five hundred speeches . . . addressing thirty to forty million people . . . traveling 18,000 miles in four swings around the country."[1] One scholar wrote of the Republican candidate that this was a classic case of a "modern advertising campaign." Cartoons, posters, and inscriptions were turned out by the carloads, more than "120 million campaign documents" were distributed to the people, and "an army of 1,400 trained speakers" was engaged to speak in favor of the candidate.[2] The Republicans canvassed voters and targeted specific ethnic groups with campaign literature written in German, Spanish, French, Italian, and Yiddish, as well as other languages.[3]

That campaign story may seem familiar. The campaign strategies and hoopla may remind you of recent races you have witnessed or seen on television. Yet the campaign took place one hundred years ago, in 1896, when the Democratic presidential candidate, William Jennings Bryan, ran against Republican William McKinley.

Rallies, use of the media, and appeals to special interests remain a basic part of modern-day campaigns and elections, and the intensity and excitement have stayed the same. The electoral system itself is quite different, however. An array of regulations, restrictions, and constitutional amendments has changed the way candidates are nominated, how campaigns are run, and who is eligible to vote. Unlike McKinley or Bryan, today's candidates for president have to contend with presidential primaries, campaign spending limits, and an expanded voting population. In 1896, most voters were middle- and upper-class white men. Today, candidates must appeal to men and women, African-Americans and whites, rich and poor, and young and old.

Despite the excitement of the campaigns and the widespread media coverage, the American public has some misgivings about the election process. Voter turnout has declined in the United States since the early 1960s, with only 49 percent of the eligible electorate voting in the 1996 presidential race. In 1960, the Kennedy-Nixon race attracted 63 percent of the vote.

Poll findings also suggest that Americans do not believe that their elected representatives respond to their demands and expectations. For example, when asked whether "public officials care much what people like me think," 66 percent of those questioned said that public officials do not care.[4] In a recent survey of citizens who call in to radio talk shows, 87 percent indicated that "generally speaking, elected officials in Washington lose touch with the people pretty quickly."[5] And when asked whether they felt that things in this country were generally going in the right direction, two out of three voters felt we were on the wrong track.[6]

The public also strongly disapproves of the way candidates run their campaigns, particularly the way they finance them. Such views are reinforced when, for example, the public learns that congressional candidates in 1996 spent more

Hoopla and Campaigns

Every campaign has included advertising posters, cartoons, and campaign literature. When William McKinley ran for president in 1896, his campaign literature emphasized his link to prosperity, prestige, and economic well-being.

than $765 million on primary and general election campaigns. Expenditures on individual races also attract a great deal of attention. In 1994, Senator Diane Feinstein, a Democrat, and her Republican challenger, Michael Huffington, set a new record for the most expensive Senate campaign in history, with total combined expenditures reaching almost $40 million.[7] In 1996, more than $3 million was raised by each of thirty-four Senate candidates, and more than seventy-five House candidates raised over $1 million for their campaigns.[8]

Why have so many Americans come to doubt the usefulness of elections? Why do so many citizens stay home on election day? One myth seems to be at the root of public criticism of the electoral process. The *myth of broken promises* holds that elections do not affect government policies—that candidates, once elected, fail to keep the promises they made during their campaigns.

The reality of the election process, however, differs from that myth. We demonstrate in this chapter that politicians seek to achieve not only their own career goals but also the social and political goals of their campaigns. In addition, we show that although money is very important in elections because it buys television time, polls, consultants, and the like, a variety of other factors also have a significant impact on who wins office.

Nominations: The Selection Process

Every year thousands of individuals decide to run for political office. Before they can get on the ballot, many must be selected, or nominated, by a political party, often after a costly, time-consuming, and exhausting primary campaign. What motivates these individuals?

Seeking Political Office

"The stakes are too high for government to be a spectator sport," former representative Barbara Jordan from Texas told a commencement audience. Few who run for office would disagree. Both personal ambition and policy goals motivate people to enter the proverbial election ring. Personal satisfactions include the power that elective office confers and the prestige of holding public office.[9] These rewards often drive politicians to climb what Joseph Schlesinger refers to as the **opportunity structure:** the political ladder of local, state, and national offices that can bring greater prestige and power as one moves toward the presidency at the very top.[10]

Politics is more than a career, however. Candidates also have a commitment to public service and to policy goals. For example, during his election campaign in 1996, President Clinton promised an increased role by the federal government in supporting primary, secondary, and higher education programs, a position he promoted after his re-election by sending to Congress educationally related legislation.

The Caucus

Ambition and commitment alone are not enough to ensure election, however. Anyone who wants to run for political office in most partisan elections, including the presidency, must first secure a party nomination. One of the oldest nomination methods is the **caucus** (the word means "meeting"). A diary entry written by John Adams in 1763 gives a less-than-flattering description of the process:

> This day learned that the caucus club meets at certain times in the garret of Dawes. . . . There they smoke tobacco till you cannot see from one end of the garret to the other. There they drink flip* . . . and they choose a moderator who puts questions to the vote regularly; and selectmen, assessors, collectors, fire wardens, and representatives are regularly chosen before they are chosen in the town.[11]

Until the Progressive Era, a period of political reform starting around the turn of the century, most party nominations were decided by caucuses or conventions. These meetings were closed to the public, and party leaders usually chose the nominees. Contemporary caucuses are local meetings open to all who live in the precinct. These citizens "caucus"—that is, meet and discuss—and then vote for delegates to district and state conventions. These delegates then nominate candidates for congressional and statewide offices. In about a third of the states, representatives to the national presidential conventions are also chosen by the caucus-convention method. Many of these delegates are committed in advance to a particular presidential candidate. Some, however, choose to run as uncommitted delegates, awaiting the national convention to declare their candidate preference.

The most celebrated of modern presidential caucuses takes place every four years in Iowa, where candidates compete for victory in their respective parties for the Democratic or Republican presidential nomination. Traditionally the Iowa caucus is the first of the presidential campaign year, and candidates are anxious to do well in order to demonstrate their appeal to both the voters and individuals who are potential campaign contributors and who want to support a winner.

Primaries

WWW•
For more information on primaries and the nomination process, see the **Gitelson/Dudley/ Dubnick** web site.

Except in presidential nominations, caucuses are relatively uncommon in contemporary politics. As we pointed out in Chapter 6, most national, state, and local nominees for the Democrats and Republicans are chosen in a **primary:** an election in which party members (and sometimes nonparty members) select candidates to run for office under the party banner. The first recorded primary was held in Crawford County, Pennsylvania, in 1842, but the first statewide primary system was not enacted until 1903, in Wisconsin. In about two-thirds of the states, delegates to the Democratic and Republican national conventions are chosen by primary.

In 1968, in response to a contentious national convention, the Democrats changed the party rules to make the nomination system more democratic. One result was an increase in the number of primaries, which rose from a low of twelve in 1912 to a high of forty-three in 1996.

*For the curious and those with a cast-iron stomach, flip is a hot mixture of beer, cider, sugar, egg, and nutmeg—an excellent eye opener.

The **open primary,** in which any qualified registered voter may participate, regardless of party affiliation, now prevails in twelve states.[12] On entering the polling place, voters choose a Democratic, Republican, or other ballot and vote for the listed candidates. A variation on the open primary is the blanket primary, found in three states—Alaska, Washington, and Louisiana—where voters do not disclose their party affiliation and where they may participate in the Democratic primary for one office and the Republican primary for another office.[13]

The **closed primary,** used in thirty-five states and Washington, D.C., allows voters to obtain only a ballot of the party in which they are registered.[14] In a **partisan primary,** candidates run for their own party's nomination. In a **nonpartisan primary,** candidates are listed on a ballot with no party identification. All presidential primaries are partisan, whereas many local primaries and the Nebraska state primary are nonpartisan.

In most states, the winning candidate is the one receiving the most votes. In ten southern states, a majority (more than 50 percent) of the vote is needed to win; if no candidate receives a clear majority, a **run-off primary** between the top two vote getters determines the party's candidate in the general election.

In presidential election years, the first presidential primary is always held in New Hampshire. Although the state is small and not necessarily representative of the nation's population as a whole, this primary plays a significant symbolic role in the nomination process. New Hampshire citizens are given the first opportunity to express their preferences for Republican and Democratic presidential hopefuls. As in the case of the first caucus held in Iowa, victory in the New Hampshire primary brings a successful candidate a great deal of media coverage and the visibility to attract campaign donations. Also worth noting is that this first primary attracts attention from the media and from the candidates and their entourage. This means not only prestige and honor for New Hampshire, but additional revenue for the state, too. It is no wonder that New Hampshire jealously guards the honor of initiating the primary season.

Presidential Nominating Conventions

When Hubert Humphrey was nominated by the Democratic party in 1968, he had entered no primaries, counting instead on support from President Lyndon B. Johnson and other party leaders. His defeat in the November election ended a century-old tradition in which the presidential and vice-presidential candidates were in effect chosen every four years at their party's national convention by delegates from the fifty states, the District of Columbia, and (in the case of the Democrats) offshore territories and Americans abroad.

The rise of the presidential primary has meant that the national party conventions no longer select the candidates, but rather ratify the presidential and vice-presidential choices already made in statewide presidential primaries and caucus–conventions.[15] In 1996 alone, thirteen Democratic and Republican presidential aspirants spent more than $223 million on their nomination campaigns.[16] Conventions still serve a number of traditional functions, however. They give the party faithful a place to transact business, which includes changing rules and writing the party platform. When the conventions are run smoothly, with minimal disputes and conflicts, they serve as an important "media event," publicizing the party's candidates and the issues to a nationwide audience.

Until the rule reforms of the late 1960s and early 1970s, state and local party leaders appointed most convention delegates. The delegates were largely well-educated, white, male professionals. One survey in the 1940s showed that nearly 40 percent of them were lawyers.[17] By 1996, a majority of delegates to the Democratic and Republican conventions were elected through primaries.[18] Delegates still tend to come from elite groups: they tend to be well educated, have relatively high family incomes, and are predominantly white. Democrats attract more African-Americans, young people, union members, and women to their conventions, whereas Republican delegates tend to be older, white, and predominantly Protestant. Loyal supporters of one of the major candidates, most delegates stand for election in a primary or caucus in that candidate's name.

Although for both parties the nomination process is critical to the success of any presidential aspirant, apparently it matters less to most voters. In 1996, only a fraction of the eligible voters cast ballots in the presidential primaries—8 million in all of the Democratic primaries (President Clinton was contested by only one minor candidate for the Democratic nomination), and 14 million in Republican primaries—compared with 96 million in the general election.[19] Primary voters consisted mainly of well-educated and older voters with higher-than-average incomes.[20]

Who Gets Nominated?

In the past, almost all the Democratic and Republican presidential nominees were white, male, wealthy Protestants. The barrier against Catholics fell with the Democratic nomination of Al Smith in 1928, but Protestant candidates still remain the rule. Furthermore, with the exception of General Dwight D. Eisenhower, a World War II hero who was elected in 1952, all successful presidential candidates for the last hundred years have held some high elective office—the vice-presidency, a seat in the U.S. Senate, or the governorship of a state. These elected positions give candidates the visibility and prestige necessary to attract campaign financing and to mount a national campaign.

Social barriers to the nomination of women, African-Americans, Jews, and other ethnic candidates seem to be weakening. For example, thirty-eight African-Americans served in the 105th Congress. Jesse Jackson, a well-known African-American minister and civil rights activist, ran an impressive, although unsuccessful, campaign for the Democratic presidential nomination in 1988, and another African-American, Governor Douglas Wilder of Virginia, ran unsuccessfully for the Democratic presidential nomination in 1992. In 1984 Democratic congressional Representative Geraldine Ferraro from New York became the first woman nominated for vice president by a major party. A poll taken in 1996 indicated that 91 percent of Americans would vote for a qualified female presidential

For most of our history, women have struggled to get nominated and elected to political office. In 1994 Diane Feinstein declared her win over Michael Huffington in the U.S. Senate race in California.

candidate.[21] Ferraro's nomination may have marked a breakthrough for women in politics. By the 105th Congress (1997–98) a record number of women were serving in Congress: fifty-one in the House of Representatives and nine in the Senate. These figures show, however, that women are still significantly underrepresented in Congress.

The Race for Office

Campaign watching is a favorite pastime for many Americans. A controversial candidate, a close race, or any presidential campaign brings headlines, television interviews and debates, and other media coverage. The public may be skeptical about the value of elections and the way they are financed, but it still enjoys the excitement of campaigns.

Financing Campaigns

WWW•

For more information
on campaign financing,
see the **Gitelson/Dudley/
Dubnick web site.**

Much of the public regards the financing of many, if not most, campaigns as suspect. The feeling prevails that campaigns consume far too much money. This perception is not just a contemporary impression of the world of campaign financing. In 1895, Senator Mark A. Hanna, a Republican from Ohio regarded as one of the most powerful party leaders in the nation, said that "There are two things that are important in politics. The first is money, and I can't remember what the second one is."[22] While reality tells us that Hanna's observations are an exaggeration, campaign financing, particularly in federal elections, remains a major issue of concern among the American public.

Candidates can face lucrative offers of campaign contributions in return for favors. No doubt, some candidates accept such offers; others do not. One would-be contributor to Edmund Muskie's 1972 presidential campaign offered $200,000 with the following stipulation: "You understand, there will be a quid pro quo. I want to be an American ambassador. Not a big country, you understand, not France or England. I couldn't afford those anyway. But can you give me a little one, Switzerland or Belgium?"[23] Muskie summarily dismissed the offer.

Of course, financing campaigns can be an expensive proposition, especially given the cost of television and the high fees charged by pollsters and various campaign strategists. Between 1964 and 1996 campaign costs in all elections in the United States rose from around $200 million to over $4 billion. In the 1996 elections, 2,605 congressional candidates spent more than $765 million on their general election campaigns.[24] In 1972, the major presidential candidates spent more than $100 million on the general election alone. At that time federal laws governing campaign contributions and expenditures were loosely written and, for all practical purposes, unenforceable.* Spending on all federal elections has tripled in twenty years, hitting $2.65 billion for the 1996 election cycle.

The Federal Election Campaign Act.   In 1971, and again in 1974 and 1979, Congress stepped in to limit the amount of money presidential candidates could receive and spend. The problem Congress tried to solve was not the overall size of campaign expenditures but rather the imbalances created when some individuals and groups could afford to contribute far more than others. The new law ensured that a single individual would no longer be able to directly contribute $2.1 million to a presidential campaign, as did W. Clement Stone, a Chicago businessman, to Nixon's campaign in 1972.

The new law, the Federal Election Campaign Act of 1971, as amended in 1974 and later, created a system to monitor the flow of funds and set limits on

---

*Until 1971, the Corrupt Practices Act of 1925 (43 Stat. 1053, ch. 368, sec. 301–319) regulated disclosure of Senate and House of Representatives campaign receipts and expenditures. What weakened the law was that it did not apply to committees set up by the candidates to collect and distribute funds, nor did it apply to presidential and vice-presidential campaigns.

contributions made by individuals. It also provided for public financing of campaigns and restricted total spending by those candidates who accept federal funding. The spending limits, however, apply only to presidential campaign finances. Congress has never restricted its own election expenditures.

The act, along with its amendments, has four key features:

- It set up the Federal Election Commission, a bipartisan, six-member commission, to administer and enforce federal regulations regarding the contribution and expenditure of campaign funds. The limits on contributions apply to congressional as well as presidential candidates.

- It limits individual contributions to $1,000 per candidate per election (primary, runoff, and general elections are regarded as autonomous elections), to $5,000 per year to any one political action committee (PAC), and to $20,000 per year to a national party committee. The total amount of contributions per year by an individual must not exceed $25,000. PACs can contribute up to $5,000 per candidate per election. There is no ceiling on the total contributions a PAC can make. In a 1976 Supreme Court case, *Buckley* v. *Valeo,* the court ruled, under the First Amendment right of freedom of speech, that no limitation could be placed on contributions to the campaign by candidates or their families.

- It provides for public funding of the major parties' presidential election costs, including the Democratic and Republican national conventions.

- It places important controls on the amount of money that can be spent in presidential primaries and general elections. In primaries, presidential hopefuls who receive federal funding are required to conform with a number of federal regulations, including a ceiling on the amount of money they may spend in each state as well as for the entire pre-convention campaign (an amount lower than the sum of the cumulative total state limits). Candidates must record all donations of $50 or more. In return, the federal government matches individual contributions of up to $250 each, with a ceiling in total matching grants for a candidate in 1996 of no more than $15.4 million. The Democratic and Republican candidates for the presidency receive federal funding for the general election.

Congress, however, did not intend to reduce the importance of money in the election process. In 1996, candidates for the House of Representatives and the Senate collectively spent more than $765 million. That year each presidential candidate received $62 million in public funding for the general election. By election day, "parties, PACs, and candidates for federal office managed to raise a total of $1.7 billion, not including a variety of other groups' independent expenditures."[25] Expenses covered by campaign funds included the rental and furnishing of campaign headquarters, communication and transportation costs, polls, television and newspaper advertisements, political consultants, and of course accountants to keep track of how the money was collected and spent. In a competitive Senate race, one political observer has estimated that between 70 and 80 percent of campaign expenditures go for television advertisements. However, Herbert Alexander, a student of campaign financing, has pointed out that only about half of the candidates for the House of Representatives use television in their campaigns.[26]

While the campaign expenditure figures that we have discussed are, indeed, quite substantial, keep in mind that the $4 billion spent on all elections in 1996 is relatively small when compared, for example, with the advertising budgets of many large companies. To illustrate, the advertising budgets for Procter & Gamble, General Motors, and Philip Morris each exceed $2 billion a year. In 1995, advertising budgets in the fast-food industry topped $2 billion, led by McDonald's ($490 million), Burger King ($252 million), Taco Bell ($172 million), and Pizza Hut ($164 million).[27] Furthermore, no matter how much a candidate spends, he or she may still lose. For example, in 1994, California Republican challenger Michael Huffington spent more than $28 million on a race for the Senate but still was defeated by the Democratic incumbent, Senator Diane Feinstein, who spent about $12 million.[28] In the 1996 congressional races, over seventy-five candidates for the House of Representatives each spent $1 million or more on their campaigns, led by Michael J. Coles, the unsuccessful Democratic challenger to House Speaker Newt Gingrich (R-Ga.). Coles spent more than $3 million in his losing race.[29]

Sources of Campaign Funding.   Where does the money come from? Some wealthy candidates finance their own campaigns or lend themselves the needed funds. This can give them an advantage over their opponents because there are no limits on that kind of contribution. Most candidates, however, must solicit gifts and loans from interested individuals, their party, or other groups, including political action committees (PACs).

One major consequence of the Federal Election Campaign Act has been the rise of the PACs. They were set up to bypass a provision of the act that prohibits unions, corporations, and other groups from contributing directly to candidates for national office. Loopholes in a 1907 law prohibiting corporations from contributing to national elections, as well as those in the Smith-Connally Act of 1944 prohibiting labor unions from the same, made these laws essentially unenforceable. PACs distribute voluntary contributions from such groups to candidates. During the 1995 through 1996 election cycle, PACs contributed more than $201 million to congressional candidates.[30]

PACs (and individuals) can legally spend any amount of money on candidates as long as they do not coordinate their spending efforts or otherwise cooperate with the candidate's campaign. Thus their participation can circumvent the spending and contribution limits of the campaign act. As important as PACs have become, however, they are overshadowed by individual contributors, who supply the bulk of election funds.[31]

Does Money Buy Victory? Since 1976 the federal government has funded presidential campaigns, giving the Democratic and Republican candidates equal support. As a result, the major party candidates have entered the race for president, at least initially, on a more or less equal financial footing. This has reduced but not entirely controlled the amount of money spent in presidential campaigns, because unlimited spending by private individuals and groups is still permitted as long as those efforts are not coordinated with the candidate's campaign. In addition, individuals, corporations, and unions may make unlimited contributions to the national parties; this "soft money" can be spent on party-building activities like get-out-the-vote endeavors. These efforts at helping the overall party ticket can have an impact on the presidential race and are therefore viewed as a way of circumventing the contribution limits set by the Federal Election Campaign Act. Such soft-money contributions are regarded as a major loophole in the federal campaign laws because get-out-the-vote activities can, and often have been, clearly directed toward partisan endeavors. In effect, the loophole allows many wealthy individuals to avoid federal limitations on campaign contributions. While such a tactic is legal, it adds to the public's justifiable skepticism of laws that supposedly limit the influence money has on campaigns and eliminate "fat cat" contributors. In 1996, it was estimated that the Republican party raised and spent over $141 million and the Democratic party raised and spent over $122 million in soft-money contributions.

Money plays a large part in congressional campaigns, which are not funded by the federal government. In 1996, for example, campaign spending for all congressional races totaled more than $765 million. Individual big spenders include North Carolina Senator Jesse Helms who spent more than $7 million and Massachusetts Senator John Kerry who spent more than $10 million on their winning campaigns. Mark Warner of Virginia spent more than $11 million on his unsuccessful Senate bid. An estimated seventy-five House candidates spent more than $1 million each on their campaigns. For many candidates, specifically challengers of incumbents, money is a passport to visibility—or at least to the television exposure needed to mount an effective challenge.

Money is unquestionably a very important factor in many campaigns, and it affects more than just the election outcome. First, both incumbents and challengers must spend a considerable amount of time raising funds for a congressional election, time that takes them away from campaigning and, for incumbents, governing and policymaking. An average competitive Senate race will cost in excess of $4 million, requiring a senator running for re-election to raise a minimum of $15,000 every week of her or his six-year term. Second, the need to raise large sums of money to campaign for Congress (as well as many other offices) prevents many citizens from even contemplating a run for political office. Third, the large sums of money spent on campaigns often gives the public the impression that contributors can buy the favor of elected officials.

However, it is important to recognize that money is not the only factor determining the outcome of congressional elections. Who wins also depends on the circumstances of the race, particularly whether one of the candidates is an **incumbent**—that is, in office at the time of the election. Incumbents are hard to beat because they are usually well known to voters and because they have already served the state or district. The retention rate of incumbent members of the House of Representatives running for re-election in 1996 was over 90 percent.

Spending has the greatest impact on elections in which no incumbent is in the race and the outcome is uncertain. That is known as an **open race.** Still, a strong, competitive challenger with sufficient funds to mount an effective campaign may have a chance against an incumbent.[32] Unfortunately for such challengers, their incumbent opponents may find it relatively easy to raise funds. Indeed, incumbents get the lion's share of campaign contributions. Unless the challenger can raise enough money—anywhere from $200,000 to more than $1 million, depending on the district—to create name recognition, the race may be lost before it begins.

Thus the reality is that money is a necessary, but not a sufficient, factor in a successful bid for many political offices. As Gary G. Jacobson has pointed out,

> Money is not sufficient because many factors quite apart from campaigns . . . affect election outcomes: partisanship, national tides, presidential coattails, issues, candidates' personalities and skills, scandals, incumbency, and many others. Money is necessary because campaigns do have an impact on election results, and campaigns cannot be run without it.[33]

Campaign Finance Reform.   Although money may not be the only important factor in a successful campaign, many people believe that even the appearance of indiscretions on the part of candidates in raising campaign funds is reason enough for reforming the system. The millions of dollars contributed to political parties in soft money, charges during the 1996 election campaign of illegal fundraising by the Clinton administration, and earlier charges against Speaker of the House Newt Gingrich by the House Ethics Committee regarding the raising of PACs funds have made voters uneasy about the role of money in campaigns. As perceived by 82 percent of the public, the campaign funding system is "broken and needs to be replaced" or "has problems and needs to be changed."[34]

Many reforms have been suggested. They have ranged from spending limits for candidates and the elimination of soft money to restrictions on PAC contributions, an increase in the size and enforcement powers of the Federal Election Commission, and the public financing of elections. Still, the future of campaign finance reform remains uncertain. What is clear is that the issue will not disappear. Just months after their successful 1992 campaigns, senators were already gearing up for their 1998 re-election races. For example, by 1996, a full two years before his re-election bid in 1998, Senator Alfonse D'Amato (R-N.Y.) had already spent close to $3 million dollars on his 1998 campaign and had cash reserves of almost $7 million. During that same period, Senator Barbara Boxer (D-Calif.) had spent almost $2 million on her 1998 re-election bid and had slightly more than $1 million in reserve for the campaign.[35] Only time will tell whether the pressures for reform by the public will have an impact on elected officials both at the state and national levels of government.

Organizing Campaigns

In Boston and its suburbs in the weeks before any election, busy street corners and highway overpasses are crowded with silent partisans holding signs that promote their candidate. This unusual ritual, commonplace to Boston natives, assures the wavering voter that the candidate has support. Campaign tactics range from such homey local traditions to highly sophisticated media shows. Even though most state and local campaigns are unorganized or underorganized and lurch from one improvisation to another as the campaign progresses, most visible campaigns—including those for the presidency, the Senate, and many House seats and governorships—are highly organized.

Campaign Organizations.   John Kennedy's 1960 presidential campaign saw the first significant use of an organization recruited from outside the party structure. Kennedy hired a young pollster named Lou Harris (later head of the Harris Survey) to join his inner circle of strategists. He also relied heavily on a personally selected team of advisers and staff, including his brother Robert, to take on the major burdens of running the campaign. That model has been followed in most presidential campaigns since the 1960s and in many state and local races as well.

Candidates assemble personal staffs because the parties historically have been slow to develop polling and media consulting programs and other support systems. The presence of such staffs also reflects the growing sophistication of campaigns. Staff members write speeches, schedule appearances, plan strategy, and recruit additional talent as needed. In recent years both major parties, and especially the Republicans, have made considerable progress in providing these services. Major state and local candidates now receive sophisticated training and support. Nevertheless, presidential candidates and many congressional and statewide candidates still seek the guidance of their own professional consultants as well as that of their personal advisers.

Campaign Strategy.   A critical part of the campaign process is the development of themes (reasons why the public should support the candidate) and campaign strategies. The plausibility of such themes is critically important to a candidate's success. If voters do not believe that campaign promises will be fulfilled—if a candidate's words evoke the myth of broken promises—the election game is lost.

In most presidential, House, and Senate races, campaign strategy depends on whether the candidate is an incumbent or a challenger. Congressional incumbents generally have the advantage of name recognition and a record of accomplishments. They often start with a loyal constituency, and, as we have noted, their established position and visibility make it relatively easy for them to raise funds. Not surprisingly, then, most incumbents in the House—between 80 and 99 percent since World War II—have succeeded in their quest for re-election. In 1996, 95 percent of Senate and House incumbents were re-elected. If efforts to pass a constitutional amendment limiting terms of office in Congress are successful, incumbency will no doubt play a weaker role in the re-election process.

Incumbency is also important in presidential elections. No other office-holder in the United States has the same visibility, name recognition, prestige, and opportunity to speak to voters on the issues, and incumbent candidates take full advantage of these assets. Incumbency does not guarantee a second term, however. Since the end of World War II, six out of ten incumbent presidents have not served second terms. In 1952, Harry S Truman chose not to run for a second full term. John F. Kennedy was assassinated on November 22, 1963, in the third year of his presidency. In 1968, his successor, Lyndon B. Johnson, exhausted and overwhelmed by the problems of the Vietnam War, dropped out of the presidential race and initiated peace talks. Gerald R. Ford, who took office after Richard M. Nixon's resignation, Jimmy Carter, who succeeded Ford, and George Bush, who lost to Bill Clinton in 1992, all failed to win elections to second terms in office.

Bush's opponent in 1992, Bill Clinton, selected a typical campaign strategy: he challenged Bush's effectiveness and convinced the voters that his leadership and positions on issues would be more effective. Challengers always emphasize a past record of accomplishments and a record that may already have given them visibility and a constituency base. Incumbents are most vulnerable when domestic or foreign policy problems call their leadership qualities into question. That was Bush's predicament. Not only was the economy weak, but Bush faced considerable criticism for focusing on foreign policy rather than on a number of important domestic issues. Clinton's campaign hit hard at those issues. In 1996, Bill Clinton became only the fourth president since World War II to win re-election to the presidency.

Differences among election outcomes reflect something more than incumbency, however. Winners and losers alike are profoundly affected by the political environment: the partisan leanings of the electorate; the candidates' experience, personality, and leadership skills; and the candidates' positions on policy issues. Most candidates try to ensure that none of these factors polarizes the electorate and drives away potential supporters. Thus they are unlikely to take either strongly conservative or strongly liberal stands, although on balance Republican candidates are more conservative than Democratic ones.

The New Campaign Style. The tools, and subsequently the style, of many campaigns have changed over the years. One major innovation has been the use of polls, an expensive and relatively new campaign tool that can dramatize or

CLOSER TO HOME

7.1 Campaign Financing: Is It Cheaper Closer to Home?

Much of the news about campaign financing has focused in recent years on the federal level, where hundreds of millions of dollars are spent every election cycle on congressional races alone. But what about closer-to-home elections—the state and local ones? Are they also costly events?

Clearly, the expenses of both state and local elections can be significant. In one recent election year, 279 candidates in thirty-six states collectively spent more than $345 million to run for the office of governor. Not surprisingly, hotly contested campaigns in two of the largest states in the nation, California ($53.2) and Texas ($50.5), accounted for about a third of those expenditures.

A state legislative contest, too, may be very costly, running up hundreds of thousands of dollars. Indeed, in a recent state legislative election in Illinois, one candidate spent about $1 million on her successful campaign for office. Whereas many mayoral and town or city council campaigns involve relatively small campaign budgets, similar large-city campaigns in New York, Chicago, Los Angeles, Dallas, Philadelphia, Boston, and Atlanta consume millions of dollars.

Efforts to regulate and control campaign fundraising and spending have varied from state to state. All fifty states have some form of campaign finance reporting procedures. Twenty-six have instituted commissions to supervise and regulate state and local campaigns, with California, Connecticut, Florida, and New Jersey leading the way. Some have established limits on contributions to state campaigns by corporations, unions, and individuals (New York and Florida), whereas others prohibit all corporate and labor union contributions (Arizona, Connecticut, North Dakota, Pennsylvania, and Texas). Colorado, Illinois, Missouri, and Utah do not limit contributions. In most states, there are no restrictions on state campaign spending, but, as noted earlier, essentially all states provide, by law, for the reporting of all candidate expenditures on campaigns. Michigan is one of the few states that uses state taxes to fund the governor's race; it limits total expenditures to a maximum of $1 million plus an additional $200,000 for other specified costs.

Are we likely to see public funding of state elections in the future? As two students of state and local government, Ann O'M. Bowman and Richard C. Kearney, have pointed out, almost half the states have begun experimenting with the public funding of statewide campaigns. Plans vary from state to state. They may include voluntary contributions to a state fund, a checkoff system on state tax forms, allowing taxpayers to designate a specified amount of their taxes to a campaign fund, and direct state legislative appropriations to a central fund earmarked for statewide campaigns.

All in all, campaign funding and spending is a hot issue. It is relevant not only in congressional and presidential races, but also closer to home—in our states, counties, cities, towns, and villages.

Sources: For a discussion of this topic and additional sources, see Ann O'M. Bowman and Richard C. Kearney, *State and Local Government,* 3rd ed. (Boston: Houghton Mifflin, 1996), pp. 135–138.

The Advantages of Incumbency

In many campaigns, the incumbent may have the advantage over his or her challenger because of the prestige of the office, name recognition, and a record of past accomplishments. In the 1996 presidential campaign, Bill Clinton, here boarding the presidential helicopter, sought to use incumbency to his advantage.

establish proof of the viability of a candidate for major office.[36] In Chapter 5, on public opinion, we looked at the way candidates use polls to evaluate their strengths and weaknesses, assess the relevance of specific issues, and determine the campaign's impact on the voters. Positive poll results can energize a campaign and draw new support and funding.

Professional pollsters, such as Republican Robert Teeter and the Democratic team of Hickman–Maslin, have established strong reputations for the accuracy of their estimates of candidates' standings and the voters' views on the issues. A pollster's services are now almost universally used in presidential and many congressional and statewide races. Costs depend on the size of the state and the kind of polling. A statewide poll can run from $25,000 to $50,000. Even if polls do not change the outcome of an election, they certainly heighten the hoopla and intensify the horse-race nature of the contest.

The Campaign Trail

Every election year, thousands of candidates campaign for political office across the nation. Here, local hopefuls in Cambridge, Massachusetts seek support from the electorate.

Another "miracle" of modern campaign technology is computer-assisted, direct-mail fundraising and advertising. A candidate or party buys mailing lists from state motor vehicle registration departments, magazines, membership organizations, and a variety of other sources. Then advanced data- and word-processing techniques are used to send letters soliciting campaign funds and providing information on the candidate. The letters can also be individualized, focusing on the interests of a specific audience. For example, a voter on the membership list of an environmental-protection group might get an original-looking, personally addressed letter that focuses on the candidate's desire to support the acquisition of park land or some other environmental cause. The signature is often the work of a machine that produces perfect replicas of the candidate's handwriting.

Technological changes over the past three decades have added new dimensions to campaigns. The new technologies have been accompanied by the rise of a new political animal—the **political consultant.** These individuals, often trained in public relations, media, or polling techniques, have replaced the traditional campaign manager in the most visible elections. Some consultants organize all aspects of the race, from the physical appearance of the candidate to the strategies that the candidate adopts in presenting positions on issues. Most consultants specialize in certain aspects of the campaign, such as polling, fundraising, or the media.[37] David Axelrod, a prominent Democratic campaign consultant based in Chicago who has worked on many statewide and national campaigns, best exemplifies the modern-day campaign consultant who serves as a "hired gun," generally to work exclusively for either Democratic or Republican candidates. His record of successful campaigns suggests either that he associates with many likely winners or that campaign consultants can be effective managers of campaigns. In all probability, the success of campaign consultants is a mixture of both.

The Media and Campaigns

Use of the media, particularly television, has almost become a way of life in recent presidential, congressional, and gubernatorial races. A campaign is often organized around media coverage. Candidates make decisions about trips, rallies, and press conferences with an eye to attracting the press and meeting its schedules. Because advertising costs so much, campaign managers work hard to maximize free television-news as well as radio and newspaper coverage to promote their candidates' virtues. Consequently, a candidate's speeches and rallies before large crowds are often scheduled so as to appear on the evening local and network news programs.

www.

For more information on the media and campaigns, see the **Gitelson/Dudley/Dubnick** web site.

The media also manipulate the coverage of important campaigns in order to maximize the attention of their audience. Media people try to structure election news to attract and hold the biggest audience possible. Often that means highlighting and even promoting conflict. Candidates are encouraged to attack one another's policies, and television debates, especially among presidential candidates, have become contests with "winners" and "losers." The Kennedy-Nixon debates in 1960 marked the beginning of face-to-face discussion between presidential candidates. The televised debates gained a new dimension in 1984 with the debate between the vice-presidential candidates, Geraldine Ferraro and George Bush. The innovation has been retained. In 1996 not only did the presidential candidates, Bill Clinton and Bob Dole, debate one another, but their vice-presidential counterparts debated each other as well.

Of course, candidates do not rely on free coverage alone. Advertising is also a crucial part of campaigns. Media consultants, such as Republican adviser Don Ringe and Democratic adviser Peter Fenn, provide their clients with a full range of services, from the production of television spots to the purchase of advertising time on local and network stations. Because television advertising is so expensive—a 30-second political campaign spot that airs during a local news show may cost as much as $5,000 in a big-city market[38]—it is used primarily in visible and well-funded campaigns.

The high cost of network television advertising has been tempered somewhat in recent years by the significant growth in cable television. Many local cable outlets provide local candidates with relatively inexpensive access to the public through their airwaves. Instead of paying for a political advertisement that may reach hundreds of thousands of viewers outside the local area, candi-

MYTHS IN POPULAR CULTURE

7.1 Campaigns, Elections, and Political Scum

Few movies treat political campaigns gently. Most films that have political themes focus on the corruption in politics and the unscrupulous, degenerate means by which one gets into public office—the campaign process. No film better depicts that theme than *The Candidate,* the 1972 classic starring Robert Redford. In one of his earliest film roles, Redford plays the part of Bill McKay, a lawyer who heads a California legal aid office that provides services to the poor. When McKay is enticed to run for political office, he is spurned and rejected by his colleagues as having sold out to a corrupt system. As one worker puts it, "Politics is bullshit." After all, remarks a political activist, "Politicians don't talk, they make sounds."

This cynical view of politics and the corrupt campaign process permeates the film. In reality, many campaigns do involve the unpleasant and, some would argue, corrupting task of raising funds for the campaign. In turn, particularly with high-visibility offices, candidates and members of the electorate often feel controlled and manipulated. Furthermore, they find the orchestrated quality of the campaign process lacking in substance and loaded with glitz, glamour, and distortion. As one newsreporter in the film states, these candidates are "selling themselves like an underarm deodorant." Such was the image depicted in *The Candidate.*

While reality suggests that such campaigns do take place, mythmaking also argues that the movie, as a form of popular culture, can and does misrepresent the campaign process. During the four years between presidential elections, more than 500,000 elections take place in the United States, and they are preceded by much more than a million political campaigns. Most campaigns are run by candidates and small staffs who work hard to establish policy positions despite relatively little money. *The Candidate* magnifies and distorts the problems of the campaign process. It also becomes a means of generating myths about the nature of many campaigns in the United States.

dates can use cable television to advertise their campaign to their prospective constituents. Such access can be cost-effective when cable television advertising rates are low.

An innovation during the 1996 elections was the first broad-based attempt to promote political campaigns over the World Wide Web. Candidates running for offices at the national, state, and local levels set up websites promoting their campaigns through access by computer. One unsuccessful Republican presidential hopeful, Senator Phil Gramm, established a website for only $8,000 and found that it was accessed almost 200,000 times.[39] Websites were even used by candidates in the 1997 city council elections in Evanston, Illinois.

The efforts to access and inform potential voters about campaigns by using the computer are still in their early stages. According to postelection polls, only between 6 and 10 percent of the public claimed to have sought or received campaign information from the World Wide Web during the 1996 elections.[40] But as the public grows more familiar with computers and Web access becomes cheaper, the use of this information source is likely to expand.

The evidence regarding the impact of the media on campaigns and elections is still very sketchy. Clearly, the use of television has increased the costs of running presidential, congressional, and gubernatorial campaigns, as well as races for other highly visible public offices. Media advertising probably has a greater impact on motivating and encouraging a candidate's supporters to go to the polls than on changing the minds of already committed opponents of a candidate. Media news coverage and advertisements are effective with marginal voters. Because such voters lack strong or even moderate commitment to a candidate, they are more open than partisan voters to the opinions and influence of a news anchorperson or reporter or to the appeals of a paid political advertisement. Finally, the media help shape the issues or nonissues that candidates will focus on in an election, thus serving as an agenda-setting force in a campaign. This can have a dramatic effect by determining the quality of debate throughout the race. (See Chapter 9 for a more far-reaching discussion on the role of media in politics.)

Campaigns and Political Parties

By using the media, as well as independent campaign consultants, computers, and polls, many high-visibility office seekers have been able to bypass the traditional roles that political parties historically played in the campaign process. Presidential, congressional, gubernatorial, and mayoral candidates are now no longer dependent on party volunteers or party campaign-funding events to jump-start their campaigns. That change has shifted the focus from **party-centered campaigns** (where the party coordinates activities, raises money, and develops strategy) to **candidate-centered campaigns** (where paid consultants or volunteers coordinate campaign activities, develop strategies, and raise funds for the campaign).

But as we suggest in Chapter 6, the role of parties in the campaign process is still evident at most levels of government. In recent years, parties have learned to adapt to the changing strategies of the campaign process, providing candidates at the national, state, and local levels with consultants, advisers, and workshops on campaign funding and strategy, and, as political brokers, with access to PACs and individual contributors who seek out the party's advice in coordinating their campaign contributions. That last function is critical for candidates who rely on the party to direct individual and PAC contributions to their campaigns.

Political parties are unlikely to return to the center of many political campaigns, but evidence suggests that the parties have adapted to the new campaign style as well as to the "new kids on the block"—political consultants who play a central role in the shaping of that style.

Voting and Elections

Voting rules and regulations have changed considerably in the past two hundred years. Until 1920, women could not vote in most states. African-Americans and women faced voting restrictions for much of the country's history. Although the vote has now been extended to all adult citizens, everyone does not choose to exercise that option. Therefore, it is important to look at who votes and why.

Who Is Permitted to Vote?

The Constitution originally left the decision on voting qualifications to the individual states. Article I, Section 4, specifies that Congress may regulate by law only the time, place, and manner of federal elections. Any extension of voting rights by the federal government must come in the form of a constitutional amendment or a federal law.

Representative Democracy at Work

Ultimately, political campaigns come down to attracting as much voter support as possible to the polls. This Texas citizen takes advantage of his right to select our government representatives as he votes on election day.

State leaders in the 1780s had little sympathy for the idea of universal voting rights. Indeed, John Jay, a New York delegate to the Constitutional Convention, summed up the view of many of the founding fathers when he wrote in 1787 that "the mass of men are neither wise nor good—those who own the country ought to govern it."[41]

All thirteen states restricted voting rights to white males, and only three of the new states—New Hampshire, Pennsylvania, and Georgia—admitted adult males into the electorate without a property requirement. In those states, however, the voter without property had to be a taxpayer. As a result, in 1789, only some 10 percent of the population could cast ballots.[42]

Over the past two centuries, voting rights have been extended to those who do not own property and to African-Americans, Native Americans, women, and young people aged eighteen to twenty. But equality was not achieved without an intense struggle. It took a civil war to give citizenship to African-Americans. And although passage of the Fifteenth Amendment in 1870 gave African-American males the right to vote, they struggled another hundred years before most barriers to voting came down.

Women fought for half a century for voting rights. In 1878, human-rights activist Susan B. Anthony managed to introduce in Congress a proposed constitutional amendment that said, "The right of citizens of the United States to vote shall not be denied or abridged by the United States or any state on account of sex." The wording of the Nineteenth Amendment, which finally became part of the Constitution in 1920, is identical.

In 1971, passage of the Twenty-sixth Amendment lowered the voting age in national, state, and local elections from twenty-one to eighteen. Several states already had similar regulations. There is nothing in the Constitution that prohibits states from setting their own voting standards, as long as these regulations do not violate the Constitution or federal law. Thus women in Wyoming had the vote some forty years before the Nineteenth Amendment enfranchised women in other states. For the same reason, a state can establish any minimum voting age.

Congress has intervened several times to break down barriers set up by the states to prevent African-Americans and others from voting. The 1970 extension of the 1965 Voting Rights Act banned the use of literacy tests and similar qualifying devices. Then the 1975 extension of the act increased the opportunities for participation for Hispanics. When the act was strengthened and extended for twenty-five years in 1982, it resulted in increased electoral participation by southern African-American voters and other minorities, including Eskimos. Poll taxes were eliminated in 1964 with the adoption of the Twenty-fourth Amendment. Finally, Supreme Court decisions have laid the remaining voting restrictions to rest. During the 1960s, the Supreme Court struck down property ownership requirements and shortened residency requirements. Today a citizen needs only to have resided in a state for thirty days in order to vote in national elections and in most state elections.

Who Votes?

Americans are proud of their electoral system. Indeed, many citizens would argue that the freedom to select political leaders is one of the most important differences between a democracy and a fascist or communist government. Yet, as we saw in Chapter 5, on public opinion and political participation, relatively few Americans vote. On the average, about 50 percent of Americans can be counted on to take part in presidential elections. In the 1996 presidential elections, only 49 percent of the eligible electorate voted, the lowest turnout since 1920. By contrast, 95 percent of Australians regularly go to the polls, and the turnout in other democracies ranges from 67 percent in Japan to 92 percent in Belgium.

Comparisons are not entirely fair, however, because voting is easier and simpler in other nations. Americans face much longer ballots and relatively brief and inconvenient polling schedules. In many European countries, voting takes place on weekends. Many European nations also have automatic universal registration, which is not widespread in the United States. As a final incentive to ensure voting, some European countries levy fines on stay-at-homes.

WWW•

For more information on voting behavior and elections, see the **Gitelson/Dudley/Dubnick web site.**

Demographics and Voter Turnout. In Chapter 5, we also learned about the social and economic factors that influence political participation patterns, particularly voter turnout. Individuals who vote regularly are more likely to be white

Registering to Vote

Low voter turnout in the United States has instigated numerous efforts by the political parties and government officials to register more of the electorate and, thus, to increase the number of eligible voters in many states. It is not unusual to find door-to-door registration drives like this one in Austin, Texas.

and have higher educational backgrounds, larger incomes, and better jobs than nonvoters. Education seems to be the key to voter turnout.[43] As political scientists Raymond Wolfinger and Steven Rosenstone point out, education "imparts information about politics . . . and about a variety of skills, some of which facilitate political learning. . . . Educated people are more likely to be well informed about politics and to follow the campaign in the mass media."[44]

In addition, for non-English-speaking citizens, including those of Puerto Rican, Mexican, Cuban, Russian, and Vietnamese extraction, education provides fluency in English, a tool necessary for following and participating in the electoral process. In 1996, the Hispanic population represented 5 percent of the vote. There is some evidence, however, that Hispanics are turning out in growing numbers, particularly in large urban areas.

Younger citizens are less likely to vote than older Americans (except those who are infirm and therefore have difficulty getting to the polling booths). For example, citizens between the ages of twenty-four and thirty are 30 percent less likely to vote than those aged thirty-seven to sixty-nine.[45] In 1996, 24 percent of the votes were cast by individuals sixty years of age and older.[46] The reasons for that pattern are complex. Young people are frequently preoccupied with the demands of school, military service, or new careers. They also tend to believe that they have little impact or influence on the political system.

In the past, turnout for women trailed behind that for men. Today, however, women vote in slightly higher percentages than do men.

The Disappointed Electorate.   As indicated earlier, barriers such as preregistration requirements and long ballots reduce the numbers of citizens who vote. But another obstacle is the myth of broken promises. Many Americans do not take part in elections because they do not believe that government in general and elected officials in particular can solve the country's problems. They also question the honesty and integrity of many political leaders.[47]

This lack of confidence in government is relatively new. As you may recall from our earlier discussion, the Vietnam War in the 1960s undermined confidence in government, and the Watergate scandal diminished it still further in the early 1970s. The energy crisis, high unemployment, inflation, and crime in the late 1970s destroyed the remaining confidence. Today citizens find little reason for trust as they contemplate the government's apparent inability to cope with world terrorism, maintain an effective public education system, or even help the average American fulfill a traditional dream—the purchase of a home.

In this atmosphere of cynicism, many potential voters doubt that their vote would matter and simply stay home on election day. Several studies have clearly documented the reasons for failure to vote. First, many people believe that government cannot resolve the nation's problems. In addition, as we pointed out in Chapter 6, people are less likely than before to strongly identify with one political party, an identification that once got out the vote. Finally, some people have even begun to question whether it makes any difference who wins elections.[48]

Should we be concerned about the disappointed voter? Some observers say yes, arguing that low turnout undermines representative government, which, they argue, depends on full electoral participation. Others disagree, suggesting that ill-informed people may make poor choices when they vote. It has even been argued that low levels of voter turnout are a sign of a healthy system—that is, they show that people are satisfied with their government.

Voter Choice

What draws voters to the polls? What influences their choices of candidates? Why did voters pick a Democrat for president and Republicans for Congress in 1996? Obviously, Clinton's supporters thought he was a better candidate, and in 1996 a majority of voters felt a Republican Congress would better serve their interests. But that is not the full answer. A number of factors influence voter choice.

Issues.   Political observers often accuse American voters of focusing on frivolous aspects of campaigns. On the contrary, many American voters do, in fact, pay attention to issues and often take them into account in making their choices. Of course, no one can review all the positions of every candidate who is running for office. Given the thousands of issues that arise at the local, state, and national level each year, no one could possibly follow or even have an interest in most of them.

However, in presidential elections there seems to be some relationship between the issues citizens support and the candidates they vote for.[49] In the 1996 presidential elections, voters viewed Clinton more favorably than Dole on the leading issue of the state of the economy. Other domestic issues that were important to voters in choosing a president included the candidate's stand on abortion, crime, illegal drugs, education, and health care.

Candidate Image.   The candidate's personal qualities, particularly experience and leadership, also count. Furthermore, voters ask themselves how well the candidate represents their own interests and whether the candidate is honest, trustworthy, and approachable by the electorate. One observer labels this process "politics by psychoanalysis."

In 1976 and in 1980, the voting public viewed Gerald Ford and Jimmy Carter as weak leaders. In 1980 and 1984, Reagan looked determined and effective, and voters liked his image as an optimistic, honest, and approachable person. In 1988, the public perceived Bush as having more experience than Michael Dukakis and as being a stronger leader. In 1992, George Bush's image had significantly deteriorated since his high performance evaluations by the public during the 1991 Persian Gulf crisis. By contrast, Bill Clinton had a positive image particularly regarding his positions on health care and the deficit. The majority of Bill Clinton's supporters felt he would bring about needed change.[50]

By 1995, Clinton, as president, was struggling with his image as both a leader and a policy initiator, particularly in regard to his inability to get a national health care bill passed by Congress. He also faced a negative public reaction because of questions about his personal character. Charges continued to be leveled at him concerning the Whitewater affair and his financial dealings as governor of Arkansas. In addition, a former employee made allegations that he had sexually harassed her. Despite these accusations, Clinton was still able to win re-election based on both his leadership qualities and the healthy state of the economy.

Party Identification.   As we saw in Chapter 6, party identification gives voters a general sense of how candidates are likely to approach various issues and policies. Such identification can be misleading because opinions within the parties are quite diverse. Nevertheless, in a world in which voters may know nothing about many of the candidates, the party label serves as an approximate cue to policy positions. Indeed, according to one poll conducted on election day, 1996, many individuals voted along party lines in making their presidential choice.[51]

Retrospective Voting.   When individuals base their votes on candidates' or parties' past performance, that process is called **retrospective voting.**[52] Incumbents are judged on their records in the office; challengers may be judged on previously held offices. In effect, voters are looking at the past to evaluate the future—one rational way to make judgments.

Is retrospective voting common? Poll findings suggest that it is. In 1980, for example, the public was dissatisfied with Carter's performance in office; 63 percent saw the outcome of that election as a rejection of Carter.[53] In contrast, only 24 percent of the public believed that the election was a mandate for winner Reagan's conservative philosophy. In 1984, many voters supported Reagan because of their perceptions of his record. When asked, for example, who would best keep the country prosperous, 60 percent of the voters said Reagan would, as compared with 32 percent who expressed greater confidence in the Democratic candidate, Walter Mondale. In 1988, as Reagan's political heir, Bush inherited the incumbent's mantle at a time when Reagan's popularity had a resurgence and when a majority of Americans seemed content with the general state of the economy. Bush benefited directly from Reagan's popularity. By 1992, however, a majority of voters were dissatisfied with Bush's record and his unkept promise of not raising taxes. Bill Clinton benefited from that retrospective discontent. In 1996, peace and prosperity assured the public that Clinton should be re-elected to a second term. Obviously, the public's opinions are directly influenced by its perception of an officeholder's recent record.

Group Support.   As seen in Figure 7.1, people from different gender, racial, age, educational, and political backgrounds vote in similar and also different ways for political candidates. In the 1996 election, for example, Bill Clinton drew strong support from college-educated voters. Because educational level is related to participation, the Democrats profited in 1996 from this demographic pattern.

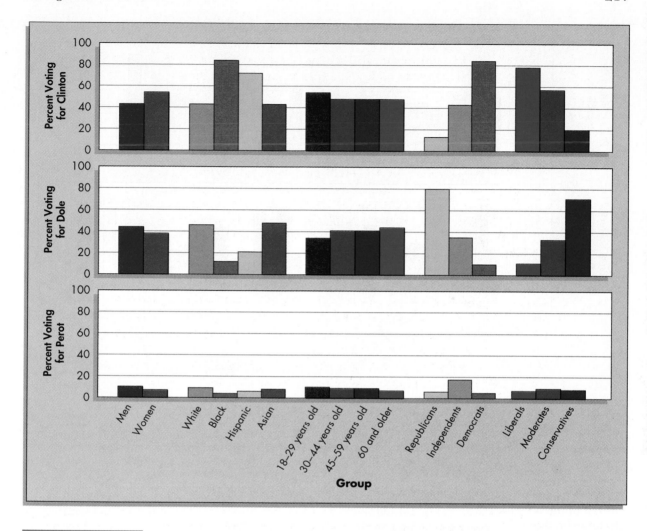

FIGURE 7.1

Group Support in
the 1996 Presidential
Election

Who you are has a major impact on how you vote. As you consider these figures, keep
in mind that party identification, candidate characteristics, and issues also explain voter
choice.

Source: Based on data from the *New York Times,* November 10, 1996.

Democrat Clinton received a majority or plurality of the vote in the three-
way contest with Bob Dole and Ross Perot from all age groups and many of the
traditional Democratic coalition members: the poor, Catholics, Jews, African-
Americans, Hispanics, liberals, moderates, independents, and union members.
Dole did well among white male Protestants, conservatives, the wealthy, and

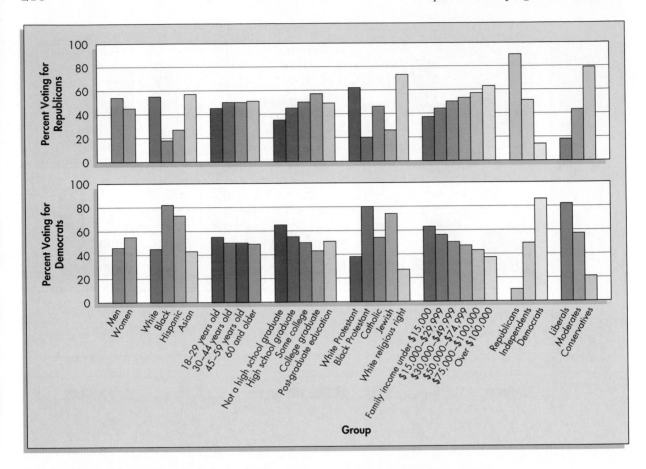

FIGURE 7.2

Portrait of the
Electorate in the
1996 Congressional
Elections

Group support in the 1996 Congressional elections paints a portrait of the electorate
that favored the Republican party.

Source: Based on data from *New York Times,* November 7, 1996.

rural voters. The gender gap was clearly evident in the 1996 presidential elections, with an 11 percent overall advantage for Clinton among female voters. Ross Perot, the Reform party presidential candidate, performed well below his 1992 presidential election showing, when he had received 19 percent of the vote. In 1996, his support declined to 8 percent of the vote; it was strongest among independents and high school graduates, although at levels significantly below his 1992 race.

But the 1996 congressional elections dampened any positive expectations the Democrats may have had of controlling both the executive and the legislative branch of government. Republicans maintained their hold on both houses of Congress, winning majority support from white males, Asian-Americans, college graduates, white Protestants, the religious right, the wealthy, and conservatives (see Figure 7.2). The Republican party also could boast thirty-two of the fifty gubernatorial seats, although in thirty-one states control was divided, with a governor of one party facing a state legislature where at least one house was controlled by the other party.

These data raise some important questions about future voting patterns. In 1992, with Ross Perot's strong showing among voters, it appeared that the American people might be ready for an independent, third-party movement. However, Perot's less impressive 8 percent share of the presidential vote in 1996 seemed to brake, at least temporarily, the movement toward a third party in the nation. Nevertheless, the high level of antiparty, antigovernment disaffection on the part of millions of Americans, who are fed up with "politics as usual," raises a question: will the Republicans, Democrats, or possibly even a third party be most effective in building new and stronger voter coalitions as the year 2000 approaches?

The Electoral College

The constitutional environment in which presidential campaigns take place is the **electoral college.** Although the founders believed in representative government, they hesitated to place the selection of the president directly in the hands of the people. The system that evolved provides for the popular election by the people of electors in each state equal to the number of U.S. senators and representatives representing that state in Congress. For example, Texas's congressional delegation includes two U.S. senators and thirty members of the House. Thus, in presidential elections, that state's voters elect thirty-two electors to the electoral college.

This system of electing the president is confusing for most Americans, who think that when they vote for their presidential preference they are directly voting for the candidate. They are instead really voting for the slate of electors (equal to the size of the state's congressional delegation) who have committed their support to that presidential candidate. In only twelve states do the names of the actual electors appear on the ballot next to the presidential candidate's name. State law determines how a person becomes an elector. In Pennsylvania, the presidential candidates select their electors. In thirty-eight states, the electors are nominated at state party conventions. In most of the remaining states, electors are selected in primaries or by state party committees.

The presidential candidate winning a plurality of the vote in a state receives all its electoral college votes. (The two exceptions are Maine and Nebraska. Maine awards two of its electoral college votes according to the statewide vote and two according to which candidate wins in each of the two congressional districts. Nebraska, with 5 electoral college votes, shares a similar system.) Members of the electoral college in each state meet in December after the November general election and vote for the president. The votes in each state are forwarded to Congress, where an official count takes place on the first day of the congressional session in January. Only after completion of that vote count is an official winner of the presidential election declared. A total of 538 electoral college votes are cast in the fifty states and the District of Columbia; the presidential candidate receiving the majority of the votes wins the election. The vice president is selected in the same manner.

At least two problems associated with the electoral college have evolved over the past two hundred years. In twenty-one states, the electors whose party candidate wins a plurality of the state's popular vote are required to vote for that candidate. In the remaining twenty-nine states, an elector is not required by law to support the candidate who has won the popular vote in the state. Disloyal electors have voted for a candidate other than the winner of the popular vote in seven elections since World War II, although the final outcomes of those presidential elections were not affected by their actions. In 1988, one disaffected West Virginia Democrat who was an electoral college elector voted for Lloyd Bentsen for president. Bentsen was the running mate of the Democratic presidential candidate, Michael Dukakis.

A second problem is the possibility that a president may be elected by a majority of the electoral college vote without having a majority of the national popular vote. That was the case in 1888, when Benjamin Harrison was elected president with 233 electoral college votes, whereas his opponent, Grover Cleveland, received more popular votes. A number of reforms have been proposed to deal with the problem, including the selection of the president by direct popular vote. Yet no consensus for a constitutional amendment has emerged, and thus the indirect election of presidents through the electoral college has remained intact.

When campaigning for the presidency, candidates are well aware that gaining a majority of the popular vote is not enough. A candidate must be successful in garnering plurality votes sufficiently distributed among the states to ensure receiving a majority of the electoral college vote (see Figure 7.3). Not surprisingly, most candidates focus much of their attention on the larger states, such as California, New York, Texas, Pennsylvania, Illinois, Ohio, Florida, and Michigan—states that have significant numbers of electoral college votes.

Promises, Promises: The Link Between Campaigns and Public Policy

As we noted earlier, poll results show a public that doubts whether a candidate's promises made in a campaign have any bearing on the policies that candidate follows once in office. We believe that this perception of broken promises is a myth—a simplification of the facts.

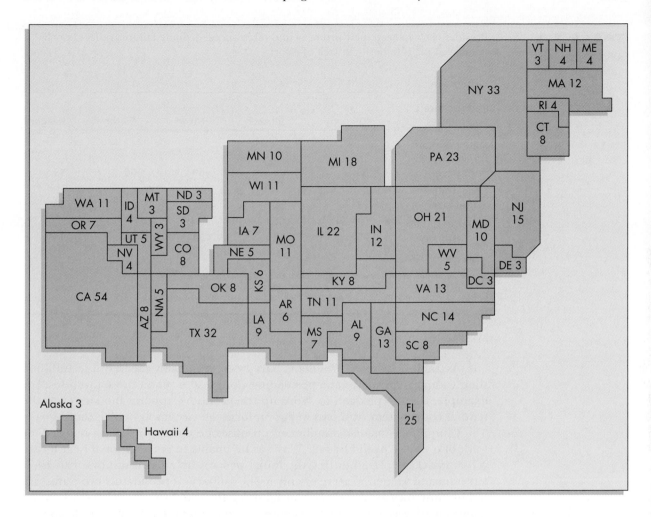

FIGURE 7.3

The United States According to Electoral College Votes

This distorted map will give you a sense of the electoral power of the most populous states, such as California, New York, Texas, and Pennsylvania.

Source: The United States According to the Electoral College Votes Chart, September 29, 1984 (with updated changes). Reprinted courtesy of *The Boston Globe*.

Of course, candidates do not fulfill all the promises they make. How could they? The collective wish list of Americans, let alone the candidates, is endless. But candidates try hard to keep many of their promises.[54] Party platforms are, in effect, their agreements with the electorate. It is as if they were saying: "This is what I think. This is what I will try to do. If you agree with what I think, at least on many of the issues, then vote for me." (A slight variation of that monologue is, "Even if you don't agree with me, give me a chance. I'm right.")

TABLE 7.1

A Score Card on
Campaign Promises

Presidents try to keep their promises and often succeed. Some failures reflect poorly
conceived plans rather than lack of effort.

Percentage

Performance on Promises	Kennedy	Johnson	Nixon	Carter	Reagan*
Full or partial fulfillment of promises	68	63	59	66	53
Little or no action taken	23	24	36	22	30
Promises turned into legislation	53	62	34	41	44

*Data through February 1984.

Source: Jeff Fishel, *Presidents and Promises: From Campaign Pledge to Presidential Performance* (Washington, D.C.: Congressional Quarterly Press, 1985). Recalculated from Table 2.3, p. 39, and Table 2.4, p. 42. Reprinted by permission of Congressional Quarterly, Inc.

As Table 7.1 shows, presidents have been reasonably successful in fulfilling their campaign promises and persuading Congress to act on those promises. For example, Clinton pledged to shore up the economy, appoint moderates to the federal court system, and pass welfare reform. He accomplished all those goals.

Clinton also made a number of promises he could not keep—but not for want of trying. Why did he fail? Why was he unable to get a national health care reform package passed during the initial years of his administration or to allow gay men and women to serve openly in the military? A president's programs can fail because they are poorly conceived or ineffective. Programs also fail because Congress refuses to cooperate. Clinton faced strong opposition from Congress, including members of his own party, regarding the rights of gays in the military. Sometimes one or both houses are controlled by the opposition party. Sometimes the president is not able to persuade his own party to support his programs. Regarding his campaign promises, then, Clinton was successful in some areas and unsuccessful in others.

In short, the politics of implementation is complex, but successful candidates try and often manage to deliver on many of their promises. These promises are not made in a vacuum and more often than not represent the genuine intentions of the candidates. While voters are often disappointed in the slow processes of government and the incomplete realization of platform agendas, voters also often "win" when they place their wishes, desires, and expectations in the hands of our elected officials. For the voters, elections do more than just select our representatives. They provide for citizen empowerment.

Conclusion: Do Elections Matter?

Americans are ambivalent about elections. The public acknowledges their importance in the democratic process but takes part in elections in relatively low numbers, compared with many western European democracies. To understand the election process better, we have examined in this chapter the facts behind the myth that candidates break their campaign promises. Although that myth contains some truth, it is by and large inaccurate and misleading.

What is the reality? First, although some campaign promises are not fulfilled, many are. Furthermore, although candidates run for office for personal reasons—power is a strong motivator—they also run in order to implement promised policies. And they are often successful in achieving that goal. An analysis of presidential performance, for example, shows that recent presidents have managed to fulfill a majority of their promises either partially or completely.

We also examined the relationship of a number of variables to election campaigning and voting behavior, particularly the influence of money. Money is a very important—indeed, a necessary—part of most campaigns, but it is not the decisive factor in most elections. Other elements, such as incumbency, issues, personalities, skills, national trends, and partisanship, strongly influence election outcomes. The voters' characteristics—religion, ethnic identity, race, age, and so forth—also appear to affect how voters view the political world and for whom they cast their ballots.

Summary

1. Elections begin with the nomination of candidates. Those who run for office are motivated by personal ambition and by a commitment to policy goals.

2. Candidates are nominated in open meetings (caucuses) and, most commonly, in primary elections.

3. Presidential nominations take place at national conventions, which frequently ratify the outcome of often-complicated primary and caucus campaigns.

4. The escalation of campaign costs in recent years has led Congress to pass the Federal Election Campaign Act, which sets limits on contributions and expenditures in federal elections. The law has given rise to a growing source of funds from political action committees (PACs).

5. Most highly visible election campaigns—including those for the presidency, the U.S. Senate and House, and governorships, as well as for many statewide and large-city mayoral races—are highly organized, with staffs that include professional consultants and personal advisers. The campaign's outcome can depend on whether the candidate is an incumbent and on other factors in the political environment, particularly the presence of the media. Campaigns have increasingly become candidate centered instead of party centered.

6. All women and nonwhite males have faced voting restrictions for most of the nation's history. Voting rights have been extended to these groups and to young people between the ages of eighteen and twenty by constitutional amendment and by federal law.

7. Voter turnout for U.S. elections is low compared with that in other countries. Wealthy, well-educated, older individuals are more likely to vote than other groups. Low turnout has been at-tributed to laws and institutional factors (such as preregistration requirements and long ballots), as well as to voters' loss of faith in government.

8. People base their choice of candidate on issue preferences, on the personal qualities and past records of the candidates, and on their party and social identity. The candidates' positions are not idle promises. Once elected, candidates try to fulfill their campaign pledges.

Key Terms and Concepts

Opportunity structure The political ladder of local, state, and national offices that brings greater prestige and power as one moves toward the presidency.

Caucus A forum closed to the public until the Progressive Era; contemporary caucuses are local party meetings, which are open to all who live in the precinct and in which citizens discuss and then vote for delegates to district and state conventions.

Primary An election in which party members select candidates to run for office under the party banner.

Open primary A primary election in which any qualified voter may participate, regardless of party affiliation. The voter chooses one party ballot at the polling place.

Closed primary A primary election that allows voters to obtain only a ballot of the party for which they are registered.

Partisan primary A primary in which candidates run for their own party's nomination.

Nonpartisan primary A primary in which candidates are listed on a ballot with no party identification.

Run-off primary An electoral contest between the top two primary vote getters that determines the party's candidate in a general election. It is held in the ten southern states, where a majority of the vote is needed to win the primary.

Incumbent A candidate who holds the contested office at the time of the election.

Open race An election in which there is no incumbent in the race.

Political consultant An individual, trained in public relations, media, or polling techniques, who advises candidates on organizing their campaign.

Party-centered campaign A campaign in which the party coordinates activities, raises money, and develops strategies.

Candidate-centered campaign A campaign in which paid consultants or volunteers coordinate campaign activities, develop strategies, and raise funds. Parties play a secondary role.

Retrospective voting The process by which individuals base their votes on the candidates' or parties' past record of performance.

Electoral college The system set up by the Constitution that provides for the people to elect a number of electors in each state equal to the number of U.S. senators and representatives for that state. The presidential candidate winning the plurality vote in a state receives all its electoral college votes.

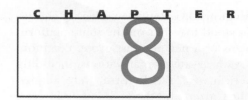

Interest Groups

- **Types and Structure of Interest and Other Advocacy Groups**
  Interest Groups: Economic, citizen activist, government related
  Lobbyists: Definition and description
  Political Action Committees (PACs): Funding campaigns

- **Resources and Problems of Interest Groups**
  Size: Potential source of power
  Unity: Internal cohesion
  Leadership: Important to success
  Information and Expertise: Major resource of lobbyists
  Money: Fundraising tactics; the free-rider problem

- **Interest Group Tactics**
  Lobbying: Definition and description
  Electioneering and Policymaking: Contributions, endorsements, scorecards
  Building Coalitions: Cooperative lobbying efforts
  Grassroots Pressure: Influence from constituents
  Litigation: Using the courts
  Hard-line tactics: Civil disobedience

- **Interest Groups and Democracy**
- **Conclusion: Corrupt or Constructive?**

MYTH & REALITY

Are all interest groups corrupt and self-serving?

WWW•
See **Political Science** at
http://www.hmco.com/college

t was an engrossing sight in Washington, D.C. Representatives of conservative and liberal advocacy groups stood together on the same platform highlighting the program and plans of a new interest group coalition, called "Stop Corporate Welfare." Conservative organizations, including the National Taxpayers Union and Americans for Tax Reform, were aligned with liberal advocacy groups such as Public Citizen and the U.S. Public Interest Research Group and with environmental advocates such as Friends of the Earth —all in an effort to end $11.5 billion in questionable governmental business subsidies. Allied with a number of leading Republican and Democratic members of Congress, the coalition was proposing the creation of a nine-member Corporate Subsidy Reform Commission, which would recommend the reform or discontinuation of dubious government programs and tax loopholes in the corporate sector.[1] The motives of the different organizations varied. The liberal ones sought deeper cuts in corporate welfare as a matter of equity, whereas the conservative groups focused on reducing government waste. However, coalitions that link interest groups are, in many respects, as American as apple pie.

Indeed, Stop Corporate Welfare represents only one of many different interest groups in Washington, where some twenty thousand lobbyists represent the interests of various groups and individuals before the members and staff of Congress and before executive officials. Although a special-interest group such as Stop Corporate Welfare projects a respectable image, most Americans see interest groups and lobbyists in a different and harsher light. They see lobbyists as wheeler-dealers and government as being influenced by a relatively few big in-

Interest Group Lobbying

Whenever Congress is in session, you will find lobbyists seeking access to our elected officials in order to try and influence their decisions. Here, hundreds of interest-group representatives wait outside the congressional hearing room, where hearings on national health care policy are being held, awaiting the results of their lobbying efforts.

terests. They suspect interest groups of dishonesty and of corrupting the political process by unduly influencing government, most often by "buying" members of Congress through campaign contributions. Past polls have reflected such skepticism. In one national poll, 76 percent of the respondents agreed that government is pretty much run by a few big interests looking out for themselves.[2] Another survey found that 57 percent of those responding thought that limiting the money spent on congressional campaigns is one way to keep members of Congress from being bought by special interests.[3] Many of those beliefs are reflected in the opinions of Americans who continue to question the roles of special interest groups and lobbyists in government activities.

Apparently, a majority of Americans believe in the *myth that interest groups are a corrupting influence in politics.* Though interest groups have undoubtedly taken center stage in the American policymaking process, whether they are a corrupting influence is open to question. We take up this issue at the end of the chapter. Before we can evaluate the myth and reality of interest groups, however, we must look at the role they play in American politics and at the resources and techniques they use to influence politics.

Types and Structure of Interest and Other Advocacy Groups

Our first task is to define three key terms: interest groups, lobbies, and political action committees (PACs).

Interest Groups

WWW•

For more information on interest groups, see the **Gitelson/Dudley/ Dubnick** web site.

A political **interest group** is any organized group of individuals who share common goals and who seek to influence government decision making.[4] Such diverse groups as the National Rifle Association, the Sierra Club, the U.S. Chamber of Commerce, and the League of Women Voters all fit this definition. Even college students are represented by interest groups—for instance, the Coalition of Independent College and University Students and the United States Student Association.

Interest groups differ from political parties.[5] In Chapter 6, on parties, we emphasize that parties are broad-based coalitions, with policies that cover a wide range of issues. The party's ultimate goal is to contest and win elections in order to control and operate government. In contrast, interest groups put forth a limited set of demands.* Although they sometimes try to affect the outcome of

---

*Some interest groups, such as Common Cause and the Liberty Federation, support a wide range of issues. Even these two groups, however, usually focus on a few key issues and direct their resources to them.

certain elections, interest groups do not run candidates for office or attempt to control or operate government. Their primary concern is to influence policy that affects their own area of interest.

Differing in size and make-up, interest groups pursue varying objectives. They also serve as organizational links between their members and elected and appointed government officials. What justifies the existence of interest groups in a democratic, representative form of government is their role in making members of the executive, legislative, and judicial branches of government more aware of the needs and concerns of various segments of the population. Many people join interest groups to promote their own economic well-being or to effect political and social change. They believe that common goals are best served by collective action.

Economic Interest Groups.   Among interest groups, business, labor, professional, and agricultural groups are the most enduring and powerful types. That fact is hardly surprising, given the intensity of most people's preoccupation with their own economic welfare.

More than three thousand individual corporations and businesses employ lobbyists, or spokespersons for corporations and businesses, in Washington.[6] The concerns of this fastest-growing type of group depend on the business in question and on the political climate. Tax laws, government subsidies, antitrust laws, tariffs on imported goods, and consumer product and environmental regulations may all affect the cost of doing business. In recent years, issues like the North American Free Trade Agreement, the General Agreement on Tariffs and Trade, and a national health care insurance program have increased lobbying efforts by the business community.

Business and trade associations are another type of economic interest group. Under the umbrella of business associations are the large and influential U.S. Chamber of Commerce, with a membership of more than 250,000 individuals and companies; the Business Roundtable, made up of approximately 200 of the largest industrial, commercial, and financial businesses in the nation; and many other groups. These associations represent some of the collective interests of corporate America.

The trade associations, which represent entire industries, also have widely divergent interests, ranging from government regulation of food and drugs to the regulation of the import of beef from Argentina. These groups are interested in government regulations that may affect the way a company does business. The National Cable Television Association, for example, closely monitors government regulations covering the cable industry—regulations that may have an impact on its cost of operations and earning capacity. Even the individuals who make their living representing interest groups, the lobbyists, have a trade association: the American League of Lobbyists.

Another important economic interest group comprises labor organizations. The American Federation of Labor and Congress of Industrial Organizations

Interest Group Protest

Joined by other labor groups, Teamster union members protest the enactment of the North American Free Trade Agreement with Mexico and Canada. Despite the strong alliance between labor unions and the Democratic party, President Clinton signed the agreement in 1993.

(AFL-CIO), an umbrella organization of ninety-six labor unions, has more than 17 million members. Along with the United Auto Workers, the Teamsters, and many other labor organizations, the AFL-CIO has for many years represented the interests of labor in the state capitals and in Washington. Individual labor unions also lobby independently of the umbrella groups. Thus, for example, the Independent Federation of Flight Attendants keeps on top of airline industry issues, and representatives of the International Brotherhood of Boilermakers, Iron Ship Builders, Blacksmiths, Forgers & Helpers focus attention on related legislative interests, including shipbuilding, tool making, and constructing nuclear and fossil-fuel plants.

Professional associations also bring the economic interests of their particular membership to the government's attention. Two of the most powerful—the American Bankers Association and the Association of Trial Lawyers of America—have large lobbying budgets as well as full-time staffs in Washington and in many state capitals. Smaller, less-powerful associations, such as the Clowns of America, have fewer resources but also try to protect their members' interests in regard to workers' compensation, tax laws, and other legislation affecting their professions.

Farmers, as an economic interest group, are a relatively strong economic force in contemporary American politics, with upwards of 20 percent of the work force directly or indirectly employed in agribusiness. One of the major goals of agricultural interest groups is protection from fluctuating prices for meat, grain, fruit, and other produce, which affect the income of individual farmers.

Citizen Activist Groups.   Not all shared interests are purely economic. In the last three decades there has been a proliferation of citizen activist groups, which rely on public opinion to back up their demands and expectations. Some of these groups try to represent what they deem to be the interests of the public at large and so are referred to as **public interest groups.**[7] Other organizations focus on specific causes or serve as advocates for those who are not able to represent themselves.[8]

Public interest groups such as Common Cause—a grassroots organization supported by member dues—and Public Citizen, Inc.—a loose affiliation of groups formed by the consumer activist Ralph Nader and supported by foundation grants—were part of an explosion of citizen lobbies in the 1960s. These groups have always tried to represent what they see as the public's interests on such issues as civil rights, consumer protection, campaign reform, and environmental regulation.

A cause group with an extremely narrow focus becomes known as a **single-issue group.** For example, the major goal of the Bass Anglers' Sportsman Society is to further the interests of bass fishing. The National Rifle Association (NRA) and the Gun Owners of America work to preserve the right of Americans to own handguns and rifles. The National Abortion Rights Action League (NARAL) fights for legislation and court decisions that protect the right of women to have abortions.

Environmental Activism

Would Abe Lincoln have approved? Two members of the environmental group Earth First hold a sign in front of the Lincoln Memorial to protest the destruction of the earth's rainforests. The risks to interest group demonstrators can be high. The two protesters were arrested by police.

Some citizen activist groups serve as advocates for persons who may be unable to represent their own interests individually.[9] For instance, the National Association for the Advancement of Colored People (NAACP), the Child Welfare League of America, and the American Cancer Society assist their target populations by lobbying, providing the public with information, and taking cases to court. Other advocacy groups focus on such issues as women's rights, gay rights, and racial equality, as well as the rights of Hispanics, various ethnic and religious groups, college students, and senior citizens. Many of their supporters do not benefit directly from their advocacy role but believe in the goals of the group.

Government-related Interest Groups.   Governments not only receive pressure from lobbyists; they also act as lobbies. San Francisco, Baltimore, Chicago, Chattanooga, and Newark are only a partial list of cities that have lobbyists representing their interests in Washington on concerns ranging from budget and appropriation legislation to welfare, Medicare, housing, and transportation. Indeed, the offices of hundreds of cities and states are listed in the *Washington Representatives Directory*.

In addition, a number of associations of government officials represent the collective interests of their members. These organizations include the U.S. Conference of Mayors, the International City Management Association, the National League of Cities, the National Association of Counties, the Council of State Governments, and the National Governors' Association. As local and state governments have come to depend on Washington for funds, the need for effective representation has increased and lobbies have become the principal means of achieving that representation.[10]

Even foreign nations have lobbyists looking after their interests. Such nations as Turkey, Jamaica, Guinea, and the African Republic of Transkei have lobbyists in the United States that represent their countries' interests before Congress and the executive branch. Those interests can range from military and economic assistance programs to foreign assistance authorization and appropriation bills. This globalization of interest group activity extends to the private sector, too. Groups like Amnesty International, a worldwide watchdog organization, lobby against any government's unjust repression and physical and mental torture of its citizens. The group has offices in the United States, Great Britain, and throughout the world.

Lobbyists

Who does the work for an interest group? A **lobbyist** is an individual who works for a specific interest group or who serves as the spokesperson for a specific set of interests. Lobbyists engage in the act of lobbying—that is, they try to affect government decision making by influencing legislators and members of the executive branch to support or reject certain policies or legislation.

Whereas some interest groups maintain their own staff of full-time lobbyists, other groups hire a lobbying firm to represent them in Washington or in various state capitals. Increasingly, lobbying has become a professional, full-time occupation. Many lobbyists are lawyers, former members of the executive branch or of Congress, and former employees of the hundreds of federal agencies. Government experience and contacts, along with an accumulated expertise, are valuable assets of the lobbying game.

As we shall see when we discuss the tactics of interest groups later in this chapter, the effective role of the lobbyist as spokesperson for an interest group is generally central to the success of that interest group's goals.

Political Action Committees

WWW•

For more information on Political Action Committees (PACs), see the **Gitelson/Dudley/Dubnick** web site.

If the myth of corruption has tainted interest-group politics in recent years, a major source of that concern has been **political action committees (PACs)**. As you learned in Chapter 7, these independent organizations are set up to collect campaign contributions from individuals who support the PAC's goals and to pass those contributions on to candidates. PACs resulted from a change in campaign finance laws designed to limit interest groups' financial involvement in elections.[11]

The change came about in the 1970s when Congress, pressured by public-interest groups, passed the Federal Election Campaign Act. The act provides for a rigid reporting system covering PAC money raised and spent for campaigns; it drastically restricts campaign contributions and prohibits corporations and labor unions from directly raising funds for or making contributions to political campaigns. However, Congress permitted unions and corporations to set up and administer independent organizations designed to collect and disburse campaign contributions (see Electioneering and Policymaking, p. 241).

Unions invented PACs, but as you can see in Figure 8.1, corporations rapidly surpassed union-sponsored PACs in numbers. Now almost every kind of group uses PACs. Trade and professional groups (for example, the American Institute of Certified Public Accountants), unions (such as the American Federation of Teachers Committee on Political Education), corporations and businesses (for example, the American Dental Political Action Committee), and cooperative groups (such as the Committee for Thorough Agricultural Political Education of Associated Milk Producers, Inc.) solicit and contribute money to political campaigns.

A PAC need not be affiliated with an interest group. Unaffiliated groups (such as the Fund for a Conservative Majority and Voters for Choice) have grown in numbers over the past ten years, often representing strongly held ideological positions on the political spectrum. The number of personal PACs has also grown; these are established by officeholders or would-be officeholders who raise money for their own campaigns, for self-promotion, or to assist in the election or re-election of partisan or ideological colleagues. Some of the leading personal PACs include the National Congressional Club (Senator Jesse Helms, R-N.C.), Effective Government Committee (Representative Richard A. Gephardt, D-Mo.), New Republican Majority (Senator Trent Lott, R-Miss.), and Fund for a

FIGURE 8.1

An Explosion of PACs

Unions invented them but corporations forged ahead with them when political action committees were in their infancy. Corporate, union, and trade PACs have tended to support candidates, whereas non-affiliated PACs have worked on negative campaigns.

Source: Federal Election Commission press release, January 24, 1997.

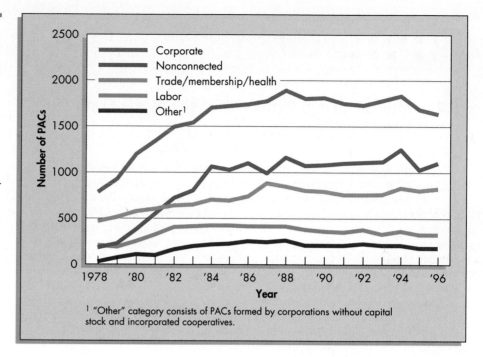

Number of PACs

Corporate
Nonconnected
Trade/membership/health
Labor
Other[1]

[1] "Other" category consists of PACs formed by corporations without capital stock and incorporated cooperatives.

Democratic Majority (Senator Edward Kennedy, D-Mass.). Many of these personal PACs are funded by friends and supporters of the individual or by other PACs.

Resources and Problems of Interest Groups

What accounts for the success of interest groups? What problems do they experience or create? In this section, we focus on five factors that strengthen or weaken interest group activity: size, unity, leadership, information and expertise, and money.

Size

Size is a major resource in establishing an interest group's base of power. Large organizations, such as the AFL-CIO or the U.S. Chamber of Commerce, have the potential collectively to mobilize vast resources of money, information, time, and energy in the service of an issue. The success of unions' defense of federally mandated minimum wages is a measure of the importance of size as a component of

**CLOSER
TO HOME**

8.1   Interest Group Politics: Diversity at the State and Local Levels

Few institutions in American politics have attracted as much attention in recent years as interest groups. When a major policy issue is debated in Congress, interest groups are sure to be spirited actors in shaping public policy. Although state and local interest groups share many of the attributes of national lobbying groups, political scientists Ann O'M. Bowman and Richard C. Kearney remind us that the interest-group environment often differs from one state to another.

With an estimated 42,500 registered lobbyists in the fifty state capitals, this situation is hardly surprising. In Florida, Louisiana, and South Carolina, for example, interest groups play a dominant role in the policymaking process. In California, Texas, Illinois, Kansas, Ohio, and Virginia, their role is either dominant or it complements that of political parties, depending on the issues. Interest groups in Delaware, Minnesota, Rhode Island, South Dakota, and Vermont, on the other hand, tend to have less influence on the policymaking process than those in the other forty-five states.

A specific interest group's policy agenda may vary from state to state, depending on the cutting issues. One recent study of the state legislative agendas of the large and powerful American Association of Retired Persons (AARP) found significant variations in state lobbying programs. In Colorado, AARP emphasized reform of the ballot initiative system and of campaign financing, but in Montana it focused on medical and long-term care in the state health plan, tax reform, and auto insurance rates. In Wyoming, it sought funding of local senior services, health care insurance, and the updating of the probate code. Its chief concerns elsewhere included drivers' training pro-

grams in North Dakota; health care reform and laws prohibiting discrimination on the basis of age in South Dakota; and increasing the severity of punishment for crimes against the elderly, as well as improving state highways, in Utah.

Clearly, then, the diversity of the fifty states and thousands of local communities in our nation is matched by the diversity in the power and influence of interest groups. It is also matched by the scope of issues and programs for which these groups lobby closer to home, at the state and local level.

Source: Ann O'M. Bowman and Richard C. Kearney, *State and Local Government* (Boston: Houghton Mifflin, 1996), pp. 121–132; see also Ronald Hrebenar and Clive S. Thomas, "Lobbying Through the Courts by State Interest Groups: A Fifty State Comparison," presented at the Western Political Science Association, Albuquerque, N. Mex., March 1994; Clive Thomas and Ronald Hrebenar, "Overview of Findings from the Spring of 1994 Update on Interest Group Power in the Fifty States," in *Politics in American States: A Comprehensive Analysis,* ed. Virginia Gray and Herbert Jacob, 6th ed. (Washington, D.C.: Congressional Quarterly Press, 1995).

political force. The success of the U.S. Chamber of Commerce's efforts in support of the North American Free Trade Agreement with Mexico and Canada is a gauge of the political influence of the Chamber's membership and size.

The ranking of the importance of size varies among interest groups. The largest types of interest groups, that is, corporate interest groups, which are not membership organizations, and trade associations, which generally have relatively few members, obviously need not pay much attention to membership size. On the other hand, unions and citizens' groups, which traditionally claim large membership and mass representation, do place a high value on membership size.[12]

In evaluating the impact of size, the key word is *potential*. Many large interest groups have little or no influence over the political opinions and participation of their membership. Indeed, a large constituency is often an organizational burden—difficult both to manage and to influence.[13] But if the leaders of large interest groups such as the AFL-CIO or the U.S. Chamber of Commerce can convince elected officials, administrators, and congressional staff that they can mobilize their membership behind a policy, size becomes very important.

Unity

A group's power is also strongly influenced by its level of internal cohesion. The AFL-CIO was sure, for example, that its large membership was united in recent legislative battles to raise the federal minimum hourly wage. Such unity gives the AFL-CIO enormous strength. Congress, the president, and the bureaucracy cannot ignore the intense preferences of millions of organized individuals who are united by a common goal.

When an interest group lacks unity on an issue, its influence on the policy-making process drops considerably, even if the group is large. Internal disagreements often work against group cohesion. For example, agreement is rare across the petroleum industry, where companies differ in size from giants such as Mobil and Exxon to the smaller, independent "wildcat" companies. One lobbyist for the American Petroleum Institute, a trade association representing oil interests, suggested that consensus on some issues was a "long time coming." When such consensus is lacking, the Institute often takes "no stand" at all, even if the issues affect its membership across the board.[14]

Leadership

Size and group unity do not necessarily ensure success, however. Interest groups must also have leaders who command respect and who can articulate and represent the issues and demands of the organization. Without such leadership, the interest group is "headless" and, more often than not, ineffective in pushing its goals.

One example of effective leadership is Marian Wright Edelman, head of the Washington-based Children's Defense Fund, which lobbies for health and social service issues on behalf of children. Highly respected by many members of

Interest Groups Without Powerful Representation

Many interest groups representing less powerful constituencies must fight for the attention of elected officials, particularly on issues like those supported by the Children's Defense Fund, a child advocacy group. One way of grabbing that attention is through the use of posters and catchy slogans.

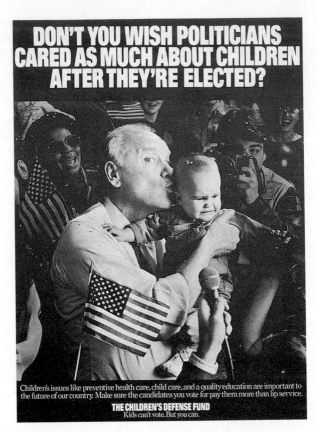

Congress, she and her organization have been instrumental and highly effectual in supporting many programs that have an impact on the lives of children.

Information and Expertise

What lobbyists know—their ability to collect information, evaluate its importance, and pass it on to appropriate government officials—is critical to their success. Faced with decisions on a variety of issues, public officials need credible and trustworthy information. Thus an interest group that can present its expertise cogently and convincingly has a distinct advantage over less-informed and less-articulate organizations. Patrick Healy, formerly the powerful and successful chief lobbyist for the National Milk Producers' Federation, argues that facts are the major resource of lobbying and that being able to provide accurate information to members and staff in Congress is the key to a lobbyist's success. Few of his colleagues would disagree with him.

The effectiveness of a group's expertise and delivery of information also depends on the perception of the group's motives. The American Medical Association's position on smoking is presumed to be economically disinterested and hence is heeded by Congress and the public. But its stand against national health insurance for all citizens is viewed with some skepticism, for it may stem from doctors' economic self-interest.

Money

Lobbying, collecting information, and other activities cost money. Besides the lobbyists' salaries, expenses include office space, support staff, telephones, office equipment, and travel. Some groups hire professional lobbying firms to conduct their business, and the costs of these services can be significant. Thus a large budget may not be the most critical resource of interest groups, but adequate funding is essential.

Fundraising tactics differ from group to group. Citizen activist groups, such as the Sierra Club, rely on an annual membership fee. For these groups, finding enough members to maintain the organization can be a problem. A hiker or camper need not join the club in order to benefit from its achievements in improving environmental conditions and preserving national parks. To get around this problem of **free riders**—those who benefit from the actions of interest groups without spending time or money to aid them—groups often seek foundation support and offer special services and resources to help recruit members.[15] They may provide members with free publications, technical journals, informative newsletters, reduced insurance rates, and even the opportunity to combine business with pleasure at annual meetings held in vacation resorts. For example, the American Association of Retired Persons provides its members with low-cost health insurance policies, a money market fund, and a mail discount pharmacy program.[16] The members of the National Rifle Association can buy ammunition, handguns, and rifles at discount prices.

Economic groups often have easier access to funds. Groups such as the U.S. Chamber of Commerce and the National Association of Manufacturers receive dues from their corporate and individual members. Many companies use corporate funds to pay for the cost of maintaining a staff lobbyist or hiring a lobbying firm. Still others can count on financial support from members, who must join the organization in order to keep their jobs. This is typical of many trade and industrial jobs and even some professions. Carpenters and plumbers must join their unions, and physicians, lawyers, and other professionals find themselves under pressure to join.

Finally, a number of interest groups, including the National Council of Senior Citizens, the National Governors' Association, and the American Council on Education, rely on government grants for financial assistance.

Interest Group Tactics

Interest groups are as powerful as their size, unity, leadership, expertise, and funds enable them to be. All of these resources need not be present, but the more, the better. Of course, no single resource can make or break a group. More often than not, success comes from effectively combining organizational resources and the tactics used to influence policymaking.

"You don't lobby with hundred-dollar bills and wild parties. You lobby with facts," says former lobbyist Patrick Healy. As you will see, however, money counts, although it is only one of many tools used by interest groups to influence government.

Lobbying

As you learned earlier in this chapter, **lobbying** is the act of trying to influence government decision makers. Named after the public rooms in which it first took place, lobbying now goes on in hearing rooms, offices, and restaurants—any spot where a lobbyist can gain a hearing and effectively present a case.

Lobbyists' stock in trade is their relationships with government officials and their staffs (see Table 8.1). That relationship is not maintained with bribes and favors, as the myth of corruption implies, but with data—technical information that members of Congress and bureaucrats need to carry out their committee and administrative assignments. Their work demands a level of expertise that few can muster, and so they come to depend on lobbyists' information and recommendations regarding the thousands of issues on which they must decide.

Once an interest group proves itself as a source of dependable information, it has easier access to officials. Lobbyists also share that expertise at congressional hearings, presenting research or technical information or discussing the impact of a bill on national, state, or local interests. Knowing how important constituents' concerns are to legislators, lobbyists are quick to point to the impact of a bill on a representative's home district or state. Whenever they can, interest groups mobilize the folks at home to write and call members of Congress to stress the importance of particular issues.

In one of the most famous cases of constituent mobilization in the 1990s, unions faced off against many corporations in a battle over the passage of the North American Free Trade Agreement (NAFTA). The unions, which opposed the trade agreement with Mexico and Canada, fearing loss of American jobs, and many corporations, which supported the bill believing that it would strengthen trade benefits for the United States, mobilized and encouraged citizens to contact their members of Congress to reject or pass NAFTA. Members of Congress received millions of letters and telephone calls from constituents. The tactic, which was part of a larger strategy for those opposing or supporting the act, was critical to the outcome of NAFTA, which Congress eventually passed.

TABLE 8.1

What Lobbyists Do

Despite the myth of corrupting influence, lobbyists do not spend all of their time "endorsing candidates" or contributing to their campaigns. As these data demonstrate, disseminating information is a major focus of their work.

Type of Technique	Percentage of Organizations Using Technique
Testifying at congressional hearings	99
Contacting government officials directly to present your point of view	98
Engaging in informal contacts with officials over lunch, and so on	95
Presenting research results or technical information	92
Helping to draft legislation	85
Mounting grassroots lobbying efforts	80
Alerting congressional representatives of the effects of a bill on their district	75
Filing suit or otherwise engaging in litigation	72
Publicizing candidates' voting records	44
Contributing work or personnel to electoral campaigns	24
Making public endorsements of candidates for office	22
Engaging in protests or demonstrations	20

Source: From *Organized Interests and American Democracy* by Kay Lehman Schlozman and John T. Tierney. Copyright © 1986 by Kay Lehman Schlozman and John T. Tierney. Reprinted by permission of HarperCollins Publishers, Inc.

Lobbyists even draft legislation, write speeches, and help plan legislative strategy. For most lobbyists, however, presenting research results or technical information to public officials is the most important and time-consuming part of their jobs.[17]

Clearly, the existence of unethical lobbyists supports the realistic side of the myth of corruption that many citizens perceive. In the early years of the republic, presenting gifts to or bribing willing legislators were not uncommon ways of influencing the passage of a specific bill. Indeed, in 1833, as prominent a senator as Daniel Webster was on retainer to the Bank of the United States, which was fighting for its survival. Webster wrote to the bank president: "My retainer has not been renewed or refreshed as usual. If it is wished that my relation to the Bank should be continued, it may be well to send me the usual retainer."[18]

Despite their reputation for bribery and corruption, most interest groups function within the law. Nevertheless, Congress has found it necessary to pass laws regulating the groups and their representatives. In 1887, Congress first required lobbyists to register with the House of Representatives. Additional laws

Lobbying at the Highest Level

Not surprisingly, our highest elected officials often lobby the public to gain their support on issues of the day. Here Vice President Al Gore speaks to a group at Harvard's Kennedy School of Government, advocating policies supported by the Clinton administration.

mandate that lobbyists file reports listing their clients, as well as describing their activities and recording the amount of money spent on them. The 1946 Federal Regulation of Lobbying Act is the most recent comprehensive attempt to regulate interest groups. Under the 1946 act, however, lobbying is vaguely defined and the regulations are minimally enforced. Of the estimated twenty thousand lobbyists active in Washington, D.C., only fifty-five hundred are actually registered. One reason is a loophole in the law: only individuals paid to lobby for someone else must register. Thus, for example, an official who works directly for a corporation and lobbies for the interests of that company need not register. In addition, only lobbyists who have direct contact with members of Congress must register. A great deal of the lobbying that goes on, however, targets the staff people who work for and advise members of Congress.

The norm of behavior for the vast majority of lobbyists is to act within the law, and their actions are governed by one major rule: a lobbyist should never lie. As one member of Congress put it, "It doesn't take very long to figure which lobbyists are straightforward, and which ones are trying to snow you. The good ones will give you the weak points as well as the strong points of their case. If anyone ever gives me false or misleading information, that's it—I'll never see him again."[19] When 175 lobbyists were asked which resources were most important to their success, an overwhelming majority singled out the reputation for being credible and trustworthy.[20]

Electioneering and Policymaking

Participating in the election process—**electioneering**—is an important tactic of many interest groups. As part of that tactic, both interest groups and political action committees have become very important to candidates.

During the 1996 election cycle, PACs spent over $400 million in direct contributions and other costs related to Senate and House races. Few congressional candidates, incumbent or not, refuse PAC funding of their expensive campaigns. (See Table 8.2 for a list of major PAC contributors.)

PACs' patterns of giving reflect their partisan persuasions. In 1996, for example, labor-sponsored PACs, traditionally strong supporters of the Democratic party, channeled their contributions primarily to Democratic candidates. Corporate-sponsored PACs, on the other hand, directed much of their support to Republican candidates.

Do PAC contributions influence politicians' decisions? Do the recipients of campaign funds support the donors' programs? Apparently, interest groups think they do. In one study, 58 percent of interest group representatives said that they used campaign contributions as a means of influencing the policymaking process.[21] Despite that belief, there is limited evidence that campaign contributions guarantee support or votes on a bill.[22] In general, what a gift may ensure is easier access to elected officials or their staff. This is important in itself, for such access allows lobbyists to present and argue their positions and to influence the agenda of Congress.

While some studies claim that campaign contributions by PACs influence the policymaking process, other studies assert that there is no clear link between money and policymaking. Many legislators argue that the PAC funds they receive are not intended to buy congressional votes but rather to support the positions that a legislator has already committed to. As Congressman Jack Fields said in responding to allegations of PAC influence through financial contributions, "I haven't changed my philosophy in the fifteen years I've been in Congress. My philosophy has always been free enterprise and to support whatever creates jobs, and those who want to contribute to me are free to do so."[23] Nevertheless, the 1996 presidential and congressional elections saw both record PAC contributions—over $217 million to federal campaigns—and a growing skepticism among citizens as to the role that money plays in the campaign and policymaking process.

TABLE 8.2

Top Fifteen PAC
Contributors

These PACs (political action committees) contributed the largest amounts of money to candidates between January 1, 1995 and December 31, 1996.

1.	Democratic Republican Independent Voter Education Committee	$2,611,140
2.	American Federation of State, County, and Municipal Employees —PEOPLE, Qualified	2,505,021
3.	UAW-V-CAP (UAW Voluntary Community Action Program)	2,467,319
4.	Association of Trial Lawyers of America Political Action Committee	2,362,938
5.	Dealers Election Action Committee of the National Automobile Dealers Association	2,351,925
6.	National Education Association Political Action Committee	2,326,830
7.	American Medical Association Political Action Committee	2,319,197
8.	Realtors Political Action Committee	2,099,683
9.	International Brotherhood of Electrical Workers Committee on Political Education	2,080,587
10.	Active Ballot Club, A Department of United Food & Commercial Workers International Union	2,030,795
11.	Machinists Non-partisan Political League	1,999,675
12.	Laborers' Political League	1,933,300
13.	United Parcel Service of America, Inc. Political Action Committee	1,788,147
14.	Committee on Letter Carriers Political Education (Letter Carriers Political Action Fund)	1,715,064
15.	American Institute of Certified Public Accountants Effective Legislation Committee (AICPA)	1,690,925

Source: Federal Election Commission news release, April 22,1997, p. 19.

According to the Federal Election Campaign Act, PACs can donate no more than $5,000 per candidate per election (primaries and general elections count as separate elections), a restriction motivated by a history of interest group contributions that sometimes reached tens of thousands of dollars for a single candidate. Because candidates must now seek out more contributors to their campaigns to ensure sufficient funding, a single group's influence on a candidate may be less than it expects. However, the $5,000 restriction per candidate makes it possible for PACs to support more candidates, for the number of campaigns to which a PAC may contribute is unlimited. This outcome disturbs many reformers, who had hoped to restrict, not increase, the involvement of interest groups in campaigns.

Interest group activity in campaigns has given rise to other concerns as well. Interest groups (and individual contributors) have found a way to bypass the Federal Election Campaign Act restrictions on PAC contributions in federal elections. PACs may contribute what is known as "soft money" to political parties. These contributions, which are unlimited, may be used only for party-building activities, such as voter registration drives and get-out-the-vote efforts. There is a fine line, however, between these activities and political campaign endeavors. The 1996 presidential campaigns raised serious questions as to how soft-money contributions had been collected and distributed by both parties—although the Democratic party and President Clinton came under specific attack for allegedly receiving inappropriately solicited contributions from different sources. As a scholar who has studied interest groups, Jeffrey Berry, has pointed out, "Expanding the role of interest groups in campaign finance has not . . . restored public confidence in the integrity of the political process. Rather, it has heightened concern about the role of interest groups in a democracy."[24]

Interest groups support campaigns in other ways besides PAC contributions. Labor, trade, and professional associations supply candidates with volunteers and offer public endorsements. The AFL-CIO, the Americans for Democratic Action, and the American Conservative Union are just three of the many interest groups and PACs that provide their members and the public with voting scorecards on candidates they support or target for defeat. By listing key votes, the cards can praise or damn the candidate. The National Congressional Club PAC specializes in the so-called negative campaign, or putting down the opposition. The group has spent large sums in the past, particularly on television advertisements, in an effort to defeat liberal candidates.

Interest groups do not limit their activities to congressional races. Besides pressuring the major parties to include their goals in the presidential party platforms, an interest group may turn out in force at the national conventions. Of the 4,320 delegates at the 1996 Democratic National Convention, 34 percent were members of labor unions, including 11 percent who were members of teacher unions. Not surprisingly, the party took strong platform positions on education and labor concerns.

Building Coalitions

An interest group tactic that has gained increasing importance is **coalition building**—the bringing together of diverse interest groups in a common lobbying effort. Such cooperative action has proved very successful. In 1994, a coalition of organizations, including the American Medical Association, the National Federation of Independent Business, and the Business Roundtable—all of which are powerful interest groups—lobbied against the employer-sponsored health insurance mandate advocated by the Clinton administration's plan for national health care insurance.[25] Their efforts paid off when national health care insurance failed to pass during the 103rd Congress.

Coalitions are often temporary alliances keyed to a particular issue. For instance, the Quaker Oats Company, interested in keeping down the price of grains used in many of its cereal products, and Common Cause, the public

Coalition Building

One of the most effective interest-group tactics is coalition building—the bringing together of diverse interest groups in a common lobbying effort. Here, consumer advocate Ralph Nadar speaks at a news conference announcing a "hit list" of "corporate welfare" programs as Congressman Edward Royce (R-Cal) in background and John Kasich (R-Ohio) look on.

interest group seeking to control the retail cost of food, have at times testified jointly against certain farm support bills. Yet Quaker Oats and Common Cause have been on opposite sides of the fence on other issues. When Quaker Oats owned Fisher-Price Toys, it was at odds with Common Cause regarding federal safety laws regulating the manufacture of children's toys.

Most signs point to an increasing use of coalition building by interest groups and PACs in an effort to influence the policymaking process.

Grassroots Pressure

The word *grassroots* is a people-centered term. In interest group politics, **grassroots pressure** refers to lobbying by rank-and-file members of an interest group who use such tactics as letter writing and public protests to influence government.

When the National Beer Wholesalers Association wanted to be exempted from antitrust legislation, it mobilized grassroots support for a massive letter, telephone, and telegram campaign. Truly a "bottoms-up" effort to stimulate pressure from the grassroots level, the campaign was supported by political contributions from the association's political action committee—which no doubt you have guessed is called SIXPAC.[26]

Grassroots activity includes face-to-face meetings between members of Congress and selected constituents, as well as demonstrations and protests. During the recent debate in Congress over a national health care program, the tobacco industry mobilized thousands of tobacco growers and workers to Washington to lobby against a proposed cigarette tax increase to fund the program. That attempt at putting a human face on the industry and reminding members of Congress of the large number of people employed in the tobacco industry had the impact of significantly reducing the proposed size of the cigarette tax.[27] When interest groups mobilize grassroots mail and telephone campaigns, they tend to focus on narrow issues and to direct their efforts toward specific members of Congress. On any given issue, "lobbyists understand intuitively what political scientists have demonstrated empirically: members of Congress are more influenced by their constituents than by Washington lobbies."[28] For that reason, many interest groups stress grassroots efforts.

These efforts have become highly sophisticated, as illustrated by the activities of the U.S. Chamber of Commerce. The group maintains a closed-circuit television network linking local affiliates all over the nation. When it wants to mobilize support for or against a bill, it can beam its views to congressional and community leaders as well as to its members.

Indeed, grassroots mobilization has evolved into a highly professional undertaking. *Campaigns and Elections* magazine has estimated that "professional grassroots lobbying has become an $800 million industry. . . . The planned orchestrated demonstration of public support through the mobilization of constituent action is . . . one of the hottest trends in politics today. . . . Interest groups that don't play the game risk becoming political eunuchs."[29] An interest group representative may call members of the public, solicit their opinion on a topic, and if those opinions coincide with the position of the interest group, the individuals are offered immediate and direct telephone hookup with their members of Congress. In this way, interest groups try to ensure that grassroots opinions favorable to them reach the appropriate legislators. As *Washington Post* correspondents Haynes Johnson and David Broder point out, "there's nothing spontaneous about this kind of operation." It has been called "astroturfing"—a reference to the synthetic grass used on many football, soccer, and baseball fields.[30] Unlike spontaneous grassroots activity generated by citizens concerned about an issue, astroturfing is "public opinion" systematically organized and generated by an interest group.

Litigation

Many pressure groups, particularly public interest and advocacy groups, also use the courts to influence policy. They bring direct suit, challenge existing laws, or file briefs as "friends of the court" to support one side in cases already before the court.

Though it is expensive and time consuming, litigation can bring about remarkable political change. Perhaps the outstanding example is the use of the courts by the National Association for the Advancement of Colored People (NAACP)

**MYTHS
IN POPULAR CULTURE**

8.1   How Politicians Sell Out to the Interest Groups

If you wanted to dramatize the corruption of politicians and interest groups, you couldn't do a better job than making the 1994 film *The Distinguished Gentleman*. The film stars Eddie Murphy as Jeff Johnson, a political neophyte who is elected to Congress through a series of bizarre flukes. The movie is actually a comic version of the 1939 drama *Mr. Smith Goes to Washington*. Murphy and the film's director take every opportunity to depict most elected members of Congress as contemptible and vile—totally devoted to selling their vote to the highest-bidding lobbyist.

As the plot unfolds, Jeff Johnson mainly goes to Washington, D.C., because "That's where the money is." His dream comes true when he arrives in the Capitol and finds lobbyists whose "whole point in life is to buy you off." When Johnson asks one of the lobbyists, "With all of this money coming in from all sides, how can anything get done," the ready response is that "it doesn't; that's the genius of the system."

As with all myths about politics, strains of truth can be found in some of the film's portrayals. In re-ality, observers are increasingly concerned, as are members of Congress, with the escalating cost of elections and the dependence on lobbyists and political action committees to help finance campaigns. An uncomfortable relationship can exist between the donors and the receivers of campaign contributions in which policy may be influenced. But *The Distinguished Gentleman* goes too far in distorting the governing process and the methods used to debate and write laws.

Most members of Congress, as well as most elected officials in our state and local legislative bodies, cannot be bought by lobbyists as portrayed in this film. Policymaking is a complex process influenced not only by interest groups but by the constituents, principles, and policy preferences of our legislators. That interest groups can and do influence the policymaking process, to the detriment of some policies, is indeed true. That they are a constant and overwhelming force of corruption in the policymaking process is a myth generated and reinforced by movies like *The Distinguished Gentleman*.

---

in the 1940s and 1950s. In a series of cases, culminating in the *Brown* v. *Board of Education* decision in 1954, NAACP lawyers argued and the Supreme Court affirmed that school segregation is illegal in the United States. Women's groups, consumer groups, environmental groups, religious groups, and others have followed the lead of the civil rights movement in taking their causes to the courts. Corporations and trade associations have also engaged in litigation. However, the high cost restrains many groups. One interest group, the Women's Equity League, could not appeal a court ruling against it in an important case because it could not afford the $40,000 necessary to pay for copies of the trial transcript.[31]

One way to get around the problem of cost is to threaten a lawsuit; often that is enough to dissuade opponents from acting. In another approach, groups try to influence the philosophy of the Supreme Court by opposing or supporting judicial nominees. In 1991, President George Bush's nominee to the Supreme Court, Clarence Thomas, was strongly opposed by liberal groups, such as the National Abortion Rights Action League and People for the American Way, because of Thomas's conservative stand on many issues. Other organizations opposed Thomas because of questions raised by sexual harassment charges made against him by a former employee. A number of conservative groups supporting Thomas countered with campaigns among their members to influence the acceptance of Thomas as a member of the Court, and indeed the Senate eventually confirmed him. (See Chapter 12 for further discussion on the Thomas appointment.)

Hard-line Tactics

In recent years, a number of interest groups have used hard-line tactics, including civil disobedience and illegal action, to make their cause known. During the 1970s, discontented farmers, angry about federal agricultural policies that they felt harmed their economic well-being, created major traffic jams in Washington, D.C., during a "tractor march" on the Capitol. In the 1980s and 1990s, groups like ACT UP have drawn public attention to the plight of AIDS victims by disrupting public events, and organizations like Operation Rescue have received a great deal of attention because they advocate violent protests against abortion clinics. Hard-line tactics appear to be a growing mechanism for presenting an interest group's cause.

Interest Groups and Democracy

Interest groups pose a number of problems for a democratic society. James Madison argued in the "Federalist No. 10" that the rise of factions is inevitable in a democracy. Although he believed that factions could destroy the policymaking process, he did not want to prohibit them, for that would undermine the basic tenets of a participatory republic. Instead, Madison hoped that the divisiveness of factions would be tempered both by built-in checks and balances and by a political system that would ensure the creation of competing factions.

Interest groups do, to some degree, distort the democratic process, mainly because their membership is clearly biased toward the upper half of the socioeconomic ladder. The groups that have the most clout in Washington are dominated by business and professional lobbies working on economic issues that benefit the already advantaged in society. The indigent have less interest group representation. Thus the haves gain more, while the have-nots remain unrepresented or underrepresented. To the extent that the business, labor, and professional groups have exceptional influence, policy is similarly distorted.

Interest groups and PACs are essentially middle- and upper-class institutions representing middle- and upper-class values in the policymaking process. Though they may intend to serve the nation's interests, they generally design their goals and limit their commitments to suit a relatively small group of private interests.

Conclusion: Corrupt or Constructive?

Unquestionably, interest groups have come to wield increasing political power, and Americans' fear of these groups has some basis in reality. With large treasuries to disburse and an inside track with public officials, they are potentially a distorting influence on the functioning of the political system. Broad national interests can be lost in the clamor of pressure-group activity and narrow self-interests. Interest groups also work out of public view, thus encouraging the popular belief that the public cannot adequately scrutinize their activities.

Not every group with a shared interest is self-interested, however. As with the proverbial concept of beauty, an interest group's "goodness" or "badness" often rests in the eyes of the beholder. To see only the biasing effects of interest groups is to perpetuate the myth of corrupting influence. Interest groups are also a healthy feature of and a positive force in the political process. They are organizations that give voice to the voiceless and represent the unrepresented. Advances for African-Americans, the poor, the young, the aged, and others who are disadvantaged, as well as farmers, laborers, and owners of small businesses, can be attributed, in part, to the effective activities of interest groups. Increasing numbers of interest groups support and fight for programs that benefit and contribute to our democratic process. They serve to supplement our representative body of elected officials by giving citizens an additional voice in government.

Few, if any, citizens are not represented directly or indirectly by an interest group, whether that group is concerned with economic, social, or environmental issues. For example, a coalition of environmental groups, including the Sierra Club, the Wilderness Society, and the National Resources Defense Council, have, for more than two decades, lobbied effectively for federal and state laws regulating air and water pollution; forest, rangeland, and coastal land management; strip-mining; and the production and use of pesticides and toxicants.

Madison warned of the pitfalls of interest groups. He also argued that they are an inevitable cost in any democratic system. We argue that the groups link citizens and public officials through corporate, labor, trade, and professional associations and through citizen activist groups. Such linkage may be worth the price of real (and imagined) distortions that inevitably occur when interest groups are active in the policymaking process. Certainly, the groups are too useful to dismiss by invoking the myth of corrupting influence.

Summary

1. Interest groups are organized groups of individuals who share one or more common goals and who seek to influence government decision making.

2. Political parties deal with both specific and general policy development. Interest groups usually focus on narrow policy areas.

3. Although they may attempt to influence the outcome of certain elections, interest groups do not run candidates for elective office, their names do not appear on the ballot, and they do not attempt to control or operate government.

4. Types of interest groups include economic interest organizations, citizen activist groups, and government-related interest groups.

5. A lobbyist is an individual who works for a specific interest group or who serves as the spokesperson for a specific set of interests. Lobbyists engage in the act of lobbying—that is, they try to influence government decision making by persuading legislators and members of the executive branch to support certain policies or legislation.

6. Political action committees (PACs), cousin organizations of interest groups, serve as affiliated or independent organizations with the prime function of collecting and disbursing campaign contributions. Candidates, particularly for Congress, have become increasingly dependent on this source of campaign support.

7. Interest groups rely on resources from within their groups to strengthen their roles in the policymaking process. These resources include strength in numbers, group cohesion, strong leadership, information and expertise, and money. In general, however, given different issues and different political environments, no single resource determines the success of an interest group. A group's influence is usually strongest when a combination of organizational resources is brought to bear on the policymaking process.

8. Interest group tactics include the use of pressure from the grassroots as well as lobbying, electioneering (which includes financing and supporting campaigns through affiliated PACs), coalition building, and litigating.

9. Interest groups can pose problems for a democratic society because they often represent narrow interests that are biased toward the higher economic groups.

10. Interest groups are important to the political process because they can and do enhance our representative process, focusing our attention on important issues.

Key Terms and Concepts

Interest group Any organized group of individuals who share common goals and seek to influence government decision making.

Public interest groups Citizen activist groups that try to represent what they deem to be the interests of the public at large.

Single-issue group Any activist group that seeks to lobby Congress on a single or narrow range of issues.

Lobbyist An individual who works for a specific interest group or who serves as the spokesperson for a specific set of interests.

Political action committees (PACs) Organizations that interest groups set up solely for the purpose of contributing money to the campaigns of candidates who sympathize with their goals. A PAC need not be affiliated with an interest group but can be unaffiliated, representing an ideological position or even a candidate or officeholder.

Free riders Those who benefit from the actions of interest groups without spending time or money to aid the groups.

Lobbying Named after the public rooms in which it first took place, lobbying is the act of trying to influence government decision makers.

Electioneering Participating in the election process by providing services or raising campaign donations.

Coalition building The bringing together of diverse interest groups in a common lobbying effort.

Grassroots pressure Lobbying by rank-and-file members of an interest group who use such tactics as letter writing and public protests to influence government.

C H A P T E R

9

Media and Politics

Do the media have the power to influence public opinion?

See **Political Science** at
http://www.hmco.com/college

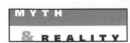

A s the fog lifted off the Potomac River on the cool September morning in 1993, pedestrians along Pennsylvania Avenue encountered a bewildering sight. Spread out across the usually serene, manicured White House lawn were scores of tents, tons of electronic equipment, and hundreds of people. What looked like a cross between a rock festival and a besieging army, which in some ways it was, turned out to be an assemblage of some two hundred radio talk show hosts with their entourage and gear. This was the morning after President Bill Clinton delivered his health care message to a joint session of Congress and millions of television viewers. Armed with an invitation from the president and a promise of access to administration aides, the talk show hosts descended on Washington to ply their special blend of entertainment and public affairs.

Why would President Clinton, who had often disparaged the media, and radio talk show hosts in particular, invite them to his very doorstep? Clearly, he hoped to sway the talk show hosts, who, he assumed, would then persuade their millions of listeners to support his policy. On a more basic level, the president was simply acknowledging the importance of the media. As many observers of American politics have noted, the media have come to play a crucial role in American politics. But in what ways? On that subject there is much disagreement and perhaps misunderstanding.

In part, the popular views of the power of the media rest on the *myth of media manipulation:* that television, radio, and the print media dominate and direct the public's thinking about politics. The myth of media manipulation is not confined to any particular group in society; it is shared by Americans of widely varying political perspectives. Conservatives worry about the effects on the public of what they see as a liberal conspiracy, and critics on the left often describe the media as a capitalist plot serving the interests of the wealthy. In their defense, journalists say they are simply reflecting the world as it is—a mirror to society. They just cover the story. Thus Roan Conrad, political editor for NBC News, argued nearly two decades ago that "the news is what happens. . . . The news is not a reporter's perception or explanation of what happens; it is simply what happens."[1]

As you will see in this chapter, although the choice of stories does much to define public concerns, the relationship between the media and public opinion is not as straightforward as the myth suggests. The media cannot dictate the political beliefs of the country. At the same time, journalists are not simply passive instruments through which events, called news, are transmitted. Interestingly, the standards by which journalists decide what is newsworthy often work to the advantage of officials and candidates who use the media to achieve policy and electoral goals.

The Rise of the Media

Americans buy nearly 60 million newspapers and keep their television sets on an average of more than six hours each day. Simultaneously, they can choose among ten thousand or so weekly and monthly periodicals and almost nine thousand radio stations. The attentive media watcher faces an incessant flow of information on topics ranging from foreign affairs to domestic scandals. Yet it has not always been this way. A mere 150 years ago news of Washington or the state capital arrived, if at all, days, weeks, or even months after the events occurred.

The Early Days

Before 1830 the American press consisted of specialized publications designed to reach elite audiences. Many papers were simply organs of political parties or individual candidates. Appearing once or twice a week, these partisan papers rallied the party faithful and denounced political opponents, often through vicious personal attacks. The only alternative sources of news were commercial papers, which appealed to merchants and traders. Although short on politics, the commercial papers provided extensive accounts of business activities. Covering shipping dates, commodity prices, and business transactions rather than local news, the commercial press made no attempt to reach a wide audience.

With the publication in 1833 of the *New York Sun,* American publishing entered the age of mass journalism. Capitalizing on technological advances that made printing relatively fast and cheap, the *Sun* was the first paper that appealed successfully to the public at large. It was sold on street corners for a penny a copy,

Read All About It

The modern mass media were born in America with the creation of the penny press. Sold on street corners by young boys and girls, like those pictured here, the penny press specialized in sensationalism.

and its many imitators (together they became known as the **penny press**) cultivated readerships in the thousands. A breezy style and an emphasis on local news, especially scandalous events, ensured the papers' popularity. Each vied fiercely with the others to produce the most sensational stories. At one point the staff of the *Sun* invented a hoax about life on the moon.[2]

Toward the end of the nineteenth century, the emphasis on sensationalism became even more pronounced. Joseph Pulitzer, a crusading spirit who owned the *New York World,* and William Randolph Hearst, owner of the *New York Journal,* created **yellow journalism**—named for the "Yellow Kid" comic strip that appeared in the *World* and then in the *Journal.* Yellow journalism utilized large bold headlines, illustrations, cartoons, and color features to promote its tales of scandal and corruption. Not content with reporting the news, both Pulitzer and Hearst often made news by committing the considerable resources of their papers to various political causes. For instance, Hearst is usually credited with arousing in the American public the strong anti-Spanish feelings that led to the Spanish-American war. Just before the war, Hearst sent an artist to Cuba to cover the conflict between Spain and Cuba. When the artist wired that war did not seem likely, Hearst replied, "Please remain. You furnish the pictures. I will furnish the war."[3] Many people believe that he did just that.

While Hearst and Pulitzer inflamed public opinion with their sensational appeals, a new style of journalism was developing. A conservative paper, the *New York Times,* attacked the excesses of yellow journalism as indecent and stressed objectivity in its reporting. Newspapers, according to Adolph Ochs, owner of the *Times,* had the responsibility to "give news impartially, without fear or favor, regardless of any party, sect or interest involved."[4] Although its circulation was small compared with that of the yellow journalism press, the *Times* became a standard by which journalism was judged, and objectivity became the goal of journalists. As any trip to the supermarket will show, however, yellow journalism did not die; it just became less prevalent.

The Broadcast Media

Even as newspapers were undergoing change, the technology of the broadcast media was being developed. The first regularly scheduled radio station, KDKA in Pittsburgh, began operation in 1920. Its owner, Westinghouse, the nation's leading manufacturer of home receivers, initially viewed it as a means of creating a market for home receivers. Entertainers such as Bob "Pepsodent" Hope (Pepsodent being the sponsor of Hope's popular radio show) soon demonstrated that advertisements linked with entertainment could be immensely popular and profitable.

Although broadcasters stressed entertainment, government leaders were quick to grasp the political potential of radio. President Franklin D. Roosevelt employed the medium skillfully during the Great Depression to deliver his famous fireside chats. Speaking in a warm and informal manner, Roosevelt sought to reassure millions of Americans by making his broadcasts sound like friendly discussions. Roosevelt demonstrated the vast possibilities of radio, as well as its potential for overt manipulation. During the 1944 election, for instance, Roosevelt learned that his opponent, Thomas Dewey, had purchased airtime immediately following his own. Although scheduled to speak for fifteen minutes, Roosevelt stopped after fourteen. Millions of puzzled listeners turned their dials away from the silence and missed Dewey's address.

Despite the interest shown by political leaders, most broadcasters resisted programming the news until the fledgling CBS network entered the business. Its owner, William Paley, saw news as a cheap source of programming and a means of competing with NBC, the more established radio network. His team of journalists, including Edward R. Murrow and Eric Sevareid, quickly established reputations for superior news coverage. Murrow's broadcasts from London during World War II captured the imagination of the entire country, making Murrow a national celebrity.

Like radio, television was from the beginning a commercial venture that stressed entertainment and advertising. (Appropriately, Philo T. Farnsworth, the inventor of television, used a dollar sign as his first test pattern.) Throughout the 1950s each of the three television networks—CBS, NBC, and ABC—provided one 15-minute news program five evenings a week. Even CBS, which had pioneered radio news, was reluctant to use valuable airtime for news and public affairs, preferring the popular and extraordinarily profitable quiz shows.

In 1960, however, the situation changed when all three networks televised the debates between presidential candidates John F. Kennedy and Richard M. Nixon. Although there is still disagreement over which candidate won, the debates definitely enhanced television's news potential. By drawing an audience of 60 to 75 million viewers, the debates demonstrated the commercial potential of news and public affairs programming. News programs ceased to be viewed simply as a means of improving a network's public image. Instead, the networks began competing to produce the most highly rated news programs, using such advanced technology as small hand-held cameras, wireless microphones, and satellite transmissions. As news coverage broadened, their audiences grew into the millions, and a majority of Americans came to depend on television as their prime source of news. Moreover, for the majority of Americans, television is the most believable source of news.[5]

Diversity and Concentration

Although the media present a staggering array of choices, merely reciting the number of outlets can be deceiving. The real issue, say media critics, is the increasing concentration of ownership in a few hands—a change that threatens to limit diversity of expression. About two-fifths of all daily newspapers published in the United States belong to the twelve largest chains. The largest of all, Gannett, owns approximately seventy-five newspapers, including *USA Today*. (Gannett also owns television stations.) Furthermore, even though the number of newspapers has stayed about the same in recent years, newspaper competition has decreased markedly. Only 2 percent of American cities have more than one newspaper.[6]

Concentrated ownership and influence are even greater in the television markets. About 85 percent of the nation's commercial television stations are affiliated with ABC, CBS, or NBC.[7] All three major networks are, in turn, owned by large conglomerates with multiple media interests that combine publishing, broadcasting, and Hollywood production studios.

All is not well for the networks, however. The rise of the Fox network and more importantly the growth of cable television have substantially eroded network dominance. Since 1980 the networks have lost more than a quarter of their prime-time audience to these new competitors. Cable television, which began as a means of bringing over-the-air broadcasts to remote communities, has been particularly aggressive at drawing the audience away from the networks. In 1980 only about a tenth of American homes were served by cable, but by 1990 the number stood at more than 55 percent.[8] As the audience for cable has grown so has its offerings. Although cable systems still carry local network affiliates, they also offer a variety of channels and cable-based networks, such as Turner Broadcasting, Music Television (MTV), and Home Shopping Network.

News and public affairs programs are also supplied by cable operators through C-SPAN and the more widely watched Cable News Network (CNN), which offers 24-hour-a-day news broadcasts worldwide. (More than 75 million households currently receive CNN, 17 million of these outside the United States.)

The enormous growth of cable, direct satellite transmissions, and a host of developing technologies that combine video and computer processing with microwave transmissions suggest a future of almost infinite choices. But who will control these outlets? Many observers believe that the technological revolution is destroying the centralized and concentrated media, which are characterized by the major networks, and paving the way for a more democratic means of information production.[9] Others, however, view the future much like the past as major corporations become multimedia giants that will control the worldwide production, distribution, and technology of the new media. This future, many claim, can be seen by looking at Time Warner, which, among its many holdings, owns in whole or in part Turner Broadcasting, CNN, Warner Brothers Motion Pictures, HBO, Cinemax, Comedy Central, eight book publishers, twenty-four magazines, the multimedia CNN Interactive (website), and cable franchises serving more than 11 million subscribers.

www•
For more information on media ownership and concentration, see the **Gitelson/Dudley/Dubnick web site.**

Government Regulation

The American mass media are freer of government restrictions than those in any other nation. Nevertheless, the government exercises some control, especially over radio and television. In the case of printed materials, regulation applies only to obscenity and libel (see Chapter 4, on rights and liberties).

**News Twenty-
Four Hours a Day**

The growth of cable
television has spawned
an array of specialized
programming, includ-
ing Cable News Net-
work (CNN) which
provides news and
public affairs informa-
tion twenty-four hours
a day. Created in 1980,
CNN has become a
leading source of
news. Pictured here
is reporter Bernard
Shaw at work in the
CNN Washington
bureau.

Government Licensing.   Because of the limited number of frequencies over
which radio and television signals can be transmitted, Congress created the Federal Communications Commission (FCC) in 1934 to monitor and regulate the
use of the airwaves. Besides assigning frequencies so that stations' signals do not
interfere with each other, the FCC issues licenses, which must be renewed every
five years for television and every seven years for radio. According to statute, license renewals depend on "satisfactory performance" that "serve[s] the public
interest, convenience, and necessity." The vagueness of that mandate gives the
FCC tremendous discretion in awarding or denying license renewals, but as a
matter of practice it has denied few applications and has exercised little control
over broadcasting content. Illustrative of the FCC position is its refusal, in the
face of heavy lobbying by advocacy groups, to require television broadcasters to
limit early evening hours to family programs accepting instead a rating system
created and managed by the networks.

Equal Time.   The most significant FCC requirement is the **equal-time rule.** This
provision stipulates that broadcasters who permit a candidate for political office
to campaign on the station (including through paid advertisements) must allow
equal time at identical rates to all other candidates for the same office. Recently,
industry leaders and others have argued for the relaxation or elimination of this
rule because the increased competition among the numerous radio and television stations ensures access for all points of view. Indeed, critics of the rule note

that electronic media are far more competitive than newspapers. Very few cities in the United States are served by more than one newspaper, but most citizens have several choices among stations, especially since the introduction of cable television. Although the Reagan administration supported this argument for deregulation, Congress has not significantly altered the equal-time rule.

What Is News?

Prominently displayed on the front page of the *New York Times* is the company motto: "All the News That's Fit to Print." Admirable as this sentiment may be, it is not, nor can it be, true. Indeed, a more accurate rephrasing of the motto

Covering the Crime

A horrifying crime and a famous defendant provides an event sure to attract media attention. Although the civil trial against O. J. Simpson was not televised live, it, like the criminal trial, received considerable media attention. Here the Goldman family, is pictured leaving the courtroom during the civil action they brought against Simpson.

might be "all the news that fits." The view that the news is simply what happens is unrealistic. No form of mass media can carry every newsworthy event; all are constrained by costs and availability of space and time. For instance, the average daily newspaper fills approximately 62 percent of its space with advertising, leaving a mere 38 percent (called the news hole) for news accounts, along with human interest stories and pure entertainment features.

Network television news is even more limited. Each half-hour program contains only 22 minutes of news and human interest stories. The news is not simply out there; it must be picked from a multitude of events, only a few of which will ever be covered. What then is news? Perhaps the best explanation is that "news is what reporters, editors, and producers decide is news."[10]

Although the basis of news judgment often seems vague and unarticulated, it is possible to identify criteria most often used in selecting stories.[11]

- Newsworthy stories must be *timely and novel*. They must be what reporters call breaking stories, which display the unusual. The routine is considered unworthy of coverage even though it may have a significant impact on people's lives. As a former editor of the *New York Sun* put it, "When a dog bites a man, that is not news, because it happens so often. But if a man bites a dog, that is news."

- Newsworthiness is heightened by *the presence of violence, conflict, disaster, or scandal.* Violent crime, for example, was a staple of the penny press and continues to dominate contemporary news. Even nonviolent conflict makes news. Larry Speakes, deputy press secretary during the Reagan administration, once noted that no one pays attention when one hundred members of Congress come out of a White House meeting and say that the president's program is great. "But if one says it stinks, that's news."

- *Familiarity* is also an important element of newsworthiness. Events are more likely to be covered if they involve individuals whom the public already knows. Approximately 85 percent of the domestic news stories covered by television and news magazines involve well-known people—mostly those holding official positions.[12] Unknown people are most newsworthy as victims of crime or natural disasters.

To the above list might be added the availability of individuals for interviews. Reporters rely almost exclusively on interviewing and only occasionally on reading documents. The dependence on the interview results partly from the need to personalize the news. Interviews with adversaries also increase the sense of conflict, adding a dramatic element to the narrative while preserving the reporter's image of objectivity by presenting the story in the familiar point-counterpoint format. Whatever the cause, the result is a bias in favor of those willing and able to provide the pithy comment.

These criteria mainly stress ways of keeping the audience interested. Because media outlets make their profit from selling their audience to advertisers, they must keep their ratings or circulations high. Indeed, cynics often claim that news is "that which is printed on the back of advertisements."[13] As you will see, this concern for audience appeal has an impact on the way politics is conducted in the United States.

The Effects of the Mass Media

For many citizens, concern about media manipulation stems from a belief that the media have an extraordinary effect on public opinion. Critics of television have been particularly prone to imagine it as dictating the attitudes of a largely passive audience. Indeed, the argument goes, if the media were not influential, why would companies spend so much money on advertisements? Social scientists who have examined the issue are far less certain of the media's impact. In fact, contrary to the myth, most research suggests that the media by and large fail to change people's settled political beliefs. More precisely, individuals who already hold beliefs on particular issues or candidates are unlikely to change in the face of contrary evidence presented by the media.

The media's power to change established political beliefs is limited because people exercise selective exposure, absorbing only information that agrees with their existing beliefs.[14] Such information is more easily incorporated than data that contradict preconceived ideas; those data may be dismissed or entirely ignored. Existing beliefs also influence the way people interpret what they see— a process known as selective perception. Thus a candidate's actions may demonstrate complete integrity to supporters, while showing complete dishonesty to opponents.[15]

Nevertheless, the media do sway individual beliefs. In matters where a person has neither experience nor a firmly held opinion, the information and interpretation supplied by the media may shape that person's political attitude. Lacking knowledge on a particular subject, citizens often adopt the views expressed by media commentators.[16] More importantly, television news is a particularly significant force in shaping the public's attribution of responsibility. Whom the public blames when things go wrong is influenced by the way television frames (presents) the issues. For instance, televised coverage of political issues is either predominately episodic or thematic. Episodic coverage of an issue, exemplified by live on-the-scene reporting that focuses on the individual (e.g., a homeless person or the victims of terrorism), encourages the public to attribute responsibility to the private individuals involved. Thematic reporting, on the other hand, puts the issue in a larger, more abstract context. Unlike the live on-the-scene reporting characteristic of episodic reports, the thematic story provides in-depth background on the issue. Stories framed in the thematic style lead the public to attribute responsibility to societal forces or the motives and actions of public officials. Thus perceptions about whether public officials should be

MYTHS IN POPULAR CULTURE

9.1 Is It Real or Is It Tape?

A few days after the 1992 riots in Los Angeles the then vice president, Dan Quayle, delivered an address in which he blamed the riots on what he called the "poverty of values" in American society. Warming to the subject, the vice president punctuated his support of "family values" and his attack on what he called the "cultural elite" by alluding to a popular television sitcom. "It doesn't help matters," he declared, "when prime-time TV has Murphy Brown—a character who supposedly epitomizes today's intelligent, highly paid, professional woman—mocking the importance of fathers by bearing a child alone and calling it just another lifestyle choice."

Because the vice president had sounded these themes many times, the substance of the speech was not by journalistic standards particularly newsworthy. The reference to Murphy Brown, however, generated a frenzy of news coverage. By using the *Murphy Brown* show as an example, the vice president attempted to link Hollywood (one of the sources of what he called the "cultural elite") to a decline in traditional values. Moreover, because the Murphy Brown character is a reporter, the vice president was also generally viewed as assailing real reporters, another element he frequently identified as a part of the "cultural elite."

Whatever his intentions, the vice president's attack on a fictional character in a sitcom known for its frequent allusions to real people set off a bizarre chain of events in which reality and fiction became blurred. Shortly after the vice president's speech, the producers of *Murphy Brown* responded by dedicating the show's Emmy award to all single parents and intoning to them, "Don't let anybody tell you you're not a family." But the Emmy award was only the first shot.

As the new television season approached, rumors that the fictional character would reply to the vice president abounded. The only unknown was how Murphy would respond. Attempting to deflect the coming attack, the vice president, on the morning before the broadcast, sent a stuffed elephant to Murphy Brown's fictional baby. Accompanying the elephant was a handwritten note in which the vice president promised that he and President Bush would work to assure prosperity for all children. The show's producers publicly thanked the vice president but announced that they were sending the gift to a real child.

When the long-awaited show finally aired, it began with Murphy trying to quiet her crying baby while watching Quayle attack her. "I'm glamorizing single motherhood?" she screams at the televised image of the vice president. "What planet is he on?" Thus the vice president was reduced to a fictional character embedded in video. Meanwhile, Murphy's newsroom colleagues are seen reading copies of the *New York Daily News* (a real newspaper) with its prominent headline, "DAN QUAYLE TO MURPHY BROWN: YOU TRAMP." (Blurring the distinction between fact and fiction even more, the following day's *New York Daily News* ran a photograph of the cast holding up the newspaper headline.) Finally, the show closed with Murphy Brown on the set of "FYI" (the show within the show) delivering a strong rebuke to the vice president and urging him to recognize that "families come in all shapes and sizes."

Quayle tried to deflect the criticism by inviting the press to watch him watching the show. Surrounded by a multicultural mix of single mothers, Quayle demonstrated good humor as the episode unfolded, but it was to little avail. The vice president had become a fictional character. The distinction between reality and fiction erased, the vice president resembled the private investigator in *Who Framed Roger Rabbit?*—a real person defined by a fictional world.

held responsible for problems are influenced not only by what television reports but also by how the issue is covered.[17]

Setting the Agenda

Increasingly, the media also influence the political agenda and the conduct of politicians. When deciding what to cover, journalists focus on some aspects of public life and ignore others. Because the media's choices often constitute the public's only source of knowledge, what journalists do not report as news may as well not happen. As Austin Ranney suggests, the appropriate riddle for the media age may well be this: "If a tree falls in a forest but the event is not video-taped or broadcast on the nightly news, has it really happened?"[18]

When the public knows events and issues well, the press has less impact on its attitudes. For example, in a study conducted in 1981 and 1982, individuals exposed to stories alleging that the nation's defenses were weak grew more concerned about national defense. Stories about inflation, however, had little effect on their opinions, undoubtedly because inflation affects everyone personally.[19] Thus the media wield the most influence in shaping the public agenda when the events and issues are either outside an individual's experience or new to the society.

Of particular importance is the effect that agenda setting by the media has on the public's evaluation of candidates and public officials. Studies examining the effect of media have identified a process called **priming,** which "refers to the capacity of the media to isolate particular issues, events, or themes in the news as the criteria for evaluating politicians."[20] The more attention given by the media to an issue, the greater its weight in the formation of public evaluations of candidates and public officials. By highlighting some issues and ignoring others the media influence the standards by which people judge governments, public officials, and candidates.

Conducting Politics in the Media

Politicians are much more attuned to the media than is the public. The conduct of politics is changing in the United States as candidates and public officials increasingly tailor their activities to meet journalists' needs. Thus they plan and time speeches, rallies, and personal appearances to win maximum media coverage, especially on television. To further facilitate coverage, campaign staffers supply the media with daily schedules, advance copies of speeches, and access to telephones and fax machines. If managed well, the campaign exploits the reporters' need for a story and influences the content of news coverage.

All these efforts are in vain, however, if the campaign cannot get reporters to cover the candidate. To attract reporters, campaigns routinely create **pseudo-events**—staged events, intended to produce media coverage. Pseudo-events are often staged with the special needs of television in mind. Knowing that television

To get their message across, political candidates stage events with strong visual appeal. Here Governor Christine Todd Whitman of New Jersey visits a neonatal unit of a hospital to show her concern with children's health issues.

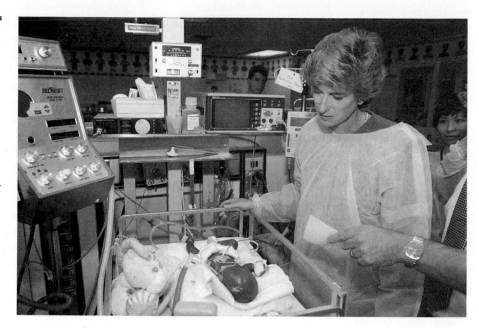

producers dislike "talking heads" (scenes of the candidate simply delivering a speech), campaign organizers work to provide interesting and symbolic visuals for the evening news. Whether candidates visit farms to indicate their concern for the family farmer or retirement centers to emphasize their commitment to aging Americans, the picture is the thing.

Of the many pseudo-events in American politics, few rival the national party nominating conventions. Obviously, a convention in which the outcome is questionable contains enough drama to attract widespread attention. Since 1952, however, the parties have nominated their presidential candidates on the first ballot. To compensate for the lack of suspense, the parties carefully stage their conventions, hoping to retain media attention. As Ken Reitz, manager of the 1980 Republican National Convention, said, "The whole idea is to make the event into a TV production instead of a convention. The most important thing we can get out of our convention is TV coverage."[21]

Despite the parties' efforts to cater to television, the major television networks are becoming increasingly reluctant to broadcast even an hour a night of party activities. Complaining that there was no news to report, Ted Koppel and his *Nightline* crew left the Republican convention of 1996 before it ended. Even more symptomatic of the networks' views was NBC's decision to forgo the acceptance speech of the Republican vice-presidential nominee, Jack Kemp. Instead, the network aired a *Seinfeld* rerun. Faced with a declining audience (only 12 percent of the nation's homes tuned in to the 1996 conventions) and what they see as a lack of news, the major networks are threatening to end live coverage of the conventions.

Even with all the planning, candidates have become increasingly frustrated with media coverage. Although the coverage is extensive, candidates are given little direct access to the public by the established media. As political scientist Thomas Patterson has pointed out, the candidates have become voiceless: "for every minute that the candidates spoke on the evening news in 1988 and 1992, the journalists who were covering them talked 6 minutes." Between Labor Day and Election Day in 1992, George Bush and Bill Clinton were heard on the evening news a total of 20 minutes each; Ross Perot was heard a total of 8 minutes.[22] Most of that time comprised ten seconds or less, known as sound bites.

In order to reach the public directly, political candidates have adopted a variety of techniques designed to bypass the established media. One such technique, the video news release (VNR), is a newslike report or interview paid for by the candidate and delivered to local television stations. By renting time on a satellite transponder, for instance, a candidate can be interviewed by local television reporters all over the country without leaving a studio. The local stations get the chance, at no cost, to interview a national political figure, and the candidate covers several cities quickly. The campaign also benefits because local anchors, who are seldom as hard on candidates as the national reporters covering the campaign, are more likely to let the candidate talk directly to the audience.

Besides making extensive use of VNRs, the presidential candidates are turning to what have been called "the new media": radio call-in shows; early morning television programs; televised town meetings; and late-night entertainment productions. Ross Perot, for instance, announced both his entry and re-entry into the 1992 race on *Larry King Live.* Clinton became a master at this new media, appearing not only on *Larry King Live,* but also on MTV, *Donahue, 20/20,* and numerous call-in radio programs. At one point in the 1992 campaign, Clinton, wearing dark "Blues Brothers"–style sunglasses, played the saxophone on the *Arsenio Hall Show.* Although initially reluctant to use these new forms of communication, George Bush eventually joined in; he even granted an interview to Tabitha Soren of MTV.

For the candidates, these new media offered irresistible opportunities to circumvent the press and speak directly to the American people. President Clinton described the advantages of the new media best in March 1993 when he told a group of radio and television correspondents, "You know why I can stiff you on press conferences? Because Larry King liberated me by giving me to the American people directly."[23]

Besides affecting the candidates' conduct, media-oriented politics also diverts attention from issues and toward campaign strategies. Because journalists define news as involving conflict and the unexpected, they pay special heed to the "horse-race" characteristics of elections. Media attention focuses on who is winning and why. When issues are discussed, the question is how the candidate's position will help or hurt the campaign. For reporters, elections are simply games in which candidates devise tactics to defeat their opponents. Foremost among the tools for reporting campaign strategy is the public opinion poll. Even though polls are of little value to voters other than those making book, the

**CLOSER
TO HOME**

9.1   If It Bleeds, It Leads

With their extravagantly paid anchors, armies of celebrated reporters, and sizable bureaus around the world, network news broadcasts are the embodiment of television journalism. Despite a declining audience for news programming, especially among the young, the major networks still draw millions of viewers each evening. Often overlooked, however, are the more than eleven hundred local commercial television stations around the nation. Less celebrated for their journalistic endeavors, the local stations nevertheless draw an even larger share of the audience for news than their national counterparts. Far from being a journalistic backwater, local newscasting is a highly competitive industry, producing abundant profits for station owners. Indeed, at some stations revenues from local news bring profit margins as high as 50 percent.

Not surprisingly, given their profitability, local stations continue to extend their news programming. Since the early 1960s the major networks' nightly news broadcasts have been limited to one 30-minute program each evening. (Network executives have tried several times to expand to a 60-minute program, but their affiliate stations have always blocked these efforts.) Local stations, on the other hand, keep increasing the time devoted to newscasts. For several years local newscasts were 30-minute programs, designed to lead into prime time entertainment shows. Now 60- and even 90-minute news programs preceding prime time are common, and usually the stations also offer 30 minutes of late evening news. One Los Angeles station provides three hours of news programming, from 8:00 P.M. to 11:00 P.M. five nights a week.

Many local stations have also begun to compete directly with the national broadcasters by independently reporting on national and international affairs. Stations in larger markets have developed their own bureaus in Washington and elsewhere; those in smaller cities often supplement their resources with video wire services such as CONUS (standing for continental United States), which can, at little cost, provide live coverage of national issues specifically tailored to a subscribing station.

Of course, matters close to home are the bread and butter for the local stations. Most of their newscasts consist of weather forecasts, sports news, entertainment features, and human interest stories—all interspersed with cheerful banter among the reporters and with promotions for upcoming stories. Consequently, very little time is left for public affairs programming. Moreover, as media critics point out, when public affairs issues are covered, they mostly have to do with crime, accidents, and fires—stories that often provide good visuals and feature ordinary people as helpless victims. These stories of individuals as victims are given less airtime than the weather and sports, but they tend to cluster in the first third of the newscast. Crimes, accidents, and fires are so likely to start off the program that some wags claim that in local broadcasting "If it bleeds, it leads."

Sources: Stephen Ansolabehere, Roy Behr, and Shanto Iyengar, *The Media Game: American Politics in the Television Age* (New York: Macmillan, 1993); and Gerald Stone and Dwight Jensen, "Local TV News and the Good Bad Dyad," *Journalism Quarterly,* 64 (Spring, 1987), 37–44.

media saturate their audience with frequent and often hyped results. The public opinion poll is the press's version of the pseudo-event; the press creates and pays for polls and then covers them as news.[24]

Illustrative of the horse-race coverage is the 1988 presidential election. According to Marjorie Hershey, from September to election day 1988, almost two-thirds of the campaign coverage in the print media dealt with campaign strategy. Indeed, more than in any previous election, the campaign managers, media consultants, and image makers became the story as they provided details of their strategy to reporters ever eager for information on the craft of election management.[25] A great deal of the election coverage then was about how the campaign was being covered.

Of course journalists defend this preoccupation with strategy by arguing that the audience prefers to hear about the campaign rather than about the issues. Whether they are correct or not, it is also apparent that campaign strategies appeal to reporters, editors, and producers for several reasons. Horse-race stories are easier to do than more substantial reports because reporting on campaign tactics requires little knowledge of complex political issues. Indeed, horse-race stories can easily be reduced to the simple question of winners and losers. More importantly, reporting on strategy and mechanics provides the kind of dramatic themes that keep an audience interested.

Although there is no unanimity on the effects of horse-race coverage, many observers believe that the emphasis on elections as games has a detrimental effect on public opinion. By highlighting tactics and strategies—described earlier as priming—the media present a consistent image of candidates as political opportunists interested solely in winning elections. The constant repetition of that vision, according to many observers, simply increases the public's mistrust of candidates.

The Uneasy Alliance Between Government and the Media

Government officials and journalists are often portrayed as adversaries locked in combat, each trying to best the other. This is an accurate picture when their goals conflict—when, for instance, journalists, wanting the big scoop on governmental waste, fraud, or incompetence that will bring them instant fame, confront government officials, who want the press to present their actions in the most favorable light possible. At other times journalists' and officials' goals overlap, and the two groups cooperate. Journalists court officials to obtain the information that is their livelihood, and government officials woo the media in order to build public support for their policies. As veteran newscaster Walter Cronkite once remarked, "Politics and media are inseparable. It is only the politicians and the media that are incompatible."[26]

Government officials, more than the general public, are consumers of journalism, and this fact creates additional incentives for cooperation. The mass media provide an important communications link among officials, informing them of what others in and out of government are doing and saying. When, for instance, King Hussein of Jordan wanted to respond to American criticism that he was favoring Iraq in the Gulf War, he bypassed normal diplomatic channels and responded to President Bush by appearing on CNN.

Given this mutual dependence, the media and government form an uneasy alliance. Journalists report the actions of government officials, particularly the president and to a slightly lesser degree members of Congress, while government officials attempt to shape the content of news.

Covering the President

Nowhere is the uneasy alliance between the media and government more apparent than in the coverage of the White House. Almost everything the president does becomes news. Even trivial events, such as the wanderings of Socks, the Clintons' cat, receive wide coverage. For presidents, this extensive coverage represents a valuable means of reaching the American public on a daily basis, but it also constitutes a source of frustration. Moreover, the frustration undoubtedly

Covering the President

Presidential activities, even recreational activities, receive media attention. Here President Clinton is photographed while playing a round of golf on a state visit to Australia.

increases throughout a president's term. As political scientist Fred Smoller has demonstrated, television portrayal of presidents becomes more negative as their terms progress.[27] John Kennedy undoubtedly spoke for all presidents when, in response to a question concerning some particularly critical accounts of his administration, he claimed to be "reading more and enjoying it less."[28]

Because the media provide the vital link between the president and the public, and because from the president's perspective journalists cannot be counted on to get their stories right, the White House goes to great lengths to put its view across to the media. Indeed, about one-third of the high-level White House staff are directly involved in media relations.[29]

Most of the responsibility for dealing with the media falls to the president's press secretary, who gives the daily briefing to some seventy-five reporters and photographers who regularly cover the White House. Under constant pressure from editors to file stories on the president, these reporters rely extensively on the briefings and press releases provided by the press secretary. On occasion, the press secretary may also arrange interviews with the president or provide photographers with photo opportunities—a chance to take photographs of the president but not to ask questions. Most White House reporters simply repeat the information given them by the press secretary. According to Bill Moyers, who was press secretary during Lyndon Johnson's administration, the White House press corps "is more stenographic than entrepreneurial in its approach to news gathering."[30] As a result, presidents are less subjects of news coverage than they are sources of news.

Press Conferences.   Presidents communicate with the public through the press conference. Although press conferences often seem spontaneous, they are in fact highly structured events that allow presidents a great deal of control. Typically, these 30-minute affairs begin with a short statement. This enables the president to speak directly to the public; it also reduces the time available for questioning and focuses the audience's attention on a subject of the president's choosing.

Careful preparation and rehearsal further strengthen presidential control of press conferences. Days, even weeks, before a press conference, the president's staff prepares a list of questions most likely to be asked and then provides written answers so that the president can study and rehearse them. Ronald Reagan, for instance, held mock news conferences. Furthermore, presidents can and do frequently call on reporters known to be friendly to their administration. Such reporters are far more likely than others to ask easy questions or even ask questions furnished (planted) by the White House. At Reagan press conferences, reporters thought to be sympathetic to the administration, called the "known friendlies," were seated in front and to the president's right. If a line of questioning became uncomfortable, Reagan needed only to "go to the right."[31]

Though press conferences can be a valuable tool, they still pose risks. Even with a high level of control over what questions are asked and by whom, presidents cannot avoid embarrassing or politically charged queries. Few presidents are satisfied with press conferences as an institution, and most take part in them with some misgivings. Indeed, during its first year in office, the Clinton administration sought to avoid the traditional press conference by combining new technologies and the new media, which proved so useful in the election. For instance, the White House quickly implemented methods of making the full text of speeches and presidential proposals available electronically (through the Internet) to circumvent the filtering influence of press summaries. The administration also makes frequent use of satellite press conferences with local journalists across the country and satellite media tours during which top administration officials give 5-minute interviews to local reporters.

WWW•

For more information on news sources, see the **Gitelson/Dudley/Dubnick web site.**

Leaks to the Press.   The frequent appearance of stories based on information provided by unnamed sources further strains relations between presidents and the media. Such leaked stories have angered many presidents. President Reagan, for instance, dealt publicly with the problem by opening a news conference in January 1982 with these words: "I was going to have an opening statement, but I decided that what I was going to say I wanted to get a lot of attention so I'm going to wait and leak it."[32] A year later an angrier Reagan declared, "I've had it up to my keister with these leaks."[33]

Presidents typically react in this fashion when leaks divulge information they would prefer the public not to know. Yet they applaud others. In fact, it is not unusual for the president or someone acting on his instructions to be the source of many leaks. During a 1992 press conference President Bush reproached the press for relying on anonymous sources and appealed to the American people to "please ask for a name to be placed next to the source so that I can get mad at the guy who's doing this." The next morning, Marlin Fitzwater, the White House press secretary, announced that Assistant Secretary of State Edward P. Djerejian would be available to brief the press on the president's meeting with King Hussein of Jordan. Fitzwater specified, however, that Djerejian was to be identified only as a senior administration official. When reporters pointed to Bush's statement of the previous day, the briefing was canceled.

Often presidents plant stories with reporters as trial balloons. A story is leaked about a proposal under consideration. If the public or Congress reacts negatively, the president can disclaim the story and drop the proposal. Thus leaks can be quite useful. Of course, because the president has no monopoly on leaks, they may also be a source of embarrassment and frustration.

Covering Congress

The press and the media do not seem to pay as much attention to Congress as to the executive branch. To some extent, this apparent imbalance is due to the nature of the institution itself. Unlike the presidency, Congress has no single leader who can be expected to speak authoritatively, although its members are generally more willing to talk and far less secretive than officials of the executive branch. Reporters cope with the multiple voices of Congress by concentrating their attention on party leaders, committee chairs, and others who hold key leadership positions or are clearly identified as experts on a particular issue. As a result, many senators and representatives receive little or no national media attention. To political scientist Stephen Hess, such focus suggests that "Where You Sit Determines How Often You Will Be Photographed."[34]

Another reason for the apparent difference in coverage is that the media have difficulty reaching Congress. The House of Representatives did not permit radio and television coverage even of its committee hearings until the 1974 impeachment hearings of Richard Nixon. In 1979, the House finally allowed live coverage of floor action, though with restrictions. For example, cameras must focus solely on the representative who is speaking. The Senate has allowed some committee hearings to be broadcast since the 1950s, but not until 1986 was floor action open to television coverage.

Despite these constraints, the media do not ignore Congress. In fact, individual members of Congress may receive extensive coverage by their home-state media, which often depend heavily on the local senators and representatives to provide a regional perspective on national issues. Many members even become regular contributors to the local media, writing news columns and producing broadcast-quality radio and television tapes for distribution within their constituency.

Covering the Courts

The branch of government least covered by the media is the courts. Although specific decisions of the U.S. Supreme Court may receive substantial media attention, most go unreported. When decisions are reported, the discussion is often superficial, concentrating on who won and who lost.

The complex nature of the decisions and the specialized knowledge necessary to interpret them make judicial opinions particularly subject to misinterpretation by journalists, and justices often complain about such misinterpretation. Nevertheless, justices also remain indifferent to the needs of journalists. For instance, they do not hold press conferences or grant interviews to explain their decisions. Reporters are expected to read the decisions and draw their own conclusions. Most justices accept former Justice William Brennan's observation that their opinions "must stand on their own merits without embellishment or comment from the judges who write or join them."[35]

Conclusion: The Great Manipulator?

We began this chapter by noting the general belief that the mass media have dramatically altered the conduct of American politics. But the increasingly sophisticated technology that made possible inexpensive newspapers and then the transmission of voice and images over the airwaves also changed the media. Slowly, newspapers began to emphasize objective reporting of public events. Similarly, radio and television turned into important sources of news, but only when it became apparent that there was an audience for such programming.

Along with the development of the mass media has come the fear, expressed as the myth of the manipulative media, that Americans are in danger of being indoctrinated by journalists. The fears expressed as the myth of the manipulative media exaggerate the power of the mass media to alter established political opinions. Citizens are not so susceptible to being told what to think as the myth suggests; they are not uncritical receptors of the media product. Nevertheless, the media do play an important role in framing the issues and setting the political agenda. Journalism may not change political attitudes, but it does have a significant effect on what people think is important and how they form political judgments. The choices that journalists make in many cases define the political reality.

Furthermore, the mass media have greatly affected the conduct of political campaigns and government business. The media do not simply hold up a mirror to these processes; the reporters and cameras are not invisible observers. On the contrary, media coverage introduces distortions. But again there is little evidence that the distortions are journalistic attempts to manipulate the news. In fact, journalists often feel that they are being manipulated when political candidates and public officials attempt to use them to get their stories across to the public.

Summary

1. Early American newspapers were either organs of the political parties or commercial papers that reported business news to merchants. True mass media did not come into being until the 1830s, with the rise of the sensationalist penny press.

2. The American mass media consist of thousands of alternative outlets. Nevertheless, critics worry that the increasingly concentrated ownership of media outlets threatens the diversity of information.

3. Television and radio are subjected to government regulation by the Federal Communications Commission (FCC), which has been reluctant to control the content of broadcasts.

4. Journalists do not just find news; they apply identifiable criteria for selecting stories. The criteria include high impact, conflict, familiarity, proximity, timeliness, and novelty.

5. The power of the media to change public opinion is limited because many people accept only the information that confirms their previous beliefs. The less familiar the issue, the more likely it is that the media will have an impact on people's attitudes.

6. American political candidates orient their campaigns to ensure media exposure. Candidates often create pseudo-events solely for the purpose of attracting media attention. Journalists, in turn, are more likely to cover the horse-race elements of political campaigns than the policy issues.

7. Government officials use the media to build public support for their programs, but reporters are often viewed as adversaries that must be controlled.

8. The president is the prime focus of media coverage. Presidential administrations expend a great deal of time and effort in dealing with the media.

9. Congress is a more difficult institution for the national media to cover, but members of Congress receive a great deal of local media coverage. The Supreme Court is the least covered institution of American government, in part because the justices are not particularly attentive to the needs of journalists.

Key Terms and Concepts

Penny press The term for the first generation of newspapers with mass popular appeal. The name comes from the *New York Sun,* which was sold for a penny a copy in the mid-1800s.

Yellow journalism A type of journalism that originated in the late nineteenth century and whose popularity was based on sensationalized stories of scandal and corruption.

Equal-time rule A Federal Communications Commission rule that requires a broadcaster who permits one candidate to campaign on the station to provide equal time at identical rates to all other candidates for the same office.

Priming The capacity of the media to isolate particular issues, events, or themes in the news as the criteria for evaluating politicians.

Pseudo-events Events, such as speeches, rallies, and personal appearances, that are staged by politicians simply to win maximum media coverage.

CHAPTER 10

Congress

Is Congress ineffective and buried under partisan bickering?

See **Political Science** at
http://www.hmco.com/college

Bleary-eyed from the round of inaugural functions the night before, members of the House of Representatives filed onto the House floor on January 21, 1997, to begin a grueling and at times highly acerbic partisan debate. Ninety minutes later, with the debate concluded, the House voted to reprimand Speaker Newt Gingrich and fine him $300,000 for engaging in financial practices that brought discredit on the House and for giving the House ethics committee false information.

It was the first time in its 208 years that the House had voted to sanction its speaker. Thus the event took on historic proportions. The vote was all the more remarkable because only two years earlier Gingrich had led the Republicans to majority party status in the House, after their forty years as a minority. His fellow Republicans had hailed his election to the speakership in 1995 with chants of "Newt! Newt! Newt!" "It's a whole Newt world." Moreover, his 1995 acceptance speech had stressed the need to restore public faith in Congress.

Whatever one might think of Speaker Gingrich's activities, the reprimand did little to restore public confidence in Congress. To many people the whole episode looked like so much partisan wrangling; to others it simply confirmed their view of Congress as a body of self-serving individuals in pursuit of power instead of the public interest. Rather than restore public confidence, the incident fueled dissatisfaction with Congress. But that dissatisfaction goes deeper than a simple unhappiness over the most recent scandals.

A Bad Day for the Speaker

Only two years after ascending to the speakership, Representative Newt Gingrich was reprimanded and fined $300,000 for giving the House ethics committee false statements.

Many Americans see Congress as an inefficient, ineffective, and excessive institution. Television commentator David Brinkley, discussing the possibility of congressional passage of an important measure in a month, summarized the electorate's frequent disgust with Congress when he observed, "It is widely believed in Washington that it would take Congress thirty days to make instant coffee work."[1] The image of Congress paralyzed by its own internal bickering and lack of effective leadership pervades almost all discussion of the institution. Consequently, public opinion polls routinely find that the American public lacks confidence in the Congress. It is rare to find a poll that reports even half the people approving of the way Congress is doing its job.

Consequently, a rather widely held *myth of Congress as the broken branch,* an institution incapable of effective action, is hardly surprising. That image of Congress seems easy to support by listing the pressing national problems that remain unsolved. The huge national debt, homelessness, the collapse of savings and loan institutions, and the countless other problems plaguing society at any given time could be solved, so the myth assumes, if only Congress were more effective. Putting aside the possibility that, in the short run at least, the problems may be insolvable, the myth does an injustice to the complex nature of Congress as an institution.

As you will see, the myth rests on the perception of Congress as solely a policymaking body, but that view ignores the full range of congressional responsibilities and their often contradictory nature. For instance, it is important to note at the outset that Congress is a representative institution as well as a policymaking one. Congress does not just make laws for the nation; its members are also expected to represent the interests of the states and the districts they serve. Congress must find ways to reconcile these different interests to produce national policy. Moreover, Congress was designed as a deliberative body that would act to change the status quo only if a broad consensus favored change. Efficiency was never the goal. A look at how Congress is organized should help illustrate these points.

Who Serves in Congress and the Paths That Lead There

Article I of the Constitution specifies only three criteria for membership in the U.S. Congress. Before taking office, senators must have reached the age of thirty, must have been citizens of the United States for at least nine years, and must reside in the states from which they are elected. Representatives may enter office at the age of twenty-five and after only seven years of citizenship. Members of the House must also reside in the states from which they are chosen, but the Constitution does not require residence in the districts they represent.

Who Serves in Congress?

www•

For more information on the make-up of Congress, see the **Gitelson/Dudley/Dubnick** web site.

Despite these rather minimal requirements, a group portrait of Congress reveals an institution composed of individuals drawn from the upper levels of American society. The typical member is a middle-aged, highly educated white male previously employed in a high-status occupation that has earned him an income well above the national average.

Education and Occupation.   As befits an elite, virtually all members of Congress hold a college degree, and a majority have completed some form of graduate work. Senators and representatives come from several different occupations, but lawyers outnumber all other professions. When the 105th Congress convened in 1997, 41 percent of the members were lawyers. Although that percentage is lower than it was in the 1970s, it nevertheless demonstrates that the legal profession is still a steppingstone to Congress. Next to law, business and banking are the most common occupations of legislators. Members of such occupational groups as manufacturing workers, farm laborers, and domestic servants are rarely found in Congress.

Race and Sex.   In the period immediately after the Civil War, more than twenty blacks (all of them Republicans) served in Congress. By the late nineteenth century, restrictions on the voting rights of blacks had eliminated their congressional representation entirely. No black Americans served in Congress from 1900 until 1928, when Oscar DePriest, a Republican from Chicago, was elected to the House of Representatives. During the next twenty-five years only three more blacks entered Congress.

In the 1970s the number of black legislators increased significantly, and in 1997 thirty-eight blacks served in Congress (all but one of them Democrats), including one African-American in the Senate. Despite recent gains, blacks, who constitute about 11 percent of the population, are still underrepresented in Congress.

Faring slightly better by comparison is the Hispanic community, which had eighteen representatives—almost 4 percent of the seats in the House—in 1997. Though this is a fourfold increase since 1980, when the House contained only four Hispanics, it still underrepresents what amounts to 5 percent of the population. The 1992 elections produced the first Native American senator in sixty years.

The first woman to serve in Congress, Representative Jeannette Rankin, a Montana Republican, was elected in 1916, four years before the Nineteenth Amendment guaranteed women the right to vote. Although defeated in 1918 when she sought the Republican nomination for a Senate seat, she returned to Congress for one term in 1940. Since Rankin's election, slightly more than a hundred women have served in Congress.

During the 1970s and 1980s, women made incremental gains in winning seats in Congress. Between 1980 and 1991, for instance, women gained only

A Growing Number

Although women still constitute a small portion of the House of Representatives their numbers are growing. Pictured (on the right) is Representative Carolyn McCarthy (D–New York). Elected in 1996, Representative McCarthy, whose husband was killed by a gunman, indiscriminately firing an automatic rifle on a commuter train, campaigned as a passionate advocate of gun control.

seven congressional seats. But in 1992, which many dubbed the "Year of the Woman," women won a record-breaking forty-seven House seats. Since then the pace has slowed again, but women continue to make some gains. When the 105th Congress convened in January 1997, fifty-one women took their seats in the House and nine women were serving in the Senate.

Getting Elected

Despite the myth of Congress as the broken branch, the American public demonstrates considerable faith in individual members by consistently re-electing incumbents—proving, as Albert Cover put it, that "one good term deserves another."[2] Since 1946 more than 90 percent of the House incumbents who sought re-election won, while slightly over 80 percent of the incumbent senators seeking re-election were victorious.

Remarkably, incumbents did well even in 1994. The 1994 election marked a historic change in Congress as the Republicans gained fifty-three seats and took control of the House for the first time in forty years. Several highly prominent members of the House were defeated, including Thomas S. Foley, the Speaker of the House in the 103rd Congress. (Foley became the first Speaker defeated in a re-election bid since 1860). But the election was not simply the product of anti-incumbent fever. House members who sought re-election generally did well. Overall, slightly more than 90 percent who sought re-election won. Of course, the losses were not distributed equally between the parties. Not one Republican was defeated, whereas thirty-five incumbent Democratic representatives and two Democratic senators lost their seats. Yet even in that seemingly bad year for Democratic incumbents, 84 percent of them were returned to Congress.

The 1996 election trimmed some of the 1994 Republican gains in the House. Over a dozen first-term Republicans were defeated, cutting the size of the Republican majority in the House. (In the Senate, the Republicans gained two seats.) Nevertheless, overall the incumbent re-election rate exceeded the post–World War II average. Despite the incumbents' success in keeping their seats, Congress has experienced substantial turnover. More than half of the House members and 40 percent of those in the Senate have arrived since 1992. High re-election rates notwithstanding, many members decide against seeking re-election. Some retire because of age, others weary of the workload, and still others believe they cannot win re-election.

Just why incumbents do so well is the subject of much speculation. One frequent explanation is that House incumbents are "safe by design"—that is, they run in districts that have been drawn to maximize their voter strength. The process of designing districts does, in fact, have a major impact on political power within Congress. Every ten years, in response to the census, House districts are redrawn by state legislatures and House seats are redistributed among the states. The Supreme Court has held that in drawing the new boundaries state legislatures must create districts approximately equal in population.[3] Furthermore, the districts may not be designed to dilute minority voting strength.[4] On the other hand, so-called majority-minority districts, districts that create political majorities for racial or ethnic minorities, are, the Supreme Court ruled in *Miller v. Johnson* (1995), unconstitutional if race was the "predominant factor" in drawing the boundaries. Thus if districts are designed with the intent of giving an advantage to a racial or ethnic group, they are likely to be unconstitutional. Nevertheless, legislatures have considerable freedom to engage in the practice of **gerrymandering**—the drawing of district boundaries in ways that gain political advantage.

The party controlling state government generally attempts to draw boundaries that maximize the number of seats it can win. It tries to concentrate opponents in the fewest possible districts and to create majorities of supporters in as many districts as possible. In 1981, for instance, Indiana Republicans, who controlled the state legislature and the governor's office, produced a reapportionment plan that placed three Democratic incumbents in the same district and required all five Democratic incumbents to move their residences.[5]

Clearly, some incumbents benefit from these practices, but gerrymandering alone cannot explain the success of incumbents. Incumbents have been receiving larger percentages of the vote even in states that did not redistrict.[6] With or without gerrymandering, they have a variety of resources on which to draw. They find it easy to get their names before the public, and they are almost always better known and viewed more favorably than their challengers. Former Speaker of the House Jim Wright may have been correct when he said that outside their districts, members of the House are individuals of "widespread obscurity," but within their districts they are conspicuous.[7] This visibility is the result of hard work and the skillful use of the resources of office. As one observer noted, "When we say Congressman Smith is unbeatable, we mean Congressman Smith is unbeatable as long as he continues to do the things he is doing."[8]

Members of Congress have a wide array of official resources that can be used to pursue re-election. For example, incumbents can send out mail free of charge. Using this **franking privilege** for newsletters or questionnaires enables them to cultivate a favorable image among constituents. A long-distance WATS line, shared use of a completely equipped television studio, an allowance to maintain district offices, and a travel allowance sufficient to permit weekly visits to the district further help incumbents enhance their name recognition. The dollar value of these services and privileges is conservatively estimated at more than $1 million over a two-year House term.

Sitting members of Congress also have opportunities to engage in "credit claiming"—taking credit for benefits constituents receive from the national government.[9] Whether a representative or senator is announcing an award of federal money for a new dam, a highway extension, or an important defense contract, the effect is to portray him or her as someone working hard for the district and getting results. Legislation appropriating funds for local projects is often referred to as **pork-barrel legislation.** Securing such benefits for the districts is "bringing home the bacon."

Finally, incumbents' success depends on what political scientist Richard Fenno has called their **home style,** or the way incumbents present themselves to their constituents. As Fenno observed, "It is the style, not the issue content, that counts most in the re-election constituency."[10] Although incumbents may differ in how they present themselves, their purpose is the same: to win the voters' trust. This kind of bond does not develop overnight; it takes time and constant attention, but the rewards can be great. An incumbent trusted by the voters is relatively safe from political attack and likely to find constituents sympathetic to occasional political mistakes. In the brief time span of a campaign, challengers find it difficult to establish this kind of relationship.

Although incumbents have a strong advantage, they are not invincible. Challengers can win, but they generally have to spend a great deal of money. Just how much varies from race to race. As we mentioned in Chapter 7, on campaigns and elections, money does not buy elections, but it may buy the name recognition that is essential to competing against a well-known incumbent.[11] Unfortunately for the challengers, incumbents have a decided advantage in raising campaign contributions, particularly those from political action committees.

The electoral advantage enjoyed by incumbents has given rise to a call for term limits. Since 1990, 23 states have passed legislation or amended their constitution to limit the tenure of members of Congress. In 1995, however, the Supreme Court declared such limits unconstitutional. Writing for a sharply divided court in *U.S. Term Limits Inc.* v. *Thorton,* Justice John Paul Stevens argued that the states do not have the constitutional authority to regulate the tenure of federal legislators. Limiting congressional terms requires, the majority argued, a constitutional amendment.

The Work of Congress

Even though the Constitution establishes a government in which three branches share power, the framers were united in the belief that the legislature should play the central role in governing. As a result, Congress is charged with several different kinds of duties.

Making Laws

Article I of the Constitution charges Congress with making binding laws. In addition, Section 8 of Article I lists a series of specific powers, known as the *enumerated powers*—for example, the power to establish post offices and to coin money. Section 8 also gives Congress the power "to make all laws which shall be necessary and proper for carrying into Execution the foregoing Powers, and all other Powers vested by this Constitution in the Government of the United States. . . ." This "necessary and proper" clause has been interpreted by the Supreme Court in such sweeping terms that Congress can legislate in nearly every aspect of American life.[12]

The Power to Tax

Foremost among the duties of Congress is the setting of taxing and spending policies for the nation. According to the Constitution, bills raising revenue (taxes) are to originate in the House, but because the Senate may amend these bills, the distinction is not particularly significant.

Tax policies—always an important issue—took on still greater prominence in 1981 as Congress, at the urging of President Ronald Reagan, passed what was at the time the largest tax cut in U.S. history. But in 1982 concern over the growing national deficit led to changes that constituted the largest peacetime tax increase in U.S. history. Congress followed these measures with the Tax Reform Act of 1986, a bill that completely overhauled the federal income tax system. Hailed by supporters, including Reagan, as promoting a simpler tax system, the bill cut individual tax rates, dramatically reduced the number of income tax brackets, and eliminated many deductions.

Despite or because of the 1986 reforms, tax policy remains a controversial issue in Congress, with an increasing number of leaders calling for the creation

Uncle Sam's Red Ink

Concern over deficit spending by the national government has led to demands for a constitutional amendment requiring a balanced budget. Here members of the Concord Coalition, a citizens' group advocating reduced deficits, dramatically illustrates the growing debt burden that results from yearly deficits.

of a flat tax—one tax rate, with few or no deductions, for everyone regardless of income. With the 1995 accession of Republican majorities in both the House and the Senate, tax policies once again took center stage in Congress. In order to assure Americans that they would not raise taxes, House Republicans passed a resolution requiring a three-fifths majority to pass any bill or amendment increasing income tax rates.

Producing the Budget

Equally controversial are the spending decisions (appropriations) made yearly by Congress and incorporated as the federal budget. Throughout most of the nation's history, Congress had no means of coordinating the federal budget. The budget was simply the total of the separate appropriations made to each department of government. For several years, however, Congress has attempted to centralize the budget process and place restraints on overall spending levels.

With the passage in 1974 of the Budget and Impoundment Control Act, Congress established a new budget committee in each house. These committees receive the president's budget and an analysis provided by the Congressional Budget Office (CBO), which was created to provide Congress with the expertise possessed by the executive branch. The CBO analyzes the president's budget, identifies changes in spending levels, and estimates the expected revenue from taxes and other sources. It also projects the cost of **entitlements,** which are payments to any person or government meeting the requirements specified by law—for example, social security benefits and military pensions. On the basis of that information, the budget committees recommend to their respective houses spending ceilings for major funding categories. These recommendations constitute the **First Concurrent Budget Resolution,** which must be passed by both the House of Representatives and the Senate by April 15.

As various appropriations committees of the two houses formulate the funding bills for specific departments and programs, they are expected to follow the overall spending guidelines set by the budget resolution. If the guidelines are exceeded, the appropriations must be reduced or the House and Senate must agree to amend the amounts in the first budget resolution.[13] This process, known as *reconciliation,* has to be completed by the passage of a second budget resolution in September.

The act created a new sense of coherence in the budgeting process, but it did not reduce the budget deficit. It was simply too easy for Congress to ignore the first budget resolution and pass a second one that merely totaled up the various appropriations bills. In the 1980s, combinations of tax cuts and spending increases brought record deficits. In response, Congress passed, in 1985, the Gramm-Rudman-Hollings law, which set a series of deficit reduction targets that were supposed to produce a balanced budget in 1993. The head of the congressional General Accounting Office, the comptroller general, was empowered to sequester expenditures—withhold funds already appropriated—if Congress and the president had not enacted either spending cuts or tax increases sufficient to meet the year's target. The Supreme Court quickly ruled that the delegation of such power to the comptroller general was unconstitutional, forcing Congress to turn the power over to the Office of Management and Budget, an executive branch agency.

Central to the workings of Gramm-Rudman-Hollings was the assumption that the threat of sequestrations would force Congress to make the tough decisions necessary to reduce the deficit. But in 1990, the sequestrations demanded by the law were so drastic that the process lacked credibility. According to one estimate, the sequestration process demanded by Gramm-Rudman-Hollings would have required "a halving of military forces, the closing of many air traffic control installations, the end of meat inspections for five months, a halt in new cleanups of toxic waste sites, and cancellations of vaccinations against childhood diseases for one million children."[14]

After months of battling between the Congress and the president, Congress avoided the sequestration by passing the Budget Enforcement Act of 1990, which once again reformed the budgeting process. This new act largely displaces Gramm-Rudman-Hollings by establishing more flexible deficit targets. Instead of focusing on deficit targets, it divides discretionary spending into three categories (defense, domestic, and international), with spending caps on each. If spending in any of the categories exceeds the cap, it will trigger automatic cuts in that category. Moreover, savings in one category may not be used to offset expenditures in another. Finally, the 1990 act stipulates that changes in eligibility requirements for entitlement programs that increase expenditures must be offset by either decreases in other entitlement programs or tax increases. This pay-as-you-go feature of the new act was invoked in 1991, when Congress extended eligibility requirements for unemployment compensation. In accordance with the act, Congress included in the extension new taxes to pay for the benefits.

Despite changes in the legislative process, the massive federal deficit has continued to allude congressional control. Indeed, the failure of the various reform efforts to contain the deficit has led to renewed calls for a balanced-budget amendment to the Constitution. In both 1995 and 1997, however, constitutional amendments requiring a balanced budget failed by one vote in the Senate.

In the wake of the failed constitutional amendments Congress and the President announced, in 1997, a bipartisan plan to balance the budget within five years. Aided by a growing economy with high employment and a low inflation rate, the plan provided targeted tax and spending cuts. Although heralded by its supporters as the first realistic effort to balance the budget, its success depends on continued economic growth. Since most of the deficit reduction occurs in the fifth year of the plan, an economic downturn could derail the bipartisan agreement and drive deficits back up.

Casework

Besides representing constituents on policy questions, members of Congress are expected to provide constituents with personal services, called **casework.** Senators, representatives, and their staffs spend a great deal of time and energy helping constituents through the maze of federal programs and benefits. For instance, are you leaving the country and need a passport in a hurry? Contact your representative. Maybe you need help with a small-business administration official who will not return your phone call? Or you're having problems getting a Veterans Administration or social security check? Perhaps you have a son or daughter in the army who has not written home in several weeks? Call the district office of your representative or senator.

Many members of Congress complain that casework reduces them to the role of an errand runner, but few refuse to do the work. Instead, most members have accommodated the demand for casework by enlarging their district or state offices. Between 1972 and 1987, for instance, the total number of staff assigned by members of the House to their district offices more than doubled, and the number of Senate staffers located in the state offices more than tripled.[15]

Though it may be tiresome, casework is good electoral politics. As Morris Fiorina pointed out some fifteen years ago, "The nice thing about casework is that it is mostly profit; one makes many more friends than enemies."[16] But casework is more than simply good politics; it is also a form of representation. Richard Fenno reminds us that constituents may want "good access or the assurance of good access as much as they want good policy."[17] Contrary to the myth of Congress as the broken branch, members of both the House and the Senate are quite effective at providing that access. However, service to their constituencies undoubtedly diminishes the capacity of members and their staffs to engage in policymaking.

Congressional Oversight

The passage of a law rarely ends congressional involvement in the matter. Congress is responsible for overseeing the activities of the executive agencies charged with implementing policy. This process of legislative oversight, which has become a crucial aspect of congressional work, takes many forms. For instance, casework can sometimes direct a member to the weakness or ineffective administration of a program.[18] Congress may also engage in oversight by requiring executive officials to prepare periodic, detailed reports of their activities. In the 1996 Department of Defense appropriations act, for instance, Congress mandated so many reports that it took the Pentagon 111 pages just to list them. Often, however, the oversight function is performed as part of the appropriation process. The hearings to consider agency budgets give members of both houses an opportunity to question executive officials extensively. As one member of the House Appropriations Committee remarked, "You keep asking questions just to let them know someone is watching them."[19]

More dramatically, Congress may exercise oversight by conducting committee investigations. Committees of both houses can compel testimony and

Overseeing the Executive Branch

Congress performs much of its oversight function in committee hearings where executive branch officials are questioned about administration policies. Pictured here is FBI director Louis Freeh testifying before a Senate panel on the Clinton administration's antiterrorism measures.

evidence from government officials and private citizens for the purpose of proposing new legislation. Thus Congress used its committee oversight function in 1997 to investigate various campaign financing issues surrounding President Clinton's re-election campaign.

In the 1970s Congress increasingly relied for oversight on the **legislative veto**—a device in a bill that allowed Congress or a committee of Congress to veto the actions of an executive agency or the president in an area covered by the bill. Using the legislative veto, Congress would pass a statute granting the president or an administrative official wide discretion in formulating specific policies, but these policies would be subject to congressional approval. Thus, in the War Powers Resolution of 1973, Congress gave the president the authority to send troops into a hostile situation for sixty days. The troops would have to leave at the end of that period unless Congress declared war or provided specific statutory authorization.

In 1983 the Supreme Court declared the legislative veto unconstitutional.[20] Nevertheless, Congress is reluctant to give up this form of oversight. Because the language of the Supreme Court opinion is not entirely clear, Congress has continued to include the legislative veto in statutes. Whether these laws will also be declared unconstitutional by federal courts remains to be seen.[21]

The Organization of Congress

The U.S. Congress is an example of a **bicameral** legislature: a legislature divided into two separate houses. Our Congress differs markedly from bicameral legislatures in other countries. Unlike most two-house assemblies, Congress contains bodies of nearly equal power. That arrangement was set up to divide power and to strike a balance between the large and small states. Furthermore, Congress is "an assembly of equals,"[22] in which each senator and representative has his or her own constituency to represent, and consequently each member of Congress has an equal claim to legitimacy. The effect of this egalitarianism in Congress is to further fragment and decentralize power, which must be structured in some manner if the institution is to make policy.

Bicameralism

The founders designed the two houses to represent different elements in American society. The House of Representatives, with its membership based on frequent and popular elections, was to be the voice of public opinion. James Madison saw the House as "the grand repository of the democratic principles of government." In contrast, senators, originally chosen by state legislatures, were expected to curb the radical tendencies of House members. Perhaps George

Washington best described the purpose of the Senate. When asked by Thomas Jefferson why the Constitutional Convention had agreed to the second body, Washington replied, "Why did you pour that coffee into your saucer?" "To cool it," responded Jefferson. "Even so," said Washington, "we pour legislation into the senatorial saucer to cool it."[23]

The Seventeenth Amendment, ratified in 1913, changed the mode of electing senators so that they too would be chosen by the mass electorate. Although the founders' expectations for the two bodies may not have been completely fulfilled, the bicameral structure is still an important feature of the American legislative system. Because the two houses are nearly equal in power, public policies are the product of two distinct legislative processes, with two sets of rules, politics, and internal dynamics. These differences fragment power, and Congress has a decentralized organization.

Congressional Leadership

Although the Constitution does not mention political parties, congressional leadership is party leadership, for the political parties organize Congress.

Leadership in the House.   The most powerful position in the lower body is that of the **Speaker of the House.** The speaker is the presiding officer of the House, the leader of its majority party, and second in line, behind the vice president, to succeed the president. The only House position created by the Constitution, the speaker was supposed to be elected by the entire body but is actually chosen by a vote of the majority party.

Because the speaker serves as majority party leader and presides over the House, the position is the most powerful in Congress. Nevertheless, the speaker's power has greatly diminished. In the early 1900s speakers dominated the business of the House. The last of the truly powerful speakers, Joseph "Uncle Joe" Cannon, assigned members of both parties to committees, appointed and removed committee chairs at will, controlled the flow of bills to the floor, and exercised complete authority to recognize members' right to speak on the floor. Cannon's almost dictatorial control of the House precipitated the 1910 "revolt against the speaker," which stripped the office of all committee assignment powers and drastically limited the power of recognition. Modern speakers have regained some power.

www•

For more information on the powers of the speaker, see the **Gitelson/Dudley/Dubnick web site.**

The holder of the second-ranking party position, the **majority leader,** schedules floor action on bills and guides the party's legislative program through the House. The majority leader also works with the speaker and other party leaders to develop the legislative agenda for the party. The majority leader generally succeeds the speaker; at least this has been true of the last five Democratic speakers. Not surprisingly, the contest for majority leader in the Democratic party is often intense. Former Speaker of the House Jim Wright of Texas was elected majority leader in 1977, beating the last of three other candidates by a single vote.

CLOSER TO HOME

10.1 Legislating in the States

In the late eighteenth and early nineteenth centuries, when states drafted their constitutions, legislatures were the center of government. Powerful assemblies were seen as the greatest protection against autocratic executives. These early constitutions placed high expectations and very few restraints on their assemblies. The early constitutions, for instance, provided for frequent legislative sessions, because it was widely assumed that the more often the legislators met, the more responsive they would be to the voters.

By the middle of the nineteenth century, the faith in legislatures began to wane, however. Mired in corruption and scandal, state legislatures came to be seen as a threat to democracy rather than as its guardian. As a result, state constitutions were rewritten or revised to limit the power and authority of legislatures. By the beginning of the twentieth century, almost all states had significantly curtailed legislative power. Symptomatic of the effort to curb power were the numerous restrictions on the frequency and duration of legislative sessions. A legislature infrequently in session and then only for short periods could not cause much trouble.

Under pressure from various reform groups, the pendulum began to swing back toward legislative power in the late 1960s. In recent decades many states have modernized and empowered their assemblies, extending their sessions and providing legislators with salaries and support services. Nevertheless, distrust dies hard, and few state legislatures even approach the professionalism of the U.S. Congress.

The frequency and length of state legislative sessions illustrate these differences. Eight states still restrict their legislatures to biennial sessions and thirty-seven states limit the length of sessions. In Kentucky, legislative sessions can be held only in even years and can last only 60 days. In one of the largest states, Texas, the state constitution limits the legislature to 140 days every 2 years. (Some critics would have liked the constitution to specify that the legislature meet every 140 years for 2 days.)

Because Americans have long favored citizen legislators, compensation in state assemblies has been low—hardly enough to attract those lacking independent means. Historically, state legislators were paid on a per diem basis. Indeed, thirteen states still use this system of payment. Alabama legislators meet for a maximum of thirty days each year and receive $10 a day. Thirty-seven states now pay an annual salary, but in most of them the level of compensation is set by the constitution, making it difficult to change. New York legislators receive more than $57,000 a year—still far short of congressional salaries. Most states pay considerably less, with New Hampshire paying the least—$100 a year.

State legislators also lack the staff resources that have become so common in Congress. In an effort to modernize, states have, in recent years, increased the availability of legislative staff. Still, few states provide for any personal staff beyond the secretarial, and even the secretarial staff generally has to be shared. Maine, for example, allocates one secretary for every forty-five members of its House of Representatives. Elsewhere, too, the numbers are usually small, although all but two states do provide staff for at least some of their standing committees. Lacking staff resources, state legislators must often rely on executive branch employees and lobbyists for information.

Increasingly, state legislators are also being subjected to term limits. In the 1995 case of *U.S. Term Limits, Inc.* v. *Thorton,* the U.S. Supreme Court ruled that states could not impose term limits on their congressional delegations, but the ruling did not apply to state legislators. Twenty states now have limits on legislative service, but there is little uniformity in applying them. Several states treat service in each chamber separately, allowing members to serve the maximum limit in both chambers, whereas some other states restrict the total length of service in the legislature. Oklahoma, for instance, permits only twelve years of total service.

The working conditions in state legislatures are likely to become a larger issue in American politics as federal lawmakers pursue a policy of devolution, shifting more responsibilities from the national government to the states. It remains to be seen whether state legislatures are equipped to handle the new responsibilities.

Sources: Ann O'M. Bowman and Richard C. Kearney, *State and Local Government,* 3rd ed. (Boston: Houghton Mifflin, 1996), and *The Book of the States, 1994–95 Edition,* vol. 30 (Lexington, Ky.: Council of State Governments, 1994).

For more information on state legislatures, see the Gitelson/Dudley/Dubnick web site.

The **minority leader** heads the opposition party in the House and represents its interests. The minority leader also consults with the speaker and the majority leader over the scheduling of bills and rules for floor action. Like their counterparts in the majority party, minority leaders are generally seasoned legislators. When Robert Michel of Illinois, minority leader in the 102nd Congress (1991–1992), was first elected to that post in 1981, he had already served twenty-four years in the House. The majority and minority leaders have the assistance of the **party whips,** who support the party leaders by communicating the party positions to the membership and keeping the leaders informed of members' views.

Senate Leadership.   The Constitution makes the vice president of the United States president of the Senate. This is largely a ceremonial position; the Senate's presiding officer votes only to break a tie. Of greater importance are the positions of majority and minority leaders. Much like their counterparts in the House, the majority and minority leaders of the Senate are expected to organize support for party initiatives. Furthermore, the majority leader is expected to manage floor activity, whereas the minority leader represents the "loyal opposition." The Democratic majority leader heads the party in the Senate and chairs the committees that assign members to committees and schedule floor debates. In the Republican party, these tasks are assigned to three different senators. The Senate also has whips, although they have fewer responsibilities than House whips.

The Committee System

Party leaders in both houses struggle to bring organization to a fragmented institution. In their efforts to manage the Congress, they must contend with a committee system that distributes power to many others because work in the

The White House Comes to the Hill

As work on a bipartisan budget agreement progressed, President Clinton traveled to Capital Hill to meet with congressional leaders. Pictured here President Clinton (center) meets with (from left to right) House Speaker Newt Gingrich (R–Georgia), Senate Majority Leader Trent Lott (R–Mississippi) and House Minority Leader Richard Gephardt (D–Missouri).

modern Congress is mostly carried out in committees and subcommittees. These "little legislatures," as Woodrow Wilson referred to them, screen the thousands of bills introduced in each session and decide which should be recommended for consideration by the larger body. The few bills that the committees recommend for floor action define the congressional agenda. Bills passed over by committees rarely reach the floor.

It has not always been that way. In the early days of Congress, temporary committees considered specific legislative proposals and then disbanded.[24] These committees possessed little independent power and could not withhold a bill from floor consideration. Only gradually did Congress come to rely on permanent committees.

Types of Committees.   The most important committees in Congress are the **standing committees.** These are permanently established committees that consider proposed legislation in specified policy areas and decide whether to recommend passage by the larger body. It is to the standing committees that nearly all legislation is referred. Table 10.1 lists the standing committees of the 105th Congress.

Subcommittees of the standing committees are increasingly important in the work of both the House and the Senate. Each subcommittee covers a portion

TABLE 10.1

Standing Committees of the House and Senate, 105th Congress (1997–1998)

Almost all of these committees have subcommittees. The number of members ranges from ten to sixty-one.

Committees	Number of Subcommittees
House	
Agriculture	5
Appropriations	13
Banking and Financial Services	5
Budget	None
Commerce	5
Education and the Workforce	5
Government Reform and Oversight	7
House Oversight	None
International Relations	5
Judiciary	5
National Security	7
Resources	5
Rules	2
Science	4
Small Business	4
Standards of Official Conduct	None
Transportation and Infrastructure	6
Veterans' Affairs	3
Ways and Means	5
Senate	
Agriculture, Nutrition and Forestry	4
Appropriations	13
Armed Services	6
Banking, Housing and Urban Affairs	5
Budget	None
Commerce, Science and Transportation	7
Energy and Natural Resources	4
Environment and Public Works	4
Finance	5
Foreign Relations	7

(continued)

TABLE 10.1

Standing Committees of the House and Senate, 105th Congress (1997–1998) *(continued)*

Committees	Number of Subcommittees
Senate	
Governmental Affairs	3
Indian Affairs	None
Judiciary	6
Labor and Human Resources	4
Rules and Administration	None
Small Business	None
Veterans' Affairs	None

Source: "Players, Politics and Turf of the 105th Congress," *Congressional Quarterly,* March 22, 1997.

of the policy area controlled by its larger committee. Having their own staff and jurisdiction, subcommittees often function as small standing committees. In fact, most decisions about proposed bills come out of subcommittees. Some parent committees routinely approve and send to the floor any proposal passed to them by their subcommittees. As a result, small groups of members have great power in extremely specialized areas, which fragments the work of the larger body.

Select, or special, committees are temporary committees established by the House or Senate to study particular problems. For instance, in 1986 both the House and the Senate created select committees to investigate the Reagan administration's sale of arms to Iran and the diversion of funds from the sale to forces seeking the overthrow of the government of Nicaragua. There are also four permanent **joint committees,** composed of an equal number of members from both houses. One of these is the Joint Library Committee, which oversees the activities of the Library of Congress. Finally, temporary **conference committees** are formed to reconcile differences between House and Senate versions of a bill. Sometimes called the "third house of Congress," conference committees are composed of members of both bodies. Because a bill may be sent to the president only if passed in identical form by both houses, the conference committees often take on great importance in shaping legislation.

Committee Size and Membership. Questions of committee size and the number of Democratic and Republican members are settled by negotiations between the party leaders. Both houses can adjust the size of their committees from session to session, and many committees have grown larger to satisfy congressional members who are seeking good assignments.

Determining the ratio of majority to minority party members on each committee causes far more controversy than committee size. Generally, the allocations reflect party strength in the full House or Senate. On occasion, however, the majority party may be unwilling to accommodate the opposition. In 1981, for instance, House Democrats refused to readjust the ratio on certain key committees, despite the substantial gains made by the Republicans in the 1980 elections. Although the Democrats held only a 5-to-4 advantage in the 1981–1982 House, they insisted on a 2-to-1 ratio on the all-important Rules Committee. (As you will see later in this chapter, no bill goes to the floor of the House without favorable action by the Rules Committee.) Fearing that such an unfavorable mix would stifle the Reagan administration's legislative program, Republicans took the matter to the House floor. Their efforts were defeated by a straight party vote, with only one Democrat defecting.

Committee Assignments. The House and Senate rules specify that the full membership is responsible for electing individuals to committees. By custom, however, the parties make the assignments, and the chambers simply ratify their choices.

Because of the key role committees play in controlling the flow of bills to the floor of Congress, competition for places is often keen. Junior members struggling for a desirable assignment seek allies among the senior members as well as among outsiders who have an interest in the committee's area. For example, in 1981 Democratic Representative Phil Gramm (now a Republican senator) enlisted the aid of fellow Texan Jim Wright (at that time majority leader) in his bid for a seat on the House Budget Committee. Wright persuaded members of the steering committee to award the seat to Gramm, though he came to regret his assistance when Gramm supported Reagan's economic policies. House Democrats pursuing a seat on the Education and Labor Committee commonly seek recommendations from organized labor.

In addition, the members' goals play an important part in committee assignment. Legislators seeking re-election and constituency service choose committees that serve their districts' interests. Members who want to acquire influence in the House show a different set of committee preferences. Still others may pick committees that allow them to pursue certain policy objectives.[25]

Committee Leadership. Following the principle that the parties organize Congress, chairs of committees and subcommittees are always members of the majority party in the body. Furthermore, the committee leadership reflects the **seniority system,** a tradition through which the member of the majority party with the longest continuous service on a committee becomes its chair. Similarly, the most senior member of the minority party is generally the ranking minority member.

Prior to the 1970s, the seniority system gave extraordinary power to Democratic members from safe districts in the South, who achieved re-election easily. In the early 1970s, liberals, dissatisfied with the system, altered it by requiring the election of committee chairs and ranking minority members. Similarly, in 1995 the House Republicans, at the recommendation of Speaker Gingrich, did promote a few less-senior members to committee chairs. Nevertheless, these changes have proven to be the exception; seniority still prevails.

In 1995 House Republicans instituted major reforms of the committee and subcommittee system designed to rein in the dispersion of power. Although seniority remains the general rule, no committee or subcommittee chair may be held for more than three consecutive terms. Moreover, with the exception of the Appropriations and Government Operations Committees, no House committee may have more than five subcommittees.

The Nonofficial Groups

Informal groups within Congress also help shape its public policy goals. The modern era of nonofficial groups began in 1958, with the formation of the Democratic Study Group (DSG) to enhance the power of Democratic liberals. The DSG has its own whip system, publishes a newsletter to keep its members informed, and even provides them with campaign and fundraising assistance.[26] Conservative Democrats have countered with the less-organized Conservative Democratic Forum. Not unexpectedly, the number of groups with a single-issue focus has increased significantly. Groups such as the Steel Caucus, the Rail Caucus, the Copper Caucus, and the Mushroom Caucus are linked to outside interests and often receive financial support from them.

Although these unofficial groups represent an effort to compensate for the fragmented committee system, they have actually made things worse, for they have increased the decentralization of the House and increased the importance of single-issue politics. As Burdett Loomis noted, "While members decry the increases in single-issue politics, they have only to consider their own behavior."[27] It may be that former Speaker of the House Thomas "Tip" O'Neill was correct when he complained that the "House has over-caucused itself."[28]

In 1995, however, the House Republicans created a storm of controversy by prohibiting the use of public money for unofficial groups. Under the resolution passed in the early days of the 104th Congress, these unofficial groups were denied House office space, and members were prohibited from supporting the organizations out of the office expense accounts. Although this measure affected several unofficial groups (e.g., the Democratic Study Group), it had no effect on the those groups funded by interest groups and industries.

The Congressional Staff

At the beginning of this century, representatives had no personal staff and senators had only thirty-nine personal assistants. By 1987, however, the number of personal assistants allocated to members had mushroomed to more than eleven thousand.[29] Although most of these assistants spend their time providing constituency service and casework, staffers also participate in the legislative process.

Members of both the House and the Senate have come to rely heavily on their personal staff to conduct research, write questions to be posed to witnesses in committee hearings, write speeches, draft bills and amendments to bills, and prepare briefs on pending legislation. Moreover, much of the negotiation among members is conducted not by the members themselves but by staff assistants representing their respective employers.

In addition to the personal staff, more than two thousand people are assigned to the various committees and subcommittees of Congress. With little responsibility for constituency service, committee staff are involved in drafting legislation and conducting committee investigations. Because they provide needed technical expertise, committee staffers often play a vital role in forming policy. In fact, committee staff often act as policy entrepreneurs, developing new initiatives and then persuading the committee to accept them.

Congress has also created three major support agencies to furnish technical advice. The staffs of the Congressional Research Service, the General Accounting Office, and the Congressional Budget Office are responsible for providing detailed policy analysis.

With all these staff resources, Congress has become better informed on technical matters and far less dependent on the expertise of the executive branch. Moreover, individual members, faced with more complex issues and busier schedules, naturally find their staffs invaluable. But the growing staff size has come at a cost. With staffers taking so much responsibility, Congress becomes further decentralized as the pool of politically relevant participants grows larger. As Senator Fritz Hollings, a South Carolina Democrat, put it, "Everybody is working for staff, staff, staff, driving you nutty, in fact. It has gotten to the point where the senators never actually sit down and exchange ideas and learn from the experience of others and listen."[30]

Having campaigned on the promise to streamline Congress, the Republicans of the 104th Congress reduced the number of staff positions by a third. Significantly, however, the reductions came solely from committee and subcommittee staff. No cuts were made in members' personal staffs. Thus the constituency service function of the members was not affected by the cuts.

How a Bill Becomes Law

The most obvious congressional function, lawmaking, is also the function that Congress has the most difficulty performing. For those who wish to pass legislation, the congressional process is an obstacle course.[31] The maze of complex rules and multiple points of power overwhelmingly favors the opponents of legislation. Ignoring the old saying that the public should never see the making of sausages or legislation, we now will look at the making of laws. Figure 10.1 shows the process schematically.

FIGURE 10.1

How a Bill Becomes
a Law

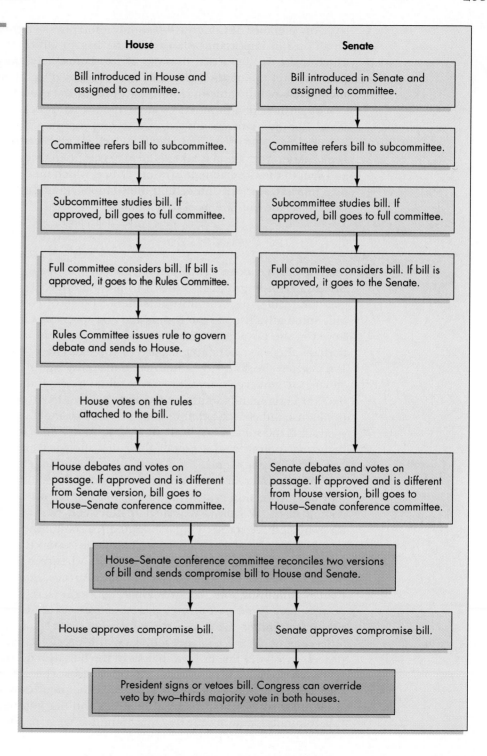

Any member of Congress—but only a member—may introduce legislation. To aid in this important task, each house has an Office of Legislative Counsel, which assists in the actual drafting of legislation; members need only present their ideas to the counsel. Some of the bills introduced may have been drafted elsewhere—by constituents, interest groups, or the presidential administration.

Regardless of a proposal's source, the formal process of introduction is the same. Representatives simply drop the proposal in a box called the "hopper." Senators hand the proposed law to a clerk for publication in the *Congressional Record*. After that action is taken, the bill is numbered (by order of introduction) and sent to the Government Printing Office, which makes multiple copies for future referral. An "HR" preceding the number identifies bills introduced in the House; Senate bills are marked with an "S."

Committee Consideration

After a bill has been properly introduced, the Speaker of the House or the Senate's presiding officer refers it to a committee. Because both houses have elaborate rules that restrain the leaders' choice of committee, most proposed bills automatically go to the committee that specializes in the area. On occasion, however, the presiding officer may be able to choose among rival committees. Perhaps the most notable example of the exercise of this option occurred in 1963, when the Kennedy administration's civil rights bill was referred to the Senate's Commerce Committee rather than to the Judiciary Committee, which had a predominantly southern membership. In the House, the bill was given to the House Judiciary Committee, whose chair strongly supported civil rights legislation. If the subject is broad enough, proposed bills may be referred to more than one committee. But under the rules, the speaker may refer a bill only to one committee at a time.

When a bill reaches a committee, it is usually referred to the subcommittee that has jurisdiction in the matter. For the vast majority of bills, that is the final resting place. Woodrow Wilson best described the fate of bills in committee when he said: "As a rule, a bill committed [to committee] is a bill doomed. When it goes from the clerk's desk to a committee room, it crosses a parliamentary bridge of sighs and dim dungeons of silence whence it will never return."[32]

If the subcommittee chooses to hold hearings, then members of the president's administration, congressional colleagues, representatives of interest groups, and (time permitting) private citizens are invited to testify. Afterward the subcommittee meets in what is called a *markup session,* in which it votes on amendments to the bill and settles on the precise language. Sometimes that process involves a line-by-line analysis of the bill, with debate on the language or intent of virtually every sentence. In other cases, the subcommittee may substitute an entirely new version of the bill. Subsequently, most bills go to the full committee, where the process of hearings and markup may begin again or the full committee may accept the subcommittee version. The full committee may also take no action, thus killing the bill, or it may send the bill back to the sub-committee for further work.

If the committee orders the bill reported—that is, votes to approve it—the bill is sent for consideration to the body from which it first came. A committee report accompanies it, explaining the bill and justifying the committee action. These reports can be crucial because for some members of Congress they may be the main source of information about a bill. Senators and representatives not on the committee are unlikely to have a great deal of expertise in the subject matter. Thus they often look to the committee reports for guidance.

Floor Action

When a committee orders a bill reported, it is placed on a calendar. What happens next differs in the House and in the Senate.[33]

The House Floor. In the House, the Rules Committee determines the scheduling of controversial bills that are unlikely to receive unanimous consent from the floor or bills requiring the expenditure of public funds. This committee grants motions that specify the time allocated for debate and any limitations on amendments. The committee may, for instance, attach a rule prohibiting amendments from the floor; such a rule is known as a *closed rule.* In formulating the rules for a bill, the committee may conduct hearings of its own or kill the bill by doing nothing.

The actions of the Rules Committee are stated in a resolution that must be approved on the House floor before the bill can be considered. Often the battle over the resolution is the most important floor action. In 1981, for instance, a fierce struggle developed over the rule for Reagan's budget cuts. A Democratic-sponsored rule would have required the House to vote on individual spending cuts separately. Republican leaders opposed it, fearing that a majority would not vote to cut popular social programs if they were separated from the larger package. With the help of conservative Democrats, Republicans managed to reject the resolution and substitute one that permitted the cuts to be voted up or down as a whole.

Once a rule is accepted, the House can begin debate, which is strictly limited by the rules adopted. The time allotted for debate ranges from an hour or two for a noncontroversial bill to ten hours for difficult legislation. Votes on amendments, if permitted under the rules, are crucial because they can alter the bill sufficiently to attract or lose supporters. Once debate is over, the full House votes on the bill and any amendments that have been attached to it.

The Senate Floor. Because the Senate is a smaller body than the House, the floor procedures are considerably more casual. The Senate has no counterpart to the House Rules Committee. Bills come off the Senate's calendars when the majority leader schedules them. The Senate also allows its members to engage in unlimited debate. This privilege of unlimited debate can lead to a **filibuster**—a prolonged debate intended to prevent a vote on a bill and thus kill it. Filibusters can be broken, but only with difficulty, because the rule for **cloture**—or ending of debate—requires a vote of at least sixty senators to cut off the discussion. When it comes to the filibuster, no one has yet topped the performance of South Carolina Republican Strom Thurmond, who, while leading the opposition to the 1957 Civil Rights Act, held forth for twenty-four hours and eighteen minutes.

Conference Work

Before a bill can be sent to the president, it must be passed by both houses of Congress in identical form. Usually this requirement poses little difficulty. If the last house to act on the bill makes only slight changes, it is generally sent back to the originating house for approval. When the two versions differ significantly, a conference committee is appointed to work out the differences.

If the members of this committee cannot reach agreement, the legislation may die in conference. More commonly, the committee reports a compromise bill that must then be accepted by both houses. At that point, so much work has gone into producing the legislation that rejection of the bill and the committee report is infrequent. The bill is then sent to the president, who either signs or vetoes it.

As we noted earlier, the lawmaking process is an obstacle course studded with complex rules and multiple points of power. In fact, many of these rules reflect the original intent of the founders, which was to create a legislative system that works slowly and is not unduly influenced by the passions of a few. As it has evolved, the system is best designed for preventing the passage of legislation and so has reinforced the myth of Congress as the broken branch. Yet Congress does make the system work, and not just in small matters. One has only to think of the civil rights bills of the 1960s to recognize that Congress can and does respond when a consensus forms in society.

Influences on Congressional Voting

Members of Congress cast thousands of votes every year on a staggering array of issues. Understanding how they vote and why they vote as they do has long been a preoccupation of students of Congress. This task is made difficult because each vote represents not one choice but a set of choices. As one observer noted, "The predicament of the legislator is that every vote is a dozen votes upon as many issues all wrapped together, tied in a verbal package, and given a number of this bill or that."[34] In addition, legislators are routinely asked to vote on an incredibly broad range of subjects.

MYTHS IN POPULAR CULTURE

10.1 Good and Evil in the U.S. Senate

Among the many movies portraying the U.S. Congress, none has received the acclaim and lasting popularity of director Frank Capra's *Mr. Smith Goes to Washington*. Although released more than fifty years ago, the film is an American classic that still attracts large audiences when it appears on television. The film's appeal is founded on a strong cast of actors supporting a brilliant performance by Jimmy Stewart.

But *Mr. Smith Goes to Washington* has lasted all these years because it also touches on widely held views about the U.S. Congress. Mr. Jefferson Smith (Jimmy Stewart), a naive young man who leads an organization of children called the Boy Rangers, is appointed to fill the unexpired term of a deceased U.S. senator. Given his inexperience and naiveté, Mr. Smith is expected to simply ratify the actions of his senior colleague from the state.

Initially, Mr. Smith behaves as expected. Awed by the Senate and his colleagues, Mr. Smith goes along, completely unaware that he is being used by a corrupt political machine from his home state. In fact, the idealistic Mr. Smith is surrounded by corrupt senators, interested only in being re-elected. Even his single senatorial staffer, a holdover from the previous senator, is initially jaded and corrupted by congressional politics. The fact that Mr. Smith has no idea how Congress does its work is proof of his goodness; it demonstrates that he has not been debased by Washington. Mr. Smith is simply too good, too honest for Washington.

But of course, even Mr. Smith figures it out eventually. When his proposal to build a summer camp for children conflicts with the bosses' desire to build a dam, Mr. Smith takes the courageous stand. Shocked by the corruption that he sees around him, Mr. Smith vows to fight the bosses and stand up for the children of the nation. Unable to persuade him to go along with their plans, the bosses frame Mr. Smith by forging his signature on deeds of land that make it appear as though he plans to make a profit on the camp.

Accused of wrongdoing and disgraced before the children he championed, Mr. Smith prepares to depart Washington without a fight. At the last minute, however, he is persuaded by his now loyal staffer to fight the corruption. What follows is a classic confrontation of good versus evil, as one man takes on the sinister forces of the U.S. Senate. Mr. Smith blocks senate action on the dam and his own expulsion by launching a filibuster. As his speaking marathon drags on, even the decadent press corps begins to side with good. Rather than the obstruction of majority will by a minority, the filibuster is described by the movie characters as "democracy's finest show" and "democracy in action."

In the end, of course, good triumphs. Mr. Smith faints in the twenty-fourth hour of his filibuster, and the senior senator from his state, overcome with remorse, confesses to the corruption. Evil is defeated, but, according to the movie, it takes an outsider to restore goodness.

Except in selecting its leaders, Congress rarely engages in straight party-line voting. Nevertheless, the party remains the single best predictor of how a member will vote. On the average, the members support party positions on better than two out of three votes. Given the extensive party organizations within

Congress, this outcome is not surprising. Of course, since members of the same party are likely to attract the same kinds of supporters, they may vote alike out of loyalty to these supporters rather than to their party.

Does the constituency influence legislative decision making? The answer is difficult to determine, in part because constituents' views are not clearly expressed. When an issue arouses deep feelings, the constituency may well sway a senator's or representative's decision. In most instances, however, members of Congress receive little or no instruction from their districts. Even so, a district's majority usually exerts at least indirect influence because most members of Congress share their constituents' views. That is why they were elected to begin with.

The threat of electoral defeat also ensures a measure of constituency influence. A single vote in Congress rarely ends a career, and a senator or representative—particularly one who has cultivated an effective home style—can now and then take a position at odds with constituents' views. But some issues are a danger for every member. Few members of Congress relish votes on particularly controversial issues because such issues may in fact be very costly to their re-election efforts. Issues such as abortion and gun control may well spell defeat for members who cross their constituency, or at least the organized elements in their constituency. Moreover, members are constantly concerned with what use future opponents may make of their floor votes. As Senator Thomas Daschle, a Democrat from South Dakota, said, "I dare say the first thing that comes to my mind in a vote is: Can it (the issue) pass the 30-second test, [and] how successful will my opponent be in applying it to a 30-second ad? It's a screen that comes up whenever there is a vote."[35] Hence few members of Congress frequently vote against the wishes of their districts.

Given the time constraints under which senators and representatives operate, no member can be fully informed on every issue. Therefore members turn to each other for information and guidance on how to vote. Most members develop a set of colleagues with whom they are in general agreement and who can be trusted to provide honest and knowledgeable advice. These experts are often members of the subcommittee or committee in charge of the area in question. Thus members are usually extremely well informed when they vote on the narrow range of issues with which they are familiar but heavily dependent on trusted colleagues in regard to other legislation.

Conclusion: Is Congress the Broken Branch?

We began this chapter by noting that Congress is generally perceived as the broken branch. This is not a recent perception, but rather a long-standing complaint. For instance, the nineteenth-century House of Representatives struck Woodrow Wilson as "a disintegrated mass of jarring elements."[36]

Yet individual members of Congress seem to satisfy their constituents. While bemoaning the conditions of Congress in general, voters return the same members to that institution election after election. Despite the myth of Congress as the broken branch, then, voters seem satisfied with the incumbents. That situation is no accident. Incumbent members of Congress are safe because they work hard at carrying out their constituents' wishes for personal services. In that area of activity, surely Congress cannot be deemed a failure.

Congress works slowly, in part because it was designed that way. Its complex rules and maze of procedural hurdles were set up to frustrate immediate responses. George Washington's talk of cooling legislation in the Senate might well describe the entire legislative process. But the lawmaking function of Congress is also filtered through the representational function. Responding to the demands of constituents enhances the representative nature of Congress, but it also diminishes the capacity of members to engage in policymaking. Moreover, the representative function encourages members to view policy in local terms instead of national needs. Nevertheless, Congress is capable of fomenting great change when a nationwide consensus develops.

Summary

1. Members of Congress tend to be wealthier and better educated than the public they represent. Furthermore, Congress includes proportionately fewer minority-group and women members than the general population.

2. Despite the public's seeming dissatisfaction with Congress, incumbents are greatly favored in congressional elections. Incumbents use the opportunities and resources available to them to win the voters' trust.

3. Members of Congress perform many roles. For example, Congress is responsible for the creation of taxing and spending policies for the nation. The members are also expected to represent the interests of their constituents and oversee the actions of the executive branch.

4. As a bicameral institution, Congress is highly decentralized. The two houses of Congress have developed their own rules and internal dynamics.

5. The most powerful position in the House of Representatives is that of the Speaker of the House. Elected by the majority party, the speaker is assisted by the majority leader and the majority party whips. Leadership of the minority party in the House falls to the minority leader and minority party whips.

6. Although the Constitution makes the vice president the presiding officer of the Senate, the majority and minority party leaders are of greater importance.

7. Most of the work of Congress is done in its committees and subcommittees. The reliance on committees and subcommittees results in decision making by highly specialized members.

8. Committee leaders are generally those members of the majority party who have the greatest seniority on the committee. In the 1970s, Congress instituted reforms that gave the majority party the right to elect committee leaders, but the seniority rule is still strong.

9. Nonofficial groups with a single-issue focus, as well as a large number of congressional staff assistants, have greatly added to the number of forces in the policymaking process.

10. A bill becomes law only after it has passed through a maze of complex procedures. Though they resemble an obstacle course, these rules and procedures are in keeping with the founders' intent that Congress not act in haste.

11. Members of Congress make decisions on a broad range of issues. In so doing, they take into account the desires of party leaders and constituents. The members also accept and seek out the advice of trusted colleagues who have expertise in the subjects under consideration.

Key Terms and Concepts

Gerrymandering The practice by the party controlling the state legislature of drawing congressional district boundaries to maximize the number of seats it can win.

Franking privilege The power of members of Congress to send out mail free of charge; this allows incumbents to cultivate a favorable image among constituents.

Pork-barrel legislation Legislation that appropriates funds for local projects in an area that a member of Congress represents.

Home style The way in which incumbent members of Congress present themselves to their constituents in an attempt to win the voters' trust.

Entitlements Payments to any person or government meeting the requirements specified by law, such as social security benefits and military pensions.

First Concurrent Budget Resolution The recommendation for spending ceilings in major funding categories. It is submitted to the House and Senate by their respective budget committees and must be passed by April 15.

Casework Work done by members of Congress to provide constituents with personal services and help through the maze of federal programs and benefits.

Legislative veto A device in a bill that allowed Congress or a congressional committee to veto the actions of an executive agency or the president in an area covered by the bill. It was declared unconstitutional by the Supreme Court in 1983.

Bicameral Refers to a legislature that is divided into two separate houses, such as the U.S. Congress.

Speaker of the House The only House position created by the Constitution. The speaker is chosen by a vote of the majority party and is the presiding officer of the House, the leader of its majority party, and second in line to succeed the president.

Majority leader The second-ranking party position in the House (and the first in the Senate). The majority leader schedules floor action on bills and guides the party's legislative program through the House.

Minority leader The head of the minority party in the Senate. Also the leader of the minority party in the House, who represents its interests by consulting with the speaker and majority leader over the scheduling of bills and rules for floor action.

Party whips Members of Congress who support the party leaders in the House and Senate by communicating the party positions to the membership and keeping the leaders informed of members' views.

Standing committees Permanently established committees that consider proposed legislation in specified policy areas and decide whether to recommend passage by the larger body.

Select, or special, committees Temporary committees established by the House or Senate to study particular problems.

Joint committees Congressional committees that are usually permanent and consist of an equal number of members from both houses.

Conference committees Temporary joint committees that are formed to reconcile differences between House and Senate versions of a bill. Such committees often play a critical role in shaping legislation.

Seniority system A tradition through which the member of the majority party with the longest continuous service on a committee automatically becomes its chair.

Filibuster A prolonged debate in the Senate that is intended to kill a bill by preventing a vote.

Cloture The rule for ending debate in the Senate that requires a vote of at least sixty senators to cut off discussion.

C H A P T E R

11

The Presidency

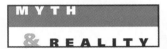

Is the president all-powerful?

See **Political Science** at
http://www.hmco.com/college

While touring tornado-damaged College Station, Arkansas, in 1997 President Clinton ran into six-year-old Vernita Peaster, who, on recognizing the president, said: "You make the laws." The amused president responded: "I do. I abide by the laws and I make the laws, Congress has to help me." The six-year-old's lack of political sophistication is understandable. As children we identify government with authority figures like presidents and police officers. But as we mature, our ability to discern the various features of American government increases. Nevertheless, the special status accorded the presidency never quite disappears.

Presidents are set apart not only from average citizens but also from other leaders because, for many citizens, the president is American government. When things go well, it is because the president is exercising leadership; when they go badly, it is because the president is weak or incapable. Somehow, if we could just get the right president—perhaps another Lincoln or a Roosevelt—all would be well. Whether called the "textbook presidency,"[1] the "imagined presidency,"[2] or the "savior" model of the presidency,[3] that view projects the *myth of the all-powerful president*. Its imagination fueled by legends of great presidents, the public has come to believe that all of the country's problems—social, economic, and international—can be solved by the immense power available to the president. Even presidents succumb to this myth. Jimmy Carter once contended that "the President is the only person who can speak with a clear voice to the American people and set a standard of ethics and morality, excellence and greatness."[4]

In this chapter, we consider the expectations placed on presidents and the powers at their disposal. We begin by examining the evolution of the presidency, for even though the Constitution has changed little with respect to presidential power, the modern presidency is a far different institution than it was in the nineteenth century.

The Growth of the Presidency

On April 30, 1789, General George Washington stood before the assembled Congress and repeated the oath of office administered by Robert Livingston. The oath completed, Washington lifted the Bible to his lips as Livingston cried out, "It is done." But just what had been done must have been a mystery to all present, for none could be sure what shape the presidency would take or what influence presidents would have. Nor did the character of the modern presidency develop in an instant. Rather, the office evolved over the course of two centuries, and during that period the balance of power moved back and forth between the presidency and Congress.

The First Presidents

As the first president, Washington was keenly aware that he was building a new institution and that his every act created a precedent. Although he respected the need to cooperate with others, he was careful to protect the dignity and strength of the office. Once, while on a visit to Boston, Washington was informed that John Hancock, the governor of Massachusetts, was ill and would be unable to call on the president. Believing that governors should defer to the office of the president, Washington canceled his dinner engagement at the governor's mansion and proceeded to outwait Hancock. The next day an apologetic Hancock, carried by four men, appeared at Washington's door to pay his respects.

During his presidency, Washington gave a notably broad interpretation to executive power. Although he stayed aloof from congressional politics, he was quite active in formulating legislation. Using his secretary of the treasury, Alexander Hamilton, to build congressional support, Washington successfully steered his program of economic development through Congress.

Washington also established a number of presidential roles and customs, including the practice of meeting with the heads of his executive departments as a cabinet. His response to international threats established a dominant role in foreign affairs for the presidency. Finally, by refusing to seek a third term, Washington eased fears that the presidency might become a monarchy, and in the process he created the precedent, not broken until 1940, of a two-term limit.

Washington's strength contrasted sharply with the weakness of his successor, John Adams. Although Adams was one of the great American patriots (during the American Revolution, he was known as the "Atlas of Independence"), his presidency was marked by failure. At odds with the opposition party (the Jeffersonians) and with members of his own Federalist party, Adams lasted only one term as president. He lost his re-election bid to Thomas Jefferson.

As the leader of the Jeffersonians (the predecessors of the modern Democratic party), Jefferson advocated restrictions for the national government. Yet as president, he enlarged the powers of the office and skillfully used the political party in Congress. During his presidency, he planned his party's legislative strategy and worked diligently to elect party faithful to Congress. By these actions, he greatly enhanced the president's effectiveness as a legislative leader. Furthermore, without consulting Congress, he doubled the landmass of the United States through the Louisiana Purchase of 1803. Jefferson's immediate successors were comparatively unsuccessful at leading their party. The so-called era of good feelings (1812–1824) was a period of congressional and one-party governance.

The Jackson Presidency.   With the election of Andrew Jackson in 1828, the United States had its first president who was truly elected by the people. Until then state legislatures appointed most members of the electoral college, but by 1828 only Delaware and South Carolina refused to select delegates by popular vote. At the same time, the elimination of the requirement that only property owners could vote significantly expanded the eligible electorate.

Capitalizing on his popularity, Jackson established a popular base for the presidency and strengthened the executive's role. He styled himself as the only representative of all the people and appealed over the heads of congressional leaders directly to the public, which supported him in confrontations with Congress. He vetoed twelve acts of Congress, more than all his predecessors combined. More important, he claimed the right to veto legislation simply because he disagreed with Congress; previous presidents had vetoed bills only when they thought them unconstitutional. Commenting on his battles with Congress, critics complained that the presidency had become an elected monarchy. The president, claimed Daniel Webster, "carries on the government; all the rest are subcontractors."[5]

Congress Reasserts Power

Although Jackson offered little by way of policy initiatives, he profoundly influenced the office by demonstrating that a strong and independent presidency could be founded on popular support. Few of his successors could apply the lessons, however. For the next hundred years, presidents, with a few exceptions, remained in obscurity.

As soon as Jackson retired, Congress re-established its power over the less flamboyant Martin Van Buren (1837–1841)—a man so famous for his political evasiveness that the noun *noncommittalism* was coined to describe his usual public stance.[6] Van Buren, a Democrat, was no match for his opponents in the Whig party. The Whig theory of presidential power held that Congress is the center of government and that the president's job is simply to execute the laws.

Van Buren was not alone in his failure to maintain an independent presidency. The years between Jackson's presidency and Lincoln's were marked by a string of remarkably mediocre presidents. Even their names are difficult to remember. The reputation of Millard Fillmore (1850–1853) illustrates the lack of power of these presidents; his only claim to fame, that he installed the first bathtub in the White House, is not even true. The one exception was James Polk (1845–1849), who annexed Texas through war with Mexico and obtained Oregon Territory by peaceful means from the British. When he left office, the nation was half again as large as when he entered.

In Abraham Lincoln (1861–1865), however, the nation found a president of immense influence. Although Lincoln was a Republican when elected president, he had earlier been elected to Congress from the Whig party. As a Whig, he had continually challenged executive authority, even attacking the war with Mexico as an unconstitutional act initiated by Polk. (Indeed, Polk had provoked the Mexican army into an attack.)

On taking office, Lincoln used the powers of the presidency in new and extraordinary ways. He blockaded southern ports, called up the militia, closed opposition newspapers, ordered the arrest of suspected traitors, closed the mail to "treasonable correspondence," and issued the Emancipation Proclamation—all without prior congressional approval. Throughout the war, Lincoln did

**A President
of Mythic
Proportions**

No president in
American history
more clearly symbol-
izes the all-powerful
president than
Abraham Lincoln.
Here Lincoln meets
with General George
McClellan at the battle
of Antietam.

whatever he thought necessary to win. In conducting the war, he demonstrated that in times of national emergency the American presidency possessed virtually unlimited powers.

Lincoln, like Jackson, was followed by a series of weak, readily forgotten presidents—known collectively as the Bearded Presidents—who were easily dominated by Congress. So complete was congressional control that for the next forty years all important legislation, including the decision to enter the Spanish-American War (1898), was initiated in Congress.

Only the vigorous administrations of Theodore Roosevelt and Woodrow Wilson briefly interrupted the era of congressional government. Viewing the presidency as a "bully pulpit" from which he could educate and appeal to the American public, Roosevelt skillfully used public opinion to build support for his actions. He articulated the "stewardship theory" of presidential power: that the president, as the only official elected by the entire nation, has the duty to take whatever action is necessary as long as it is not specifically forbidden by the Constitution or law. Taking a similar view of the presidency, Wilson was the first president to propose a comprehensive legislative program.

The Modern Presidency

Theodore Roosevelt argued for a strong presidency, but it was Franklin D. Roosevelt who infused the office with power. Confronting the Great Depression and then World War II, the second Roosevelt rallied the American people to accept his leadership and, in the process, the legitimacy of the powerful president. Immediately after his inauguration in 1933, Roosevelt called Congress into special session and in the First One Hundred Days introduced fifteen major pieces of legislation. A willing Congress passed all of them. (One of the most important of these, the administration's banking bill, passed in just seven hours.)

World War II helped expand Roosevelt's power still further. The mobilization effort needed to fight a total war led to such a spectacular growth in government size and authority that the federal government became involved in every aspect of life. Struggling to deal with the emergency of war, Congress willingly turned to the president for policy leadership. By the end of the war, political power had dramatically shifted from Congress to the White House, and the Whig theory of the active Congress dominating the passive president was dead. More important, the heroic image of Roosevelt rescuing the nation so changed the presidency that the nation came to expect action from its vigorous presidents as the norm. As one scholar put it, rather than being a threat to democracy, the strong executive was its "savior."[7] The argument was simple: The more power the executive had, the more good he could do.

Ironically, the "savior" quickly turned into what one critic has called a "Frankenstein monster"[8] when Lyndon B. Johnson and Richard M. Nixon used their power to prosecute an increasingly unpopular war in Southeast Asia. Revelations of secret bombings of Cambodia and the Watergate scandal led to a general disenchantment with the presidency. Suddenly, presidential government seemed harmful to the republic. Many of the same scholars who had glorified the expanded presidency of Franklin D. Roosevelt began to argue that the office had grown too strong. Arthur M. Schlesinger, Jr., whose biographies of Andrew Jackson, Franklin D. Roosevelt, and John F. Kennedy had done so much to build myths around the presidency, began to warn of the dangers of the *imperial presidency*—the increased authority and decreased accountability of the presidency in the 1960s.[9]

In the wake of these concerns, leadership passed to two successive presidents who were anything but imperial. Gerald Ford assured the nation that he was "A Ford, not a Lincoln," and Jimmy Carter, with his cardigans and blue jeans, sought to reduce the pomp surrounding the president. Failing to project an image of a strong leader, both were rejected by voters, and presidential observers began to worry about the *tethered presidency*—a presidency too constrained to be effective.[10]

The election of Ronald Reagan in 1980 seemed to confirm the concerns over the tethered presidency. Elected on the promise to dismantle much of the federal government, Reagan seemed unlikely to manifest the characteristics of the strong president. His first term saw major legislative victories on tax and budget reductions, but deepening economic problems soon overshadowed these triumphs. Midway through Reagan's first term, the number of unemployed reached 11 million, and the president could command only a 37 percent approval rating in the Gallup poll.

Yet those who wrote off Reagan as another one-term president obviously misjudged the situation. Riding the wave of an economic recovery, Reagan scored a landslide victory in 1984. At the beginning of his second term, Reagan garnered higher public opinion approval ratings than had the popular Dwight D. Eisenhower, the last president to serve two full terms. Often defying the image of a lame-duck president, Reagan took strong positions on some issues and backed them by vetoes and threats of vetoes. But the second term was also marred by the Iran-Contra affair, which resulted in the forced resignations and criminal convictions of some of the president's closest advisers, and a much enlarged federal deficit.

As Reagan's political heir, George Bush, in his campaign for the office, benefited directly from Reagan's popularity. But Bush, unlike Reagan, was forced to begin his administration with both houses of Congress controlled by the Democrats. Recognizing this, President Bush called for a "new engagement" between the president and Congress, one characterized by cooperation and mutual respect. Both the invasion of Panama and the war with Iraq were perceived by the public as great successes, and Bush's popularity soared. Buttressed by approval ratings as high as 90 percent, Bush aggressively assailed Congress with a series of vetoes that Congress could not override. In his fourth year, however, the president's popular approval dropped below 40 percent, as the economy suffered through a recession. As a result, Bush became another one-term president.

Although elected with only 43 percent of the popular vote, President Bill Clinton initially had the advantage of taking office with his party controlling both houses of Congress. At times, however, that advantage was more apparent than real. The administration did have some early successes in Congress, most notably the passage of the North American Free Trade Agreement, but the president was also rebuffed by Congress on several occasions. As Clinton fell in the polls and, after the 1994 elections, had to cope with a Republican-controlled Congress, his re-election seemed doubtful. However, the president dealt with Congress skillfully and even succeeded in blaming its extremist elements for the two government shutdowns. As a result, Clinton was able to win re-election in 1996 with 49 percent of the popular vote. But much of the momentum from the victory quickly dissipated as the administration found itself immersed in a series of campaign financing scandals.

Presidential Roles

Tethered or free, presidents are perceived as central to American politics, and perhaps the strongest evidence of their eminence is the variety of roles that they are expected to play. When combined, these roles create the appearance of what has been called "the awesome burden" of the presidency. Indeed, as one scholar has pointed out, "All that is missing is Mover of Mountains and Raiser of the Dead."[11]

Chief of State

Presidents are not just celebrities; they are the American version of royalty.[12] Lacking a royal family, Americans look to the president to symbolize the uniqueness of their government.

As chiefs of state, presidents entertain foreign dignitaries and prominent Americans, throw out the first baseball of the season, review parades, issue proclamations, and carry out other ceremonial duties. To some, these activities may seem a waste of valuable time, but presidents view them as enhancing prestige. Ever mindful of the value of pageantry, Washington regularly rode through the streets of Manhattan (New York then being the nation's capital) in an elaborate carriage pulled by six cream-colored horses. On the days when he chose to ride horseback, he mounted a white steed draped in leopard skin and a saddlecloth bound in gold. His flair for pomp and circumstance was such that John Adams once said of Washington, "If he was not the greatest President, he was the best actor that we ever had."[13]

Chief Executive

Article II of the Constitution clearly specifies that "the executive power shall be vested in a President of the United States of America" and that the president shall "take care that the laws be faithfully executed." On the surface, then, the president appears all-powerful as a chief executive. After all, no other official shares executive authority. Yet the notion that one person can manage an executive branch of some three million civilian employees is an illusion. Presidents quickly discover that management is a considerably more difficult and time-consuming function than they had imagined. Indeed, they often neglect management functions as they find themselves facing more immediate and rewarding political concerns.

Powers to Appoint and Remove.   Given the president's role as the chief executive, it stands to reason that he would possess enormous power to staff the executive branch. Such is not the case, however. Because the vast majority of federal employees are protected by the civil service (see Chapter 12, on the bureaucracy), the president has fewer than two thousand positions to fill by appointment. Moreover, many of these appointments require senatorial approval, which may on occasion be denied. The fate of President Clinton's nomination of Anthony Lake to head the CIA illustrates the Senate's power. After days of grueling questioning about his role in foreign policymaking during Clinton's first term, his personal stock investments, and his management abilities, Lake, the former national security adviser, withdrew his nomination.

Likewise, the president has limited power to remove officials—an issue on which the Constitution is silent. The president can hire and fire agency heads and others who perform purely executive functions. Officials who perform legislative or judicial functions, however, are protected by Congress from presidential discharge, although the line between purely executive functions and those that are legislative or judicial is somewhat unclear.[14]

Power to Pardon.   The president's power to grant pardons and reprieves is one of the few executive powers that Congress may not limit. It may be used to correct what the president sees as mistaken convictions or, as Alexander Hamilton put it, to "restore the tranquility of the commonwealth." Reagan demonstrated the first of these uses when, in 1981, he granted pardons to two FBI agents who had been convicted of burglarizing the homes of Americans suspected of harboring terrorists. Reagan claimed that the agents had acted in good faith, believing their actions were legal. In contrast, after the Civil War, President Andrew Johnson used the power to restore tranquility to a divided nation by granting full amnesty to all Confederate veterans except those guilty of treason or felonies. Similarly, President Ford justified his pardoning of Richard Nixon as necessary to shift national attention away from what he referred to as our "long national nightmare" and toward the economic problems of the nation.

Executive Privilege.   Even though the Constitution makes no mention of this power, presidents since Washington have claimed **executive privilege**—the right to withhold information from the legislature. Justifying their claims either by the need for secrecy in foreign affairs or by the necessity of keeping advice confidential, presidents exercised the power without serious congressional challenge for almost two hundred years.

The issue came to a head, however, when the Nixon administration greatly expanded the meaning of executive privilege. As the events of Watergate began to unfold, Nixon tried to deflect inquiry by claiming that executive privilege applied to all executive officials. At one point, Nixon even claimed the privilege for all who had worked for the executive branch in the past.

The Nixon version of executive privilege was challenged in court when the Watergate special prosecutor requested tape recordings of White House conversations. The president, citing executive privilege, refused to turn over the tapes, and the special prosecutor pursued the matter in federal court. In the case of *United States* v. *Nixon* (1974), the Supreme Court ruled that presidents could rightfully claim executive privilege but not when facing a criminal investigation.[15] Thus although the Court recognized the need for executive privilege, it also set limits on this power.

Chief Diplomat

According to Article II of the Constitution, the president is authorized to make treaties with the advice and consent of the Senate; to receive foreign ambas-

President Clinton
looks on as the Pales-
tine Liberation Orga-
nization's chairman
Yasser Arafat (left)
shakes hands with
Israeli Prime Minister
Benjamin Netanyahu
at the conclusion
of an Israelian-
Palestinian Summit
at the White House.

sadors and ministers; and, with the advice and consent of the Senate, to nominate and appoint ambassadors, ministers, and consuls. As chief diplomat, the
president plays a leading role in shaping U.S. foreign policy, but he is seldom
free to do as he wishes. Although President Harry Truman once claimed, "I
make foreign policy," presidents have found their role as chief diplomat far more
constrained than it appears.

Treaties.   The power to make treaties illustrates the limits of the role. A literal
reading of the Constitution suggests that both the president and the Senate are
to take part in all phases of the treaty process. Such was Washington's initial understanding, but he soon changed his mind. While negotiating a treaty with the
Indians, Washington appeared before the Senate and requested advice on certain provisions. The Senate, however, withdrew to discuss the matter without
Washington. Angered by the Senate's refusal to engage in face-to-face discussions, Washington reversed his position.

Since Washington's time, no president has appeared before the entire Senate seeking advice on treaty provisions. Nevertheless, presidents do consult
prominent senators. As former secretary of state Dean Acheson said, "Anybody
with any sense would consult with certainly some of the members of the ratifying
body before he got himself out on the very end of a limb from which he could
be sawed off." [16] At times individual senators are even included in the delegation

appointed by the president to negotiate a treaty. The 1963 nuclear test ban treaty was negotiated in the presence of a panel of senators. In contrast, President Woodrow Wilson did not include senators in the delegation to the conference that created the League of Nations at the end of World War I. Many observers believe that this oversight angered members of both his own and the opposition party and led the Senate to reject U.S. membership in the new international organization.

Consulting leading senators is imperative because every treaty must be approved by two-thirds of the Senate before it can take effect. Even if the Senate does not reject the treaty, it can modify it in ways that may not be acceptable to the president. President Carter, for instance, won the necessary Senate support for his Panama Canal treaties only after agreeing to several Senate modifications that he initially opposed.

Executive Agreements.   To avoid the uncertainties associated with treaty ratification, presidents frequently turn to **executive agreements,** agreements with other nations made by the president without the Senate's consent. Such accords have all the legal force of treaties but, unlike treaties, are not binding on succeeding presidents.

Even though the Constitution does not provide for executive agreements, presidents since Washington have used them more and more, for both trivial and important matters (see Table 11.1). Because executive agreements can be made quickly and secretly, presidents use them to avoid rejection by the Senate. Thus in 1905, when Senate Democrats, fearful of foreign commitments, blocked consideration of a proposal for American operation of customhouses on the Caribbean island of Santo Domingo, Theodore Roosevelt implemented the proposal as an executive agreement.[17]

Legally, anything the president and the Senate can do through treaty can be accomplished by executive agreement. The political reality is sometimes quite different, however, since the implementation of executive agreements often requires congressional action. Executive agreements, for instance, generally need appropriated money, which means that both the House and the Senate become involved in the implementation. Recently, presidents have made use of an innovative method, known as the **congressional-executive agreement**—an agreement (usually a trade agreement) with a foreign nation negotiated by the president and then submitted to both houses of Congress for approval. By submitting the agreement to the Senate and the House, the president can win the assent of those who would be needed to carry out the agreement, and yet avoid the constitutional requirement of a two-thirds vote in the Senate needed for treaty ratification. (Congressional-executive agreements need only a majority vote in each house for approval.) President Clinton successfully used this procedure to win approval for the North American Free Trade Agreement (NAFTA), which probably would not have received the necessary votes in the Senate if it had been submitted as a treaty.

WWW•
For more information on congressional executive agreements, see the **Gitelson/Dudley/Dubnick web site.**

TABLE 11.1

Treaties and Executive
Agreements Approved
by the United States
Senate, 1789–1994

Year	Number of Treaties	Number of Executive Agreements
1789–1839	60	27
1839–1889	215	238
1889–1929	382	763
1930–1932	49	41
1933–1944 (F. Roosevelt)	131	369
1945–1952 (Truman)	132	1,324
1953–1960 (Eisenhower)	89	1,834
1961–1963 (Kennedy)	36	813
1964–1968 (L. Johnson)	67	1,083
1969–1974 (Nixon)	93	1,317
1975–1976 (Ford)	26	666
1977–1980 (Carter)	79	1,476
1981–1988 (Reagan)	125	2,840
1989–1992 (Bush)	67	1,371
1993–1994 (Clinton)	41	594

Source: Harold W. Stanley and Richard Niemi, *Vital Statistics on American Politics,* 5th ed.
(Washington, D.C.: CQ Press, 1995), p. 260. Reprinted with permission of Congressional Quarterly Inc.

Power of Recognition. As an element of their constitutional power to receive foreign ambassadors and ministers, presidents possess the power of recognition. The simple act of receiving a foreign diplomat signifies the official recognition of the sponsoring government. As one observer noted, "Throughout the entire course of our national history the President has performed dozens of acts of recognition of new governments without consulting, or being expected to consult, Congress."[18] Thus Washington granted recognition to the new French Republic without consulting Congress. Similarly, within hours of Soviet President Mikhail Gorbachev's resignation, President Bush extended recognition to Russia and five other republics of what had been the Soviet Union.

Diplomatic Appointments. A final aspect of the president's role as chief diplomat is the power to make diplomatic appointments. According to Article II of the Constitution, the president "shall nominate, and by and with the advice and consent of the Senate, shall appoint ambassadors, other public ministers and consuls." By and large, the Senate automatically approves the nominees, allowing the president to fill diplomatic posts with people who share his views. On occasion, however, members of the Senate delay and even obstruct a confirmation as a way of expressing displeasure with administration policy. In reaction to Nixon's efforts to normalize relations with the People's Republic of China, several senators used confirmation hearings to block the administration's initiative. Nevertheless, David Bruce and George Bush, Nixon's liaisons to Beijing, were eventually confirmed.

Commander in Chief

Of all the president's roles, the most controversial is that of commander in chief. Under the provisions of Article II of the Constitution, the president is the "Commander in Chief of the Army and Navy of the United States, and of the Militia of the several States, when called in the actual service of the United States." The Constitution, however, clearly assigns the power to declare war to Congress, and not to the president. Alexander Hamilton, in the "Federalist No. 69," stressed this division of responsibilities when he said of the role of commander in chief, "It would amount to nothing more than the supreme command and direction of the military and naval forces, as first general and admiral of the confederacy." Thus the president was to command the troops once they were committed to battle, but Congress was to make the decision to wage war.

Addressing the Troops

As commander in chief, presidents generally exercise wide latitude in deploying troops. Here President Clinton address U.S. soldiers stationed in Tuzla, Bosnia as part of peace-keeping mission.

Although the founders restricted the role of commander in chief, presidents have come to view this power quite expansively. In fact, presidents have regularly committed troops to action without asking Congress to formally declare war. Usually these actions have been small in scale, as when Jefferson sent ships against the Barbary pirates in 1805. Sometimes, however, presidents have unilaterally embarked on major war efforts. Convinced that he possessed all the powers necessary to win the Civil War, Lincoln undertook a series of extraordinary actions that included the blockade of southern ports, the expenditure of $2 million from funds not appropriated by Congress, and the drafting of 300,000 militiamen. All of this was done without explicit statutory authorization, although later Congress did approve most of the president's actions.

In the period preceding American entry into World War II, Franklin D. Roosevelt issued several orders of doubtful constitutionality. The most famous of these was his "shoot at sight" order given to U.S. naval vessels transporting military material to Great Britain. Roosevelt's directive, issued without congressional approval, empowered the U.S. naval forces to fire at German submarines even though the United States had not yet entered the war. A formal declaration of war did not come until three months later, after the attack on Pearl Harbor.

Roosevelt's successor, Harry S Truman, went a step further in exerting presidential power when he ordered U.S. troops to repel an attack on South Korea by North Korean troops. On learning of the North Korean assault, Truman did not seek a congressional declaration of war but immediately committed thousands of American soldiers to combat in what was called a "police action." Truman moved with such haste that his order to the troops preceded both the South Korean and the United Nations requests for intervention. Later the administration justified American actions as necessary to fulfill the U.S. commitment to the United Nations. However, a State Department publication of the time noted that the dispatching of military forces was really based on the "traditional power of the president to use the Armed Forces of the United States without consulting Congress." [19]

Presidents have taken over the power to make war because Congress and the public, particularly in the face of the perceived threat of the Cold War, have let them do so. Even though specific presidential actions have at times generated controversy, Congress has been willing to surrender its constitutional authority to the president. Not until the U.S. involvement in Vietnam divided the nation did Congress begin to reassess its own role.

Johnson's and Nixon's continuation of that war led Congress and the public to question presidential power to make war. Yet the initial commitment of American military forces to Vietnam had followed a familiar pattern of executive leadership and congressional docility. In August 1964, Johnson reported to Congress that the USS *Maddox* had been attacked while patrolling in international waters off the coast of North Vietnam. At the president's request, Congress responded to the event by passing, with only two dissenting votes, the Gulf of Tonkin Resolution, which authorized the president "to take all necessary measures to repel any armed attack against the forces of the United States and to prevent further aggression." Thus, with little knowledge of the actual events and only nine hours of debate, Congress provided the president with a blank check to increase American involvement as he saw fit.

Nine years after the Gulf of Tonkin Resolution, Congress moved to limit the war-making powers of the president by passing the War Powers Resolution of 1973. Enacted over Nixon's veto, the War Powers Resolution provided that the president could send troops into hostile territory for a period not to exceed sixty days (Congress can provide a thirty-day extension). If within that time Congress does not approve the actions or if by resolution it votes to withdraw the troops, they must be removed. Another important provision of the resolution requires the president "in every possible instance" to consult with Congress before dispatching troops into hostile or potentially hostile situations.

Years after its enactment, the effectiveness of the War Powers Resolution remains questionable. Gerald Ford, the first president to initiate actions that could be said to fall under its provisions, refused to acknowledge its legitimacy. In 1975, he ordered air and ground forces to rescue an American ship, the *Mayaguez,* and its crew from Cambodian communists. Ford did not consult with members of Congress before committing the troops but merely informed Congress of actions already under way.

A more serious challenge to the War Powers Resolution came in 1982, when Reagan detailed a "peace-keeping" force of marines to Lebanon. Like Ford, Reagan refused to acknowledge the validity of the resolution and therefore did not formally notify Congress of his actions. One year after the introduction of the marines, Reagan and congressional leaders worked out a compromise that allowed the marines to stay in Lebanon for eighteen months on the understanding that the president would recognize the legitimacy of the resolution.

Reagan then became the first president to invoke the resolution, but only in this one instance. In 1983, he informed Congress about the invasion of Grenada after it was over, and late in his term he refused to invoke the resolution in his decision to provide U.S. naval escorts for foreign ships operating in the Persian Gulf, even though these ships often engaged in hostilities. Similarly, although George Bush informed Congress of the 1989 invasion of Panama, he refused to acknowledge the legitimacy of the War Powers Resolution. Some members of Congress objected to Bush's refusal to invoke the resolution, but the quick collapse of armed resistance and the evidence of public support for the invasion stilled congressional resistance.

Most telling of all, however, is the insignificant role that the War Powers Resolution played in the war with Iraq. Following the Iraqi invasion of Kuwait, Bush deployed troops to Saudi Arabia without informing Congress. As the mission changed from defending Saudi Arabia to driving Iraq out of Kuwait, some members of Congress began to protest. Eventually Bush requested and received congressional support for his actions, but only after he became convinced that he had strong support in Congress. By joint resolution in January 1991, Congress approved what amounted to a declaration of war when it authorized the president to use "all means necessary" to force Iraq out of Kuwait. Neither Congress nor the president, however, invoked the War Powers Resolution, and the president claimed, even as Congress was voting on the joint resolution, that he needed no congressional authorization. For some analysts, the minor role played by the War Powers Resolution in the Gulf War suggests that it is no longer viable.[20]

Indeed, President Clinton paid little heed to the resolution in his 1994 planned invasion of Haiti. Claiming that presidential power was sufficient, Clinton, without congressional authorization, directed the army's Eighty-second Airborne Division to invade Haiti. As it turned out, negotiations with Haitian leaders resulted in a last-minute compromise. The assault unit en route to Haiti was then ordered back and a forceful invasion of the island was avoided, although more than eleven thousand troops were peacefully inserted onto the island.

Chief Legislator

These days the mass media, the public, and even members of Congress look to the president as a kind of grand legislator who initiates public policy and then guides it through Congress. As soon as they take office, presidents are expected to formulate and present a well-defined legislative program that promises to solve all that ails the nation. As the chairman of the House Foreign Affairs Committee told an Eisenhower administration official in 1953, "Don't expect us to start from scratch on what you people want. That's not the way we do things here. You draft bills and we work them over."[21]

These assumptions suggest that the president possesses broad legislative powers, but such is not the case. Article II of the Constitution gives the president only four rather narrow legislative duties: (1) to "convene both Houses, or either of them" in special sessions; (2) to adjourn Congress if the two houses cannot agree on adjournment; (3) to "from time to time give Congress Information of the State of the Union"; and (4) to recommend such measures "as he shall judge necessary and expedient." In addition, Article I arms the president with a veto.

The president no longer uses his powers to convene and adjourn Congress, mostly because of the extended length of the legislative year. Congress was last called into special session on July 26, 1948—the day turnips are planted in Missouri. President Truman barraged this so-called turnip Congress with one reform proposal after another. When, as expected, Congress failed to act, Truman had the issue for his 1948 campaign. Running against the "do-nothing, good-for-nothing" Eightieth Congress, Truman defeated his Republican opponent, Thomas E. Dewey, and scored the biggest political upset of the century.

Recommending Legislation.   The weak presidents of the 1800s offered Congress few specific policy proposals for fear of appearing to meddle with the legislative process. Modern presidents show no such reluctance, and this attitude certainly contributes to the myth of their unlimited power. The State of the Union message delivered each January illustrates the change in presidential dealings with Congress. During the 1800s presidents typically offered nothing more than a routine report on the work of the previous year. Today this message is a major political statement addressed to the entire nation. The president exalts the administration's achievements and presents legislative goals for the coming year. Carefully crafted to hold the attention of the radio and television audience (a detailed written report is provided a few days after the oral message), the contemporary State of the Union message gives the president an opportunity to mobilize congressional and public support.

The president presents legislative proposals in less conspicuous ways as well. Numerous statutes require the president to submit detailed reports and even specific legislation. Each year, for instance, the president, as directed by the Budget and Accounting Act of 1921, presents a proposed federal budget for congressional consideration. Similarly, the president reports annually on the nation's economic condition, as required by the Employment Act of 1946.

As you will soon see, initiating legislation and mobilizing sufficient support to secure passage are two different matters. Members of Congress expect presidential initiatives; they even demand them. That does not mean, however, that the president's program will pass.

The Veto Power.   The president's ultimate weapon is the veto. After passing both houses of Congress, bills are submitted to the White House for the president's signature. A presidential signature is not necessary for a bill to become law, however. If the president fails to act within ten days of receiving the bill (Sundays excepted), the bill becomes law without presidential approval.

During the last ten days of a session, the president's failure to sign has the opposite effect: it kills the bill. The action, known as a **pocket veto,** is particularly effective because Congress, which has gone out of session, has no way to fight back. When presidents exercise their ordinary veto power by sending bills back to the originating house, their vetoes can be overridden by a vote of two-thirds of those present in both houses.

In practice, Congress overrides few vetoes, giving presidents a substantial advantage. Nixon's veto of the War Powers Resolution at the height of the Watergate scandal shows how hard it is for Congress to muster its forces for an override even when a president is in disgrace. Though the scandal seriously undermined the president's public support, the House was able to override his veto by only a four-vote margin.

Because Congress succeeds in overriding vetoes so rarely, presidents can wring concessions from it through the threat of a veto. In such instances, the House and Senate drop provisions that run counter to White House priorities and sometimes even withhold entire bills rather than face certain veto. But to make the threat credible, the president must occasionally use the veto. At one time Franklin Roosevelt is said to have pleaded with his staff to "give me a bill that I can veto" so that Congress would be convinced of his willingness to use the power.[22]

For several years presidents have complained that the veto power is too blunt an instrument to prevent wasteful spending. Since the president must sign or veto the entire bill, Congress has often attached **riders:** provisions opposed by the administration. Thus the president must accept the objectionable parts or veto the entire bill. In most cases the president signs the bill.

After years of debate, Congress, in 1996, finally passed legislation bestowing on the president the **line-item veto:** the power to veto portions of a bill while signing the rest. Under the terms of the act, which became effective January 1, 1997, the president may sign a bill, but strike out individual spending provisions. The president may also cancel any tax break that applies to a hundred or fewer taxpayers. There are some limitations, however. The president may not cut out spending for entitlement programs such as social security or Medicare. Moreover, a spending item can be eliminated only if it reduces the budget deficit. Money saved by the use of the line-item veto may not be transferred to another program.

Congress can restore the canceled provisions by passing a bill disapproving the cuts. The president, however, can veto that legislation, and Congress can override that veto only by a two-thirds vote in both chambers.

Whether the line-item veto will actually reduce spending remains to be seen. What is clearer is that the act represents a major transfer of power from the legislative to the executive branch. As opponents of the bill argue, it is likely that presidents will use the threat of a veto as leverage against members of Congress. By targeting home-state spending, presidents may coerce members into supporting administration proposals.

Since Congress created the line-item veto by legislation rather than through a constitutional amendment, its constitutionality is questionable. Within hours of passage several members of Congress filed suit to prevent its use, but since the act had not yet been invoked the Supreme Court refused to rule on the issue.

WWW•

For more information on the line-item veto, see the **Gitelson/Dudley/ Dubnick web site.**

Impoundment.   Presidents have also tried to create an item veto by **impounding** (withholding) funds appropriated by Congress. As far back as Jefferson, presidents have claimed the right to impound funds either by deferring spending to some later date or by forbidding agencies to spend money. Jefferson postponed spending $50,000 on gunboats in 1803 so that he could purchase a more advanced model the following year.

Traditionally, impoundment power has been used cautiously to avoid confrontation with Congress; in most cases the money was eventually released. Taking impoundment further than any previous president, Nixon provoked a series of confrontations with the Democratically controlled Congress. After failing to get Congress to agree to cut spending, Nixon simply impounded appropriated funds, arguing that he had a right not to spend money that he had not requested from Congress. Nixon used the technique to eliminate whole programs that he disliked. By signing the bills that created the programs but refusing to spend the money to implement them, he fashioned a veto that could not be overridden. His strategy was more than a method of controlling spending: it was a means of controlling Congress.

Congress responded by limiting the president's impoundment power. In the Budget and Impoundment Control Act of 1974, it set forty-five days as the maximum time that funds may be impounded. During that time Congress must pass a new act—a rescission bill (as in *rescind,* or repeal)—to cancel the spending, or the funds must be spent.

The Seamless Web

For the sake of easier discussion, it is useful to partition presidential responsibilities into distinct roles. Yet presidential activity is not so neatly divided. In fact, the various roles form a "seamless web" of overlapping connections in endless combinations, and doing well in one role may be essential to performing another.[23] For instance, successful performance as chief of state can often benefit a president seeking to fulfill other roles. Similarly, when diplomatic actions involve the threat or use of force, the distinction between chief diplomat and commander in chief may all but disappear.

The Institutional Presidency

According to the standard organizational charts reproduced in textbooks, the president is the boss of some 3 million civilian employees—the largest administrative organization in the country. Obviously, no single person can control an organization of such size, yet that is exactly what is expected of presidents. But the president does not perform the task alone, for the modern president is surrounded, perhaps even engulfed, by layers of presidential advisers, known collectively as the institutional presidency.[24] Included in that group are members of the cabinet and of the Executive Office of the President, the White House staff, and the vice president.

The Cabinet

The original advisory group is the cabinet. Not provided for in the Constitution, the cabinet by tradition comprises the heads of the major executive departments and other officials whom the president designates. George Washington created the cabinet by meeting frequently with his attorney general and the secretaries of state, treasury, and war. (James Madison gave those meetings with Washington the title of the "president's cabinet.") The modern cabinet consists of the fourteen department heads, the ambassador to the United Nations, and the director of the Office of Management and Budget. In 1996, President Clinton elevated the director of the Federal Emergency Management Agency to the cabinet.

As a collective unit, the cabinet has seldom functioned as an effective advisory body for the president. Because it is not provided for in the Constitution, its role in decision making is defined by the individual presidents, who rarely find it useful. Many presidents have undoubtedly found themselves in the position of Lincoln when he asked his assembled cabinet for advice. As Lincoln went around the table, each member voted against the president's position. Undisturbed, Lincoln announced, "Seven nays and one aye, the ayes have it."

Most candidates for the presidency have high hopes for the cabinet and promise to revitalize it when elected. Early in the first term there is usually a great show of cabinet meetings, but the president soon grows weary of that approach. Acting on his promise to create a strong cabinet, Carter held sixty such meetings during his first two years in office. By the spring of 1979, he was so disenchanted that he asked all of his cabinet secretaries to resign. (He accepted four of the resignations.)

In 1980, Reagan promised to restore cabinet government. Because Reagan attached great importance to the budget, he added the director of the Office of Management and Budget to the cabinet. Even this did not prevent the inevitable disillusionment. By the end of Reagan's first year in office, cabinet meetings had become largely ceremonial events, with policy developments coming out of the White House.

Even though collectively the cabinet does not often act as an effective advisory body to the president, its members may perform important advising functions. In any cabinet, for instance, there are likely to be individuals who are close to the president. (John F. Kennedy's reliance on his brother, Attorney General Robert Kennedy, is an obvious example.) By virtue of the departments they head, members of what Thomas Cronin calls the "inner cabinet" (the secretaries of state, defense, and the treasury and the attorney general) are most likely to serve as important counselors to the president. The secretaries of the clientele-oriented agencies (that is, the secretaries of health and human services, education, labor, housing and urban development, the interior, agriculture, commerce, transportation, energy, and veterans affairs) generally constitute a kind of "outer cabinet," whose members often have little direct contact with the president.[25] Indeed, the pressures to represent the interests of their clientele often put secretaries of these departments at odds with the president.

The Executive Office of the President

In 1939, the President's Commission on Administrative Management reported: "The President needs help." Acting on the commission's recommendations, Franklin D. Roosevelt issued an **executive order**—a rule or regulation that has the effect of law—creating the Executive Office of the President (EOP). The

Advising the President

Modern presidents are surrounded by layers of advisers that constitute the institutional presidency. However, few presidential advisers have been more influential than Robert Kennedy, who served as attorney general in his brother's administration. In addition to his responsibilities as attorney general, Robert Kennedy served as the president's closest confidant on a variety of issues not directly related to the Department of Justice. Robert Kennedy is shown here meeting with President Kennedy.

EOP is not so much an office as an umbrella for a hodgepodge of organizations performing a wide variety of tasks for the president. Currently, it is composed of fourteen separate organizations, the most important of which are the Office of Management and Budget, the Council of Economic Advisers, and the National Security Council.

The Office of Management and Budget. The Office of Management and Budget (OMB), until 1971 known as the Bureau of the Budget, is the largest of the organizations within the Executive Office of the President. The OMB's primary function is to prepare the president's budget for presentation to Congress each January. The departments and agencies of the executive branch each submit their budget requests to the OMB, which screens these requests for fidelity to the president's program and impact on the economy. Because no agency can request appropriations from Congress without clearance from the OMB, the director of the office, who is appointed by the president with senatorial confirmation, serves as an important means of controlling the budget and making policy through budgetary power. Although originally the OMB was viewed as a professional organization producing independent analysis, it has in recent years become an institutional advocate for the president's initiatives, a status that often puts it in direct conflict with other departments, particularly those that compose the "outer cabinet."

In addition to its budgetary responsibilities, the OMB routinely reviews all legislation proposed by the executive departments and agencies to make sure that the proposals are consistent with the president's program.[26] Agencies proposing laws and regulations with projected costs of $100 million or more must justify the expense. The OMB cannot reject the proposal on the basis of such a cost-benefit analysis, but it can recommend that the president do so. Occasionally, it even conducts cost-benefit analyses on its own. Although these procedures help evaluate the effectiveness of new programs and regulations, they heighten tension between the departments and the Executive Office of the President.

The Council of Economic Advisers.   Legislated into existence by the Employment Act of 1946, the Council of Economic Advisers (CEA) consists of three members, generally professional economists, appointed by the president with senatorial confirmation. Its small but highly competent staff advises the president on the full range of economic issues: unemployment, inflation, taxes, federal spending levels, and the value of the dollar abroad. The council also prepares an annual report that contains analyses of current economic data and economic forecasts. Given its wide-ranging responsibilities, the council often finds itself competing for influence in economic policymaking with the director of the Office of Management and Budget, the chairman of the Federal Reserve Board, and the secretaries of the treasury, commerce, and labor.

The National Security Council.   Created by the National Security Act of 1947, the National Security Council (NSC) advises the president on foreign and defense policy. By statute, the NSC consists of the president, the vice president, and the secretaries of state and defense. In addition, the heads of the Central Intelligence Agency and the Joint Chiefs of Staff are statutory advisers. The president may also request the attendance of other officials.

The role of the NSC depends greatly on the president's preference. President Eisenhower met weekly with the council, but succeeding presidents have preferred to rely on informal groups of advisers and the special assistant for national security affairs. Originally, the job of special assistant for national security affairs was little more than the secretary of the NSC. But President Kennedy, in order to limit his dependence on the State Department, placed greater authority in McGeorge Bundy, the special assistant, encouraging him to create a "Little State Department." President Nixon's special assistant, Henry Kissinger, rivaled the secretary of state in power. Using an enlarged staff and his considerable political skills, Kissinger soon eclipsed Nixon's secretary of state, William P. Rogers, as foreign policy adviser to the president. Ultimately, Rogers resigned, and Kissinger took on both jobs.

During Reagan's second term, the National Security Council became the subject of controversy over its direction of undercover operations in Iran and Nicaragua. In an effort to secure the release of Americans held hostage in the Middle East, NSC employees arranged for the sale of weapons to Iran. Profits from these sales were then diverted to Contra rebels attempting to overthrow the government of Nicaragua, despite a congressional ban on such aid. In this instance, rather than serving as an advisory body, the NSC took on policy implementation.

The White House Office

Technically, the White House Office is part of the Executive Office of the President, but in an important sense the two organizations are separate. The White House Office is composed of staff members who are located in the White House and serve the president's political needs. Smaller than the Executive Office of the President, it is nevertheless a sizable organization in its own right—for example, in the Clinton administration, it employs more than four hundred people. The White House Office includes assistants, special assistants, counselors, special counselors, and consultants of varying titles who owe almost total loyalty to the president. Originally, the staff was limited to coordinating executive branch activities, but increasingly presidents, frustrated by their inability to control the bureaucracy, have tried to centralize power by relying on the White House Office to develop and implement policy initiatives. Indeed, much to their chagrin, cabinet secretaries often find that policies affecting their departments are developed in the White House Office.

The actual structure of the office depends on the president's organizational preferences. Some presidents have favored a rather loose structure in which several aides report directly to the president. Sometimes referred to as the "wheel," this highly personalized approach is designed to assure the president access to information. The best-known exponent of this organizational style was Franklin D. Roosevelt, who often assigned the same task to different aides. The fierce competition among his aides, each wanting recognition from the boss, maximized the information available to the president and allowed him to extend his influence.

Although valuable as a means of gaining information, the wheel may create confusion and conflict among staff members, creating the impression that the president cannot manage his own office. Carter's early efforts to implement the wheel style of organization led to public battles among his aides and contributed to his image as an ineffectual leader. On the other hand, Reagan's use, in his first term, of a modified version of the wheel style proved generally successful.

Some presidents have favored a tight structure, with staff responsibilities and reporting procedures clearly detailed. Under this organizational style, which resembles a pyramid, only one or two key aides have access to the president. Eisenhower, with his military background, clearly preferred this type of arrangement, delegating much authority to his chief aide, Sherman Adams. Nothing could come to the president unless it was initialed by Adams. Carrying the pyramid style a step further, Nixon used his chief of staff, H. R. "Bob" Haldeman, and his domestic adviser, John Ehrlichman, to seal him off from the rest of government. Haldeman had such tight control over the president's daily schedule that not even members of the president's family could see him without Haldeman's permission.

Pyramid structures can reduce the president's burden, allowing concentration on those issues that truly require a president's time. But the relief may come at some cost. Staff members may limit their communications to what the president wants to hear, cutting off dissenting viewpoints. The aides may make important decisions before the questions reach the president. As two critics have observed, "presidential assistants can become assistant presidents."[27]

The Vice President

Benjamin Franklin once suggested that the vice president be called "His Superfluous Majesty," and Daniel Webster, saying that "he did not propose to be buried until he was already dead," refused to accept nomination for the office.[28] Although fourteen vice presidents have become presidents, esteem for the office

A Role for the Vice President

Recent presidents have assigned several responsibilities to their vice presidents. Here President Clinton applauds as Vice President Gore announces plans to reorganize the federal bureaucracy. The vice president's recommendations, known as "reinventing government," were a centerpiece of the Clinton administration.

has never been high. The reason rests with the Constitution: it provides the vice president with little to do. The vice president's only constitutionally prescribed task—presiding over the Senate—offers little real power, except to cast a tie-breaking vote. The vice president has no role in the day-to-day business of that body.

The vice president does, of course, become the president if the president dies in office, resigns, or is impeached and removed from office. Furthermore, since the adoption of the Twenty-fifth Amendment, the vice president can assume the presidency if the president decides that he is disabled, or if the vice president and a majority of the cabinet declare the president to be disabled. For instance, Reagan, before undergoing cancer surgery, wrote a letter empowering Vice President George Bush to take over the functions of the presidency while Reagan was under the anesthetic.

Because the Constitution does not specify the vice president's duties, they are determined by the president. Typically, presidents send their vice presidents to advisory panels and ceremonial functions that they want to avoid. Perhaps the most striking example of a distant relationship between a president and a vice president was provided by Franklin D. Roosevelt. Although it was known for months that the president was dying, Truman was not briefed on the existence of the atomic bomb until after he became president, a mere four months before he made the decision to use it.

In part, presidents have been reluctant to delegate too much power to their vice presidents for fear of creating a political rival. Generally, vice-presidential candidates are chosen with an eye to drawing to the ticket the additional supporters that the presidential candidates need; thus they are potential competitors for the limelight. The vice president is also a constant reminder of the president's own mortality. Indeed, Lyndon Johnson likened the vice president to "a raven hovering around the head of the president." [29]

Recently, however, presidents have delegated more responsibilities to their vice presidents. Carter signaled a change in the role of the office by allowing his vice president, Walter Mondale, to influence the selection of several high officials in the administration. Presidents since Carter have continued to assign expanded responsibilities and greater visibility to their vice presidents. Vice President Al Gore, for instance, was given the responsibility of spearheading the Clinton administration's task force on reinventing and streamlining government operations.

Presidential Influence

To those outside the office, the myth of the all-powerful president seems compelling. Yet presidents themselves stress the frustrations of holding office. For instance, Truman, describing what it was going to be like for his successor, Eisenhower, said: "He'll sit here, and he'll say, Do this! Do that! And nothing will happen. Poor Ike—it won't be a bit like the army."[30] Similarly, Lyndon Johnson once complained that the only power he had was nuclear, and he could not use it.

The point of these remarks is that presidential desires are not automatically translated into government policy. Power is shared in the American system. Congress, with its different constituency interests, often checks presidential initiatives. The bureaucracy seems to have endless opportunities to circumvent presidential directives. According to political scientist and former presidential adviser Richard Neustadt, for a president to be effective, he must become adept at persuasion, convincing others that what he wants of them is in their own interest.[31]

Persuading Congress

Perhaps the greatest and most persistent problem facing any president is working with Congress. According to Lyndon Johnson, "There is only one way for a President to deal with Congress, and that is continuously, incessantly, and without interruption. If it's really going to work, the relationship between the president and Congress has got to be almost incestuous."[32] As you may recall from Chapter 10, on Congress, presidential initiatives are only a starting point for congressional action. Obtaining congressional support is crucial. In pursuing this goal, presidents have three primary resources: party loyalty, staff lobbyists, and personal appeal.

Party Loyalty.   At the heart of a successful strategy for dealing with Congress is the political party. Presidents must retain the support of members in their own party while gaining the support of as many of the opposition party as possible. Historically, party loyalty has been fairly strong in the Republican party, and less so among Democrats in Congress. Clearly, presidents cannot take their own partisans for granted, but they can assume that most members of the opposition party will oppose them. Having a majority of seats in Congress is no guarantee of an administration's success, but it is easier than dealing with a Congress controlled by the opposition.

Lobbying Staff.   Before 1953, contacts between the president and Congress were informal and largely based on personal relationships. Some presidents relied on frequent social occasions to discuss their concerns with members of Congress. Jefferson used that tactic with particular success. His elaborate dinner parties were planned as much for their lively talk as for the superb cuisine. In 1953, however, Eisenhower created the Office of Congressional Relations to formalize the administration's lobbying efforts. (That did not, of course, replace the social occasions; rather, it provided the president with a structure to coordinate lobbying activities.)

Because Eisenhower offered few major legislative proposals, the office was small and mostly concerned with heading off the passage of legislation that he opposed. During the Kennedy and Johnson years, however, the office began to grow substantially as these administrations took a more aggressive legislative posture. Johnson, in particular, used the office to inform members of Congress of the administration's position on issues and to solicit congressional support. More important, Johnson expanded the role of the office by instructing the administration's lobbyists to help members of Congress with personal services for constituents.

Although talented lobbyists can be quite effective in persuading members of Congress to support administration proposals, they must have presidential involvement to succeed. According to Bryce Harlow, legislative liaison chief under both Eisenhower and Nixon, "for real effectiveness a White House congressional man must be known on Capitol Hill as a confidant of the president; he must be in the know."[33] As if to underscore the point, Harlow resigned as Nixon's liaison chief because he lacked the necessary access to the president.

During Carter's first year as president, his Office of Congressional Relations was notorious for virtually ignoring Congress. Complaints of phone calls not returned and a staff of inexperienced aides aggravated tensions between the White House and Congress. Much was made of the fact that Carter's chief liaison officer, Frank Moore, had no Washington experience, but the real problem was that Carter paid little attention to Congress. Congressional relations were not a high priority of the early Carter administration.

Personal Appeal.   A president's ability to appeal personally to members of Congress can be vital to his success. A little flattery and attention from a president

Healing the Wounds

In times of crisis Americans often look to the president for leadership. Here President and Mrs. Clinton attend a memorial service for the victims of the Oklahoma City federal office building bombing.

11.1 The View From the Governors' Mansions

As the governor is the chief executive of a state, it may be tempting to view that office as analogous to the office of president, but on a smaller scale. The analogy breaks down, however, on examination of the legal and constitutional authority that governors have. When it comes to gubernatorial power, expectation and reality are often far apart.

The nation's first governors, as representatives of the British Crown, commanded broad powers—except in Rhode Island and Connecticut, where they were elected by the people. Colonial governors commanded the armed forces, appointed judges as well as most other officials, vetoed legislation, and even convened and dissolved the legislature. Indeed, the powers of the governors became a focal point of antiroyalist protests.

Not surprisingly then, the first state constitutions formulated after the country had gained independence constrained executive authority. Five of the original states created plural executives, with the governor being simply the presiding officer over an executive council. Only two of the original state constitutions (New York and Massachusetts) granted the governor a veto, and all but three limited the governor's term to one year, often without the possibility of succession. Frequently, too, governors were appointed by the legislature rather than elected. Northern states tended to create more powerful governors than the southern states, but weak governors were the rule throughout the nation.

When the Jackson presidency revived executive authority, governors benefited as well. State constitutions began to expand executive power. Many states lengthened the term of governors, restored the veto power, and, most important, provided for elected chief executives. Slowly, governors began to emerge from the shadows of state legislatures. But the era's emphasis on the election rather than appointment of public officials (characterized by the long ballot) impeded gubernatorial power. Surrounded as they were by administrative officials who were also elected statewide, governors often lost control over their own administrations.

Today's governors generally enjoy substantial advantages over those who served only a few decades ago. For instance, in all but one state, gubernatorial terms are now four years. (The exception is New Hampshire, where the governor's term is two years.) Furthermore, all states except Virginia allow governors to be re-elected. Most states limit the governor to two consecutive terms, but some, like Texas, do not restrict the length of service.

In forty states, the governors have full responsibility for proposing the budget, and, to the envy of most recent presidents, forty-one states have given their governors some version of the line-item veto.

Nevertheless, modern governors are still constrained by the number of elected officials serving in the executive branch. The governor is the sole elected executive official in only three states: Maine, New Hampshire, and New Jersey. North Dakota, on the other hand, elects twelve officials statewide. Coordinating activities is difficult in an administration populated by many elected officials, but it is even more complex when, as is true in several states, only the governor's right to succession is restricted. In North Carolina, for instance, the governor can serve only two consecutive terms, whereas the secretary of state, the treasurer, the attorney general, and the heads of four major departments face no limits on consecutive terms of service. Under these conditions, entrenched executives often view the governor as a temporary interloper.

Most troubling to some governors is their relationship to the lieutenant governor. In nineteen states, the governor and lieutenant governor are elected separately. This often creates difficulties as the two officials may disagree on significant policy questions. Former Democratic governor of Arkansas Jim Guy Tucker, for one, discovered the pitfalls of leaving the state in the hands of an elected lieutenant governor. While Governor Tucker was on a medical visit to Minnesota, Lieutenant Governor Mike Huckabee, a Republican, signed a Christian Heritage Week proclamation that Tucker had previously rejected.

Yet clearly, the governors' power in American politics is rising. The fact that three of the last four presidents had been governors indicates the new-

found respect the office carries. Still, most governors and many observers worry that the office is not equipped to perform the demanding tasks of modern state governments. Reform efforts aimed at modernizing gubernatorial authority will continue as the states take on responsibilities previously borne by the national government.

Sources: Thad L. Beyle, "The Executive Branch: Organization and Issues, 1992–93," in *The Book of the States*, vol. 30 (Lexington, Ky.: Council of State Governments, 1994); and Larry Sabato, *Goodbye to Good-time Charlie: The American Governorship Transformed* (Washington, D.C.: Congressional Quarterly Press, 1983).

For more information on your state's governor, see the **Gitelson/Dudley/Dubnick** web site.

can go a long way in persuading members of Congress. Reagan used this personal approach to great advantage, offering frequent invitations to breakfast at the White House and the gift of cuff links bearing the presidential seal in his persistent effort to cultivate relations with Congress. On important bills, the president often made phone calls to wavering members, personally soliciting their support. But even Reagan's personal appeal had its limits. Although he demonstrated great success in securing congressional support early in his first term, his success rate declined markedly after 1982. A little flattery may go a long way, but too much dilutes its effectiveness.

Public Opinion

Lincoln once said, "Public sentiment is everything. With public sentiment nothing can fail, without it nothing can succeed." Although Lincoln overstated the importance of public approval, popularity is an important tool of persuasion. One political scientist has argued that members of Congress try to predict the public's reaction to their behavior toward the president and often decide on that basis what tack they should take.[34] Lacking precise information about public attitudes, they look to the president's popularity as a guide. Popularity does not guarantee presidential success, however. "When [a member of Congress] is confronted by a choice between supporting a popular president and the clear interests of his constituents, the president's public prestige is a poor match for his or her constituents' interests."[35]

FIGURE 11.1

Presidential Approval, 1982–1997

Every president experiences a decline in public approval as the term of office progresses.

Sources: 1982–1988: *The Gallup Report* (July 1988), 19–20; the Gallup poll, "Reagan Regaining Public Confidence," press release, October 9, 1988; and the Gallup Library, 1994–1997, from the Gallup web page http://www.gallup.com/ratings.

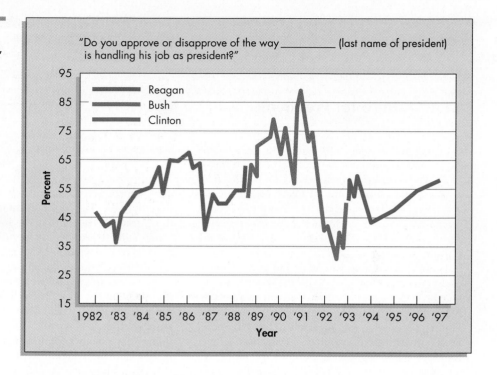

"Do you approve or disapprove of the way _____ (last name of president) is handling his job as president?"

Naturally, presidents are well aware of the importance of public popularity. (When the polls were good, Lyndon Johnson used to carry the results in his breast pocket, ready to show anyone who needed convincing.) Recent presidents have increasingly tried to translate their popularity into political strength by taking their policy proposals directly to the public. Many of Reagan's early successes in cutting the budget were attributed to his skillful use of this strategy. His televised appeals to the nation for help in cutting taxes put pressure on Congress to act.[36]

As a method of influence, going public has its drawbacks, however. First of all, there is always the danger of overuse. A president who calls for public response too many times may find the audience losing interest. More fundamentally, the effectiveness of public appeals depends on the president's general popularity, and presidential popularity tends to decline during the term of office.

At the beginning of their term, presidents traditionally enjoy a honeymoon period of broad public support and favorable media coverage. Indeed, with the exception of Ronald Reagan, a substantially larger percentage of Americans have approved of newly elected presidents than were willing to vote for them. By the third year in office, however, public approval declines significantly (see Figure 11.1). President Bush's drop from a 90 percent approval rating immediately after the Gulf War to 39 percent at the beginning of his fourth year serves as a reminder of the likelihood of decline.

MYTHS IN POPULAR CULTURE

11.1 A Hero for President

In the summer of 1996, millions of Americans flocked to their local theaters to see director Roland Emmerich's science fiction thriller *Independence Day*. With its mix of heavy prerelease advertising, excellent special effects, and predictable melodramatic plot, including three separate love stories, *Independence Day* became a major hit of the summer season.

As the film opens, we are treated to an eerie vision of the American flag planted on the moon's surface being covered by the shadow of an alien spacecraft. A few minutes later the scene shifts to the White House and the fictional president, Tom Whitmore. President Whitmore, seeming so much like John F. Kennedy, is a young, handsome Gulf War hero, with an attractive wife and a small child. He is also a president under attack. Criticized from all sides for his lack of success, his public approval ratings slipping below 40 percent, the president is described by a real-life newswoman, Cokie Roberts, as a wimp.

The wimp president, however, is transformed back into the hero as the alien spaceships descend on the earth's major cities. Rising to the challenge, he addresses a frightened nation, urging calm and stressing American desire for peace. When, despite his peace overtures, the alien ships start destroying the earth (some marvelous special effects show the White House being blown up), the president is forced to act. On the Fourth of July, he redeems himself and saves the world by once again becoming a hero.

Entertaining as it is, the movie offers a pastiche of several well-worn themes regarding American politics. Take, for instance, the characterization of President Whitmore as a wimp. Why is he a wimp? His aide tells him that he has become a politician. He compromises too much, and compromise is beneath a true leader. If he would just stick to his principles, he could once again become a great leader.

The movie also develops the theme of government conspiracy, so successfully used in the television drama *X Files*. In the midst of the alien attack, the president learns that for forty years the government has been secretly spending billions of dollars at a place called Area 51. Managed by the CIA and the Department of Defense, Area 51 houses an alien spacecraft and its former occupants, as well as the obligatory mad scientist. (We all know about this place because that is where those famous alien autopsy films were made.) Of course, all these doings have been kept secret from the American people and their idealistic president by venal bureaucrats, who form an inside-the-beltway shadow government.

In the end, the aliens are defeated by the technical wizardry of a cable television technician/environmentalist (Jeff Golblum) and a squadron of fighter planes, manned by civilians (a kind of high-tech civilian militia) recruited and led by the president. Here then is a president who lives up to the job. No longer encumbered by politics or bureaucrats (he fired his secretary of defense), President Whitmore disdains compromise and transcends the status of a politician, becoming a leader.

More important, President Whitmore restores America to its place as the world leader. Not just Americans, but the whole world has been waiting for the president to lead the attack. Addressing the squadron before the assault, President Whitmore delivers a rousing speech, in which he notes that henceforth our national holiday will be the world's holiday. America behind a true leader saves the world, or what's left of it anyway, and inspires ordinary people to rise to the challenge. This is truly the president as savior.

The existence of this decline in presidential popularity is part of what political scientist Paul Light calls the "cycle of decreasing influence." According to Light, as the term progresses, a president's political capital (that is, public approval and partisan support), time, and energy diminish, seriously eroding his influence over public policy. Moreover, Light argues that in a president's second term the cycle is more pronounced. Re-election gives the president a brief burst of resources, but the falloff is more rapid than in the first term.[37] Given this cycle, presidents may even suffer from these initially high ratings. When inflated ratings drop, as they inevitably do, "the fall can be all the more devastating."[38]

High levels of public approval may also be a trap for modern presidents. As a president's popularity surges, expectations of successful leadership also escalate. Indeed, the more popular the president, the more the myth of the all-powerful president seems a reality. But, as we have seen, presidents are not the government, and while high public approval ratings may give presidents some leeway, they do not automatically translate into power. A highly popular president who does not translate high approval ratings into visible legislative successes runs the risk of looking like a failure.

Conclusion: The All-Powerful President?

According to the myth of the all-powerful president, modern presidents possess awesome powers that, if mobilized, could enable them to solve all the country's problems. Although that myth has not always prevailed, it has colored public expectations of the presidency in the latter half of the twentieth century. As the office evolved to its current state, the course of change has not been smooth. Presidential power has increased at times of grave emergency and great stress. In calmer periods, Congress has generally reasserted its role by reining in the president.

The broad range of roles ascribed to the president further enhances the myth of presidential power. Yet presidents often find that the duties ascribed to these roles are more difficult than they imagined. And Congress is hardly a silent spectator in the process of governing.

To give him support in his various roles, the president has acquired a multitude of advisers—in the cabinet, the Executive Office of the President, and the White House Office. In fact, presidents are surrounded by a bureaucracy of advisers who constitute the institutional presidency. Thus the president does not lack counsel, but with the growth of the institutional presidency, the problem has become that of managing the advisers.

Finally, we have also examined presidential power as persuasion. Although the office itself is generally seen as all-powerful, presidents find that their wishes do not automatically become policy. In this system of shared powers, the president must convince others that what he wants lies in their interest as well.

Invoking party loyalty, effective lobbying, and personal appeal are all potential means of persuasion, but the support of the public is particularly useful. Although popular approval does not guarantee presidential success, it makes it more likely.

Summary

1. The powers of the presidency have expanded significantly since the adoption of the Constitution. American history has witnessed periods of presidential dominance, usually in times of emergency, followed by congressional efforts to reassert the power of Congress by limiting that of the president.

2. The importance of the modern presidency is seen most clearly in the variety of roles that the incumbent is now expected to play. As chief of state, for example, the president is the ceremonial head of the government.

3. As chief executive, the president must "take care that the laws be faithfully executed" and manage an executive branch composed of some 3 million employees. To perform the duties of chief executive, the president has the power of appointment, the power to grant pardons, and the power of executive privilege, but none of these is unlimited.

4. As chief diplomat, the president, with the advice and consent of the Senate, can negotiate treaties and make diplomatic appointments. The president also has the power to extend diplomatic recognition to other countries and can make executive agreements with other nations without Senate approval.

5. As commander in chief, the president is supreme commander of the military forces. Presidents have also used that role to claim the power to make war.

6. As chief legislator, the president can convene special sessions of Congress and adjourn Congress if the two houses cannot agree on a date of adjournment. The president is also required to give Congress "from time to time" information on the "State of the Union" and to recommend measures for congressional action. Furthermore, the president has the power to veto acts of Congress, although the veto is subject to override.

7. The modern president is assisted by several advisory groups: the cabinet, the Executive Office of the President, the White House Office, and the office of the vice president. These groups constitute the institutional presidency.

8. The cabinet, consisting of the fourteen department heads, the ambassador to the United Nations, and other officials whom the president designates, is the original presidential advisory group. But the cabinet does not often function effectively, and most presidents hold cabinet meetings for purely ceremonial purposes.

9. Created by an executive order of Franklin D. Roosevelt, the Executive Office of the President (EOP) contains ten separate organizations, including the Office of Management and Budget, the Council of Economic Advisers, and the National Security Council.

10. Also within the EOP is the smaller White House Office, which includes assistants, special assistants, counselors, special counselors, and consultants, who perform a wide variety of personal and political duties.

11. The vice president presides over the Senate but votes only to break a tie. The vice president assumes the presidency if the president dies, resigns, is removed by impeachment, or is unable to function because of a disability.

12. To be effective, presidents must be skilled at persuasion. In dealing with Congress, presidents can rely to some extent on party loyalty, but they must also assemble an effective lobbying staff and use it well. Skillful use of personal appeals to legislators is often effective and necessary.

13. Presidents are more successful at persuasion when their public popularity is high, but popularity often eludes them as their term progresses.

Key Terms and Concepts

Executive privilege The traditional right, claimed by presidents since Washington, to withhold information from Congress.

Executive agreements Agreements with other nations made by the president without the Senate's consent. They have all the legal force of treaties but, unlike treaties, are not binding on succeeding presidents.

Congressional-executive agreement An agreement with a foreign nation negotiated by the president and then submitted to both houses of Congress for approval.

Pocket veto An action whereby the president fails to sign a bill during the last ten days of a term and thus effectively kills the bill.

Riders Provisions that Congress knows the president opposes but that Congress attaches to bills the president otherwise desires.

Line-item veto The power to veto portions of a bill but sign the rest of it. The president was given this power in 1997.

Impoundment When a president withholds funds that have been appropriated by Congress for a bill. Used in place of an item veto, a power so far denied the president. See *item veto*.

Executive order A rule or regulation issued by the president that has the effect of law.

12

Bureaucracy

• A Profile of the Federal Bureaucracy

Who Are the Bureaucrats? Political appointees, merit systems, and wage systems

What Do Federal Bureaucrats Do? Direct policy implementation and proxy administration

Where Do They Work? Executive Office of the President, the cabinet departments, independent executive branch agencies, regulatory commissions, government corporations, and other agencies

A Diverse Institution: Large and complex

• Growth of the American Bureaucracy

Overview of Bureaucratic Growth: Rapid expansion since late 1800s

Explaining the Growth of the Bureaucracy: Several causes

• Bureaucratic Power

The Sources of Bureaucratic Power: External support, expertise, discretion, longevity in office, and skill and leadership

Limiting Bureaucratic Power: Self-restraint and limited resources, the White House, Congress, the courts, other restraints; increased responsiveness

• Bureaucratic Problems and Reforms

Bureaucratic Pathologies: Clientelism, incrementalism, arbitrariness, parochialism, and imperialism

Calls for Reform: Various approaches; presidential reform efforts

• Conclusion: Expectations and Government Operations

MYTH & REALITY

Are Washington bureaucrats unresponsive and incompetent?

WWW•

See **Political Science** at
http://www.hmco.com/college

Until the summer of 1994, Glenwood Springs, Colorado, was best known for its mineral springs' swimming pool and a turn-of-the-century hotel that attracts several thousand tourists each year. Although lacking the glamour and facilities of Aspen, Vail, and the other ski resorts that dot Colorado's mountainous terrain, Glenwood Springs has a charm enhanced by the beauty of the juniper- and piñon-lined canyons that surround it. Located 180 miles west of Denver, it is the kind of place where Coloradans escape for a summer weekend away from the smog-filled and crowded cities that have blossomed along the eastern range of the Continental Divide.

All that relative peace and calm changed in July 1994 when a wildfire flared up on Storm King Mountain, which rises to form the western border of the community of 6,500 residents. The fire was initially confined to an uninhabited area along the Colorado River, five miles from Glenwood Springs. By July 5, however, the situation called for action by federal officials who had jurisdiction over the lands.

On Wednesday afternoon, July 6, fifty-two firefighters—most of them members of the U.S. Forest Service's "Hot Shot" team—were busy digging trench lines along a slope located about a half-mile from a major highway that curves

MYTH & REALITY

Dangerous Enough for Government Work

Many federal employees do not fit the typical stereotype of the gray-suited bureaucrat sitting at some desk in Washington, D.C. Pictured is a federal firefighter who survived the tragic fire in Glenwood Canyon, Colorado, that took the lives of fourteen of his colleagues.

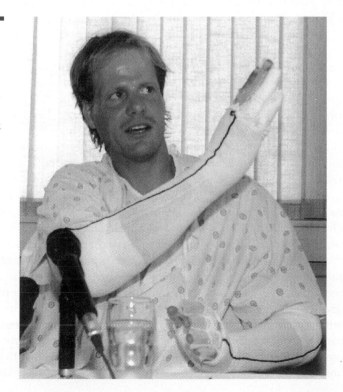

along the Colorado River through Glenwood Canyon. This was a mundane task, and there seemed little danger from the well-contained blaze situated hundreds of yards away.

Suddenly unforecasted wind gusts shot through the canyon, turning the blaze into a firestorm that rushed up the mountain slope at more than 1,000 feet per minute until it reached the lowest crest. The fifty-acre fire would quickly expand to consume 2,110 acres along the Storm King slopes. As the flames and heat (estimated to have reached temperatures of 1,600 to 2,000 degrees Fahrenheit) headed up the slope, crew members began to either run for safety or seek protective cover in "pup tent" shelters specially designed for such circumstances. Eight of those who used the metal-lined pup tents survived, while another thirty who tried to outrun the flames survived by following a previously dug fire line or racing to reach the slope's crest. Fourteen others, however, were not as lucky. It took two days to recover their bodies.

Among the fourteen dead were two firefighters from Colorado, two from Idaho, one from Montana, and nine members of the Hot Shot crew from the small town of Prineville, Oregon. In a few moments, that community lost four women and five men. On July 9, the same day the fire was being brought under control, the people of Prineville held their annual rodeo parade. At the end of the procession walked eleven surviving members of the local Hot Shot crew. They marched beside nine riderless horses while the people of Prineville stood in silent tribute.[1]

When Americans think about government bureaucracy, they rarely consider the Hot Shots or the thousands of others who risk—and sometimes give—their lives in public service. Instead, they picture incompetent or unresponsive pencil pushers, sitting behind their desks in Washington, D.C., wasting the taxpayers' money. Those are the images fed by the popular media and built on a foundation of two pervasive myths: the *myth of bureaucratic incompetence* and the *myth of the unresponsive bureaucracy*.

Behind the myth of bureaucratic incompetence is a widely held belief that the management of government programs should not be significantly different from private-sector management. According to that view, governments can and should be as efficient and effective as businesses. The myth of bureaucratic incompetence has emerged because most government programs do not seem to live up to private-sector standards. For most Americans, the federal bureaucracy seems too large and cumbersome—bloated by wasteful practices and inefficiencies.

Public opinion polls illustrate the growing popularity of the myth of bureaucratic incompetence. Since at least the mid-1960s, of those Americans surveyed, most felt that government was wasteful.[2] In 1992, 70 percent of 3,517 Americans agreed with the statement that "When something is run by the government it is usually inefficient and wasteful." Sixty-four percent of that sample also agreed that "Dealing with a federal government agency is often not worth the trouble."[3] Another 1992 survey (of 1,387 registered voters) found that only 14 percent of those polled believed they could trust government to do what is right most of the time, and only 28 percent agreed with the statement "If government acts to solve a problem, I can count on it to be effective."[4] The growing negative assessment of bureaucratic competence is made worse by the fact that it reinforces a trend toward overall distrust of government. In a survey conducted in late 1995, 80 percent of those who had expressed a distrust of the federal government said inefficient and wasteful government was a major reason for their negative views.[5]

The myth of an unresponsive bureaucracy is also reflected in survey results. Many Americans assume that individual agencies and bureaucrats do as they please, despite popular or political wishes. At the heart of this myth is the idea that government bureaucracies appear accountable to no one but themselves. As a consequence, the actions of many federal agencies seem to serve the self-interest of the bureaucrats rather than the public. That is clearly illustrated in Figure 12.1. Those agreeing with the statement that government "is pretty much run by a few interests looking out for themselves" increased from 29 percent in 1964 to nearly 76 percent in 1994, while 51 percent of those surveyed in 1994 believed that "quite a few of the people running government are crooked." Twenty years earlier only 29 percent agreed with that statement.[6] Given the widespread belief in the myth of the unresponsive bureaucracy, it is little wonder that the American public is suspicious about the work of federal government agencies.

FIGURE 12.1

Is Government Run for the Benefit of All? 1964–1994

Source: National Election Studies, "Support for the Political System: Is Government Run for the Benefit of All? 1964–1994." http://www.umich.edu/~nes/nesguide/toptables/tabs5a–2.htm, April 28, 1996.

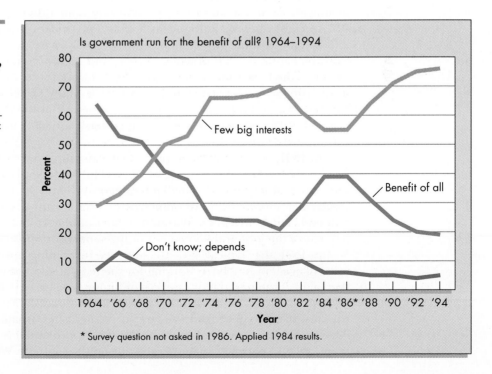

A Profile of the Federal Bureaucracy

The myths of an incompetent and unresponsive federal bureaucracy result in part from a lack of knowledge about the agencies and the people who make up the administrative machinery of our government. We often hear complaints about *the* bureaucracy as though it were a monolithic beast that could be found in some central location in the middle of Washington, D.C.—just like Congress or the White House or the Supreme Court. As we shall see, the facts offer an entirely different picture.

Who Are the Bureaucrats?

Technically, a **bureaucracy** is any large, complex organization in which employees carry out specific job responsibilities within a hierarchy. For most Americans, however, the term bureaucracy is commonly used to describe both government agencies and the people who work in them. For our purposes, the term applies to the 2.9 million nonelected civilian federal employees working in the United States and abroad. Although we will focus on these civilian federal workers, we should keep in mind that another 1.7 million uniformed individuals are in the military and 15.9 million work for state and local governments.

Four of every five federal civilian workers are employed in full-time clerical, technical, service, managerial, professional, and other white-collar positions. That includes people working in a wide range of occupations. For example, in 1991 the federal government employed 766 creative arts therapists, 2,136 microbiologists, 12,924 practical nurses, and 23,953 general attorneys. Equally diverse is the blue-collar federal government work force, which includes carpenters, maintenance workers, and a variety of other skilled and unskilled jobs. In 1991, for instance, the federal government employed 10,948 sheet metal workers, 9,715 electricians, 8,995 pipefitters, and 668 water treatment plant operators.[7]

In 1991, 56 percent of all federal civilian employees were men and 44 percent were women. The number of women in the federal government has been increasing rapidly, but not in all job categories. Thus, 49.1 percent of all federal white-collar employees were women, with a significant portion of them holding low-level clerical positions. Within the ranks of blue-collar workers, men held 90 percent of the jobs and 95 percent of the supervisory positions.

In 1991, the "typical" federal employee (excluding postal workers) was 42.5 years of age and had been working for the federal government 13.5 years. More than a third had a bachelor's degree or higher, and earned an annual base salary of $34,100. Members of minority groups constituted 27.7 percent of all federal workers: 16.8 percent African-American, 5.4 percent Hispanic, 3.6 percent Asian-American, and 1.9 percent Native American. Approximately 28 percent were veterans, with 15 percent having served during the Vietnam War.[8]

MYTHS IN POPULAR CULTURE

12.1 Hollywood Bureaucrats . . . and other Myths

The myths surrounding bureaucracy find their expression in many parts of America's popular culture, but especially in its movies. On any given evening, Americans can select from among dozens—if not hundreds—of home videos that entertain by using myth-based images of government bureaucracy.

Those with a hankering for some comic relief can find movies that spoof incompetent, bungling, or overzealous government officials. The U.S. Environmental Protection Agency is the inept source of problems in the film *Ghostbusters.* In the 1993 release *Coneheads,* agents of the U.S. Immigration and Naturalization Service are overeager and self-serving in their pursuit of the strange, pointy-headed "aliens."

Those who prefer action and adventure movies may find the messages about government bureaucracy more mixed. In the 1993 movie *Cliffhanger,* starring Sylvester Stallone, the heroism of a National Park Service mountain rescue team soon makes you forget the corruption of a federal offi-

cial that resulted in the hijacking of a shipment of Treasury notes. And while most people who saw *In the Line of Fire* will remember how Clint Eastwood's Secret Service character stopped a presidential assassination, they will also recall the negative image of his superiors, who constantly questioned his competence.

The same double message about government employees comes through in the film version of Tom Clancy's novel *Clear and Present Danger.* The hero, Central Intelligence Agency deputy director Jack Ryan (played by Harrison Ford), stands out as a bureaucrat with professional integrity who will not give in to the political pressures of Washington, D.C. In stark contrast is the behavior of Bob Ritter, another deputy director who supports the bad political decisions and regards Ryan as a hopeless "boy scout." Rarely, if ever, is the motion-picture image of the public servant unambiguous. In most instances that image portrays the contrasting myths about public administrators.

Political Appointees. The federal government has adopted several different personnel systems to manage this large and diverse work force. The most visible consists of **political appointees,** who occupy the most strategically important positions in government. At the top of this group are the members of the president's **cabinet,** an official advisory board comprising the heads of the fourteen major departments responsible for carrying out most of the federal government's policies and programs (see Chapter 11, on the presidency). The heads of these departments have the title of secretary, except at the U.S. Department of Justice, where the chief officer is called the attorney general. Below them are assistant and deputy department secretaries, deputy assistant secretaries, counselors, and a variety of other appointive positions.

Under President Bill Clinton, 347 cabinet officials hold the top formal appointments made by the president that had to be confirmed by the U.S. Senate. The president makes another 272 Senate-confirmable political appointments to fill other leading positions in his administration, primarily to head independent agencies and regulatory commissions such as the Environmental Protection Agency and the Federal Trade Commission (see below). In addition to these, Clinton (like his predecessors) appointed nearly two thousand other individuals who were not subject to Senate confirmation. All these appointees owe their loyalty to the president, and with few exceptions their tenure in office hinges on how the White House evaluates their performance.

At one time in our history, political appointees made up a vast majority of the federal bureaucracy. **Patronage**—a system in which you receive a government position based on whom you know rather than what you know—was commonplace. Thomas Jefferson used patronage in 1801 when he replaced many government workers loyal to John Adams and the Federalist party. But the first wholesale application of patronage followed Andrew Jackson's election nearly three decades later. Jackson believed in the **spoils system,** that is, giving government jobs at all levels to members of the winning party ("to the victor go the spoils"). That reflected more than a desire to reward his friends: Jackson was committed to opening up government positions to ordinary American citizens, and the political appointment process was his means of promoting democracy.

The Jacksonian spoils system influenced the design and operation of the federal government for several decades. Under the system, the federal bureaucracy was probably more than usually responsive to the president's wishes, because loyalty to the White House was the key to getting the job in the first place. But there was another important outgrowth of this patronage approach. Because no one stayed for very long in any position, government jobs had to be redesigned and standardized so that anyone could step in to fulfill the tasks of the position. Thus the job of being a postal clerk or a customs tax collector was made much simpler and less demanding. Instead of seeking people with special skills for special jobs, government agencies hired less-skilled people and then trained them to do the tasks demanded by the simply designed positions.[9]

Merit Systems.   But the spoils system inevitably led to undesirable outcomes, such as widespread political corruption in the administration of Ulysses S. Grant and the assassination of President James Garfield in 1881 by a disgruntled office seeker. These events led to calls for reforms, and in 1883 Congress passed the **Pendleton Act,** which reduced the number of political appointments a president could make and established a merit system for about 10 percent of existing federal jobs. A **merit system** stresses employee ability, education, experience, and job performance; political factors are not supposed to be considered. Hiring and promotion depend on competitive examinations or job performance evaluations, usually overseen by a civil service commission or professional personnel office.

The national government's merit system now applies to almost 95 percent of all federal civilian jobs. Many of these come under the **general civil service system,** which covers government positions from weather forecasters to financial analysts and from librarians to civil engineers. Many of these federal workers obtain their jobs through a competitive process. Almost all positions under this personnel system are ranked according to a General Schedule (GS), which ranges from GS-1 through GS-15 (see Table 12.1).

The highest ranks in the general civil service system (GS-15 and above, often called the "supergrades") overlap the **Senior Executive Service (SES),** a select group of federal public administrators who specialize in managing public agencies. Most of the civil servants in the elite SES have made their mark as effective supergrade managers in the highest positions within individual agencies. In joining the SES, those managers agree to make themselves available for transfers to other agencies that need their talents. In exchange, they receive higher salaries (see Table 12.1) and the possibility of greater rewards. Before the Civil Service Reform Act of 1978 established the SES, the best executive talent in the federal government could not be efficiently or effectively used because moving from one agency to another was too difficult. Now, along with a small group of

TABLE 12.1

Meritorious Service: The Pay Scale for Federal Employees

Salaries for bureaucrats range from somewhat above minimum wage to salaries comparable to those of executives in private industry.

General Civil Service

Grade: Salary Range for 1997

1:	$12,669–15,844	9:	29,577–38,451
2:	14,243–17,928	10:	32,571–42,345
3:	15,542–20,204	11:	35,786–46,523
4:	17,447–22,685	12:	42,890–55,760
5:	19,520–25,379	13:	51,003–66,303
6:	21,758–28,283	14:	60,270–78,351
7:	24,178–31,432	15:	70,894–92,161
8:	26,777–34,814		

Senior Executive Service (SES)

ES-1:	$ 97,000	ES-4:	111,900
ES-2:	101,600	ES-5:	115,700
ES-3:	106,200	ES-6:	115,700

Source: Salary table no. 97-GS. U.S. Office of Personnel Management, 1997.

presidential appointees, SES and supergrade personnel fill the major manager-ial positions in federal agencies.

Besides the general civil service and the SES, there are **career service per-sonnel systems** for highly specialized agencies, such as the Forest Service and the Coast Guard. Perhaps the best known of these career service systems is the For-eign Service, which includes more than 13,000 State Department officials who serve in American embassies throughout the world. The Department of Veterans Affairs (formerly the Veterans Administration) operates the largest career serv-ice system, employing more than 36,000 physicians and surgeons. Altogether, ap-proximately 125,000 federal civilian employees occupy positions in these career service systems.

Wage Systems.   Finally, more than a million workers can be classified as part of the federal government's **wage systems.** Included in this group are those with blue-collar and related jobs, ranging from pipefitting to janitorial work. More than 623,000 full-time and 167,000 part-time postal workers make up the largest single organized group in this category. Many of the workers in these wage sys-tems are paid by the hour, and a great many are represented by unions or other associations that have limited bargaining rights under current civil service laws.

What Do Federal Bureaucrats Do?

The primary role of the national bureaucracy is to implement the policies of the federal government. In that sense, the work of federal agencies touches almost every aspect of American lives. Sometimes these agencies carry out the policies themselves. For example, the Federal Aviation Administration employs air traffic controllers to oversee the growing volume of aviation in America's skies, and fed-eral rangers protect and manage national parks and forests throughout the country. We also deal with federal employees directly when the U.S. Postal Serv-ice delivers our mail, when we have questions about social security benefits, or when we have problems with our federal taxes.

At other times the federal bureaucracy carries out its implementation tasks indirectly through a variety of tools that one analyst has termed "government by proxy." **Proxy administration** of government programs includes such things as government contracts, grants-in-aid, loan guarantees, and the establishment of government-sponsored enterprises to carry out government programs.[10]

Many government activities are carried out through *government contracts* with private firms. The U.S. Department of Defense makes use of this approach when it hires private companies to build weapons systems or supply food for the troops. In 1995, for example, McDonnell Douglas, a St. Louis–based company, earned more than $8.5 billion from government contracts. Although that may seem like a significant amount of business, the federal government purchased more than $200 billion in goods and services from private companies during that same year.[11]

Doing the Public's Business

Many private firms conduct the public's business under government contracts. Among the biggest contractors are aircraft manufacturers.

The intergovernmental relations system and its *grant programs,* discussed in Chapter 3, on federalism and intergovernmental relations, offer another indirect means of implementation. For instance, through grants to states and localities, the U.S. Department of Education can get local school districts to offer special-education courses for children with learning disabilities. Similarly, the U.S. Department of Transportation provides funds to states for highway construction and maintenance through a special trust fund.

The federal government also uses other indirect means to carry out some of its policies. Through bank *loan guarantees,* for example, some federal agencies are able to get local financial institutions to lend money to home buyers, students, or farmers who might not otherwise qualify. These guarantees cost the taxpayers nothing until and unless the borrower defaults on the loan—something that was happening with greater frequency for student loans during the 1980s.

In some cases, the federal government has established special *government-sponsored enterprises,* which, among other functions, make credit more easily available to special populations for specific purposes without relying on loan guarantees. Though created by the government, these organizations often operate as if they were privately owned and operated. For example, the federal government created the Student Loan Marketing Association (known as "Sallie Mae"), which promotes low-cost loans to students by arranging to "buy" student bank loans from lending institutions and then selling them to investors. Similar organizations exist for home loans (such as the Federal National Mortgage Association, known as "Fannie Mae") and loans to farmers.

Federal bureaucracies also play an important role in making government policies. They often provide expert advice to policymakers, especially in the design of special policies and highly technical programs. Agencies such as the Bureau of Reclamation and the Army Corps of Engineers develop plans for water diversion and storage projects, which then go to the White House and Congress for revision and adoption as official government programs. At other times Congress and the president establish the general outlines of policies and leave specific policy decisions to designated agencies. That approach is commonplace with defense policies, in which program details are left to civilian and military experts at the Pentagon.

Where Do They Work?

Federal civil servants work in literally hundreds of agencies, ranging from those closest to the president to agencies with a great deal of independence from the White House (see Figure 12.2).

Executive Office of the President.   Faced with the task of managing the federal bureaucracy, the president relies on several agencies that collectively make up the **Executive Office of the President (EOP)** (see Chapter 11, on the presidency). Among the most important of the EOP agencies is the **Office of Management and Budget (OMB).** The OMB is the president's principal link to most federal agencies. Almost all federal agencies report to the OMB on matters relating to program and budget requests. A smaller (but no less important) group of EOP employees is located in a variety of offices known collectively as the **White House Office.** These staff members include the president's key advisers, as well as those who help the chief executive deal with the day-to-day business of the presidency.

Also found in the EOP are various council and staff members specializing in particular policy areas. These agencies include the *Council of Economic Advisers,* the *National Security Council,* and the *Office of National Drug Control Policy.* The number of these agencies changes with each presidential administration. For example, in 1981 President Ronald Reagan eliminated the Council on Wage and Price Stability, which was created ten years earlier by President Richard Nixon to oversee anti-inflation policies. In 1989 President George Bush established a National Space Council in the EOP to deal with issues related to the nation's space policy; a similar agency had been eliminated years earlier by Nixon during his administration. When Bill Clinton took office, he eliminated the National Space Council. At the same time, President Clinton created a National Economic Council to assist in the coordination of economic policy and changed the mission of the Office of National Service to promote his initiative for providing college students an opportunity to volunteer for community service as a means for repaying educational loans.

The importance of EOP agencies also varies over time. For many years, the Special Representative for Trade Negotiations was an obscure office in the EOP.

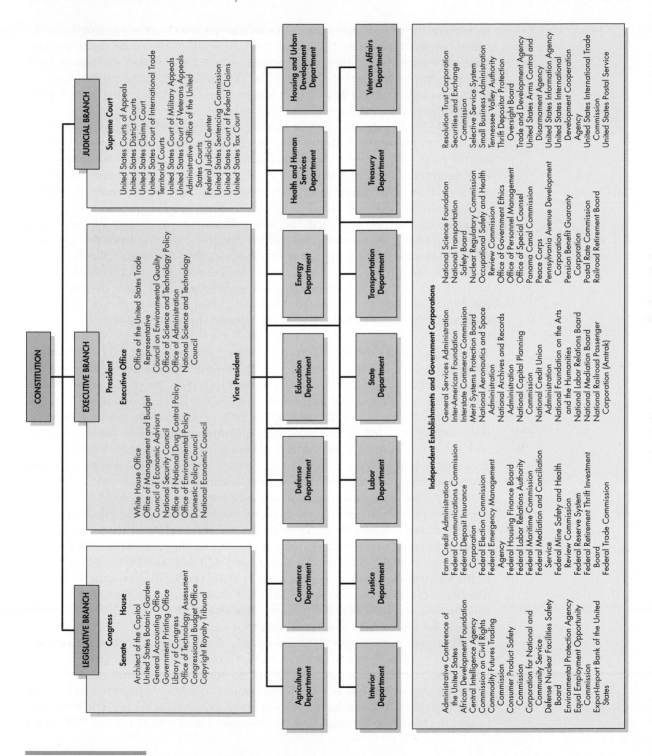

FIGURE 12.2   Government of the United States

As foreign trade and international economic policy became a major factor in American life during the 1970s and 1980s, the job of the trade representative grew more important. The agency, now called the *Office of the United States Trade Representative,* became increasingly visible. The choice of a person to head the office was as significant as any cabinet appointment for Presidents Jimmy Carter, Ronald Reagan, and George Bush.

EOP agencies are designed to play key roles in formulating, but not in carrying out, public policy. Under the Reagan administration, however, some members of the National Security Council staff crossed the boundary into implementation when they arranged to sell arms to a hostile government in Iran and illegally transfer funds to support rebel groups in Central America. The resulting scandal, which surfaced in 1986, led to several resignations and a political crisis that nearly paralyzed the White House. In 1989 one of those staff members, Oliver North, was convicted on charges stemming from that episode. In 1990 John Poindexter, Reagan's national security adviser and North's immediate superior, was tried and convicted of charges related to what became known as the Iran-Contra affair. Although those convictions were later overturned by the courts on technical grounds, the investigation and prosecution of government officials involved in the scandal continued through 1992.[12]

The Cabinet Departments.   The most visible agencies in the executive branch are the fourteen cabinet departments. As we have already noted, they are the major bureaucratic institutions responsible for carrying out most of the federal government's policies and programs (see Table 12.2). Each department is headed by a secretary, or, in the case of Justice, an attorney general. Some of these departments are in charge of basic government functions, such as defense and foreign relations. Others address the needs of special groups—for example, agriculture, veterans affairs, and labor; or they coordinate federal programs in education, energy, health and human services, and other areas.

Each cabinet department is composed of smaller units, called bureaus, offices, services, administrations, or divisions. For example, among the major units in the U.S. Department of the Treasury are the Internal Revenue Service (IRS), the U.S. Customs Service, the Bureau of the Public Debt, the Financial Management Division, the U.S. Mint, the Bureau of Engraving and Printing, the Office of the Comptroller of the Currency, the U.S. Secret Service, and the Bureau of Alcohol, Tobacco, and Firearms. Many of these units are divided into even smaller subunits. The IRS, for instance, has several regional offices, more than sixty district offices, and nearly two hundred local offices.

There is no particular logic underlying the way cabinet departments are organized. In fact, cabinet agencies often face the challenging task of coordinating their efforts with agencies found in other cabinet departments. Thus, when the Department of Interior's Bureau of Land Management (BLM) needs to fight wildfires, it often has to rely on other agencies to do so. Hot Shots who fought the Glenwood Springs fire, for example, actually work for the U.S. Forest

TABLE 12.2

The Cabinet
Departments

The growth of government over the past two hundred years is evident in this list. Originally responsible for foreign policy, finances, defense, and the law, the executive branch agencies now oversee a wide range of activities.

Department	Year Created	Number of Employees[a] (1996, in thousands)
State	1789	22.9
Treasury[b]	1789	151.1
Defense[c]	1789	778.9
Justice[d]	1789	103.8
Interior	1849	66.7
Agriculture[e]	1889	100.7
Commerce[f]	1913	33.8
Labor	1913	19.1
Health and Human Services	1953	57.2
Housing and Urban Development	1965	11.4
Transportation	1966	62.4
Energy	1977	19.1
Education[g]	1979	4.7
Veterans Affairs	1989	221.9

[a]Civilian employees.
[b]One agency, the Internal Revenue Service, employs nearly 75 percent of Treasury Department workers.
[c]Originally called the Department of War.
[d]Originally called the Office of the Attorney General.
[e]Although created in 1862, the Department of Agriculture did not achieve cabinet status until 1889.
[f]The U.S. Census Bureau employs nearly 45 percent of all Commerce Department workers during census-taking years.
[g]Prior to 1979 the Department of Health and Human Services and the Department of Education were combined in the Department of Health, Education, and Welfare.

Source: Data from *Budget of the United States Government: Analytic Perspectives, Fiscal Year 1998* (Washington, D.C.: U.S. Government Printing Office, 1997).

Service (which is part of the Department of Agriculture). The number of active wildfires in 1994 even led to the use of U.S. Army and Marine personnel (from the Department of Defense) as firefighters. In addition, the BLM must also rely on the National Weather Service, which is part of the Department of Commerce, for detailed information on atmospheric conditions at the blaze site. When faced with the prospect of evacuating private property or dealing with the aftermath of the wildfires, the BLM turns to the Federal Emergency Management Agency (FEMA), an independent agency (see below).

Independent Executive Branch Agencies.   A great many federal bureaucrats work for the more than two hundred **independent agencies** that exist outside both the EOP and the cabinet departments. Many of these agencies carry out important government functions. The *Federal Emergency Management Agency,* for instance, helps coordinate national, state, and local government responses to major disasters. The *Environmental Protection Agency (EPA)* regulates air and water quality, as well as the use of pesticides, disposal of hazardous wastes, and other human challenges to our ecology. The *National Aeronautics and Space Administration (NASA)* runs the civilian space program. The administrators who head these independent executive branch agencies report directly to the president and do not have to work through a cabinet department bureaucracy.

There is no specific rationale for why some agencies are independent while others are part of cabinet departments. Sometimes the nature of what they do calls for this special status. In other instances, the political importance of an agency's programs at the time it was created has made the difference. Both factors were present when the *Social Security Administration (SSA)* was made an independent agency in 1994. Formerly part of the Department of Health and Human Services, SSA implements a variety of important social programs, including federal old age and disability insurance (see Chapter 14, on domestic policy and policymaking). SSA is a very large and important agency; furthermore, financing SSA programs has been a politically sensitive issue over the past two

NASA's Shuttle Missions

In recent years, the primary project of the National Aeronautics and Space Administration (NASA) has involved space shuttle missions. Pictured is the liftoff of the space shuttle Columbia on a successful two-week mission conducted in March 1994.

decades.[13] Efforts to reform social security programs have often led to charges of partisanship on the part of SSA administrators. The Social Security Independence and Program Improvements Act—signed on August 15, 1994, exactly fifty years and one day after Social Security was established—made SSA an independent agency. Under the new act, the Commissioner of Social Security is appointed for a term of six years and can be removed only by the president "for cause." Thus, not only was SSA taken from under the jurisdiction of the secretary of the Health and Human Services Department but its head was given some protection from being removed from office arbitrarily or for political reasons.

Of special note are those independent agencies that play a housekeeping and human resource management role in the federal government. For example, the *General Services Administration (GSA)* acts as the government's landlord and maintenance team, and the *Office of Personnel Management (OPM)* has responsibility for overseeing several of the federal government's personnel systems and the training and development of all civilian personnel.

Regulatory Commissions. Employing large professional staffs, **regulatory commissions** make policies affecting various sectors of the American economy. Although their members are appointed by the president, regulatory commissions are formally independent of the White House: that is, they exist outside the cabinet departments and have a special legal status (provided by Congress and supported by the Supreme Court) that protects them from excessive presidential interference. For example, the president cannot fire commission members for political reasons—only for corruption or a similar cause. Of course, the president has considerable influence over many of the commissions; because he appoints their members and designates their chairpersons, he can choose individuals whose decisions are likely to accord with his views.

Regulatory commissions have a special legal status in the federal bureaucracy because they are empowered to do more than enforce the law or implement public policy. Most have the authority to formulate rules that regulated companies or individuals must adhere to. In this sense, regulatory agencies are performing lawmaking, or **quasi-legislative, functions.**[14] For example, in 1972 the Federal Trade Commission issued regulations requiring that all billboard and magazine advertisements for cigarettes contain a warning from the surgeon general's office about the health hazards of smoking. Along with enforcing and making rules, these commissions also have **quasi-judicial functions** because they sit in judgment of those companies or individuals accused of violating the regulations. Violators of commission rules get their first court-like hearing before commission officials. A company or person found guilty of such violations may appeal directly to the federal court system.

Government Corporations. A unique form of bureaucracy, the **government corporation** is designed to act more like a private business than a part of government. As we have already noted, some are actually government-sponsored enterprises that are created and launched by the government to perform special functions but that are effectively private organizations. For example, the Communication Satellite Corporation (COMSAT) was established by an act of Congress in 1962 to facilitate the launching of telecommunications satellites. Up to 50 percent of COMSAT could be owned by the private-sector firms that use the agency's services. Three members of COMSAT's fifteen-member board of directors are appointed by the president, but in most other respects the organization acts like a private corporation.[15]

Another group of government corporations are located within cabinet departments, although they tend to operate somewhat independently. For example, the Commodity Credit Corporation—the organization through which farm subsidy programs are funded—is part of the U.S. Department of Agriculture. But perhaps the best known of these organizations, the *Tennessee Valley Authority (TVA)* and the *U.S. Postal Service (USPS)*, exist separately from other federal agencies.

Most government corporations carry out specific economic or service functions, such as generating electric power or delivering the mail. Most are intended to be self-financing agencies, but that does not always work out as planned. The *Corporation for Public Broadcasting (CPB)* helps promote and fund the *Public Broadcasting System (PBS)* and *National Public Radio (NPR)*. In the past, the CPB has provided significant subsidies for public radio and television, either through government grants or by raising funds privately. That support has decreased in recent years, leaving PBS- and NPR-affiliate stations with the task of raising money through donations and sponsorships.

The *Federal Deposit Insurance Corporation (FDIC)* insures savings accounts in many local banks and was always intended to be self-funding through the fees it assesses member banks. Since the late 1980s, however, the onus of member bank failures put pressure on FDIC officials to borrow money from the federal treasury and to consider actually asking Congress for tax dollars to help save it from insolvency. To help it deal with those problems, Congress authorized the creation of still another government corporation, the *Resolution Trust Corporation (RTC)*. The RTC assumes control of the assets of banks declared insolvent by the FDIC and attempts to reduce the government's losses by selling that property to private bidders.

Other Agencies.   Besides these five types of federal agencies, literally hundreds of boards, commissions, institutes, foundations, endowments, councils, and other organizations make up the federal bureaucracy. They range in importance from the Federal Reserve System (better known in the news media as the "Fed"; see Chapter 14, on domestic policy and policymaking) and the National Science Foundation (NSF) to the National Telecommunications Information Administration and the U.S. Metric Board.

A Diverse Institution

Our profile of the federal bureaucracy makes it clear that we are not discussing a single-minded, monolithic institution. Instead, we see that the federal bureaucracy is composed of hundreds of distinct organizations employing millions of individuals—a powerful institution so large and complex that to the uninformed citizen it seems to be a maze of structures and people. Given its size and complexity, it is not surprising that many Americans are suspicious of public agencies. Typically, their suspicions take the form of concerns about both the growth and the power of the federal bureaucracy. As we see in the sections that follow, those concerns are also built on myths.

Growth of the American Bureaucracy

Many Americans believe that the government bureaucracy has grown too large and has become a burden on the American public. According to the myths of bureaucracy, bureaucratic growth is an inevitable result of the incompetence and unresponsiveness of government agencies. An incompetent bureaucracy wastes resources. If government workers were more productive, they would use fewer resources and the result would be smaller but more efficient public agencies. To many Americans, excessive bureaucratic growth is also related to unresponsive government agencies. Unresponsive agencies are more likely to serve their own needs—including the need to grow and expand. A truly responsive bureaucracy would aim to serve the general public's wishes for less, not more, government intrusion.

Has bureaucratic growth been excessive? Is that growth a result of bureaucratic incompetence and unresponsiveness?

Overview of Bureaucratic Growth

The framers of the Constitution left little indication of how they thought the policies of the newly established republic should be administered. We do know that they considered bureaucracy a vital institution in our constitutional system. For instance, in the "Federalist No. 70," Alexander Hamilton acknowledged that a badly administered government "must be . . . a bad government."

The Constitution makes the president responsible for ensuring that the laws and policies of the national government are carried out. The tasks that the framers foresaw for the national government were relatively few and easy to implement. Executing the law meant keeping the peace, defending the country from foreign intruders, collecting import duties and other taxes, and delivering the mail. To the framers, charging a single individual with overseeing the administration of government did not seem unreasonable. Consequently, in Section 2 of Article II, they made the president both commander in chief of the armed forces and the chief executive officer to whom the heads of all administrative departments would report.

Initially, the framers' assumptions about the administration of the government were correct. The federal bureaucracy was small and its functions simple enough to permit the president to oversee most national government tasks.[16] In 1802, for example, there were fewer than ten thousand civilian and military federal employees. Almost all the civilian employees were tax collectors or postal workers. But those were simpler times. The country was rural and the people more self-sufficient. When Americans did turn to government for help in building roads or establishing schools, it was usually to state and local governments rather than the nation's newly settled capital in Washington, D.C.

Of course, the number of federal workers did grow during these early years. By the 1820s the national government's civilian bureaucracy had more than doubled. However, that growth did not represent a major expansion of government activities. No major new agencies were created during this early period. Most of the growth in federal government jobs took place in the Post Office Department, where nearly 75 percent of the federal work force was employed.

A different pattern began to emerge after the Civil War, as Americans demanded more and better government services from elected officials at all levels. During the last half of the nineteenth century the number of federal agencies doubled. The major agencies established during that period included the Department of Agriculture and the Interstate Commerce Commission. Federal workers were being hired not just to deliver the mail but also to regulate railroads, assist farmers, manage the federal government's vast land holdings, survey and help settle newly acquired territories in the West, and promote American commerce overseas. The changing nature of government is evident when considering the relative size of the post office. In 1861, the post office accounted for 80 percent of all federal civilian jobs; by 1901 post office positions made up only 58 percent of such jobs.

Rapid bureaucratic expansion continued through the first decades of the twentieth century. Between 1901 and 1933 the number of major federal agencies had increased from 90 to 170. Responding to the economic and social problems of the Great Depression, President Franklin D. Roosevelt helped create many new federal programs and agencies, especially in employment and business regulation. Federal employment jumped under Roosevelt's New Deal, and the demands of World War II led to further growth in the bureaucracy and the expansion of government responsibilities in domestic and foreign affairs.

Putting that growth in perspective, although the size of the federal civilian work force numbers in the millions, it constitutes a relatively small—and shrinking—part of the total U.S. labor force. For example, within the total U.S. labor force, federal civilian workers accounted for 2.7 percent of all employed individuals in 1987. That is, fewer than 3 of every 100 employed Americans worked for the federal government. During World War II that figure had been as high as 4.7 federal workers for every 100 Americans, and even as recently as 1970 there were 3.7 civilians on the federal payroll for every 100 people in the U.S. labor force. Thus, when viewed as part of the U.S. labor force, the federal bureaucracy does not look quite as big and may not be growing as much as many people believe.

Nor does the size of the federal bureaucracy seem too big when compared with the number of civilian workers employed by state and local governments. In 1993, the federal government employed fewer than one out of every four government workers in the United States. That year, state and local governments employed 15.9 million people while Washington employed 4.7 million. When federal military personnel are subtracted from the totals, the size of the federal work force is even smaller relative to those at the state and local levels. Furthermore, the relatively shrinking size of the federal civilian work force has been part of a significant trend for at least three decades (see Figure 12.3).

In other words, while 2.9 million federal employees may seem like a large number, in relative terms the federal bureaucracy is not as big as it appears at first glance. Nevertheless, 2.9 million is a great many people, and the question of why there are so many federal bureaucrats is unavoidable.[17]

Another indicator of bureaucratic expansion is the growing federal budget. George Washington ran the government for about $1.5 million a year. By the time Andrew Jackson took office in 1829, the federal budget had increased tenfold, to

FIGURE 12.3

Relative Size of the Federal Bureaucracy

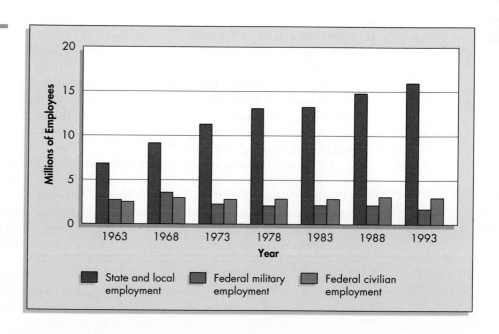

over $15 million. By 1940 the budget had climbed to $9.5 billion, and in 1960 the U.S. government spent a little over $92 billion. The greatest growth in federal expenditures, however, took place over the next quarter-century. In January 1987 President Reagan submitted the first trillion-dollar budget proposal to Congress, and federal government spending has continued to climb under Presidents Bush and Clinton (see Chapter 14, on domestic policy and policymaking). By 1996, the federal budget had exceeded $1.56 trillion and was projected to be $1.9 trillion by the year 2002!

Explaining the Growth of the Bureaucracy

What accounts for the growth of bureaucracies and bureaucrats since the late 1800s? Was all this growth the result of bureaucratic incompetence and unresponsiveness? Many observers believe that the growth can be attributed directly to the expansion of the nation itself. There are a great many more of us—more than 248 million in 1990, compared with fewer than 5 million in the 1790s—and we are living closer together. Not only do the residents of cities and suburbs require many more services than did the predominantly rural dwellers of the early 1800s, but the challenges of urban and industrial life have intensified and outstripped the capacity of families or local and state governments to cope with them. Thus the American people have increasingly turned to their national government for help.

There is considerable evidence that the growth of bureaucracies is "of our own making."[18] Public opinion polls indicate widespread public support for expanding federal involvement in a variety of areas (see Chapter 14, on domestic policy and policymaking). Even when public support for new programs is low, pollsters find Americans unwilling to eliminate or reduce existing programs. Furthermore, the public's expectations about the quality of service it should receive are constantly rising. The public wants government to be more responsive, responsible, and compassionate in administering public programs. Officials have reacted to these pressures by establishing new programs and maintaining and improving existing ones.

The federal bureaucracy has also expanded in response to sudden changes in economic, social, cultural, and political conditions. During the Great Depression and World War II, for example, the federal bureaucracy grew to meet the challenges these situations created. Washington became more and more involved in programs providing financial aid and employment to the poor. It increased its regulation of important industries and during the war imposed controls over much of the American economy. As part of the general war effort, the federal government also built roads and hospitals and mobilized the entire population. When these crises ended, the public was reluctant to give up many of the federal welfare and economic programs implemented during the time of emergency.

Political leaders, too, foster bureaucratic growth. Government bureaucracies are often enlarged by presidents running for re-election so they can leave their mark on history. We have noted the large expansions of federal bureaucracies that occurred under Franklin Roosevelt's New Deal and Lyndon Johnson's Great Society programs. Congress, however, is no innocent bystander. Bowing to pressure to "bring the bacon" back to the folks at home, even the most conservative members of Congress find themselves voting for new or larger programs to serve their constituents.[19]

There is also considerable evidence that the bureaucracy itself plays a role in developing and expanding government programs.[20] Some analysts point out that expanding agency programs and budgets are among the few personal rewards that bureaucrats can seek, since compensation for public employees is limited and opportunities are very limited. The role of bureaucrats in government growth, however, is not merely self-serving. For example, a 1970 report by Department of Labor staff members found that many Americans were needlessly exposed to work-related illnesses and injuries. Although state and national policies should have dealt with the consequences of work-related disabilities, the staff found no significant program designed to prevent on-the-job ailments or accidents. As a result of that study, Congress created the Occupational Safety and Health Administration (OSHA), which oversees the regulation of workplace conditions.

Thus a number of factors have contributed to the growth of the federal bureaucracy. Although bureaucratic incompetence and unresponsiveness may play a part in governmental expansion, most of the evidence points to the other factors we have discussed.

Bureaucratic Power

The effective operation of government requires that it employ qualified personnel and possess the financial resources needed for these employees to carry out their jobs. Another critical ingredient, however, is **bureaucratic power.** Government agencies require power if they are to be competent. This requirement is so great that one student of American public administration has called power the "lifeblood of administration."[21] Without sufficient power, government agencies would be bound to live up to the myth of bureaucratic incompetence, for they would not be able to accomplish their tasks effectively or efficiently.

In spite of the importance of bureaucratic power, the public is very suspicious of the role it plays in American government. Inherent in the myth of an unresponsive bureaucracy is a fear of bureaucratic power and a widespread belief that federal bureaucrats are misusing or even abusing this power. The U.S. constitutional system is rooted in the idea that the people should govern, if not directly, then at least indirectly, through their elected representatives. Yet over the past two centuries, more and more government power has been placed in the hands of bureaucrats. Those who believe in the myth of an unresponsive bureaucracy are likely to worry about the existence and use of bureaucratic power.

Taken to extremes, the public concern about bureaucratic power can turn deadly. On April 19, 1995, a nine-story office building in downtown Oklahoma City, housing federal government agencies, exploded, killing 168 federal workers and citizens who happened to be in or near the building at the time. The scale of the tragedy was magnified by the death of many children, who attended a day care facility on the second floor of the building, just a few yards from the explosive device. Law enforcement officials traced the bomb to individuals who had ties with antigovernment groups that had formed in twenty-six states. Many of those groups—often called "militias"—feared the tyranny of the federal government. Some members of these groups regarded the Bureau of Alcohol, Tobacco, and Firearms (BATF), the Federal Bureau of Investigation (FBI), and other federal agencies as the enemy. Law enforcement officials investigating the tragic attack on the federal building in Oklahoma City argued that those involved in the bombing saw their actions as a preemptive attack on the tyrannical federal bureaucracy.

The Sources of Bureaucratic Power

Where do bureaucracies get the power they need to function? Some of it is derived from the legitimacy of the laws they are required to enforce or from the policies they are asked to implement (see Chapter 2, on the Constitution). But often neither the legitimacy of laws nor the policies are enough. There are other key sources to look for.[22]

External Support.   A major source of bureaucratic power is the support that government agencies receive from the general public, special-interest groups, the media, Congress, or the White House. The greater an agency's external support, the more power it is likely to wield. Throughout the 1950s and 1960s, for example, the Federal Bureau of Investigation (FBI), under Director J. Edgar Hoover, had a great deal of support from the general public. After Hoover's death and a series of revelations about questionable actions taken by the FBI and its agents, the agency's reputation and support declined. The directors who succeeded Hoover worked for many years to restore public confidence and to rebuild the agency's power.

Another form of external support comes from coalitions formed between bureaucracies and other actors in the American political arena. Thus agencies sometimes participate in political alliances that might include their clientele group, other agencies, lobbyists for special interests, and members of Congress who preside over relevant committees and subcommittees.[23] Analysts call these alliances **policy subgovernments** because the actors effectively exercise authority in a narrowly defined policy area.

The Tragic War on Government

The April 19, 1995, terrorist bombing of a federal office building in Oklahoma City has been traced to domestic extremists who believe government agencies are part of a conspiracy to take away the freedom of American citizens. The blast killed 168 people, including 19 children.

In their most extreme forms, often called **cozy triangles,** these subgovernments can be powerful coalitions (see Chapter 8, on interest groups). The success of any cozy triangle coalition depends on its members' ability to limit participation to a few "insiders" and to maintain a low public profile. Until recently, one of Washington's most successful cozy triangles was the tobacco subgovernment, which focused on policies related to promoting the consumption of tobacco products. The three main sets of actors in that subgovernment were members of Congress from tobacco-growing states (for example, North Carolina, South Carolina, and Kentucky) who sat on the Agriculture and Appropriations committees; lobbyists representing tobacco growers and cigarette-manufacturing companies; and bureaucrats from tobacco-related programs at the Agriculture and Commerce Departments. Meeting regularly to work out policies favorable to tobacco products, these actors created programs that helped tobacco farmers and the giant tobacco industry to fend off attacks from those who sought policies contrary to their interests.

In 1964, the cozy world of the tobacco subgovernment began to fall apart. That year the surgeon general of the United States issued a report linking cigarette smoking to lung cancer, heart disease, and emphysema. The report was followed by a Federal Trade Commission proposal that cigarette packages and advertising contain health warnings. The cozy triangle no longer had the low visibility that made it so effective before the surgeon general's announcement. Nevertheless, the tobacco subgovernment remains intact today, although its members can no longer easily set public policies related to tobacco. For years they fought a constant battle to maintain what remained of their subsidy and international marketing programs.[24] More recently, members of Congress, in conjunction with a variety of federal agencies—from the Public Health Service and the Environmental Protection Agency to the Food and Drug Administration—have led a direct attack on the tobacco industry that indicated a future of greater regulation of cigarette production and consumption.[25]

At the opposite extreme from cozy triangles are subgovernments organized as **issue networks.** Issue networks involve a large number of participants with different degrees of interest in and commitment to the policies and problems that bring them together. An issue network is an open and at times highly visible subgovernment. Those who take part in it may come and go constantly, and often there is neither the time nor the leadership to develop shared attitudes toward policy. Bureaucrats also play a role in issue network subgovernments, but that role often depends on their grasp of the issues and their willingness to dive into the open policymaking process.[26]

Environmental policymaking is a classic example of an issue network in action. It has been highly visible since the mid-1960s. The challenge of environmental protection has attracted a multitude of actors, including dozens of members of Congress, hundreds of interest groups with varying points of view, and a host of media and academic observers. In the middle of that issue network sits the Environmental Protection Agency (EPA), which was created in 1970 to coordinate the implementation of federal environmental policy. The EPA quite successfully maintained a leading role in the environmental issue network during the 1970s. Beginning in 1981, however, the agency's situation changed as it experienced a crisis.

The Reagan administration came to office intent on changing the direction of environmental policy through deregulation and reform. It planned to use the EPA to implement these changes by instituting new agency policies and radically altering the way established programs enforced environmental regulations. The administration's strategy virtually ignored the interests of major actors in the existing environmental policy issue network. Incensed at the EPA's positions, environmental interest groups formed alliances to defeat Reagan's EPA initiatives in a variety of program areas. A coalition of conservationists and others concerned about environment policy used direct lobbying and the media to press the White House and Congress for major changes in the Reagan approach. In 1983 the administration acknowledged defeat by replacing the controversial head of the EPA, Ann Gorsuch Burford, with William Ruckelshaus, an individual highly regarded by environmental interest groups who had been the first administrator of the agency when it was created during the Nixon presidency.[27] Ruckelshaus spent two years undoing the administrative changes made during Burford's tenure and re-establishing the EPA's credibility among the members of the environmental issue network.

Whether taking the form of public support or coalitions with special-interest groups, external support plays an important role in shaping and directing bureaucratic power. The cases of the tobacco and environmental policy subgovernments indicate just how significant that support can be for individual agencies.

Expertise.   An agency's power can also stem from its expertise. In matters of national defense, America's top policymakers often turn to experts at the Pentagon for advice. On issues involving the public's health, they ask the opinion of the surgeon general or the Centers for Disease Control and Prevention. On international subjects, the Central Intelligence Agency (CIA) is regarded as the primary source of expert information. As long as such expert information is deemed accurate and reliable by those who use it, it enhances the power of the agency. But if the credibility of that information is brought into question—as happened to the CIA in the late 1980s and early 1990s when it failed to accurately predict the collapse of the Soviet bloc (see Chapter 15, on foreign and defense policies)—the public immediately questions the competence of that agency and its officials. Once the credibility of a bureaucracy's expertise is put in doubt, its influence and power are likely to deteriorate.

Discretion.   In performing their administrative tasks, bureaucrats are often permitted to use their own judgment in carrying out public policies and programs. Congress and the White House frequently formulate policies in ambiguous and vague terms. When President John F. Kennedy issued a mandate to the National Aeronautics and Space Administration to land an American on the moon by 1970, he could not tell the agency exactly when and how to do it: those details were left to the discretion of NASA officials. Discretion can be an important source of power, for it gives some personnel within a bureaucracy considerable flexibility in deciding how to do their jobs.

Longevity in Office.   The merit system, which protects most federal employees from being fired for political reasons, provides still another source of bureaucratic power. Because it is extremely difficult to dismiss a federal civil servant without a good, nonpolitical cause, civil servants usually last long in their jobs. Presidents and members of Congress come and go, as do the presidential appointees who head federal agencies, but the average bureaucrat serves through several presidential and congressional terms in office. As a result, elected officials and their appointees often find themselves relying on career civil servants to keep the agencies functioning. Thus longevity in office can mean considerable power for the experienced bureaucrat.

Skill and Leadership.   External support, expertise, discretion, and longevity in office will not accomplish much by themselves. Potential wielders of bureaucratic power must have the talents and will to use those resources. That is as true for agencies as it is for individuals. Without skills and leadership, even the most resource-rich federal agency will not be able to accomplish its objectives.

The Defense Department, for all its potential power and influence, would fail in its search for White House and congressional support if the secretary of defense did not provide effective leadership. During the Reagan administration, for example, Secretary of Defense Caspar ("Cap") Weinberger gained a reputation as a successful advocate for increasing defense expenditures. When some members of the Reagan administration proposed reductions in the defense budget, Weinberger managed to convince the president that defense "is not a budget issue. You spend what you need." In most instances, Weinberger was able to get the president to protect his department's budget.[28]

In short, power is the fuel that gives bureaucracies the energy to carry out their missions. A bureaucracy without power or the potential to exercise power is truly a waste of public resources. The question is not whether bureaucratic power exists or should exist, but whether that power is responsive to the wishes of the American public and its elected representatives.

Limiting Bureaucratic Power

The American political system does provide effective means to limit bureaucratic power and keep it responsive. It offers a variety of internal and external checks designed to contain bureaucratic influence and authority within acceptable bounds.

Self-Restraint and Limited Resources.   Some of the curbs come from bureaucratic self-restraint. In the mid-1970s certain regulatory commissions took the initiative of beginning to relax the controls they had previously exercised over sectors of the American economy. For example, the Civil Aeronautics Board (CAB) intentionally eliminated many barriers to competition among the nation's major airlines. That initiative proved so popular that in 1978 Congress formally deregulated the airline industry and in 1985 eliminated the CAB altogether. Although no other regulatory commission has been abolished, most exercised similar self-restraint during the late 1970s and throughout the 1980s.

The quantity and quality of available resources also put limits on bureaucratic power. The Internal Revenue Service (IRS), for example, does not have enough auditors and agents to review everyone's tax return and investigate all suspected cases of tax fraud. In fact, it has been estimated that the IRS is able to investigate only a small percentage of the returns filed each year. Therefore, the competence of its auditors and agents determines how effectively the IRS collects taxes, as does the agency's increasing use of computers to process tax returns. Ultimately, however, the IRS's best tool is the individual taxpayer's fear that his or her return might be one of the few subjected to a detailed audit.

The White House.   As the formal head of the executive branch, the president can also exercise some control over the federal bureaucracy by carefully selecting those he appoints to office or promotes. Before taking office in 1981, Reagan established an appointment system that chose for office only people who would be loyal to him and willing to pursue forcefully his objectives of reduced government activity.[29] In addition, the Reagan administration functioned through a system of what one observer termed "jigsaw puzzle management," under which agency managers were told to carry out policies and programs while being kept in the dark about the overall strategy being pursued. The impact of these strategies was to reduce the overall effectiveness and influence of federal bureaucrats while enhancing the power of administration officials.[30]

The White House can also influence the funding of federal agencies and their programs. Typically, federal agencies make their budget requests through the Office of Management and Budget, which evaluates and often modifies the agencies' proposals to conform with presidential priorities. Even after funds and other resources have been appropriated to agency programs by Congress, the White House retains control over the allocation of funds from the Treasury Department. In addition, the president can require that federal agencies adopt certain management methods and budgetary techniques. In 1965, for example, President Johnson ordered all federal agencies to adopt an agency-planning technique that originated in the Department of Defense. When Jimmy Carter became president in 1977, he ordered federal agencies to adopt a budgeting approach that he had used when he was governor of Georgia. In both instances, the management techniques were intended to give the president greater control over agency decisions.

Congress.   Congress can also impose limitations on the power of federal agencies. The Constitution authorizes Congress to establish public programs and arrange for their implementation. Yet it has never been clear how detailed and explicit Congress must be in its instructions to federal agencies. Vague legislation has led many critics to argue that Congress is not working hard enough to limit or control bureaucratic power, and bureaucrats themselves have complained about the lack of specificity. In 1979 one administrator openly criticized a congressional act that, in a single line of statutory language, required his agency to establish a program to protect the rights of the handicapped—with no details or guidance. "They're frequently very unhappy with what we do after they give us a mandate like that," he noted. "But the trouble is, the mandate is broad, they deliberately are ambiguous where there is conflict on details, and they leave it to us to try to resolve the ambiguities."[31]

Implied in such criticism is the belief that Congress has a right to exercise much more legislative control than it does today by expanding or narrowing an agency's authority to take action. In a few instances, Congress has tried to provide detailed instructions for federal agencies. The Clean Air Act Amendments of 1970, for instance, set a number of specific deadlines for action by the Environmental Protection Agency (EPA). By April 30, 1971, the EPA was to establish a set of rules and regulations that would reduce air pollution. By June 30, 1972, it was to have received and reviewed state plans for dealing with air pollution. By

1975 it was to have made certain that automobile companies reduced carbon monoxide and hydrocarbon emissions by 90 percent. These were challenging goals and ultimately proved too difficult to reach on schedule. Delays and postponements were common. Critics of too much congressional interference in the implementation process point to those problems when asked why Congress often shies away from supplying many details in its legislation.[32]

Although Congress finds it difficult to control or limit bureaucratic power through detailed legislation, it has other tools with which to accomplish these ends.[33] Each year Congress reviews agency budget requests and can use that opportunity to scrutinize agency operations. Almost every congressional committee has jurisdiction over a group of federal agencies, and they sometimes exercise their oversight responsibilities by holding public hearings on agency operations. In 1988, for example, Representative Douglas Barnard, Jr., from Georgia, chairman of the House Government Operations consumer subcommittee, launched a two-year investigation of the operations of the IRS. That investigation eventually led to administrative changes within the agency, including the establishment of an IRS ethics program.[34]

Individual members of Congress often intercede with specific agencies in behalf of their constituents. Members of Congress can also order the General Accounting Office to conduct an audit or investigation of any federal program. Finally, the role of the U.S. Senate in confirming political appointments provides that chamber with a unique opportunity to review bureaucratic actions.

The Courts.   The courts also play a role in limiting the power of the federal bureaucracy. Until 1937 the judiciary had often agreed to hear cases challenging the authority given to federal agencies by Congress. Today the courts are much less likely to entertain such cases; nevertheless, they pay considerable attention to complaints that a federal agency has exceeded its authority or acted in an arbitrary or unreasonable way when carrying out its duties.

> For public administrators the reach of the courts is broad and deep. When administrators are challenged by parties affected by their decisions, courts can decide whether the administrator interpreted the law correctly, whether the administrator was required to act and failed to do so, whether the administrator acted within or beyond the authorized power, whether the administrator acted capriciously, whether the evidence was adequate to support the administrator's decision, and whether the administrator violated the individual's right to "due process" and equal protection of the law.[35]

Some of the courts' power over the federal bureaucracy stems from specific provisions of the U.S. Constitution, such as the prohibition against "unreasonable searches and seizures" or guarantees that citizens shall not be deprived of "life, liberty, or property without due process of law." These powers were reinforced by the Federal Tort Claims Act of 1946, which permits (with a few specified exceptions) Americans to sue the federal government for damages incurred through government actions.[36] Congress has even made special provisions for taking legal action against specific agencies. Under provisions of the 1988 tax laws, for example, a taxpayer may sue any IRS employee for damages if the agent seeks to collect taxes in a reckless way or with intentional disregard of tax laws. The prospect of being challenged in court has proven an effective means of control.

The courts also play a role in shaping the relationships between the bureaucracy and the other branches of government. From time to time in our history, controversies have arisen about whether government agencies were subject to presidential or congressional control. Sometimes these have taken the form of court cases. In some of these, the courts have sided with Congress, and at other times they have deferred to the White House. The Supreme Court has tended to favor the presidency in recent cases,[37] but there has been no firm answer in the past two hundred years to the question of who runs the bureaucracy. The answer is often the subject of legal controversies. Thus, the courts remain a major factor in the life of the federal bureaucracy.

Other Restraints.   *Agency competition* among federal bureaucracies is another source of limits on bureaucratic power. Many agencies have competitors in the federal government—agencies that vie for the same set of authorizations or appropriations. The different branches of the armed forces, for instance, compete with each other for a bigger slice of the defense budget. Although such competition may seem inefficient, it does help impose restraints on the power of the military bureaucracies by having each keep an eye on the activities of the other.

A strong sense of *professionalism* and responsibility among public-sector employees can act as a brake on bureaucratic power, especially when someone within an agency exposes inappropriate, unethical, or questionable activities. Ernest Fitzgerald, a civilian analyst at the Defense Department, went public with his concerns about major cost overruns on the purchase of C5-A transport planes by the U.S. Air Force. His complaints led to an investigation of those cost overruns and several new management policies. People like Fitzgerald, who risk their careers to halt bureaucratic misconduct, are called **whistle-blowers.** Whistle-blowers usually pay a high price for their honesty and candor. In many instances, blowing the whistle on an agency can make one an outcast in the organization and end one's career.[38] Today whistle-blowers have some protection under federal personnel laws, and at least one agency (the National Aeronautics and Space Administration) has arranged to have a special telephone number that whistle-blowers can call for action. Each agency also has an **inspector general's** office,[39] which can investigate complaints or suspicious behavior.

By investigating leads that might uncover major problems, an alert press corps can also restrain bureaucratic power. The Freedom of Information Act and other public disclosure laws restrain bureaucratic power as well. Citizen lobbies, such as Common Cause and Ralph Nader's Public Citizen (see Chapter 8, on interest groups), perform much the same function at times.

Limits and Responsiveness.   As we have seen, although it is impossible to guarantee that bureaucratic power will not be misused or abused, the mechanisms for limiting that power do exist. In the face of all these potential and actual restraints, bureaucratic power in the federal government has a good chance of being controlled.

In many respects, the limits work to make government agencies more, rather than less, responsive. Thus, what many Americans perceive as an "unresponsive" bureaucracy may in fact be just the opposite. The problem is that being responsive to one constituency group often means being perceived as unresponsive by others. Consumer groups, for example, often criticize the Department of Agriculture for being too supportive of farming interests and not sufficiently attentive to the needs of consumers. Similarly, many businesses complain that the Environmental Protection Agency and other regulatory agencies fail to take their interests and needs into account, whereas those who support regulation believe the regulators are on the right track.

Bureaucratic Problems and Reforms

If the myths of bureaucratic incompetence and unresponsiveness do not reflect reality, then why do so many Americans continue to complain about the way government operates? This is somewhat of a mystery in itself, for students of public administration find that many citizens are quite satisfied with most of their routine encounters with bureaucracies.[40] The complaints that most Americans have about the federal bureaucracy may reflect more what they hear about others' ordeals than what they have experienced themselves. There are, however, problems with the bureaucracy that help keep the myths alive.

Bureaucratic Pathologies

At their best, federal bureaucracies serve the public interest. At their worst, they seem to conduct themselves in ways that feed the myths of incompetence and unresponsiveness. Students of American government describe these behaviors as **bureaucratic pathologies**—or "bureaupathologies," for short.[41]

Clientelism.   In very general terms, public agencies attempt to work in behalf of the public interest. On a day-to-day basis, however, bureaucracies must deal with those served by the programs being implemented—the agency's clientele. The Department of Agriculture works with farmers, the Department of Education with educators, and so on. This daily contact with clientele groups is an absolute necessity for many government employees if they are to be responsive to the needs of those they serve. But this constant contact can become pathological when bureaucrats begin to display favoritism toward their clientele's interests, even if those interests may not serve the public good.

The case of the tobacco subgovernment discussed earlier is a classic example of clientelism at work. Bureaucrats within the Department of Agriculture who worked with tobacco farmers for decades supported their clients' interests even though they were contrary to emerging government policies against smoking.

Similarly, the staffs of government regulatory commissions are sometimes accused of being "captured" by those they regulate. For many years the now defunct Civil Aeronautics Board issued policies and decisions that clearly favored the interests of the nation's major airlines rather than those of airline passengers.

Incrementalism. Federal agencies are created to carry out programs, and we expect them to do so with consistency and fairness. But the conditions under which agencies operate competently are not stagnant. Conditions and circumstances change—sometimes quite swiftly. One would expect public-sector agencies to adapt to those changes as quickly as possible, but often they resist change or make only small, incremental adjustments. At times this response may be intentional. For example, Secretary of Defense Richard Cheney and others in the Bush administration resisted calls for radical reductions in the Pentagon's 1991 federal budget, despite major changes occurring in the former Soviet Union and Eastern Europe (see Chapter 15, on foreign and defense policy).

Incrementalist behavior can become pathological when it threatens the very program or service that the agency is supposedly providing. The U.S. military has often been plagued by pathological incrementalism. The navy was slow to recognize the importance of air power in the 1920s until a maverick army general, Billy Mitchell, sank a warship in a widely publicized demonstration of the point. It was equally difficult to convince many army leaders to abandon the horse cavalry units during that same period. Bureaucracies tend to move cautiously and slowly, and sometimes a snail's pace can prove much too dangerous and costly.

Arbitrariness. A competent bureaucracy is one that does its job effectively and efficiently. To achieve this condition, the agency often must adopt **standard operating procedures,** often called "SOPs." There are times, however, when regularized procedures can interfere with responsiveness or replace common sense, and then arbitrariness becomes a factor. For example, there are stories about people losing their welfare or unemployment benefits because they failed to show up for an appointment with a social worker or forgot to file a certain form on time. A bureaucrat who is unwilling to listen to excuses or explanations can hardly be faulted for sticking to the rules, but he or she can be faulted for being too arbitrary and losing sight of why a program or procedure exists. Bureaucracies often serve people with special needs or individuals facing special circumstances. Even if the aim is efficiency, arbitrary behavior can prove harmful under such conditions.

Arbitrariness also arises when a bureaucrat acts without legal authority. While a police officer has the authority to stop a driver whose vehicle is swerving dangerously, he or she cannot use a nightstick to beat the car's driver or occupants without cause.[42]

Parochialism.   In order to perform their functions effectively, some government agencies believe it is necessary to focus attention on the job at hand. Such concentration on getting the job done can result in another pathological behavior—parochialism.

For example, the job of the army's Rocky Mountain Arsenal was to produce and store chemical and biological weapons, and for most of its thirty-year existence that organization carried out its work without paying too much attention to the damage it was doing to its surroundings. That parochial attitude had both short-term and long-term effects. During the early 1970s a series of earth tremors in the Denver region was traced by one geologist to a weapons disposal process being used at the arsenal. After months of denying any link between its activities and the disturbances, the arsenal temporarily halted the operation. The tremors came to an end, and the army finally agreed to discontinue the process permanently. Years later, when the army closed the arsenal, state and federal environmental protection investigators found the land in and around the weapons facility to be so contaminated that it might remain unusable for hundreds of years. Taken to its extreme, this type of pathological behavior can prove deadly.

Imperialism.   As we noted earlier, bureaucracies need power in one form or another to carry out their jobs. Therefore, bureaucrats often seek to obtain the resources they need to accomplish their assignments. At times this means expanding agency operations and taking on more responsibilities and personnel. In some agencies this drive for expansion becomes an end in itself—a key sign of the pathological behavior we call bureaucratic imperialism.

Imperialism may involve getting a bigger slice of the federal budget pie, or it may mean starting new programs or even taking over another agency's functions. Whatever form it takes, expansion for its own sake is not regarded as a desirable feature of bureaucratic operations by most Americans. During the 1950s and 1960s, for example, the U.S. Army built up its "aviation" units through the acquisition of enough helicopters to make it the third-largest air force on earth, after the U.S. Air Force and the air forces of the Soviet Union. The army leadership rationalized the growth of its aviation units as a means for improving the mobility and effectiveness of land troops. This upset air force generals, who were constantly arguing that they should have exclusive control of all airborne military equipment and personnel.[43]

Calls for Reform

These pathological behaviors help explain why the myths of incompetent and unresponsive bureaucracies remain popular today. Americans perceive these

CLOSER TO HOME

12.1 Government as Innovator!

The media often pay a great deal of attention to what is wrong with government and to horror stories about bureaucratic errors. The good news about government—the accomplishments, devotion, and hard work of government workers—is rarely mentioned and almost never celebrated. State and local bureaucracies, particularly, suffer this type of neglect, for the national media tend to focus on federal programs and the agencies that implement them.

Although working in obscurity, state and local bureaucracies have frequently developed interesting and innovative approaches to governmental problems. To help highlight and reward the good work occurring at these less visible levels of government, the Ford Foundation and the Kennedy School of Government at Harvard University established the Innovations in American Government Program, which annually honors the ten most innovative approaches to administrative tasks. Some of the winning innovations include the following.

- In 1991, the city of Philadelphia received an award for its anti-graffiti program. Initiated in January 1984, the effort involved three strategies: public education and community awareness; quick and persistent removal of graffiti; and increased detection and punishment of vandals.

- A 1992 award went to the Automated Traffic Surveillance and Control (ATSAC) system in Los Angeles. An elaborate system started just before the 1984 Olympics, it will cover more than four thousand of the city's congested intersections by 1998. According to studies, the system has eliminated some 8 million car stops for red lights per day, reduced air emissions by 26 percent, and enhanced fuel consumption by 13 percent. It cuts vehicle delays by fifty thousand hours per day, a 32 percent reduction. Roughly one-third of those who live and work in Los Angeles on a typical day have benefited from this system.

- Anoka County, Minnesota, won recognition in 1994 for its Parents' Fair Share program. Targeting divorced or separated parents who failed to provide child support because they lacked jobs or enough income, the program was an alliance among various agencies to help get job training and employment for those who required it. The result in the first two years of operation (1992–1994) was a significant increase in the number and amount of child support payments.

- In 1995, an award honored Genesis, a social service program developed in Boulder County, Colorado. It focuses local resources on comprehensive services to pregnant teens and teenage parents of infants. Established in 1990, Genesis seeks to help those youngsters become nurturing parents, attain the education and skills needed for self-sufficiency, and expand opportunities for their children.

- One of the 1996 winners was the Florida Healthy Kids, Inc., program, established in 1990 by the Florida legislature. This voluntary program provided comprehensive health care coverage to more than twenty thousand children in eleven school districts across the state in 1996. In 1997, it was expanded to five additional sites and will cover forty-five thousand children by 1998. Its $26 million cost is paid by a combination of state funding (50 percent), family premiums (33 percent), and contributions from school districts, hospital authorities, children's services councils, and community groups (17 percent). Administratively simple, the program had greatly reduced the burden on local hospital emergency rooms and did not lead to overutilization of other medical resources.

Just as important as these individual examples is the fact that such efforts often become models for other jurisdictions facing similar problems. Florida's Healthy Kids program, for example, has been copied in several other states, and proposals for a national program gained bipartisan support in the 105th Congress when they were introduced in March 1997.

Source: From the "Innovations in American Government" homepage at http://ksgwww.harvard.edu/~innovat/index.html.

problems as the rule rather than as the exception. It is not surprising, therefore, to hear calls for bureaucratic reform.

Various Approaches.   Those who focus on the need to deal with bureaucratic incompetence advocate the elimination of certain government programs and agencies. Others stress the need to reduce agency size and adopt more efficient management techniques. Still others suggest that the work of government agencies should be turned over to the private sector—a strategy called **privatization.**[44]

Some reformers believe that government agencies must be made more responsive, more open, and more aware of potential problems. They advocate holding public hearings or establishing an agency **ombudsman** office to hear citizen complaints or other problems related to agency programs. Others believe that government agencies would be more responsive if they relied more on marketplace strategies. For example, instead of having some government agency build and operate public housing units, why not provide qualified families with either the money or the housing vouchers they would need to find appropriate rental space themselves within the local private housing market? A similar voucher approach has been advocated for primary and secondary education.[45]

A number of reformers believe that problems of incompetence and unresponsiveness can be solved through agency reorganizations. Some reorganization plans call for increased centralization within federal agencies to enhance coordination and efficiency. Other reorganizations require agency decentralization in an effort to enhance responsiveness and citizen participation.

Still other reforms focus on agency personnel policies, such as hiring practices or compensation levels. For instance, a major accomplishment of reformers during the past 150 years has been the adoption of a merit-based personnel system and the elimination of political appointments within federal agencies. Reformers have also pressed for increasing the pay of government employees to help the federal agencies attract more qualified people to public service.[46]

Presidential Reform Efforts.   The current efforts to reform the federal bureaucracy have a nearly century-long history. The most visible reforms have been led by the White House—often in an attempt to gain greater control over the bureaucracy.

For example, in 1905 President Theodore Roosevelt asked an assistant secretary of the Treasury, Charles H. Keep, to chair a Commission on Department Methods. Over the next four years, the Keep Commission brought about significant changes in record keeping and accounting procedures used by federal agencies. Between 1910 and 1913, President William Howard Taft's Commission on Economy and Efficiency sought to bring more budgetary and managerial coordination to the federal bureaucracy. Although no major commissions were formed by either President Woodrow Wilson or his immediate successors, major legislation and congressional initiatives for reform were enacted and implemented.

Under Franklin Roosevelt, a President's Committee on Administrative Management (known as the Brownlow Committee, after its chair, Louis Brownlow) advocated a major transformation of the federal bureaucracy, which would greatly enhance the president's role as the chief administrative officer of American government. Under both Harry S Truman and Dwight D. Eisenhower, commissions chaired by former President Herbert Hoover called for still more reforms. Kennedy and Johnson relied more on task forces within their administration to recommend and implement managerial reform. Nixon appointed a council headed by businessman Roy Ash (who later became the head of the Office of Management and Budget) to assess the federal bureaucracy. Gerald Ford was not in office long enough to undertake any significant reform effort, but Carter came into office seeking major changes in the way business was conducted in Washington. Reagan sought advice from a presidentially appointed but privately funded commission, chaired by Peter Grace. The Bush administration took few initiatives in the area of administrative reform, but it did work toward implementing and extending many of the privatization and similar efforts begun under Reagan.

WWW•

For more on "goring" the bureaucracy, see the **Gitelson/Dudley/Dubnick web site.**

As one of his first acts as president, Clinton put his vice president, Al Gore, in charge of an effort—the *National Performance Review (NPR)*—to improve the performance of the federal bureaucracy. Influenced by the writings of David Osborne and Ted Gaebler,[47] the NPR effort called for the "reinvention" of the federal bureaucracy. This approach of **reinventing government** was to "put people first" by having agencies cut unnecessary spending, serve their "customers," empower their employees, help communities solve their own problems, and foster excellence in the public service.

The NPR effort differed from past presidential reform initiatives in several important ways. First, it did not stress enhancement of presidential power over the bureaucracy. In fact, its emphasis on empowering government employees and communities seemed contrary to past efforts at centralization. Nor did NPR focus obsessively on cutting the size of government; instead, it sought to improve performance. Furthermore, NPR's strategy was to push reform from the inside—making government employees the force of reform instead of trying to impose changes from outside or from the top.

It is too early to tell how successful this effort of reinventing government will be in improving the operation of the federal bureaucracy. Some critics have charged that the changes being made are superficial and will not have a lasting impact. Others contend that the NPR approach will ultimately fail. That is, public sector agencies have legal and constitutional obligations that must be fulfilled, and some reforms—no matter how sensible or well-intentioned—do not fit well into the American legal framework. Still others regard it as just another White House attempt to control the bureaucracy. The jury is still out.

Conclusion: Expectations and Government Operations

Although these efforts to reform the federal bureaucracy are well-meaning, most are based on the two myths we have examined in this chapter. The reforms aim at making government agencies either more competent or more responsive, or both. Yet there is little evidence to support the contention that bureaucratic incompetence and unresponsiveness are pervasive problems in federal agencies. Instead, the problems of our national bureaucracy may be rooted in the constant effort of federal employees to competently respond to the expectations made of them.

Americans are demanding citizens. They want government to be efficient and keep costs to a minimum while insisting that agencies spare no resources to get the job done. They want government workers to treat everyone equally but feel that bureaucrats should consider the special needs of individual citizens. They want public officials to increase the quantity and quality of public services while insisting that program budgets be cut back. Put bluntly, the principal problems facing our national bureaucracy lie in what the American people expect from it.

Expectations are important for bureaucrats because federal workers spend most of their time trying to live up to the expectations of others—expectations as varied and diverse as the programs they administer.[48] Many of the problems surrounding bureaucratic institutions can be traced to those efforts. If we are going to criticize the performance of those bureaucrats and accuse them of being too wasteful or too unresponsive, then we must remember that most federal government employees are often responding to our demands.

Summary

1. The federal bureaucracy comprises diverse groups of people who occupy a variety of white-collar and blue-collar positions. They are organized under several personnel systems, including political appointees, the general civil service system, career personnel systems, and wage systems.

2. Much of what federal bureaucrats do is hidden from public view. Nevertheless, they play important roles in the policymaking process—roles that go beyond merely administering government programs.

3. Organizationally, federal bureaucrats work in hundreds of agencies, including the Executive

Office of the President, cabinet departments, independent executive branch agencies, regulatory commissions, government corporations, and other types of agencies.

4. The federal bureaucracy has grown in size and changed in nature over the past two centuries, mostly because of increasing demands by the public and changing conditions in American society.

5. Bureaucracies need power to function in the American political system. They derive that power from a variety of sources, such as external support, expertise, bureaucratic discretion, longevity, and skill and leadership.

6. There are many limits to bureaucratic power. These limits come from the legal and political controls exercised by the presidency, Congress, the courts, and various agencies.

7. In their operations, bureaucracies sometimes adopt pathological behavior patterns. They may give excessive attention to the interests of those they serve (clientelism), oppose change (incrementalism), tend to be arbitrary and capricious (arbitrariness), take an overly narrow view of the world (parochialism), and yield to an urge to expand (imperialism).

8. Such behaviors stimulate a variety of reform efforts, many of which focus on reorganizations and changes in personnel policies. Ultimately, however, bureaucracies must meet the expectations of the public in accomplishing their jobs. In many instances those expectations are in direct conflict with the standards of businesslike performance.

Key Terms and Concepts

Bureaucracy Any large, complex organization in which employees have specific job responsibilities and work within a hierarchy. Often used to refer to both government agencies and the people who work in them.

Political appointees Government officials who occupy the approximately three thousand most strategically important positions in the federal government and who are appointed by the president. About six hundred of these formal appointments must be confirmed by the Senate.

Cabinet An official advisory board to the president, made up of the heads (secretaries) of the fourteen major departments in the federal government.

Patronage A system of filling government positions in which whom a person knows is more important than what a person knows.

Spoils system A patronage-based system of giving government jobs at all levels to members of the party that has won the top political office.

Pendleton Act A law passed in 1883 that established the first merit-based personnel system for the federal government.

Merit system A system that stresses the ability, education, and job performance of government employees rather than their political backgrounds.

General civil service system The merit-based system that covers most white-collar and technical positions in the federal government.

Senior Executive Service (SES) The highest category of federal civil service employees, composed of a select group of public administrators who specialize in agency management.

Career service personnel systems Separate personnel systems for highly specialized agencies like the Coast Guard and the Foreign Service.

Wage systems A federal personnel system covering over a million federal workers who perform blue-collar and related jobs and are largely represented by unions or other associations with limited bargaining rights.

Proxy administration The government's use of indirect means to deliver public goods and services, such as contracting, grants-in-aid, loan guarantees, and government-sponsored enterprises.

Executive Office of the President (EOP) The collective name for several agencies, councils, and staff members that advise the president and help manage the federal bureaucracy. The EOP was established in the 1930s; the number and type of agencies that constitute it change with each presidential administration.

Office of Management and Budget (OMB) An EOP agency that acts as the president's principal link to most federal agencies. The agency supervises matters relating to program and budget requests.

White House Office An EOP agency that includes the president's key advisers and assistants who help him with the daily requirements of the presidency.

Independent agencies More than two hundred agencies that exist outside the EOP and the cabinet departments. Reporting directly to the president, they perform a wide range of functions, from environmental protection (Environmental Protection Agency) and managing social programs (Social Security Administration) to responding to disasters (Federal Emergency Management Agency), conducting the nation's space policy (National Aeronautics and Space Administration), and helping the president manage the federal government (the General Services Administration and the Office of Personnel Management).

Regulatory commissions Federal agencies led by presidentially appointed boards that make and enforce policies affecting various sectors of the U.S. economy. Formally independent of the White House to avoid presidential interference, these agencies employ large professional staffs to help them carry out their many functions.

Quasi-legislative functions Lawmaking functions performed by regulatory commissions as authorized by Congress.

Quasi-judicial functions Judicial functions performed by regulatory commissions. Agencies can hold hearings for companies or individuals accused of violating agency regulations. Commission decisions can be appealed to the federal courts.

Government corporations Public agencies that carry out specific economic or service functions (such as the U.S. Postal Service, which delivers the mail, and the Tennessee Valley Authority, which provides power and other services to its namesake region) and are organized in the same way as private corporations. Other examples include the Corporation for Public Broadcasting (as well as the Public Broadcasting System and National Public Radio), the Federal Deposit Insurance Corporation, and the Resolution Trust Corporation.

Bureaucratic power The power of government agencies derived from law, external support, expertise, discretion, longevity in office, skill, leadership, and a variety of other sources.

Policy subgovernments Alliances among specific agencies, interest groups, and relevant members of Congress. In their most extreme forms, called **cozy triangles,** these alliances might effectively exercise authority in a narrow policy area, such as tobacco price supports. Other forms of subgovernments, called **issue networks,** involve a large number of participants with different degrees of interest.

Whistle-blowers Employees who risk their careers by reporting corruption or waste in their agencies to oversight officials.

Inspector general An official in a government agency assigned the task of investigating complaints or suspicious behavior.

Bureaucratic pathologies Behaviors by bureaucrats that feed the idea that the bureaucracy is incompetent and unresponsive. They include clientelism, incrementalism, arbitrariness, parochialism, and imperialism.

Standard operating procedures (SOPs) Regularized procedures used in public agencies to help conduct administrative business effectively and efficiently.

Privatization The process of turning the work of government agencies over to the private sector.

Ombudsman The person in a government agency responsible for hearing citizen complaints or problems related to government programs and policies.

Reinventing government An approach to bureaucratic reform adopted by the Clinton administration that emphasized empowerment and decentralization in order to enhance the performance of government agencies and programs.

Courts, Judges, and the Law

MYTH & REALITY

Are judicial decisions
completely objective and
final?

WWW•

See **Political Science** at
http://www.hmco.com/college

Frustrated by the course his life had taken, a young man from Boulder, Colorado, filed suit against his parents. Claiming that they had neglected his physical and psychological needs, the young man asked the court to award him $350,000 for something he termed "malpractice of parenting." Halfway across the country another man, professing that the world hated him, brought suit for unspecified damages against the Supreme Court and the world.

Although extreme in their triviality, the parties to these cases demonstrated a basic American belief: that courts can resolve almost any kind of dispute. In large measure, the uniqueness of the American political system stems from the role played by the courts. No other nation grants so much authority and political power to the judiciary; nor are people of other nations quite as willing to entrust their fate to courts as are Americans. Yet for all their faith in courts, most citizens know very little about the legal system. They may be familiar with the local traffic court or entertained by Judge Wapner's version of small-claims court. (In a 1989 poll, the *Washington Post* found that 54 percent of its sample knew that Wapner presides over television's *The People's Court,* but only 9 percent could correctly name the chief justice of the U.S. Supreme Court.) Nevertheless, when pressed to elaborate on what courts do and why they do it, people fall back on some vague notions about the law.

Thus the image of the courts is shrouded in symbolism and myth. Pomp and circumstance surround even the lowliest of courts. Only in a courtroom will you find a black-robed individual looking down from a raised platform. No other public official is allowed such trappings. In fact, a mayor or senator bedecked in a black robe would seem a pompous fool. Yet when a judge puts on those same robes, no one laughs or even thinks it odd: instead the robes evoke respect. The same is true of the myths that surround the American courts: if they were attributed to any other political institution, they would seem preposterous.

Perhaps the most widespread of the illusions surrounding the courts is that they are above politics. In contrast to the compromise and partisanship of the political world, the *myth of the nonpolitical courts* represents the judiciary as operating with the certainty and objectivity that comes from the application of a body of specialized knowledge. Members of Congress may act out of self-interest; judges simply apply the law. It is the fate of courts to be characterized as the defenders of the rule of law as opposed to the rule of ordinary men and women.

As comforting as this myth may be, it distorts reality. In the pages that follow, you will see that even the act of creating the federal courts was fraught with political conflict. Similarly, not only is the process of selecting judges mired in political controversy, but those chosen are often active participants in politics.

The idea that courts have special powers also gives rise to the *myth of finality,* which assumes that once a court—especially the Supreme Court—has spoken, the decision is implemented. This tendency to view court decisions as an endpoint in the political process makes courts seem more powerful than they actually are. Final authority does not rest with the Supreme Court, nor should it in a

**The Ultimate
Punishment**

Although executions
have become more
common, the im-
position of capital
punishment remains
controversial. Here,
demonstrators protest
the planned execution
of convicted murderer
Gary Graham. Despite
the protests, the state
of Texas executed
Graham.

representative democracy. Courts cannot compel anyone to comply with decisions. Their orders become effective only with the aid of others—aid that is not
always provided.

We begin our discussion of the role of courts in American society by distin-
guishing the various sources of law. Then we look at the structure of the court
system and the way that judges are appointed and removed. We conclude the
chapter with an examination of the workings of the Supreme Court and the
question of compliance.

The Origins and Types of American Law

As you may recall from Chapter 2, on the Constitution, the oldest source of law
applied by U.S. courts is common, or judge-made, law, which dates from medieval England. A comparatively modern and increasingly important source of
law is *statutory law,* which originates from specifically designated lawmaking bodies (for example, Congress and state legislatures).

The distinction between civil and criminal actions is also important in understanding the legal process. **Civil actions** involve a conflict between private
persons and/or organizations. Typical of these cases are those involving disputes

over contracts, claims for damages resulting from a personal injury, and divorce cases. In a civil case, the person bringing the suit is called the plaintiff, and the person being sued is the defendant.

Criminal law, on the other hand, applies to offenses against the public order and provides for a specified punishment. Acts in violation of criminal law are specifically detailed in governmental statutes. The party demanding legal action (the national, state, or other government) is called the prosecution. Most of these cases arise in state courts, although there is a growing body of federal criminal law dealing with such issues as kidnapping, tax evasion, and the sale of narcotics.

The Structure of the Court Systems

When most people think about courts, the U.S. Supreme Court immediately comes to mind. As the highest court in the land, the Supreme Court symbolizes the American judiciary. Yet it is only one of more than eighteen thousand American courts, most of which are the creations of the various states. Each state, as well as the Commonwealth of Puerto Rico, has its own independent court system. Because most crimes and civil disputes involve state laws, these are the courts that most affect the average citizen. For example, the motorist accused of driving under the influence of alcohol will be brought before a court in the state in which the violation occurred.

Obviously, among fifty-two court systems there is bound to be a great deal of variability; in fact, no two systems are exactly alike. Nevertheless, two types of courts can be found in all systems.

Trial courts, the lowest level of a court system, are the "courts of first instance," possessing **original jurisdiction** (the power to be the first court to hear a case). These courts take evidence, listen to witnesses, and decide what is true and what is not. Trial courts handle both criminal and civil matters.

Trial court decisions may be made by a single judge (a procedure known as a *bench trial*) or by a jury composed of citizens selected from the community. The Constitution provides for jury trials in all criminal cases and in civil cases where the value contested exceeds $20. Most state constitutions contain similar provisions for jury trials. Nevertheless, jury trials tend to be the exception rather than the rule. The desire for quick decisions encourages many defendants to waive the time-consuming jury selection process in favor of the faster decision by a judge. Parties to particularly complicated civil litigation may also assume that members of a jury are less capable of following the detailed arguments than a judge. In criminal cases, a high percentage of defendants enter into plea-bargaining agreements, in which the accused, with the consent of the prosecutor, pleads guilty to a lesser crime or a less severe punishment and so avoids a trial.

In contrast, **appellate courts** are charged with the responsibility of reconsidering decisions made by trial courts if the losing party requests it. The appellate review is designed to ensure that there is no error in judicial procedures or interpretations of the law. Because appellate courts simply review the written record of lower courts, they do not use juries.

The Federal and State Court Systems

On paper, the federal court structure appears to be a relatively simple and eminently rational arrangement. After all, the system is composed of a single Supreme Court, several intermediate appellate and trial courts, and a limited number of specialized trial courts (see Figure 13.1). But behind the judicial system's facade of orderliness is a history of intense political struggle that contradicts the myth of the nonpolitical courts.

Lower Courts

Article III of the Constitution creates only one court, the Supreme Court, leaving to Congress the power to create such "inferior courts" as it deems necessary. This peculiar approach to court structure was the direct result of the bitter struggle between the Federalists and the Antifederalists at the Constitutional Convention. The Antifederalists, in order to protect the power of the states, wanted a system in which all cases, even those involving the national government, would be heard by the state courts. The Federalists argued for a national court system, which would establish the supremacy of the central government and limit the biases of the local courts.[1] Unable to reach agreement, the delegates finally compromised by creating the Supreme Court and leaving to Congress the responsibility for filling in the details of the system.

The organization of federal courts remains a divisive political issue, however. For example, it took twenty years of struggle between conservative white southerners and civil rights groups to create a court of appeals for the eleventh circuit, or judicial territory. In the 1960s southerners proposed moving conservative southern judges from one circuit to another, creating a Deep South court. Convinced that such restructuring would weaken civil rights enforcement, civil rights groups, principally the National Association for the Advancement of Colored People (NAACP), managed to block the reorganization. In 1980 civil rights groups and liberal members of Congress finally agreed to split an old circuit into two new southern circuits. The NAACP withdrew its opposition only after the appointment of some black judges to the circuits—demonstrating that even the apparently technical questions of court structure are matters of sharp political conflict.

U.S. District Courts.   As trial courts of general jurisdiction for the federal system, district courts hear trials in all federal criminal and civil cases. The district

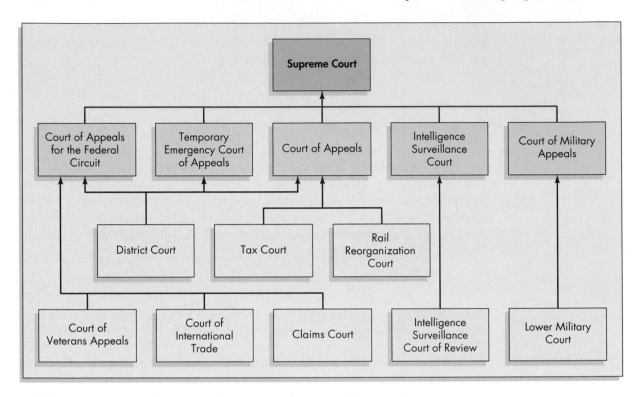

FIGURE 13.1

Organization of the
Federal Court System

The lines and arrows show the routes of cases through appeals and Supreme Court
grants of hearings.

Source: From Lawrence Baum, *American Courts: Process and Policy,* 2nd ed., p.27. © 1990 by Houghton Mifflin
Company.

courts also hear what are known as *diversity cases:* suits between parties from different states when the amount in controversy exceeds $50,000. In addition to
their trial duties, the district courts are also responsible for the naturalization of
aliens, the approval of passports, and the granting of parole to federal prisoners.

The Judiciary Act of 1789, the first Senate bill introduced in the First Congress, created a national judiciary that included the district courts. Although
these courts resulted from the Federalist impulse to establish a strong national
judiciary, they were also shaped by the Federalists' need to compromise with the
Antifederalists. Thus the Federalist forces attained their goal of a national court
system, but the Antifederalists insisted on district boundaries identical with state
borders—a situation that remains to this day. By requiring district court and state
boundaries to be the same, the Antifederalists achieved a decentralized structure
committed to local political values.

New Citizens

In addition to conducting trials, U.S. district courts are responsible for naturalization of aliens. Pictured here is a naturalization ceremony.

Currently, ninety-four U.S. district courts are distributed in the fifty states, the District of Columbia, and the four territories. Twenty-four states contain more than one district, and the remaining states and territories have one district court each.

District court cases are usually heard by a single judge, who presides over both civil and criminal trials. The district courts have a total of 632 judicial positions, but the number of judgeships assigned to each district varies from 1 to 28. The state of Vermont, for example, constitutes a single judicial district, staffed by one judge. In contrast, the Southern District of New York, which includes Manhattan and the Bronx, has twenty-eight judges assigned to it.

To most Americans, the district courts may seem to be the least important of the federal courts. If the Supreme Court is not more important, it is certainly more noticeable. Yet district courts hear more than two hundred thousand cases each year, and fewer than 10 percent of them are appealed to a higher court. Of those that are appealed, only a small fraction are reversed. For most litigants, the district court decision is the final decision.

Courts of Appeals.   Courts of appeals, or **circuit courts,** as they are sometimes called, serve as the major appellate courts for the federal system. They review all cases—civil and criminal—appealed from the district courts. Moreover, on occasion these courts review decisions of the independent regulatory agencies and departments. For example, decisions of the Federal Communications Commission involving the renewal of radio and television licenses can be appealed only to the District of Columbia Circuit.

There are twelve U.S. courts of appeals, one for the District of Columbia and eleven others covering regional groupings of states (see Figure 13.2). Although the circuits include more than one state, no state is in more than one circuit. A thirteenth court of appeals, the U.S. Court of Appeals for the Federal Circuit, is an appellate court charged with hearing patent and trademark cases.

The twelve courts of appeals of general jurisdiction have 179 authorized judgeships. But, as in the district courts, these judges are unevenly distributed among the circuits. Individual circuits have anywhere from 6 to 28 judges assigned to them. The number is determined by Congress and is supposed to reflect the workload of the circuit. Ordinarily, the courts of appeals hear cases in panels of three judges, and these panels vary in membership from case to case.

The Supreme Court

The Constitution is remarkably vague even with regard to the Supreme Court. In comparing Article I with Article III, it becomes evident how detailed Article I is concerning the make-up and duties of Congress, and how such details are lacking in Article III about the Court.

How many justices serve on the Supreme Court? The answer is nine, but you will not discover that from reading the Constitution. The Constitution does not designate a size for the Court; that is up to Congress. Since 1869 the Court has been staffed by a chief justice and eight associate justices. Until 1869, however, Congress made frequent changes in the size of the Court. Often these changes were thinly disguised efforts to serve partisan political purposes. During the Civil War, for instance, Congress created a tenth seat on the Supreme Court, assuring President Abraham Lincoln a solid majority on the Court.

According to the Constitution, the Supreme Court has both original and appellate jurisdiction. Original jurisdiction, as stated earlier, means that a court is empowered to make the first decision in a particular kind of dispute; it is the court of first instance. Article III limits the Court's original jurisdiction to cases involving foreign ambassadors and those in which a state is a party. Suits under original jurisdiction account for a very small portion of the Supreme Court's workload: about 150 such cases since 1789.

The chief labor of the Supreme Court is appellate. For much of the nation's history, the Court was mandated by Congress to hear all cases that came to it. Then complaints by the justices that the workload was unmanageable led Congress to pass the Judiciary Act of 1925. Under the provisions of this act, the Court has tremendous latitude in selecting the cases it wants to hear.

Of the more than seven thousand cases brought annually to the Supreme Court, approximately 90 percent come by way of a request for a **writ of certiorari**—a request that the Supreme Court order the lower court to send up the record of the case. Cases are accepted for review by means of the *rule of four,*

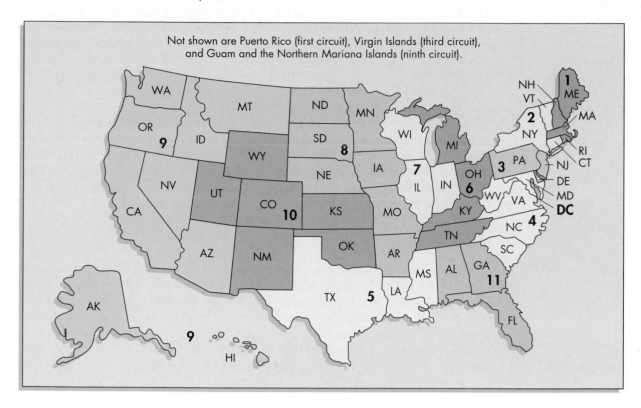

Not shown are Puerto Rico (first circuit), Virgin Islands (third circuit), and Guam and the Northern Mariana Islands (ninth circuit).

FIGURE 13.2

U.S. Circuit Courts of Appeals

At the base of the federal court system are ninety-four district (or trial) courts. Each state has at least one district court, and larger states have more. Judgments from district courts can be appealed to one of twelve circuit courts of appeals. Only a fraction of the cases decided in district courts ever come before the appeals courts, and only a tiny fraction of these are reviewed by the Supreme Court.

that is, four justices must vote to consider the case. In more than 95 percent of requests for writs of certiorari, appeal is denied, normally without explanation. The Court simply notes that certiorari is denied and that the decision of the lower court stands. Cases can also come to the Court by **appeal,** which states that the litigants have some right under the law to have their cases reviewed. In practice, appeals are treated in the same discretionary way as certiorari.

Because the Court receives many more petitions each year than it can possibly process, the freedom to accept a limited number of cases is essential to its effective operation. But there are also political advantages to the screening process. By carefully selecting cases for review, the justices can and do advance their policy preferences. Moreover, the ability to deny review to cases without explanation can be used to avoid particularly controversial political issues. Thus the Supreme Court avoided ruling on the constitutionality of the undeclared war in Vietnam by refusing, without explanation, to grant certiorari to cases raising the issue.

Specialized Courts

In addition to the federal courts that we have discussed, Congress has also created a few specialized courts. One of them is the U.S. Court of Federal Claims, created to litigate disputes involving government contracts. Other special courts include the U.S. Court of Military Appeals, the U.S. Court of International Trade, and the U.S. Tax Court. Staffed by judges with expertise in a particular area, these courts reduce the workload of the general courts.

State Court Systems

All states have at least one appellate court that serves as the highest tribunal. These courts are not always identifiable by title, however. For example, in the state of New York the highest court is called the court of appeals, and the trial courts are designated as the supreme courts. Whatever their name, nearly every state possesses one court that reviews the decisions of all other courts. (Both Texas and Oklahoma have two high courts—one for civil litigation and one that handles only criminal appeals.) Slightly more than half the states also make use of an intermediate appellate court to hear appeals from the trial court decisions.

Questioning the Expert

A major part of a trial court judge's job is to determine the admissibility of evidence. Pictured here is California Superior Court Judge Stanley Weisberg questioning, outside the presence of the jury, forensic psychiatrist William Vicary who testified as an expert witness in the notorious Menendez brothers trial.

Such courts permit the parties to appeal without overburdening the highest court.

The most numerous state courts, the trial courts, are divided into two types: those with limited jurisdiction and those with general jurisdiction. Trial courts of **limited jurisdiction** are empowered to hear only a narrowly defined class of cases. These specialized courts often process a large number of routine cases involving minor issues. Among the most common courts in this category are traffic courts and small-claims courts.

On the other hand, trial courts of **general jurisdiction** have authority over a broader class of issues. Ordinarily, such courts hear all civil cases involving non-trivial monetary value and all cases involving serious criminal matters. Although the courts of general jurisdiction are not as specialized as the courts of limited jurisdiction, it is not unusual to find general jurisdiction courts divided into criminal and civil courts, especially in metropolitan areas with heavy caseloads.

Interactions Among Court Systems

The existence of so many court systems obviously complicates the interactions among them. Often the litigants (parties involved in a suit) can choose among several different courts. Indeed, it is common for the plaintiff (the party bringing suit) to shop around for a court, hoping to find one favorable to his or her side.

This complexity is heightened by the fact that both state and national courts may have jurisdiction over the same issues—a situation known as *concurrent jurisdiction*. For example, Congress has granted to the federal district courts the right to hear the so-called diversity cases—cases involving citizens of different states contesting a sum greater than $50,000. In doing so, however, Congress did not deny the state courts the right to hear such cases; it merely established an additional forum for resolving them.[2]

Although the complex network of multiple court systems provides the opportunity to shop around for a favorable court, once the case has been tried, appeals must be made within the same court system. Occasionally, decisions of a state's highest court are successfully appealed to the U.S. Supreme Court, but this can occur only when the state's highest court has rendered a decision interpreting provisions of the U.S. Constitution, a treaty, or a federal law. Decisions of a court in one state may never be appealed to a court of another state. Nor is it possible to appeal a federal court decision to a state court.

Recruiting and Removing Judges

In contrast to nations such as Italy, the United States does not have a career judiciary; there is no special training required for judges. In fact, the U.S. Constitution does not even require legal training as a qualification for service on the Supreme Court. All 108 justices who have served on the Court have been lawyers, but it was not until 1957 that all members of the Court had earned law degrees.

There is an old adage in American politics that a judge is a lawyer who knew a senator or governor. Though something of an overstatement, the saying indicates that beyond the formal requirements of constitutions and statutes lies a selection process that is highly political. The myth of the nonpolitical courts suggests that judicial selections are or should be based on merit. The reality is that the choices are always political.

Federal Judges

According to Article II of the Constitution, the president shall nominate and, with the "advice and consent of the Senate," appoint justices of the Supreme Court. The president proposes a candidate to the Senate; if a majority of the Senate approves, the nominee takes office. This same formal method is used to appoint judges to the courts of appeals and district courts. But the constitutional requirements do not describe the political complexity of the selection process. Besides, informal methods of selection have evolved alongside the formal process.

Appointment to the District Courts.   The president, in conjunction with others, has the power to make nominations to the district courts. Most administrations establish guidelines detailing the qualities the president expects in a nominee and then leave the search for candidates to the U.S. Department of Justice. In Ronald Reagan's administration, for instance, the Justice Department's Office of Legal Policy was chiefly responsible for nominations to the federal district court. To ensure that the nominees shared the president's political philosophy, attorneys in the Office of Legal Policy reportedly subjected judicial candidates to extensive interviews, said to last six or more hours. The most controversial aspect of the Reagan administration's screening was the reported use of abortion as a litmus test. Throughout Reagan's term complaints surfaced that Justice Department officials routinely questioned prospective nominees on their views on abortion and rejected those who did not conform to the administration's position. Though Reagan was certainly not the first president to consider the ideology of his nominees, his administration represents "the most systematic, most coordinated effort at the use of appointment power to maximize the president's agenda and to maximize the president's influence on the appointment process."[3]

In nominating candidates for the district courts, however, the executive branch must always be mindful of the power of individual senators. Under the terms of the unwritten rule of senatorial courtesy, the Senate as a whole will reject the nomination of any candidate opposed by a senator of the president's party from the nominee's state. In recent years senatorial courtesy has been exercised at the committee stage by use of the "blue slip." When it receives a nomination to a federal court, the Senate Judiciary Committee notifies the senators by means of a blue slip. The failure by a senator of the president's party and from the nominee's state to return the blue slip kills the appointment. The committee will simply refuse to take any action until the nomination is withdrawn.

Rather than provoke confrontations with the Senate, presidents have as a rule accepted advice from appropriate senators. Often this translates into formal nomination by the president but informal nomination by a senator. In fact, the prominence of senatorial courtesy led one former assistant attorney general to remark, "The Constitution is backwards. Article II, Section 2, should read: 'the Senators shall nominate, and by and with the consent of the President, shall appoint.'"[4]

Appointment to the Courts of Appeals. In making appointments to the courts of appeals, the president and the Justice Department have a freer hand than they do in the case of district courts. Because the circuits contain more than one state, no senator can unambiguously claim senatorial courtesy. Because it is generally assumed that each state in a circuit should have at least one judge on that circuit's appellate bench, the president is constrained by having to maintain the proper balance of state representation.

Appointment to the Supreme Court. The Supreme Court is a national institution, with no special ties to states or regions. Thus the president need not worry about individual senators exercising senatorial courtesy, although senators from the nominee's state are asked to serve as sponsors. The Senate is not irrelevant to the nomination process, however, and has considered itself free to reject candidates for a variety of reasons. Reagan's nomination of Judge Robert Bork, for instance, failed in the Senate because of widespread opposition to his restrictive views on the right to privacy and equal rights for women.

In the nineteenth century the Senate was more likely than it is today to disapprove a presidential nomination on purely partisan grounds. Before the Bork nomination, the two most recent nominations to fail in the Senate, those of Judges Clement Haynsworth and G. Harrold Carswell, were opposed by Senate liberals for ideological reasons, but both candidates had other serious disadvantages. Haynsworth came under attack for purchasing stock in a company that had been a party in a case before him; he bought the stock after the decision had been made but before it was announced. Carswell was criticized for lacking the professional qualifications expected of a Supreme Court justice. His fate was probably sealed when one of his defenders, Republican Senator Roman Hruska from Nebraska, argued that "there are a lot of mediocre judges and people and lawyers. They are entitled to a little representation, aren't they, and a little chance?"[5]

None of these battles, not even the failed Bork nomination, matched the furor over President George Bush's 1991 nomination of Judge Clarence Thomas, however. Nominated by the president to replace Thurgood Marshall, the Court's only African-American justice, Thomas initially appeared assured of Senate confirmation. Like Marshall, he had overcome segregation and poverty. But from

Appointment to the Supreme Court requires nomination by the president and confirmation by the Senate. Here Ruth Bader Ginsburg appears before the Senate Judiciary Committee confirmation hearings. Ginsburg was easily confirmed by the Senate.

www.

For more information on the Supreme Court justices, see the **Gitelson/ Dudley/Dubnick web site.**

the beginning Thomas's conservatism, particularly on issues of affirmative action, troubled Senate liberals and leaders of the major civil rights organizations.

After five days of hearings, during which Thomas recanted many of his previous writings and refused to discuss his opinions on abortion, the Senate seemed set to confirm his nomination. As the Senate was about to vote, however, allegations of sexual harassment were leaked to the press. Although the allegations made by Professor Anita Hill, a former government employee who had worked for Thomas, had been presented to the committee, they had not been part of the public record. Embarrassed by the leak, the Senate postponed the floor vote on the nominee, and the Senate Judiciary Committee reconvened for an extraordinary set of weekend hearings. With the hearings covered live on television, the Judiciary Committee heard testimony from Hill, Thomas, and others concerning the nominee's behavior. Following this second round of hearings, the committee sent the nomination to the Senate floor without a recommendation—the committee had divided 7 to 7 over whether Thomas should be confirmed. Eventually the Senate confirmed him by the closest vote of any successful nominee in this century, but the battle polarized the nation and left many senators questioning the confirmation process. Several senators, including the chair of the Judiciary Committee, vowed to seek changes in the Senate procedures, but no changes have been made.

Because justices of the Supreme Court are appointed for life and occupy such a prominent position in the American system of government, most presidents are quite careful to choose justices whose ideological views seem to be in harmony with theirs. If fate provides enough vacancies, presidential appointments can reshape the judiciary to reflect the administration's views, perpetuating the president's philosophical positions long after the administration has left office (see Table 13.1).[6]

Of course, presidents are not always successful in predicting what a candidate will do once in office. Perhaps the most famous example of a president frustrated by his own appointment is Theodore Roosevelt, who nominated Justice Oliver Wendell Holmes. Before forwarding the Holmes nomination to the Senate, Roosevelt had assured himself that the candidate shared his views on the antitrust statutes. When Holmes immediately voted against the president's view in an antitrust case, Roosevelt quipped that he could "make a judge with a stronger backbone out of a banana."[7] Similarly, President Dwight D. Eisenhower came to regret his appointment of Earl Warren as the chief justice. Eisenhower had made the appointment expecting Warren to express the president's own middle-of-the-road political views. Instead, the Warren Court (1953–1969) became known as the most liberal Supreme Court in U.S. history. Eisenhower referred to the appointment as "the biggest damned-fool mistake I ever made."[8]

TABLE 13.1

The Rehnquist Court

Justice	Year Born	Year Appointed	Appointing President	Political Party
Rehnquist, William	1924	1971	Nixon	Rep.
		1986*	Reagan	
Stevens, John	1920	1975	Ford	Rep.
O'Connor, Sandra	1930	1981	Reagan	Rep.
Scalia, Antonin	1936	1986	Reagan	Rep.
Kennedy, Anthony	1936	1988	Reagan	Rep.
Souter, David	1939	1990	Bush	Rep.
Thomas, Clarence	1948	1991	Bush	Rep.
Ginsburg, Ruth Bader	1933	1993	Clinton	Dem.
Breyer, Stephen G.	1938	1994	Clinton	Dem.

*Appointed chief justice.

Nominations to the Supreme Court also give presidents a chance to recognize important constituent groups, especially social groups that have been unrepresented. President Lyndon B. Johnson broke the Supreme Court's color barrier by appointing Thurgood Marshall, the first black justice. President Reagan appointed Sandra Day O'Connor, the first woman to serve on the Court. Obviously, the appointment of a woman or minority member to the Court is unlikely to have a substantive impact on decisions, but representation for those groups traditionally excluded from the process has great symbolic value.

Who Becomes a Federal Judge?

WWW•

For more information on federal justices, see the **Gitelson/Dudley/ Dubnick** web site.

No recruitment system is ever neutral. Any system will favor certain skills and opportunities and downplay others. The process of selecting Supreme Court justices favors individuals from socially advantaged families. As an observer has noted, "The typical Supreme Court Justice has generally been white, Protestant (with a penchant for a high social status denomination), usually of ethnic stock originating in the British Isles, and born in comfortable circumstances in an urban or small-town environment."[9] What is more, almost two-thirds of the justices came from politically active families. Finally, those appointed to the Court were by and large politically active themselves, with the vast majority having previously held political office.

When we examine the judiciary in the lower federal courts, we see a similar, although less pronounced, pattern of upper- and middle-class appointees. Compared with Supreme Court justices, judges on the courts of appeals, for instance, are slightly less likely to come from politically active families and more likely to be educated at less prestigious law schools. These courts also manifest greater gender and racial diversity than does the High Court. This diversity peaked under President Jimmy Carter, who appointed more women and minorities to the federal courts than any other president.

Because appointments are for life, the federal courts are an especially rich source of political patronage, and presidents are under some pressure to reward the party faithful by such appointments. Although presidents occasionally nominate a member of the opposition party, most have selected at least 90 percent of the appointees from their own party. Staffing the courts with partisans ensures a foothold in the government for a party, even when the party is out of favor with the voters. Aside from patronage, relying on members of their own party allows presidents to choose judges who most likely share their political outlook. Thus the bias toward fellow party members serves two goals, both of which clearly contradict the myth of nonpolitical courts.

Removing Judges

In the early days of the republic, one of the most important problems facing the federal courts was attracting and retaining judges. As strange as it may seem,

President George Washington had problems filling positions on the Supreme Court. For example, John Rutledge, one of Washington's first appointees, resigned before the Court ever met to become the chief justice of the South Carolina supreme court—apparently a more attractive position. As the prestige of the federal courts increased, recruitment problems diminished, although attracting and retaining lower-court judges is sometimes difficult because the salaries are low compared with what many members of the judiciary would earn in private law practice.

The prestige and power of a judgeship occasionally create the need to remove an ill or incompetent judge who refuses to retire. This problem is particularly thorny in the federal courts because the only constitutional means for removing judges is the impeachment process, which requires evidence of "Treason, Bribery, or other high Crimes and Misdemeanors."

Over the years there have been few impeachment trials. In 1986, however, Congress, in its first such trial in fifty years, did impeach and convict U.S. District Court Judge Harry E. Claiborne of Nevada. Claiborne had previously been convicted of evading the payment of more than $90,000 in income taxes. At the time of his impeachment trial, he was serving a two-year sentence in federal prison but continuing to draw his salary as a federal judge. In 1989 Congress impeached and convicted two more district court judges. Judge Walter Nixon of Mississippi was removed from the bench on the grounds that he had committed perjury. At the time of his Senate conviction, Nixon was serving a five-year prison sentence for knowingly making false statements to a grand jury. More controversial was the 1989 impeachment and conviction of Judge Alcee L. Hastings of Florida. Hastings was removed for accepting a bribe in a criminal case. Unlike Claiborne and Nixon, he had been acquitted in a criminal trial on related charges, but the Senate concluded that Hastings had lied and presented false evidence at the criminal trial. These two impeachment trials in a single year prompted several members of Congress to seek alternatives to the time-consuming process. Suggested constitutional amendments to provide for an easy removal procedure were introduced in 1990, but no action has been taken on them.

Even if impeachment were easier, it would probably not be deemed appropriate in situations where a judge suffers from illness or senility. A case in point is that of Utah District Court Judge Willis Ritter. Ritter first drew national attention when he ordered court officials to arrest noisy plumbers who were making repairs near his courtroom.[10] He also engaged in such eccentric behavior as hissing throughout an attorney's presentation to the court. But although this behavior is clearly odd, it does not seem to fit the definition of an impeachable offense—"Treason, Bribery, or other high Crimes and Misdemeanors."

Lacking an effective means of removing judges, Congress has turned to providing pension programs as an incentive. Under a 1954 act of Congress, judges can opt for the status of senior judge. Senior judges receive a pension equal to full pay, and they may participate, where needed, in as many cases as they choose. This option allows a judge to enjoy a reduced workload without completely retiring. Senior judges have become essential for the operation of many of the more overworked lower federal courts. Because judges do not have to accept senior status, Congress has also provided a mechanism for denying case assignments to sitting judges on the lower federal courts.[11] The judge retains the post and the salary but receives no work.

The Supreme Court at Work

The Supreme Court term begins the first Monday in October and runs through June or into early July, depending on the workload. The term of the Court is designated by the year it begins, even though very few decisions will actually be handed down in October, November, and December of that year. Throughout the term, the Court alternates between two weeks of open court, called sessions, and two weeks of recess, the time when the justices read petitions and write opinions.

Oral Argument

During the weeks that the Court is in session, the justices meet Monday through Wednesday to hear oral arguments. These sessions begin at 10 A.M. and last until 3 P.M., with a one-hour break for lunch. Ordinary cases are allotted one hour for arguments, and the time is evenly divided between the parties. If the case is especially important or involves multiple parties raising a variety of issues, the Court may permit longer presentations.

The attorneys presenting oral arguments are reminded of their time limitations by two lights on the lectern. When the white light appears, they know that they have five minutes left. The flash of the red light signals that their time is up, and they must cease speaking unless the chief justice grants an extension. Most often the parties are held strictly to their allotted time. Chief Justice Charles E. Hughes (1930–1941) was so rigid in enforcing the time limit that he is said to have stopped an attorney in the middle of the word *if.*

Because all parties have prepared written **briefs** (documents containing a summary of the issues, the laws applying to the case, and arguments supporting counsel's position), the Court discourages attorneys from reading prepared statements. Indeed, the Court's rules state that "the Court looks with disfavor on any oral argument that is read from a prepared text." Generally, the justices expect the attorneys to discuss the case and not to deliver a lecture. Often the attorneys spend their allotted time answering questions posed by the justices, and the justices often use the questions as a means of debating with each other. On one occasion, as Justice Felix Frankfurter repeatedly questioned a nervous attorney, Justice William O. Douglas repeatedly responded with answers helpful

to the attorney. Finally, a frustrated Frankfurter, directing his remarks to the attorney, said, "I thought you were arguing this case." The attorney responded, "I am, but I can use all the help I can get."[12]

In addition to the arguments of the lawyers for the parties to the case, the Court may also consider the positions taken by interested third parties. Any individual or organization, with the consent of the parties involved in the case or by Court permission, may submit written arguments known as **amicus curiae** (friend of the court) briefs. Occasionally, amicus participation may even include the offering of oral arguments. For instance, in the 1989 abortion case of *Webster* v. *Reproductive Health Services,* seventy-eight amicus briefs were filed and the Court allowed the federal government, acting as amicus, ten minutes of oral argument.[13] Amicus participation has become an important means of interest-group lobbying before the courts.

Conference Work

Though oral argument may be dramatic, the crucial work of the Court is done in conference. Twice a week, when the Court is in session, the justices gather in the conference room to discuss and decide cases. No one else is admitted—not even secretaries or law clerks to help the justices. If a justice needs anything from outside the room, the junior justice (least senior in terms of service, not the youngest) must go to the door and summon a messenger. In the past the junior justice was even responsible for pouring the coffee, a practice rumored to have ended with the appointment of Justice Sandra Day O'Connor.

Generally, the justices first decide which petitions should be accepted. Before the conference, the chief justice, with the aid of law clerks, prepares and circulates to the other justices a "discuss" list: a list of cases that the chief justice thinks worthy of discussion. Any case not on the list will be automatically denied review unless another justice requests that it be added to the list. Apparently, as many as 70 percent of the requests for review are denied without any discussion.[14]

Cases that make the list are not automatically accepted for review, however. Instead, each case is considered and voted on by the justices. Only the cases that receive four votes (the rule of four) are accepted and scheduled for further action, and the number of such cases is usually quite small.

After deciding which cases to accept for review, the Court moves on to the cases being argued that week. The chief justice begins the discussion of each case by outlining and commenting on the main issues. Then each justice, in order of seniority, comments on the case. If the votes of the justices are not clear from the discussion, the chief justice calls for a formal vote. Most questions, however, require no vote since the justices' positions will be clear from their initial comments. These conference votes are only tentative votes, however. As Justice John Harlan explained, "The books on voting are never closed until the decision actually comes down."[15]

After the vote, the chief justice, if he is in the majority, assigns the writing of the opinion. If the chief justice is not in the majority, then the majority's most senior justice makes the assignment. The assignment of an opinion writer is important because it will determine the grounds for the Court's decision and perhaps even the size of the majority, since the conference vote was tentative. The justice who assigns the writing of the opinion may decide to write the opinion himself or herself, or give the task to the member of the majority closest to his or her views. As rumor has it, when Warren Burger was chief justice, he frequently let his turn in the discussion of important cases pass so that he could remain free to join the majority at the end and therefore pick the opinion writer. This practice reportedly became so common that Justice Potter Stewart is said to have drawn a tombstone for Burger with the words, "I'll Pass for The Moment."[16]

WWW•

For more information on the Supreme Court decision process, see the **Gitelson/Dudley/Dubnick web site.**

Writing and Announcing the Opinion

Once the writing of the opinion has been assigned, the justice given this task begins work on a draft that expresses his or her own ideas and also takes into account opinions expressed by others in the conference. At the same time other justices may be drafting separate **concurring opinions** (opinions that agree with the conclusion but not with the reasoning of the majority) or **dissenting opinions** (opinions that disagree with the majority conclusion).

As the drafts are completed, they are circulated so that all justices can see and have an opportunity to comment on them. As justices suggest changes in wording and reasoning, negotiations begin. The justice who has drafted the majority opinion, as well as any justices working on any concurring or dissenting opinions, may have to make changes in order to satisfy the others. Sometimes conflicting views among the justices make this process extremely difficult and time consuming. More important, the need to compromise may produce vague decisions that offer little guidance to lower courts. For instance, many Court observers have attributed the extraordinarily vague command of *Brown* v. *Board of Education II* (1955) to desegregate with "all deliberate speed" to the chief justice's desire for a unanimous decision.[17]

Occasionally, the justice assigned to write the majority opinion will change positions and become a dissenter or vice versa. Justice William Brennan described the process when he noted: "I have had to convert more than one of my proposed majority opinions into a dissent before the final opinion was announced. I have also, however, had the more satisfying experience of rewriting a dissent as a majority opinion of the Court."[18]

The opinion-writing stage does not end until all the justices decide which opinion to join. Once they do so, the Court announces the opinion. Throughout much of the Court's history, the justices have read their opinions—majority, concurring, and dissenting—publicly. Currently, the opinion writers read only short statements describing the issues and the disposition.

Interpreting the Constitution

As Chief Justice Hughes quipped, "We are under a Constitution, but the Constitution is what the judges say it is." Of course, as you learned in Chapter 2, on the Constitution, judges are not the sole interpreters of that document. Nevertheless, judges, and particularly justices of the Supreme Court, do play a leading role in interpreting the Constitution, largely because of the power of **judicial review:** the power of courts to declare an act of a legislature constitutional or unconstitutional.

Nowhere in the Constitution is the U.S. Supreme Court specifically granted such authority. Instead, judicial review was inferred by the Court in the 1803 case of *Marbury* v. *Madison*.[19] After the election of 1800, which saw Thomas Jefferson and his fellow partisans win control of the White House and both chambers of Congress, the incumbent president, John Adams, and the Federalist party attempted to maintain a foothold in government by using the time between the election and inauguration to fill the judiciary with Federalists. First John Marshall, secretary of state in the Adams administration, was named the new chief justice of the Supreme Court. Congress then created fifty-eight additional judgeships to be filled by loyal Federalists. (Because these appointments came in the last days of the Adams administration, they became known as the "midnight appointments.")

So great was this haste that the Adams administration failed to deliver the commissions of four newly appointed justices of the peace for the District of

Columbia. Undelivered, the four commissions were returned to the secretary of state's office, where James Madison, the new secretary of state, found them. On orders of President Jefferson, Madison refused to deliver the commissions, prompting William Marbury, one of the four whose papers were withheld, to bring suit in the Supreme Court. Marbury requested that the Court issue a writ of *mandamus* (an order to a government official to carry out a duty of his or her office) compelling Madison to deliver the commission. The case was filed with the Supreme Court directly because a congressional statute, the Judiciary Act of 1789, empowered the Supreme Court to issue such writs as an act of original jurisdiction.

Marbury's suit placed the Court in a difficult and politically charged situation. Congress had already served warning on the Court by canceling the 1802 term of the Court, requiring that Marbury's case be put off until 1803. The Court was faced with two choices, neither of which seemed attractive. The justices could have issued the writ and ordered Madison to deliver the commission, but that would have been to no avail. Madison would most certainly have defied the writ, making the Court look powerless. On the other hand, the Court could have refused to issue the writ, but that would have amounted to an admission of impotence.

Chief Justice Marshall, however, devised a third alternative. After writing an opinion that attacked the administration for neglecting constitutional duties, the Court ruled that it could not issue the writ. According to Marshall, Madison clearly breached his sworn duties, but the Court could not constitutionally issue the writ of mandamus. The Court was powerless in this instance, Marshall argued, because the provision of the Judiciary Act of 1789 that granted original jurisdiction to issue such writs was unconstitutional. Article III of the Constitution specifies the circumstances under which the Court possesses original jurisdiction, but the issuance of writs of mandamus is not included. Therefore, argued Marshall, the Judiciary Act of 1789, by adding such writs to the Court's original jurisdiction, was actually attempting to alter the Constitution by simple statute rather than the prescribed method of amendment. Since Congress may not do this, Marshall concluded that the act was null and void and the Court was without power to grant Marbury a writ of mandamus.

As a political document, Marshall's decision was a masterpiece. By arguing that Madison was obligated to deliver the commission, Marshall attacked the Jefferson administration. Yet by refusing to issue the writ, he avoided a confrontation with the president, which the Court was sure to lose. More important, Marshall created for the Court the power of judicial review and insulated that power from attack. The only loser in the case was Marbury, who was sacrificed to Marshall's larger political design.

The political brilliance of Marshall's opinion is unquestionable, but the legal reasoning employed remains to this day subject to debate. In a straightforward manner, Marshall simply stated that (1) the Constitution is superior to any statute; (2) the Judiciary Act of 1789 contradicted the Constitution; and (3) therefore the Judiciary Act of 1789 must be unconstitutional. As an exercise in logic, the conclusion seems inescapable.

To many critics, however, Marshall's logic misses the point. Why is it the job of the Court, composed as it is of life-tenured appointees, to decide whether an act conflicts with the Constitution? Why, ask Marshall's critics, should this power not belong to elected officials?[20]

Although judicial review has become an element of American politics, its use remains controversial. Those judges and legal scholars who find Marshall's reasoning unconvincing advocate **judicial restraint**—the limited and infrequent use of judicial review. Practitioners of judicial restraint argue that the frequent use of judicial review substitutes the judgment of unelected, life-tenured officials for that of elected representatives and is therefore undemocratic. Indeed, the frequent use of judicial review, according to some critics, creates an "imperial judiciary," which makes decisions best left to the elected branches of a democratic government.[21] Opposing judicial restraint are those judges and legal scholars who believe in **judicial activism:** that the Court has a right, and even an obligation, to exercise judicial review. In our day activism is usually justified by liberals in the defense of political minorities, but the frequent use of judicial review and the numerous precedents overturned by the Rehnquist Court demonstrate that conservatives may also be activists.

A more recent judicial argument concerns how the Constitution is to be interpreted. One perspective on constitutional interpretation demands that justices adhere to a literal reading of the Constitution or, if the language is not specific, the intent of the provisions' authors. During the 1980s this view, known as original intent, was forcefully advocated by President Reagan's attorney general, Edwin Meese. Meese repeatedly argued that the justices should restrict themselves to the Constitution's original intent and not its spirit. Original intent assumes that judges do not make law, but rather find it ready-made by others—those who authored the Constitution.

Opponents of that view—a loose collection of scholars and judges, conservatives, and liberals—contend that many of the Constitution's most important provisions are "deliberate models of ambiguity."[22] Although these opponents often disagree among themselves as to the preferred interpretation of constitutional provisions, they are united in their belief that judging involves choosing among competing values and not simply finding the law.[23]

The Implementation of Court Decisions

The pomp and circumstance surrounding the announcement of a Supreme Court decision lends credibility to the myth of finality. Yet this ceremony seldom settles the matter. Rather than being the final decision, the Court's announcement is only the beginning of a long process of implementation.

Court orders are not self-executing, and the Court needs the cooperation of others to carry out the announced policy. It cannot force compliance: it cannot call on an army or police force to carry out its orders; nor can it levy taxes to fund their implementation. Even if a previous decision is not being implemented, the Court cannot act until someone brings suit in a lower court. Unlike the other agencies of government, courts must await cases; they cannot seek them out. Their only recourse is to signal their willingness to consider cases involving particular issues by the language that they use in deciding cases before them.

Compliance by Other Courts

Compliance is not just a matter of getting the parties in the cases to go along with the decision. When the Supreme Court overturns the decision of a lower court, it generally sends (remands) the case back to the lower courts for a decision "not inconsistent" with its opinion. But lower courts do not always follow the Supreme Court's wishes.

For instance, lower courts may find it difficult to carry out an ambiguous Supreme Court decision. If multiple concurring and dissenting opinions accompany a decision, the lower court may find it difficult to interpret. In *Furman* v. *Georgia* (1972), for example, five justices ruled that the death penalty was unconstitutional as applied in that particular case, but they could not agree on the reason.[24] Consequently, each justice wrote a separate opinion. Lower courts cannot interpret such a decision easily, and in such situations lower-court judges find it easier to substitute their own values and beliefs.

Because lower federal and state courts are independent of the High Court, they can—and occasionally do—defy the Court's rulings. There is little that the Court can do in such cases. The judges of these lower courts are sworn to uphold the U.S. Constitution but not the opinions of the Supreme Court, and the Court lacks the power to fire even the most disobedient judge. Thus the Supreme Court's power to reverse lower-court decisions is limited both by its inability to police lower courts and by time constraints (it cannot review every lower-court decision).

Of course, reversal by a higher court is sometimes welcomed. Judges who are caught between the mandates of the Supreme Court, located in far-off Washington, and the strong contradictory desires of their neighbors may find the displeasure of the High Court easier to bear than the anger of the community. Elected state judges may be especially reluctant to enforce Court orders that risk voter ire, even if they personally agree with the High Court. In the 1950s federal district court judges were deeply embroiled in the school desegregation issue— a conflict of national versus local values. Many communities resisted, often vehemently, Court-ordered desegregation. Those district judges who enforced the *Brown* v. *Board of Education* (1954) decision found themselves cut off from their own communities, as old friends and colleagues fell away. Many were threatened and even physically harmed.[25]

13.1 O.J., Matlock, and Criminal Justice

Throughout the spring of 1995 millions of Americans eagerly watched their televisions as the drama of the O. J. Simpson trial unfolded. From the police chase involving Simpson's white Ford Bronco, to the pretrial hearing and finally to the trial itself, television provided live coverage. Like a sporting event, the coverage was generously supplemented with commentary from famous criminal lawyers, who analyzed and critiqued every move of the contending attorneys.

Although some thought that the trial's publicity played to a morbid curiosity of Americans, most media pundits hailed the reporting as a great civics lesson. The recounting of each phase of the trial was supposedly teaching us about the workings of criminal trials and the constitutional safeguards that accompany them. Americans could, we were assured, learn how real trials differed from the courtroom dramas that have long been a staple of television.

Obviously, the Simpson trial was different from television drama. This was neither Matlock nor Perry Mason. The trial was not wrapped up in an hour, and no witness conveniently broke down on the stand and confessed to the crime. What television gave us in the Simpson trial was a far cry from the way Hollywood usually scripts a trial, but it was also a far cry from the normal criminal trial. Indeed, most criminal defendants do not even go to trial; instead, in more than 90 percent of the cases, they plead guilty. Often the defendants participate in a criminal-justice system labeled by its critics as "slaughterhouse justice." As one public defender described disposing of seventeen cases, "I met 'em, pled 'em, and closed 'em—all in the same day."

But even when a trial does take place, it seldom resembles the Simpson trial because few criminal defendants have the resources to hire a phalanx of highly skilled attorneys and investigators. Many defendants in most communities are indigent and thus unable to afford even basic representation. These defendants must depend on court-appointed counsel. Although these lawyers may be highly skilled, they seldom have the investigative resources available to the state or a wealthy defendant. In New Orleans, for instance, the public defenders' office has three investigators to handle more than seven thousand cases a year.

Moreover, the quality of appointed counsel varies tremendously. Most courts provide legal services to indigents by appointing private counsel to serve the defendant—generally only the largest communities have a public defender service. Because fees paid to court-appointed counsel are commonly less than they receive for other services, experienced lawyers are reluctant to accept such assignments. Thus court-appointed counsel are often inexperienced lawyers who lack an interest in criminal law but need even the small fees that the court pays. In Philadelphia, for instance, one study found that the appointed counsel were so bad that "even officials in charge of the system say they wouldn't want to be represented in traffic court by some of the people appointed to defend poor people accused of murder." Even more illustrative may be the woman in Alabama who, while standing trial for murdering her abusive husband, had the trial delayed by a day when the judge found her appointed counsel in contempt for showing up drunk. The following day the attorney and his client were both led into the courtroom—from jail. The trial proceeded, and the defendant was found guilty and sentenced to death. Never did the court-appointed lawyer produce hospital records documenting the injuries suffered by the woman and her children.

In many ways it may well be that by covering the Simpson trial television has substituted one mythic view of criminal justice for another. The Simpson trial was real, but not representative.

Source: Quotes from Stephen B. Bright, "Counsel for the Poor: The Death Sentence Not for the Worst Crime but for the Worst Lawyer," 103, *The Yale Law Review* (1994), 1835–1883.

Congress and the President

Just as the Supreme Court must depend on the so-called inferior courts to implement decisions, so too must it rely on the cooperation of Congress and the president. Both institutions have the power to aid or hinder the implementation of Supreme Court decisions.

The most important power that Congress has is its control of public funds. By providing or withholding the funds necessary to carry out Court policy, Congress can significantly affect implementation, as the history of school desegregation amply illustrates. During Lyndon Johnson's administration, Congress authorized the U.S. Department of Health, Education, and Welfare to withhold federal funds from school systems that refused to desegregate—providing a strong incentive for the local communities to comply with the Supreme Court's 1954 ruling. In 1975, however, Congress, disturbed by court-ordered busing, diminished the incentive by prohibiting the withholding of funds from school districts refusing to implement busing.

The actions of individual members of Congress may also advance or impede Court policy. Whether important political leaders defend or attack a Court decision may have much to do with the willingness of others to accept the judgment. Clearly, the cause of school desegregation was not helped when, in 1956, ninety-six members of Congress signed the Southern Manifesto, a document attacking the *Brown* decision. Those who believed that the Supreme Court was wrong could always point to distinguished members of Congress as sharing their view. Furthermore, the support of so many in Congress undoubtedly gave hope that the decision would someday be overturned.

Congress may also use its powers to directly counteract Court decisions. Court decisions interpreting the Constitution may, for example, be overturned by a congressionally initiated constitutional amendment. Although the process is cumbersome and difficult, it has been used on five occasions. Most recently, the Twenty-sixth Amendment, in lowering the voting age to eighteen, overturned the decision in *Oregon* v. *Mitchell* (1970).[26] (In the *Mitchell* decision, the Court ruled that Congress could by statute lower the voting age to eighteen in national, but not state, elections.) The Court's decision prohibiting prayer in public schools has generated hundreds of proposals for constitutional amendments. To date none of these proposals has passed both houses of Congress.

Occasionally, Congress tries to pressure the Court into reversing its decisions. In 1964, for instance, angered by a series of Warren Court rulings that required reapportionment of state legislatures solely on the basis of population, Congress gave the justices a smaller pay raise than other top-level officials. To underscore the point, Republican Representative Robert Dole from Kansas proposed that the pay increase be contingent on reversal of the decision.[27]

The president and the executive branch can also vitally affect the fate of Supreme Court decisions. On the average, a president appoints a new justice every twenty-two months. Thus a two-term president has the potential to reshape the Court, which can then negate a troublesome policy. Certainly, Richard Nixon intended to do just that when, in 1968, he campaigned for the presidency on the promise to appoint justices who would be tough on criminal defendants. Much of Nixon's 1968 presidential campaign was an attack on the liberal Warren Court. His four appointments to the Supreme Court, including a new chief justice (Warren Burger), managed to stem much of the liberal trend set by the Warren Court and reverse some previous liberal decisions.

Similarly, Reagan attempted to alter several Court decisions through careful selection of nominees. Reagan's appointments of associate justices Sandra Day O'Connor, Antonin Scalia, and Anthony Kennedy, as well as his elevation of William H. Rehnquist to the post of chief justice, were designed to create a Supreme Court ideologically compatible with the administration. Bush's appointment of Clarence Thomas to replace Thurgood Marshall was seen by observers as a continuance of the Reagan administration's strategy.

As the most visible public official, the president may influence public opinion by his willingness to accept a decision. His silence, on the other hand, may encourage disobedience or delay implementation. President Eisenhower's initial refusal to endorse the *Brown* decision gave support to those who opposed the Court. Although in 1957 Eisenhower dispatched troops to enforce court-ordered desegregation of the schools in Little Rock, Arkansas, many commentators have argued that his initial reluctance to support the decision encouraged avoidance of Court orders. Indeed, a Supreme Court justice of that period, Tom C. Clark, observed that "if Mr. Eisenhower had come through, it would have changed things a lot."[28]

As the head of the executive branch, the president may also order the U.S. Department of Justice to prosecute noncompliance vigorously or to make only a token effort. President Johnson's vigorous use of the department to prosecute segregated school districts was very important in implementing *Brown*. President Nixon, on the other hand, slowed the process of desegregation by curtailing the department's prosecutorial activities.

CLOSER
TO HOME

13.1   Selecting State Court Judges

Although all major courts in the federal system are staffed by judges appointed by the president, with the advice and consent of the Senate, the fifty states use a variety of selection systems. Indeed, many states have established different selection methods for different levels of courts. Nevertheless, five methods dominate.

• *Gubernatorial Appointment.* This holdover from the colonial experience allows the governor to make the appointment, but in virtually all instances such appointment must gain legislative confirmation—usually by the state senate. Confined largely to northeastern states, this system attempts to ensure a judiciary independent of popular sentiment or political pressure.

• *Legislative Election.* Three states—Rhode Island, South Carolina, and Virginia—authorize the legislature to elect judges. In Rhode Island, only the Supreme Court justices are elected by the legislature; all other judges are appointed by the governor with the consent of the senate. Like the gubernatorial system, legislative election stresses a politically independent judiciary.

• *Partisan Election.* In this system judicial candidates run on a partisan ballot, after winning nomination, usually by way of a partisan primary. A product of the Jacksonian era's emphasis on democratic accountability, partisan elections are intended to ensure that judges are not insulated from popular opinion. Partisan election systems are most commonly found in southern and lower midwestern states—states that entered the union during the Jacksonian era.

• *Nonpartisan Elections.* When states use this system, candidates' names appear on the ballot without party labels attached. This method of selection aims to create a judiciary responsive to the people. A product of the Populist and Progressive movements' reaction to partisan abuses of power, the nonpartisan election system is found most often in the upper midwestern and western states.

• *Merit Selection.* Also known as the Missouri Plan, for the state that first adopted it, merit selection attempts to blend independence and accountability. There are several nuances, but in general the following procedure applies: a nominating commission composed of three lawyers selected by a state bar association, three nonlawyers selected by the governor, and an incumbent judge submit a short list of candidates (usually three) to the governor. The governor makes the appointment from the list. After a brief term of service, the new judge faces the electorate in a retention election. There is no opponent; the electorate simply chooses whether or not to retain the judge. If the electorate prefers not to retain the judge, the process starts over again. Since 1940, when Missouri adopted the system, most states that have altered their selection system have adopted some version of merit selection.

Does it matter which system a state adopts? Most political scientists who have looked at judicial recruitment have found no substantial differences in the personal characteristics of judges that can be attributed to the selection method. Merit systems tend to produce slightly higher proportions of Protestant judges than other selection systems, and women and minorities are somewhat favored by gubernatorial systems. Even the length of service varies little. Judges in partisan election states have slightly shorter careers than those in states using gubernatorial selection, but again the differences are small.

Sources: Lawrence Baum, *American Courts: Process and Policy,* 2nd ed. (Boston, Mass.: Houghton Mifflin, 1990); Henry R. Glick and Craig F. Emmert, "Selection Systems and Judicial Characteristics: the Recruitment of State Supreme Court Justices," *Judicature,* 70 (December–January, 1987), 228–235; and Robert L. Dudley, "Turnover and Tenure on State High Courts: Does Method of Selection Make a Difference?" *The Justice System Journal,* 19 (1, 1997), 1–16.

For more information on your state's court, see the **Gitelson/Dudley/Dubnick web site.**

Conclusion: The Courts Are Not What They Seem

This brief discussion of the American legal system demonstrates that, no matter how much we may wish it to be otherwise, the courts are political institutions. As soothing as it may be, the myth of the nonpolitical courts simply does not reflect the American legal process. Although the conflict that produced the basic structure of the federal courts occurred long ago, the potential for political discord still exists, and we should not be blind to this fact. Nor can we ignore the link between partisan politics and the courts inherent in the system of judicial selection. Because judicial positions go to those who demonstrate faithful service to the party, courts are staffed by individuals of considerable political experience.

The myth of finality likewise fails to capture the reality of American courts. The implementation of court decisions requires the participation and cooperation of many in the political system. A simple pronouncement from a court does not suffice.

Summary

1. Civil actions cover conflict between private individuals or organizations; criminal law concerns wrongs done to the public.

2. The United States has fifty-two court systems, one for the national government, one for each state, and a separate system for the Commonwealth of Puerto Rico.

3. The ninety-four U.S. district courts are the trial courts for the federal system. Approximately two hundred thousand cases a year are heard by the district courts, and fewer than 10 percent of their decisions are appealed.

4. The twelve U.S. courts of appeals handle most of the appellate work in the federal system. Organized into state groupings known as circuits, the courts of appeals hear all appeals from the federal district courts and some independent regulatory agencies and departments.

5. Cases are appealed to the Supreme Court primarily either by an appeal or by a writ of certiorari. The Court has great latitude in deciding which cases it wants to hear.

6. The Constitution requires that federal judges be nominated by the president and appointed with the advice and consent of the Senate. Appointment procedures vary considerably, however, depending on the level of the court involved. The nomination of district court judges often originates with the senator or senators of the president's party from the nominee's state. These senators may exercise senatorial courtesy. Because courts of appeals are organized into circuits that cross state boundaries, no senator is entitled to exercise senatorial courtesy over these appointments.

7. Because federal judges are appointed for life, occasionally the need arises to remove an ill or incompetent judge. Because the Constitution provides for removal only by impeachment, Congress has created the position of senior judge as a means of encouraging judges to retire.

8. The public phase of the Supreme Court's business consists of oral arguments presented before the justices. These are very formalized procedures conducted under tight time constraints.

9. The most important part of the Court's work takes place in its conferences, which are closed to all but the justices themselves. In these conferences, the justices discuss and vote on the cases.

10. Once a vote has been taken on a case, the chief justice, if he is in the majority, or the senior justice in the majority assigns the writing of the opinion. The justice assigned to write the opinion must then circulate drafts of the decision to the other justices. No opinion is final until at least a majority of the Court agrees on it.

11. Justices who disagree with the majority opinion are free to write dissenting opinions explaining why they cannot accept the majority decision. Justices who agree with the majority opinion but not its reasoning may write concurring opinions.

12. Judges are often involved in interpreting the Constitution, though controversy exists over how aggressively the courts should pursue such judicial review.

13. Lower courts do not necessarily comply with Supreme Court decisions. Often they find the decisions sufficiently ambiguous to make compliance extremely difficult. When Supreme Court decisions conflict with locally held values, lower-court judges may be reluctant to displease their communities by enforcing the High Court's rulings.

14. Congress also possesses a great deal of power because the implementation of Supreme Court decisions often requires the appropriation of public funds, a function controlled by Congress. Congress can also propose constitutional amendments to overturn Supreme Court decisions.

15. The successful implementation of Supreme Court decisions also requires the cooperation of the president, or at least his acceptance of the policy. A president's willingness to accept a particular Court opinion will serve to influence public opinion. More important, a president may seek to reshape the Court through the appointment process.

Key Terms and Concepts

Civil actions Cover conflicts between private persons and/or organizations and typically include disputes over contracts, claims for damages, and divorce cases.

Criminal law Covers offenses against the public order and provides for a specified punishment. Most criminal law cases arise in state courts.

Trial courts Courts at the lowest level of the system. They possess *original jurisdiction*.

Original jurisdiction The authority to hear a case before any other court does.

Appellate courts Courts that reconsider the decisions rendered by trial courts, at the request of the losing party seeking to appeal.

Circuit courts The federal courts of appeals that rank above the district courts and serve as the major appellate courts for the federal system. They review all cases, both civil and criminal, and the decisions of independent regulatory agencies and departments.

Writ of certiorari A request that the Supreme Court order the lower court to send up the record of a case.

Appeal A route for cases to reach the Supreme Court. By that route, litigants have some right under the law to have their cases reviewed.

Limited jurisdiction The power of certain trial courts that are allowed to hear only a narrowly defined class of cases.

General jurisdiction The power of trial courts to hear cases from a broad class of issues, ordinarily including all civil cases involving nontrivial monetary value and all cases involving serious criminal matters.

Briefs Documents submitted to the court by attorneys that contain a summary of the issues, the laws applying to the case, and arguments supporting counsel's position.

Amicus curiae Written briefs submitted to the Supreme Court by third-party individuals or organizations that want their opinions to be considered in a case. The term is Latin for "friend of the court."

Concurring opinions Opinions written by Supreme Court justices that agree with the conclusion but not with the reasoning of the majority opinion.

Dissenting opinions Legal opinions written by Supreme Court justices that disagree with the majority conclusion.

Judicial review The power of the courts to declare an act of a legislature constitutional or unconstitutional.

Judicial restraint Limited and infrequent use of judicial review—advocated on the grounds that unelected judges should not overrule the laws of the elected representatives.

Judicial activism The concept that the Court has a right and obligation to practice judicial review, especially in defense of political minorities.

Domestic Policy and Policymaking

MYTH & REALITY

Does the national government do too much or too little to solve America's economic and social problems?

See **Political Science** at
http://www.hmco.com/college

In 1995 you didn't need the *Farmer's Almanac* to know that American agriculture was in for several months of stormy political weather. Anyone familiar with U.S. farm policy saw indications of the emerging tempest in the election results of November 1994. The voters created a high-pressure system for policy change by giving the Republican party control of both chambers of the U.S. Congress for the first time in forty years. Just as significant was a low-pressure system that had been building among groups with a special interest in U.S. farm policy. These groups had been engaging in an ongoing debate for at least a decade over the future of government support of agriculture.

The federal government has had policies on agriculture since at least the Civil War, but from the 1930s through the mid-1980s programs were developed that would become the primary determinants of the success or failure of America's agricultural economy. Although the details of the programs would change occasionally, there were essentially three types:[1]

Farm loan programs provided eligible farmers with funds for planting and harvesting for the coming year, with the projected value of production or yield being used as collateral. If all went well, the farmer would repay the low-cost loan and arrange for the next year's loan. However, if the annual yield or farm prices fell below projected levels, the farmer could turn over his or her crop to the government and consider the loan paid.

Deficiency payment programs complemented loan programs by having the government establish a "target price" for different farm commodities, such as wheat, feed grains, or cotton. Farmers participating in the program would have to meet certain conditions, such as promising to limit their production of the designated crop. If the actual market price for their crops was below the targeted price at harvest time, they would receive the difference in "deficiency payments" made by the U.S. government. If the market price exceeded the target price, participating farmers would reap the benefits.

Marketing order programs involved having the producers of a certain commodity in a given region of the country (e.g., dairy farmers in Wisconsin) enter into a government-supervised agreement to limit their production levels in order to guarantee higher prices—and therefore, higher average incomes—for all.

From the beginning these programs were surrounded by controversy. Within the farm community, debates raged among producers of different commodities over the amount of support each was receiving. Even within specific commodity-producing communities controversy existed over how the programs favored the wealthiest producers and led to the demise of many smaller farm operations. Outside the agricultural community, purchasers of farm products—from giant corporations like Coca-Cola and General Foods to consumer advocates—were increasingly fighting for changes in programs that kept commodity and food prices artificially high.

Nineteen eighty-one was a watershed year in the debate over farm programs.[2] The Reagan administration offered a farm bill that would significantly reduce federal funding of the major farm programs. After some acrimonious debate, Congress passed a bill that did just the opposite—increased financial support through program modifications that favored participating farmers. The disastrous results became evident by 1985 as a major recession hit the agricultural economy. Exports declined, inflationary commodity prices offset the intended impact of various programs, and the value of American farmland dropped significantly. Congress reviewed their farm policies that year and promised to make major corrective changes. The 1985 bill greatly reduced price supports through loan programs, thus forcing many farmers to sell their yields in the marketplace rather than to the government. At the same time, more money was shifted to deficiency payment programs as a means of offsetting the shift in policy. Further changes made in a 1990 farm bill were intended to decrease spending through more reductions in loans and in deficiency payments.

Two problems emerged despite these efforts to cut back. First, market conditions were uncooperative, and as a result annual program costs have increased rather than declined. Although expecting to pay farmers only $7.1 billion in 1991, the government actually spent $10.1 billion. In 1992 program costs exceeded expected costs by $1.2 billion, and in 1993 the United States expended $7.3 billion more than it had projected. To make the situation worse, the structure of the programs reduced the level of U.S. farm product exports at a time when America's role in the world economy was becoming a major concern (see Chapter 15, on foreign and defense policies).

By 1994 it was evident to all that something had to be done to deal with the problems generated by the government's farm policies. With the farm bill coming up for reauthorization in Congress in 1995, two positions emerged even before the November 1994 elections. One side advocated further reducing price supports while maintaining a significant government role in the agricultural sector. Because they focused primarily on cost reductions, they became known in Washington as the "fiscalists." The other side believed it was time to make fundamental reforms in U.S. farm policy. "We think it is time for bold reform," stated one influential interest group lobbyist. From that perspective, it is necessary for government to do less and not merely spend less, and for farmers to rely more on the marketplace. Given the sweeping changes they proposed, this group was dubbed the "radicals."

When the new 104th Congress gathered in Washington in January 1995, it had to confront the farm bill, which would also mean confronting two myths that have become increasingly prevalent in American politics. Those who support continued involvement of the government in agricultural policy are likely to believe in the *myth of too little government*. According to this myth, government has an obligation to meet the needs of the American public in general, and certain "needy" groups in particular. Those believing in that myth might differ about what the public needs (e.g., economic stability, security) or which groups should be defined as "needy" (e.g., the poor and homeless, the family farmer), but they are likely to agree that government must do more—not less—to fulfill its obligations. Belief in this myth leads to calls for government to do as much as possible to meet its obligations—or, during hard economic times, to at least maintain its commitments in various policy areas. This was the position represented by the agricultural policy fiscalists.

In contrast stand those who believe in the *myth of too much government,* which says that big government has become the major threat to the well-being and future of American society. If government has any obligations, it is to stay out of such areas as agriculture and let market forces do their work. Belief in this myth in part reflects fears that government will interfere in our personal lives and the choices we can make.

As with other myths, these two are based on many stories that Americans hear about what can happen when government does too little or too much. Stories surrounding the Great Depression tell of how the American economy worsened because President Herbert Hoover did nothing to rescue the U.S. economic system after the great stock market crash of 1929. The myth of too little government is enhanced by stories of how the active intervention of government under Franklin D. Roosevelt helped alleviate the most insufferable consequences of the Depression.[3] In contrast, critics of America's welfare policies during the 1960s frequently tell stories of how these programs failed and left a legacy of social deprivation among the poor. The critics support their view of too much government by pointing to stories of success among those who avoided or escaped the welfare system, or by citing a link between those programs and high crime rates or civil disorders.[4] As with other stories and the myths they generate, people can find facts to support each example.

For the American public, deciding whether the government is doing too much or too little often depends on the specific issue or program being discussed. In May 1992 pollsters asked Americans whether the government was spending too much, too little, or the right amount on "assistance to the poor." Sixty-four percent responded "too little," while only 13 percent said "too much" and 16 percent said "the right amount." As Figure 14.1 shows, the responses were quite different when the word "welfare" was substituted for assistance to the poor. Only 23 percent said "too little" was being spent while 27 and 44 percent, respectively, said "the right amount" and "too much." Similarly, while 62 percent of those surveyed in 1993 believed that it was government's responsibility to "take care of people who can't take care of themselves," a full 80 percent agreed with the contention that "poor people have become too dependent on government assistance."[5]

Is the government doing too much? Is the government doing too little? Those questions, rooted in the two widely held myths, are central to much of the ongoing debate among politicians and policymakers. As we can see in the following discussion of economic and social welfare policies, the questions have no definitive answers. Nevertheless, the myths are important for the dynamic role they play in shaping public perceptions and giving force and direction to the deliberations of public policymakers.

FIGURE 14.1

The Answer Depends
on the Question

Americans believe we
spend too much on
"welfare," but too little
on "assistance to the
poor." This interesting
contrast says a great
deal about the myths
of too much/too little
government.

Source: Copyright © 1992
by the New York Times
Company. Reprinted by
permission.

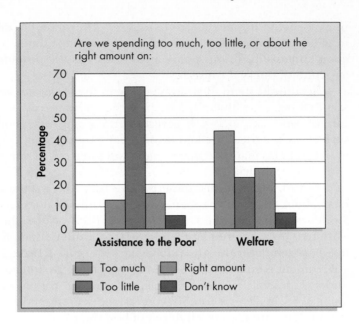

Making Public Policy

Public policies are actions taken by government officials in response to problems
and issues raised through the political system. At the national level, public policies can emerge from each of the major institutions of government. Congress
makes policy by enacting laws, such as the 1964 Civil Rights Act (see Chapter 4,
on rights and liberties). Presidents can issue executive orders (see Chapter 11,
on the presidency), as President John F. Kennedy did in 1961 to create the Peace
Corps. As discussed in Chapter 13, on the judiciary, judges also make policy
through court decisions and orders, such as the famous *Brown* v. *Board of Education* (1954) case, which led to the desegregation of southern schools. Even
bureaucracies are involved in public policymaking through developing and publishing rules and regulations. None of these institutional actions, however, occurs in a vacuum. Each is the product of formal and informal interactions
among hundreds of participants inside and outside government.[6]

Stages in the Policymaking Process

Public policymaking can be pictured as a six-stage process (see Figure 14.2). In
the first stage, **issue identification,** some event, person, or group calls attention

FIGURE 14.2

The Six Stages of
Policymaking

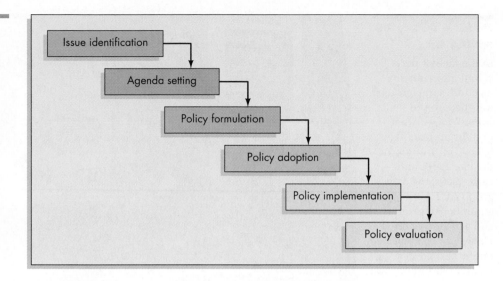

to a problem that needs government action. During the early 1980s, for example, the increasing number of deaths attributed to acquired immune deficiency syndrome (AIDS) brought demands for money to fund research into the cause of the deadly disease. Health care professionals, the surgeon general of the United States, and groups representing homosexual men (who were at high risk for the disease) used every opportunity they could to get the attention of policymakers at all levels of American government.[7]

In a second stage, **agenda setting,** the issue or problem is seriously considered by the policymaking institution. Not all the problems identified in the first stage of the process get this far. In mid-November 1953, for instance, a thick cloud of dirty air settled on New York City, causing headaches, itchy eyes, nausea, and other physical ailments. The incident lasted long enough to draw the media's attention, for the clouded atmosphere interfered with football games, astronomical observations, and other outdoor activities. No action followed, however, since the immediate impact of the air pollution was not regarded as serious. Nine years later a review of public health records showed that the incident was linked to approximately two hundred deaths in the New York area.[8] By the early 1960s environmental pollution was on the agenda of national policymakers, and problems similar to New York City's "cloud"—for example, the smog that hangs over Los Angeles and other major cities—began to get serious attention.

The fact that an issue on the government's agenda gets serious attention does not necessarily mean that a policy will emerge immediately. Someone must develop a proposal or program that can address the issue. This third stage of the policymaking process, **policy formulation,** may take years to complete as policymakers and their staffs deliberate the pros and cons of each issue.

Making Policy by Acting Up

In the face of perceived government inaction, some groups will "take to the streets" to get attention for an issue they believe in strongly. In the late 1980s and early 1990s, the activist group ACT UP staged a number of protests and acts of civil disobedience to focus public and government attention on the emerging AIDS epidemic.

Many policy responses are formulated within government agencies, in Congress, and by groups outside the national government, working separately and together. Both the White House and Congress looked to the federal Centers for Disease Control and Prevention for policy proposals to deal with AIDS. A major reform of the U.S. welfare system, the 1988 Family Support Act, was formulated by a group of governors working with the staff of the National Governors' Association.[9] In 1993, a White House task force involving dozens of government officials took nine months to come up with a comprehensive health care proposal. As the health care debate unfolded over the next year, a variety of alternative proposals emerged. By the summer of 1994, anyone attempting to follow the debate needed a guidebook to help sort out all the different proposals that had been formulated to deal with America's health care crisis.[10]

The next step, **policy adoption,** includes efforts to obtain enough support so that a proposal can become the government's stated policy. At this point, most policy proposals—particularly congressional legislation—go through a process of bargaining and compromise and emerge significantly changed. When Congress considers tax reform proposals, what may begin as an attempt to close large tax loopholes may wind up creating more or different loopholes.[11] When members of Congress propose amendments to bills, they can radically change the intent of a bill or give it added meaning. In 1987, a bill funding highway projects included an amendment authorizing states to raise the maximum speed limit on interstate highways to 65 miles per hour in rural areas. In 1988, a bill intended to create a new cabinet post—the Department of Veterans Affairs—became the vehicle for passing a law giving veterans the right to sue their government.[12]

Policy adoption is no less complex in the executive branch. Executive orders, vetoes of legislation, and other presidential actions are not made arbitrarily, for the White House cannot operate in a political vacuum. After President Kennedy used an executive order to set up the Peace Corps in 1961, he did not go to Congress for funding but paid for its operation for nearly six months through a special discretionary account. During that period administration officials worked to build congressional support for the program. Although Kennedy was eventually successful, some members of Congress questioned his use of executive powers to establish and operate a brand-new program without congressional authority.

Decisions of the Supreme Court are special types of public policies, for they are often rooted in legal doctrines. Nevertheless, even policy adoption in the Supreme Court involves some political give-and-take among its members, which has an impact on the resulting policies (see Chapter 13). In recent years we have learned a great deal more about what takes place when the justices of the Supreme Court decide an important case. Conferences involving all the Court's members are held regularly, and supposedly the discussions in those closed meetings sometimes focus on the political, as well as the legal, implications of a case.[13]

The policy-adoption stage can last quite a long time. National air pollution laws were first passed in 1960, and they did little more than authorize the surgeon general to study the problem. Three years later Congress set up a technical committee to monitor air pollution problems and to provide assistance to state and local governments that chose to develop and maintain antipollution programs. In 1965 and 1967 Congress required states and localities to develop air pollution programs and required federal agencies to set emission standards for new automobiles. In 1970 President Richard M. Nixon created the Environmental Protection Agency (EPA), acknowledging the importance of environmental problems. A few weeks later Congress gave the EPA significant powers to clean America's air. Additional amendments followed during the 1970s and 1980s, and policy adoption in this area continued with passage of Clean Air Act amendments in 1990 and 1995.

Critical to the policymaking process is the stage of **policy implementation**—the carrying out of policy mandates through public programs and actions. Usually, the national bureaucracy performs this task (see Chapter 12, on the bureaucracy), although many policies involve the cooperation of state and local officials and individuals outside government. For example, Congress passed an income tax law and created the Internal Revenue Service (IRS) to implement it, but the government still relies on the American people to do most of the paperwork. Washington also depends on state and local officials to enforce a variety of environmental laws. As noted in Chapter 3, on federalism and intergovernmental relations, most domestic policies require the cooperation of private individuals or the intergovernmental relations system.

The final stage in public policymaking often involves **policy evaluation**—looking at government actions and programs to see whether goals have been achieved or to assess a policy's effectiveness and efficiency. Changes in the policy may then be instituted quickly, slowly, or not at all. A major plane crash caused by poorly maintained equipment is likely to result in new directives being issued immediately by the Federal Aviation Administration. A report indicating that public schools are not giving students an education appropriate for the changing world economy will not result in quick changes, but it might generate plans for major long-term changes in high school curriculum and instruction. Another report indicating that interstate highway speeds in excess of 40 miles per hour result in thousands of additional deaths each year is unlikely to result in policy changes in most states because of popular pressure to keep or even raise current speed limits.

Models of Decision Making

As outlined above, the stages of the policymaking process seem both sequential and logical. What actually takes place however, is rarely so neat. During each stage, policymakers must reach many decisions about how the issue will be handled or how an adopted policy will be implemented or evaluated. Ideally, a policymaker should carefully analyze the issues being addressed, consider all alternative actions that can be taken to address those issues, accurately evaluate those alternatives, and finally select one as the government's policy. This ideal process is called the **rational model of decision making.** It assumes that the policymaker has a clear objective and all the information needed for a sound and reasoned decision, resulting in the selection of the policy alternative that offers the most efficient and effective way to achieve the desired goal.

Few of the conditions required for rationality exist in the real world of public policy. Policymakers rarely have enough information to analyze alternatives. And no matter how much they know, there is always some doubt about the future. This uncertainty affects not only members of Congress and people on the White House staff, but also the advisers in the scientific community and elsewhere.

Furthermore, large groups of decision makers usually have trouble reaching a consensus on goals. There are some exceptions, of course. In May 1961 President Kennedy had broad political support when he declared that the aim of U.S. space policy was to land an American on the moon by the end of the decade.[14] With such a clear and widely accepted goal, decision making in the National Aeronautics and Space Administration (NASA) seemed close to the rational model. But the NASA programs of the 1960s were unique. In most cases, the objectives of public policies are too vague and controversial, making the rational model inappropriate.

Is there a model that explains how policymakers really make their decisions? One possibility is the **incremental model of decision making.** According to this model, public policy is a process by which, little by little, decisions add to or subtract from the policies that already exist. Each year, for example, the national government reconsiders the amount of money it will spend on highways and education. Rarely, however, do the White House and Congress start their annual deliberations with a clean slate. Instead, in most cases executive officials and members of Congress begin by assuming that most current highway and education programs will remain intact; usually, the major issues are whether to expand or reduce spending for these programs and, if so, by how much. Sometimes this leads to marginal changes in the policies as well. For instance, each time a major program such as social security comes up for reauthorization before Congress, amendments are added to meet the new or special needs of recipients that have emerged since the law was last revised. Thus public policies and programs develop and change from year to year through marginal adjustments.

Other models of decision making trace public policies back to certain groups or classes of people. The **elite model of decision making** holds that public policies are made by a relatively small group of influential leaders who share common goals and points of view. President Dwight D. Eisenhower may have had this model in mind when, in his 1961 farewell address to the nation, he warned against the emerging influence of the "military-industrial complex," in which high-level military and industry leaders make decisions that have widespread effects throughout the rest of the country and the world.

In contrast, the **pluralist model of decision making** attributes policy outcomes to pressures exerted by different interest groups. Specific policies reflect the relative influence these interests possess at given points in the decision-making process (see Chapter 8, on interest groups). Thus, although environmentalists might have the upper hand in Congress, advocates of deregulation might be more influential in the White House or at the EPA. This model assumes that public policies are the product of bargains and compromises among the various interests and policymakers.

The models may differ, but on one issue all observers agree: public policies result from a dynamic process involving a variety of participants and a wide range of factors. One constant feature of the process is the debate between those who believe strongly in the myth of too much government and those who have adopted the myth of too little government. That debate has an impact on almost all domestic policies, especially in two major areas of concern: economic and social welfare policies.

Economic Policy

What should government's role be in managing the economy? Those who think government interferes too much in economic matters view most public policies as needlessly restricting the operations of the marketplace and damaging the nation's economic health. Those who fault government for doing too little believe it should be more active in guiding the American economy. They argue that because the private marketplace cannot meet the basic needs of many citizens, the government must step in and correct its imperfections.

Behind this debate is the fact that the national government has been engaged in economic policymaking for most of its history. Government intervention in the marketplace can be traced to colonial times.[15] Colonial governments offered payments (called bounties) to businesses making large investments in the manufacture of certain products or promoting increases in the exportation of locally produced goods. In 1640, for example, Massachusetts offered bounties for the production of wool products. In 1661 Virginia awarded bounties of large quantities of tobacco to shipbuilders and ship owners for every vessel they docked in the colony. Other forms of business support were available as well. Many colonies provided public instruction to train young men in tanning, silk production, lumbering, and similar trades. Colonial governments even owned and operated businesses and banks. Many of these activities continued long after the Revolution as states and local governments actively promoted their economies with tax breaks, low-cost loans, grants-in-aid, and franchises to certain businesses.

Alexander Hamilton, the first secretary of the treasury, and others tried to give the national government a major role in the economy during the presidencies of George Washington and John Adams. Hamilton felt that the young nation's future depended on a strong economy, and he believed that the national government should play a major role in shaping that economic future. But Thomas Jefferson and his successors (especially Andrew Jackson) strongly opposed any form of central controls. They believed that economic policy matters should be left to local and state governments. This opposition, however, did not stop some national policymakers. Between 1816 and the early 1830s, members of Congress from the northeastern states won passage of banking and tariff legislation favorable to their small but growing manufacturing and trade businesses. During the 1830s the power in Congress shifted toward agricultural interests in the South and West. With that shift came lower tariffs and other economic policies favoring farmers and plantation owners. Railroads were important to agrarian America, and between 1850 and 1857 Congress turned over more than 25 million acres of public lands to railroad companies.

After the Civil War, Congress became much more involved in the nation's economy by promoting westward expansion and the growth of business and by establishing regulatory agencies to control and monitor certain industries. But in spite of these efforts, the economy was subject to boom-and-bust cycles in the late nineteenth and early twentieth centuries, which culminated in the Great Depression of the 1930s.

The Great Depression experience became a watershed era, as President Franklin D. Roosevelt's administration responded with a series of popular programs known as the New Deal to help promote recovery and stabilize the economy. Two major dimensions of national economic policy emerged during this period: monetary policies, involving control of the money supply, and fiscal policies, involving changes in government spending and tax rates.

Monetary and Fiscal Policies

Two major tasks of the national government that resulted from the Great Depression were to maintain stable prices and orderly growth. A key factor in meeting these goals has been the national government's ability to manage the supply of money circulating in the economy.

Monetary Policies.   Economists talk of tight and loose money supplies. A *tight money supply* exists when the amount of money circulating in the economy is low relative to the demand for money by consumers and investors. Basic economics teaches that when the money supply is tight, interest rates (the cost of using someone else's money) tend to be high and the cost of most goods and services is likely to fall. A *loose money supply* exists when the amount of money is high relative to the demand. During these periods, interest rates decline and prices of goods and services increase. Thus economists attribute periods of both high and low interest rates, deflated and inflated prices, and a variety of related economic conditions to the supply of money circulating in the economy.

   Monetary policy—the manipulation of the money supply to control the economy—has become a major tool of economic management for government. The principal mechanisms for making monetary policies are in the hands of the Federal Reserve System, also known as "the Fed" (see Figure 14.3). The Federal Reserve System, established in 1913, consists of twelve regional banks and a Federal Reserve Board, which is empowered to regulate the circulation of currency in the U.S. economy. When the economy is sluggish—when not enough money is being invested to maintain economic growth or when unemployment is high—policymakers at the Fed can stimulate economic activity by increasing the supply of money. With more money in circulation, people will be likely to make purchases or investments, which, in turn, will generate business activity and jobs. If policymakers think that the economy is overheated and generating too much inflation, they can reduce the supply of money and slow down economic activity.

   The Fed's policies are often influenced by recent history.[16] The "double-digit" inflation of the late 1970s and early 1980s was still fresh in the minds of monetary policymakers who sat on the Federal Reserve's governing board as the U.S. economy began to pull out of its long recession during 1993 and 1994. While most Americans welcomed the signs of recovery, the Fed's policymakers saw them differently. Fearing the return of inflation, they began raising interest rates to help keep inflation in check. Advocates of more rapid economic recovery openly criticized these decisions, for they felt higher interest rates would slow down investment and perhaps stall economic growth.

FEDERAL RESERVE BANKS

Twelve banks representing the nation's twelve Federal Reserve districts. The twelve manage the day-to-day needs of the banking system by maintaining a stable flow of money.

The banks, by districts:

1 Boston	7 Chicago
2 New York	8 St. Louis
3 Philadelphia	9 Minneapolis
4 Cleveland	10 Kansas City
5 Richmond	11 Dallas
6 Atlanta	12 San Francisco

What They Do

• Act as lender of last resort to banks, savings associations, and credit unions in trouble
• Keep reserves deposited by depository institutions
• Supply currency and coins to banks
• Destroy worn-out bills, coins
• Operate clearinghouses for checks
• Serve as fiscal agent for the U.S. Treasury
• Conduct domestic and foreign monetary operations through the New York Federal Reserve Bank as agent for the Federal Open Market Committee

BOARD OF GOVERNORS

Seven members appointed by the president and confirmed by the Senate. Terms are 14 years. The president names one member as chairman for a four-year term. The board is based in Washington, D.C.

What It Does

• Helps carry out policy for regulating the supply of money and credit by:
  –Setting reserve requirements for the depository institutions
  –Setting the discount rate on the Fed's loans to banks
• Makes margin rules for purchases of securities on credit
• Oversees major banks by regulating the nation's bank holding companies
• Inspects and regulates state-chartered banks that are members of the reserve system
• Monitors the economy
• Deals with international monetary problems
• Enforces consumer-credit laws
• Supervises Federal Reserve banks

FEDERAL OPEN MARKET COMMITTEE

Twelve members: The seven Federal Reserve governors and the president of the New York Federal Reserve Bank plus four of the presidents of the other eleven Federal Reserve banks on a rotating basis.

All twelve bank presidents attend the FOMC meetings, held every five to eight weeks.

What It Does

• Sets overall policy for regulating the supply of money and credit in the country
• Helps carry out that policy by directing the "trading desk" of the Federal Reserve Bank of New York to buy and sell government securities in the open market

FIGURE 14.3

The Long Reach of the Federal Reserve

Source: Copyright, Jan. 27, 1986, *U.S. News & World Report.*

Fiscal Policies.   During the Depression, policymakers discovered that changes in how much the government spent and the taxes it collected could influence overall economic performance. The use of these **fiscal policies** became still another way to manage the general condition of the economy. During sluggish periods, the federal government can stimulate economic activity through its purchases of goods and services. By reducing taxes, it can put money in the hands of consumers, who can stimulate economic activity through increased purchases and investments. If the economy is overheating, the government can cut spending and raise taxes, which slows down the economy and takes money away from consumers and others who might otherwise spend it.

How Should the Economy Be Managed?   The debate over how to manage the economy has raged between those who believe the government should be using monetary and fiscal tools to manage the overall direction of the economy and those who believe in a much more limited government role. The advocates of government activism include the **Keynesians**—the followers of John Maynard Keynes (pronounced "canes"), a British economist. His theory of deficit spending during periods when the economy is sluggish provided the rationale for fiscal policies from the 1930s through the 1960s. The Keynesian approach is reflected in the *Employment Act of 1946,* which made national government officials responsible for ensuring maximum production, high employment, and increased purchasing power in the American economy. The sustained period of relative prosperity from the late 1940s until the late 1960s led many to assume that such government intervention had made the threat of stagnation and major recessions a thing of the past.[17]

The **monetarists,** a group of prominent economists led by Milton Friedman, reject the argument that constant government intervention in the economy can bring either constant prosperity or stability. They believe that the economy kept growing between 1946 and 1970 in spite of government fiscal and monetary policies, not because of them. Not only is government intervention in the economy not a solution; it has held back even stronger economic growth. They argue that government intervention should be limited to maintaining a consistent growth in the nation's money supply in order to control inflation. During the 1970s and early 1980s, when the U.S. economy went through a period of both high inflation and rising unemployment, the country's economic policymakers gave greater attention to the monetarists' argument that government was doing too much through fiscal policies.[18]

Economic Development Policies

In addition to monetary and fiscal policies to manage the economy and help stabilize it, policymakers have used **economic development policies** to help the economy grow. In the second half of the nineteenth century, Congress adopted policies intended to protect and promote the growth of American businesses. It also promoted westward expansion by providing land grants to railroads and potential settlers. And it passed steadily higher import **tariffs**—taxes on goods brought into the United States from abroad. These tariffs were intended to protect growing industries from foreign competition.

Tariff and Free Trade Policies.   For much of U.S. history, our national economic development policies were closely associated with our tariff policies. American business developed behind a wall of high protective tariffs on imported goods and services. From the turn of this century until 1929, tariffs continued to increase slowly. But they took a big leap with enactment of the Hawley-Smoot Tariff of 1929. Today Hawley-Smoot is often viewed as a major cause of the Great Depression because it created turmoil in international markets. Consequently, Congress has been reluctant to pass protective tariff legislation during the past half-century. Most policymakers believe that **free trade** (the abolition of tariffs and other trade barriers) is the best policy to follow.[19]

The free trade policy raised little controversy from the 1940s through the 1970s. During those years the U.S. **balance of trade**—the net difference between the value of what Americans bought and sold overseas—ran a surplus as Americans exported more goods and services than they imported. In 1975, for example, the United States had exported $18 billion of merchandise more than it imported. By contrast, in 1994 Americans imported over $170 billion more in goods and services than they exported—the highest trade deficit in the nation's history. Furthermore, by 1985 the United States had become a debtor nation: the value of foreign investment in America exceeded U.S. overseas investment by more than $110 billion.[20]

Autos Driving the Trade Deficit

The balance-of-trade deficit has become a major issue shaping this country's economic policies, especially efforts to open world markets for U.S. products. Under pressure from the U.S. government, Japan has increasingly opened its auto market to American auto manufacturers.

CLOSER TO HOME

14.1 An Economic War Between the States?

Like the national government, states and local communities have actively engaged in economic development policies throughout their history, mostly as a means of protecting local businesses from outside competition. These protective endeavors have since been replaced by state and local efforts to attract industries and jobs to their jurisdictions. Such programs have been labeled "smokestack chasing."

Ironically, aggressive government programs to attract jobs to local areas had their start and greatest success in the South—a region traditionally associated with antigovernment sentiments. The probusiness attitude of many southern politicians offset any reluctance to use government's economic development powers.

The first statewide program to promote smokestack chasing emerged in Mississippi during the 1930s. By the 1970s, several southern states had demonstrated a willingness and aptitude for providing the tax breaks, subsidies, and employment programs needed to get major corporations to shift some of their operations below the Mason-Dixon line. The trend continues today, but the efforts are no longer limited to southern states.

Some people worry, however, that the competition among states and localities for business has gone too far. Indeed, some state officials have even called on the U.S. Congress to regulate the most abusive forms of smokestack chasing. The Ohio state senate, for example, passed a resolution in May 1996 asking the federal government to consider putting a halt to the use of federal block grant funds for economic competition. This is a major development, considering that Ohio is one of the more successful states in attracting business. What concerned the Buckeye State legislators was

the misuse of federal resources in the competition among the states.

What else could the federal government do? Some have advocated national rules that would require each state and community to provide full disclosure of what they offered a company targeted for relocation or expansion. Others have suggested that Congress change tax and welfare laws to help level the competitive playing field (or some would say "battlefield") among the states.

The likelihood of federal government intervention is not great. There seem to be too many economic development weapons available to states and localities. How far will states go to draw a new business to their borders? Although North Carolina was willing to subsidize Mercedes-Benz to the tune of $100 million if it would locate there, the state lost out to Alabama, which offered three times as much. Besides tax breaks and subsidies, many states have established funds that can be used as venture capital to attract new businesses, while other states promote business start-ups through "small business incubator" programs. State governments have also created special enterprise zones, where sales taxes and even wage rates can be lower in order to attract business to the area. In Oregon, a portion of the proceeds from the state lottery is earmarked for statewide economic development projects. Other states have allocated more and more of their general revenue funds for similar programs.

Are there alternatives to this ongoing war besides federal regulation of state economic policies? A legislator from Maryland has advocated negotiated agreements among the states to halt or moderate the competition—the equivalent of treaties that would bring peace to the war-torn economies of the most competition-driven states. Another tactic has been legislation, proposed in several midwestern states, that would prohibit company-specific efforts, such as those targeted at Mercedes-Benz. Instead, each state would be restricted to broad-based programs that lowered taxes across the board or provided employment training for all—not just for those who worked for a designated company.

Students of state economies see this last proposal as the latest step in a three-stage evolution of economic development policies. During the initial stage—or "first wave"—efforts focused on business-specific programs as a means of bringing estab-

lished companies to the area. The "second wave" saw a shift toward local business development efforts, supported by more state services for new enterprises. The "third wave" is taking a new direction: developing policies that make the regional environment friendly to new and existing business—policies that will foster success and facilitate growth. Time will tell if the achievements will be real or merely wishful thinking.

Sources: Ann O'M. Bowman and Richard C. Kearney, *State and Local Government*, 3rd ed. (Boston, Mass.: Houghton Mifflin, 1996), chap. 14; also visit a site developed by the Federal Reserve Bank of Minneapolis to promote discussion of this issue (http://woodrow.mpls.frb.fed.us/sylloge/econwar/conf.html).

Responding to these conditions, some members of Congress advocated raising tariffs or taking other policy measures to protect U.S. industries and jobs from foreign competition. The Reagan administration and other advocates of free trade opposed such proposals, insisting that free and open international markets are the answer to trade deficits. The problem, they contended, was rooted in the barriers to free trade imposed by other countries, especially Japan. Instead of protective tariffs, they undertook diplomatic and other kinds of political pressures to persuade those nations to lower their barriers to the importation of U.S. goods and services. In most instances, the Bush and Clinton administrations continued to follow diplomacy rather than retaliate, and economic policy has become intertwined with America's post–Cold War foreign policy (see Chapter 15, on foreign and defense policies).

Tax Incentives.   Tax breaks, too, can promote economic activity in certain industries. For example, the home-building industry has benefited greatly over the past several decades from a provision allowing Americans to deduct their home mortgage interest costs from their personal income taxes. Another well-known but less-popular tax break was an oil depletion allowance. Introduced during the 1920s, this tax break absolved owners of oil- or gas-producing properties from paying taxes on more than a fourth of their income. Experts estimate that this tax break saved these property owners as much as $2.5 billion annually. The tax break promoted oil and gas exploration, but many critics thought its benefits were excessive and much too costly. It took more than fifty years, however, to get the tax break eliminated.

Industrial and Supply-Side Policies.   During the 1980s, economic policy discussions often centered on a debate between two strategies. Adopting the myth of too little government, some analysts argued that policymakers must develop a comprehensive economic development strategy for restructuring the economy. This approach, known as **industrial policy,** would let the United States abandon certain industries in which labor costs are too high for successful competition with other nations. At the same time, it would rescue other industries and make them competitive in the world market. Most advocates of industrial policy also call for investments in new high-technology and service industries.

By contrast, advocates of **supply-side economics** believe in giving more attention to policies that promote increased production of goods. Thus supply-siders have supported cutting taxes to help stimulate investment, lifting regulations in the marketplace, and eliminating other government restraints on private business initiatives. Supply-siders claim that past government intervention in the economy relied too much on consumer demand to stimulate economic growth and imposed too many obstacles to private investment. According to supply-side advocates, only through policies that increase suppliers' incentives will jobs be created and the economy grow.

Economic Regulatory Policies

Along with economic development policies, Congress also expanded the scope of economic policy in the late 1800s to include **economic regulatory policies,** through which government monitors and controls critical industries and sectors of the economy. The **Interstate Commerce Act of 1887** established the first regulatory commission, the *Interstate Commerce Commission (ICC),* and authorized it to regulate prices and standards of service for interstate rail companies.[21]

Regulatory Agencies.   During the next fifty years, Congress established other major economic regulatory agencies (see Chapter 12, on the federal bureaucracy). The *Food and Drug Administration (FDA)* came into being in 1906 to protect consumers from health-threatening products. The *Federal Trade Commission (FTC)* was formed in 1914 to provide safeguards against unfair methods of competition or deceptive practices in the marketplace. In the depths of the Great Depression during the 1930s, Congress created several other agencies. The *Federal Communications Commission (FCC)* was established to regulate interstate telephone, telegraph, radio, and other telecommunications industries; the *Securities and Exchange Commission (SEC)* was to oversee the activities of businesses in the securities and investment markets; and the Federal Power Commission (now called the *Federal Energy Regulatory Commission, FERC)* was to regulate the interstate production and distribution of electric power and natural gas. Reacting to widely publicized episodes of violent confrontations between workers and business, Congress also established the *National Labor Relations Board (NLRB)* to regulate workplace relations between employers and their employees who sought to unionize.

Antitrust Laws.   Congress also passed **antitrust laws** intended to promote greater economic competition. The *Sherman Antitrust Act of 1890* made it illegal for businesses to restrain trade or to monopolize a market for some product or service. The *Clayton Antitrust Act of 1914* outlawed business practices that might diminish competition or promote monopolies in a market. In 1936 the Clayton Act was amended to prevent corporate mergers that would reduce competition in a sector of the economy.

Criticisms of Regulation.   As early as the 1950s, however, critics argued that the major economic regulatory agencies seemed to be serving the interests of those they regulated rather than the public interest.[22] In addition, studies conducted in the 1960s and 1970s showed that consumers often paid a higher price for goods and services produced by a regulated industry than they would have if the industry were unregulated. The call for economic deregulation eventually led to legislation in 1978 that phased out the Civil Aeronautics Board.

Under both the Carter and Reagan administrations, Congress and the commissions lowered restrictions on natural gas producers, banks, trucking companies, interstate buses, and railroads. The Securities and Exchange Commission deregulated stockbroker commissions. The Federal Communications Commission permitted ownership of television and radio stations by local newspaper companies. Agencies charged with enforcing antitrust policies (the Federal Trade Commission and the Antitrust Division of the U.S. Department of Justice) relaxed their criteria for approving corporate mergers.[23]

For more information on the hidden costs of deregulation, see the **Gitelson/Dudley/Dubnick web site.**

By the early 1990s some observers argued that economic deregulation had gone too far too fast. The elimination of airline and bus service to many communities, a wave of corporate buyouts and mergers, a stock-market crash in 1987, the specter of a bailout for failing savings-and-loan banks that would cost American taxpayers hundreds of billions of dollars, and other events led some to call for re-regulation. Regulatory reform, they felt, had "turned out to be an exercise in national self-deception."[24] Nevertheless, deregulation and antiregulatory policy efforts remained an important part of the U.S. public policy agenda.

The National Debt Debate

Nowhere do issues of economic policy create more heat than in the ongoing debate over the size and growth of the national debt.[25] The **national debt** is the total amount of money the federal government owes as a result of spending more funds than it receives in revenues. Each year the federal government accumulates either a **budget surplus** (when its revenues or receipts exceed spending, or expenditures) or a **budget deficit** (when expenditures exceed revenues). During most of the 1980s the federal government had recorded yearly deficits of between $73 billion and $221 billion. In 1992 the deficit increased to a record level of $290 billion, though it declined to $255 billion a year later. Since then, the annual deficit has declined further. By the end of fiscal year 1996, it had decreased to $107 billion—less than half of its 1993 levels. Despite that improvement, by October 1996 the national government's outstanding debt was approaching $3.7 trillion (see Figure 14.4).

Why is the national debt so high? There are several reasons that any government goes into debt. First, a government must sometimes respond to emergency situations, such as a war or major economic depression. When Franklin D. Roosevelt became president in 1933, he inherited a national debt of $22.5 billion. By the time the United States entered World War II, the national debt had climbed to $48 billion. During that war the federal government financed about 60 percent of its spending through debts. At the completion of the war, the national debt stood at $280 billion.

Second, the national debt is high because we expect government to make large-scale capital investments that generate little or no return in the short term, and even in the long term. Unlike the private sector where investments in buildings and equipment are expected to generate income and pay for themselves over time, the government's investments include highways, weapon systems, airports, and school buildings—all important **infrastructure projects** that are

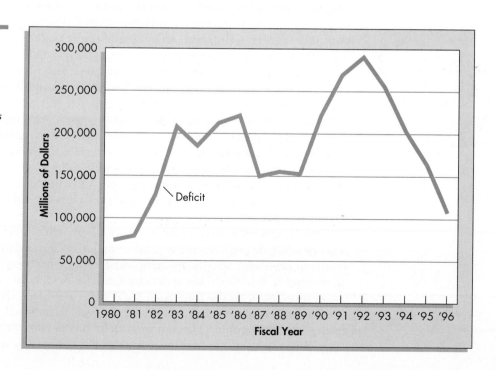

FIGURE 14.4

The Federal Budget Deficit, 1980–1996

Source: U.S. Office of Management and Budget, *Budget of the United States Government, Fiscal Year 1998,* Historical Tables, tb. 1.1.

necessary for national economic health but do not bring in revenues sufficient to offset their costs. Many of these projects take years to complete, and many have a lifespan of several decades. Unlike state and local governments, which assume long-term debt to finance such capital projects, the federal government pays for them as they are being constructed. Funding capital projects with current-year budgets places an added burden on the federal government's budget and tends to increase the annual deficit.

A third reason for government indebtedness is the growth of mandatory spending, especially for **entitlement programs.** These programs, such as social security and unemployment benefits, commit the government to supplying funds or services to all citizens who meet set eligibility requirements. Because the amount of money spent depends on the number of people who meet those standards, such spending is uncontrollable from year to year. As more people reach retirement age or as more become unemployed during a recession, government spending increases without any congressional or executive action. By 1996, social security and other entitlement programs accounted for $784.9 billion, and it was estimated that this figure would climb to $1.07 trillion by fiscal year 2002. Also in fiscal year 1996, the federal government paid over $344 billion in interest on the national debt—more than seven times what it paid in interest in 1976. As Figure 14.5 shows, the upward trend in government spending has been driven by the growth of mandatory obligations. Thus, as the federal government attempts to maintain its spending on entitlement and other domestic programs, the pressure builds to finance the increases in uncontrollable spending through deficits. In 1994, a special Bipartisan Commission on Entitlements and Tax Reform reported that unless significant policy changes were made soon, mandatory spending will comprise 72 percent of the federal budget in 2003.

A fourth reason for the growing national debt is rooted in the myths of too little and too much government, for the American public sometimes demands more goods and services than it is willing to pay in taxes or special fees. Politicians rarely advocate tax increases, and in recent years many elected officials have felt the impact of "taxpayer revolts" at the voting booths. That same public, however, is reluctant to support government officials who propose reductions in popular programs. The heads of families with college-age children, for instance, may lead the fight to reduce a local property tax increase or defeat a state sales tax measure while insisting that state colleges keep tuition costs low and guarantee admission to their sons and daughters.

Finally, governments can get into debt when policymakers decide to fund current spending through borrowing rather than through taxes in order to sustain or stimulate economic activity. Helping the economy has been the primary reason used to justify the huge federal deficits that have been piling up in recent years. It is a strategy based on the Keynesian fiscal policy approach described earlier.

Regardless of what has caused the large U.S. national debt, its size is staggering to most people. The national debt has become a major public policy issue. But other aspects besides its size worry many policymakers and analysts.

FIGURE 14.5

Mandatory and Discretionary Spending, 1980–1996

Most of the increase in the federal budget has been linked to the growth in mandatory spending.

Source: U.S. Office of Management and Budget, *Budget of the United States Government, Fiscal Year 1998,* Historical Tables, tb. 8.1.

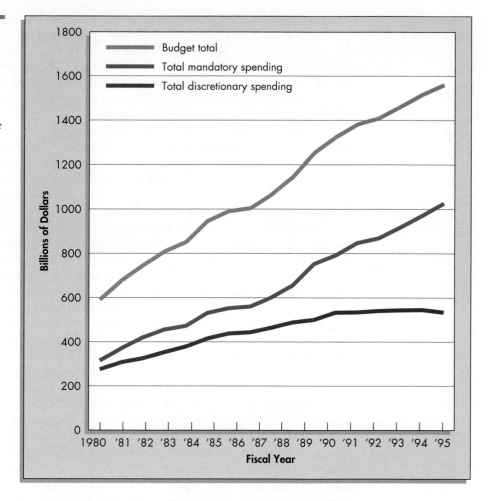

Some believe that it is not fair to burden future generations with debts that finance our current consumption of public goods and services. Others see the debt as inflationary—that is, causing higher prices for the private-sector goods and services we buy today. Still others argue that financing the national debt is pushing all interest rates higher, thus making it more difficult for consumers and businesses to borrow money.[26]

Other analysts and policymakers argue that critics of the national debt are wrong. Relatively speaking, the public debt is low. For example, the private-sector debt in 1991 stood at $7.57 trillion—twice as much as the $3.6 trillion in debt accumulated by all governments (national, state, and local) by the end of that year.[27] Nor is the national debt too large when measured against the country's assets or the annual gross national product. Some point out that whereas the national government's debt is large and growing, state and local governments often run budget surpluses each year that offset the national debt. Others stress the fact that most of the national debt (more than 75 percent) is owed to ourselves—to the millions of Americans who directly or indirectly hold U.S. savings bonds, Treasury notes, and long-term Treasury bills. And many of these analysts emphasize that the health of the American economy frequently depends on the stimulus provided by government deficits.[28]

By the mid-1980s, however, even those analysts who had felt little concern about the national debt in the past began to worry about both the annual growth of the deficit and its impact on the U.S. economy. The national debt approached $2 trillion in 1985, fueled in part by the Reagan administration's supply-side policy of dealing with the deficit by cutting taxes while increasing spending for defense. That year Congress passed the Gramm-Rudman-Hollings Act, which included a plan for reducing the annual deficit to zero by 1993. Enacted with much fanfare, the legislation expressed the intent of policymakers, but at first it had little impact. By the late 1980s, however, a number of unforeseen events had helped reduce the growth of the annual deficit. A major stock-market crash in October 1987 created a panic on world financial markets and led to greater cooperation among Washington policymakers in an effort to keep government spending in check. A series of droughts during the late 1980s raised the prices for farm products, decreasing the need for costly agricultural price support payments. Thus, although the Gramm-Rudman-Hollings law did help lower the federal deficit for a few years, it was only a partial solution that was aided by other events.

By the spring of 1990 the deficit again became a major issue. Although many in Washington looked forward to a post–Cold War peace dividend, the Bush administration and many members of Congress were concerned about their inability to meet the requirements of the Gramm-Rudman-Hollings law. The White House and congressional leaders developed another plan to bring the deficit under control, and after considerable debate it was put into effect for the 1992 budget. That agreement separated the overall budget into two categories, domestic and military. Any proposals for establishing new programs or expanding existing ones in either category would have to be funded through savings within the same category. Thus, whatever peace dividend would emerge from the end of the Cold War could only be used for other military expenditures or to reduce the deficit. Less than a year later, however, a deepening recession and upcoming presidential elections led the White House to seek a modification of the agreement so that some of the peace dividend could be used to pay for domestic policy initiatives. Reducing or eliminating the national debt played a major role in the 1992 presidential race. Independent candidate H. Ross Perot made the issue the focus of his campaign, calling for higher taxes and spending cuts. Stressing the need to stimulate the economy, Democratic candidate Bill Clinton offered a plan combining some tax increases with an "investment" strategy. And President George Bush presented a debt-reduction strategy built on a promise of no new taxes and spending cuts.[29]

Once in office, Clinton proposed a $500 billion deficit reduction plan as part of his first budget. Congress passed the plan, but only after a very close vote in both the House and Senate. By November 1994 the annual deficit was declining and the economy was on the rebound. The deficit had declined from $290 billion in fiscal year (FY) 1992 to $255 billion in FY 1993 and $203 billion in FY 1994. As indicated in Figure 14.4, the deficit continued to drop through fiscal year 1996.

As concern about the deficit has grown, so has public and congressional support for a **balanced budget amendment** in the U.S. Constitution that would force Congress to keep annual expenditures below government revenues (see Chapter 2, on constitutional foundations). Proposals for such an amendment had been introduced in Congress every year since 1936, but it was considered seriously only once.[30] In 1994 several amendment proposals were considered, but all went down in defeat.

In 1995 the Republican-led Congress placed a balanced budget amendment high on its agenda in fulfilling its "Contract with America."[31] The Republican-dominated House of Representatives took swift action and passed a resolution that went to the U.S. Senate, where it was defeated by one vote. The balanced budget amendment was brought before the Senate again in 1997—and once again lost by a single vote.

Social Welfare Policy

Social welfare policies, like economic policies, have deep roots in American history. America's earliest social policies were based on England's **poor laws**—enacted in the early 1600s—which made local communities responsible for taking care of their own needy and sick. Each town selected an overseer for the poor, who was to dispense charity to the needy and to provide able-bodied men with work. State governments became involved in aiding the needy during the 1800s. Many states abolished local debtor prisons, instituted child labor laws, mandated public education, and supported creation of institutions to care for the orphaned, insane, blind and deaf, epileptic, destitute, and others in need. These state and local efforts continued to expand into the twentieth century.[32]

Except for a few small federal grant-in-aid programs to the states described in Chapter 3, on federalism and intergovernmental relations, the national government did not become actively involved in social policy until the Great Depression. Many national programs followed the tradition of state and local efforts to help meet the needs of the poor or to improve their circumstances. Beginning in the 1930s, national social policy focused on promoting the general welfare through social programs for all Americans, regardless of their income level.[33] Thus, when discussing social policy, we must address at least two types of government programs: those that provide benefits and services only to the poor and those that help meet the needs of the general public.[34]

Aiding the Poor

Federal policies aimed explicitly at helping those in need went through a major overhaul in 1996 with passage of the **Personal Responsibility and Work Opportunity Reconciliation Act.** To appreciate the significance of those changes, we must understand the welfare system that the 1996 act replaced.

The Old Welfare System.   Under the previous system of aiding the poor, federal welfare policies took three distinct forms:[35] *general assistance,* given in cash (such as emergency assistance) or food and other commodities (such as food stamps) to those in need; *work assistance,* offering jobs or job-training programs; and *categorical assistance,* targeted at specific populations (for example, aid to families with dependent children and supplemental assistance to children with disabilities). Almost all programs in these categories were intergovernmental programs, involving state and local funding and participation. (See Chapter 3, on federalism and intergovernmental relations.) The resulting welfare system amounted to a complex arrangement of programs that drew criticism from all corners of the political arena. Among those criticisms, three stood out and helped shape the 1996 reforms.

First, the system was perceived as *too centralized and inflexible.* Many of the federal programs were designed to guarantee that those needing help had roughly equivalent access to minimal welfare benefits whether they resided in New York City or Jackson, Mississippi. This goal required that the national government establish basic program standards and ensure the implementation of minimal eligibility requirements throughout the country. It did so through specific provisions attached to the categorical grants it provided to the states to carry out the various programs. While the level of benefits for different federally funded programs might vary from state to state, program standards and a minimal level of benefits were set and enforced in Washington.

Initially, many Americans accepted this centralized system as necessary in order to guarantee some minimal assistance to the poor, no matter where they lived. By the 1980s, however, critics were successfully arguing that program centralization had gone too far and hindered state and local efforts to deal with the special circumstances and needs of local residents. Attempts to modify or adapt federal programs to local circumstances through special waivers allowed under existing law were often rejected or severely limited. Starting in 1993 the Clinton administration invited and sanctioned a great many more waivers to states, but the process was unwieldy and allowable innovations were restricted by existing laws.

The second criticism of the older welfare system was that it created *too much dependence* on government programs among the poor.[36] A growing chorus of critics from the political left and right noted that existing welfare programs provided little, if any, incentive for recipients to seek employment or job-related training. Instead, the system seemed to create a culture of poverty that increased the dependence of welfare recipients on government programs. Together with changing economic conditions, welfare programs were producing a social and economic underclass, which had no incentive to break out of the cycle of impoverishment.

The large and growing costs of the existing welfare system gave rise to the third criticism. The system was proving *too expensive* for a nation increasingly concerned about the climbing national debt. Entitlement programs—programs in which all eligible individuals had a right to the program's benefits (see page 63)—dominated the welfare approach, requiring open-ended funding. In other words, regardless of what federal, state, and local governments might budget for these programs in any given year, they were obligated to spend as much as necessary to meet the needs of those entitled to the benefits. This obligation created uncertainty and anxiety about future expenditures—especially as projections indicated a steep rise in entitlement costs by the year 2000.

These and related criticisms of the welfare system helped to fuel reform efforts, which eventually led to passage of the Personal Responsibility and Work Opportunity Reconciliation Act; President Clinton signed it into law on August 22, 1996. What had also spurred elected officials to action was the growing political popularity of reform. When he was running for the presidency in 1992, Clinton promised to "end welfare as we know it." The Republican majority in the 104th Congress was also anxious to overhaul the welfare system before facing the voters in November 1996. These political pressures created the incentive for policymakers to make the most significant changes in American welfare policies in over three decades.

The New Welfare System.[37]   The 1996 welfare reform legislation addressed the three major criticisms of the previous system. It gave more power to the states, focused on the goal of reducing dependence on welfare, and placed limits on government spending for welfare programs.

Empowering the states. We have already noted in Chapter 3, on federalism and intergovernmental relations, that the Personal Responsibility and Work Opportunity Reconciliation Act changed federalism as much as it changed the welfare system. To replace many of the highly centralized and inflexible categorical programs of the past, the 1996 reforms created a block grant titled **Temporary Assistance for Needy Families (TANF),** funded by monies previously allocated to Aid to Families with Dependent Children (AFDC), emergency assistance, and work assistance programs. TANF provides each state with resources to accomplish the legislation's four basic goals: (1) assisting needy families so that children may be cared for in their own homes or in the homes of relatives; (2) ending the dependence of needy parents on government benefits by promoting job preparation, work, and marriage; (3) reducing the incidence of out-of-wedlock pregnancies and establishing annual numerical goals for preventing

Changing Welfare as We Knew It

In August 1996, President Clinton signed a welfare reform act that significantly changed assistance to the poor.

such pregnancies and thus reducing their number; and (4) encouraging the formation and maintenance of two-parent families.

While giving states considerably more power to shape their own welfare policies and programs, the Congress did set some limits. To receive federal funding under TANF, states had to submit an acceptable welfare assistance plan to the national government by July 1, 1997. In that plan each state had to demonstrate that its efforts will be equal to at least 80 percent of what it spent on federally funded programs in fiscal year 1994. The plan also had to include provisions that would require most recipients to seek at least part-time employment after two years, as well as provisions that would end eligibility for TANF-funded programs for most recipients after five years. In addition, each state had to promise that it would hold the administrative costs of any programs funded under TANF to 15 percent or less of budget.

Ending dependence. Instead of establishing a federal work-assistance program, TANF requires the states to develop their own assistance programs that would offer incentives and opportunities for welfare recipients to obtain employment as a means for getting off federally funded welfare. For example, the funding was set up so that by 1999 in 90 percent of two-parent families still receiving TANF-related assistance at least one adult would be gainfully employed or engaged in job-assistance training programs.

The law also contains provisions allowing states to reduce or cut off assistance to a variety of groups. For example, the states can refuse support for teenage parents who do not participate in training or educational programs or who refuse to live in their parent's home. Anyone who refuses to help determine the paternity of children receiving aid can also lose some or all assistance. Furthermore, states can withhold additional support for children born to unwed mothers already on welfare. Persons convicted of drug-related felonies are not eligible for any federally funded cash or food stamp assistance under the new law, although states can aid their families if they so choose. These and other provisions of the 1996 act reflect the goal of ending welfare dependence.

Capping the costs of welfare. In funding the TANF program, Congress limited federal spending to $16.4 billion through fiscal year 2002, thus stopping the open-ended funding of the past. In addition, the law expressly states that the programs funded under TANF are not entitlements, and both eligibility and benefits can be adjusted to stay within spending limits. The law also includes some additional funding provisions for states facing special circumstances, but even this amount is set at a specific level. Individual states can, of course, spend as much as they wish on other programs, but they would have to do so without the hope of federal financial assistance. Most analysts agree that without the incentive of receiving help from Washington most states are unlikely to provide a great deal more assistance to the poor. In short, the 1996 act is expected to rein in the growth of spending on welfare at all levels of government.

Other provisions. While the 1996 act changed the structure of AFDC and other major entitlement programs, it did not make radical changes in some other parts of the welfare system. For example, the **Supplemental Security Income (SSI)** was created in 1972 to provide direct monthly benefits from the federal government to the aged, blind, and disabled, regardless of the level of assistance they receive from other programs. Although not eliminated in 1996, a major portion of the program, affecting disabled children (and often used to supplement assistance to poor families), was modified to tighten eligibility requirements.

Another major entitlement program, **food stamps,** was also left mostly intact. Begun in 1961 as an experiment, the program slowly expanded until it became the primary source of food assistance for the poor. By 1994 more than 27 million people—about one-tenth of the U.S. population—were receiving some level of food stamp support. Since eligibility for food stamps was often tied to AFDC and other programs replaced by TANF, some parts of the program were modified. For example, to receive food stamps, able-bodied recipients must fulfill work requirements. State are also permitted to simplify the operation of the food stamp program and related programs.

In the case of both SSI and food stamps, the 1996 act expressly makes almost all noncitizens ineligible for either program. This particular provision of the act proved very controversial, especially in urban areas and populous states, where large numbers of elderly legal immigrants reside. Without access to these and related federal entitlement programs, meeting the needs of poor noncitizens is likely to be a major burden for states and localities in the future.

Social Programs

Head Start is one of the most successful federal social programs to emerge from President Lyndon Johnson's Great Society agenda.

In the area of health care, **Medicaid** remained the primary program for aiding the poor. Established in 1965 as part of the social security system (see below), it provided some form of assistance to over 31 million Americans by 1994. Among those receiving Medicaid, about half were children and another 25 percent were the elderly or disabled.

Although the 1996 act did not have a direct impact on Medicaid, its provisions significantly affected Medicaid eligibility, which had been automatically linked to AFDC and other welfare programs. The 1996 act severed that automatic link, and eligibility for Medicaid was modified to maintain the entitlement based on mostly pre-TANF standards. The law also gave states the right to modify eligibility standards slightly and even to refuse Medicaid assistance to some who refused to find work. For the most part, however, Medicaid was left as a major entitlement program in America's welfare system.

Many other federally funded programs—including housing assistance, child nutrition, child care, and child support—were linked in some way to programs modified by the 1996 act, and each was affected in some way by the legislation. The true impact and long-term implications of welfare reform on these and other programs will become clearer as the new act is implemented.

Too Little Government?   From the perspective of those who favored more federal government involvement in meeting the needs of the poor, the 1996 welfare reform act was a major victory for the opposition. President Clinton's decision to sign the law drew harsh criticism from many liberals, and several prominent members of his administration resigned in protest. Even as he signed the legislation, Clinton commented that details of the law were not quite what he desired, and he promised to work hard to make changes when the new Congress met in January 1997. Several months into that year, however, it became evident that no major changes would be made until the new welfare system has had a chance to work.

Meeting the Needs of the General Public

Although welfare programs for the poor have been a major part of America's social policies, many other policies have addressed the needs of all Americans, regardless of the level of income. We will focus on two types of programs: social insurance and social regulation.

Social Insurance.   Many people try to save for that rainy day when they cannot count on their paychecks; few, however, actually set aside enough income to deal with such crises. **Social insurance programs** are intended to cover income losses caused by long-term illnesses, unemployment, retirement, and other interruptions. Funding for these benefits comes from contributions (actually involuntary taxes) levied on both employers and employees and placed in special trust funds. Once a person has made a minimum number of payments into that trust fund, he or she is entitled to participate in the program's benefits.[38]

Among major industrialized nations, the United States was one of the last to adopt such a plan. Unemployment insurance and retirement benefits were established by the Social Security Act of 1935. Under social security, employees and employers contribute a certain portion of employees' earnings to several trust funds administered by the *Social Security Administration (SSA)*. The SSA is supposed to use those funds to pay unemployment claims or monthly pension checks when a worker retires. At the outset, the system assured most American workers at least minimal coverage when they were temporarily unemployed or when they retired.

Over the years social insurance programs have grown considerably. In addition to unemployment and old-age pension insurance, social security now applies to the disabled and the survivors (widows, widowers, and children) of deceased contributors. The number of Americans covered by social security's general social insurance programs has expanded. In 1940 social security covered only 20 percent of the U.S. work force. By 1993, the old-age, survivors, disability, and related federal programs covered 95 percent of the American labor force. A smaller portion, approximately 90 percent, was protected by unemployment insurance.[39]

With the passage of Medicare in 1965, the federal government also began providing health insurance for the elderly and disabled. The basic Medicare program provided insurance for hospitalization, as well as extended care and home health services. It also contained a voluntary supplementary medical insurance program to help offset the costs of physicians' fees, lab tests, medical supplies and appliances, and related payments. By 1994, 32.1 million elderly Americans were enrolled in the basic hospital insurance program, and 31.4 million paid an additional monthly premium to take part in the supplementary health insurance program. An additional 4.1 million disabled Americans under the age of sixty-five were covered under the basic program, with 3.7 million nonelderly disabled signed up for the supplemental program.[40]

Despite steady increases in the number of participants who contribute, social insurance programs under social security—especially old-age pensions and Medicare—remain critically underfunded for the long-term future. For decades contributions to the SSA trust funds had typically equaled or exceeded the amount paid out in benefits (see Figure 14.6), but by the mid-1980s it was evident that significant problems were emerging. The American population was growing older, and policymakers had expanded and increased social security benefit levels for years. Critics warned of a pending crisis, but they were generally ignored until 1982, when the old-age and survivors insurance trust fund— the largest of SSA funds—had to borrow billions of dollars from other SSA trust funds (for instance, the disability and hospital trust funds) in order to maintain a minimal level of reserves for the future.

This episode caused concern among policymakers, who took several steps to ensure SSA's solvency in the near future. For example, in 1983 Congress raised the retirement age for eligible beneficiaries from the current sixty-five to sixty-seven by the year 2027. Those choosing to retire before the age of sixty-five will have a cut of 20 to 30 percent in their benefits.[41] In addition, policymakers have been increasing the amount that each American contributes to social security insurance. The social security tax rate for all participating employees increased from 4.8 percent in 1970 to 6.13 percent in 1980, and then to 7.65 percent in 1990. Furthermore, in 1970 only the first $7,800 of income was taxed; by 1997 the maximum taxable earnings had increased to $65,400 for old-age, survivors, and disability insurance, with additional taxes applied for Medicare insurance.[42] All this is being done in an attempt to keep the program solvent until the year 2021, when the last of the post–World War II baby boomers reach the age of sixty-five. Experts predict that another major revision of the way Americans finance the social security system must be undertaken to deal with the years beyond, for unless changes are made the system will run out of money in the year 2029.[43]

Social Regulation.   Protecting citizens from the major social hazards and problems associated with life in a highly industrialized economic system has also become a policy focus.[44]

The first federal **social regulation programs** emerged in the early 1900s in response to problems of adulterated food and the deceptive advertising of drugs. Stirred to action by research conducted at the Department of Agriculture and investigations by muckraking journalists, Congress passed the Pure Food and Drug Act of 1906 and the Meat Inspection Act of 1907. These and other **consumer pro-**

FIGURE 14.6

Social Security Contributions and Benefits

The difference between social security contributions and benefit payments created a funding crisis during the late 1970s and early 1980s, leading Congress to modify the system in an effort to enhance its long-term financial health. With these changes, contributions will stay ahead of benefit payments—at least for the short run.

Source: Social Security Administration, *Social Security Bulletin, Annual Statistical Supplement, 1996,* tb. 4.A3.

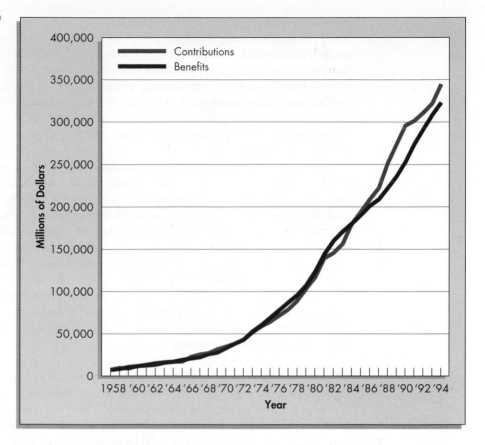

tection policies established federal agencies to deal with questions related to the safety and quality of food and drug products sold in the American marketplace. Over the years the laws have been modified to meet new problems and demands. Other forms of social regulation have followed similar patterns.

Many of the economic regulatory agencies mentioned above continue to play a role in these policy areas. The Food and Drug Administration regulates a wide range of consumer products, including drugs, cosmetics, medical devices, and food (except for meat and poultry), to ensure their safety, purity, and effectiveness. For drugs and medical devices, FDA approval is needed before a product can be marketed. The FDA investigates complaints about the safety or purity of food and cosmetics. If a product is found to be unsafe or adulterated, the FDA can order its removal from the marketplace. Overseeing the processing of meat and related products is the responsibility of the Food Safety and Inspection Service of the Department of Agriculture.

The government also looks out for the traveler and the purchaser of consumer products. The Interstate Commerce Commission has been involved in regulating passenger ground transportation industries for more than a century. Until its demise during the 1980s, the Civil Aeronautics Board regulated air passenger service. The Federal Aviation Administration continues its oversight of air traffic and safety. On the consumer side, the Federal Trade Commission (FTC) tries to keep businesses from deceiving consumers with false advertising. During Jimmy Carter's presidency, the FTC and related regulatory agencies strove to keep business in line and protect the consumer. During the Reagan and Bush administrations, however, the activity at the FTC and other consumer protection agencies had abated.[45]

Through **worker protection programs,** the federal government has extended its reach into the workplace as well, especially in the areas of discrimination, worker rights, and occupational safety and health. **Equal employment opportunity** programs prohibit workplace discrimination on the basis of race, sex, religion, national origin, or handicapped status. In addition, the federal government has required companies doing business with it to undertake affirmative action, aimed at improving employment and promotion opportunities for minorities, women, the handicapped, and other groups that have traditionally suffered from workplace discrimination. Although these antidiscrimination programs have been in place for nearly two decades, they remain extremely controversial and are constantly being challenged in the courts (see Chapter 4, on civil rights and civil liberties).

The best-known occupational safety and health program was established in 1970, under the Occupational Safety and Health Act. The primary goal of this legislation is "to assure so far as possible every working man and woman in the Nation safe and healthy work conditions." The act created the **Occupational Safety and Health Administration (OSHA)** to implement this policy through regulations and on-site inspections. OSHA's regulations and enforcement programs have been controversial from the start. Many critics found its early regulations to be both trivial and costly. By 1986, however, OSHA had issued standards that would eliminate or minimize worker exposure to a variety of highly suspect materials, such as asbestos, vinyl chloride, arsenic, benzene, lead, ethylene oxide, and cotton dust. The agency also set workplace standards for construction sites, grain elevators, and chemical plants, where hazardous materials were handled. Although still subject to criticisms, OSHA remains an important part of federal policies dealing with worker protection.

Besides OSHA, several other agencies are involved in workplace safety and health regulation. For example, agencies such as the Mine Health and Safety Administration and the Nuclear Regulatory Commission have jurisdiction over workplace conditions in specific industries. Overall, these agencies and programs represent a federal commitment to protecting the general population of workers from workplace hazards.

Critics of Government Interference.   Social regulation policies have not been without their critics, who claim that current efforts have not worked. Some accuse the government of interfering too much in the workings of the open

MYTHS IN POPULAR CULTURE

14.1 Murder, They Wrote

Among the most significant domestic policy issues for Americans during the first half of the 1990s was crime. In the 1994 elections, 25 percent of those who voted said crime was the issue that mattered most to them, and of those voters more than half voted Republican. Crime rated consistently high among the American public's concerns in public opinion polls throughout the first half of the 1990s. Of all major issues, only the economy received as much public attention.

It is little wonder that both the White House and Congress were willing to increase expenditures for law enforcement and prisons even as they discussed cutting back on everything from highways to defense and welfare.

What made this growing concern for crime interesting to many observers was that in recent years crime rates had declined for most major categories of criminal activity. The crime rate for violent crimes (including murder, forcible rape, robbery, and aggravated assault) had declined slightly in recent years, while rates for crimes against property (e.g., burglary, larceny—theft, motor vehicle theft) had dropped even more. Nevertheless, anxiety about crime continued to climb. We were, in one analyst's words, "doing better, but feeling worse."

There are many explanations for this seeming paradox. For one thing, while crime rates have been declining in recent years, the public's feelings probably reflect the significant increase in criminal activity over the past several decades. Violent crime rates had increased by more than 40 percent between 1983 and 1992, and property crime had grown by nearly 6 percent during that same period. Between 1955 and 1995, the crime rate for robberies increased sixfold. Such statistics are certainly cause for concern. In addition, some analysts say the recent minor declines are due to the public being more cautious as a result of their growing fear of crime. They point to the fact that spending for private security in 1990 stood at $52 billion—a good deal more than the $20 billion spent on security by individuals and private sector firms in 1980.

Some analysts, however, argue that the public's focus on the crime issue has more to do with how that issue is portrayed in the popular media than what the reality is out on the streets. One detailed analysis—by S. Robert Lichter, Linda Lichter, and Stanley Rothman—of prime-time television shows aired since the mid-1950s concluded that violent crime "is far more pervasive on television than in real life. . . ." Between 1955 and 1964, for instance, there were 7 murders for every 100 characters seen on television—a murder rate some 1,400 greater than the actual U.S. murder rate during the same period. Other violent crimes were committed at a rate of 40 per 1,000 TV characters during that decade, while the real-world rate was only 2 per 1,000. During the study's second decade (1965–1974), violent crime rates on television rose to 140 per 1,000, while real-world crime grew to 25 per 1,000.

Those trends changed slightly in the mid-1970s, when prime-time TV schedulers reacted to criticisms of television being too violent by reducing the violent crime rate on TV. Thus, as violent crime declined on television, real-world violent crime rates continued to increase. However, the study found that the incidence of nonviolent (property) crimes on TV sharply increased after 1975, which more than compensated for the decline in TV violence.

In broader perspective, the Lichter, Lichter, and Rothman study counted 2,228 crimes on 620 prime-time TV shows—an average of 3.6 crimes per episode, or nearly 50 crimes a night. Even more bothersome, however, was their finding that among those 50 were typically a dozen murders and about 20 robberies, rapes, and other violent acts. "So television is not just more crime-ridden than real life. It also highlights the most violent and serious crimes." Furthermore,

> . . . television presents crime in a context that bears little relation to reality. This context suggests that violence flows not from anger or passion, but from premeditated avarice. Crimes are layered on one another to create the scariest combinations. When businessmen commit crimes, they are not the nonviolent white-collar crimes they might commit in reality. Instead, they murder for the sake of the company or in the interest of career success. It is not enough for the TV rapist simply to assault his victim; he must brutally murder her as well. In short, video crime is unlike reality in its frequency, severity, and motivation.

It remains an open question as to whether the image of crime found on television over the past forty years has had any impact on the way Americans view the issue of crime. Perhaps the typical viewer gets his or her fears and anxieties about criminal activity—its frequency, its severity, and its premeditativeness—from watching the "boob tube" rather than from the real world. In that sense, the issue of crime may be built on a popular culture myth—one that might be very different from actual problems of crime. The result could be law enforcement policies that address mythical rather than actual problems.

Sources: S. Robert Lichter, Linda S. Lichter, and Stanley Rothman, *Prime Time: How TV Portrays American Culture* (Washington, D.C.: Regnery, 1994), especially chap. 8; quotes are from pp. 277–278, 299. Also see Paul H. Robinson, "Moral Credibility and Crime," *Atlantic Monthly,.* 275, No. 3 (March 1995).

marketplace through these regulations. They consider the laws of supply and demand to be the best means of protecting consumers and workers, and worry about the costs of social regulatory policy. As one critic put it, "The public does not get a 'free lunch' by imposing public requirements on private industries. Although the costs of government regulation are not borne by the taxpayer directly, they do show up in higher prices of the goods and services that consumers buy."[46]

Those who support social regulations, however, complain that the rules are too few or that they are not enforced stringently enough. Consequently, consumer advocates such as Ralph Nader and Michael Pertschuk have been calling for a revival of the consumer protection movement that achieved so much in the 1960s and 1970s. On worker protection issues, some advocates of a comprehensive industrial policy for the United States have urged legislation that would establish a higher minimum wage, protect the jobs of workers from unannounced plant closings, and increase worker participation in corporate decisions.

Conclusion: The Dynamic Myths of American Public Policy

We have touched on only two of the major domestic policy arenas in which the federal government is involved today. In addition to economic and social welfare policies, the federal government has been extremely active in many other areas, including efforts to provide for health care, support public education, construct new highways, promote the conservation of our natural resources, deal with energy shortages, and clean up and protect our environment. Although each of those policy arenas has its own distinctive characteristics, all share the two fundamental popular myths we have discussed in this chapter: the myths of too much and too little government activity.

These myths are closely related to ideological beliefs about the proper role of government, national versus state power, individual initiative versus concern for others, taxes, and other issues affecting domestic policy. People who hold strong ideological positions tend to see questions of policy through their own perspective instead of looking at them from a more objective viewpoint. The reality behind these myths is that public policies and the problems that they address are more complicated than either myth will allow. Government activity is not determined solely or primarily by how the public or policymakers feel about the level of government activity. Rather, government activity is typically a response to a problem.

The myths play a central role in helping shape the policies and programs that emerge from the policymaking process. Sometimes these policies and programs may tend to go in a zigzag direction of too much and then too little. But any decision maker will take into account the real or potential criticisms of those who argue that a policy proposal goes too far or not far enough. Similarly, officials who implement the policy may try to strike some balance between those who believe the policy is being enforced too stringently and those who feel it is not being enforced strictly enough. Even policy evaluations, whether formal or informal, are likely to weigh the policy's achievements against charges that the government is doing too much or too little.

Equally important, the myths serve a useful function by offering members of the general public, as well as policymakers, numerous opportunities to "mouth off" about the action or inaction of public officials. These debates and discussions invigorate the policymaking process. The pressures of the two myths thus shape the outcomes of the policymaking process and provide checks against extremes in either direction.

Summary

1. There are two major myths associated with American public policy: one reflects a widely held belief that government does too much when it gets involved in domestic matters, and the other holds that government gets involved too little.

2. The policymaking process in the United States is difficult to summarize because so many different policies emerge from so many different institutions. However, the overall process can be described in six stages: issue identification, agenda setting, policy formulation, policy

adoption, policy implementation, and policy evaluation.

3. Within each stage, the method of decision making varies. Ideally, decisions would be made rationally, but in reality decisions are often made incrementally—that is, through additions to and subtractions from current policies and programs. According to the elite model, decisions are made by a relatively small group of influential leaders who share a common perspective and common goals. Finally, many students of public policy have adopted a pluralist model, which holds that decisions are made as the result of pressures from a diverse population of interest groups.

4. In the economic policy area, the federal government has focused its attention on monetary policies, fiscal policies, economic development, and economic regulation. In each of these endeavors, the government's efforts have been shaped by the pressures created by the two myths of "too much" and "too little" government intervention. Nowhere is this more evident than in the debate over the national debt.

5. Social welfare policy covers government action providing aid to low-income Americans and promoting the general welfare of all Americans. As with economic policies, each of these government undertakings has been criticized both for being too much and too little.

6. No area of American domestic public policy escapes the pressures generated by the two myths. This is not necessarily bad, since policy debates and discussions invigorate the policymaking system. In addition, policies are often shaped and implemented in response to real or potential criticisms.

Key Terms and Concepts

Public policies Actions taken by government officials in response to problems and issues raised through the political system.

Issue identification The first of six stages in policymaking, in which some event, person, or group calls attention to a problem that needs government action.

Agenda setting The second stage of policymaking, in which the issue or problem is seriously considered by the policymaking institution.

Policy formulation The third stage of policymaking, in which policymakers and their staffs deliberate the pros and cons of each issue in a process that may take years to complete.

Policy adoption The fourth stage of policymaking, which is usually a fight to gain government support for a policy that demands much bargaining and compromise.

Policy implementation The carrying out of policy mandates through public programs and actions— the fifth stage in the policymaking process.

Policy evaluation The final stage in the policymaking process: looking at government actions and programs to see whether goals have been achieved or to assess a policy's effectiveness and efficiency.

Rational model of decision making The ideal process whereby a policymaker has a clear objective and all the information needed to make a sound and reasoned decision, resulting in the selection of the best way to achieve the desired goal.

Incremental model of decision making A more realistic model of decision making which sees public policy as a process of making decisions at the margins of current policies by adding to or subtracting from current policies.

Elite model of decision making The theory that public policies are made by a relatively small group of influential leaders who share common goals and points of view.

Pluralist model of decision making A theory that attributes policy outcomes to pressures exerted by different interest groups.

Monetary policy The manipulation of the money supply to control the economy. The Federal Reserve System, or "Fed," is the principal mechanism for making monetary policy.

Fiscal policy The management of government expenditures and tax rates as a means for conducting national economic policy. Policymakers raise or lower government spending and taxes to execute fiscal policy.

Keynesians Followers of economist John Maynard Keynes. They advocate government spending when the economy is sluggish (even if a deficit exists) in order to revive the economy.

Monetarists A group of economists who reject the argument that constant government intervention in the economy can bring either sustained prosperity or stability.

Economic development policies Policies intended to promote and protect businesses in order to enhance overall economic growth.

Tariffs Taxes on goods brought into the country from abroad that are often intended to protect growing industries from foreign competition.

Free trade An international economic policy that calls for the abolition of tariffs and other barriers so that goods and services may be exchanged freely among nations.

Balance of trade The net difference between the value of what Americans buy and sell overseas.

Industrial policy A comprehensive strategy for using government policies to restructure the nation's economy.

Supply-side economics An economic policy strategy that advocates increasing the production of goods by cutting taxes to help stimulate investment, lifting regulations in the marketplace, and eliminating other government restraints on private business initiatives.

Economic regulatory policies Economic policies through which government monitors and controls critical industries and sectors of the economy.

Interstate Commerce Act of 1887 Legislation that established the first regulatory commission, the *Interstate Commerce Commission (ICC)*, and authorized it to regulate prices and standards of service for interstate rail companies.

Antitrust laws Laws intended to promote greater economic competition. Among the major examples in U.S. history are the *Sherman Antitrust Act of 1890* and the *Clayton Antitrust Act of 1914*.

National debt The total amount of money the government owes as a result of overspending.

Budget surplus The case when budget revenues exceed expenditures.

Budget deficit The case when expenditures exceed revenues.

Infrastructure projects High-cost government projects such as highways and school buildings that are provided to support and enhance the economic health of the nation.

Entitlement programs Programs such as social security that commit the government to supply funds or services to all citizens who meet set eligibility requirements.

Balanced budget amendment A constitutional amendment proposed as a means of forcing Congress to deal with the national debt problem.

Poor laws British laws enacted in the early 1600s that made local communities responsible for taking care of their own needy and sick. Used as the basis for American social policies early in the nation's history.

Personal Responsibility and Work Opportunity Reconciliation Act of 1996 Welfare reform legislation that significantly changed the structure of government assistance to the poor.

Temporary Assistance for Needy Families (TANF) A block grant created by the 1996 welfare reform act, which replaced or changed most of the previous federal welfare system.

Supplemental Security Income (SSI) Established in 1972, this program provides monthly benefits for the aged, blind, and disabled, regardless of the level of assistance they receive from state governments.

Food stamps A federal public assistance program begun in the early 1960s and run by the U.S. Department of Agriculture through which eligible persons receive stamps redeemable at participating food stores.

Medicaid Established in 1965 as part of several major amendments to the Social Security Act, this program is designed to provide federal funding for specific medical services offered to qualified low-income recipients by participating states.

Social insurance programs Social policy programs, administered by the *Social Security Administration (SSA)* and intended to cover income losses due to long-term illnesses, unemployment, retirement, and other interruptions.

Social regulation programs Social policy programs intended to protect consumers from the hazards of life in a highly industrialized economic system.

Consumer protection policies Government laws and programs developed to deal with the safety and quality of consumer products, as well as to protect consumers from deceptive business practices.

Worker protection programs Government programs that protect the worker in areas of discrimination, worker rights, and occupational safety and health.

Equal employment opportunity Federal programs developed under civil rights legislation that prohibit workplace and other forms of discrimination on the basis of race, sex, religion, national origin, or handicapped status.

Occupational Safety and Health Administration (OSHA) Agency established to enforce legislation passed in 1970 and intended to reduce safety and health hazards in the workplace.

Foreign and Defense Policy

MYTH & REALITY

Is the United States still vulnerable in the post–Cold War world?

WWW●
See **Political Science** at
http://www.hmco.com/college

A hundred years from now, when students of world history read about the late twentieth century, a great deal of attention will be paid to the period from December 1988 to December 1991. On December 7, 1988, the leader of the Soviet Union, Mikhail S. Gorbachev, announced to a meeting of the United Nations that his country would unilaterally reduce its armed forces by half a million troops and withdraw and disband six tank divisions that were then stationed in East Germany, Czechoslovakia, and Hungary. Furthermore, he told the assembled leaders from around the world that his country would operate under a new military doctrine stressing defense rather than offense. Six months later, convinced that Gorbachev and the Soviet leadership were serious in their commitments, President George Bush publicly acknowledged that the Cold War was coming to an end. As confirmation for this, in November 1989 the Berlin Wall came down, thus reducing to rubble the most prominent symbol of the Cold War era. A little over two years later, the Soviet Union itself dissolved in the face of political turmoil that resulted from a foiled attempt to seize power from Gorbachev several months earlier.

The end of the Cold War was welcomed by all Americans, for it immediately reduced the anxiety that most had felt during the previous forty years as the threat of nuclear war hovered over the world stage. At first, many hoped for sharp cutbacks in military spending, which would create a huge "peace dividend" that could be used to solve social problems or reduce the burgeoning federal deficit. Even when it became clear that such a dividend was unlikely to

MYTH & REALITY

The Wall Comes Tumbling Down

For many Americans, the tearing down of the Berlin Wall in November 1989 symbolized the end of the Cold War era and the beginning of a new period in U.S. foreign policy.

materialize, there still remained the hope that in a post–Cold War world America could turn away from its forty-year reliance on power politics and pursue instead a "New World Order" based on America's most cherished values.

In the early 1990s, a belief that a New World Order was possible was not merely the fantasy of some naive idealists. To the contrary, some of America's most influential foreign policy decision makers spoke of completely reorienting international relations. Among the first to articulate a vision of such a New World Order was George Bush. In an address before the United Nations in October 1990, President Bush spoke about a

> new partnership of nations that transcends the cold war; a partnership based on consultation, cooperation and collective action, especially through international and regional organizations; a partnership united by principle and the rule of law and supported by an equitable sharing of both cost and commitment; a partnership whose goals are to increase democracy, increase prosperity, increase the peace and reduce arms.[1]

In June 1992, Joseph R. Biden, Jr., Democratic senator from Delaware and a senior member of the Senate Foreign Relations Committee, expressed a slightly different image of the New World Order by proposing "four pillars" of U.S. foreign policy for post–Cold War America. First and foremost among Biden's pillars was the promotion of democracy, followed closely by containment of the spread of dangerous weapons. The third pillar was greater reliance on collective, multilateral military action through international and regional organizations. Finally, Biden called for policies that promoted Third World economic development while protecting the global environment.[2]

Despite these grand images of a new direction for American foreign policy, the reality that emerged by the mid-1990s has been somewhat different. While no one would argue with the fact that American foreign and defense policies have changed significantly, it is also clear that the underlying theme that has guided those policies for generations has not. As we will discuss in this chapter, both before and during the Cold War American foreign and defense policies reflected a common perspective that is summarized in the *myth of American vulnerability*. According to this myth, despite what might seem like positive changes in the world situation, the United States must guard constantly against challenges to its territorial, political, and economic integrity.

"We are and have always been a nation preoccupied with security," argue James Chace and Caleb Carr.[3] For decades, this preoccupation led to an urge to achieve "absolute security" in the face of immediate and potential challenges— both real and perceived. One would assume that, as the one remaining superpower in the post–Cold War era, Americans would feel less vulnerable and more secure. But as we shall see, that has not been the case. Instead, both the myth of American vulnerability and the realities of the post–Cold War world have made U.S. policymakers less concerned with creating a New World Order and more focused on maintaining security and promoting America's national interests.

There has always been some truth to the myth of a vulnerable America. From the outset, the new nation was subject to threats from both its British enemies and French allies. The British attack on Washington during the War of 1812 provided substantial support for the worst fears of the American public. Those concerns have changed over the years, but they are no less important today. The nuclear age reinforced the idea of American vulnerability to military attacks.[4] The ending of the Cold War has reduced, but not completely eliminated, that fear. More important, however, has been the emergence of concerns about the economic vulnerability of the United States.

Immediately after World War II, the United States was the dominant country in the world economy outside the communist bloc nations. From the late 1940s to the early 1970s, the United States seemed invincible as an economic power. "The American economy was truly a leading indicator of where the world economy was going," observes Michael E. Porter; and it became "the world's center of innovation."[5] The first signs of economic vulnerability began to appear in 1971, when the U.S. balance of trade figures showed that, for the first time in the twentieth century, Americans had imported more than they had exported. A second indicator emerged in 1973 and 1974, when an oil embargo by Arab nations and a subsequent quadrupling of oil prices by member nations of the Organization of Petroleum Exporting Countries (OPEC) led to increasing turmoil in the American economy. A third sign came during the mid-1980s, when the United States became the world's largest debtor nation. It was becoming increasingly obvious that American companies were losing their ability to compete effectively with the emerging economic powers such as Japan, Korea, and Germany. In fact, they were growing more dependent on investors from those nations.[6]

The new economic vulnerability was dramatically brought home on Monday, October 19, 1987, when American stock markets took a major plunge, which cost investors half a trillion dollars in a single day. A former American trade official summarized the view of many other observers:

> The bell that sounded the end of the trading session on Bloody Monday 1987 signaled as clearly as any bugle call the most serious defeat the United States has ever suffered. . . . [T]he defeat was a most unusual one. There were no military weapons and no armed troops. There were casualties but no blood; tears, but no one missing in action. It was an economic rather than a military defeat, partially self-inflicted, and partially at the hands of friends and allies. . . .[7]

Whether the threat to American economic interests was real or not, the sense of vulnerability among Americans and their policymakers has played an important role in the shaping of the country's foreign and defense policies in the post–Cold War period.

Thus, there is little doubt that the United States has always been and remains to some extent militarily and economically vulnerable. The myth of vulnerability, however, often leads the public and policymakers to seek solutions in foreign and defense policies that can prove costly and unwise in the long term.[8] In this chapter, we examine the history and the making of U.S. foreign and defense policies from the perspective of that powerful myth.

From Isolationism to World Leadership

Historically, Americans have always shied away from excessive involvement in world affairs. During the 1800s policymakers followed the basic principles advocated by George Washington, who believed that the U.S. government should seek commercial relations with other countries while avoiding political alliances and maintaining a strong defense against foreign threats. These views led to the adoption of isolationism and unilateralism, which, combined with the myth of vulnerability, eventually created an atmosphere conducive to a policy of expansionism.

1800–1914: Isolationism, Unilateralism, and Expansionism

During the nineteenth century, American leaders pursued policies that deliberately isolated the United States from many of the intrigues and entanglements of world politics. At the time, Europe was the center of international power. Under **isolationism,** policymakers attempted to maintain American neutrality and avoid any direct involvement in European affairs that might drag the new nation into commitments that might make it politically or militarily vulnerable.

Isolationism characterized many American foreign and defense policies until World War I. But we should not conclude that the United States did not take part in world affairs at all during the 1800s. Our nation maintained an army and navy, engaged in diplomatic relations, and even took military actions to protect its neutrality and assert its interests in the international arena. Policymakers were particularly concerned with protecting American interests in the Western Hemisphere. What characterized these actions was a second tenet of U.S. foreign policy: **unilateralism.** Under unilateralism, Americans "went it alone" in world affairs and avoided political or military alliances.

Isolationism and unilateralism were both at work in U.S. policies toward our Latin American and Caribbean neighbors. In 1823, President James Monroe announced that America would keep out of the affairs of European nations so long as those countries, in turn, did not blatantly interfere in the Western Hemisphere. Yet the **Monroe Doctrine** did not stop the United States from pursuing its own territorial expansion during the 1830s and 1840s.

Expansionism also emerged as a major factor in American policies during the 1800s; the drive to expand U.S. boundaries from the Atlantic to the Pacific often influenced foreign affairs. During that period the United States purchased the Louisiana Territory from France, Alaska from Russia, and portions of the Southwest from Mexico. Territorial expansion also played a role in American wars with Mexico (1846–1848), with a number of Native American tribes in the West, and with Spain (1898). The Spanish-American War turned out to be an important turning point, for as part of the conflict's settlement, Spain gave the United States its first colonial possessions: Puerto Rico, Cuba, Guam, and the Philippines. Earlier agreements and actions had extended U.S. control in Alaska, Hawaii, and the Sandwich Islands in the Pacific. Furthermore, during the 1890s and early 1900s, American presidents intervened politically and militarily in Nicaragua, Panama, the Dominican Republic, Haiti, and other Central American and Caribbean nations.

To some degree, U.S. expansionism was a response to a sense of vulnerability among Americans in the nineteenth century. Efforts to extend American jurisdiction over the Great Plains, southwestern, and western territories were often justified as a means of enhancing the security of U.S. borders and reducing the influence of European powers.[9] American involvement in the Pacific and Caribbean reflected a growing belief that without such holdings, the United States would remain both militarily and economically exposed to the imperial designs of Great Britain, Germany, Japan, and other world powers.[10]

1914–1960: America Emerges as World Leader

Between 1914 and 1917, American policymakers faced growing pressures to enter World War I. In 1916, isolationist pressures remained so strong that President Woodrow Wilson ran for re-election using the popular slogan "He kept us out of war!" The neutrality of the United States, however, was rooted in the belief that America should not get involved unless its own security was threatened. In 1917, publication of a secret German telegram proposing a military alliance with Mexico, and the sinking of ships carrying American passengers by German submarines led President Wilson and others to conclude that the United States must get involved in the conflicts on the side of Great Britain and its allies.

With the war over, Wilson believed that the United States could no longer barricade itself behind an isolationist strategy. He was also convinced that the United States would remain vulnerable as long as there were barriers to popular rule in the world. Thus he played a major role in writing the treaty to end the war and helped design the League of Nations and the World Court. When Wilson returned home from Paris, however, he was criticized for his internationalist policies. Although he campaigned for ratification of the peace treaty throughout the United States, isolationist attitudes remained powerful and the Senate refused to ratify.

Isolationism persisted through the 1920s and 1930s. Many Americans blamed their economic problems and the Great Depression on too much contact with Europe. They believed increasing contacts would only expose the United States to more economic aggravation. Even when the rise of militarism in Europe and the Pacific grew threatening, many Americans opposed involvement in another international war that did not seem to threaten them directly. It took the Japanese attack on the U.S. Naval base at Hawaii's Pearl Harbor—for many, the ultimate proof of vulnerability—to launch the United States into that conflict.

World War II and its aftermath finally convinced many Americans that the United States must play a major role in world affairs. The United States emerged from that war as the world's industrial and military giant. As the world entered the nuclear age, Americans also began to realize just how vulnerable they were to events in the international arena.

At the outset, America's leaders were hopeful about the prospects for an era of peace. The wartime alliance among the Big Three powers—the United States, Great Britain, and the Soviet Union—was peaceful and seemed likely to last. The United States played a major role in creating the United Nations to promote world cooperation and peace. By 1946, however—only a year after the war had ended—the international scene had changed. The Soviet Union tightened its political hold on Eastern Europe, North Korea, and other occupied areas. It also challenged Britain's influence in Greece, Turkey, and the Middle East.

At first the United States tried to mediate between its two former allies, but before long it decided to openly support the British. Events came to a head in early 1947, when the British realized they could no longer afford to meet their commitments to Greece or Turkey. Within several weeks, President Harry S Truman called for a policy that supported the efforts of "free peoples who are resisting attempted subjugations by armed minorities or by outside pressures." He advocated providing economic and financial aid to countries whose political and economic stability was threatened. This general policy marked the beginning of the Cold War.

The **Cold War** is a term applied to the international situation between 1947 and the late 1980s, characterized by hostile, yet for the most part peaceful, relations between a Western alliance led by the United States and an Eastern alliance led by the Soviet Union. During most of the Cold War era, the U.S. public and many policymakers tended to perceive the world as **bipolar:** they saw nations as being allied with either of the two "poles" represented by the United States and the Soviet Union.

For most Americans, Cold War battles raged primarily on the level of ideology: the "democracies" of the West against the "totalitarian regimes" of the East, the capitalism of the West against the communism of the East, and so on. Sometimes the Cold War became hot and bloody, but these conflicts were typically limited in scope. The Korean War (1950–1952), for example, pitted the United States and its allies against North Korean and Chinese troops (see below). In addition, on several occasions the world held its breath as the two major powers confronted each other in crisis situations.

In 1947, for example, the U.S. and its allies challenged a ground-based blockade of Berlin by the Soviet Union by airlifting supplies into the city. The Soviets eventually backed off. In 1961, Soviet leaders demanded that the Allies negotiate their withdrawal from the city. President John F. Kennedy responded that the survival of West Berlin was not negotiable. The Soviets responded, in turn, by constructing a wall around the city that physically isolated it and would become a symbol of the Cold War until its destruction in 1989. Only a ground and air corridor through East Germany linked West Berlin to its support in West Germany. As in the case of the 1947 blockade, the Allies, led by the United States, held fast and demonstrated their resolve not to abandon their commitments to West Berlin.

Perhaps the "hottest" Cold War encounter between the United States and the Soviet Union came in October 1962, when Kennedy demanded that the Soviets dismantle the offensive missile sites they had placed in Cuba and halt the shipment of additional missiles to that Caribbean island. The world stood on the brink of nuclear war for thirteen days as Kennedy and Soviet Premier Nikita Khrushchev bargained back and forth in what became known as the **Cuban missile crisis.** Kennedy ordered a blockade of Cuba, and the U.S. Navy was told to make certain that no ships carrying additional missiles would sail into Cuban ports. One ship was boarded, and other Soviet vessels turned back rather than confront the blockade. In the meantime, the American and Soviet leaders exchanged heated messages. Finally, on October 28, 1962, the crisis ended when the Soviets agreed to dismantle the missile sites in return for assurances that the United States was in the process of removing some of its missiles from Turkey and Italy.

While these specific confrontations played an important role in the Cold War, the United States followed a more general policy of containment during the period. According to proponents of **containment,** the Soviet Union was not seeking immediate victories. Instead it exercised patience, caution, and flexibility in pursuit of expansionist goals. Only through a policy of "long-term, patient, but firm and vigilant containment" would U.S. efforts succeed in countering the Soviet Union's unrelenting commitment to conquer the capitalist world.[11] In that sense, containment was a further extension of the American belief in the myth of vulnerability: unless the Soviets were contained, they would soon extend their dominance throughout Europe, Asia, and the Americas.

Containment led to significant changes in American foreign and defense policies. It resulted in greater U.S. expenditures for foreign aid to countries vulnerable to Soviet influence. It also caused a major shift in America's defense policies. In 1949 President Truman signed a treaty establishing the **North Atlantic Treaty Organization (NATO),** thus formally ending a long-standing commitment of American policymakers to unilateralism during peacetime. NATO was a response to the perceived threat of communist expansion in Europe. It closely tied American security to political conditions in Europe by guaranteeing the maintenance of Western European governments, and it committed the United States to ongoing military collaboration with the armed services of other NATO member nations. Most important, the establishment of NATO signified a break with policies of the past and reflected American determination to halt communist expansion.[12]

The policy of containment took on more obvious military dimensions in 1950, when President Truman ordered American forces to South Korea after that country was invaded by North Korean troops. More than 34,000 American lives were lost in that "police action," and another 103,000 U.S. personnel were wounded. Throughout the conflict, Truman maintained the limited objective of forcing the North Koreans and their Chinese allies back across the border and out of South Korea.

Under Truman's successor, Dwight D. Eisenhower, the United States avoided direct military actions while getting more involved in formal alliances with other nations. By 1960 it was committed to the defense of nations in almost every region of the world, especially those bordering on Soviet bloc states.

Eventually, however, the containment policy was tested when U.S. policy-makers viewed the defense of South Vietnam as an opportunity to demonstrate America's commitments. A communist-led insurgency in South Vietnam against an American-supported government grew stronger in the late 1950s and early 1960s. Presidents Eisenhower, Kennedy, Lyndon B. Johnson, and Richard M. Nixon backed U.S. commitments with foreign aid, military assistance, and eventually with American fighting forces. Between 1964 and 1973, nearly 9 million American military personnel had served in Vietnam. At least 47,355 Americans died as a result of the Vietnam conflict, and more than 300,000 were wounded. These costs proved too much for the American public, and the United States was forced to withdraw from Vietnam in 1975 as North Vietnamese entered South Vietnam's capital, Saigon (now called Ho Chi Minh City).[13]

1960s–1980s: Containment in a Changing World

By the early 1960s international conditions were rapidly changing. Third World nations emerged as important actors in world affairs. Poor, less-industrialized countries, such as India, Kenya, and Indonesia, sought aid from the industrialized world while avoiding excessive dependence on either the United States or the Soviet Union. Furthermore, both the American and the Soviet alliances experienced growing dissent. In NATO, France developed a more independent foreign and defense policy. In the East, policy disagreements between the Soviet Union and the People's Republic of China weakened that fragile alliance, as did the desire of some Eastern European countries (for example, Albania, Yugoslavia, and Romania) to conduct their own foreign policies.

The seeming failure of the containment policy in Vietnam and the negative reaction of the American people to that war effort also led to major changes in

The Period of Détente

President Richard Nixon used a policy of détente in his relations with the Soviet Union. Here he is pictured with Soviet Premier Leonid Brezhnev during one of several summit meetings.

U.S. foreign policy—changes that shaped America's role in world affairs from 1975 until the late 1980s. Richard Nixon's administration established a policy of **détente**—or relaxation of tensions—reflecting a more cooperative approach to dealing with Soviet bloc nations while enhancing U.S. security arrangements with its allies. It was a period of negotiations with the Soviets, bringing an end to direct American involvement in the Vietnam conflict, establishing diplomatic relations with the People's Republic of China, strengthening NATO and other alliances, and providing indirect assistance to nations threatened by communist takeovers.[14]

Behind these events was a new way of dealing with the sense of vulnerability: the **balance of power strategy** was advocated and implemented by Henry A. Kissinger, who served as Nixon's top adviser on foreign policy and eventually as his secretary of state. Kissinger believed that American foreign policy in the past had been too idealistic and not cold-blooded and calculating enough. Foreign policy, Kissinger argued, was not intended to promote idealistic causes but to protect America's national interests, and that could be done only through a foreign policy that focused on maintaining an international balance of power. To accomplish this meant following one principle: "No nation could be permitted to be preeminent, however fleetingly, over the combination of forces that could be arrayed against it, for in the fleeting moment of neglect independence and identity could be irrevocably lost."[15] At times that might mean taking steps to offset the power of an increasingly powerful nation by supporting regimes and leaders whose behavior might otherwise be deplorable to many Americans. Thus

Nixon and Kissinger believed it was necessary to take unprecedented steps to counter the growing strength and influence of the Soviet Union. One such step was to open diplomatic relations with mainland China, despite a long-standing commitment not to abandon the anticommunist Chinese allies based in Taiwan. Reflecting on negotiations with communist China, Kissinger argued that the "many different strands that made up American thinking on foreign policy have so far proved inhospitable to an approach based on the calculation of the national interest and relationships of power. . . . We in the Nixon Administration felt that our challenge was to educate the American people in the requirements of the balance of power."[16]

Although the balance of power approach seemed to ease the sense of American vulnerability to perils generated by the Soviet Union and China, it could not stop the anxiety that came from the Middle East and other parts of the oil-producing world. Under the banner of the Organization of Petroleum Exporting Countries (OPEC), oil producers began raising the price and reducing the supply of crude oil during the early 1970s. By April 1973, the Nixon administration publicly declared that the United States had to take steps to reduce its vulnerability to the threat posed by the policies of OPEC and its member states. Then in October 1973 events in the Middle East elevated the situation to a foreign policy crisis. War had broken out between Israel and its Arab neighbors on October 6. In response to U.S. support for Israel, Arab member states of OPEC unilaterally made dramatic increases in the price of crude oil, and on October 20 declared an embargo of oil shipments to the West. Eventually, the embargo ended, but the nature of world affairs and U.S. foreign policy had significantly changed by the end of 1973. The embargo marked the high point of an international energy crisis that brought home to Americans just how vulnerable the U.S. economy was to developments in the international arena.

The OPEC embargo was not the only time embargo was used in international affairs. American policymakers also used that tactic when the Soviet Union invaded Afghanistan in 1979. At that time President Jimmy Carter ended the era of détente by imposing a grain embargo. In addition, Carter canceled cultural exchange programs and withdrew U.S. teams from the 1980 Olympic Games scheduled to take place in Moscow. Carter also pursued more formal relations with China, helped negotiate a peace agreement between Israel and Egypt, concluded a treaty to give Panama control over the Panama Canal, and took other actions that helped adjust U.S. foreign and defense policies to the changing international scene of the 1970s. The continuing energy crisis and events in Iran, however, had the most impact on the Carter administration. In 1979, Iranian revolutionaries seized the U.S. embassy in Tehran and took more than a hundred Americans hostage. This and similar terrorist actions against American citizens added to the general public feeling that America was once again vulnerable. The Iranian hostage crisis preoccupied Americans during 1980, adding to the public's sense of vulnerability in an election year. The crisis lasted more than a year, ending on the day President Ronald Reagan was sworn into office in 1981.

Iran Hostage Crisis

In the late 1970s, international crises such as the seizure of U.S. embassy personnel in Tehran increased the feeling of vulnerability among Americans.

At the outset, the Reagan administration stressed military superiority over the Soviet Union and the need to strengthen America's leadership in the Western world. Underlying the Reagan approach was the assumption that the United States must operate from a position of strength. Anything less, administration officials believed, would make the United States susceptible to the designs of Soviet leaders. Reagan supported stepped-up military spending and increased American involvement in the Middle East, Latin America, and other international "hot spots."[17] In many respects, his policies resembled the containment policies of the Cold War, but the changing realities of world affairs eventually posed major challenges to that approach.

At the center of those challenges were changes taking place in the Soviet Union and Eastern Europe. Gorbachev's emergence as the leader of the Soviet Union in 1985 created a situation that even hard-line cold warriors in the Reagan administration could not ignore. The shift was dramatic, especially for President Reagan and the American public. In 1985, Reagan had called the Soviet Union an "evil empire." The American people seemed to support that belief; in 1983, nearly two-thirds of those polled regarded the Soviets as a real and immediate military threat to the United States. But by 1987, Reagan was walking through Moscow's Red Square with Gorbachev, waving and shaking hands with Soviet citizens; meanwhile, the number of Americans concerned about the Soviet military threat decreased to less than one in three.[18] Even then, few observers could predict the coming end to the Cold War.

Policymakers in the Bush administration were extremely pleased with the events that unfolded between 1988 and 1991, despite some setbacks and disappointments, such as the brutal suppression of China's student demonstrators in Beijing's Tiananmen Square in June 1989. Nevertheless, major changes were clearly in the wind. American-Soviet relations were the pivotal feature that had shaped U.S. foreign policy since World War II; significant changes in those relations were bound to affect other foreign policy areas. America's NATO allies were especially eager to build on those improved relationships. This was particularly true in West Germany, where Gorbachev was popular and where there was considerable pressure for reunification with East Germany and for arms reductions. By May 1990, every Eastern European nation had new, more liberal leadership or policies. A more cooperative Soviet posture in Latin America, the Middle East, Africa, and other potential regional "hot spots" provided still more proof that real changes were taking place in the context of U.S. foreign policy.

1990s: Rethinking Foreign and Defense Policies

Shifting Contexts.   Developments started to turn sour as early as August 1990. Many of the new governments of Eastern Europe were beginning to face the hard realities of making the transition to democracy and free-market economies. In the Soviet Union, Gorbachev became anxious about the rapid pace of the changes he had initiated and began to turn his back on the reform movement. Equally ominous was the successful Iraqi invasion of Kuwait early that month. The outlook for the post–Cold War era seemed suddenly bleaker.

In 1991, however, hope returned in several arenas. The Persian Gulf War launched by U.S.-led allies against Iraq was quickly and decisively concluded. In August, several of Gorbachev's hard-line allies staged an abortive coup, and by the time the dust settled in December of that year, the Soviet Union was no more. There were other positive developments: in the Middle East, a U.S. initiative on peace talks began to take hold; in South Africa, progress was being made toward ending apartheid and establishing a majority-rule regime; and in Central America, peace talks in El Salvador were being brought to a successful conclusion. But this newly regained sense of hope was now tempered by the realization that the post–Cold War era was not without its uncertainties, despite the many changes that had occurred.

Bush Strategy.   It was in this context that the Bush administration began to articulate a foreign and military strategy based on new assumptions.[19] Central to this strategy was the sense that the United States, even as the one remaining world superpower, was still vulnerable to forces it could not control. It should therefore develop a strategy that would attempt to deter aggression and defend the nation's vital interests in an uncertain world.

Although not specific in content, the Bush foreign policy strategy was based on four general principles. First, it assumed that American interests would be best served if the United States took a regional focus, as opposed to a more global perspective that ignored unique regional issues. Second, it stressed strong alliances within that regional framework rather than unilateral activities. Third, building on the model of the Persian Gulf War, the Bush administration would give preference to multinational joint operations when military action was required. Finally, the Bush strategy took into account the need to maintain the U.S. capability to act alone if necessary to protect the nation's vital interests. When presenting their revised strategic plans, Bush administration officials would always emphasize the uncertainties facing the United States and its vulnerability to unexpected challenges.

The myth of vulnerability also remained active in several key domestic issues facing U.S. policymakers that had important foreign policy implications. For example, the War on Drugs, declared by President Bush, was based in part on strategies to cut off the supply of cocaine and other drugs from Latin America. Environmental concerns had international repercussions. Canada's leaders, for example, put considerable pressure on Presidents Reagan and Bush to address the problems caused by the acid rain produced by U.S. industries. Global warming was by its very nature an international issue, as was popular concern about the destruction of the Amazon rain forests by Brazil. In these and related cases, policymakers felt that their ability to deal effectively with problems was dependent on others—a situation that extends America's vulnerability in world affairs.

But it was in the area of economic policy that the greatest concerns emerged. During most of the Cold War, economics and national security were perceived as separate concerns, and when the two came in conflict, it was national defense that took priority.[20] However, in the early 1980s economic concerns prompted President Reagan to appoint a National Commission on Industrial Competitiveness. In its 1985 report, the commission noted that the U.S. economy's "ability to compete internationally faces unprecedented challenge from abroad. Our world leadership is at stake, and so is our ability to provide for our people the standard of living and opportunity to which they aspire."[21] Although not drawing a significant amount of public attention, the commission was expressing a theme about America's economic vulnerability that would become increasingly important over the next decade.

Clinton Presidency. The Clinton foreign policy team has refocused the country's attention from issues of military vulnerability to those of economic security. The United States must remain an international leader, they have argued, but not because of any military threat. "Today . . . the defense of the national interest requires a more subtle examination of the dangers and opportunities in a new world." To meet those new challenges, the Clinton administration gave top priority to integrating "a healthy American economy into a healthy global economy. . . ." Relatedly, the next foreign policy priority was "creating and expanding democratic governance and free markets overseas. . . ." By 1994, the more tradi-tional Cold War objectives of national security "through skilled diplomacy and a strong, ready military" were relegated to the third item on the administration's list of priorities.[22]

Making Foreign and Defense Policy

The end of the Cold War not only led to a major shift in the priorities of Amer-ican foreign and defense policies, but also transformed the way foreign and defense policies are made.

During the Cold War, there was a broad consensus that the primary objec-tive of American foreign policy was to protect our nation and its allies from the military threats posed by the Soviet Union and its allies. Thus foreign policy was closely tied to military and defense policies—that is, national security policy. Under those conditions, foreign policy decision making was relatively central-ized and isolated from the hurly-burly politics that characterize domestic policy-making (see Chapter 14 on domestic policy and policymaking). It was an arena dominated by the president, his national security advisers, and military experts.[23]

After the Cold War, foreign policy has taken on many of the characteristics of domestic policymaking. The Congress and a growing number of interest groups have become increasingly involved, and American public opinion is now more divided over specific foreign policy issues. Presidential leadership now de-pends more on developing policies that satisfy a wide range of constituencies, and the State and Defense Departments must work closely with other cabinet offices, including those from the Treasury and Commerce, as well as the Office of the U.S. Trade Representative.

The President and the White House

The president's role in foreign and military affairs is rooted in constitutional provisions giving that officeholder the power to make treaties, appoint ambas-sadors, receive diplomatic representatives from other nations, and serve as com-mander in chief of the armed forces (see discussion on these roles in Chapter 11, on the presidency). Thus, although Congress shares some of the responsi-bility for shaping, funding, and implementing our foreign and defense policies, the lion's share of the power in these arenas traditionally and constitutionally be-longs to the president of the United States.[24]

Prior to the Cold War, much of the foreign policymaking was conducted by the secretary of state. With the advent of the Cold War, however, formulating and implementing foreign and defense policies became a complex affair, and the president increasingly relied on special advisers. The National Security Act of

1947 authorized the president to establish the **National Security Council (NSC),** comprising the president, the vice president, the secretaries of defense and state, and other officials the president wished to invite, such as the secretary of commerce, the director of the Central Intelligence Agency (CIA), or the chairman of the Joint Chiefs of Staff. The NSC's primary functions were to advise the president on national security issues and to coordinate the implementation of policy. It was not intended to be a decision-making body, but its members were called on for their opinions and advice during times of crisis.

The NSC staff also played an important role in shaping U.S. foreign and military policies. Typically, the staff consisted of experts who monitored the world situation for the White House, prepared analyses and policy options for the president's consideration, and oversaw the coordination of foreign and defense policies.

The special assistant to the president for national security affairs, often called the **national security adviser,** headed the staff. Under some presidents, the national security adviser strongly influenced foreign and defense policies. In the Nixon administration, for instance, Henry Kissinger played a central role in negotiating agreements with the Soviets, as well as in efforts to end the Vietnam War and to open relations with the People's Republic of China. Eventually, Nixon appointed Kissinger to serve simultaneously as secretary of state and national security adviser.

Recent national security advisers have been less well known to the general public. President Clinton, for example, appointed Anthony Lake as his adviser during his first term. Lake intentionally kept a low profile, and some in Congress distrusted him. His successor, Samuel Berger, came to the job almost completely unknown outside of Washington, but he promised to be more visible and accessible than Lake.

As an indication of the policy shift toward economic security concerns, President Clinton established a **National Economic Council (NEC)** when he entered office. Modeled after the NSC, the NEC was given responsibility to coordinate and integrate U.S. foreign trade and domestic economic policy. In establishing the position of **national economic council adviser** to coordinate NEC activities, Clinton gave that official equal status with the administration's national security adviser. The two advisers—Robert Rubin (later appointed secretary of Treasury) at the NEC and Anthony Lake at the NSC—worked closely together during Clinton's first two years in office. In addition, several other key advisers on economic policy served on the staff of both the NSC and NEC, further supporting the idea that economic security had become a major priority in the U.S. foreign policy arena.

The Bureaucracies

Outside the White House, the president typically relied on several agencies to help formulate and implement foreign and defense policies during the Cold

Madame Secretary

Madelein Albright is the first woman to hold the position of Secretary of State—and thus the first to formally head the U.S. foreign policy-making team.

WWW•

For more information on military rules and American values, see the **Gitelson/Dudley/Dubnick** web site.

War—especially the Departments of State and Defense and the Central Intelligence Agency. The post–Cold War emphasis on economic security, however, has given a number of other bureaucracies important roles in the international relations arena.

The **Department of State** is the oldest agency associated with the conduct of foreign affairs. Its personnel manage the day-to-day operations of American foreign relations. They operate American embassies, look after U.S. interests abroad, conduct formal negotiations between the United States and other nations, and provide advice and assistance to the president and other foreign policymakers. At the heart of the State Department is the **Foreign Service,** consisting of approximately thirty-five hundred people with expertise and training in foreign diplomacy.

The **Department of Defense** (also called the Pentagon, after its five-sided office complex) is the agency most closely linked to military policymaking. Actually, it comprises three subordinate agencies—the Departments of the Navy, Army, and Air Force—which are responsible for managing their respective branches of the armed services. The civilian leaders of the Defense Department strive to integrate the policies and programs of the different military branches. In those tasks they are assisted by the **Joint Chiefs of Staff,** a group of high-ranking military officers representing the navy, army, air force, and marines. The Joint Chiefs of Staff also advise the president and the National Security Council when requested.[25]

No foreign or defense policymaking can take place without information provided through intelligence-gathering agencies. These agencies obtain much of the needed information from newspapers, magazines, public documents, and other openly available material. When seeking more detailed or hard-to-get information, policymakers often rely on the U.S. **Central Intelligence Agency (CIA).** With a staff of fifteen thousand at the height of the Cold War, the CIA could both gather needed intelligence and provide analyses of the data. It also conducted covert, or secret, operations. In 1961, for example, the CIA supplied and trained the anti-Castro troops who took part in the ill-fated invasion of Cuba. During the 1980s, CIA operatives helped pro-U.S. forces in Central America.

The CIA is not the only U.S. intelligence agency. In fact, it was estimated that in 1995 the CIA spent only 10 percent of all the expenditures for intelligence. The **National Security Agency (NSA),** a highly secretive unit located just outside Washington, uses sophisticated technologies to obtain intelligence. The Defense Department operates the NSA as well as other intelligence-gathering units to collect needed information for military purposes.

The end of the Cold War brought much discussion about reorganizing, consolidating, and refocusing intelligence-gathering functions. In its 1995 budget proposals, the Clinton administration noted that it wanted the size of the intelligence community reduced by 20 percent by 1999, and it gave priority to refocusing the attention of the various agencies to regional and economic security concerns as well as support for military operations.

Other agencies that were important during the Cold War included the *Arms Control and Disarmament Agency,* which conducted negotiations on nuclear arms limitations with the Soviets and monitored compliance with existing agreements. The *United States Information Agency (USIA)* helped coordinate educational, cultural, and media programs to provide a positive image of the United States in foreign nations. In addition, the *Agency for International Development (USAID)* helped organize economic aid programs to Third World nations and, in the post–Cold War era, to Eastern Europe and the republics that emerged from the breakup of the Soviet Union.

The end of the Cold War also increased the importance of several agencies that had previously played a relatively small role in the foreign and defense policy arenas. The *Office of the U.S. Trade Representative* has taken on a pivotal role in U.S. trade policy.[26] Treated as a cabinet-level agency, the Trade Representative's office has been at the center of efforts to promote free trade through negotiated treaties. Two such agreements—the 1993 *North American Free Trade Agreement (NAFTA)* and the 1994 *General Agreement on Tariffs and Trade (GATT)*—became major issues during the first two years of the Clinton presidency. NAFTA lowered most trade barriers among the United States, Canada, and Mexico, and GATT made significant progress toward worldwide free trade. Both, however, had significant implications for domestic policy interests, and their passage was in doubt until votes were cast in Congress (see below).

Similarly, due to the increased emphasis on economic security, the *Treasury Department* and the *Commerce Department* have emerged as major foreign policymaking agencies in the post–Cold War era. In recent years, top officials from both departments have spent as much time promoting U.S. trade interests overseas as they have dealing with domestic policy concerns.

The Congressional Role in Policymaking

Edward Corwin, one of this century's foremost authorities on the U.S. Constitution, described the provisions relating to foreign policy as "an invitation to struggle for the privilege of directing American foreign policy."

> What the Constitution does, *and all that it does*, is to confer on the President certain powers capable of affecting our foreign relations, and certain other powers of the same general kind on the Senate, and still other such powers on Congress; but which of these organs shall have the decisive and final voice in determining the course of the American nation is left for events to resolve.[27]

Congress can rely on several mechanisms when seeking to influence both foreign and defense policies.[28] The Senate can affect presidential policies through its power to ratify treaties negotiated by the White House. The Senate can also express its displeasure with White House policies indirectly by delaying or rejecting confirmation of a presidential appointment to a high-level post in the foreign or defense policy bureaucracies or to an ambassadorship.

Both the House and the Senate can influence foreign and defense policies through direct legislation. In 1973, for example, Congress approved the War Powers Resolution Act, limiting the president's power to commit U.S. troops overseas without congressional authorization (see Chapter 11, on the presidency). The act's provisions have rarely been applied as intended, especially the requirement that Congress be consulted prior to committing U.S. forces.[29]

Congressional control of the nation's purse strings provides an additional source of influence over foreign and defense policies. In 1974, for example, Congress passed a budget authorization bill for military assistance that included a provision urging the president to substantially reduce assistance to any government that violated "internationally recognized human rights." Over the years, similar and often stronger provisions have been included in military aid and economic assistance budget authorizations, and in 1983 Congress denied a specific Reagan administration request for aid to Guatemala, citing the oppressive policies of that nation's leaders.[30] That same year, congressional opponents of Reagan's policies toward Nicaragua imposed a $24 million limit on funding to support military efforts aimed at overthrowing that nation's government.[31]

When considering legislation or appropriations, members of Congress have an opportunity to question key foreign or defense policymakers. The secretaries of state and defense, the director of the CIA, and other agency chiefs or their assistants often appear before congressional committees and subcommittees to answer questions that can cover a broad range of policy concerns. Congress also uses its investigative power to influence foreign and defense policies. Thus in

1987 both houses of Congress selected special committees to investigate the charges that members of Reagan's National Security Council staff had violated a 1985 congressional action, which prohibited the U.S. government from assisting rebel forces fighting the government of Nicaragua.[32] The right to conduct these and similar investigations gives Congress leverage in shaping U.S. foreign and defense policies.

In general, however, congressional involvement in foreign and defense policies was very limited during the Cold War period. Rarely were major policy decisions debated, and when they were the result was typically overwhelming support for the position of the president.[33] In part, this was due to the constitutional preeminence of presidential powers in foreign and defense matters; but it was also a result of the nature of the Cold War itself, where the "enemy" was clearly defined and there existed widespread support for the objective of containment. Analysts have been unable to predict whether the congressional tendency to defer to the White House in foreign and defense matters will endure in the post–Cold War era.

The Mass Media and Attentive Publics

The media influence foreign and defense policymaking in several ways. In their search for stories to stir the interest of their readers and listeners (see Chapter 9, on media and politics), news reporters constantly monitor American involvement in world affairs. News reports from Vietnam, for example, greatly affected public attitudes toward that war. The lessons of Vietnam and similar events have not been lost on foreign and defense policymakers. The White House is especially sensitive to the need to gain and hold the attention of the American public on important policy matters. "You don't let the press control the agenda," noted Dick Cheney, George Bush's secretary of defense. "They like to decide what's important. But if you let them do that, they're going to trash your presidency."[34]

The task of *media management* in foreign affairs has involved three major objectives: defining events, dominating the news, and silencing critics.[35] Defining events involves being able to influence the way conditions or actions are depicted in the media. Several days prior to ordering an invasion of Haiti in 1994 to reinstate that country's deposed president, President Clinton called several news reporters into his office to show them gruesome pictures of murdered critics of the nation's current leaders. As the time for decision neared, the media were briefed by other officials on the deteriorating conditions in that Caribbean nation. Although the invasion was eventually called off after an agreement was reached with Haiti's leaders, the effort to define the conditions helped justify the sending of troops to assist in implementing the accord.[36]

Similarly, the White House's ability to dominate the news is substantial. Through news conferences, speeches, staged events, and international trips, the president can provide a sense of leadership as well as draw attention to the administration's foreign policy priorities. That helps accomplish the third goal, which is to silence critics of the president's policies. In the foreign and defense policy arenas, critics of presidential policies have rarely gotten the attention accorded to the White House. The media's attention, in short, can be focused in a way that effectively keeps the voices of critics and doubters subdued.

Most students of American foreign policy point to the 1991 Persian Gulf War against Iraq as a classic case in which media management was masterfully used as a policy tool by both the White House and Defense Department. Press coverage of the military buildup and invasion was limited and at times tightly controlled in the name of security. After the conflict, the press learned just how much it had been misled, and it reacted bitterly to being manipulated. Policymakers had learned many lessons from their experience in Vietnam. As one veteran reporter wrote, "If Vietnam was in a sense the media's war, Iraq was the military's."[37]

The main audience for most media coverage of foreign and defense policies is not the mass public, but the segments of the public that are normally more interested in, as well as informed on, relevant issues. Called **attentive publics,** these groups typically make up less than one-fifth of the American public and yet play an important role in the shaping of U.S. policies. Much of what the general public (see below) knows and thinks about foreign and defense policies comes from contacts with these attentive publics.

An important characteristic of the attentive publics is that many of them join and support organizations and groups with specific positions on U.S. foreign and defense policies. Although these interest groups do not play a formal role in deciding national security policy, they are often highly influential.

The activities of interest groups in the foreign and defense policy arenas have been extremely diverse. Groups such as the influential Council on Foreign Relations have worked to increase citizen awareness of foreign and defense policy issues. Others have promoted a specific ideological perspective, such as defeating international communism or establishing a world government. Still others have advocated particular goals, such as support for the United Nations or promoting human rights. Many more are devoted to advancing specific community or business interests. Greek-American organizations, for example, have lobbied actively for U.S. policies that favor Greece and give less support to its long-time foe, Turkey. Trade associations representing almost every sector of the U.S. economy—from farmers seeking international markets for their surplus crops and automobile manufacturers seeking protection from Japanese imports to defense contractors wanting Congress to fund a new weapons system—have also frequently become involved in the foreign policymaking process. There are even lobbyists representing foreign governments and seeking favorable policies from the White House and Congress.[38]

Over the past three decades, one of the most influential interests in the foreign policy arena has been the pro-Israeli lobby. Of particular significance have been the activities of the American-Israel Public Affairs Committee (AIPAC), which has been able to influence important provisions of U.S. policy in the Middle East. In the late 1970s, for example, efforts to shore up U.S. relations with Saudi Arabia by selling that nation armaments were subject to considerable debate in Congress because several members felt the weapons would be used against Israel. AIPAC's access to members of Congress was enhanced by the numerous campaign contributions it had made over the years, as well as its ability to mount major grassroots lobbying campaigns in key regions of the country. Although it was unable to halt the arms deal with the Saudis, through its lobbying AIPAC was able to impose severe restrictions on the conditions of the sale. Such power did not go unnoticed, of course, and in the early 1980s the Arab-American community formed a group to counter AIPAC's influence—the National Association of Arab Americans (NAAA).[39]

The Role of Public Opinion

Students of public opinion often note that the general American public does not show a deep or enduring interest in foreign and defense policies. For most Americans, domestic policy concerns and personal affairs overshadow interest in world affairs. Most look to the president and other policymakers for leadership in foreign and defense matters. When it is aroused, the mass public's interest in foreign and defense policies usually focuses on some immediate threat or crisis.[40]

For example, few Americans, until the Arab oil embargo of 1973, knew how heavily the United States relied on imported oil. Nor could most Americans point to Vietnam on a world map until thousands of American troops were sent to that Southeast Asian country in the early 1960s. When the general public does pay attention to a national security issue, its responses are often highly volatile and based on scant information.

The volatility of public opinion poses a dilemma for policymakers. To gain public support in foreign and defense affairs, they must often oversell the challenges being faced or the need for the administration's programs. Examples abound. Presidential trips abroad and summit meetings with leaders of other nations become media events that dominate the news for weeks. Throughout the Cold War, the Pentagon would issue annual reports showing the growing threat of Soviet military superiority. The dramatization of such events helps rouse the public out of its normal passivity in matters of foreign affairs and defense.[41]

Some analysts believe that the mass public's main influence on policy derives from its attitude, or "mood," regarding U.S. involvement in world affairs. According to this **mood theory,** the general public has very little direct impact on specific foreign and defense matters. But its perceived willingness to accept certain views, tactics, and programs carries considerable weight in policy decisions.[42]

Historically, the public's mood has fluctuated between a willingness to accept greater U.S. involvement in world affairs and a contrary urge to withdraw from the international scene. When the public mood favors involvement, policymakers find it easier to engage in diplomacy or military ventures. When the

MYTHS IN POPULAR CULTURE

15.1 Comments on the "Big One"

Popular music frequently allows people to escape the problems and tensions of the real world. Instead of focusing on economic conditions and the threat of war or social devastation, they can, through music, contemplate the more personal problems of love and individual identity—or just lose themselves in the beauty of the sounds.

Yet there are times when some popular musicians address more worldly concerns. The threat of nuclear war, for example, was the subject of several popular artists. How they addressed the topic, however, varied from artist to artist.

In 1972, singer-songwriter Randy Newman, well known for his tongue-in-cheek approach to life, wrote a piece aptly titled "Political Science," in which he took a rather unusual approach to U.S. foreign policy. "No one likes us," he complains, "I don't know why. We may not be perfect, but heaven knows we try." With lyrics claiming that other nations are spiteful and hateful, when they should be grateful, he puts forth his proposal. "They don't respect us, so let's surprise 'em," Newman suggests. "We'll drop the big one, and pulverize 'em."

> Boom goes London,
> Boom Paree.
> More room for you,
> And more room for me.

In 1989, rock star Sting took a more serious approach to the issue of nuclear war. Using a musical theme suggested by the Russian composer, Sergei Prokofiev, Sting provided lyrics to his song "Russians," which expressed a hopeful attitude that human common sense will overcome the threats and counterthreats issued by national leaders. "Mr. Khrushchev said we will bury you," he states, referring to the Soviet leader of the early 1960s who was well known for his threatening statements. "I don't subscribe to this point of view. It'd be such an ignorant thing to do, if the Russians love their children too." He is equally harsh on Ronald Reagan for keeping the threat of nuclear war alive. The theme emerging throughout the song, however, is an optimistic one:

> We share the same biology
> Regardless of ideology
> Believe me when I say to you
> I hope the Russians love their children too.

Sources: Composition "Political Science" by Randy Newman. Copyright © 1969 Unichappell Music, Inc. (BMI). All rights reserved. Used by permission. Warner Bros. Publications U.S. Inc., Miami, FL 33014. "Russians" written and arranged by Sting. © 1985 Magnetic Publishing Ltd. (PRS) & Boosey & Hawkes represented by Regatta Music LTD. (BMI) on behalf of Magnetic Publishing LTD. Administered by Irving Music, Inc. in the U.S. and Canada. All rights reserved. Intl. copyright secured. Used by permission.

public mood favors withdrawal, policymakers are reluctant to sign treaties, increase foreign aid, or commit U.S. troops abroad. President Carter faced such a public mood during his term in office. After the Vietnam War, most Americans were leery of new diplomatic initiatives or military ventures on foreign soil. By 1986, however, President Reagan found the American public more willing to support increasing U.S. commitments abroad. The Reagan administration responded by calling for increased defense spending and a greater commitment in Central America.[43]

The Bush administration faced still another challenge in the shifting public mood accompanying the end of the Cold War and the growing American discomfort with the United States' deteriorating position as a world economic power. In early 1991, strong public support for his actions in the Persian Gulf War gave Bush the highest ratings in public opinion polls ever achieved by a sitting president. Less than a year later, however, Bush's popularity declined as the public turned its attention to domestic problems. During the presidential campaign of 1992, conservative columnist Patrick Buchanan ran against President Bush in several Republican state primaries, stressing the need for an "America first" attitude in the White House. Although he attracted less than one-third of the votes in those primary contests, Buchanan was trying to tap the isolationist attitudes that were once the dominant feature of the public mood. His overall lack of success reflected the fact that during the Cold War a constant majority of Americans had developed positions that accepted active U.S. involvement in world affairs—positions that they did not relinquish after the Cold War ended (see Figure 15.1). Nevertheless, the public's growing concern with domestic issues and the end of the Cold War may have set the stage for the reemergence of a more isolationist public.

President Clinton's focus on domestic affairs during his first two years in office was, in part, a response to greater public concern about economic problems. As he reached the midpoint in his term, however, Clinton began to pay greater

FIGURE 15.1

Preferred U.S. Role in World Affairs

Americans have consistently favored an active role for the United States in world affairs since the end of World War II. This has remained true during the post-Vietnam and post–Cold War periods as well.

Source: Data from the *CCFR: American Public Opinion Report–1995* by The Chicago Council on Foreign Relations.

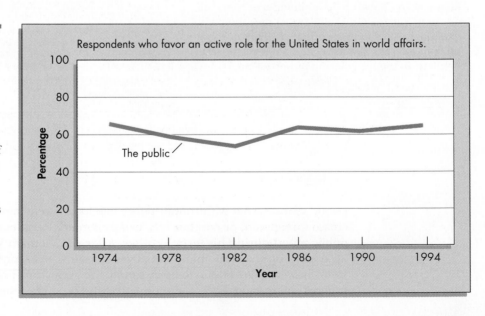

attention to international affairs. The devastating defeat suffered by the Democrats in the 1994 elections did not send any clear message regarding foreign and defense policies, nor did public opinion polls during that same period provide clear signals about the public's mood. Yet it has become increasingly obvious to foreign and defense policymakers that mood and opinion can mean a great deal more in a post–Cold War period, in which there no longer exists a "common enemy," such as the Soviet Union provided.[44]

Diplomatic Tools

The public mood is just one of many factors that have helped shape U.S. foreign and defense policies over the past two centuries. Still other factors are the diplomatic tools and the military capabilities available to our foreign and defense policymakers.

Like all nations, the United States uses several diplomatic tools in its relations with other countries (see Chapter 11, on the president as chief diplomat). One of the most common tools is **formal recognition** of another nation. For the United States, formal recognition means that the president publicly accepts and acknowledges the sovereignty of another nation and receives its ambassador in Washington as that country's official representative. Granting or withdrawing formal recognition can have great bearing on foreign policy. In 1948, President Truman formally recognized the State of Israel within hours of receiving word that the new nation had been formed. Because controversy and violence accompanied Israel's birth, diplomatic recognition by the United States was critically important and helped establish a close relationship between the two countries. Similarly, as the Soviet Union collapsed in 1991, many of the emerging republics immediately sought recognition from the United States as a signal of their legitimacy to the rest of the world.

In contrast, when the United States fails to recognize a nation or breaks off formal diplomatic relations, it clearly signals its views on that country's leadership. American policymakers were often reluctant to extend recognition to communist countries even before the Cold War era. Although the Russian Revolution took place in 1917, the United States did not establish formal relations with the Soviet Union until 1933. Similarly, after a communist regime took over in China, nearly thirty years passed before the United States and the People's Republic of China agreed to exchange ambassadors.

Breaking off diplomatic relations is an extreme step in international affairs and is usually a response to some dramatic event. The United States ended its formal recognition of Cuba in 1961 when Fidel Castro seized American property without compensation and entered into a close relationship with the Soviet Union. In 1979, President Carter broke off formal ties with Iran after the American embassy was seized and its employees taken hostage.

In other cases, however, the United States has maintained formal relations with a country even if it objected to that country's policies. President Reagan, for example, did not sever American ties with the Nicaraguan government during the 1980s, even though his administration openly supported rebel groups (the *contras*) seeking to overthrow that nation's leadership. Reagan officials believed that by maintaining those relations the United States was able to provide more effective public support for the Nicaraguan opposition groups, who eventually won major elections in February 1990. Similarly, the United States maintained its relations with South Africa throughout the 1970s and 1980s, despite widespread public condemnation of that country's apartheid policies. Many members of Congress and others urged President Bush to sever diplomatic relations with China when that government violently crushed a student movement for democratic reforms in June 1989. Bush, who once served as the American envoy to China, decided against taking such drastic measures.

Foreign aid is another major diplomatic tool. It usually takes the form of a grant of money or supplies to another nation, although it can also be a low-interest loan. As a tool of U.S. foreign policy, the best-known example of foreign aid was the **Marshall Plan.** Proposed in 1947 by the then secretary of state George C. Marshall, the plan provided financial aid and low-cost loans to help America's allies rebuild and strengthen their economies after World War II.

As Third World nations emerged in the 1960s and 1970s, the United States provided an increasing amount of direct and indirect assistance for economic development in these poor nations. Foreign aid was also used to support and reward friendly governments threatened by internal rebellions or hostile neighbors. Most such aid was intended to strengthen the military capabilities of recipient governments. President Reagan, for example, supported sending billions of dollars of military aid to El Salvador and other Central American nations as "security assistance," to help them withstand what the Reagan administration saw as the spread of Soviet influence in the region. Very little of that assistance was devoted to building schools and highways or promoting effective health care and birth control programs.[45] The withholding of aid can also prove to be an effective tool. The Reagan administration showed its displeasure with the Nicaraguan government by halting U.S. aid to that nation. Many people believe that cutting off this aid contributed to the economic problems that eventually led Nicaraguan voters to elect the opposition to office in 1990.

In the post–Cold War era, foreign aid has taken on new roles. Humanitarian aid was sent to the Kurdish people of Iraq after the Persian Gulf War and to the Ethiopian people, who suffered from both war and drought during the 1980s. The Bush administration also provided some assistance to republics emerging from the former Soviet Union as a means of supporting the move toward democracy and free-market economies in that region. When hundreds of thousands of Rwandans escaped to Zaire in 1994 following ethnic conflict that resulted in the slaughter of thousands, the U.S. joined other nations in a major effort to provide shelter and clean water.

A third major tool of diplomacy, **treaties,** are legally binding pacts by which two or more nations formalize an agreement reached through negotiation. Some treaties form the basis of international or regional organizations, for example, the United Nations Charter. Others establish standards of behavior among the nations that sign them. In 1986 the United States signed an international treaty outlawing genocide, or the mass murder of a group of people, such as occurred in Hitler's Germany during World War II. Other agreements address the treatment of prisoners of war and refugees. Treaties can also reflect solutions to disputes or problems arising between two or more nations. The United States and the former Soviet Union signed a number of treaties after 1960 dealing with such issues as the proliferation of nuclear weapons, the use of nuclear weapons in outer space, the testing of nuclear weapons in the atmosphere, and arms limitations. The best-known use of treaties, however, relates to agreements about defense issues, such as NATO. During the early 1990s, treaties relating to the promotion of free trade (e.g., NAFTA and GATT) have drawn the most attention.

Covert actions can also have a considerable impact. As the phrase implies, covert actions involve activities intentionally hidden from public view. Sometimes these are justified on the grounds that the operation cannot be successfully conducted in full public view. At other times they are justified by the need to protect the lives of those involved. Nevertheless, the secrecy surrounding covert actions frequently raises questions about their legality. Covert actions range from gathering intelligence through bugging devices to paying an informant or planning the overthrow or assassination of another nation's leaders. The CIA played a major role in such activities as the 1961 Bay of Pigs invasion of Cuba, which sought to overthrow Castro; the training of a hundred thousand Laotian troops who fought in the Vietnam War; the funding of striking truckers in Chile to destabilize that country's government in the early 1970s; and the training and funding of Nicaraguan rebel forces through most of the 1980s.

Aside from the moral and legal questions, covert activities pose a difficult dilemma for American policymakers. In 1987 a special presidential commission appointed by President Reagan to study the covert actions of the National Security Council staff concluded that such operations greatly burden policymaking in a free society. Disclosure of some covert operations might jeopardize their effectiveness and embarrass government officials. Yet democratic and free societies traditionally thrive on openness and access to information.[46]

Military and Defense Strategies

Foreign and defense policies were closely related during the Cold War era. American policymakers were convinced that the greatest threat posed by the Soviet Union and its allies was primarily military in nature. They believed that communist influence could only expand through military conquest or insurgent revolutions backed by the Soviet Union or China. It is little wonder that so much attention was focused on military and defense strategies as part of American foreign policy.

Two issues dominated debate about America's military expenditures throughout the Cold War period and after. One was the amount of money spent on defense, which is at the heart of the "guns-or-butter" debate—a debate between those who believe in higher defense expenditures and those who think additional funds should be spent on consumer goods and social services. The second issue is how to allocate the dollars being spent on defense.

Guns or Butter?

The key question in the guns-or-butter debate is how much of our nation's resources should go for defense. Before the Cold War, peacetime military spending in the United States remained relatively low compared with that in European nations. Our military expenditures consumed only a small portion of our economic resources—usually about 1 percent of the gross domestic product (GDP).

All that changed in the late 1940s. By 1950 the United States was a world power, and its leadership of the Western alliance made a large and costly military establishment necessary. That same year the Cold War became even more costly when the United States sent troops to help South Korea repel an attack by North Korea. The defense budget more than tripled, from $12.2 billion in 1950 to about $43 billion just five years later. During the 1960s—the years of the Vietnam War—defense spending climbed to more than $80 billion and consumed nearly 9 percent of the nation's GDP.

After American forces withdrew from Vietnam in the early 1970s, defense expenditures continued to grow, though at a slower rate. When Ronald Reagan took office in 1981, military spending had reached $157.5 billion, but that represented only 5.3 percent of the nation's Gross Domestic Product (see Table 15.1). Within four years, however, Reagan administration policies had increased defense expenditures to nearly $252.7 billion.

Those who supported more spending for defense usually argued that the United States needed a strong military capability in the face of a constant Soviet military buildup. They pointed out that in 1982 the Soviet Union spent an estimated $952 per capita on its military, whereas the United States spent only $846 per capita. According to the U.S. Arms Control and Disarmament Agency, more than 15 percent of the Soviet Union's GDP was devoted to military expenditures—more than twice the figure for the United States. If we were to catch up to the Soviets on military spending, the argument ran, we must be willing to make as great an effort as they do.

During the late 1980s, Gorbachev's reforms in the Soviet Union undermined that justification, and the collapse of the Soviet regime in 1991 seemed to have eliminated that threat as a major factor in U.S. military policy. Nevertheless, advocates for maintaining high levels of U.S. defense spending pointed out that

TABLE 15.1

Federal Spending for Defense, 1948–1996

Although the actual dollars spent on national defense increased during most of the Cold War period, the pattern of defense spending has had its ups and downs relative to non-defense spending (that is, as a portion of the total budget) and the nation's economy as measured by the gross domestic product (GDP). Prior to the Reagan and Bush administrations, the most significant increases in defense spending were associated with U.S. war efforts (e.g., Korea and Vietnam). Total defense spending seemingly nearly doubled under Reagan and Bush; however, in relative terms it increased during most of Reagan's years in office and shows a pattern of decline under Bush and Clinton.

		Defense Spending as % of	
Fiscal Year	Total Defense Spending (billions of dollars)	Federal Budget	Gross Domestic Product
1948	9.1	30.6	3.7
1951	23.5	51.8	7.5
1954	49.2	69.5	13.4
1957	45.4	59.3	10.4
1960	48.1	52.2	9.5
1963	53.4	48.0	9.1
1966	58.1	43.2	7.9
1969	82.5	44.9	8.9
1972	79.2	34.3	6.9
1975	86.5	26.0	5.7
1978	104.5	22.8	4.8
1981	157.5	23.2	5.3
1982	185.3	24.8	5.9
1983	209.9	26.0	6.3
1984	227.4	26.7	6.2
1985	252.7	26.7	6.4
1986	273.4	27.6	6.5
1987	282.0	28.1	6.3
1988	290.3	27.3	6.0
1989	303.6	26.5	5.9
1990	299.3	23.9	5.5
1991	273.2	20.6	4.8
1992	298.4	21.6	5.0
1993	291.1	20.7	4.6
1994	281.6	19.3	4.1
1995	272.1	17.9	3.8
1996	265.7	17.0	3.6

Source: U.S. Office of Management and Budget, *Budget of the United States Government, Fiscal Year 1998,* Historical Tables, tb. 6.1.

15.1   When Guns Were Like Butter. . . .

The Cold War did more than shape American foreign and defense policy for nearly forty years. It has also shaped and sustained the economies of many states and localities through the post–World War II era. When the Soviet threat came to an end, so did the recession-free economies of many communities.

At the height of the Cold War, there were more than five hundred major military installations located in the United States. In the mid-1980s, however, the Department of Defense realized that it needed to shut down some of these facilities as part of an effort to modernize and streamline the armed services. Deciding which installations to close was not easy, especially since any rumors of base closings generated political opposition among some very powerful people who had a stake in protecting bases in their states and districts. To make the task somewhat less political, in 1988 Congress created a process by which a blue-ribbon commission, the Commission on Base Realignment and Closure (BRAC), would review proposed base closings and submit its findings to Congress. Congress had two choices: to approve or disapprove the package of recommendations from BRAC.

The first round of BRAC closures was not without controversy, but the system worked so well that it was used again in 1991, 1993, and 1995. With the Cold War ended and budgetary pressures mounting, the number of military facilities closed or modified grew significantly. By the end of the 1995 round, BRAC's decisions had resulted in 548 "actions," which will eventually save U.S. taxpayers an estimated $56.7 billion.

Of those 548 actions, 97 resulted in the closing of military installations, and each of those closures had a potentially devastating impact on the economies of nearby cities and towns. Not surprisingly, local officials testified against the closures that would hurt them. It was estimated that 226,000 jobs would be lost as a direct consequence of the closures and many more losses would result indirectly. Communities heavily dependent on military spending were bracing for the worst. At one hearing, for example, the mayor of Charleston, South Carolina, said that the planned shutdowns would be like dropping a nuclear bomb on his city.

Perhaps the end of the Cold War hit no other city as hard as it hit Long Beach, California. Between 1990 and 1994, that city lost fifty-six thousand jobs when both Long Beach Naval Station and the naval shipyard facility were closed. "We faced a crisis," explained the city's mayor. In five years Long Beach had lost $1.7 billion in wages and contracts—and an estimated $4 billion in local economic activity.

But by 1997, the Long Beach economy was making an impressive comeback. Supported by nearly $3.5 billion in public and private investment, Long Beach has redeveloped itself into a tourist and shopping center for the region. It is estimated that the revitalized local economy will generate eighty-five thousand new jobs to replace those lost in the closures—an increase of more than twenty-five thousand positions. The key to the turnaround was an aggressive economic development campaign that focused on positive strategies for growth.

Not all communities were as lucky. Studies indicate that rural communities have had less success in replacing the economic losses from the base closures. Also, those cities that did not develop a proactive and unified economic growth strategy or spent most of their efforts fighting the closures have not bounced back with the vigor of Long Beach.

Despite its success in becoming less dependent on American defense spending, Long Beach faced a crisis in April 1997, which reminded its leaders that their city's economy would always be affected by international developments and national security concerns. As part of a plan to make more efficient use of the abandoned military base and shipyard, the Long Beach Harbor Commission approved the construction of a $200 million cargo facility, which was to be leased to the China Ocean Shipping Company—a company owned by the Chinese government. The proposal met stiff opposition from a variety of sources, including several members of Congress, who thought the sale would let an enemy power establish a communist beachhead on American shores. The opponents successfully got a court order to halt the project and the political haggling continued.

Sources: See James Kitfield, "Baseless Concerns," *National Journal,* 29, No. 15 (April 12, 1997), 703–705.

international threats remained—if not from the Soviets, then from the growing number of nuclear-armed Third World nations, international terrorists, and leaders such as Iraq's Saddam Hussein.[47]

In contrast, a growing chorus of analysts and policymakers claimed that Americans neither needed nor could afford to spend more on defense. Even before the dramatic changes in the Soviet bloc, doubts were raised about the need for spending more on defense. In 1980 former secretary of state Cyrus Vance contended, "America's military strength is formidable. I know of no responsible military official who would exchange our strategic position for that of any other nation."[48] Furthermore, the money for increased defense spending would have to come from one of three sources: higher taxes, greater government debt, or funds that would otherwise be spent on nondefense programs. Raising taxes would mean leaving the taxpayer with less money for consumer items and for investing in the U.S. economy. Funding higher military expenditures through greater government debt, or deficit financing—that is, by having the government borrow the money it needs—would add to a huge public debt, which many observers believe has already caused major economic problems (see Chapter 14). In its efforts to increase defense spending, the Reagan administration adopted the third approach: increasing the funds for military expenditures by reducing federal spending for economic, social, and other domestic programs.

The realization that the Cold War was over initially changed the nature of the guns-and-butter debate in two ways. First, there was general agreement that less will be spent on guns. A key question is "How much less?" The Bush administration's plans called for a 25 percent reduction in military forces between 1992 and 1997. In its budget proposal for 1998, the Clinton administration called for spending levels that would be over $50 million lower than the amount spent on the military in 1989, the last year of the Cold War.

A second issue revolved around what to do with the "peace dividend" generated by decreased defense spending. Should the government provide more

The Costs of Peace

In its new role in the post–Cold War world, the United States has had to pay a heavy price to sustain regional peace. In 1996, for example, nineteen American military personnel were killed in a terrorist bombing of a U.S. outpost in Dhahran, Saudi Arabia.

butter—that is, should the savings on defense result in more spending on domestic programs—or should it use the dividend to reduce the deficit or federal taxes? By late 1994, however, policymakers realized that the hoped-for peace dividend was not going to materialize. A few days after the November elections, the Clinton administration announced that it would have to increase its projected budget requests for defense spending in the future. The estimated savings from force reductions and base closings made just a year earlier had proven too optimistic, and it would take much more money to reconfigure the U.S. military for its post–Cold War missions.[49] As it turned out, the United States still had to pay the price of its continuing vulnerability. (See Table 15.2).

Alternative Military Strategies

Given the realization that the post–Cold War world would still require a militarily prepared United States, the issue of how to allocate defense expenditures remains an important one. Throughout most of the Cold War era, the debate over how to allocate defense spending focused on what mix of nuclear and conventional forces would best meet the challenge posed by the Soviet Union. As difficult as that debate was, it was based on a consensus that the primary objectives of military strategy revolved around the containment of the Soviet threat. Today that consensus is gone, and the debate is more difficult.

The first and only use of nuclear weapons in time of war occurred in 1945, when the United States dropped atomic bombs on the Japanese cities of

TABLE 15.2

Military Actions in a Post–Cold War Year, 1994

The post–Cold War period has not necessarily meant little action for the military. In 1994, 118,892 American troops were sent to undertake or join in various operations.

Operation	Place	Troops	Purpose
Deny Flight	Bosnia	8,679	No-fly zone enforcement
Distant Haven	Suriname	496	Refugee care
Korea	South Korea	1,150	Crisis response
Marine Intercept	Iraq	8,000	Enforcing sanctions
Provide Comfort	Northern Iraq	1,400	Humanitarian assistance
Provide Promise	Bosnia	725	Humanitarian assistance
Safe Haven	Panama	3,525	Refugee care
Sea Signal	Haiti and Cuba	7,705	Refugee care
Sharp Guard	Adriatic Sea	2,531	Enforcing sanctions
Southern Watch	Southern Iraq	14,000	No-fly zone enforcement
Support Hope	Rwanda	2,364	Humanitarian assistance
UNOSOM II	Somalia	2,000	Peace enforcement
UNPROFOR	Croatia-Macedonia	897	Peacekeeping
Uphold Democracy	Haiti	32,761	Intervention
Vigilant Warrior	Southern Iraq	28,952	Crisis response
Wild Fire	Western U.S.	3,707	Disaster relief

Source: Adapted from table "The Faraway Places That Draw U.S. Troops" in David C. Morrison, "Republicans at War with Peacekeeping," *National Journal,* March 11, 1995, p. 616. Used with permission.

Hiroshima and Nagasaki. Nevertheless, the new weapon changed the nature of war and military strategy. A special report prepared in 1950 by the National Security Council staff underscored that change. It argued for a **deterrence strategy** based on the buildup of nuclear and conventional (nonnuclear) forces, so that any potential enemy would hesitate to attack the United States or its allies.

At first the council's appeal for a strategy based on both nuclear and conventional forces was ignored. During the 1950s the principal defense strategy emphasized nuclear weapons. Called **massive retaliation,** this strategy required stockpiling nuclear weapons and warning the Soviet Union and its allies that any confrontation with the United States and its allies could wipe out Moscow and other major cities. The enormous buildup of the Soviet nuclear arsenal during the 1950s and 1960s focused attention on the dangers of massive retaliation as a policy. Given the development of intercontinental ballistic missiles (ICBMs), multiple independently targeted re-entry vehicles (MIRVs), and other delivery technology, the Soviet Union could also devastate American cities. A new strategy emerged based on **mutual assured destruction (MAD):** Each of the nuclear powers would hold the other in check by maintaining the ability to annihilate the other in any major confrontation.

Massive retaliation and its MAD variant were very risky and controversial strategies. By spending so much on nuclear weapons, the policymakers had let conventional forces deteriorate. By 1960, many felt that the United States had lost its capacity to respond effectively to small, localized conflicts. Thus during the 1960s, the emphasis shifted to a strategy of **flexible response,** which called for the buildup of America's nonnuclear, limited-war capabilities. Advocates of this strategy believed that strengthened conventional troops would make deterrence more credible, for the United States could counter enemy aggression with the right amount of force.

Throughout the 1970s, American policymakers stressed the need for keeping our nuclear weapons force at a level roughly equivalent to that of the Soviet force. In other words, nuclear equality, rather than nuclear superiority, would suffice. We would be safe—that is, invulnerable—if our enemies knew that we could retaliate effectively when attacked. As for nonnuclear forces, during the 1970s the U.S. defense strategy shifted to improving conventional weapons systems and training all-volunteer armed forces. Most military leaders, however, became reluctant to have American forces engaged in any type of long-term, land-based operation that might lead to the kind of war we fought in Vietnam.[50]

During the 1980s, the United States concentrated on strengthening both its nuclear and its nonnuclear forces. On the nuclear side, President Reagan called for maintaining a weapons force to provide a margin of safety over the Soviets. The Reagan administration also sought more spending on new, more sophisticated nonnuclear weapons. But it was the *Strategic Defense Initiative (SDI)* that drew most of the attention during the latter part of the Reagan years. Also termed "Star Wars," it was a proposed $90 billion space-based weapons system that would render nuclear threats "impotent and obsolete."[51] It came the closest to reflecting the urge for absolute security embodied in the myth of vulnerability.

In the post–Cold War era, attention focused on the development of a "balanced" approach that would allow the United States to deter aggression and provide for the protection of the nation's "vital interests in an uncertain world."[52] In April 1992, the Joint Chiefs of Staff put forward four themes as the basis for future military policy. First, the post–Cold War strategy would retain a *strategic deterrence* component. That would involve maintaining a combination of nuclear and conventional forces, although at significantly reduced levels. A second feature of the revised military strategy would retain an American *forward presence* in key locations around the world, such as Europe and the Pacific. The number of Americans stationed overseas would be reduced, but that reduction would be offset by a *crisis response* strategy that would call for U.S.-based forces to be ready to react to international situations as needed. Finally, the post–Cold War strategy included plans for the *reconstitution* of deactivated forces in a relatively short time if needed, which would be accomplished by maintaining some reserve units, as well as "cadre divisions" composed of military officers ready to recreate and re-equip entire military units.

While accepting the general principles outlined in those four themes, the Clinton administration has developed a more specific guideline for determining the future configuration of U.S. military forces. The key premise has been the need to maintain a military capacity to fight and win "two nearly simultaneous major regional conflicts" anywhere in the world. Using that mission as a standard, Clinton has ordered a "bottom-up review" of the armed services and has started the process of restructuring American military forces.

Conclusion: The Reshaping of Foreign and Defense Policy

American foreign and defense policies have undergone many periods of change, reflecting the many changes that have taken place in the world arena. The intrigues of European politics played a central role in shaping U.S. foreign and defense policies during the 1800s. Pressures created by European imperialism and America's own urge to extend and protect its economic influence helped mold those policies at the turn of the century. World wars and shifting international power helped define U.S. international activity until midcentury, and the mantle of leadership passed to American presidents during the Cold War. Throughout the history of the nation, however, there has been a constant urge to protect the country from the dangers of political, military, and economic vulnerability.

Current changes in the international arena are reshaping U.S. foreign and defense policies. A great deal has already changed. Nevertheless, the myth of vulnerability remains a powerful factor in guiding America's policymakers. The consequences of attachment to the myth can be positive or negative. On the positive side, the myth creates a sense of caution that can result in more thoughtful decisions. On the negative side, the danger is that the urge for absolute security will distort the perspectives and choices of America's policymakers.

Summary

1. American foreign and defense policies have been influenced by a myth of vulnerability and a resulting urge to minimize insecurity.

2. Initially, American policies were guided by principles of isolationism and unilateralism established by George Washington and other early presidents. Combined with a sense of vulnera-

bility, these principles led to American expansionist policies during the 1800s.

3. Although U.S. involvement in world affairs increased significantly from the 1890s through the 1930s, not until World War II did American policymakers and the American people accept the nation's role as an international leader. After

World War II, U.S. international involvement continued—but in response to the perceived threat of Soviet expansionism. That involvement took the form of a policy of containment. The Cold War put an end to unilateralism, and the United States entered into formal alliances with the nations of Western Europe to form NATO. Other alliances followed.

4. In more recent years the United States has adapted its foreign and defense policies to changes in world affairs. Among the most important changes have been the emergence of Third World nations and an end to the bipolar world situation, as countries such as France and the People's Republic of China broke from their respective alliances.

5. Most recently, the collapse of the Soviet Union has had a significant impact on the conduct of foreign policy under the Bush and Clinton administrations. One major transformation has been the greater emphasis now placed on economic security as a primary goal of U.S. foreign policy.

6. The making of U.S. foreign and defense policies involves a distinct set of policymaking institu-

tions, although many factors help determine decisions in each arena. During the Cold War era, the crucial decision makers in foreign and defense matters were part of an inner circle centered in the White House. However, the moods and attitudes of the general public also influenced the decisions made in both arenas. In the post–Cold War era, the nature of foreign and defense policymaking has been changing, with a greater role for both Congress and the public.

7. U.S. policymakers have a variety of foreign policy tools at their disposal. These include formal recognition, foreign aid, treaties, and covert actions.

8. Two issues have marked American defense policies since the start of the Cold War: how much money to spend on defense and which defensive strategies to rely on. The end of the Cold War has not closed that debate, but rather has changed the nature of the issues and questions being raised.

9. Despite recent changes in world affairs, the myth of vulnerability remains a powerful force in shaping America's foreign and defense policies.

Key Terms and Concepts

Isolationism A basic tenet of American policy before World War I that advocated American neutrality and avoidance of direct involvement in European affairs.

Unilateralism The pre–World War I American policy of taking action independently in foreign affairs, avoiding political or military alliances.

Monroe Doctrine An American policy, established in 1823, that warned European nations not to interfere in Latin America while promising that the United States would not interfere in European affairs.

Expansionism The pre–World War I American policy that led the United States to extend its boundaries to the Pacific while extending its influ-

ence in other areas of the world, for example, the Pacific islands, the Caribbean, and Asia.

Cold War The post–World War II period characterized by ideological and policy confrontations between the American-led West and the Soviet-led East.

Bipolar In the eyes of many U.S. policymakers, the state of the world during the Cold War, with nations being allied either with the United States or with the Soviet Union, the two "poles."

Cuban missile crisis A 1962 Cold War confrontation between the U.S. and the U.S.S.R. involving the locating of Soviet nuclear missiles in Cuba. Often regarded as a watershed event in the history of the

Cold War, it has been examined in detail as a classic case study of foreign and defense policymaking.

Containment The foreign policy, pursued by the United States throughout the Cold War, that called for preventing the Soviet Union from making further expansionist moves in its effort to conquer the capitalist world.

North Atlantic Treaty Organization (NATO) A 1949 treaty tying U.S. security interests to those of Western European and other member nations. It represented a major break in the U.S. commitment to unilateralism.

Détente The relaxation of tensions between nations. It became the name for President Nixon's policy of taking a more cooperative approach in dealing with Soviet bloc nations while enhancing U.S. security arrangements with its allies.

Balance of power strategy A "realist's" approach to foreign policy, based on the need to offset any imbalance in international relations where one nation might become too powerful. Advocated by Henry Kissinger, it was the central premise of American foreign policy for most of the 1970s.

National Security Council (NSC) A council created by Congress in 1947 to advise the president on foreign policy and to coordinate its implementation.

National security adviser The head of the National Security Council staff, who may sometimes have a strong influence on foreign and defense policies.

National Economic Council (NEC) A council patterned after the NSC created by President Clinton to coordinate foreign and domestic economic policy matters. It is headed by the **national economic council adviser,** who is expected to facilitate coordination of relevant policy concerns.

Department of State The cabinet department responsible for the day-to-day operation of embassies, the protection of U.S. interests abroad, formal negotiations between the United States and other nations, and the provision of advice and assistance to the president.

Foreign Service The core personnel system of the State Department, consisting of some thirty-five hundred people with expertise and training in foreign policy.

Department of Defense The agency most closely linked with military policymaking. It includes the Departments of the Army, Navy, and Air Force.

Joint Chiefs of Staff The high-ranking military officers who represent the army, navy, air force, and marines. They provide advice to the president and coordinate military actions undertaken by U.S. forces.

Central Intelligence Agency (CIA) The agency responsible for gathering and analyzing information for policymakers.

National Security Agency (NSA) A highly secret intelligence-gathering agency operated by the Defense Department.

Attentive publics The segment of the population that is normally more interested, as well as better informed, about relevant issues than the general public. These groups are the main audience for media coverage of foreign and defense policies.

Mood theory The theory that the public's main influence on policy is indirect; the public's perceived willingness to accept certain programs carries weight in policy decisions.

Formal recognition The act whereby the president publicly accepts and acknowledges the sovereignty and government of another nation and receives its ambassador in Washington as that country's official representative.

Foreign aid Assistance provided by the United States to another country. This usually takes the form of a grant of money or supplies, but it can also be a low-interest loan.

Marshall Plan A plan proposed in 1947 by Secretary of State George Marshall to provide financial aid and low-cost loans to help rebuild Europe after World War II.

Treaties Legally binding pacts by which two or more nations formalize an agreement reached through negotiation.

Covert actions Activities—ranging from gathering intelligence to assassinating foreign leaders—that are intentionally hidden from public view and may be of questionable legality.

Deterrence strategy The buildup and maintenance of nuclear and conventional forces and large stockpiles of weapons to discourage any potential enemy from attacking the United States or its allies.

Massive retaliation The military strategy favored by the United States during the 1950s, which warned the Soviet Union and its allies that any military confrontation could produce an annihilating nuclear attack on Moscow and other Soviet cities.

Mutual assured destruction (MAD) The strategy that evolved in the 1960s whereby each of the nu-clear powers would hold the other in check by maintaining the ability to annihilate the other in any major nuclear confrontation.

Flexible response The military strategy adopted by the United States during the 1960s that shifted emphasis from solely nuclear weapons to increasing the United States' ability to engage in limited, conventional wars in order to make deterrence more credible.

Illustration Credits

Chapter 2: p. 25 (L), Gilbert Stuart, *James Madison*, c. 1821, Ailsa Mellon Bruce Fund, © 1995 Board of Trustees, National Gallery of Art, Washington; p. 25 (R), Gilbert Stuart, *Thomas Jefferson*, c. 1821. Gift of Thomas Jefferson Coolidge IV in memory of his great-grandfather, Thomas Jefferson Coolidge, his grandfather, Thomas Jefferson Coolidge II, and his father, Thomas Jefferson Coolidge III. © 1995 Board of Trustees, National Gallery of Art, Washington; p. 29, The Bettman Archive; p. 50, J.P. Laffont/Sygma.

Chapter 3: p. 67, Culver Pictures; p. 83, AP/Wide World Photos; p. 85, AP/Wide World Photos.

Chapter 4: p. 97, Rob Nelson/Black Star; p. 99, UPI/Bettman Newsphotos; p. 108, UPI/Bettman Newsphotos; p. 115, Bettman Archive; p. 120, Naviv/SABA.

Chapter 5: p. 132, David Young Wolff/Photo Edit; p. 136, Bob Daemmrich/The Image Works; p. 143, AP/Wide World Photos; p. 151, Greenberg/Seattle Post Intelligencier, 1997; p. 156, Ira Wyman/Sygma; p. 158, Bob Daemmrich/Stock Boston.

Chapter 6: p. 164, Jean Marc Giboux/Gamma Liaison; p. 168, AP/Wide World Photos; p. 170, Jeff Stahler reprinted by permission; p. 176, The Library of Congress/from Photo Researchers; p. 183, AP/Wide World Photos.

Chapter 7: p. 192, Library of Congress; p. 197, Gary Wagner/Stock Boston; p. 206, Reuters/Bettman Archive; p. 207, Peter Southwick/Stock Boston; p. 211, Bob Daemmrich; p. 213, Bob Daemmrich/The Image Works.

Chapter 8: p. 226, Dennis Brack/Black Star; p. 229, Bill Horsman/Stock Boston; p. 230, UPI/Bettman Newsphoto; p. 236, Reprinted with permission of the Children's Defense Fund; p. 240, Jane Tyska/Stock Boston; p. 244, Ray Lustig/TWP.

Chapter 9: p. 253, Library of Congress; p. 257, Douglas Kirland/Sygma; p. 258, Axel Koester/Sygma; p. 263, Allan Tannenbaum/Sygma; p. 267, Dirck Halstead/Gamma Liaison.

Chapter 10: p. 274, Dennis Brack/Black Star; p. 277, Richard Ellis/Sygma; p. 281, Richard Ellis/Sygma; p. 284, Reuters/Pool/Archive Photos.

Chapter 11: p. 308, Corbis/Bettmann; p. 313, L. Downing/Sygma; p. 316, Peterson/Gamma Liaison; p. 324, UPI/Bettman Newsphoto; p. 327, Cynthia Jackson/Gamma Liaison; p. 330, Diana Walker/Gamma Liaison.

Chapter 12: p. 339, Bettmann; p. 347, Eric Sander/Gamma Liaison; p. 352, NASA; p. 361, Bettmann.

Chapter 13: p. 379, Bob Daemmrich/Stock Boston; p. 383, Carol Guzy/Miami Herald; p. 386, Reuters/Kim Kulish/Archive Photos; p. 390, AP/Wide World Photos; p. 395, Market/Gamma Liaison.

Chapter 14: p. 414, Rick Maiman/Sygma; p. 422, Jon Burbank/Image Works; p. 434, R. Ellis/Sygma; p. 436, Michael D. Sullivan/Texa Stock.

Chapter 15: p. 448, Stephen Ferry/Gamma Liaison; p. 456, Laffont/Sygma; p. 458, A. Mingam/Gamma Liaison; p. 463, Sygma; p. 478, Gamma Liaison.

Appendixes

The Declaration of Independence in Congress July 4, 1776

The unanimous declaration of the thirteen United States of America

When, in the course of human events, it becomes necessary for one people to dissolve the political bands which have connected them with another, and to assume, among the powers of the earth, the separate and equal station to which the laws of nature and of nature's God entitle them, a decent respect to the opinions of mankind requires that they should declare the causes which impel them to the separation.

We hold these truths to be self-evident: That all men are created equal; that they are endowed by their Creator with certain unalienable rights; that among these are life, liberty, and the pursuit of happiness; that, to secure these rights, governments are instituted among men, deriving their just powers from the consent of the governed; that whenever any form of government becomes destructive of these ends, it is the right of the people to alter or to abolish it, and to institute new government, laying its foundation on such principles, and organizing its powers in such form, as to them shall seem most likely to effect their safety and happiness. Prudence, indeed, will dictate that governments long established should not be changed for light and transient

causes; and accordingly all experience hath shown that mankind are more disposed to suffer, while evils are sufferable, than to right themselves by abolishing the forms to which they are accustomed. But when a long train of abuses and usurpations, pursuing invariably the same object, evinces a design to reduce them under absolute despotism, it is their right, it is their duty, to throw off such government, and to provide new guards for their future security. Such has been the patient sufferance of these colonies; and such is now the necessity which constrains them to alter their former systems of government. The history of the present King of Great Britain is a history of repeated injuries and usurpations, all having in direct object the establishment of an absolute tyranny over these states. To prove this, let facts be submitted to a candid world.

He has refused his assent to laws, the most wholesome and necessary for the public good.

He has forbidden his governors to pass laws of immediate and pressing importance, unless suspended in their operation till his assent should be obtained; and, when so suspended, he has utterly neglected to attend to them.

He has refused to pass other laws for the accommodation of large districts of people, unless those people would relinquish the right of representation in the legislature, a right inestimable to them, and formidable to tyrants only.

He has called together legislative bodies at places unusual, uncomfortable, and distant from the depository of their public records, for the sole purpose of fatiguing them into compliance with his measures.

He has dissolved representative houses repeatedly, for opposing, with manly firmness, his invasions on the rights of the people.

He has refused for a long time, after such dissolutions, to cause others to be elected; whereby the legislative powers, incapable of annihilation, have returned to the people at large for their exercise; the state remaining, in the mean time, exposed to all the dangers of invasions from without and convulsions within.

He has endeavored to prevent the population of these states; for that purpose obstructing the laws for naturalization of foreigners; refusing to pass others to encourage their migration hither, and raising the conditions of new appropriations of lands.

He has obstructed the administration of justice, by refusing his assent to laws for establishing judiciary powers.

He has made judges dependent on his will alone, for the tenure of their offices, and the amount and payment of their salaries.

He has erected a multitude of new offices, and sent hither swarms of officers to harass our people and eat out their substance.

He has kept among us, in times of peace, standing armies, without the consent of our legislatures.

He has affected to render the military independent of, and superior to, the civil power.

He has combined with others to subject us to a jurisdiction foreign to our constitution, and unacknowledged by our laws, giving his assent to their acts of pretended legislation:

For quartering large bodies of armed troops among us;

For protecting them, by a mock trial, from punishment for any murders which they should commit on the inhabitants of these states;

For cutting off our trade with all parts of the world;

For imposing taxes on us without our consent;

For depriving us, in many cases, of the benefits of trial by jury;

For transporting us beyond seas, to be tried for pretended offenses;

For abolishing the free system of English laws in a neighboring province, establishing therein an arbitrary government, and enlarging its boundaries, so as to render it at once an example and fit instrument for introducing the same absolute rule into these colonies;

For taking away our charters, abolishing our most valuable laws, and altering fundamentally the forms of our governments;

For suspending our own legislatures, and declaring themselves invested with power to legislate for us in all cases whatsoever.

He has abdicated government here, by declaring us out of his protection and waging war against us.

He has plundered our seas, ravaged our coasts, burned our towns, and destroyed the lives of our people.

He is at this time transporting large armies of foreign mercenaries to complete the works of death, desolation, and tyranny already begun with circumstances of cruelty and perfidy scarcely paralleled in the most barbarous ages, and totally unworthy the head of a civilized nation.

He has constrained our fellow-citizens, taken captive on the high seas, to bear arms against their country, to become the executioners of their friends and brethren, or to fall themselves by their hands.

He has excited domestic insurrection among us, and has endeavored to bring on the inhabitants of our frontiers the merciless Indian savages, whose known rule of warfare is an undistinguished destruction of all ages, sexes, and conditions.

In every stage of these oppressions we have petitioned for redress in the most humble terms; our repeated petitions have been answered only by repeated injury. A prince, whose character is thus marked by every act which may define a tyrant, is unfit to be the ruler of a free people.

Nor have we been wanting in our attentions to our British brethren. We have warned them, from time to time, of attempts by their legislature to extend an unwarrantable jurisdiction over us. We have reminded them of the circumstances of our emigration and settlement here. We have appealed to their native justice and magnanimity; and we have conjured them, by the ties of our common kindred, to disavow these usurpations, which would inevitably interrupt our connections and correspondence. They, too, have been deaf to the voice of justice and of consanguinity. We must, therefore, acquiesce in the necessity which denounces our separation, and hold them, as we hold the rest of mankind, enemies in war, in peace friends.

We, therefore, the representatives of the United States of America, in General Congress assembled, appealing to the Supreme Judge of the world for the rectitude of our intentions, do, in the name and by the authority of the good people of these colonies, solemnly publish and declare, that these United Colonies are, and of right out to be, FREE AND

INDEPENDENT STATES; that they are absolved from all allegiance to the British crown, and that all political connection between them and the state of Great Britain is, and ought to be, totally dissolved; and that, as free and independent states, they have full power to levy war, conclude peace, contract alliances, establish commerce, and do all other acts and things which independent states may of right do. And for the support of this declaration, with a firm reliance on the protection of Divine Providence, we mutually pledge to each other our lives, our fortunes, and our sacred honor.

JOHN HANCOCK
and fifty-five others

The Constitution of the United States of America*

Preamble

We the people of the United States, in order to form a more perfect union, establish justice, insure domestic tranquility, provide for the common defense, promote the general welfare, and secure the blessings of liberty to ourselves and our posterity, do ordain and establish this Constitution for the United States of America.

Article I

Section 1   All legislative powers herein granted shall be vested in a Congress of the United States, which shall consist of a Senate and a House of Representatives.

Section 2   The House of Representatives shall be composed of members chosen every second year by the people of the several States, and the electors in each State shall have the qualifications requisite for electors of the most numerous branch of the State Legislature.

*Passages no longer in effect are printed in italic type.

No person shall be a Representative who shall not have attained to the age of twenty-five years, and been seven years a citizen of the United States, and who shall not, when elected, be an inhabitant of that State in which he shall be chosen.

Representatives and direct taxes shall be apportioned among the several States which may be included within this Union, according to their respective numbers, *which shall be determined by adding to the whole number of free persons, including those bound to service for a term of years and excluding Indians not taxed, three-fifths of all other persons.* The actual enumeration shall be made within three years after the first meeting of the Congress of the United States, and within every subsequent term of ten years, in such manner as they shall by law direct. The number of Representatives shall not exceed one for every thirty thousand, but each State shall have at least one Representative; *and until such enumeration shall be made, the State of New Hampshire shall be entitled to choose three, Massachusetts eight, Rhode Island and Providence Plantations one, Connecticut five, New York six, New Jersey four, Pennsylvania eight, Delaware one, Maryland six, Virginia ten, North Carolina five, South Carolina five, and Georgia three.*

When vacancies happen in the representation from any State, the Executive authority thereof shall issue writs of election to fill such vacancies.

The House of Representatives shall choose their Speaker and other officers; and shall have the sole power of impeachment.

Section 3   The Senate of the United States shall be composed of two Senators from each State, *chosen by the legislature thereof,* for six years; and each Senator shall have one vote.

Immediately after they shall be assembled in consequence of the first election, they shall be divided as equally as may be into three classes. The seats of the Senators of the first class shall be vacated at the expiration of the second year, of the second class at the expiration of the fourth year, and of the third class at the expiration of the sixth year, so that one-third may be chosen every second year; and if vacancies happen by resignation or otherwise, during the recess of the legislature of any State, the Executive thereof may make temporary appointments until the next meeting of the legislature, which shall then fill such vacancies.

No person shall be a Senator who shall not have attained to the age of thirty years, and been nine years a citizen of the United States, and who shall not, when elected, be an inhabitant of that State for which he shall be chosen.

The Vice-President of the United States shall be President of the Senate, but shall have no vote, unless they be equally divided.

The Senate shall choose their other officers, and also a President *pro tempore,* in the absence of the Vice-President, or when he shall exercise the office of President of the United States.

The Senate shall have the sole power to try all impeachments. When sitting for that purpose, they shall be on oath or affirmation. When the President of the United States is tried, the Chief Justice shall preside: and no person shall be convicted without the concurrence of two-thirds of the members present.

Judgment in cases of impeachment shall not extend further than to removal from the office, and disqualification to hold and enjoy any office of honor, trust or profit under the United States: but the party convicted shall nevertheless be liable and subject to indictment, trial, judgment and punishment, according to law.

Section 4 The times, places and manner of holding elections for Senators and Representatives shall be prescribed in each State by the legislature thereof; but the Congress may at any time by law make or alter such regulations, except as to the places of choosing Senators.

The Congress shall assemble at least once in every year, and such meeting *shall be on the first Monday in December, unless they shall by law appoint a different day.*

Section 5 Each house shall be the judge of the elections, returns and qualifications of its own members, and a majority of each shall constitute a quorum to do business; but a smaller number may adjourn from day to day, and may be authorized to compel the attendance of absent members, in such manner, and under such penalties, as each house may provide.

Each house may determine the rules of its proceedings, punish its members for disorderly behavior, and with the concurrence of two-thirds, expel a member.

Each house shall keep a journal of its proceedings, and from time to time publish the same, excepting such parts as may in their judgment require secrecy; and the yeas and nays of the members of either house on any question shall, at the desire of one-fifth of those present, be entered on the journal.

Neither house, during the session of Congress, shall, without the consent of the other, adjourn for more than three days, nor to any other place than that in which the two houses shall be sitting.

Section 6 The Senators and Representatives shall receive a compensation for their services, to be ascertained by law and paid out of the treasury of the United States. They shall in all cases except treason, felony and breach of the peace, be privileged from arrest during their attendance at the session of their respective houses, and in going to and returning from the same; and for any speech or debate in either house, they shall not be questioned in any other place.

No Senator or Representative shall, during the time for which he was elected, be appointed to any civil office under the authority of the United States, which shall have been created, or the emoluments whereof shall have been increased, during such time; and no person holding any office under the United States shall be a member of either house during his continuance in office.

Section 7 All bills for raising revenue shall originate in the House of Representatives; but the Senate may propose or concur with amendments as on other bills.

Every bill which shall have passed the House of Representatives and the Senate, shall, before it become a law, be presented to the President of the United States; if he approve he shall sign it, but if not he shall return it with objections to that house in which it originated, who shall enter the objections at large on their journal, and proceed to reconsider it. If after such reconsideration two-thirds of that house shall agree to pass the bill, it shall be sent, together with the objections, to the other house, by which it shall likewise by reconsidered, and, if approved by two-thirds of that house, it shall become a law. But in all such cases the votes of both houses shall be determined by yeas and nays, and the names of the persons voting for and against the bill shall be entered on the journal of each house respectively. If any bill shall not be returned by the President within ten days (Sundays excepted) after it shall have been presented to him, the same shall be a law, in like manner as if he had signed it, unless the Congress by their adjournment prevents its return, in which case it shall not be a law.

Every order, resolution, or vote to which the concurrence of the Senate and House of Representatives may be necessary (except on a question of adjournment) shall be presented to the President of the United States; and before the same shall take effect, shall be approved by him, or being disapproved by him, shall be repassed by two-thirds of the Senate and House of Representatives, according to the rules and limitations prescribed in the case of a bill.

Section 8 The Congress shall have power

To lay and collect taxes, duties, imposts, and excises, to pay the debts and provide for the common defense and general welfare of the United States; but all duties, imposts and excises shall be uniform throughout the United States;

To borrow money on the credit of the United States;

To regulate commerce with foreign nations, and among the several States, and with the Indian tribes;

To establish an uniform rule of naturalization, and uniform laws on the subject of bankruptcies throughout the United States;

To coin money, regulate the value thereof, and of foreign coin, and fix the standard of weights and measures;

To provide for the punishment of counterfeiting the securities and current coin of the United States;

To establish post offices and post roads;

To promote the progress of science and useful arts by securing for limited times to authors and inventors the exclusive right to their respective writings and discoveries;

To constitute tribunals inferior to the Supreme Court;

To define and punish piracies and felonies committed on the high seas and offenses against the law of nations;

To declare war, grant letters of marque and reprisal, and make rules concerning captures on land and water;

To raise and support armies, but no appropriation of money to that use shall be for a longer term than two years;

To provide and maintain a navy;

To make rules for the government and regulation of the land and naval forces;

To provide for calling forth the militia to execute the laws of the Union, suppress insurrections, and repel invasions;

To provide for organizing, arming, and disciplining the militia, and for governing such part of them as may be employed in the service of the United States, reserving to the States respectively the appointment of the officers, and the authority of training the militia according to the discipline prescribed by Congress;

To exercise exclusive legislation in all cases whatsoever, over such district (not exceeding ten miles square) as may, by cession of particular States, and the acceptance of Congress, become the seat of government of the United States, and to exercise like authority over all places purchased by the consent of the legislature of the State, in which the same shall be, for erection of forts, magazines, arsenals, dockyards, and other needful buildings;—and

To make all laws which shall be necessary and proper for carrying into execution the foregoing powers, and all other powers vested by this Constitution in the government of the United States, or in any department or officer thereof.

Section 9 *The migration or importation of such persons as any of the States now existing shall think proper to admit shall not be prohibited by the Congress prior to the year 1808; but a tax or duty may be imposed on such importation, not exceeding $10 for each person.*

The privilege of the writ of habeas corpus shall not be suspended, unless when in cases of rebellion or invasion the public safety may require it.

No bill of attainder or ex post facto law shall be passed.

No capitation, or other direct, tax shall be laid, unless in proportion to the census or enumeration herein before directed to be taken.

No tax or duty shall be laid on articles exported from any State.

No preference shall be given by any regulation of commerce or revenue to the ports of one State over those of another; nor shall vessels bound to, or from, one State, be obliged to enter, clear, or pay duties in another.

No money shall be drawn from the treasury, but in consequence of appropriations made by law; and a regular statement and account of the receipts and expenditures of all public money shall be published from time to time.

No title of nobility shall be granted by the United States: and no person holding any office of profit or trust under them, shall, without the consent of the Congress, accept of any present, emolument, office, or title, of any kind whatever, from any king, prince, or foreign state.

Section 10 No State shall enter into any treaty, alliance, or confederation; grant letters of marque and reprisal; coin money; emit bills of credit; make anything but gold and silver coin a tender in payment of debts; pass any bill of attainder, ex post facto law, or law impairing the obligation of contracts, or grant any title of nobility.

No State shall, without the consent of Congress, lay any imposts or duties on imports or exports, except what may be absolutely necessary for executing its inspection laws: and the net produce of all duties and imposts, laid by any State on imports or exports, shall be for the use of the treasury of the United States; and all such laws shall be subject to the revision and control of the Congress.

No State shall, without the consent of Congress, lay any duty of tonnage, keep troops or ships of war in time of peace, enter into any agreement or compact with another State, or with a foreign power, or engage in war, unless actually invaded, or in such imminent danger as will not admit of delay.

Article II

Section 1 The executive power shall be vested in a President of the United States of America. He shall hold his office during the term of four years, and, together with the Vice-President, chosen for the same term, be elected as follows:

Each State shall appoint, in such manner as the legislature thereof may direct, a number of electors, equal to the whole number of Senators and Representatives to which the State may be entitled in the Congress; but no Senator or Representative, or person holding an office of trust or profit under the United States, shall be appointed an elector.

The electors shall meet in their respective States, and vote by ballot for two persons, of whom one at least shall not be an inhabitant of the same State with themselves. And they shall make a list of all the persons voted for, and of the number of votes for each; which list they shall sign and certify, and transmit sealed to the seat of government of the United States, directed to the President of the Senate. The President of the Senate shall, in the presence of the Senate and House of Representatives, open all the certificates, and the votes shall then be counted. The person having the greatest number of votes shall be the President, if such number be a majority of the whole number of electors appointed; and if there be more than one who have such majority, and have an equal number of votes, then the House of Representatives shall immediately choose by ballot one of them for President; and if no person have a majority, then from the five highest on the list said house shall in like manner choose the President. But in choosing the President the votes shall be taken by States, the representation from each State having one vote; a quorum for this purpose shall consist of a member or members from two-thirds of the States, and a majority of all the States shall be necessary to a choice. In every case, after the choice of the President, the person having the greatest number of votes of the electors shall be the Vice-President. But if there should remain two or more who have equal votes, the Senate shall choose from them by ballot the Vice-President.

The Congress may determine the time of choosing the electors and the day on which they shall give their votes; which day shall be the same throughout the United States.

No person except a natural-born citizen, *or a citizen of the United States at the time of the adoption of this Constitution,* shall be eligible to the office of President; neither shall any person be eligible to that office who shall not have attained to the age of thirty-five years, and been fourteen years a resident within the United States.

In cases of the removal of the President from office or of his death, resignation, or inability to discharge the powers and duties of the said office, the same shall devolve on the Vice-President, and the Congress may by law provide for the case of removal, death, resignation, or inability, both of the President and Vice-President, declaring what officer shall then act as President, and such officer shall act accordingly, until the disability be removed, or a President shall be elected.

The President shall, at stated times, receive for his services a compensation, which shall neither be increased nor diminished during the period for which he shall have been elected, and he shall not receive within that period any other emolument from the United States, or any of them.

Before he enter on the execution of his office, he shall take the following oath or affirmation:— "I do solemnly swear (or affirm) that I will faithfully execute the office of the President of the United States, and will to the best of my ability preserve, protect and defend the Constitution of the United States."

Section 2 The President shall be commander in chief of the army and navy of the United States, and of the militia of the several States, when called into the actual service of the United States; he may require the opinion, in writing, of the principal officer in each of the executive departments, upon any subject relating to the duties of their respective offices, and he shall have power to grant reprieves and pardons for offenses against the United States, except in cases of impeachment.

He shall have power, by and with the advice and consent of the senate, to make treaties, provided two-thirds of the Senators present concur; and he shall nominate, and by and with the advice and consent of the Senate, shall appoint ambassadors, other public ministers and consuls, judges of the Supreme Court, and all other officers of the United States, whose appointments are not herein otherwise provided for, and which shall be established by law: but Congress may by law vest the appointment of such inferior officers, as they think proper, in the President alone, in the courts of law, or in the heads of departments.

The President shall have power to fill up all vacancies that may happen during the recess of the Senate, by granting commissions which shall expire at the end of their next session.

Section 3 He shall from time to time give to the Congress information of the state of the Union, and recommend to their consideration such measures as he shall judge necessary and expedient; he may, on extraordinary occasions, convene both houses, or either of them, and in case of disagreement between them, with respect to the time of adjournment, he may adjourn them to such time as he shall think proper; he shall receive ambassadors and other public ministers; he shall take care that the laws be faithfully executed, and shall commission all the officers of the United States.

Section 4 The President, Vice-President and all civil officers of the United States shall be removed from office on impeachment for, and on conviction of, treason, bribery, or other high crimes and misdemeanors.

Article III

Section 1 The judicial power of the United States shall be vested in one Supreme Court, and in such inferior courts as the Congress may from time to time ordain and establish. The judges, both of the Supreme and inferior courts, shall hold their offices during good behavior, and shall, at stated times, receive for their services a compensation which shall not be diminished during their continuance in office.

Section 2 The judicial power shall extend to all cases, in law and equity, arising under this Constitution, the laws of the United States, and treaties made, or which shall be made, under their authority;—to all cases affecting ambassadors, other public ministers and consuls;—to all cases of admiralty and maritime jurisdiction;—to controversies to which the United States shall be a party;—to controversies between two or more States;—*between a State and citizens of another State;*—between citizens of different States;—between citizens of the same State claiming lands under grants of different States, and between a State, or the citizens thereof, and foreign states, citizens or subjects.

In all cases affecting ambassadors, other public ministers and consuls, and those in which a State shall be party, the Supreme Court shall have original jurisdiction. In all the other cases before mentioned, the Supreme Court shall have appellate jurisdiction, both as to law and fact, with such exceptions, and under such regulations, as the Congress shall make.

The trial of all crimes, except in cases of impeachment, shall be by jury; and such trial shall be held in the state where said crimes shall have been committed; but when not committed within any State, the trial shall be at such place or places as the Congress may by law have directed.

Section 3 Treason against the United States shall consist only in levying war against them, or in adhering to their enemies, giving them aid and comfort. No person shall be convicted of treason unless on the testimony of two witnesses to the same overt act, or on confession in open court.

The Congress shall have power to declare the punishment of treason, but no attainder of treason shall work corruption of blood, or forfeiture except during the life of the person attained.

Article IV

Section 1 Full faith and credit shall be given in each State to the public acts, records, and judicial proceedings of every other State. And the Congress may by general laws prescribe the manner in which such acts, records, and proceedings shall be proved, and the effect thereof.

Section 2 The citizens of each State shall be entitled to all privileges and immunities of citizens in the several States.

A person charged in any State with treason, felony, or other crime, who shall flee from justice, and be found in another State, shall on demand of the executive authority of the State from which he fled, be delivered up, to be removed to the State having jurisdiction of the crime.

No person held to service or labor in one State, under the laws thereof, escaping into another, shall, in consequence of any law or regulation therein, be discharged from such service or labor, but shall be delivered up on claim of the party to whom such service or labor may be due.

Section 3 New States may be admitted by the Congress into this Union; but no new State shall be formed or erected within the jurisdiction of any other State; nor any State be formed by the junction of two or more States, or parts of States, without the consent of the legislatures of the States concerned as well as of the Congress.

The Congress shall have power to dispose of and make all needful rules and regulations respecting the territory or other property belonging to the United States; and nothing in this Constitution shall be so construed as to prejudice any claims of the United States, or of any particular State.

Section 4 The United States shall guarantee to every State in this Union a republican form of government, and shall protect each of them against invasion; and on application of the legislature, or of the executive (when the legislature cannot be convened), against domestic violence.

Article V

The Congress, whenever two-thirds of both houses shall deem it necessary, shall propose amendments to this Constitution, or, on the application of the legislatures of two-thirds of the several States, shall call a convention for proposing amendments, which, in either case, shall be valid to all intents and purposes, as part of this Constitution, when ratified by the legislatures of three-fourths of the several States, or by conventions in three-fourths thereof, as the one or the other mode of ratification may be proposed by the Congress; provided *that no amendments which may be made prior to the year one thousand eight hundred and eight shall in any manner affect the first and fourth clauses in the ninth section of the first article;* and that no State, without its consent, shall be deprived of its equal suffrage in the Senate.

Article VI

All debts contracted and engagements entered into, before the adoption of this Constitution, shall be as valid against the United States under this Constitution, as under the Confederation.

This Constitution, and the laws of the United States which shall be made in pursuance thereof; and all treaties made, or which shall be made, under the authority of the United States, shall be the supreme law of the land; and the judges in every State shall be bound thereby, anything in the Constitution or laws of any State to the contrary notwithstanding.

The Senators and Representatives before mentioned, and the members of the several State legislatures, and all executive and judicial officers, both of the United States and of the several States, shall be bound by oath or affirmation to support this Constitution; but no religious test shall ever be required as a qualification to any office or public trust under the United States.

Article VII

The ratification of the conventions of nine States shall be sufficient for the establishment of this Constitution between the States so ratifying the same.

Done in Convention by the unanimous consent of the States present, the seventeenth day of September in the year of our Lord one thousand seven hundred and eighty-seven and of the Independence of the United States of America the twelfth. In witness whereof we have hereunto subscribed our names.

GEORGE WASHINGTON
and thirty-eight others

Amendments to the Constitution*

Amendment I

Congress shall make no law respecting an establishment of religion, or prohibiting the free exercise thereof; or abridging the freedom of speech, or of the press; or the right of the people peaceably to assemble, and to petition the government for a redress of grievances.

Amendment II

A well-regulated militia being necessary to the security of a free State, the right of the people to keep and bear arms shall not be infringed.

Amendment III

No soldier shall, in time of peace, be quartered in any house without the consent of the owner, nor in time of war, but in a manner to be prescribed by law.

Amendment IV

The right of the people to be secure in their persons, houses, papers, and effects, against unreasonable searches and seizures, shall not be violated, and no warrants shall issue but upon probable cause, supported by oath or affirmation, and particularly describing the place to be searched, and the persons or things to be seized.

Amendment V

No person shall be held to answer for a capital, or otherwise infamous crime, unless on a presentment or indictment of a grand jury, except in cases arising

*The first ten amendments (the Bill of Rights) were adopted in 1791.

in the land or naval forces, or in the militia, when in actual service in time of war or public danger; nor shall any person be subject for the same offense to be twice put in jeopardy of life or limb; nor shall be compelled in any criminal case to be a witness against himself, nor be deprived of life, liberty, or property, without due process of law; nor shall private property be taken for public use without just compensation.

Amendment VI

In all criminal prosecutions, the accused shall enjoy the right to a speedy and public trial, by an impartial jury of the State and district wherein the crime shall have been committed, which district shall have been previously ascertained by law, and to be informed of the nature and cause of the accusation; to be confronted with the witnesses against him; to have compulsory process for obtaining witnesses in his favor, and to have the assistance of counsel for his defense.

Amendment VII

In suits at common law, where the value in controversy shall exceed twenty dollars, the right of trial by jury shall be preserved, and no fact tried by a jury shall be otherwise reexamined in any court of the United States, than according to the rules of the common law.

Amendment VIII

Excessive bail shall not be required, nor excessive fines imposed, nor cruel and unusual punishments inflicted.

Amendment IX

The enumeration in the Constitution, of certain rights, shall not be construed to deny or disparage others retained by the people.

Amendment X

The powers not delegated to the United States by the Constitution, nor prohibited by it to the States, are reserved to the States respectively, or to the people.

Amendment XI   *[Adopted 1798]*

The judicial power of the United States shall not be construed to extend to any suit in law or equity, commenced or prosecuted against one of the United States by citizens of another State, or by citizens or subjects of any foreign State.

Amendment XII   *[Adopted 1804]*

The electors shall meet in their respective States, and vote by ballot for President and Vice-President, one of whom, at least, shall not be an inhabitant of the same State with themselves; they shall name in their ballots the person voted for as President, and in distinct ballots the person voted for as Vice-President, and they shall make distinct lists of all persons voted for as President, and of all persons voted for as Vice-President, and of the number of votes for each, which lists they shall sign and certify, and transmit sealed to the seat of government of the United States, directed to the President of the Senate;—the President of the Senate shall, in the presence of the Senate and House of Representatives, open all the certificates and the votes shall then be counted;—the person having the greatest number of votes for President shall be the President, if such number be a majority of the whole number of electors appointed; and if no person have such majority, then from the persons having the highest numbers not exceeding three on the list of those voted for as President, the House of Representatives shall choose immediately, by ballot, the President. But in choosing the President, the votes shall be taken by States, the representation from each State having one vote; a quorum for this purpose shall consist of a member or members from two-thirds of the States, and a majority of all the states shall be necessary to a choice. And if the House of Representatives shall not choose a President whenever the right of choice shall devolve upon them, before *the fourth day of March* next following, then the Vice-President shall act as President, as in the case of the death or other constitutional disability of the President.

The person having the greatest number of votes as Vice-President shall be the Vice-President, if such number be a majority of the whole number of electors appointed; and if no person have a majority, then from the two highest numbers on the list the Senate shall choose the Vice-President; a quorum for the purpose shall consist of two-thirds of the whole number of Senators, and a majority of the whole number shall be necessary to a choice. But no person constitutionally ineligible to the office of President shall be eligible to that of Vice-President of the United States.

Amendment XIII *[Adopted 1865]*

Section 1 Neither slavery nor involuntary servitude, except as a punishment for crime whereof the party shall have been duly convicted, shall exist within the United States, or any place subject to their jurisdiction.

Section 2 Congress shall have the power to enforce this article by appropriate legislation.

Amendment XIV *[Adopted 1868]*

Section 1 All persons born or naturalized in the United States, and subject to the jurisdiction thereof, are citizens of the United States and of the State wherein they reside. No State shall make or enforce any law which shall abridge the privileges or immunities of citizens of the United States; nor shall any State deprive any person of life, liberty, or property, without due process of law; nor deny to any person within its jurisdiction the equal protection of the laws.

Section 2 Representatives shall be apportioned among the several States according to their respective numbers, counting the whole number of persons in each State, excluding Indians not taxed. But when the right to vote at any election for the choice of electors for President and Vice-President of the United States, Representatives in Congress, the executive and judicial officers of a State, or the members of the legislature thereof, is denied to any of the male inhabitants of such State, being twenty-one years of age and citizens of the United States, or in any way abridged, except for participation in rebellion, or other crime, the basis of representation therein shall be reduced in the proportion which the number of such male citizens shall bear to the whole number of male citizens twenty-one years of age in such State.

Section 3 No person shall be a Senator or Representative in Congress, or elector of President and Vice-President, or hold any office, civil or military, under the United States, or under any State, who, having previously taken an oath, as a member of Congress, or as an officer of the United States, or as a member of any State legislature, or as an executive or judicial officer of any State, to support the Constitution of the United States, shall have engaged in insurrection or rebellion against the same, or given aid or comfort to the enemies thereof. Congress may, by a vote of two-thirds of each house, remove such disability.

Section 4 The validity of the public debt of the United States, authorized by law, including debts incurred for payment of pensions and bounties for services in suppressing insurrection or rebellion, shall not be questioned. But neither the United States nor any State shall assume or pay any debt or obligation incurred in aid of insurrection or rebellion against the United States, or any claim for the loss of emancipation of any slave; but all such debts, obligations, and claims shall be held illegal and void.

Section 5 The Congress shall have power to enforce, by appropriate legislation, the provisions of this article.

Amendment XV   *[Adopted 1870]*

Section 1   The right of citizens of the United States to vote shall not be denied or abridged by the United States or by any State on account of race, color, or previous condition of servitude.

Section 2   The Congress shall have power to enforce this article by appropriate legislation.

Amendment XVI   *[Adopted 1913]*

The Congress shall have power to lay and collect taxes on incomes, from whatever source derived, without apportionment among the several States, and without regard to any census or enumeration.

Amendment XVII   *[Adopted 1913]*

Section 1   The Senate of the United States shall be composed of two Senators from each State, elected by the people thereof, for six years; and each Senator shall have one vote. The electors in each State shall have the qualifications requisite for electors of [voters for] the most numerous branch of the State legislatures.

Section 2   When vacancies happen in the representation of any State in the Senate, the executive authority of such State shall issue writs of election to fill such vacancies: Provided, that the Legislature of any State may empower the executive thereof to make temporary appointments until the people fill the vacancies by election as the Legislature may direct.

Section 3   This amendment shall not be so construed as to affect the election or term of any Senator chosen before it becomes valid as part of the Constitution.

Amendment XVIII *[Adopted 1919, repealed 1933]*

Section 1   After one year from the ratification of this article the manufacture, sale or transportation of intoxicating liquors within, the importation thereof into, or the exportation thereof from the United States and all territory subject to the jurisdiction thereof, for beverage purposes, is hereby prohibited.

Section 2   The Congress and the several States shall have concurrent power to enforce this article by appropriate legislation.

Section 3   This article shall be inoperative unless it shall have been ratified as an amendment to the Constitution by the legislatures of the several States, as provided by the Constitution, within seven years from the date of the submission thereof to the States by the Congress.

Amendment XIX   *[Adopted 1920]*

Section 1   The right of citizens of the United States to vote shall not be denied or abridged by the United States or by any State on account of sex.

Section 2   The Congress shall have power to enforce this article by appropriate legislation.

Amendment XX   *[Adopted 1933]*

Section 1   The terms of the President and Vice-President shall end at noon on the 20th day of January, and the terms of Senators and Representatives at noon on the 3d day of January, of the years in which such terms would have ended if this article had not been ratified; and the terms of their successors shall then begin.

Section 2   The Congress shall assemble at least once in every year, and such meetings shall begin at noon on the 3d day of January, unless they shall by law appoint a different day.

Section 3   If, at the time fixed for the beginning of the term of the President, the President-elect shall have died, the Vice-President-elect shall become President. If a President shall not have been chosen before the time fixed for the beginning of his term, or if the President-elect shall have failed to qualify, then the Vice-President-elect shall act as President until a President shall have qualified; and the Congress may by law provide for the case wherein neither a President-elect nor a Vice-President-elect shall have qualified, declaring who shall then act as President, or the manner in which one who is to act shall be selected, and such persons shall act accordingly until a President or Vice-President shall have qualified.

Section 4   The Congress may by law provide for the case of the death of any of the persons from whom the House of Representatives may choose a President whenever the right of choice shall have devolved upon them, and for the case of the death of any of the persons from whom the Senate may choose a Vice-President whenever the right of choice shall have devolved upon them.

Section 5   Sections 1 and 2 shall take effect on the 15th day of October following the ratification of this article.

Section 6   This article shall be inoperative unless it shall have been ratified as an amendment to the Constitution by the Legislatures of three-fourths of the several States within seven years from the date of its submission.

Amendment XXI   *[Adopted 1933]*

Section 1   The eighteenth article of amendment to the Constitution of the United States is hereby repealed.

Section 2   The transportation or importation into any State, Territory, or Possession of the United States for delivery or use therein of intoxicating liquors, in violation of the laws thereof, is hereby prohibited.

Section 3   This article shall be inoperative unless it shall have been ratified as an amendment to the Constitution by conventions in the several States, as provided in the Constitution, within seven years

from the date of submission thereof to the States by the Congress.

Amendment XXII   *[Adopted 1951]*

Section 1   No person shall be elected to the office of President more than twice, and no person who has held the office of President, or acted as President, for more than two years of a term to which some other person was elected President shall be elected to the office of President more than once. But this article shall not apply to any person holding the office of President when this article was proposed by the Congress, and shall not prevent any person who may be holding the office of President, or acting as President, during the term within which this article becomes operative from holding the office of President or acting as President during the remainder of such term.

Section 2   This article shall be inoperative unless it shall have been ratified as an amendment to the Constitution by the legislatures of three-fourths of the several States within seven years from the date of its submission to the States by the Congress.

Amendment XXIII   *[Adopted 1961]*

Section 1   The District constituting the seat of Government of the United States shall appoint in such manner as the Congress may direct:

A number of electors of President and Vice-President equal to the whole number of Senators and Representatives in Congress to which the District would be entitled if it were a State, but in no event more than the least populous State; they shall be in addition to those appointed by the States, but they shall be considered for the purposes of the election of President and Vice-President, to be electors appointed by a State; and they shall meet in the District and perform such duties as provided by the twelfth article of amendment.

Section 2   The Congress shall have the power to enforce this article by appropriate legislation.

Amendment XXIV   *[Adopted 1964]*

Section 1   The right of citizens of the United States to vote in any primary or other election for President or Vice-President, for electors for President or Vice-President, or for Senator or Representative in Congress, shall not be denied or abridged by the United States or any State by reason of failure to pay any poll tax or other tax.

Section 2   The Congress shall have the power to enforce this article by appropriate legislation.

Amendment XXV   *[Adopted 1967]*

Section 1   In case of the removal of the President from office or of his death or resignation, the Vice-President shall become President.

Section 2   Whenever there is a vacancy in the office of the Vice-President, the President shall nominate a Vice-President who shall take office upon confirmation by a majority vote of both Houses of Congress.

Section 3   Whenever the President transmits to the President pro tempore of the Senate and the Speaker of the House of Representatives his written declaration that he is unable to discharge the powers and duties of his office, and until he transmits to them a written declaration to the contrary, such powers and duties shall be discharged by the Vice-President as Acting President.

Section 4   Whenever the Vice-President and a majority of either the principal officers of the executive departments or of such other body as Congress may by law provide, transmit to the President pro tempore of the Senate and the Speaker of the House of Representatives their written declaration that the President is unable to discharge the powers and duties of his office, the Vice-President shall immediately assume the powers and duties of the office as Acting President.

Thereafter, when the President transmits to the President pro tempore of the Senate and the Speaker of the House of Representatives his written declaration that no inability exists, he shall resume the powers and duties of his office unless the Vice-President and a majority of either the principal officers of the executive department(s) or of such other body as Congress may by law provide, transmit within four days to the President pro tempore of the Senate and the Speaker of the House of Representatives their written declaration that the President is unable to discharge the powers and duties of his office. Thereupon Congress shall decide the issue, assembling within forty-eight hours for that purpose if not in session. If the Congress, within twenty-one days after receipt of the latter written declaration, or, if Congress is not in session, within twenty-one days after Congress is required to assemble, determines by two-thirds vote of both Houses that the President is unable to discharge the powers and duties of his office, the Vice-President shall continue to discharge the same as Acting President; otherwise, the President shall resume the powers and duties of his office.

Amendment XXVI   *[Adopted 1971]*

Section 1   The right of citizens of the United States, who are eighteen years of age or older, to vote shall not be denied or abridged by the United States or by any State on account of age.

Section 2   The Congress shall have power to enforce this article by appropriate legislation.

Amendment XXVII   *[Adopted 1992]*

No law, varying the compensation for the services of the senators and representatives shall take effect, until an election of representatives shall have intervened.

Federalist No. 10, 1787

To the People of the State of New York: Among the numerous advantages promised by a well-constructed union, none deserves to be more accurately developed than its tendency to break and control the violence of faction. The friend of popular governments, never finds himself so much alarmed for their character and fate, as when he contemplates their propensity to this dangerous vice. He will not fail, therefore, to set a due value on any plan which, without violating the principles to which he is attached, provides a proper cure for it. The instability, injustice, and confusion introduced into the public councils, have, in truth, been the mortal diseases under which popular governments have everywhere perished; as they continue to be the favourite and fruitful topics from which the adversaries to liberty derive their most specious declamations. The valuable improvements made by the American constitutions on the popular models, both ancient and modern, cannot certainly be too much admired; but it would be an unwarrantable partiality, to contend that they have as effectually obviated the danger on this side, as was wished and expected. Complaints are everywhere heard from our most considerate and virtuous citizens, equally the friends of public and private faith, and of public and personal liberty, that our governments are too unstable; that the public good is disregarded in the conflicts of rival parties; and that measures are too often decided, not according to the rules of justice, and the rights of the minor party, but by the superior force of an interested and overbearing majority. However anxiously we may wish that these complaints had no foundation, the evidence of known facts will not permit us to deny that they are in some degree true. It will be found, indeed, on a candid review of our situation, that some of the distresses under which we labour have been erroneously charged on the operation of our governments; but it will be found, at the same time, that other causes will not alone account for many of our heaviest misfortunes; and, particularly, for that prevailing and increasing distrust of public engagements, and alarm for private rights, which are echoed from one end of the continent to the other. These must be chiefly, if not wholly, effects of the unsteadiness and injustice, with which a factious spirit has tainted our public administrations.

By a faction, I understand a number of citizens, whether amounting to a majority or minority of the whole, who are united and actuated by some common impulse of passion, or of interest, adverse to the rights of other citizens, or to the permanent and aggregate interests of the community.

There are two methods of curing the mischiefs of faction: The one, by removing its causes; the other, by controlling its effects.

There are again two methods of removing the causes of faction: The one, by destroying the liberty which is essential to its existence; the other, by giving to every citizen the same opinions, the same passions, and the same interests.

It could never be more truly said, than of the first remedy, that it was worse than the disease. Liberty is to faction what air is to fire, an aliment without which it instantly expires. But it could not be a less folly to abolish liberty, which is essential to political life, because it nourishes faction, than it would be to wish the annihilation of air, which is essential to animal life, because it imparts to fire its destructive agency.

The second expedient is as impracticable, as the first would be unwise. As long as the reason of man continues fallible, and he is at liberty to exercise it, different opinions will be formed. As long as the connection subsists between his reason and his self-love, his opinions and his passions will have a reciprocal influence on each other; and the former will be objects to which the latter will attach themselves. The diversity in the faculties of men, from which the rights of property originate, is not less an insuperable obstacle to an uniformity of interests. The protection of these faculties is the first object of government. From the protection of different and unequal faculties of acquiring property, the possession of different degrees and kinds of property immediately results; and from the influence of these on the sentiments and views of the respective proprietors, ensues a division of the society into different interests and parties.

The latent causes of faction are thus sown in the nature of man; and we see them everywhere brought into different degrees of activity, according to the different circumstances of civil society. A zeal for different opinions concerning religion, concerning government, and many other points, as well as of speculation as of practice; an attachment to different leaders ambitiously contending for preeminence and power; or to persons of other descriptions whose fortunes have been interesting to the human passions, have, in turn, divided mankind into parties, inflamed them with mutual animosity, and rendered them much more disposed to vex and oppress each other, than to cooperate for their common good. So strong is this propensity of mankind, to fall into mutual animosities, that where no substantial occasion presents itself, the most frivolous and fanciful distinctions have been sufficient to kindle their unfriendly passions and excite their most violent conflicts. But the most common and durable source of factions, has been the various and unequal distribution of property. Those who hold, and those who are without property, have ever formed distinct interests in society. Those who are creditors, and those who are debtors, fall under a like discrimination. A landed interest, a manufacturing interest, a mercantile interest, a moneyed interest, with many lesser interests, grow up of necessity in civilized nations, and divide them into different classes, actuated by different sentiments and views. The regulation of these various and interfering interests forms the principal task of modern legislation, and involves the spirit of the party and faction in the necessary and ordinary operations of the government.

No man is allowed to be a judge in his own cause; because his interest will certainly bias his judgment, and, not improbably, corrupt his integrity. With equal, nay, with greater reason, a body of men are unfit to be both judges and parties at the same time; yet what are many of the most important acts of legislation, but so many judicial determinations, not indeed concerning the right of single persons, but concerning the rights of large bodies of citizens? And what are the different classes of legislators, but advocates and parties to the causes which they determine? Is a law proposed concerning private debts? It is a question to which the creditors are parties on one side, and the debtors on the other. Justice ought to hold the balance between them. Yet the parties are, and must be, themselves the judges; and the most numerous party, or, in other words, the

most powerful faction, must be expected to prevail. Shall domestic manufactures be encouraged, and in what degree, by restrictions on foreign manufactures? are questions which would be differently decided by the landed and the manufacturing classes; and probably by neither with a sole regard to justice and the public good. The apportionment of taxes, on the various descriptions of property, is an act which seems to require the most exact impartiality; yet there is, perhaps, no legislative act, in which greater opportunity and temptation are given to a predominant party to trample on the rules of justice. Every shilling, with which they overburden the inferior number, is a shilling saved to their own pockets.

It is in vain to say, that enlightened statesmen will be able to adjust these clashing interests, and render them all subservient to the public good. Enlightened statesmen will not always be at the helm: nor, in many cases, can such an adjustment be made at all, without taking into view indirect and remote considerations, which will rarely prevail over the immediate interest which one party may find in disregarding the rights of another, or the good of the whole.

The inference to which we are brought is, that the *causes* of faction cannot be removed; and that relief is only to be sought in the means of controlling its *effects*.

If a faction consists of less than a majority, relief is supplied by the republican principle, which enables the majority to defeat its sinister views, by regular vote. It may clog the administration, it may convulse the society; but it will be unable to execute and mask its violence under the forms of the constitution. When a majority is included in a faction, the form of popular government, on the other hand, enables it to sacrifice to its ruling passion or interest, both the public good and the rights of other citizens. To secure the public good, and private rights, against the danger of such a faction, and at the same time to preserve the spirit and the form of popular government, is then the great object to which our inquiries are directed. Let me add, that it is the great desideratum, by which alone this form of government can be rescued from the opprobrium under which it has so long laboured, and be recommended to the esteem and adoption of mankind.

By what means is this object attainable? Evidently by one of two only. Either the existence of the same passion or interest in a majority, at the same time, must be prevented; or the majority, having such coexistent passion or interest, must be rendered, by their number and local situation, unable to concert and carry into effect schemes of oppression. If the impulse and the opportunity be suffered to coincide, we well know that neither moral nor religious motives can be relied on as an adequate control. They are not found to be such on the injustice and violence of individuals, and lose their efficacy in proportion to the number combined together; that is, in proportion as their efficacy becomes needful.

From this view of the subject, it may be concluded, that a pure democracy, by which I mean a society consisting of a small number of citizens, who assemble and administer the government in person, can admit of no cure for the mischiefs of faction. A common passion or interest will, in almost every case, be felt by a majority of the whole; a communication and concert, results from the form of government itself; and there is nothing to check the inducements to sacrifice the weaker party, or an obnoxious individual. Hence, it is, that such democracies have ever been spectacles of turbulence and contention; have ever been found incompatible with personal security, or the rights of property; and have in general been as short in their lives, as they have been violent in their deaths. Theoretic politicians, who have patronized this species of government, have erroneously supposed, that by reducing mankind to a perfect equality in their political rights, they would, at the same time, be perfectly equalized and assimilated in their possessions, their opinions, and their passions.

A republic, by which I mean a government in which the scheme of representation takes place, opens a different prospect, and promises the cure for which we are seeking. Let us examine the points in which it varies from pure democracy, and we shall comprehend both the nature of the cure and the efficacy which it must derive from the union.

The two great points of difference, between a democracy and a republic, are, first, the delegation of the government, in the latter, to a small number of citizens, elected by the rest; secondly, the greatest number of citizens, and greater sphere of country, over which the latter may be extended.

The effect of the first difference is, on the one hand, to refine and enlarge the public views, by passing them through the medium of a chosen body of citizens, whose wisdom may best discern the true interest of their country, and whose patriotism and love of justice, will be least likely to sacrifice it to temporary or partial considerations. Under such a regulation, it may well happen, that the public voice, pronounced by the representatives of the people, will be more consonant to the public good, than if pronounced by the people themselves, convened for the purpose. On the other hand the effect may be inverted. Men of factious tempers, of local prejudices, or of sinister designs, may by intrigue, by corruption, or by other means, first obtain the suffrages, and then betray the interest of the people. The question resulting is, whether small or extensive republics are most favourable to the election of proper guardians of the public weal; and it is clearly decided in favour of the latter by two obvious considerations.

In the first place, it is to be remarked that, however small the republic may be, the representatives must be raised to a certain number, in order to guard against the cabals of a few; and that however large it may be, they must be limited to a certain number, in order to guard against the confusion of a multitude. Hence, the number of representatives in the two cases not being in proportion to that of the constituents, and being proportionally greatest in the small republic, it follows, that if the proportion of fit characters be not less in the large than in the small republic, the former will present a greater option, and consequently a greater probability of a fit choice.

In the next place, as each representative will be chosen by a greater number of citizens in the large than in the small republic, it will be more difficult for unworthy candidates to practise with success the vicious arts, by which elections are too often carried;

and the suffrages of the people being more free, will be more likely to centre in men who possess the most attractive merit, and the most diffusive and established characters.

It must be confessed, that in this, as in most other cases, there is a mean, on both sides of which inconveniences will be found to lie. By enlarging too much the number of electors, you render the representatives too little acquainted with all their local circumstances and lesser interests; as by reducing it too much, you render him unduly attached to these, and too little fit to comprehend and pursue great and national objects. The federal constitution forms a happy combination in this respect; the great and aggregate interests being referred to the national, the local and particular to the state legislatures.

The other point of difference is, the greater number of citizens, and extent of territory, which may be brought within the compass of republican, than of democratic government; and it is this circumstance principally which renders factious combinations less to be dreaded in the former, than in the latter. The smaller the society, the fewer probably will be the distinct parties and interests composing it; the fewer the distinct parties and interests, the more frequently will a majority be found of the same party; and the smaller the number of individuals composing a majority, and the smaller the compass within which they are placed, the more easily will they concert and execute their plans of oppression. Extend the sphere, and you take in a greater variety of parties and interests; you make it less probable that a majority of the whole will have a common motive to invade the rights of other citizens; or if such a common motive exists, it will be more difficult for all who feel it to discover their own strength, and to act in unison with each other. Besides other impediments, it may be remarked, that where there is a consciousness of unjust or dishonourable purposes, communication is always checked by distrust, in proportion to the number whose concurrence is necessary.

Hence, it clearly appears, that the same advantage, which a republic has over a democracy, in controlling the effects of faction, is enjoyed by a large over a small republic,—is enjoyed by the union over the states composing it. Does this advantage consist in the substitution of representatives, whose enlightened views and virtuous sentiments render them superior to local prejudices, and to schemes of injustice? It will not be denied that the representation of the union will be most likely to possess these requisite endowments. Does it consist in the greater security afforded by a greater variety of parties, against the event of any one party being able to outnumber and oppress the rest? In an equal degree does the increased variety of parties, comprised within the union, increase the security? Does it, in fine, consist in the greater obstacles opposed to the concert and accomplishment of the secret wishes of an unjust and interested majority? Here, again, the extent of the union gives it the most palpable advantage.

The influence of factious leaders may kindle a flame within their particular states, but will be unable to spread a general conflagration through the other states; a religious sect may degenerate into a political faction in a part of the confederacy; but the variety of sects dispersed over the entire face of it, must secure the national councils against any danger from that source: a rage for paper money, for an abolition of debts, for an equal division of property, or for any other improper or wicked project, will be less apt to pervade the whole body of the union than a particular member of it; in the same proportion as such a malady is more likely to taint a particular county or district, than an entire state.

In the extent and proper structure of the union, therefore, we behold a republican remedy for the diseases most incident to republican government. And according to the degree of pleasure and pride we feel in being republicans, ought to be our zeal in cherishing the spirit, and supporting the character of federalists.

JAMES MADISON

Federalist No. 51, 1788

To the People of the State of New York: To what expedient then shall we finally resort for maintaining in practice the necessary partition of power among the several departments, as laid down in the constitution? The only answer that can be given is, that as all these exterior provisions are found to be inadequate, the defect must be supplied, by so contriving the interior structure of the government, as that its several constituent parts may, by their mutual relations, be the means of keeping each other in their proper places. Without presuming to undertake a full development of this important idea, I will hazard a few general observations, which may perhaps place it in a clearer light, and enable us to form a more correct judgment of the principles and structure of the government planned by the convention.

In order to lay a due foundation for that separate and distinct exercise of the different powers of government, which to a certain extent, is admitted on all hands to be essential to the preservation of liberty, it is evident that each department should have a will of its own; and consequently should be so constituted, that the members of each should have as little agency as possible in the appointment of the members of the others. Were this principle rigorously adhered to, it would require that all the appointments for the supreme executive, legislative, and judiciary magistracies, should be drawn from the same fountain of authority, the people, through channels, having no communication whatever with one another. Perhaps such a plan of constructing the several departments would be less difficult in practice than it may in contemplation appear. Some difficulties however, and some additional expense, would attend the execution of it. Some deviations therefore from the principle must be admitted. In the constitution of the judiciary department in particular, it might be inexpedient to insist rigorously on the principle; first, because peculiar qualifications being essential in the members, the primary consideration ought to be to select that mode of choice, which best secures these qualifications; secondly, because the permanent tenure by which the appointments are held in that department, must soon destroy all sense of dependence on the authority conferring them.

It is equally evident that the members of each department should be as little dependent as possible on those of the others, for the emoluments annexed to their offices. Were the executive magistrate, or the judges, not independent of the legislature in this particular, their independence in every other would be merely nominal.

But the great security against a gradual concentration of the several powers in the same department, consists in giving to those who administer each department, the necessary constitutional means, and personal motives, to resist encroachments of the others. The provision for defense must in this, as in all other cases, be made commensurate to the danger of attack. Ambition must be made to counteract ambition. The interest of the man must be connected with the constitutional rights of the place. It may be a reflection on human nature, that such devices should be necessary to control the abuses of government. But what is government itself but the greatest of all reflections on human nature? If men were angels, no government would be necessary. If angels were to govern men, neither external nor internal controls on government would be necessary. In framing a government which is to be administered by men over men, the great difficulty lies in this: You must first enable the government to control the governed; and in the next place, oblige it to control itself. A dependence on the people is no doubt the primary control on the government; but experience has taught mankind the necessity of auxiliary precautions.

This policy of supplying by opposite and rival interests, the defect of better motives, might be traced through the whole system of human affairs, private as well as public. We see it particularly displayed in all the subordinate distributions of power; where the constant aim is to divide and arrange the several offices in such a manner as that each may be a check on the other; that the private interest of every individual, may be a sentinel over the public rights. These inventions of prudence cannot be less requisite in the distribution of the supreme powers of the state.

But it is not possible to give to each department an equal power of self defense. In republican government the legislative authority, necessarily, predominates. The remedy for this inconveniency is, to divide the legislature into different branches; and to render them by different modes of election, and different principles of action, as little connected with each other, as the nature of their common functions, and their common dependence on the society, will admit. It may even be necessary to guard against dangerous encroachments by still further precautions. As the weight of the legislative authority requires that it should be thus divided, the weakness of the executive may require, on the other hand, that it should be fortified. An absolute negative, on the legislature, appears at first view to be the natural defense with which the executive magistrate should be armed. But perhaps it would be neither altogether safe, nor alone sufficient. On ordinary occasions, it might not be exerted with the requisite firmness; and on extraordinary occasions, it might be perfidiously abused. May not this defect of an absolute negative be supplied, by some qualified connection between this weaker department, and the weaker branch of the stronger department, by which the latter may be led to support the constitutional rights of the former, without being too much detached from the rights of its own department?

If the principles on which these observations are founded be just, as I persuade myself they are, and they be applied as a criterion, to the several state constitutions, and to the federal constitution, it will be found, that if the latter does not perfectly correspond with them, the former are infinitely less able to bear such a test.

There are moreover two considerations particularly applicable to the federal system of America, which place that system in a very interesting point of view.

First. In a single republic, all the power surrendered by the people, is submitted to the administration of a single government; and usurpations are guarded against by a division of the government into distinct and separate departments. In the compound republic of America, the power surrendered by the people, is first divided between two distinct governments, and then the portion allotted to each, sub-divided among distinct and separate departments. Hence a double security arises to the rights of the people. The different governments will control each other; at the same time that each will be controlled by itself.

Second. It is of great importance in a republic, not only to guard the society against the oppression of its rulers; but to guard one part of the society against the injustice of the other part. Different interests necessarily exist in different classes of citizens. If a majority be united by a common interest, the rights of the minority will be insecure. There are but two methods of providing against this evil: The one by creating a will in the community independent of the majority, that is, of the society itself; the other by comprehending in the society so many separate descriptions of citizens, as will render an unjust combination of a majority of the whole, very improbable, if not impracticable. The first method prevails in all governments possessing an hereditary or self appointed authority. This at best is but a precarious security; because a power independent of the society may as well espouse the unjust views of the major, as the rightful interests, of the minor party, and may possibly be turned against both parties. The second method will be exemplified in the federal republic of the United States. While all authority in it will be derived from and dependent on the society, the society itself will be broken into so many parts, interests and classes of citizens, that the rights of individuals or of the minority, will be in little danger from interested combinations of the majority. In a free government, the security for civil rights must be the same as for religious rights. It consists in the one case in the multiplicity of interests, and in the other in the multiplicity of sects. The degree of security in both cases will depend on the number of interests and sects; and this may be presumed to depend on the extent of country and number of people comprehended under the same government. This view of the subject must particularly recommend a proper federal system to all the sincere and considerate friends of republican government: Since it shows that in exact proportion as the territory of the union may be formed into more circumscribed confederacies or states, oppressive combinations of a majority will be facilitated; the best security under the republican form, for the rights of every class of citizens, will be diminished; and consequently, the stability and independence of some member of the government, the only other security, must be proportionally increased. Justice is the end of government. It is the end of civil society. It ever has been, and ever will be pursued, until it be obtained, or until liberty be lost in the pursuit. In a society under the forms of which the stronger faction can readily unite and oppress the weaker, anarchy may as truly be said to reign, as in a state of nature where the weaker individual is not secured against the violence of the stronger: And as in the latter state even the stronger individuals are prompted by the uncertainty of their condition, to submit to a government which may protect the weak as well as themselves: So in the former state, will the more powerful factions or parties be gradually induced by a like motive, to which for a government which will protect all parties, the weaker as well as the more powerful. It can be little doubted, that if the state of Rhode Island was separated from the confederacy, and left to itself, the insecurity of rights under the popular form of government within such narrow limits, would be displayed by such reiterated oppressions of factious majorities, that some power altogether independent of the people would soon be called for by the voice of the very factions whose misrule had proved the necessity of it. In the extended republic of the United States, and among the great variety of interests, parties and sects which it embraces, a coalition of a majority of the whole society could seldom take place on any other principles than those of justice and the general good; and there being thus less danger to a minor from the will of the major party, there must be less pretext also, to provide for the security of the former, by introducing into the government a will not dependent on the latter; or in other words, a will independent of the society itself. It is no less certain that it is important, notwithstanding the contrary opinions which have been entertained, that the larger the society, provided it lie within a practicable sphere, the more duly capable it will be of self government. And happily for the *republican cause*, the practicable sphere may be carried to a very great extent, by a judicious modification and mixture of the *federal principle*.

JAMES MADISON

Presidents of the
United States

		Party	Term
1.	George Washington (1732–1799)	Federalist	1789–1797
2.	John Adams (1735–1826)	Federalist	1797–1801
3.	Thomas Jefferson (1743–1826)	Democratic-Republican	1801–1809
4.	James Madison (1751–1836)	Democratic-Republican	1809–1817
5.	James Monroe (1758–1831)	Democratic-Republican	1817–1825
6.	John Quincy Adams (1767–1848)	Democratic-Republican	1825–1829
7.	Andrew Jackson (1767–1845)	Democratic	1829–1837
8.	Martin Van Buren (1782–1862)	Democratic	1837–1841
9.	William Henry Harrison (1773–1841)	Whig	1841
10.	John Tyler (1790–1862)	Whig	1841–1845
11.	James K. Polk (1795–1849)	Democratic	1845–1849
12.	Zachary Taylor (1784–1850)	Whig	1849–1850
13.	Millard Fillmore (1800–1874)	Whig	1850–1853
14.	Franklin Pierce (1804–1869)	Democratic	1853–1857
15.	James Buchanan (1791–1868)	Democratic	1857–1861
16.	Abraham Lincoln (1809–1865)	Republican	1861–1865
17.	Andrew Johnson (1808–1875)	Union	1865–1869
18.	Ulysses S. Grant (1822–1885)	Republican	1869–1877
19.	Rutherford B. Hayes (1822–1893)	Republican	1877–1881
20.	James A. Garfield (1831–1881)	Republican	1881
21.	Chester A. Arthur (1830–1886)	Republican	1881–1885
22.	Grover Cleveland (1837–1908)	Democratic	1885–1889
23.	Benjamin Harrison (1833–1901)	Republican	1889–1893
24.	Grover Cleveland (1837–1908)	Democratic	1893–1897
25.	William McKinley (1843–1901)	Republican	1897–1901
26.	Theodore Roosevelt (1858–1919)	Republican	1901–1909
27.	William Howard Taft (1857–1930)	Republican	1909–1913
28.	Woodrow Wilson (1856–1924)	Democratic	1913–1921
29.	Warren G. Harding (1865–1923)	Republican	1921–1923
30.	Calvin Coolidge (1871–1933)	Republican	1923–1929
31.	Herbert Hoover (1874–1964)	Republican	1929–1933
32.	Franklin Delano Roosevelt (1882–1945)	Democratic	1933–1945
33.	Harry S Truman (1884–1972)	Democratic	1945–1953
34.	Dwight D. Eisenhower (1890–1969)	Republican	1953–1961
35.	John F. Kennedy (1917–1963)	Democratic	1961–1963
36.	Lyndon B. Johnson (1908–1973)	Democratic	1963–1969
37.	Richard M. Nixon (1913–1994)	Republican	1969–1974
38.	Gerald R. Ford (b. 1913)	Republican	1974–1977
39.	Jimmy Carter (b. 1924)	Democratic	1977–1981
40.	Ronald Reagan (b. 1911)	Republican	1981–1989
41.	George Bush (b. 1924)	Republican	1989–1993
42.	Bill Clinton (b. 1946)	Democratic	1993–

References

Chapter 1
Myth and Reality in American Politics, pp. 1–23

1. For the original series and related stories, see the *San Jose (Calif.) Mercury News* web site at http://www.sjmercury.com/drugs/postscript/update1115.html.
2. Benjamin I. Page and Robert Y. Shapiro, *The Rational Public: Fifty Years of Trends in Americans' Policy Preferences* (Chicago: University of Chicago Press, 1992), pp. 9–15.
3. James Oliver Robertson, *American Myth, American Reality* (New York: Hill and Wang, 1980), p. xv.
4. In recent years, the work of Joseph Campbell has done much to popularize our awareness of primitive and ancient mythologies. For example, see his four-volume work *The Masks of God,* reissued in 1987 by Penguin Books.
5. Murray Edelman, *Politics as Symbolic Action: Mass Arousal and Quiescence* (Chicago: Markham, 1971), p. 83.
6. Two popular examples are Clyde V. Prestowitz, Jr., *Trading Places: How We Are Giving Our Future to Japan and How to Reclaim It* (New York: Basic Books, 1988); and Pat Choate, *Agents of Influence: How Japan Manipulates America's Political and Economic System* (New York: Simon and Schuster, 1990).
7. See Robert B. Reich, *The Work of Nations: Preparing Ourselves for 21st Century Capitalism* (New York: Vintage Books, 1992).
8. According to H. Mark Roelofs, myths offer us a "nationally shared framework of political consciousness" by which we become aware of ourselves as "a people, as having an identity in history," and by which we are "prepared to recognize some governing regime . . . as legitimate." See his *Ideol-ogy and Myth in American Politics: A Critique of a National Political Mind* (Boston: Little, Brown, 1976), p. 4.
9. Robert C. Tucker, *Political Culture and Leadership in Soviet Russia: From Lenin to Gorbachev* (New York: W. W. Norton, 1987), pp. 22–23.
10. Robertson, p. 17.
11. See Robert C. Tucker, *Political Culture and Leadership in Soviet Russia: From Lenin to Gorbachev* (New York: Norton, 1987).
12. Murray Edelman, *The Symbolic Uses of Politics* (Urbana, Ill.: University of Illinois Press, 1964), pp. 2–3.
13. Christopher Lasch, *The True and Only Heaven: Progress and Its Critics* (New York: Norton, 1991), p. 93.
14. Quoted from FitzGerald's *Fire in the Lake,* in Robertson, p. 5.
15. The myth-as-lie has a long history, as well as some significant advocates. The most famous was Plato, who proposed the use of the "inspired lie" in his *Republic.* See Karl R. Popper. *The Spell of Plato,* vol. 1 of *The Open Society and Its Enemies* (New York: Harper and Row, 1962).
16. See Bob Woodward, *The Commanders* (New York: Simon and Schuster, 1991), pp. 306–307.
17. Arthur M. Schlesinger, Jr., *The Cycles of American History* (Boston: Houghton Mifflin, 1986), p. 219.
18. Mary Beth Norton et al., *A People and a Nation,* 3rd ed. (Boston: Houghton Mifflin, 1990), p. 218.
19. See Frank Bourgin, *The Great Challenge: The Myth of Laissez-Faire in the Early Republic* (New York: George Braziller, 1989). See also Stuart Bruchey, *The Wealth of the Nation: An Economic History of the United States* (New York: Harper and Row, 1988), especially chaps. 1–3.
20. On the distinction between myths and ideologies, see Roelofs, p. 4. For a general discussion on the concept of "ideology," see David E. Apter, *Introduction to Political Analysis* (Cambridge, Mass.: Winthrop, 1977), chap. 8.
21. See Tucker; see also Zbigniew Brzezinski and Samuel P. Huntington, *Political Power: USA/USSR* (New York: Viking, 1964), pp. 45ff.
22. Joel D. Aberbach, Robert D. Putnam, and Bert A. Rockman, *Bureaucrats and Politicians in Western Democracies* (Cambridge, Mass.: Harvard University Press, 1981), chap. 5.
23. See William S. Maddox and Stuart A. Lilie, *Beyond Liberal and Conservative: Reassessing the Political Spectrum* (Washington, D.C.: The Cato Institute, 1984).

24. E. J. Dionne, Jr., *Why Americans Hate Politics* (New York: Simon and Schuster, 1991), p. 11.
25. Roelofs, pp. 4–5.

Chapter 2
Constitutional Foundations, pp. 24–61

1. See "Federalist No. 49," in *The Federalist,* ed. Jacob E. Cooke (Middletown, Conn.: Wesleyan University Press, 1961).
2. Letter to James Madison, January 30, 1787, in *Thomas Jefferson: Writings,* ed. Merrill D. Peterson (New York: The Library of America, 1984), p. 882. See also p. 1402, letter to Samuel Kercheval, July 12, 1816.
3. From Ed Gillespie and Bob Schellhas, eds., *Contract With America* (New York: Times Books, 1994), pp. 166–167.
4. See Michael Kammen, *A Machine That Would Go of Itself: The Constitution in American Culture* (New York: Alfred A. Knopf, 1987).
5. Senator William Maclay, quoted in Walter F. Murphy, "Merlin's Memory: The Past and Future Imperfect of the Once and Future Polity," in Sanford Levinson, ed., *Responding to Imperfection: the Theory and Practice of Constitutional Amendment* (Princeton, N.J.: Princeton University Press, 1995), p. 166.
6. Ibid., pp. 166–167.
7. Robert G. Ferris and James H. Charleton, *The Signers of the Constitution* (Flagstaff, Ariz.: Interpretive Publications, 1986), pp. 14–15. For a thorough and groundbreaking treatment of the politics and ideas that led to the Convention, see Gordon S. Wood, *The Creation of the American Republic, 1776–1787* (New York: W. W. Norton, 1969).
8. Ibid., p. 19. Shays led one thousand ragtag insurgents against the arsenal, but the defeat of the uprising was made possible only after local merchants and bankers financed a defense of the weapons storehouse. The congress could not afford to do more than provide a few guards for the arsenal.
9. Martin Diamond, *The Founding of the Democratic Republic* (Itasca, Ill.: F. E. Peacock, 1981), p. 15. For an authoritative general overview of the convention, see Max Farrand, *The Framing of the Constitution of the United States* (New Haven, Conn.: Yale University Press, 1913). See also Ferris and Charleton, pp. 35–36; and Catherine Drinker Bowen, *Miracle at Philadelphia: The Story of the Constitutional Convention, May to September 1787* (Boston: Little, Brown, 1966).
10. The quoted characterizations were communicated to the French foreign ministry by the French ambassador to the United States in 1788. See Saul K. Padover, *The Living Constitution* (New York: Mentor Books, 1953), pp. 51ff. For more general biographies of the delegates, see M. E. Bradford, *Founding Fathers: Brief Lives of the Framers of the United States Constitution,* 2nd ed. (Lawrence, Kan.: University Press of Kansas, 1994); also Ferris and Charleton, part 2.
11. "Speech in the Convention at the Conclusion of Its Deliberations," in *Benjamin Franklin, Writings,* ed. J. A. Leo Lemay (New York: Library of America, 1987), pp. 1139–1141. On Franklin's health, see Ferris and Charleton, p. 35. For other supportive comments attributed to Franklin at the convention, see Farrand, p. 194.
12. For an in-depth analysis of the roots of the Constitution, see Donald S. Lutz, *The Origins of American Constitutionalism* (Baton Rouge: Louisiana State University Press, 1988). Also see Jack P. Greene, *The Intellectual Heritage of the Constitutional Era: The Delegates' Library* (Philadelphia: The Library Company of Philadelphia, 1986).
13. Charles Howard McIlwain, *The American Revolution: A Constitutional Interpretation* (Ithaca, N.Y.: Cornell University Press, 1958), p. 5.
14. It would be an error, however, to think of the American system as a mere variation of the modern British system. See Bruce Ackerman, *Foundations,* vol. 1 of *We the People* (Cambridge, Mass.: Belknap Press, 1991), especially his "dualist model" versus "monist model" argument in chap. 1.
15. A classic exposition of the development of the British constitutional system is found in Walter Bagehot, *The English Constitution* (London: Oxford University Press, 1928). His views on the use of charters are presented on pp. 247–249.
16. Later in the 1600s, as the Stuarts attempted to reassert royal authority, the Parliament joined the courts in elevating common law to "higher-law" status; see Greene, chap. 4.
17. See Ackerman; see also Sanford Levinson, *Constitutional Faith* (Princeton, N.J.: Princeton University Press, 1988).

18. See the reference to Bonham's Case and common-law tradition in Charles Rembar, *The Law of the Land: The Evolution of Our Legal System* (New York: Simon and Schuster, 1980), pp. 43–47, 286–287.

19. Compare with Thomas L. Pangle, "The Constitution's Human Vision," *The Public Interest,* 86 (Winter 1987), 79–81.

20. Lutz contends that this situation came about because for most of the seventeenth century the British were preoccupied with trying to settle their own constitutional problems. See Lutz, p. 63.

21. See Lawrence J. R. Herson, *The Politics of Ideas: Political Theory and American Public Policy* (Homewood, Ill.: Dorsey Press, 1984), pp. 28–29.

22. See Abraham I. Katsh, "Hebraic Foundations of American Democracy," in *The Hebrew Impact on Western Civilization,* ed. Dagobert D. Runes (Secaucus, N.J.: Citadel Press, 1951), especially pp. 39–52. While steeped in the Judeo-Christian tradition, the Constitution lacks any reference to God or religion. It was in that sense designed to be "godless" in content. See Issaac Kramnick and R. Laurence Moore, *The Godless Constitution: The Case Against Religious Correctness* (New York: W. W. Norton, 1996).

23. For more on Hobbes's contribution to the work of the framers, see Walter Berns, "The New Pursuit of Happiness," *The Public Interest,* 86 (Winter 1987), 68–69.

24. See Greene, chap. 2.

25. In fact, of all the philosophers and authors cited by those who debated the Constitution, Montesquieu was mentioned most often. See Greene, pp. 43–44; also Lutz, pp. 139–147.

26. See Diamond, pp. 3–6. For a controversial interpretation of the Declaration, see Garry Wills, *Inventing America: Jefferson's Declaration of Independence* (New York: Vintage, 1978).

27. For an interesting analysis of the Constitution based on a perspective that gives special standing to the constitutional mechanisms that support the legitimacy of "We the People," see Ackerman.

28. The controversy over a national bank has a long history. For more details, see Bray Hammond, "The Bank Cases," in *Quarrels That Have Shaped the Constitution,* ed. John A. Garraty, rev. ed. (New York: Harper Torchbooks, 1987), pp. 37–55. See also William Greider, *Secrets of the Temple: How the Federal Reserve Runs the Country* (New York: Simon and Schuster, 1987), chaps. 8–9.

29. James Madison, "Federalist No. 39," in *The Federalist,* ed. Jacob E. Cooke.

30. See Michael Allen Gillespie and Michael Lienesch, eds., *Ratifying the Constitution* (Lawrence, Kan.: University Press of Kansas, 1989).

31. The deadline, originally set for 1979, was later extended by thirty-nine months by congressional action.

32. For a history of the amending process, see Richard B. Bernstein, with Jerome Agel, *Amending America: If We Love the Constitution So Much, Why Do We Keep Trying to Change It?* (New York: Times Books, 1993).

33. For a critical assessment of the relative use of amendment and non-amendment means for changing the Constitution, see Stephen M. Griffin, "Constitutionalism in the United States: From Theory to Politics," in Levinson, ed., *Responding to Imperfection,* chap. 3.

34. See Hamilton's "Federalist No. 11," in *The Federalist,* ed. Jacob E. Cooke.

35. Kermit L. Hall, *The Magic Mirror: Law in American History* (New York: Oxford University Press, 1989), p. 6. Also see Cass R. Sunstein, *The Partial Constitution* (Cambridge, Mass.: Harvard University Press, 1993).

36. Sunstein, pp. 32–37.

37. For an excellent introduction to how the rule of law impacts public officials, see David H. Rosenbloom and James D. Carroll, *Toward Constitutional Competence: A Casebook for Public Administrators* (Englewood Cliffs, N.J.: Prentice-Hall, 1990).

38. See "Federalist No. 51," also in the Appendix.

39. Jack N. Rakove, *The Beginnings of National Politics: An Interpretive History of the Continental Congress* (Baltimore, Md.: Johns Hopkins University Press, 1979), pp. 394–395.

40. "Federalist No. 44," in *The Federalist,* ed. Jacob E. Cooke.

41. See Seymour Martin Lipset and William Schneider, *The Confidence Gap: Business, Labor, and Government in the Public Mind* (New York: The Free Press, 1983), pp. 15–29.

42. Samuel P. Huntington, *American Politics: The Politics of Disharmony* (Cambridge, Mass.: Harvard University Press, 1981), p. 30.

43. Theodore H. White, "The American Idea," *New York Times Magazine,* July 6, 1986, p. 13.
44. Quoted in Farrand, pp. 209–210.
45. Quoted in Levinson, p. 11.

Chapter 3
Federalism and Intergovernmental Relations, pp. 62–90

1. A detailed study of the debates of that early period is provided in Stanley Elkins and Eric McKitrick, *The Age of Federalism: The Early American Republic, 1788–1800* (New York: Oxford University Press, 1993).
2. "Can States Act Without Federal Permission?" *New York Times,* November 16, 1986, p. E5.
3. The 1981 and 1987 survey results are quoted in Morton Keller, "State Power Needn't Be Resurrected Because It Never Died," *Governing*, 2, No. 1 (October 1988), 53–57. For the 1995 survey results, see the *Washington Post,* Kaiser Family Foundation, and Harvard University Survey Project, "Why Don't Americans Trust the Government?" 1996. http://www.kff.org/kff/govt.html, February 5, 1996.
4. In a 1936 Gallup poll, 56 percent of the respondents favored the federal government over state governments. See Keller, p. 57.
5. Terry Sanford, *Storm over the States* (New York: McGraw-Hill, 1967), p. 35.
6. For a detailed survey of the concept of federalism, see S. Rufus Davis, *The Federal Principle: A Journey Through Time in Quest of Meaning* (Berkeley, Calif.: University of California Press, 1978).
7. For a general overview of the conflicting theories of federalism, see Richard H. Leach, *American Federalism* (New York: Norton, 1970), chap. 1. See also William H. Riker, *Federalism: Origin, Operation, Significance* (Boston: Little, Brown, 1964).
8. This view had its most direct expression in the Virginia and Kentucky resolutions of 1798. Written by Jefferson and Madison, the resolutions called for the "nullification" of the unpopular Alien and Sedition Acts—laws that had led to the conviction of several newspaper editors critical of American foreign policy decisions. The resolutions circulated among the states, but the election of Jefferson as president in 1800 seemed to end the controversy— since the new president was a leading advocate of this view.
9. The quote is from Justice Barbour's decision in *Miln* v. *New York* (1837); quoted in W. Brooke Graves, *American Intergovernmental Relations: Their Origins, Historical Development, and Current Status* (New York: Scribner's, 1964), pp. 319–320.
10. J. G. Randall and David Donald, *The Civil War and Reconstruction,* 2nd ed., 1961, pp. 97–102.
11. From the Supreme Court decision in Tarbel's Case, quoted in Deil S. Wright, *Understanding Intergovernmental Relations,* 3rd ed. (Monterey, Calif.: Brooks/Cole, 1988), p. 41. For a more general discussion, see Graves, pp. 321–324.
12. *Hammer* v. *Dagenhart* (1918).
13. The federal government did provide special funding for canals and similar projects earlier in the century, and the states did receive parts of a national budget surplus into the 1830s. But the first grant-in-aid program was the Morrill Act. See Graves, chap. 14.
14. See David B. Walker, *The Rebirth of Federalism: Slouching Toward Washington* (Chatham, N.J.; Chatham House, 1995), pp. 82–83.
15. *Historical Statistics of the United States: Colonial Times to 1970,* Table Y638, p. 1125.
16. See Walker, chap. 4. See also Wright, pp. 71–72.
17. Roscoe C. Martin, *The Cities and the Federal System* (New York: Atherton Press, 1965), chaps. 4 and 5. See also Advisory Commission on Intergovernmental Relations, *Public Assistance: The Growth of a Federal Function* (Washington, D.C.: ACIR, 1980), pp. 24–25.
18. See Kenneth T. Palmer, "The Evolution of Grant Policies," in *The Changing Politics of Federal Grants,* ed. Lawrence D. Brown, James W. Fossett, and Kenneth T. Palmer (Washington, D.C.: The Brookings Institution, 1984).
19. For a general overview of how the national government used this strategy, see Advisory Commission on Intergovernmental Relations, *Regulatory Federalism: Policy, Process, Impact and Reform* (Washington, D.C.: ACIR, 1984).
20. For the story of how these cuts were accomplished, see David A. Stockman, *The Triumph of Politics: How the Reagan Revolution Failed* (New York: Harper and Row, 1986).
21. See George E. Peterson, "Federalism and the States: An Experiment in Decentralization," in *The*

Reagan Record: An Assessment of America's Changing Domestic Priorities, ed. John L. Palmer and Isabel V. Sawhill (Cambridge, Mass.: Ballinger, 1984), p. 228.

22. Ibid., pp. 229–230.

23. For the latest figures on federal intergovernmental grants-in-aid, see *Significant Features of Fiscal Federalism,* an annual publication issued by the Advisory Commission on Intergovernmental Relations.

24. John Shannon, "The Return of Fend-For-Yourself Federalism: The Reagan Marks," *Intergovernmental Perspective,* 13 (Summer 1987), 34–37.

25. Clinton was prominently featured in one book that addressed the strengths of state governments in the 1980s; see David Osborne, *Laboratories of Democracy* (Boston: Harvard Business School Press, 1988).

26. In *Baker* v. *Carr* (1962), for instance, the Court forced the states to reapportion their legislative seats to guarantee equal representation for all their citizens. In *Roe* v. *Wade* (1973), the Court limited the authority states have to regulate abortion (see Chapter 4). Finally, in *Garcia* v. *San Antonio Metropolitan Transit Authority* (1985), the Court held that federal wage and hour laws apply to state and local governments. See Robert Pear, "Study Urges Fight for States' Power," *New York Times,* November 9, 1986, pp. 1, 20.

27. See Elder Witt, "On Issues of State Power, The Supreme Court Seems to Be of Two Minds," *Governing,* 4, No. 1 (October 1990), 54–64.

28. See Morris P. Fiorina, *Congress: Keystone of the Washington Establishment* (New Haven, Conn.: Yale University Press, 1977), p. 48.

29. David E. Satterfield III, representative from Richmond, Virginia, quoted in Rochelle L. Stanfield, "Federal Aid—Taking the Good with the Bad," *National Journal* (July 8, 1978), 1076.

30. See Ann O'M. Bowman and Richard C. Kearney, *The Resurgence of the States* (Englewood Cliffs, N.J.: Prentice-Hall, 1986), p. 136.

31. Ibid., pp. 25–27. See also Osborne's *Laboratories of Democracy.* Each year, *Governing* magazine publishes numerous state and local "government success stories" that rarely make headlines elsewhere.

32. Rochelle L. Stanfield, ""The New Federalism," *National Journal* (January 28, 1995), 227.

33. See ACIR, *State Government Capability.*

34. Luther H. Gulick, quoted in ACIR, *State Government Capability,* p. 1.

35. See Ira Sharkansky, *The Maligned States: Policy Accomplishments, Problems, and Opportunities* (New York: McGraw-Hill, 1972). On the waxing and waning of the role of the states in American federalism, see Keller, pp. 53–57.

36. The now defunct ACIR published the survey results throughout the 1980s as part of an annual report titled *Public Attitudes on Government and Taxes* (Washington, D.C., v.d.)

37. See ACIR, *State Government Capability.*

38. For an interesting perspective on how Americans have viewed their local governments, see Anwar Syed, *The Political Theory of American Local Government* (New York: Random House, 1966).

39. Data from preliminary Census Bureau figures published in Walker, p. 271.

40. Statistics for local areas from U. S. Department of Commerce, Bureau of the Census, *State and Metropolitan Area Data Book, 1991,* 4th ed. (Washington, D.C.: U.S. Government Printing Office, 1991), tbs. 2 and C.

41. Robert Pear, "Saying Medicaid Experiments Cut Services to Poor, Clinics Sue," *New York Times,* June 12, 1994, p. A30.

42. See Donald H. Haider, *When Governments Come to Washington: Governors, Mayors, and Intergovernmental Lobbying* (New York: Free Press, 1974). See also Alan Ehrenhalt, "As Interest in Its Agenda Wanes, a Shrinking Urban Bloc in Congress Plays Defense," *Governing,* 2, No. 10 (July 1989), 21–25.

43. See Jonathan Walters, "Lobbying for the Good Old Days," *Governing,* 4, No. 9 (June 1991), 32–37.

Chapter 4

The Heritage of Rights and Liberties, pp. 91–129

1. Quoted in Mary Ann Glendon, *Rights Talk: The Impoverishment of Political Discourse* (New York: Free Press, 1991) p. 8.

2. *Barron* v. *Baltimore,* 32 U.S. (7 Pet.) 243 (1833).

3. See Justice Black's concurring opinion in *Adamson* v. *California,* 332 U.S. 67 (1947).

4. *Palko* v. *Connecticut,* 302 U.S. 319 (1937).

5. *Milk Wagon Drivers Union* v. *Meadowmoor Dairies,* 312 U.S. 287 (1941).

6. *Schenck* v. *U.S.*, 249 U.S. 47 (1919).

7. *Gitlow* v. *New York*, 268 U.S. 652 (1925).

8. *Texas* v. *Johnson*, 491 U.S. 397 (1989).

9. *United States* v. *Eichman*, 496 U.S. 310 (1990).

10. *United States* v. *O'Brien*, 391 U.S. 367 (1968).

11. *Madsen* v. *Women's Health Center Inc.*, --- U.S. --- (1994).

12. *West Virginia State Board of Education* v. *Barnette*, 319 U.S. 624 (1943).

13. *Near* v. *Minnesota*, 283 U.S. 697 (1931).

14. *New York Times* v. *U.S.*, 403 U.S. 713 (1971).

15. *New York Times* v. *Sullivan*, 376 U.S. 254 (1964).

16. *Time, Inc.* v. *Firestone*, 424 U.S. 96 (1976).

17. *Flynt* v. *Falwell*, 485 U.S. 46 (1988).

18. *Roth* v. *U.S.*, 354 U.S. 476 (1957).

19. *Memoirs of a Woman of Pleasure* v. *Massachusetts*, 382 U.S. 975 (1966).

20. *Miller* v. *California*, 413 U.S. 15 (1973).

21. C. Herman Pritchett, *Constitutional Civil Liberties* (Englewood Cliffs, N.J.: Prentice-Hall, 1984), pp. 132–133.

22. *Everson* v. *Board of Education*, 330 U.S. 1 (1947).

23. *Lemon* v. *Kurtzman*, 403 U.S. 602 (1971).

24. *Engel* v. *Vitale*, 370 U.S. 421 (1962).

25. *School District of Abington Township* v. *Schempp*, 374 U.S. 203 (1963).

26. *Marsh* v. *Chambers*, 463 U.S. 783 (1983).

27. *Allegheny County* v. *American Civil Liberties Union*, 492 U.S. 573 (1989).

28. *Reynolds* v. *United States*, 98 U.S. 145 (1879).

29. *Braunfeld* v. *Brown*, 366 U.S. 599 (1961).

30. *Jacobson* v. *Massachusetts*, 197 U.S. 11 (1905).

31. *Wisconsin* v. *Yoder*, 406 U.S. 215 (1972).

32. *Employment Division, Dept. of Human Resources of Oregon* v. *Smith*, 494 U.S. 872 (1990).

33. *Powell* v. *Alabama*, 287 U.S. 45 (1932).

34. *Gideon* v. *Wainwright*, 372 U.S. 335 (1963).

35. *Argersinger* v. *Hamlin*, 407 U.S. 25 (1972).

36. *Escobedo* v. *Illinois*, 378 U.S. 478 (1964).

37. *Miranda* v. *Arizona*, 384 U.S. 436 (1966).

38. *Duckworth* v. *Eagan*, 492 U.S. 195 (1989).

39. *New York* v. *Quarles*, 467 U.S. 649 (1984).

40. *Arizona* v. *Fuliminante*, 111 S.Ct. 1246 (1991).

41. *Schneckloth* v. *Bustamonte*, 412 U.S. 218 (1973).

42. *Mapp* v. *Ohio*, 367 U.S. 643 (1961).

43. *Nix* v. *Williams*, 476 U.S. 431 (1984).

44. *United States* v. *Leon*, 468 U.S. 897 (1984).

45. *Robinson* v. *California*, 370 U.S. 660 (1962).

46. *Hammelin* v. *Michigan*, 111 S.Ct. 2680 (1991).

47. *Furman* v. *Georgia*, 408 U.S. 238 (1972).

48. *Woodson* v. *North Carolina*, 428 U.S. 280 (1976).

49. *Thompson* v. *Oklahoma*, 487 U.S. 815 (1988).

50. *Penry* v. *Lynaugh*, 492 U.S. 302 (1989) and *Stanford* v. *Kentucky*, 492 U.S. 361 (1989).

51. *McCleskey* v. *Zant*, 111 S.Ct. 1454 (1991).

52. *Payne* v. *Tennessee*, 111 S.Ct. 2597 (1991).

53. Charles Warren and Louis Brandeis, "The Right of Privacy," *Harvard Law Review*, 4, p. 193 (1890).

54. *Griswold* v. *Connecticut*, 381 U.S. 479 (1965).

55. *Roe* v. *Wade*, 410 U.S. 113 (1973).

56. *Webster* v. *Reproductive Health Services*, 492 U.S. 490 (1989).

57. *Planned Parenthood of Southeastern Pennsylvania* v. *Casey*, 505 U.S. 833 (1992).

58. *Compassion in Dying* v. *State of Washington*, --- U.S. --- (1997).

59. *Quill* v. *Vacco*, --- U.S. --- (1997).

60. *Cruzan by Cruzan* v. Director, *Missouri Dept. of Health*, 497 U.S. 261 (1990).

61. C. Vann Woodward, *The Strange Career of Jim Crow* (New York: Oxford University Press, 1966).

62. *Plessy* v. *Ferguson*, 163 U.S. 537 (1896).

63. Paul Oberst, "The Strange Career of *Plessy* v. *Ferguson*," *Arizona Law Review*, 15 (1973).

64. *Cumming* v. *Richmond County Board of Education*, 175 U.S. 528 (1899).

65. *Missouri ex rel. Gaines* v. *Canada*, 305 U.S. 337 (1938).

66. *Sweatt* v. *Painter*, 339 U.S. 629 (1950).

67. *Brown* v. *Board of Education of Topeka*, 347 U.S. 483 (1954).

68. *Brown* v. *Board of Education II*, 349 U.S. 294 (1955).

69. *Alexander* v. *Holmes County Board of Education*, 396 U.S. 19 (1969).

70. *Milliken* v. *Bradley*, 418 U.S. 717 (1974).

71. See Pritchett, p. 345.

72. *Chisom* v. *Roemer*, 501 U.S. 380 (1991) and *Houston Lawyers' Association* v. *Attorney General of Texas*, 501 U.S. 419 (1991).

73. *Goesaert* v. *Cleary*, 335 U.S. 464 (1948).

74. *Hoyt* v. *Florida*, 368 U.S. 62 (1961).

75. *Craig* v. *Boren*, 429 U.S. 190 (1976).

76. *Kahn* v. *Shevin*, 416 U.S. 351 (1974).

77. *United States* v. *Virginia*, --- U.S. --- (1997).

78. Quoted in Susan Gluck Mezey, *In Pursuit of Equality: Women, Public Policy, and the Federal Courts* (New York: St. Martin's, 1991), p. 97.

79. *General Electric Co.* v. *Gilbert,* 429 U.S. 125 (1976).
80. *Williams* v. *Saxbe,* 413 F. Supp. 654 (D.D.C. 1976).
81. *Meritor Savings Bank* v. *Vinson,* 477 U.S. 57 (1986).
82. *Harris* v. *Forklift,* 570 U.S. 17 (1993).
83. *Bowers* v. *Hardwick,* 478 U.S. 186 (1986).
84. *Romer* v. *Evans,* --- U.S. --- (1994).
85. *Plyer* v. *Doe,* 457 U.S. 202 (1982).
86. *Regents of the University of California* v. *Bakke,* 438 U.S. 265 (1978).
87. *Martin* v. *Wilks,* 490 U.S. 755 (1989).
88. *Wards Cove Packing Company* v. *Atonio,* 109 S.Ct. 2115 (1989).

Chapter 5
Public Opinion and Political Participation, pp. 130–161

1. *New York Times,* February 16, 1997, Section 4, p. 1.
2. Ibid., p.1.
3. Everett Carll Ladd, "The Polls: 1948 Looks Better and Better," *Christian Science Monitor,* November 17, 1989, p. 18.
4. W. H. Hartley and W. S. Vincent, *American Civics,* 4th ed. (New York: Harcourt Brace Jovanovich, 1983), p. 221.
5. V. O. Key, Jr., *Public Opinion and American Democracy* (New York: Knopf, 1961).
6. *The Public Perspective,* Vol. 5, no. 1, November/December 1993, p. 75.
7. Max J. Skidmore, *Ideologies: Politics in Action* (New York: Harcourt Brace Jovanovich, 1989), p. 7.
8. Bernard Hennessy, *Public Opinion,* 5th ed. (Monterey, Calif.: Brooks/Cole, 1985), p. 199; and Harry Holloway, with John George, *Public Opinion: Coalitions, Elites, and Masses,* 2nd ed. (New York: St. Martin's, 1986), p. 72.
9. M. Margaret Conway, *Political Participation in the United States,* 2nd ed. (Washington, D.C.: Congressional Quarterly Press, 1991), pp. 23–25; Hennessy, p. 200.
10. See John L. Sullivan et al., *Political Tolerance and American Democracy* (Chicago: University of Chicago Press, 1982); and Herbert McClosky and Alida Brill, *Dimensions of Tolerance: What Americans Believe About Civil Liberties* (New York: Russell Sage Foundation, 1983).
11. M. Margaret Conway et al., "The News Media in Children's Political Socialization," *Public Opinion Quarterly,* 45 (1981), 164–178; and M. Margaret Conway, David Ahern, and Mikel L. Wyckoff, "The Mass Media and Changes in Adolescents' Political Knowledge During an Election Cycle," *Political Behavior,* 3 (1981), 69–80.
12. Harold W. Stanley and Richard G. Niemi, *Vital Statistics on American Politics,* 4th ed., (Washington, D.C.: Congressional Quarterly Press, 1994), p. 63.
13. Harold W. Stanley and Richard G. Niemi, *Vital Statistics on American Politics,* 5th ed., (Washington, D.C.: Congressional Quarterly Press, 1995), p. 48.
14. See Daniel Elazar, *American Federalism: A View from the States,* 2nd ed. (New York: Crowell, 1972) and Robert S. Erikson, Gerald C. Wright, and John P. McIver, *Statehouse Democracy* (New York: Cambridge University Press, 1993), for two excellent discussions of political culture and public opinion.
15. For a systematic and readable review of polling and the measurement of public opinion, see Albert H. Cantrill, *The Opinion Connection: Polling, Politics, and the Press* (Washington, D.C.: Congressional Quarterly Press, 1991).
16. Survey by CBS News/*New York Times,* June 17–20, 1992.
17. *American National Election Study,* 1984, Center for Political Studies, University of Michigan, Ann Arbor.
18. Richard Morin, "The Public May Not Know Much, But It Knows What It Doesn't Like," *Washington Post National Weekly Edition,* January 23–29, 1989, p. 37.
19. Ladd, p. 18.
20. National Opinion Research Center of International Studies, Princeton University, March 1960.
21. University of Michigan National Election Studies, 1996.
22. *The Public Perspective,* Vol. 5, no. 2, January/February 1994, p. 95 and Vol. 5, no. 3, March/April 1994, p. 88; CBS News Poll, October 29–November 1, 1994, and November 27–28, 1994.
23. University of Michigan National Election Studies, 1996.
24. *The Public Perspective,* Vol. 4, no. 5, July/August 1993, p. 91.
25. The Roper Organization, Roper Report 93-2, January 9–23, 1993.

26. Linda S. Lichter, *Public Opinion* (August/September 1985), 42; *The American Enterprise* 23 (September/October 1991), 82.

27. *New York Times* Public Opinion Poll, June 1991, p. 13.

28. Ibid.

29. Poll by Yankelovich Partners, Inc., for *Time* and CNN, January 13–14, 1993.

30. *The Public Perspective* (February/March 1997), 7.

31. *American National Election Study,* 1984.

32. *Gallup Report* (May 1987), 6–7; Pat Dunham, *Electoral Behavior in the United States* (Englewood Cliffs, N.J.: Prentice-Hall, 1991), p. 31; Survey by Louis Harris and Associates, June 24–29, 1993.

33. *The Public Perspective* (August/September 1996), 26–27.

34. *The Public Perspective* (August/September 1996).

35. See, for example, Celinda Lake, "Power, Equity, and Policy Dimensions of the Women's Vote in 1984," paper presented at the annual meeting of the American Political Science Association, Washington, D.C., August 1986.

36. Stanley and Niemi, p. 163.

37. "The American Freshman: National Norms for Fall 1996," published by American Council on Education and the University of California at Los Angeles, Higher Education Institute, 1996.

38. Ibid.

39. Ibid.

40. *The Public Perspective* (February/March 1996), 21.

41. Ibid., p. 29.

42. Juan Williams and Kenneth E. John, "Blacks and Whites Are Agreeing on Key Issues Facing the Nation," *Washington Post National Weekly Edition,* October 27–31, 1986, p. 37.

43. Adam Clymer, "Poll Studies Hispanic Party Loyalty," *New York Times,* July 18, 1986, p. A1.

44. *The Public Perspective,* Vol. 4, no. 5, March/April 1993, p. 9.

45. Hennessy, p. 184.

46. Ibid., pp. 180–187.

47. Lawrence R. Jacobs, *The Health of Nations: Public Opinion and the Making of American and British Health Policy,* Ithaca, N.Y.: Cornell University Press, 1993, p. xi.

48. The latter part of the definition of participation, given in quotes, comes from Conway, pp. 3–4.

49. Quote from Everett Carll Ladd, *The Public Perspective,* Vol. 5, no. 3, March/April 1994, based on a study by Sidney Verba, Kay L. Schlozman, Henry R. Brady, and Norman H. Nie, "The Citizen Participation Project: Summary Findings," a project supported by the National Science Foundation and the Spencer, Ford, and Hewlett Foundations, with survey work done in 1990 by the National Opinion Research Center.

50. Polling data reported in *The Public Perspective,* Vol. 6, no. 3, April/May 1995, p. 23.

51. Sidney Verba and Norman H. Nie, *Participation in America: Political Democracy and Social Equality* (New York: Harper and Row, 1972), pp. 95–101.

52. Data were collected by the University of Michigan National Election Study, 1996.

53. Survey of American Political Culture, 199, Gallup Organization.

54. Norman H. Nie and Sidney Verba, "Political Participation," in *Handbook of Political Science,* ed. Fred I. Greenstein and Nelson W. Polsby (Reading, Mass.: Addison-Wesley, 1975), IV, 24–25.

55. The International Social Justice Project, 1991.

56. Reported in *The Public Perspective,* Vol. 5, no. 3, March/April 1994, pp. 16–18, 34.

57. Harold W. Stanley and Richard G. Niemi, *Vital Statistics on American Politics,* 4th ed. (Washington, D.C.: Congressional Quarterly Press, 1994), p. 87.

58. Center for the American Woman and Politics (CAWP), Eagleton Institute of Politics, Rutgers University, New Brunswick, N.J., 1995.

59. Nancy McGlen and Karen O'Connor, *Women's Rights: The Struggle for Equality in the Nineteenth and Twentieth Centuries* (New York: Praeger, 1983), p. 110, tb. 4.5.

60. Center for the American Woman and Politics (CAWP), Eagleton Institute of Politics, Rutgers University, New Brunswick, N.J., 1997.

61. *New York Times,* August 26, 1996, p. A12.

62. Harold W. Stanley and Richard G. Niemi, *Vital Statistics on American Politics,* 4th ed. (Washington, D.C.: Congressional Quarterly Press, 1994), p. 291.

63. *Congressional Quarterly Weekly Report,* February 8, 1997, p. 369.

64. Harold W. Stanley and Richard G. Niemi, *Vital Statistics on American Politics,* 5th ed. (Washington, D.C.: Congressional Quarterly Press, 1995), p. 79.

65. Ibid., p. 369.

66. Neal R. Pierce, "Minorities Slowly Gain State Offices," *National Review,* January 5, 1991, p. 33.

67. *Congressional Quarterly Weekly Report,* February 8, 1997, p. 369.

68. *Los Angeles Times,* March 4, 1997.

69. Ibid.

70. Conway, pp. 30–31.

Chapter 6

Political Parties, pp. 162–189

1. James MacGregor Burns, *The Deadlock of Democracy: Four-Party Politics in America* (Englewood Cliffs, N.J.: Prentice-Hall, 1963), p. 27.

2. See, for example, Jeff Fishel, ed., *Parties and Elections in an Anti-Party Age* (Bloomington, Ind.: Indiana University Press, 1978); and Merle Black and George Rabinowitz, "American Electoral Change: 1952–1972," in *The Party Symbol: Readings on Political Parties,* ed. William Crotty (San Francisco: Freeman, 1980).

3. Surveys by the Gallup Organization for CNN/*USA Today,* August 1996.

4. Survey by the Media Studies Center/Roper Center, February 1996.

5. Survey by *New York Times*/CBS Poll, September 1996.

6. William J. Keefe, *Parties, Politics, and Public Policy in America* (Washington, D.C.: Congressional Quarterly Press, 1994), p. 11.

7. Alan R. Gitelson, M. Margaret Conway, and Frank B. Feigert, *American Political Parties: Stability and Change* (Boston: Houghton Mifflin, 1984), p. 4.

8. For one of the most comprehensive studies of comparative party organizations, see Kenneth Janda, *Political Parties: A Cross-National Survey* (New York: The Free Press, 1980); see also Janda, "A Comparative Analysis of Party Organizations: The United States, Europe, and the World," in Crotty, pp. 339–358; and Kay Lawson, *The Comparative Study of Political Parties* (New York: St. Martin's, 1976).

9. Reference to this term can be found in Paul Allen Beck and Frank J. Sorauf, *Party Politics in America,* 7th ed. (Glenview, Ill.: HarperCollins, 1992).

10. Survey by the Gallup Organization, August 1996.

11. Various polls: CBS News/*New York Times,* NBC/*Wall Street Journal, U.S. News and World Report,* 1996.

12. For a discussion on the decline of parties from the early 1950s to the mid-1980s, see Martin P. Wattenberg, *The Decline of American Political Parties: 1952–1984* (Cambridge, Mass.: Harvard University Press, 1986).

13. See Alan R. Gitelson and Patricia Bayer Richard, "Ticket-Splitting: Aggregate Measures v. Actual Ballots," *Western Political Quarterly,* 36 (September 1983), 410–419; and Frank B. Feigert, "Illusions of Ticket-Splitting," *American Politics Quarterly,* 7 (October 1979), 470–488.

14. For an in-depth discussion of the voting patterns and beliefs of self-declared independents, see Bruce E. Keith, David B. Magleby, Candice J. Nelson, Elizabeth Orr, Mark C. Westlye, and Raymond E. Wolfinger, *The Myth of the Independent Voter* (Berkeley, Calif.: University of California Press, 1992).

15. Gitelson, Conway, and Feigert, p. 131; Harold W. Stanley and Richard G. Niemi, *Vital Statistics on American Politics,* 4th ed. (Washington, D.C.: Congressional Quarterly Press, 1994), p. 158.

16. For one of the classic defenses of the role of parties, see E. E. Schattschneider, *Party Government* (New York: Rinehart, 1942). For an equally compelling argument in support of parties by a leading proponent of the view that parties are in decline, see Walter Dean Burnham, "The Changing Shape of the American Political Universe, in *Controversies in American Voting Behavior,* ed. Richard G. Niemi and Herbert F. Weisberg (San Francisco: Freeman, 1976), pp. 451–483.

17. Allan D. Monroe, "American Party Platforms and Public Opinion," *American Journal of Political Science,* 27 (February 1983), 27–42; and Gerald M. Pomper, with Susan S. Lederman, *Elections in America: Control and Influences in Democratic Politics,* 2nd ed. (New York: Longman, 1980).

18. Pomper, with Lederman, pp. 173–174.

19. Stanley and Niemi, p. 212.

20. Woodrow Wilson, *Constitutional Government in the United States* (New York: Columbia University Press, 1961), pp. 206, 217.

21. Three excellent discussions of the development of American parties are William N. Chambers, *Political Parties in a New Nation* (New York: Oxford University Press, 1963); William N. Chambers and Walter Dean Burnham, eds., *The American Party System* (New York: Oxford University Press, 1967);

and Everett C. Ladd, Jr., *American Political Parties* (New York: Norton, 1970).

22. See Robert P. Formisano, "Federalists and Republicans: Parties, Yes—System, No," in *The Evolution of American Electoral Systems,* ed. Paul Kleppner (Westport, Conn.: Greenwood Press, 1981), p. 35; and Formisano, "Deferential Participant Politics: The Early Republic's Political Culture, 1789–1840," *American Political Science Review,* 58 (June 1984), 473–487.

23. For a concise review of the splits within the Democratic-Republican party, see Burns, chap. 3.

24. For the most comprehensive discussion of the realignment process, see V. O. Key, Jr., "A Theory of Critical Elections," *Journal of Politics,* 17 (February 1955), pp. 3–18; Walter Dean Burnham, *Critical Elections and the Mainspring of American Politics* (New York: Norton, 1970); and James L. Sundquist, *Dynamics of the Party System: Alignment and Realignment of Political Parties in the United States,* rev. ed. (Washington, D.C.: The Brookings Institution, 1983).

25. See, for example, Paul Allen Beck, "The Dealignment Era in America," in *Electoral Change in Advanced Industrial Democracies: Realignment or Dealignment?* ed. Russell J. Dalton, Scott C. Flanagan, and Paul Allen Beck (Princeton, N.J.: Princeton University Press, 1984), pp. 240–266.

26. For a review of the several theories that we discuss in this section, see Beck and Sorauf, pp. 43–47.

27. Two proponents of the institutionalist explanation for the two-party system are Schattschneider; and Maurice Duverger, *Political Parties* (New York: Wiley, 1954).

28. V. O. Key, Jr., *Politics, Parties, and Pressure Groups,* 5th ed. (New York: Crowell, 1964); and Louis Hartz, *The Liberal Tradition in America* (New York: Harcourt, Brace and World, 1955).

29. The American "Know-Nothings" party, an anti-immigrant organization, received its nickname because of its original goal of keeping its purposes secret; to all questions party members responded with the words "I know nothing." See Mary Beth Norton et al., *A People and a Nation: A History of the United States,* 2nd ed. (Boston: Houghton Mifflin, 1986), p. 365.

30. For a revealing review of state laws that restrict participation by third parties in the electoral process, see Jim McClellan, "Two-Party Monopoly: Democrats and Republicans Pass Go, Collect Millions," in *American Government 85/86,* ed. Bruce Stinebrickner (Guilford, Conn.: Dushkin, 1985), pp. 183–186.

31. For a discussion of reform club activities in the United States and their impact on the electoral system, see Alan R. Gitelson, "Reform Clubs," in *Political Parties & Elections in the United States: An Encyclopedia,* ed. L. Sandy Maisel (New York: Garland, 1991), II, 926–931.

32. See John Frendreis, Alan R. Gitelson, Gregory Flemming, and Anne Layzell, "Local Political Parties and the 1992 Campaign for the State Legislature." Paper presented at the annual meeting of the American Political Science Association, Washington, D.C., September 2–5, 1993; John P. Frendreis and Alan R. Gitelson, "Local Political Parties in an Age of Change," *American Review of Politics,* vol. 14, Winter 1993, pp. 533–548.

33. Gitelson, Conway, and Feigert, p. 82.

34. See John F. Bibby, "Party Organization at the State Level," in *The Parties Respond: Changes in the American Party System,* ed. Sandy Maisel (Boulder, Colo.: Westview Press, 1994).

35. For comprehensive reviews of party reform during the past two decades, see William Crotty, *Political Reform and the American Experiment* (New York: Crowell, 1977); William Crotty, *Party Reform* (New York: Longman, 1983); and Charles Longley, "National Party Renewal," in *Party Renewal in America,* ed. Gerald M. Pomper (New York: Praeger, 1980), pp. 69–86.

36. For an overview of the resurgent national party organizations, see Paul S. Herrnson, "Reemergent National Party Organizations," in *The Parties Respond: Changes in the American Party System,* ed. Sandy Maisel (Boulder, Colo.: Westview Press, 1994).

37. See Burnham; William Crotty, *American Parties in Decline* (Boston: Little, Brown, 1984); and Martin P. Wattenberg, *The Decline of American Political Parties.*

38. See, for example, Stanley and Niemi, pp. 166–168.

39. See Gitelson, Conway, and Feigert, chap. 15, for a discussion of the transformation of political parties.

Chapter 7

Campaigns and Elections, pp. 190–224

1. Stephen A. Salmore and Barbara G. Salmore, *Candidates, Parties, and Campaigns: Electoral Politics in*

America (Washington, D.C.: Congressional Quarterly Press, 1985), p. 28. See also Wayne C. Williams, *William Jennings Bryan* (New York: Putnam, 1936), p. 162.

2. Francis T. Russell, *The Shadowing of Blooming Grove* (New York: McGraw-Hill, 1968), p. 125. See also Salmore and Salmore, p. 29.

3. Salmore and Salmore, p. 29.

4. National Election Studies, University of Michigan, 1994.

5. "The Vocal Minority In American Politics," Times Mirror Center for the People and the Press, July 16, 1993, p. 49.

6. CBS News Poll, November 27–28, 1994.

7. Michael J. Malbin, "1994 Vote: The Money Story," in *America at the Polls 1994*, ed. Everett Carll Ladd, (Storrs, Conn.: The Roper Center for Public Opinion Research, 1995), p. 128.

8. Federal Election Commission, news release, December 31, 1996, pp. 44, 50; April 14, 1997, p. 26; *Congressional Quarterly Report*, December 21, 1997, p. 3448.

9. See Joseph A. Schlesinger, *Ambition and Politics: Political Careers in the United States* (Chicago: Rand McNally, 1966); Gordon Black, "A Theory of Political Ambition: Career Choices and the Role of Structural Incentives," *American Political Science Review*, 66 (March 1972), 144–159; and Linda L. Fowler and Robert D. McClure, *Political Ambition: Who Decides to Run for Congress* (New Haven, Conn.: Yale University Press, 1989).

10. Schlesinger, pp. 16–20. For an excellent study on political ambition that points out the limitations of Schlesinger's opportunity structure theory, see Fowler and McClure.

11. M. I. Ostrogorski, *Democracy and the Organization of Political Parties* (New York: Macmillan, 1902), XI, 4.

12. Harold W. Stanley and Richard G. Niemi, *Vital Statistics on American Politics*, 4th ed. (Washington, D.C.: Congressional Quarterly Press, 1994), pp. 37–39.

13. Ibid.

14. Ibid.

15. For a concise discussion of the presidential nomination process, see William Crotty and John S. Jackson III, *Presidential Primaries and Nominations* (Washington, D.C.: Congressional Quarterly Press, 1985).

16. Federal Election Commission, news release, August 31, 1996.

17. Barbara Farah, "Delegate Polls: 1944–1984," *Public Opinion* (August/September 1984), 44.

18. Rhodes Cook, "The Nomination Process," in *The Elections of 1988*, ed. Michael Nelson (Washington, D.C.: Congressional Quarterly Press, 1989), p. 28.

19. *Congressional Quarterly Weekly Report*, June 15, 1996, p. 1637, and January 18, 1997, p. 188.

20. Ibid.

21. Survey by Gallup Polls, 1987.

22. PoliticsNow Classroom Website, March 11, 1997.

23. George Thayer, *Who Shakes the Money Tree?* (New York: Simon and Schuster, 1973), p. 150.

24. Federal Election Commission, news release, April 14, 1997.

25. Marjorie Randon Hershey, "The Congressional Elections," *The Election of 1996*, ed. Gerald M. Pomper (Chatham, N.J.: Chatham House, 1997), pp. 221–222.

26. William J. Keefe, *Parties, Politics, and Public Policy in America*, 7th ed. (Washington, D.C.: Congressional Quarterly Press, 1994), p. 153.

27. AdAge, website release, February 20, 1997.

28. Federal Election Commission, news release, November 4, 1994.

29. *Congressional Quarterly Weekly Report*, December 21, 1996, p. 3448.

30. Federal Election Commission, news release, April 14, 1997, p. 2.

31. William J. Keefe, *Parties, Politics, and Public Policy in America*, 7th ed. (Washington, D.C.: Congressional Quarterly Press, 1994), p. 153.

32. For a discussion of the impact of spending by challengers in congressional races, see Paul R. Abramson, John H. Aldrich, and David W. Rhode, *Change and Continuity in the 1980 Elections*, rev. ed. (Washington, D.C.: Congressional Quarterly Press, 1983), p. 201.

33. Gary C. Jacobson, "Money in the 1980 and 1982 Congressional Elections," in *Money and Politics in the United States: Financing Elections in the 1980s*, ed. Michael J. Malbin (Chatham, N.J.: Chatham House, 1984), p. 65.

34. *Washington Post*, February 9, 1997, p. A22.

35. *Congressional Quarterly Weekly Report*, February 22, 1997, p. 494.

36. Alan R. Gitelson, M. Margaret Conway, and Frank B. Feigert, *American Political Parties: Stability*

and Change (Boston: Houghton Mifflin, 1984), p. 242.

37. For the most comprehensive study of campaign consultants, see Larry J. Sabato, *The Rise of Political Consultants: New Ways of Winning Elections* (New York: Basic Books, 1981).

38. *Current American Government,* Fall 1981 Guide (Washington, D.C.: Congressional Quarterly Press, 1991), p. 138.

39. Gerald M. Pomper, ed., *The Election of 1996* (Chatham, N.J.: Chatham House, 1997), p. 100.

40. Ibid., p. 100.

41. Marchette Chute, *The First Liberty: A History of the Right to Vote in America,* 1619–1850 (New York: Dutton, 1969), p. 223; for a brief but concise review of the early development of the electorate, see Bruce Campbell, *The American Electorate: Attitudes and Action* (New York: Holt, Rinehart and Winston, 1979), chap. 2.

42. Campbell, pp. 12–13.

43. See Raymond E. Wolfinger and Steven J. Rosenstone, *Who Votes?* (New Haven, Conn.: Yale University Press, 1980).

44. Ibid., p. 18.

45. Ibid.

46. *New York Times,* November 10, 1996, p. 16.

47. In one public opinion poll, close to 50 percent of the respondents disagreed with the statement that "the members of Congress are honest, decent human beings." See "Attitudes Toward Campaign Financing," p. 7.

48. Paul R. Abramson and John H. Aldrich, "The Decline of Electoral Participation in America," *American Political Science Review,* 76 (September 1982), 502–521; and Richard A. Brody, "The Puzzle of Participation in America," in *The New American Political System,* ed. Anthony King (Washington, D.C.: American Enterprise Institute, 1978).

49. Paul R. Abramson, John H. Aldrich, and David W. Rhode, *Change and Continuity in the 1984 Elections* (Washington, D.C.: Congressional Quarterly Press, 1986), p. 176.

50. William H. Flanigan and Nancy H. Zingale, *Political Behavior of the American Electorate,* 8th ed. (Washington, D.C.: Congressional Quarterly Press, 1994), p. 173.

51. *New York Times,* November 10, 1996, p. 16.

52. For the most comprehensive discussion of retrospective voting, see Morris P. Fiorina, *Retrospective Voting in American National Elections* (New Haven, Conn.: Yale University Press, 1981).

53. See Adam Clymer, "Displeasure with Carter Turned Many to Reagan," *New York Times,* November 9, 1980, p. 28; John Stacks, "New Beginnings; Old Anxieties," *Time,* February 2, 1981, p. 22; and Barry Sussman, "Americans Have Moved Away from Reagan on Key Issues," *Washington Post National Weekly Edition,* January 7–13, 1985, p. 37.

54. See Gerald M. Pomper, with Susan S. Lederman, *Elections in America: Control and Influence in Democratic Politics,* 2nd ed. (New York: Longman, 1980).

Chapter 8

Interest Groups, pp. 225–250

1. Eric Pianin and Paul Blustein, "Welfare Reformers Aim at Goliaths: Bipartisan Group Wants to End $11.5 Billion in Business Subsidies," *Washington Post,* January 29, 1997, p. A19.

2. University of Michigan, Ann Arbor, National Election Study, 1994.

3. "Attitudes Towards Campaign Financing," Civic Service, Inc., February 1985.

4. See Jeffrey M. Berry, *The Interest Group Society,* 2nd ed. (Glenview, Ill.: Scott, Foresman, 1989); Kay Lehman Schlozman and John T. Tierney, *Organized Interests and American Democracy* (New York: Harper and Row, 1986); and Allan J. Cigler and Burdett A. Loomis, *Interest Group Politics,* 2nd ed. (Washington, D.C.: Congressional Quarterly Press, 1986).

5. Alan R. Gitelson, M. Margaret Conway, and Frank B. Feigert, *American Political Parties: Stability and Change* (Boston: Houghton Mifflin, 1984), pp. 333–335.

6. Schlozman and Tierney, p. 50.

7. For an excellent discussion of public interest groups, see Jeffrey M. Berry, *Lobbying for the People* (Princeton, N.J.: Princeton University Press, 1977).

8. These categories are drawn, in part, from Schlozman and Tierney's excellent study on interest group politics, pp. 45–49.

9. Ibid., pp. 45–46.

10. Robert H. Salisbury, "Interest Groups: Toward a New Understanding," in *Interest Group Politics,* ed. Allan J. Cigler and Burdett A. Loomis, 1st ed. (Washington, D.C.: Congressional Quarterly Press, 1983), p. 364.

11. Berry, *The Interest Group Society,* p. 96.

12. See Mancur Olson, *The Logic of Collective Action* (Cambridge, Mass.: Harvard University Press, 1965).

13. See ibid. See also E. E. Schattschneider, *The Semisovereign People* (New York: Holt, Rinehart and Winston, 1960).

14. Schlozman and Tierney, pp. 103–106.

15. Ibid., p. 106.

16. Berry, *The Interest Group Society,* p. 114.

17. Schlozman and Tierney, pp. 150–151.

18. *Current American Government: Fall 1991 Guide* (Washington, D.C.: Congressional Quarterly Press, 1991), p. 150.

19. *Guide to Current American Government, Spring 1983* (Washington, D.C.: Congressional Quarterly Press, 1983), p. 48.

20. Schlozman and Tierney, p. 104.

21. Schlozman and Tierney, p. 150.

22. See John R. Wright, "PACs, Contributions, and Roll Calls: An Organizational Perspective," *American Political Science Review,* 79 (June 1985), 400–414. For an excellent account of campaign financing, see Frank J. Sorauf, *Inside Campaign Finance* (New Haven, Conn.: Yale University Press, 1992).

23. Jeffrey Taylor, "Accountants' Campaign Contributions Are About to Pay Off in Legislation on Lawsuit Protection," *Wall Street Journal,* March 8, 1995, p. 1; see also Jeffrey M. Berry, *The Interest Group Society,* 3rd ed. (New York: Longman, 1997), pp. 154–160.

24. Berry, *The Interest Group Society,* p. 161.

25. Michael Weisskopf, "Health Care Lobbies Lobby Each Other," Washington Post, March 1, 1994, p. A8.

26. Gitelson, Conway, and Feigert, p. 339.

27. Neil A. Lewis, "Gains for Tobacco in Health Care Fight," *New York Times,* June 25, 1994, p. 16.

28. Berry, *The Interest Group Society,* p. 112. See also John W. Kingdon, *Congressmen's Voting Decisions,* 2nd ed. (New York: Harper and Row, 1981).

29. Quoted in David S. Broder, "News of the Weak," *Washington Post National Weekly Edition,* January 13–19, 1997, p. 21.

30. See Haynes Johnson and David S. Broder, *The System* (Boston: Little, Brown, 1996), p. 215.

31. Karen O'Connor, *Women's Organizations' Use of the Courts* (Lexington, Mass.: Lexington Books, 1980), p. 118.

Chapter 9

Media and Politics, pp. 251–272

1. Roan Conrad, "TV News and the 1976 Election: A Dialogue," *The Wilson Quarterly,* 1 (Spring 1977), 84.

2. Ronald Berkman and Laura W. Kitch, *Politics in the Media Age* (New York: McGraw-Hill, 1986), p. 21.

3. Phillip Knightley, *The First Casualty* (New York: Harcourt Brace Jovanovich, 1975), p. 56.

4. Quoted in Berkman and Kitch, p. 25.

5. Stephen Ansolabehere, Roy Behr, and Shanto Iyengar, *The Media Game: American Politics in the Television Age* (New York: Macmillan, 1993), p. 44.

6. Doris A. Graber, *Mass Media and American Politics,* 3rd ed. (Washington, D.C.: Congressional Quarterly Press, 1989), p. 45.

7. Kathleen Hall Jamieson and Karlyn Kohrs Campbell, *The Interplay of Influence* (Belmont, Calif.: Wadsworth, 1983), p. 10.

8. Ansolabehere, Behr, and Iyengar, pp. 26–28.

9. George F. Gilder, *Life After Television* (New York: W. W. Norton, 1994).

10. Jamieson and Campbell, p. 16.

11. Graber, pp. 84–86.

12. Herbert J. Gans, *Deciding What's News: A Study of CBS Evening News, NBC Nightly News, Newsweek and Time* (New York: Vintage, 1980), p. 9.

13. John Fiske, *Television Culture* (New York: Routledge, 1995), p. 281.

14. Paul Lazarfeld, Bernard Berelson, and H. Gaudet, *The People's Choice* (New York: Columbia University Press, 1948).

15. Thomas E. Patterson, *The Mass Media Election: How Americans Choose Their President* (New York: Praeger, 1980), pp. 86–91.

16. Benjamin I. Page, Robert Y. Shapiro, and Glenn R. Dempsey, "What Moves Public Opinion," *American Political Science Review,* 81 (March 1987), 23–43.

17. Shanto Iyengar, *Is Anyone Responsible? How Television Frames Political Issues* (Chicago: University of Chicago Press, 1991).

18. Austin Ranney, *Channels of Power: The Impact of Television on American Politics* (New York: Basic Books, 1983), p. 17.

19. Shanto Iyengar, Mark D. Peters, and Donald R. Kinder, "Experimental Demonstrations of the

'Not-so-Minimal' Consequences of Television News Programs," *American Political Science Review,* 76 (December 1982), 848–858.

20. Ansolabehere, Behr, and Iyengar, p. 148.

21. Quoted in Joseph C. Spear, *Presidents and the Press: The Nixon Legacy* (Cambridge, Mass.: MIT Press, 1984), p. 14.

22. Thomas E. Patterson, *Out of Order* (New York: Alfred A. Knopf, 1993), pp. 74–75.

23. Stephen Hess, "President Clinton and the White House Press Corps—Year One," *Media Studies Journal,* 8 (Spring 1994), 4.

24. Dayton Duncan, *Press, Polls, and the 1988 Campaign: An Insider's Critique,* Joan Shorenstein Barone Center for the Press and Public Policy, John F. Kennedy School of Government, Harvard University (Cambridge, Mass.: April 1989), pp. 3, 5.

25. Marjorie Randon Hershey, "The Campaign and the Media," in *The Election of 1988: Reports and Interpretations,* ed. Gerald M. Pomper (Chatham, N.J.: Chatham House, 1989), pp. 96–99.

26. Quoted in Graber, p. 235.

27. Fred Smoller, "The Six O'Clock Presidency: Patterns of Network News Coverage of the President," *Presidential Studies Quarterly,* 16 (Winter 1986), 31–49.

28. David Wise, *The Politics of Lying: Government Deception, Secrecy, and Power* (New York: Vintage, 1973), p. 460.

29. Michael Baruch Grossman and Martha Joynt Kumar, *Portraying the President: The White House and the Media* (Baltimore, Md.: Johns Hopkins University Press, 1981), p. 116.

30. Quoted in Charles Peters, "Why the White House Press Didn't Get the Watergate Story," *Washington Monthly,* 4 (July/August 1973), 6.

31. Quoted in Joseph C. Spear, *Presidents and the Press: The Nixon Legacy* (Cambridge, Mass.: MIT Press, 1984), pp. 10–11.

32. Ibid., p. 292.

33. Quoted in Graber, p. 254.

34. Stephen Hess, *The Washington Reporters* (Washington, D.C.: The Brookings Institution, 1981), pp. 98–99.

35. Quoted in David M. O'Brien, *Storm Center: The Supreme Court in American Politics* (New York: Norton, 1986), p. 281.

Chapter 10

Congress, pp. 273–303

1. Quoted in Albert R. Hunt, "In Defense of a Messy Congress," *The Washingtonian,* 13 (September 1982), 180.

2. Cited in Barbara Hinckley, *Congressional Elections* (Washington, D.C.: Congressional Quarterly Press, 1981), p. 89.

3. Albert D. Cover, "One Good Term Deserves Another: The Advantage of Incumbency in Congressional Elections," *American Journal of Political Science,* 21 (August 1977), 523–541.

4. *Wesberry* v. *Sanders,* 376 U.S. 1 (1964).

5. See "Redistricting Procedure Has Few Rules," *Congressional Quarterly Weekly Report* (February 21, 1981), 354.

6. Gary C. Jacobson, *The Politics of Congressional Elections,* 2nd ed. (Boston: Little, Brown, 1987), p. 13.

7. Morris Fiorina, *Congress: Keystone of the Washington Establishment* (New Haven, Conn.: Yale University Press, 1977), pp. 17–19.

8. Jim Wright, *You and Your Congressman* (New York: Coward, McMann and Geoghegan, 1972), p. 22.

9. David R. Mayhew, *Congress: The Electoral Connection* (New Haven, Conn.: Yale University Press, 1974), p. 37.

10. Ibid., p. 61.

11. Richard F. Fenno, Jr., *Home Style: House Members in Their Districts* (Boston: Little, Brown, 1978), p. 61.

12. Jacobson, p. 50.

13. *McCulloch* v. *Maryland,* 17 U.S. (4 Wheat.) 316 (1819).

14. For a detailed account of the budget process, see Allen Schick, *Congress and Money* (Washington, D.C.: The Urban Institute, 1980). See also James P. Pfiffner, *The President, the Budget, and Congress: Impoundment and the 1974 Budget Act* (Boulder, Colo.: Westview Press, 1979).

15. Richard Doyle and Jerry McCaffery, "The Budget Enforcement Act of 1990: The Path to No Fault Budgeting," *Public Budgeting and Finance,* 11 (Spring 1991), 29.

16. Richard Shapiro, *Frontline Management: A Guide for Congressional District/State Offices* (Washington, D.C.: Congressional Management Foundation, 1989), pp. 1–7.

17. Morris P. Fiorina, "The Case of the Vanishing Marginals: The Bureaucracy Did It," *American Political Science Review,* 71 (March 1977), 180.

18. Fenno, p. 240.

19. See Mathew McCubbins and Thomas Schwartz, "Congressional Oversight Overlooked: Police Patrols Versus Fire Alarms," *American Journal of Political Science,* 28 (February 1984), 165–179.

20. Quoted in Barbara Hinckley, *Stability and Change in Congress* (New York: Harper and Row, 1983), p. 243.

21. *Immigration and Naturalization Service* v. *Chadha,* 103 S.Ct. 2764 (1983).

22. For a general discussion of the legislative veto and its alternatives, see Joseph Cooper, "The Legislative Veto in the 1980s," in *Congress Reconsidered,* ed. Lawrence C. Dodd and Bruce I. Oppenheimer, 3rd ed. (Washington, D.C.: Congressional Quarterly Press, 1985), pp. 364–389.

23. Hinckley, *Stability and Change,* p. 16.

24. Paul Boller, *Presidential Anecdotes* (New York: Penguin, 1981), p. 18.

25. See Steven S. Smith and Christopher J. Deering, *Committees in Congress,* 2nd ed. (Washington, D.C.: Congressional Quarterly Press, 1990).

26. Richard Fenno, Jr., *Congressmen in Committees* (Boston: Little, Brown, 1973).

27. See Mark F. Ferber, "The Formation of the Democratic Study Group," in *Congressional Behavior,* ed. Nelson Polsby (New York: Random House, 1971).

28. Burdett A. Loomis, "Congressional Caucuses and the Politics of Representation," in *Congress Reconsidered,* ed. Lawrence C. Dodd and Bruce I. Oppenheimer, 2nd ed. (Washington, D.C.: Congressional Quarterly Press, 1981), pp. 204–220.

29. Quoted in Roger H. Davidson and Walter J. Oleszek, *Congress and Its Members* (Washington, D.C.: Congressional Quarterly Press, 1981), p. 352.

30. Norman J. Ornstein, Thomas E. Mann, and Michael J. Malbin, *Vital Statistics on Congress: 1989–1990* (Washington, D.C.: Congressional Quarterly Press, 1990).

31. Quoted in Hedrick Smith, *The Power Game: How Washington Works* (New York: Ballantine, 1989), p. 287.

32. Ibid., p. 266.

33. Quoted in *Origins and Development of Congress,* p. 122.

34. For an excellent discussion of House and Senate rules, see Walter J. Oleszek, *Congressional Procedures and the Policy Process* (Washington, D.C.: Congressional Quarterly Press, 1978).

35. Quoted in William J. Keefe and Morris S. Ogul, *The American Legislative Process: Congress and the States* (Englewood Cliffs, N.J.: Prentice-Hall, 1981), pp. 259–260.

36. Quoted in Helen Dewar, "On Capitol Hill, Symbols Triumph," *Washington Post,* November 26, 1991, p. A4.

37. Woodrow Wilson, *Congressional Government,* rev. ed. (New York: Meridian Books, 1956), p. 210.

Chapter 11

The Presidency, pp. 304–337

1. Thomas E. Cronin, *The State of the Presidency* (Boston: Little, Brown, 1980).

2. Louis W. Koenig, *The Chief Executive,* 3rd ed. (New York: Harcourt Brace Jovanovich, 1975).

3. Michael Nelson, "Evaluating the Presidency," in *The Presidency and the Political System,* ed. Michael Nelson (Washington, D.C.: Congressional Quarterly Press, 1984), pp. 5–28.

4. Quoted in Koenig, p. 8.

5. Quoted in Edward S. Corwin, *The President: Office and Powers* (New York: New York University Press, 1957), p. 22.

6. Paul F. Boller, Jr., *Presidential Anecdotes* (New York: Penguin, 1981), p. 86.

7. Nelson, pp. 5–28.

8. Marcus Cunliffe, "A Defective Institution?" *Commentary* (February 1968), 28.

9. Arthur M. Schlesinger, Jr., *The Imperial Presidency* (Boston: Houghton Mifflin, 1973).

10. Thomas Franck, ed., *The Tethered Presidency* (New York: New York University Press, 1981).

11. Charles Funderburk, *Presidents and Politics: The Limits of Power* (Monterey, Calif.: Brooks/Cole, 1982), p. 7.

12. Michael Novak, *Choosing Our King* (New York: Macmillan, 1974).

13. Mary Klein, ed., *Viewpoints on the Presidency: The Power and the Glory* (Minneapolis: Winston Press, 1974), pp. 18–19.

14. *Humphrey's Executor* v. *United States,* 295 U.S. 602 (1935).

15. 418 U.S. 683.

16. Quoted in Louis Fisher, *The Politics of Shared Power: Congress and the Executive* (Washington, D.C.: Congressional Quarterly Press, 1981), p. 9.
17. Richard M. Pious, *The American Presidency* (New York: Basic Books, 1979), p. 340.
18. Corwin, p. 189.
19. Quoted in Pious, p. 395.
20. For an excellent discussion of the Gulf War and the War Powers Resolution, see Marcia Lynn Whicker, Raymond A. Moore, and James P. Pfiffner, *The Presidency and the Persian Gulf War* (Lexington: University of Kentucky Press, 1996).
21. Richard Neustadt, "The Presidency and Legislation: Planning the President's Program," *American Political Science Review,* 49 (1955), 1015.
22. Quoted in Michael L. Mezey, *Congress, the President, and Public Policy* (Boulder, Colo.: Westview Press, 1989), p. 10.
23. Clinton Rossiter, *The American Presidency* (New York: Harcourt, Brace, 1960).
24. For a complete account of the growth of presidential staffing, see Stephen Hess, *Organizing the Presidency* (Washington, D.C.: The Brookings Institution, 1976).
25. Cronin, pp. 276–278.
26. For a history of such clearance procedures, see Richard E. Neustadt, "Presidency and Legislation: The Growth of Central Clearance," *American Political Science Review,* 48 (1954), 150–158.
27. George Edwards and Stephen Wayne, *Presidential Leadership: Politics and Policy Making* (New York: St. Martin's, 1985), p. 189.
28. Barbara Hinckley, *Problems of the Presidency: A Text with Readings* (Glenview, Ill.: Scott, Foresman, 1985), p. 101.
29. Quoted in ibid., p. 105.
30. Quoted in Richard E. Neustadt, *Presidential Power: The Politics of Leadership from FDR to Carter* (New York: Wiley, 1980), p. 9.
31. Ibid., chap. 3.
32. Quoted in Doris Kearnes, *Lyndon Johnson and the American Dream* (New York: Harper and Row, 1976), p. 226.
33. Quoted in Pious, p. 189.
34. George Edwards, *Presidential Influence in Congress* (San Francisco: Freeman, 1980), p. 89.
35. Douglas Rivers and Nancy L. Rose, "Passing the President's Program: Public Opinion and Presidential Influence in Congress," *American Journal of Political Science,* 29 (1985), 187.
36. For a discussion of the strategy of going public, see Samuel Kernell, *Going Public: New Strategies of Presidential Leadership* (Washington, D.C.: Congressional Quarterly Press, 1986).
37. Paul C. Light, *The President's Agenda: Domestic Policy Choice from Kennedy to Carter* (Baltimore: Johns Hopkins University Press, 1983), pp. 36–37.
38. Paul Brace and Barbara Hinckley, *Follow the Leader* (New York: Basic Books, 1994), p. 161.

Chapter 12
Bureaucracy, pp. 338–376

1. See "Fire Traps 50 Firefighters in Colorado, Killing 11," *New York Times,* July 7, 1994, p. A-14; Timothy Egan, "Elite Crew Mourns Deaths of 12 In a Wildfire Blast in Colorado," *New York Times,* July 8, 1994, pp. A-1, A-16; Seth Mydans, "Town of Firefighters Weeps for 9 of Them," *New York Times,* July 9, 1994, pp. 1, 9; "Fatal Wildfire Contained," *New York Times,* July 10, 1994, p. 17; Dirk Johnson, "Lax Procedures Cited in Fatal Colorado Wildfire, *New York Times,* August 23, 1994, p. A-10; and "Deadly Mistakes," *Newark (N.J.) Star-Ledger,* August 23, 1994, p. 2.
2. See National Election Studies, "Support for the Political System: Do People in Government Waste Tax Money, 1958–1994." http://www.umich.edu/~nes/nesguide/toptables/tab5a_3.htm, April 28, 1996.
3. Survey conducted for the Times Mirror Center for the Public and the Press, May 28–June 10, 1992.
4. Knight-Ridder/CNN Town Meeting poll, conducted August 28 through September 2, 1992.
5. See *Washington Post,* Kaiser Family Foundation, and Harvard University Survey Project, "Why Don't Americans Trust Government?" 1996. http://www.kff.org/kff/govt.html, February 5, 1996.
6. For these and related survey results, see the National Election Studies, "Support for the Political System." http://www.umich.edu/~nes/nesguide/gd-index.htm#5, April 28, 1996.
7. The rest are employed in the legislative (approximately thirty-nine thousand) and judicial (twenty-eight thousand) branches. Civilian employment does not include figures from the Central Intelligence Agency and other intelligence-gathering

organizations. These and other detailed statistics are gathered and issued on a regular basis by the U.S. Office of Personnel Management. For a more general picture of federal employment, see the *Statistical Abstract of the United States,* an annual publication of the U.S. Bureau of the Census, which can be found at any public library.

8. In addition to the *Statistical Abstract,* the Office of Personnel Management issues a "Profile of the Typical Federal Employee" from time to time in its bimonthly *Federal Civilian Workforce Statistics: Employment and Trends* report. The data presented here were issued in its January 1992 report.

9. See Mathew Crenson, *The Federal Machine* (Baltimore, Md.: Johns Hopkins University Press, 1975).

10. See Donald F. Kettl, *Government By Proxy: (Mis?)Managing Federal Programs* (Washington, D.C.: Congressional Quarterly Press, 1988).

11. In August each year, *Government Executive Magazine* publishes a summary, "The Top Government Purchasers."

12. See Theodore Draper, *A Very Thin Line: The Iran-Contra Affair* (New York: Simon and Schuster, 1991). The overturned conviction of Oliver North has not taken him out of the spotlight. In 1994 North won the Republican Party nomination for the U.S. Senate in Virginia, but lost in the general election.

13. See Paul Light, *Artful Work: The Politics of Social Security Reform* (New York: Random House, 1985).

14. See Cornelius M. Kerwin, *Rulemaking: How Government Agencies Write Law and Make Policy* (Washington, D.C.: Congressional Quarterly Press, 1994).

15. Harold Seidman and Robert Gilmour, *Politics, Position, and Power: From the Positive to the Regulatory State,* 4th ed. (New York: Oxford University Press, 1986), pp. 309–310.

16. See Leonard D. White, *The Jacksonians: A Study in Administrative History, 1829–1861* (New York: Free Press, 1954), chap. 4.

17. Based on data from *Budget of the United States Government: Analytic Perspectives, Fiscal Year 1995* (Washington, D.C.: U.S. Government Printing Office, 1994).

18. Herbert Kaufman, *Red Tape: Its Origins, Uses, and Abuses* (Washington, D.C.: The Brookings Institution, 1977), p. 2.

19. See David A. Stockman, *The Triumph of Politics: How the Reagan Revolution Failed* (New York: Harper and Row, 1986).

20. For example, see R. Douglas Arnold, *Congress and the Bureaucracy: A Theory of Influence* (New Haven, Conn.: Yale University Press, 1979).

21. Norton E. Long, "Power and Administration," *Public Administration Review,* 9 (Autumn 1949), 257–264.

22. See Francis E. Rourke, *Bureaucracy, Politics, and Public Policy,* 3rd ed. (Boston: Little, Brown, 1984).

23. See Arnold.

24. See A. Lee Fritschler, *Smoking and Politics: Policymaking and the Federal Bureaucracy,* 3rd ed. (Englewood Cliffs, N.J.: Prentice-Hall, 1983).

25. See Margaret Kriz, "Where There's Smoke . . . ," *National Journal* (May 7, 1994), 1056–1060.

26. The concept of issue networks was first described in detail by Hugh Heclo in "Issue Networks and the Executive Establishment," in *The New American Political System,* ed. Anthony King (Washington, D.C.: American Enterprise Institute for Public Policy Research, 1978), chap. 3.

27. See Norman J. Vig and Michael E. Kraft, eds., *Environmental Policy in the 1980s* (Washington, D.C.: Congressional Quarterly Press, 1984).

28. Stockman, pp. 278, 296–297.

29. See Richard P. Nathan, *The Administrative Presidency* (New York: Wiley, 1983), pp. 74–76.

30. See Joel D. Aberbach, "The President and the Executive Branch," in *The Bush Presidency: First Appraisals,* ed. Colin Campbell and Bert S. Rockman (Chatham, N.J.: Chatham House, 1991), especially pp. 232–235.

31. Quoted in James L. Sunquist, *The Decline and Resurgence of Congress* (Washington, D.C.: The Brookings Institution, 1981), p. 320.

32. See Alfred E. Marcus, *Promise and Performance: Choosing and Implementing an Environmental Policy* (Westport, Conn.: Greenwood Press, 1980).

33. See Joel D. Aberbach, *Keeping a Watchful Eye: The Politics of Congressional Oversight* (Washington, D.C.: The Brookings Institution, 1990).

34. See Clyde H. Farnsworth, "In Hearings, I.S.R. Agent Tells of Reprisals, Gifts, and Nepotism," *New York Times,* July 27, 1989, pp. A1, D2; also "I.R.S. Has Plan to Prevent Misconduct by Its Workers," *New York Times,* January 15, 1990, p. D1.

35. Bernard Rosen, *Holding Government Bureaucracies Accountable,* 2nd ed. (New York: Praeger, 1989), p. 113. Also David H. Rosenbloom and James D. Carroll, *Toward Constitutional Competence: A Casebook for Public Administrators* (Englewood Cliffs, N.J.: Prentice-Hall, 1990).

36. Rosen, p. 111.

37. See Louis Fisher, "The Administrative World of *Chadha* and *Bowsher,*" *Public Administration Review,* 47, No. 3 (May/June 1987), 213–219.

38. Taylor Branch, "Courage Without Esteem: Profiles in Whistle-Blowing," in *The Culture of Bureaucracy,* ed. Charles Peters and Michael Nelson (New York: Holt, Rinehart and Winston, 1979), pp. 217–238.

39. See Paul C. Light, *Monitoring Government: Inspectors General and the Search for Accountability* (Washington, D.C.: Brookings Institution, 1993).

40. Charles T. Goodsell, *The Case for Bureaucracy: A Public Administration Polemic,* 3rd ed. (Chatham, N.J.: Chatham House, 1994).

41. See Gerald E. Caiden, "What Is Maladministration?" *Public Administration Review,* 51, No. 6 (November/December 1991), pp. 486–493. See also William T. Gormley, Jr., *Taming the Bureaucracy: Muscles, Prayers, and Other Strategies* (Princeton, N.J.: Princeton University Press, 1989).

42. James Q. Wilson, *Bureaucracy: What Government Agencies Do and Why They Do It* (New York: Basic Books, 1989), pp. 326–331.

43. See Frederic A. Bergerson, *The Army Gets an Air Force: Tactics of Insurgent Bureaucratic Politics* (Baltimore, Md.: Johns Hopkins University Press, 1980).

44. See E. S. Savas, *Privatization: The Key to Better Government* (Chatham, N.J.: Chatham House, 1987); for a more critical approach, see John D. Donahue, *The Privatization Decision: Public Ends, Private Means* (New York: Basic Books, 1989).

45. See Milton Friedman and Rose Friedman, *Free to Choose: A Personal Statement* (New York: Avon, 1981), pp. 140–178. See also John E. Chubb and Terry M. Moe, *Politics, Markets, and America's Schools* (Washington, D.C.: The Brookings Institution, 1990).

46. See the Report of the National Commission on the Public Service (Volker Commission), *Leadership for America: Rebuilding the Public Service* (Lexington, Mass.: D. C. Heath, 1989).

47. David Osborne and Ted Gaebler, *Reinventing Government* (Reading, Mass.: Addison-Wesley, 1997).

48. See Melvin J. Dubnick and Barbara S. Romzek, *American Public Administration: Politics and the Management of Expectations* (New York: Macmillan, 1991), especially chap. 3.

Chapter 13

Courts, Judges, and the Law, pp. 377–407

1. Richard J. Richardson and Kenneth N. Vines, *The Politics of Federal Courts: Lower Courts in the United States* (Boston: Little, Brown, 1970).

2. For a comprehensive discussion of the uses of diversity jurisdiction, see Victor E. Flango, "Attorney's Perspectives on Choice of Forum in Diversity Cases," *Akron Law Review,* 25 (Summer 1991), 1–82.

3. "CQ Law/Judiciary," *Congressional Quarterly Weekly Report* (November 26, 1988), p. 3393.

4. Quoted in Howard Ball, *Courts and Politics: The Federal Judicial System* (Englewood Cliffs, N.J.: Prentice-Hall, 1980), p. 176.

5. "CQ on the Floor," *Congressional Quarterly Weekly Report* (March 20, 1970), p. 776.

6. See Lawrence H. Tribe, *God Save This Honorable Court: How the Choice of Supreme Court Justices Shapes Our History* (New York: Random House, 1985).

7. Quoted in Stephen Wasby, *The Supreme Court in the Federal System,* 2nd ed. (New York: Holt, Rinehart and Winston, 1984), p. 89.

8. *The Supreme Court: Justice and the Law* (Washington, D.C.: Congressional Quarterly, 1981), p. 163.

9. John Schmidauser, *Judges and Justices: The Federal Appellate Judiciary* (Boston: Little, Brown, 1979), p. 96.

10. Sheldon Goldman and Thomas P. Jahnige, *The Federal Courts as a Political System* (New York: Harper and Row, 1985), p. 250.

11. See Stephen Wasby, *The Supreme Court in the Federal System,* 3rd ed. (New York: Holt, Rinehart and Winston, 1984), pp. 91–97.

12. Quoted in Henry J. Abraham, *The Judicial Process* (New York: Oxford University Press, 1980), p. 203.

13. *Webster* v. *Reproductive Health Services,* 492 U.S. 490 (1989).

14. Doris Marie Provine, *Case Selection in the United States Supreme Court* (Chicago: University of Chicago Press, 1980).

15. Quoted in David M. O'Brien, *Storm Center: The Supreme Court in American Politics,* 2nd ed. (New York: Norton, 1990), p. 283.

16. Quoted in Bob Woodward and Scott Armstrong, *The Brethren: Inside the Supreme Court* (New York: Avon Books, 1979), p. 490.

17. *Brown* v. *Board of Education II,* 349 U.S. 294 (1955).

18. William J. Brennan, "Inside View of the High Court," *New York Times Magazine,* October 6, 1963, p. 22.

19. *Marbury* v. *Madison,* 5 U.S. (1 Cranch) 137 (1803).

20. For a complete discussion of the *Marbury* decision, see Craig R. Ducat, *Modes of Constitutional Interpretation* (St. Paul, Minn.: West, 1978), pp. 1–41.

21. See in particular Nathan Glazer, "Toward an Imperial Judiciary," *The Public Interest* 47 (Fall 1975), 104–123; and Raoul Berger, *Government by the Judiciary: The Transformation of the Fourteenth Amendment* (Cambridge, Mass.: Harvard University Press, 1977).

22. Tribe, p. 42.

23. For a conservative critique of the original intent approach, see Richard A. Posner, "What Am I? A Potted Plant?" *New Republic,* September 28, 1987, 23–25.

24. *Furman* v. *Georgia,* 408 U.S. 238 (1972).

25. See Jack Peltason, *Fifty-eight Lonely Men: Southern Federal Judges and School Desegregation* (Urbana, Ill.: University of Illinois Press, 1971).

26. *Oregon* v. *Mitchell,* 400 U.S. 112 (1970).

27. Cited in O'Brien, p. 361.

28. Quoted in Richard Kluger, *Simple Justice: The History of Brown v. Board of Education and Black America's Struggle for Equality* (New York: Knopf, 1976), p. 753.

Chapter 14

Domestic Policy and Policymaking, pp. 408–446

1. For a critical summary of U.S. farm policy, see Joseph N. Belden, *Dirt Rich, Dirt Poor: America's Food and Farm Crisis* (New York: Routledge and Kegan Paul, 1986).

2. Much of the following discussion, including quotations, is drawn from Jonathan Rauch, "Plowing a New Field," *National Journal* (January 28, 1995), 212–216.

3. See Herbert Stein, *Presidential Economics: The Making of Economic Policy from Roosevelt to Reagan and Be-*
yond, rev. ed. (New York: Simon and Schuster, 1985).

4. For example, see George Gilder, *Wealth and Poverty* (New York: Basic Books, 1981).

5. Survey of 1,507 Americans taken for the Times Mirror Center for the People and the Press.

6. James E. Anderson, *Public Policymaking: An Introduction,* 3rd ed. (Boston, Mass.: Houghton Mifflin), 1997.

7. Considerable controversy and drama accompanied the "discovery" of AIDS; it is chronicled in Randy Shilts, *And the Band Played On: Politics, People, and the AIDS Epidemic* (New York: Penguin Books, 1988).

8. See Matthew A. Crenson, *The Un-Politics of Air Pollution: A Study of Non-Decisionmaking in the Cities* (Baltimore, Md.: Johns Hopkins University Press, 1971), pp. 1–2.

9. See Julie Rovner, "Welfare Reform: The Issue That Bubbled Up from the States to Capitol Hill," *Governing,* 2, No. 2 (December 1988), 17–21.

10. During the debate many newspapers and other periodicals published such analyses. There were also books published that typically reflected specific positions of Clinton's health care plan. For example, Paul Starr, *The Logic of Health Care Reform: Why and How the President's Plan Will Work,* revised edition (New York: Penguin Books, 1994).

11. See Jeffrey H. Birnbaum and Alan S. Murray, *Showdown at Gucci Gulch: Lawmakers, Lobbyists, and the Unlikely Triumph of Tax Reform* (New York: Vintage, 1987).

12. See Paul C. Light, *Forging Legislation* (New York: Norton, 1992).

13. The Court's decision-making process remains one of the mysteries of Washington. Whatever insights we have into the process come from the recollections of law clerks and others who served the justices. The only popular effort to understand what takes place inside the Court was Bob Woodward and Scott Armstrong, *The Brethren: Inside the Supreme Court* (New York: Simon and Schuster, 1979).

14. See John M. Logsdon, *The Decision to Go to the Moon: Project Apollo and the National Interest* (Chicago: University of Chicago Press, 1970).

15. For more on the early history of economic policy in the United States, see Carl Bridenbaugh, *Cities in the Wilderness: The First Century of Urban Life in America, 1625–1672* (New York: Knopf, 1964); Gerald D.

Nash, *State Government and Economic Development: A History of Administrative Policies in California, 1849–1933* (Berkeley, Calif.: Institute of Governmental Studies, 1964), pp. 10–26; and Stuart Bruchey, *The Roots of American Economic Growth, 1607–1861; An Essay in Social Causation* (New York: Harper and Row, 1965). For an interesting study of Jefferson's views, see Frank Bourgin, *The Great Challenge: The Myth of Laissez-Faire in the Early Republic* (New York: George Braziller, 1989), chaps. 7 and 8.

16. For insight into the importance and policymaking process at the Fed, see William Greider, *Secrets of the Temple: How the Federal Reserve Runs the Country* (New York: Simon and Schuster, 1987).

17. Arthur M. Okun, *The Political Economy of Prosperity* (New York: Norton, 1970), p. 37; see also Stein, *Presidential Economics.*

18. See Alan S. Blinder, *Economic Policy and the Great Stagflation* (New York: Academic Press, 1981). Also William A. Lovett, *Inflation and Politics: Fiscal, Monetary, and Wage-Price Discipline* (Lexington, Mass.: Lexington Books, 1982).

19. See I. M. Destler, *American Trade Politics: System Under Stress* (Washington, D.C.: Institute for International Economics, 1986).

20. *Statistical Abstract of the United States, 1989* (Washington, D.C.: U.S. Government Printing Office, 1989), tbs. 1354, 1356.

21. The act also provided for regulation of grain elevators. Later the Interstate Commerce Commission was given jurisdiction over other forms of interstate transport, such as trucks, water carriers, and buses.

22. See Louis M. Kohlmeier, Jr., *The Regulators: Watchdog Agencies and the Public Interest* (New York: Harper and Row, 1969).

23. Larry H. Gerston, Cynthia Fraleigh, and Robert Schwab, *The Deregulated Society* (Pacific Grove, Calif.: Brooks/Cole, 1988); see also George C. Eads and Michael Fix, eds., *The Reagan Regulatory Strategy: An Assessment* (Washington, D.C.: The Urban Institute, 1984); and Roger C. Noll and Bruce M. Owen, eds., *The Political Economy of Deregulation: Interest Groups and the Regulatory Process* (Washington, D.C.: American Enterprise Institute for Public Policy Research, 1983).

24. Susan J. Tolchin and Martin Tolchin, *Dismantling America: The Rush to Deregulate* (Boston: Houghton Mifflin, 1983).

25. For a readable and stimulating overview of the national debt issue, see Donald Kettl, *Deficit Politics* (New York: Macmillan, 1992); see also David P. Calleo, *The Bankrupting of America: How the Federal Budget Is Impoverishing the Nation* (New York: William Morrow, 1992).

26. See Calleo, 1992.

27. See the *Federal Reserve Bulletin,* 78, No. 7 (July 1992), A43, tb. 1.60.

28. A growing number of analysts contend that, although there is nothing inherently wrong with a national debt, it should be tolerated only if the indebtedness is targeted toward socially and economically beneficial "investments." See Benjamin M. Friedman, *Day of Reckoning: The Consequences of American Economic Policy Under Reagan and After* (New York: Random House, 1988).

29. For a general overview of deficit politics, see Kettl.

30. In 1986 the U.S. Senate defeated a balanced budget amendment by one vote.

31. See Ed Gillespie and Bob Schellhas, *Contract With America* (New York: Times Books, 1994).

32. See Theda Skocpol, *Protecting Soldiers and Mothers: The Political Origins of Social Policy in the United States* (Cambridge, Mass.: Belknap/Harvard, 1992). See also Sidney Fine, *Laissez Faire and the General Welfare State: A Study in Conflict in American Thought, 1865–1901* (Ann Arbor, Mich.: Ann Arbor Paperbacks, 1969), pp. 22–23, 360–361; Clarke A. Chambers, *Seedtime of Reform: American Social Service and Social Action, 1918–1933* (Ann Arbor, Mich.: Ann Arbor Paperbacks, 1963); and Robert Morris, *Social Policy of the American Welfare State: An Introduction to Policy Analysis,* 2nd ed. (New York: Longman, 1985).

33. For a general discussion of contemporary social welfare policy, see Theodore R. Marmor, Jerry L. Mashaw, and Philip L. Harvey, *America's Misunderstood Welfare State: Persistent Myths, Enduring Realities* (New York: Basic Books, 1990).

34. In recent years, growing attention has been given to what some analysts term "corporate welfare" programs. These are programs that subsidize the activies of America's large corporations and can be associated with industrial policies discussed in the previous section on economic policies. The issue of corporate welfare made it briefly onto the national agenda in late 1994 when Secretary of Labor

Robert Reich gave a speech focusing attention on such programs. The Clinton White House quickly distanced itself from such talk.

In 1997, however, a bipartisan and ideologically diverse coalition—including Ralph Nader and the National Taxpayers Union—joined forces with members of Congress to pursue an end to "corporate welfare."

35. For an overview of the "old" welfare system, see Thomas E. Patterson, *America's Struggle Against Poverty, 1900–1980* (Cambridge, Mass.: Harvard University Press, 1981); U.S. House of Representatives, Committee on Ways and Means, *Overview of Entitlement Programs: 1994 Green Book* (Washington, D.C.: U.S. Government Printing Office, July 15, 1994); and Marmor, Mashaw, and Harvey.

36. See Charles Murray's *Losing Ground: American Social Policy, 1950–1980* (New York: Basic Books, 1984). See also Nathan Glazer, *The Limits of Social Policy* (Cambridge, Mass.: Harvard University Press, 1988). For a counterargument, refer to John E. Schwarz, *America's Hidden Success: A Reassessment of Twenty Years of Public Policy* (New York: Norton, 1983). See also William Julius Wilson, *The Truly Disadvantaged: The Inner City, the Underclass, and Public Policy* (Chicago: University of Chicago Press, 1987).

37. For analyses of the 1996 act, see U.S. Department of Health and Human Services, "Comparison of Prior Law and the Personal Responsibility and Work Opportunity Reconciliation Act of 1996 (P.L. 104-193)," http://aspe.os.dhhs.gov/hsp/isp/reform.htm, n.d.; also National Conference of State Legislatures, "Analysis of the Personal Responsibility and Work Opportunity Reconciliation Act of 1996: Conference Agreement for H.R. 3734," http://www.ncsl.org/statefed/wel913.htm, n.d.

38. For a general survey of social insurance programs, see Arnold J. Heidenheimer, Hugh Heclo, and Carolyn Teich Adams, *Comparative Public Policy: The Politics of Social Choice in Europe and America,* 2nd ed. (New York: St. Martin's, 1983), chap. 7.

39. See most recent editions of the *Social Security Bulletin,* published quarterly by the Social Security Administration, for an overview of these and other programs administered by SSA.

40. U.S. House of Representatives, Committee on Ways and Means, *Overview of Entitlement Programs,* pp. 123–206.

41. On the politics of dealing with that crisis, see Paul Light, *Artful Work: The Politics of Social Security Reform* (New York: Random House, 1985).

42. As of 1997, wage earners making over $65,400 continue to contribute 1.45 percent of their pay for Medicare insurance. Self-employed workers pay a social security tax of 15.3 percent to $65,400, and then just 2.9 percent above that level.

43. Under current law, an Advisory Council on Social Security is appointed every four years to review the future of social security funding and to make recommendations. The findings of the first such coucil were issued in January 1997 and can be located on the Internet at http://www.ssa.gov/policy/adcouncilintro.html.

44. Much of the discussion in this section relies on Kenneth J. Meier, *Regulation: Politics, Bureaucracy, and Economics* (New York: St. Martin's, 1985).

45. See Richard A. Harris and Sidney M. Milkis, *The Politics of Regulatory Change: A Tale of Two Agencies* (New York: Oxford University Press, 1989).

46. Murray L. Weidenbaum, *Business, Government, and the Public,* 2nd ed. (Englewood Cliffs, N.J.: Prentice-Hall, 1981), p. 27.

Chapter 15
Foreign and Defense Policy, pp. 447–482

1. Quoted in Richard N. Gardner, "Practical Internationalism," in *Rethinking America's Security: Beyond Cold War to New World Order,* ed. Graham Allison and Gregory F. Treverton (New York: Norton, 1992), p. 272.

2. For Biden's views, as well as those of other prominent Democrats after the Clinton election victory in 1992, see Christopher Madison, "Juggling Act," *National Journal* (January 9, 1993), 62–65.

3. James Chace and Caleb Carr, *America Invulnerable: The Quest for Absolute Security from 1812 to Star Wars* (New York: Summit Books, 1988), p. 12.

4. See Michael Nacht, *The Age of Vulnerability: Threats to the Nuclear Stalemate* (Washington, D.C.: The Brookings Institution, 1985).

5. Michael E. Porter, *The Competitive Advantage of Nations* (New York: Free Press, 1990), p. 306.

6. See Richard Rosecrance, *The Rise of the Trading State: Commerce and Conquest in the Modern World*

(New York: Basic Books, 1986); also Roy Hofheinz, Jr., and Kent E. Calder, *The Eastasia Edge* (New York: Basic Books, 1982).

7. Clyde V. Prestowitz, Jr., *Trading Places: How We Are Giving Our Future to Japan and How to Reclaim It* (New York: Basic Books, 1989), p. 93.

8. For a sweeping and well-informed critique of American policies, see David P. Calleo, *Beyond American Hegemony: The Future of the Western Alliance* (New York: Basic Books, 1987).

9. Chace and Carr, chaps. 2 and 3.

10. Ibid., chap. 4.

11. The policy of containment is most closely associated with George F. Kennan, an American diplomat and scholar who was very influential in shaping U.S. strategies during the Cold War. See his *American Diplomacy, 1900–1950* (New York: Mentor Books, 1951).

12. See Stephen E. Ambrose, *Rise to Globalism: American Foreign Policy Since 1938* (Baltimore, Md.: Penguin Books, 1971), pp. 174–175.

13. For a history of the Vietnam conflict, see Stanley Karnow, *Vietnam: A History* (New York: Penguin Books, 1983).

14. Henry Kissinger, *Years of Upheaval* (Boston: Little, Brown, 1982), pp. 235–246, 339.

15. Ibid., p. 50.

16. Ibid.

17. See Congressional Quarterly, *U.S. Foreign Policy: The Reagan Imprint* (Washington, D.C.: Congressional Quarterly Press, 1986).

18. See R. W. Apple, Jr., "Poll Finds That Gorbachev's Rule Eases American Minds on Soviets," *New York Times,* May 16, 1989, pp. A1, A10.

19. This summary of Bush administration strategy is drawn primarily from public presentations and related documents presented by the Department of Defense during March 1992.

20. I. M. Destler, "Foreign Policy Making with Economy at Center Stage," in *Beyond the Beltway: Engaging the Public in U.S. Foreign Policy,* ed. Daniel Yankelovich and I. M. Destler (New York: Norton, 1994), pp. 26–42.

21. President's Commission on Industrial Competitiveness, *Global Competition: The New Reality* (Washington, D.C.: U.S. Government Printing Office, 1985), p. 1.

22. Executive Office of the President, Office of Management and Budget, *Budget of the United States Government, Fiscal Year 1995* (Washington, D.C.: U.S. Government Printing Office, 1994), pp. 213–217.

23. For an initial assessment of the changes taking place in U.S. foreign policymaking, see Arnold Kanter, "Adapting the Executive Branch to the Post–Cold War World," in *Beyond the Beltway,* pp. 131–154.

24. See Edward S. Corwin, *The President: Office and Powers, 1787–1857* (New York: New York University Press, 1957), chap. 5.

25. For an interesting and readable introduction to the operations of the defense bureaucracy under the Bush administration, see Bob Woodward, *The Commanders* (New York: Simon and Schuster, 1991).

26. See Steve Dryden, *Trade Warriors: USTR and the American Crusade for Free Trade* (New York: Oxford University Press, 1995).

27. Corwin, p. 171 (emphasis in original).

28. See Norman J. Ornstein, "The Constitution and the Sharing of Foreign Policy Responsibility," in *The President, the Congress, and Foreign Policy,* ed. Edmund S. Muskie, Kenneth Rush, and Kenneth W. Thompson (Lanham, Md.: University Press of America, 1986), pp. 35–66.

29. From its final passage to the end of the Reagan administration, there were twenty-five instances when provisions of the act might have applied, and in only fifteen did the White House bother to submit a formal report to Congress as required by the act. See Barbara Hinckley, *Less Than Meets the Eye: Foreign Policy Making and the Myth of the Assertive Congress* (Chicago: University of Chicago Press, 1994), pp. 84–92.

30. G. Calvin Mackenzie, "Resolving Policy Differences: Foreign Aid and Human Rights," in *Who Makes Public Policy? The Struggle for Control Between Congress and the Executive,* ed. Robert S. Gilmour and Alexis A. Halley (Chatham, N.J.: Chatham House, 1994), pp. 261–288.

31. These and other congressional restrictions on Reagan's policies toward Nicaragua eventually led members of the Reagan administration to develop alternative—and legally questionable—means for funding the rebel forces. The resulting scandal became known as the Iran-Contra affair. See Theodore Draper, *A Very Thin Line: The Iran-Contra Affairs* (New York: Simon and Schuster, 1991).

32. Ibid.

33. See Hinckley.

34. Quoted in James A. Nathan and James K. Oliver, *Foreign Policy Making and the American Political System,* 3rd ed. (Baltimore, Md.: Johns Hopkins University Press, 1994), p. 174.

35. See Stephen Ansolabehere, Roy Behr, and Shanto Iyengar, *The Media Game: American Politics in the Television Age* (New York: Macmillan, 1993), pp. 195–202.

36. The media strategy used by Clinton was very similar to that used by Reagan to set the stage for his invasion of Grenada in 1983. See Ansolabehere, Behr, and Iyengar, pp. 195–197.

37. Stephen Rosenfeld, quoted in Nathan and Oliver, p. 186.

38. Pat Choate, *Agents of Influence* (New York: Touchstone Simon and Schuster, 1990).

39. See Harold H. Saunders, "The Middle East, 1973–84: Hidden Agendas," in *The President, the Congress, and Foreign Policy,* ed. Muskie et al., chap. 7. Also, Nathan and Oliver, *Foreign Policy Making and the American Political System,* pp. 199–204.

40. See Gabriel A. Almond, *The American People and Foreign Policy* (New York: Praeger, 1960). Many advocates of the "mood theory" approach tend to regard the American public's opinions as "fickle and undependable." For a contrasting view, see Benjamin I. Page and Robert Y. Shapiro, *The Rational Public: Fifty Years of Trends in Americans' Policy Preferences* (Chicago: University of Chicago Press, 1992), chap. 5.

41. See Theodore J. Lowi, *The Personal President: Power Invested, Promise Unfulfilled* (Ithaca, N.Y.: Cornell University Press, 1985), pp. 170–173.

42. The mood theory concept was originally articulated by Frank L. Klingberg. See Jack E. Holmes, *The Mood/Interest Theory of American Foreign Policy* (Lexington: University Press of Kentucky, 1985).

43. Bruce Russett and Donald R. DeLuca, "'Don't Tread on Me,' Public Opinion and Foreign Policy in the Eighties," *Political Science Quarterly,* 96, No. 3 (Fall 1981), 381–387; also Congressional Quarterly, *U.S. Foreign Policy: The Reagan Imprint.*

44. See Daniel Yankelovich and John Immerwahr, "The Rules of Public Engagement," in *Beyond the Beltway,* pp. 43–77.

45. In his 1985 State of the Union address, Reagan equated this aid with defense rather than diplomacy. He argued that "dollar for dollar, our security assistance contributes as much to global security as our own defense budget." See Congressional Quarterly, *U.S. Foreign Policy: The Reagan Imprint.*

46. John Tower et al., *The Tower Commission Report: The Full Text of the President's Special Review Board* (New York: Bantam/Times Books, 1987), p. 15.

47. See Gerald F. Seib, "Prodded by Quayle and Cheney, Bush Becomes Fervent Supporter of Strategic Defense Initiative," *Wall Street Journal,* February 23, 1990, p. A12.

48. Quoted in Christopher A. Kojm, *The ABCs of Defense: America's Military in the 1980s* (New York: Foreign Policy Association, 1981), p. 3.

49. Jeff Shear, "The Numbers Crunch," *National Journal,* September 24, 1994, pp. 2213–2216.

50. This reluctance comes through quite clearly in the views of military leaders expressed in Woodward's *The Commanders.*

51. See Chace and Carr.

52. Much of what follows reflects presentations made by Bush administration officials during March and April 1992.

Suggested Readings

Chapter 1

Myth and Reality in American Politics, pp. 1–23

Darman, Richard. *Who's In Control: Polar Politics and the Sensible Center.* A readable and insightful analysis of contemporary American politics and policymaking by a key Washington "insider." His observations bring together the role played by ideology, power, and leadership in American government.

Dionne, E. J., Jr., *Why Americans Hate Politics.* New York: Simon and Schuster, 1991. This popular analysis of American politics in the 1980s argues that America's negative attitudes toward politics are rooted in the irrelevance of the mainstream political ideologies of liberalism and conservatism to the changing realities of America's problems. In the process of making this argument, Dionne offers key insights into the tenets of American ideas and their role in politics.

Greenberg, Stanley E. *Middle Class Dreams: The Politics and Power of the New American Majority.* New York: Times Books, 1995. Reflections of a political analyst with close ties to the Clinton White House on the current crisis in American politics.

Hofstadter, Richard. *The Paranoid Style in American Politics and Other Essays.* New York: Vintage Books, 1967. A noted historian's classic statement of the role conspiracy theories have played in American politics.

Medcalf, Linda J., and Kenneth M. Dolbeare. *American Ideologies Today: From Neopolitics to New Ideas.* New York: Random House, 1988. A brief history of political ideology in the United States with clear explanations and applications to contemporary politics.

Parenti, Michael. *Land of Idols: Political Mythology in America.* New York: St. Martin's, 1994. A distinctly more radical approach to the study of American politics that relies on the myths that permeate our political system.

Robertson, James Oliver. *American Myth, American Reality.* New York: Hill and Wang, 1980. A survey of myths held by Americans, including many related to government. The author explores the importance of myth in shaping the American past and present.

Tinder, Glenn. *Political Thinking: The Perennial Questions,* 3rd ed. Boston: Little, Brown, 1986. A brief but concise examination and statement of the perennial philosophical and political questions raised in the Western intellectual tradition.

Chapter 2

Constitutional Foundations, pp. 24–61

Ackerman, Bruce. *We The People.* Vol. 1, *Foundations.* Cambridge, Mass.: Belknap Press, 1991. A fresh interpretation of American constitutionalism that focuses on the uniqueness of the historical evolution of the U.S. system.

Bradford, M. E. *Founding Fathers: Brief Lives of the Framers of the United States Constitution,* 2nd ed. Lawrence, Kan.: University Press of Kansas, 1994. A classic collection of short biographies that provides some insights into the framers' backgrounds and personalities.

Cooke, Jacob E., ed. *The Federalist.* Middletown, Conn.: Wesleyan University Press, 1961. A complete collection of these important papers that have played a major role in our understanding of what the framers meant when they wrote the Constitution.

DePauw, Linda Grant. *Founding Mothers: Women of America in the Revolutionary Era.* Boston: Houghton Mifflin, 1975. An overview of the role of women in the social, economic, and political atmosphere that preceded the writing of the Constitution.

Diamond, Martin. *The Founding of the Democratic Republic.* Itasca, Ill.: F. E. Peacock, 1981. A clear presentation of the issues and ideas that influenced the framers of the Constitution.

Farrand, Max. *The Framing of the Constitution of the United States.* New Haven, Conn.: Yale University Press, 1913. A classic study, describing the people and debates at the Constitutional Convention.

Ferris, Robert G., and James H. Charleton. *The Signers of the Constitution.* Flagstaff, Ariz.: Interpretive Publications, 1986. A well-written overview of the convention and its participants by two National Park

Service historians who provide interesting insights and visual displays to bring the story of the Constitutional Convention to life.

Levinson, Sanford. *Constitutional Faith.* Princeton, N.J.: Princeton University Press, 1988. An insightful analysis of the "civil religion" that has developed around the American Constitution.

Maier, Pauline. *American Scripture: Making the Declaration of Independence.* New York: Alfred A. Knopf, 1997. A historian's study of the Declaration and the political setting in which it was written. She also addresses the emergence of the Declaration of Independence as a moral force in American politics during the 19th century.

McDonald, Forrest. *Novus Ordo Seclorum: The Intellectual Origins of the Constitution.* Lawrence, Kan.: University Press of Kansas, 1985. An intellectual history of the work of the framers by one of America's leading authorities on the founding of the republic.

Rakove, Jack N., ed. *Interpreting the Constitution: The Debate Over Original Intent.* Boston, Mass.: Northeastern University Press, 1990. A collection of essays providing various perspectives on the doctrine of "originalism," i.e., whether interpretations of the Constitution should rely on the framers' intentions rather than adapting them to suit modern needs.

Sunstein, Cass R. *The Partial Constitution.* Cambridge, Mass.: Harvard University Press, 1993. A critical analysis of contemporary constitutional law and its reliance on "status quo neutrality" rather than impartiality. This is a critical source for anyone interested in issues surrounding the "rule of law" principle.

Wood, Gordon S. *The Creation of the American Republic, 1776–1787.* New York: W. W. Norton and Co., 1969. A groundbreaking study of the issues, politics, and ideas during a tumultuous period that set the stage for the writing of the U.S. Constitution.

federal system, with emphasis on the growing influence of governors, state legislatures, and other state institutions.

Davis, S. Rufus. *The Federal Principle: A Journey Through Time in Quest of Meaning.* Berkeley, Calif.: University of California Press, 1978. A classic survey of the meaning of federalism as a constitutional and political concept in Western civilization. Focuses on the historical emergence of federalism in the United States.

Donahue, John D. *Disunited States.* New York: Basic Books, 1997. A critical assessment of "devolution" and its implications for American government.

Rivlin, Alice M. *Reviving the American Dream: The Economy, the States, and the Federal Government.* Washington, D.C.: The Brookings Institution, 1992. In a refreshing look at the burdens of public policy, Rivlin concludes that the national government is doing too much and must defer much more to the states. Rivlin's views became particularly important when President Bill Clinton appointed her deputy director, and then director, of the Office of Management and Budget.

Van Horn, Carl E., ed. *The State of the States,* 2nd ed. Washington, D.C.: CQ Press, 1993. A collection of essays that addresses the increasing role and capacities of state govenment and officials in the 1990s.

Walker, David B. *The Rebirth of Federalism: Slouching Toward Washington.* Chatham, N.J.: Chatham House, 1995. An overview of the changing nature of American federalism from one of the country's leading students of intergovernmental relations.

Wright, Deil S. *Understanding Intergovernmental Relations,* 3rd ed. Monterey, Calif.: Brooks/Cole, 1988. A comprehensive survey of the research in and issues of U.S. intergovernmental relations.

Chapter 3

Federalism and Intergovernmental Relations, pp. 62–90

Bowman, Ann O'M., and Richard C. Kearney. *The Resurgence of the States.* Englewood Cliffs, N.J.: Prentice-Hall, 1986. A survey of the increasingly important role played by the states in the American

Chapter 4

The Heritage of Rights and Liberties, pp. 91–129

Abraham, Henry J. *Freedom and the Court,* 5th ed. New York: Oxford University Press, 1988. A carefully documented analysis of Supreme Court civil rights and civil liberties decisions.

Alderman, Ellen, and Caroline Kennedy. *In Our Defense: The Bill of Rights in Action.* New York: Avon Books,

1991. Written for the layperson, this book provides vivid accounts of major cases invoking the Bill of Rights.

Cleary, Edward J. *Beyond the Burning Cross: A Landmark Case of Race, Censorship, and the First Amendment.* New York: Vintage Books, 1995. A first-person account by the lawyer who successfully challenged the St. Paul, Minnesota, hate crime ordinance.

Domino, John C. *Civil Rights and Liberties.* New York: HarperCollins, 1994. A brief analysis of the rulings on civil rights and liberties from the early Warren Court to 1994. The text emphasizes the philosophical shifts over time.

Ducat, Craig R., and Harold W. Chase. *Constitutional Interpretation,* 6th ed. St. Paul, Minn.: West, 1996. A comprehensive history and commentary on judicial enforcement of civil liberties and rights.

Kluger, Richard. *Simple Justice.* New York: Knopf, 1975. A complete account of the legal and political setting of the Supreme Court's decision in *Brown v. Board of Education.*

Mezey, Susan Gluck. *In Pursuit of Equality: Women, Public Policy, and the Federal Courts.* New York: St. Martin's, 1992. The author provides a well-written and comprehensive account of court interpretations of the issues regarding sex discrimination.

Polenberg, Richard. *Fighting Faiths: The Abrams Case, the Supreme Court, and Free Speech.* New York: Viking, 1988. An informative examination of an important free-speech case.

Chapter 5
Public Opinion and Political Participation, pp. 130–161

Asher, Herbert. *Polling and the Public: What Every Citizen Should Know,* 3rd ed. Washington, D.C.: Congressional Quarterly Press, 1995. A highly useful text explaining polling and survey methods.

Brace, Paul, and Barbara Hinckley. *Follow the Leader: Opinion Polls and Modern Presidents.* New York: Basic Books, 1992. A careful analysis of the use of polls in a modern presidency.

Conway, M. Margaret. *Political Participation in the United States,* 2nd ed. Washington, D.C.: Congressional Quarterly Press, 1991. A well-crafted and readable study of political participation. The book explores who participates, patterns of participation, the effects of participation on the political system, and the ways in which participation differs from the assumptions of classical democratic theory.

Crotty, William J., ed. *Political Participation and American Democracy.* New York: Greenwood Press, 1991. A selection of readings on the nature of political participation in a democratic system.

Erickson, Robert S. *American Public Opinion: Its Origins, Content, and Impact,* 5th ed. New York: Allyn and Bacon, 1995. A readable and comprehensive text covering the formation of public opinion in the United States.

Traugott, Michael W., and Paul J. Lavrakas. *The Voter's Guide to Election Polls.* Chatham, N.J.: Chatham House, 1996. An introductory handbook on polling, the collection of public opinion, sampling, questionnaire construction, the evaluation of polls, and the common problems associated with polling.

Chapter 6
Political Parties, pp. 162–189

Green, John C., and Daniel M. Shea, eds., 2nd ed. *The State of the Parties: The Changing Role of Contemporary American Parties.* Lanham, Md.: Rowman and Littlefield, 1996. An excellent selection of essays about the condition and future of American parties at the national, state, and local levels, as well as about independent candidates and minor parties.

Keefe, William J. *Parties, Politics, and Public Policy in America,* 7th ed. Washington, D.C.: CQ Press, 1994. A textbook overview of the structure and function of political parties.

Maisel, L. Sandy. *The Parties Respond: Changes in the American Party System,* 2nd ed. Boulder, Colo.: Westview Press, 1994. An excellent collection of essays on the present status of political parties.

Riordon, William L. *Plunkitt of Tammany Hall.* New York: Dutton, 1963. An entertaining story of an infamous member of the legendary Tammany Hall political machine of New York City.

Schlesinger, Joseph. *Political Parties and the Winning of Office.* Ann Arbor, Mich.: University of Michigan Press, 1994. An excellent analysis of the role and function of political parties in the United States, with an emphasis on the role of parties in elections.

Sundquist, James L. *Dynamics of the Party System*. Washington, D.C.: The Brookings Institution, 1983. One of the best discourses on the history, traditions, and transformation of political parties.

Chapter 7
Campaigns and Elections, pp. 190–224

Abramson, Paul R., John H. Aldrich, and David W. Rohde. *Change and Continuity in the 1996 Elections: Revised Edition*. Washington, D.C.: CQ Press, 1998. A comprehensive review and analysis of the 1996 elections.

Alexander, Herbert E. *Financing Politics: Money, Elections, and Political Reform*, 4th ed. Washington, D.C.: CQ Press, 1992. An excellent text on the impact of money on elections. Includes a historical review of campaign funding, recent campaign funding reforms, and the sources and costs of state and federal elections.

Darcy, Robert, Susan Welch, and Janet Clark. *Women, Elections, and Representation*. New York: Longman, 1987. A careful analysis and inquiry into why so few women are elected to public office. An excellent review of the workings of the American electoral system.

Fowler, Linda L., and Robert D. McClure. *Political Ambition: Who Decides to Run for Congress*. New Haven, Conn.: Yale University Press, 1990. An excellent and readable study of how and why each of a group of individuals sought the party nomination to run for a seat in the U.S. House of Representatives. This book introduces the reader to the relevance of political ambition in choosing to campaign for a political office.

Pomper, Gerald M., ed. *The Election of 1996: Reports and Interpretations*. Chatham, N.J.: Chatham House, 1997. A series of articles on the 1996 elections, with interpretation and analysis.

Sorauf, Frank J. *Inside Campaign Finance: Myths and Realities*. New Haven: Yale University Press, 1992. An excellent review of campaign finance, separating fact from fiction.

Chapter 8
Interest Groups, pp. 225–250

Berry, Jeffrey M. *Interest Group Society*. New York: Longman, 1997. A well-written examination of how interest groups operate within the context of democratic theory. The author stresses the relationship between interest groups and political parties and the changes in campaign finance practices.

Cigler, Allan J., and Burdett A. Loomis. *Interest Group Politics*, 4th ed. Washington, D.C.: Congressional Quarterly Press, 1994. An excellent collection of essays by leading scholars, focusing on the policy-making roles of interest groups, interest group participation, organizations and elections, political action committees, interest groups and the courts, and lobbyists.

Costain, Anne N. *Inviting Women's Rebellion*. Baltimore, Md.: Johns Hopkins University Press, 1992. An examination of the evolution of the women's movement in the United States.

Hrebenar, Ronald J. *Interest Group Politics in America*, 3rd ed. New York: M. E. Sharpe, 1996. A basic introductory text on the study of group power.

Schlozman, Kay Lehman, and John T. Tierney. *Organized Interests and American Democracy*. New York: Harper and Row, 1986. A skillful study broadly covering the role of organized interests in the United States. The authors draw on several sources of information, including a set of interviews with 175 Washington, D.C., interest group representatives and lobbyists.

Walker, Jack L., Jr. *Mobilizing Interest Groups in America*. Ann Arbor, Mich.: University of Michigan Press, 1991. An excellent review of the role of interest groups in the United States.

Chapter 9
Media and Politics, pp. 251–272

Ansolabehere, Stephen, Roy Behr, and Shanto Iyengar. *The Media Game: American Politics in the Television Age*. New York: Macmillan, 1993. Combining survey data and experimental results, the authors document the effects of television on politicians and voters. Highly readable and up-to-date, the authors provide a comprehensive guide to this complex subject.

Fallows, James. *Breaking the News: How the Media Undermine American Democracy*. New York: Pantheon Books, 1996. A member of the press critiques his own profession, accusing the media of destroying democracy.

Hess, Stephen. *The Government/Press Connection: Press Officers and Their Offices*. Washington, D.C.: The Brookings Institution, 1984. An examination of the production of news about government by the government itself. The author discusses the organization and staffing of government press offices and details how press briefings are prepared and conducted.

Page, Benjamin I. *Who Deliberates? Mass Media in Modern Democracy*. Chicago: University of Chicago Press, 1996. Based on a careful analysis of three case studies, the author argues that the press plays a central role in public deliberation, but that they do not always reflect the attitudes of ordinary people.

Patterson, Thomas E. *Out of Order*. New York: Alfred A. Knopf, 1993. A well-researched and provocative discussion of the role of the media in presidential elections. The author argues that the press, in taking over the functions of the political parties, has distorted the election process and poorly served the public.

West, Darrell M. *Air Wars: Television Advertising in Election Campaigns, 1952–1992*. Washington, D.C.: Congressional Quarterly Press, 1993. An informative history of the use of television ads in American elections. The author examines the effects of paid advertising on citizen awareness and democracy.

Chapter 10
Congress, pp. 273–303

Conlan, Timothy J., Margaret T. Wrightson, and David R. Beam. *Taxing Choices: The Politics of Tax Reform*. Washington, D.C.: Congressional Quarterly Press, 1990. A well-written account of how the Tax Reform Act of 1986 became law. The authors draw on more than fifty interviews to illuminate the congressional policymaking process.

Cox, Gary, and Matthew D. McCubbins. *Legislative Leviathan: Party Government in the House*. Berkeley, Calif.: University of California Press, 1993. The authors argue that observers of Congress have seriously underestimated the importance of political parties in the workings of the House of Representatives.

Davidson, Roger H., and Walter J. Oleszek. *Congress and Its Members*, 5th ed. Washington, D.C.: Congressional Quarterly Press, 1996. A comprehensive explanation of the workings of Congress. Throughout the book the authors emphasize the theme of the two Congresses.

Hibbing, John R., and Elizabeth Theiss-Morse. *Congress as Public Enemy: Public Attitudes Toward American Political Institutions*. Cambridge: Cambridge University Press, 1995. The authors argue that Americans hate Congress because it is so publicly democratic. Although the American people revere democracy in theory, they dislike it in practice.

Mezey, Michael L. *Congress, the President and Public Policy*. Boulder, Colo.: Westview Press, 1990. An engaging discussion of the interactions between the legislative and executive branches.

Chapter 11
The Presidency, pp. 304–337

Frendreis, John P., and Raymond Tatalovich. *The Modern Presidency and Economic Policy*. Itasca, Ill.: F. E. Peacock, 1994. An extensive discussion of the formulation of economic policy and the role played by presidents.

Jones, Charles O. *The Presidency in a Separated System*. Washington, D.C.: The Brookings Institution, 1994. Warning against viewing American government as presidential government, the author argues that the separated system created by the Constitution can and does work.

Kernell, Samuel. *Going Public: New Strategies of Presidential Leadership*, 2nd ed. Washington, D.C.: Congressional Quarterly Press, 1993. Through a careful analysis of existing data and an illuminating case study, the author convincingly argues that presidents have, over the last fifty years, replaced bargaining for policy outcomes with a style that emphasizes going directly to the people.

Neustadt, Richard E. *Presidential Power and the Modern President: The Politics of Leadership from Roosevelt to Reagan*. New York: The Free Press, 1990. A classic study of the elements of presidential power. The author argues that presidential power is the power to persuade and not the power to command.

Pfiffner, James P. *The Strategic Presidency: Hitting the Ground Running*. Pacific Grove, Calif.: Brooks/Cole, 1988. A well-documented study of presidential transition that offers provocative insights on the inner workings of the White House.

Rose, Richard. *The Postmodern President: George Bush Meets the World,* 2nd ed. Chatham, N.J.: Chatham House, 1991. A provocative account of presidential power in the modern era. The author contends that presidential power is greatly constrained by the need to cooperate with other nations to achieve economic and national security goals.

Skowronek, Stephen. *The Politics Presidents Make: Leadership from John Adams to George Bush.* Cambridge, Mass.: Harvard University Press, 1993. The author argues that presidents are often agents of great change, but that they also inherit a political context which shapes their actions.

Chapter 12

Bureaucracy, 338–376

Dubnick, Melvin J., and Barbara S. Romzek. *American Public Administration: Politics and the Management of Expectations.* New York: Macmillan, 1991. An introduction to the study of public administration. Stresses the role that public expectations play in shaping the work of American bureaucracies.

Goodsell, Charles T. *The Case for Bureaucracy: A Public Administration Polemic,* 3rd ed. Chatham, N.J.: Chatham House, 1994. A unique defense of bureaucracies that counters major criticisms of public administration with empirical evidence.

Gormley, William T., Jr. *Taming the Bureaucracy: Muscles, Prayers, and Other Strategies.* Princeton, N.J.: Princeton University Press, 1989. An interesting overview of the different strategies used to attempt to control and manage the bureaucracy.

Kaufman, Herbert. *Red Tape: Its Origins, Uses, and Abuses.* Washington, D.C.: The Brookings Institution, 1977. A short, readable exploration of bureaucratic red tape and its sources, showing that much red tape is of our own making.

Meier, Kenneth J. *Politics and the Bureaucracy: Policymaking in the Fourth Branch of Government,* 2nd ed. Pacific Grove, Calif.: Brooks/Cole, 1993. An overview of the federal bureaucracy as a policymaking institution.

Osborne, David, and Ted Gaebler. *Reinventing Government: How the Entrepreneurial Spirit is Transforming the Public Sector.* Reading, Mass.: Addison-Wesley, 1992. A widely cited work proposing government reforms that foster entrepreneurial approaches in public administration. Became the "bible" of the Clinton administration's National Performance Review effort.

Osborne, David and Peter Plastrik. *Banishing Bureaucracy: The Five Strategies for Reinventing Government.* Reading, Mass.: Addison-Wesley, 1997. A sequel to Reinventing Government that focuses on how to implement entrepreneurial reforms.

Rourke, Francis E. *Bureaucracy, Politics, and Public Policy,* 3rd ed. Boston: Little, Brown, 1984. A classic introduction to bureaucratic power and its role in the policymaking process.

Wilson, James Q. *Bureaucracy: What Government Agencies Do and Why They Do It.* New York: Basic Books, 1989. An overview of American bureaucracy that takes a "bottom-up" perspective and emphasizes the reasons why bureaucratic organizations behave the way they do.

Chapter 13

Courts, Judges, and the Law, pp. 377–407

Baum, Lawrence. *American Courts: Process and Policy,* 4th ed. Boston: Houghton Mifflin, 1998. A detailed description of the workings of the judicial process at both the state and national level.

Epstein, Lee, ed. *Contemplating Courts.* Washington, D.C.: Congressional Quarterly Press, 1995. An excellent collection of seventeen essays broadly covering the most recent scholarship on courts.

Rosenberg, Gerald N. *The Hollow Hope: Can Courts Bring About Social Change?* Chicago: University of Chicago Press, 1991. The author argues that the Supreme Court's influence on social change has been greatly exaggerated.

Scalia, Antonin. *A Matter of Interpretation: Federal Courts and the Law,* (edited by Amy Gutmann) Princeton, N.J.: Princeton University Press, 1997. A spirited debate between Justice Scalia and his critics over the role of the Supreme Court.

Silverstein, Mark. *Judicial Choices: The New Politics of Supreme Court Confirmations.* New York: W. W. Norton, 1994. The author discusses the modern judicial confirmation process. Focusing on recent controversial appointments, the author connects the judicial activism of the post–New Deal era to the increased politicalization of the appointment process.

Stumpf, Harry P., and John H. Culver. *The Politics of State Courts.* New York: Longman, 1992. A comprehensive guide to the role and operation of state and local courts in the United States.

Chapter 14
Domestic Policy and Policymaking, pp. 408–446

Anderson, James E. *Public Policymaking: An Introduction,* 2nd ed. Boston, Mass.: Houghton Mifflin, 1994. An introductory book on the policymaking process.

Dye, Thomas R. *Understanding Public Policy,* 6th ed. Englewood Cliffs, N.J.: Prentice-Hall, 1987. An introductory book on policy analysis that uses different models to explain the development of a wide range of policies, such as civil rights, defense, health care, education, and taxes.

Friedman, Benjamin M. *Day of Reckoning: The Consequences of American Economic Policy Under Reagan and After.* New York: Random House, 1988. A critical assessment of economic policies under the Reagan administration.

Gordon, John Steele. *Hamilton's Blessing: The Extraordinary Life and Times of Our National Debt.* New York: Walker and Co., 1997. A brief and readable history of the national debt and the role it has played in the U.S. economy over the past two centuries.

Kelman, Steven. *Making Public Policy: A Hopeful View of American Government.* New York: Basic Books, 1987. An upbeat analysis of public policymaking, focusing on the accomplishments of the process rather than its failures.

Kettl, Donald F. *Deficit Politics: Public Budgeting and Its Institutional and Historical Context.* New York: Macmillan, 1992. A short and readable overview of the deficit issue and the politics surrounding it.

Kuttner, Robert. *Everything for Sale: The Virtues and Limits of Markets.* New York: Alfred A. Knopf, 1997. A controversial assessment of the American economy, stressing the limited role of markets and the need for government intervention.

Marmor, Theodore R., Jerry L. Mashaw, and Philip L. Harvey. *America's Misunderstood Welfare State: Persistent Myths, Enduring Realities.* New York: Basic Books, 1990. An analysis of a wide range of American social welfare policies that highlights the overall success of the programs.

Murray, Charles. *Losing Ground: American Social Policy, 1950–1980.* New York: Basic Books, 1984. A critical analysis of social policies of the post–World War II era that argues that those policies have made the situation of the poor worse rather than better.

Schwarz, John E. *America's Hidden Success: A Reassessment of Public Policy from Kennedy to Reagan,* rev. ed. New York: Norton, 1987. An analysis of the Great Society programs of the 1960s, arguing—in contrast to Murray's book—that antipoverty and environmental protection policies of that period have accomplished much more than is generally thought.

Shultz, George P., and Kenneth W. Dam. *Economic Policy Beyond the Headlines.* New York: Norton, 1977. An "insider's" view of economic policymaking from two people who played a major role in that field during the Nixon and Ford administrations. Both Shultz and Dam were also active in the foreign policy area in the Reagan administration.

Skocpol, Theda. *Boomerang: Health Care Reform and the Turn Against Government.* New York: W. W. Norton, 1997. The story of the failed Clinton administration effort at health care reform. The author's analysis focuses on the context within which the story unfolds, particularly the changing public attitude toward government.

Chapter 15
Foreign and Defense Policy, pp. 447–482

Allison, Graham, and Gregory F. Treverton, eds. *Rethinking America's Security: Beyond Cold War to New World Order.* New York: W. W. Norton, 1992. A collection of essays critically assessing the prospects and possibilities for American national security under post–Cold War conditions. Includes insightful contributions by scholar-diplomats Henry Kissinger and George Ball.

Baylis, John, Ken Booth, John Garnett, and Phil Williams. *Contemporary Strategy,* 2 vols., 2nd ed. New York: Holmes and Meier, 1987. A comprehensive analysis of modern military strategies that focuses on the United States.

Callahan, David. *Between Two Worlds: Realism, Idealism, and American Foreign Policy After the Cold War.* New

York: HarperCollins, 1994. An assessment of the choices that American foreign policymakers face in the post–Cold War era, with a strong bias toward developing an "idealist" foreign policy.

Chace, James, and Caleb Carr. *America Invulnerable: The Quest for Absolute Security from 1812 to Star Wars.* New York: Summit Books, 1988. A sweeping overview of U.S. defense policy that looks to the sense of vulnerability as an underlying theme of American policy.

Dryden, Steve. *Trade Warriors: USTR and the American Crusade for Free Trade.* New York: Oxford University Press, 1995. A comprehensive history of the Office of the U.S. Trade Representative, a foreign policy agency that is playing an ever greater role in U.S. foreign policymaking.

Fry, Earl H., Stan A. Taylor, and Robert S. Wood. *America the Vincible: U.S. Foreign Policy for the Twenty-First Century.* Englewood Cliffs, N.J.: Prentice-Hall, 1994. Focusing on the changing conditions influencing American foreign and defense policies, this book assumes the continued vulnerability of the U.S. in its view of future directions.

Hinckley, Barbara. *Less Than Meets the Eye: Foreign Policy Making and the Myth of the Assertive Congress.* Chicago, Ill.: University of Chicago Press, 1994. A review of congressional actions in the Cold War era that indicates that the legislature tended to defer to the White House.

Jordon, Amos A., William J. Taylor, Jr., and Lawrence J. Korb. *American National Security: Policy and Process,* 4th ed. Baltimore, Md.: Johns Hopkins University Press, 1993. A survey of U.S. national security policy as it enters the post–Cold War age.

Karnow, Stanley. *Vietnam: A History.* New York: Penguin Books, 1983. A history of U.S. involvement in the Southeast Asian nation, which eventually led to a conflict that changed the direction of U.S. foreign and defense policies in the 1970s and 1980s.

Leffler, Melvyn P. *A Preponderance of Power: National Security, the Truman Administration, and the Cold War.* Stanford, Calif.: Stanford University Press, 1992. A prize-winning assessment of decisions by U.S. policymakers made at the outset of the Cold War. Leffler concludes that the start of the Cold War can be blamed as much on those decisions as on the actions of Stalin and the Soviets.

McDougall, Walter A. *Promised Land, Crusader State: The American Encounter with the World Since 1776.* Boston, Mass.: Houghton Mifflin, 1997. A reinterpretation of U.S. foreign policy that sees it as the product of two contrasting traditions: the image of America as the promised land of the Old Testament versus that of the crusader state of the New Testament.

Nathan, James A., and James K. Oliver. *Foreign Policy Making and the American Political System,* 3rd ed. Baltimore, Md.: Johns Hopkins University Press, 1994. Critical overview of foreign policymaking and policymakers in the Cold War era, with particular attention to the possible changes that are taking place after the fall of the Soviet Union.

Nye, Joseph S., Jr. *Bound to Lead: The Changing Nature of American Power.* New York: Basic Books, 1990. A critical but positive assessment of America's role in international affairs in the post–Cold War era.

Woodward, Bob. *The Commanders.* New York: Simon and Schuster, 1991. A readable and insightful account of what took place among the highest ranks in the Pentagon during the 1989 Panama invasion and the 1991 Persian Gulf War.

Yankelovich, Daniel, and I. M. Destler, eds. *Beyond the Beltway: Engaging the Public in U.S. Foreign Policy.* New York: W. W. Norton, 1994. A collection of essays focusing on the changing nature of American foreign policymaking in the post–Cold War era, with emphasis on the importance of economic issues and engaging the American public in the policy process.

Index to References

Index